MW00611913

The Kansas Guidebook 2

for explorers

Marci Penner & WenDee Rowe

Designer
Liz Penner King

Editor
Bobbie Pray

Photographers
Marci Penner & WenDee Rowe

Kansas Sampler Foundation

To my dad, Mil Penner.

This book is dedicated to you. You blazed the trail for me to do something
like this and although you are no longer with us, your stamp is on every page.
To my mom, VLee Penner, you are generous and strong and did all the unsung
things to help us reach the finish line. To my family and friends, your patience,
love, and support far exceeded the time it took to do this entire project.
We all did this together.
–*Marci*

To my father, Dave Rowe.

You are an explorer at heart, with a keen eye and appreciation for the unique
and unusual. You have passed your sense of adventure on to me. For your
unfaltering support, I dedicate this book to you. To my daughters, Jessica and
Samantha, and grandchildren, your sweetness and patience mean the world
to me. I can't wait to explore Kansas with you. To my siblings and friends,
your encouragement has been a precious gift throughout this journey.
–*WenDee*

Mennonite Press, Inc., of Newton, Kansas, our printer for this book and past publications,
is a proud supporter of Kansas and the Kansas Sampler Foundation's efforts to help sustain
Kansas communities and tell the Kansas story.

Copyright © 2017 by the Kansas Sampler Foundation
This publication may not be reproduced, stored in a retrieval system, or transmitted in whole or in part, in any form
by any means, electronic, mechanical, photocopying, recording, or otherwise without prior permission from the
Kansas Sampler Foundation.

Printed in the United States of America by Mennonite Press, Inc.,
Newton, Kansas.

ISBN 978-0-9765408-2-3
Library of Congress Control Number 2017937083

Kansas Sampler Foundation
978 Arapaho Road
Inman, Kansas 67546
kansassampler.org
info@kansassampler.org
620.585.2374

NW

NC

NE

SE

SC

SW

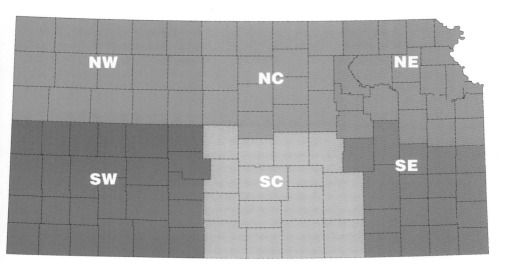

This book. This journey.

It surely was one of the greatest trips anyone could ever take, a deep dive into exploring this great state. We met Kansans in their environment, in grocery stores, in mechanic shops, and in their homes. More than once, a farmer driving down the road in his tractor stopped to see if we needed anything.

Marlene Deters, organist at the beautiful St. Mary's Church in St. Benedict, left her canning to come play "Jesu, Joy of Man's Desiring" for us. Tim Rues and Paul Bahnmaier held a mock debate in Lecompton's Constitution Hall arguing the free state or slave state side for a proposed constitution so we could feel what it was like. Terry Tietjens played piano in Abilene's Seelye Mansion for us. And there's nothing like a Jim Gray tour of the Smoky Hills or finding Patrick Haire at work in his 19th-century woodworking shop in Humboldt.

We received priceless information from city clerks, folks in the courthouse, museum curators, and "guys on the bench." We stopped in numerous barber and beauty shops, and always stopped in post offices. Sometimes we addressed an entire cafe or sale barn since we were obviously strangers in town, and they wanted to know what we were doing.

We were invited into restaurant kitchens, and were introduced to several ghosts. We found out where the liquor stash is kept in Cuba, and discovered the Prohibition gravestone in, well, we promised we wouldn't tell. We were taken into attics and clock towers in courthouses and churches and found only one bridge too scary to cross.

We ate and ate and ate. Three meals a day, three restaurants, always the locally owned ones. In one county we ate two hamburgers within an hour in two different towns—because we were told, "you have to!" And although it was over 100 degrees with a 45-mile-per-hour wind, we were still amazed by the Santa Fe Trail wagon ruts on the prairie close to Howell.

It was always the conversation with local folks that provided the highlight of any day, although sometimes the sheer beauty of grasses, wildflowers, hills, and expanse was beyond description.

You will have different experiences than we did, but yours will be special, too. Explore with a purpose, ask questions of the locals, and keep your heart open. Use this guidebook as your starting point and have fun making memories.

This book is about *your* journey.

–*Marci and WenDee*

Guidebook tips

Take a moment to glance at these tips, which will enhance your use of this book.

Abbreviations

The abbreviations we use throughout the book are listed here along with complete names.

DAR: Daughters of the American Revolution

FB: Facebook page

GAR: Grand Army of the Republic

KBBA: Kansas Bed and Breakfast Association

NRHP: National Register of Historic Places

RHKP: Register of Historic Kansas Places

WCTU: Woman's Christian Temperance Union

WPA: Works Progress Administration and also Works Projects Administration

Call ahead: This indicates it is best to call ahead to learn if a place is open. It also indicates that a place does not have regular hours, but if you call ahead it can open for you. These places do want to accommodate you.

Cell service: Many parts of Kansas do not have cell service or Wi-Fi availability.

Directions: For out-of-town roads we include only the name or number of a road. For example, 200th Road is stated as 200. Our mileage is to the nearest quarter mile. Do not always trust GPS, especially for rural locations.

8 Wonders of Kansas:

This designation means that a building, attraction, site, etc. was one of the top 8 Wonders chosen in online contests that ran from 2007 to 2010. 8wonders.org.

Groups: Especially for rural attractions and restaurants, it is a courtesy to call ahead if you have more than six in your party.

Hours: Hours listed do not reflect that some places are closed over the noon hour. Nor do we state holiday hours. Many times we list common open hours meaning some hours may be extended on certain days or times of the year. Hours often change. It's best to call ahead.

Lodging: We include bed and breakfasts and a common website, if available, for all other lodging in that town.

Made the Explorer Way: Many entries note that the chicken-fried steak is "made the Explorer Way," meaning that the steak is fresh, hand breaded, and grilled or pan fried.

Population: Populations cited are 2013 estimates from the United States Census Bureau.

Restaurants: Of the many restaurants listed, some unfortunately will close. If a restaurant is your destination, do call ahead.

Scenic Byway, Scenic Road, Back Road:

We list many beautiful scenic routes through Kansas, but we use three different descriptive titles. A Scenic Byway is an official state designated route. A Scenic Road is a paved route that we suggest. A Scenic Back Road is an unpaved route that we suggest.

Tours: Two companies organize Kansas tours. Prairie Earth Tours (prairieearthtours.com) and Sunflower State Tours (sunflowerstatetours.org).

Towns not listed: Although every town was researched, not every town is included in the book. But don't let that stop you from exploring them.

Helpful websites

8 Wonders of Kansas
8wonders.org

Flint Hills Tourism Coalition
kansasflinthills.travel

Kansas Agritourism
kansasagritourism.com

Kansas Association of RV Parks and Campgrounds
ksrvparks.com

Kansas Barn Alliance
kansasbarnalliance.org

Kansas Bed and Breakfast
kbba.com

Kansas Department of Wildlife, Parks and Tourism
travelks.com

Kansas Historic Bridges
bridgehunter.com

Kansas Historic Resources Inventory
khri.kansasgis.org

Kansas I-70 Association
kansasi70.com

Kansas RV Parks & Travel
kansasrvparks.org

Kansas Scenic Byways
ksbyways.com

Kansas State Historical Society
kshs.org

National Register of Historic Places
tinyurl.com/kshsnrhp

Northwest Kansas Travel Council
northwestkansas.org

Solomon Valley-Highway 24-Heritage Alliance
hwy24.org

South Central Kansas Tourism Region
visitsouthcentralks.com

Southeast Kansas Tourism Region
Facebook

Wild West Country
wildwestcountry.com

How to get the most out of exploring? 8 Rural Culture Elements

When Mil Penner and Marci Penner started traveling the state in 1990, they asked townspeople what their town had that could be included in a guidebook. The common answer was that they had nothing and we should move on to the next town.

This biased answer prompted Mil and Marci to create the "rural culture element" concept to help towns inventory their assets. No matter the size of a town or a community, it either has evidence or a story to tell about each element. And, everything in a town fits into one of the eight element categories.

When you're out exploring and can't find information about a town, go through the checklist of the eight elements and ask yourself these questions. They will help you see the area with new eyes.

8 Rural Culture Elements

1. Architecture: Stone, wood, iron, or brick? What materials were used to build the structures and why were they used? When were the buildings constructed? By whom? What style of architecture are they, and how have structures evolved?

2. Art: Keep your eyes and ears open for murals, music, statues, grassroots art, art museums, galleries, artists at work, and performing centers. Think textiles, literature, and dance. You may be surprised at the heritage and diversity of art in Kansas.

3. Commerce: Look for evidence of early businesses. How did they shape the community? What businesses remain and how have they survived? What are the current common types of commerce? Who are the entrepreneurs? Be aware of the ongoing drama of the rural economy.

4. Cuisine: What specialty foods, ethnic dishes, recipes, and ingredients will you find? What sorts of eateries? A home-cooking cafe, locally owned restaurant, bar and grill, something completely different?

5. Customs: Customs are seen in annual events, long-standing community practices, and sometimes in hard-to-notice daily rituals. Usually they are an action, often colorful, sometimes common, and certainly they can be quirky.

6. Geography: Anything on the natural side fits here. Landmarks, hiking trails, scenic drives, lakes, birds and wildlife, trees, wildflowers, grasses, pastures, hills, gardens, rivers and streams—and the varying natural landscapes. Notice the changes from one physiographic region to another.

7. History: Evidence of history is easy, and exciting, to find in museums, at historic sites, and on historical markers. But keep looking. You'll find it in cemeteries and in architecture. It's carved into rocks, preserved in the landscape and community events, even written on the backs of menus.

8. People: Famous citizens, historic characters, and ethnic groups—they all influence our towns and communities. But no more than have our everyday folks, both from past and present. Visit with the locals.

The Explorer Way

- Dare to do dirt

- Visit with the locals

- Eat made-from-scratch at small town cafes

- Buy local

- Get to know a town rather than judge it

- Choose a quest

- Use the 8 Rural Culture Elements to see Kansas with new eyes.

- Enjoy the journey

Kansas Explorers Club

A project of the Kansas Sampler Foundation, the Kansas Explorers Club was designed to create an audience for rural communities. Kansas Explorers have had some great fun together, from group adventures and Bring Your Own Lawn Chair events, to difference-making activities like the Whiting Cafe Makeover and helping develop the World's Largest Baseball in Muscotah. More good times are ahead!

Membership is $18.61 for individuals, $30 for families. Membership benefits include five print newsletters a year, your own Explorer number, and knowledge of the secret greeting ritual! Join us at explorekansas.org.

Connect: facebook.com/ervoyage.com, facebook.com/kansasexplorersclub, explorekansas.org.

Kansas Sampler Foundation

The Kansas Sampler Foundation's mission is to preserve and sustain rural culture by educating the public about Kansas and by networking and supporting rural communities. The Inman-based public nonprofit is a 501(c)(3) organization. Mil Penner and daughter Marci Penner established the foundation in 1993.

Board members: Christy Hopkins, Shelia Lampe, Eric Montgomery, Andrea Springer, Shari Wilson
Staff: Marci Penner, WenDee Rowe, Kim Clark

Connect: kansassampler.org, info@kansassampler.org.

Northwest Kansas

Counties: Cheyenne, Decatur, Ellis, Gove, Graham, Logan, Norton, Phillips, Rawlins, Rooks, Sheridan, Sherman, Thomas, Trego, Wallace

EXPLORER ELEMENT EXAMPLES

Architecture: Cottonwood Ranch State Historic Site, Studley

Art: Giant Van Gogh Painting, Goodland

Commerce: Fresh Seven Coffee at Union Square, St. Francis

Cuisine: Third Street Bakery, Phillipsburg

Customs: Large Fishing Pole at Cedar Bluff Lake and State Park, Trego County

Geography: Little Jerusalem, Logan County

History: Fort Wallace Museum, Wallace

People: Walter Chrysler Boyhood Home, Ellis

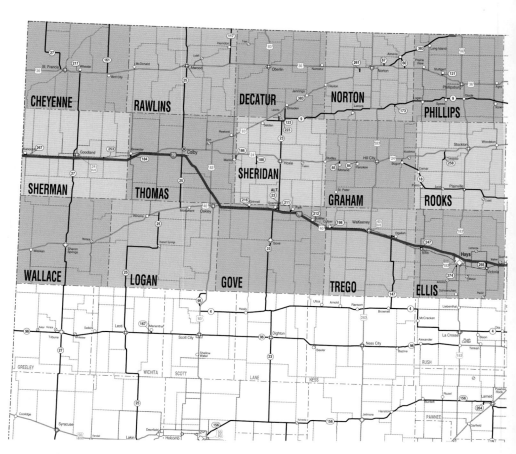

Cheyenne County

AROUND THE COUNTY

Land and Sky Kansas Scenic Byway:
For 88 miles along K-27 between Sharon Springs and Nebraska, travelers will be immersed in views of cropland, livestock, and wildlife. The route's unique features include Mount Sunflower, the highest point in the state; a giant reproduction of a Van Gogh sunflower painting; and the Arikaree Breaks. travelks.com/ksbyways.

Arikaree Breaks:
In St. Francis, from Washington, 2½ miles north on Benton (becomes 14). At the fork, stay right and continue 1 mile on 14. Watch for the numbered red-disk signs as you go 13½ miles north into Nebraska on 15 (unpaved). In Nebraska, go 8 miles west on U.S. 34 to Haigler, then, back into Kansas, continue 22 miles southeast on K-27 to U.S. 36. This breathtakingly beautiful area of rough terrain and deep canyons that stretches across the corners of Kansas and Nebraska is an anomaly in the High Plains. Water carved the rugged landscape into the wind-blown loess deposits that blanketed this area. Dominated by abundant yucca, sage, and native buffalo grass, the Breaks are simply so different from any other part of the state, you will be delighted and amazed. Dry weather roads. We recommend the self-guided driving tour brochure available at the Cheyenne County Museum or at tinyurl.com/arikbreaks. 785.332.3508.

Three Corners:
From U.S. 36, 13 miles north on K-27, 4 miles west on W, 2½ miles north on 3, 4½ miles northwest on 2, then cross a cattle guard and continue almost 3 miles northwest on a pasture driveway. The junction

of Kansas, Nebraska, and Colorado is in a cattle pasture and is marked by cattle panels surrounding a simple bronze bench mark and plaque. This entire area is on private property, so please be respectful; this gracious landowner has allowed public access to this historic landmark. Dry weather roads. 785.332.3508.

Devil's Gap:
From U.S. 36, 13 miles north on K-27, 4 miles west on W, then 2½ miles north on 3. Look for the red-disk marker. On New Year's Day 1865 American Indian tribes that had camped at Cherry Creek (see next entry) passed through here enroute to attack Old Julesburg, Colorado. The depths of the canyons at this point are astounding. Dry weather roads.

Cherry Creek Encampment:
From St. Francis, 1½ miles west on U.S. 36, then 1½ miles north on K-27. The Cheyenne survivors (83 men and 95 women and children) of the November 1864 Sand Creek Massacre came to this site to regroup. As word of the tragic and senseless massacre spread, 3,000 warriors from various tribes joined the survivors here to plan their revenge—the attack and raids near Old Julesburg, Colorado, in January 1865. The tribes then returned

here to share the plunder. The Plains Indian Wars began on this spot, culminating 12 years later in 1876 at the Battle of the Little Bighorn in Montana. At this encampment site, as a tribute to the Sand Creek Massacre survivors, local historian Tobe Zweygardt has welded and erected a series of iron figures depicting, for example, an

Indian astride his horse atop a bluff guarding a tipi. Tobe has also created a large sign listing the names of the Cheyenne who survived the massacre.

Red-Disk Markers:
In an effort to preserve area history, Fred Magley and his wife, Marsha, began creating disk-blade markers in the 1980s. The Magleys' 400 informative disks are placed throughout the county (and a few out-of-county) to mark important historic sites, one-room schoolhouses, cemeteries, and post offices.

BIRD CITY

Population 441

Street Names:
In 1886 Benjamin Bird formed a company to establish a townsite. Streets were named for town company members including Ketcham, Penn, Demick, Bird, Cave, Rich, and Burr.

WPA Projects:
Van Doren Park's sandstone and brick entrance pillars (Rich and LeBow)

and the stone shelter house and outdoor fireplace were built by the WPA in 1935. The attractive sandstone construction of City Hall (111 E. Bressler) was a 1936 WPA project.

Hometown Market:
112 W. Bressler. The Hometown Market is well managed, clean, locally supported, and welcomes you to stop in for a hometown shopping experience. Monday-Saturday 8 a.m.-6 p.m. 785.734.2050. FB.

Bird City Century II Development Foundation:
107 W. Bressler. This renovated former American Legion Hall is the office for two foundations and serves as a community center. The American Legion Memorial Flag room can be visited when the Century II office is open. Monday-Thursday 8:30 a.m.-4:30 p.m. 785.734.2556.

Sand-Green Golf: 3 miles north on K-161, 1 mile west on Q, then ½ mile north on 27. For a High Plains recreational experience, play nine holes on this sand-green course. Greens fee.

Ancient Indian Traders Trail:
From U.S. 36, ½ mile west to K-161. From this junction to the Nebraska state line, K-161 was designated the Ancient Indian Traders Trail in 2014 by the state legislature and is marked by a white disk. The trail was documented to have been used for thousands of years by various tribes traveling throughout this region for hunting, trading, tracking enemy tribes, seeking religious or sacred sites, and accessing fresh water and groves of trees in the arid climate.

Big Ed's Steakhouse:
104 W. Bressler. Big Ed's big open room greets you with murals, animal mounts, a pressed-tin ceiling, and an old wood floor—imagine the thousands of cowboy boots that have walked across it! Customers have come here for years knowing they will get a consistently good meal and fresh, hand-cut steaks. Monday-Saturday 5-10 p.m. 785.734.2475.

ST. FRANCIS

Population 1,310

St. Francis Motorcycle Museum:
110 E. Washington. If you are a vintage motorcycle fanatic or a fan of gleaming, colorful things, this museum, which opened in 2016, will certainly get you revved up. In addition to the early Indian and Harley-Davidson classics, you'll see more than 100 machines of many makes including Flanders, Cleveland, Suzuki, Yamaha, and Triumph. Daily 10 a.m.-5 p.m. Donation welcome. 785.332.2400. stfrancismotorcyclemuseum.org.

Cheyenne County Museum:
201 W. U.S. 36. A likeness of astronaut Ron Evans' Apollo 17 module is displayed outside, and inside is a small exhibit about this St. Francis native. Among other exhibits is a diorama illustrating the county's history from prehistoric days through the 1864 Cherry Creek Encampment. A display on Jack Weinstein tells this man's heroic story (see p. 11). Memorial Day-Labor Day, Thursday-Saturday 9:30 a.m.-12:30 p.m. 785.332.2504.

Cheyenne County Courthouse (NRHP):
212 Washington. Built with buff brick and limestone trim, this 1925 Modern Eclecticism structure holds center stage in the courthouse square. Monday-Friday 8 a.m.-5 p.m.

Sawhill Park (NRHP):
E. Washington. On the site of the county's first courthouse, the park and the band shell were completed in 1934 by WPA workers. Howard Sawhill, for whom the park is named, designed it around the large center fountain. But perhaps the most unique feature is the

art deco horseshoe-shaped concrete amphitheater. Sawhill, an artist by education, would be pleased to see the new modern sculptures that dot the grounds. Sawhill's case of drafting tools that he used to design the park can be seen at the Cheyenne County Museum.

Sawhill Park Art:
The Sawhill Park sculptures were created by native son Glenn Zweygardt. Two of the three pieces, *Earthen Parents* and *Stone Pass Through*, were installed in 2012.

Quincy Gallery and the Cheyenne Center for Creativity: 109 N. Quincy. "Enhancing Lives Through Creativity and the Arts," the Cheyenne Center, which opened in 2012, offers a gallery of local and regional works. Thursday-Friday 9:30 a.m.-3:30 p.m.; Saturday 9:30 a.m.-12:30 p.m. 785.332.0308. FB.

Fresh Seven Coffee at Union Square: 312 W. Washington. Travelers drive out of their way to stop at this rehabbed building for the fresh coffee and healthy food and to meet the friendly owners, Heidi and Kale, and their staff. Along with the made-from-scratch food, enjoy the hand-crafted coffee (roasted on site) or a cocktail, whatever mood strikes you. Monday-Friday 7 a.m.-7 p.m.; Saturday 8 a.m.-12 p.m. 785.772.0823. FB.

Cheyenne Bowl and Dairy King: 709 S. Quincy. A rare Dairy King combines with a bowling alley to create a doubly fun experience. Bowling, pizza, burritos, sandwiches of all kinds, and ice cream treats—who could ask for more! Monday, Thursday-Saturday 11 a.m.-10 p.m.; Sunday 12 p.m.-10 p.m. 785.332.9139. FB.

Lodging: Spencer House Bed & Breakfast (785.332.2513, thespencerhousebandb.com); Jackson Suite (785.332.5001, FB); additional lodging (tinyurl.com/staysainty).

explorer extras... In St. Francis

In 1992 the town pitched in and saved the 1949 city-owned Cheyenne Theater, 104 W. Washington, from becoming a warehouse. Movies are now showing, Friday-Sunday. 785.332.2747. cheyennetheater.com. **ee**

WHEELER

Unincorporated

Cheyenne Valley Cemetery: From U.S. 36, south ½ mile on K-27. Sergeant Jack Weinstein was bestowed the Medal of

Honor post-humously in 2014 when President Obama presented the award to Weinstein's widow, Nancy. Although he had received the Distinguished Service Cross for courageous action during the Korean War, he was one of 24 who had not been awarded the Medal of Honor because of prejudice against Jewish and Hispanic soldiers. Weinstein, who died in 2006, is buried here. His story is told at the Cheyenne County Museum. Also of interest in this cemetery are the four bronze miniature

military statues donated by Fred Magley's family to honor him and all Cheyenne County military veterans. Fred, who posted the red-disk historical markers throughout the county, also made the one in this cemetery to mark the grave of baby Grant Barnhouse who died in 1910.

Decatur County

explorer extras... In Dresden

Population 41

Mona's Market at 320 E. Main is a delightful nursery in a small town. It's accented by horse-

shoes, wooden drawers, old water pumps, and barn wood cleverly placed among the bedding plants, shrubs, trees, vegetable plants, and more. Open in season. 785.475.3921. monasmarket.com. **ee**

JENNINGS

Population 95

The Jennings entrance sign invites you to "Czech Us Out."

Czech Memorial Museum: 118 S. Kansas. A former Methodist church and the Royal Neighbors of America building are home to this museum, which contains displays about the area's Czech heritage. The buildings are connected with a covered walkway that houses a veterans memorial. 785.678.2652.

WPA Project: 121 S. Kansas. This beautifully maintained native limestone city hall was built by the WPA in 1939. At one time it housed a movie theater and currently is a community

building, senior center, and library. Monday, Wednesday 1-3 p.m.; Friday 4-6 p.m.; Saturday 9-11 a.m. 785.678.2666.

NORCATUR

Population 150

U.S. Highway 36 Association Museum:

101 S. Decatur. Opened in 2016, this museum is the depository for national and state archives and artifacts pertaining to the history of U.S. 36. The highway had its beginnings in 1913 and extends from Ohio to Colorado. Museum exhibits include tools used in building the road, construction photos, and replicas of early motels and filling stations along the route. Tuesday, Thursday, Saturday 10 a.m.-2 p.m. 785.693.4597.

OBERLIN

Population 1,761

Pioneer Sculpture:

U.S. 36 and Penn. Created in 1971 by Pete Felten, this four-member Pioneer Family "resides" on the north side of Oberlin.

Historic Bank of Oberlin (NRHP) and Landmark Inn:

189 S. Penn. Many homesteaders depended on this 1886 bank, which today houses the Landmark Inn. An impressive red-brick

structure, it's still the signature building in town and has been restored to its Victorian splendor. The Landmark Inn, elegantly decorated with antique furnishings and vintage wallpaper, offers five second-story Victorian suites, and one ground-floor modern room with a Jacuzzi. Guests can enjoy a complimentary full gourmet breakfast in the Teller Room Restaurant. 785.475.2340. landmarkinn.com.

Teller Room Restaurant:

189 S. Penn. The teller cage, high ceilings, and massive cherry-stained windows are clues that you're in for a grand experience in the Teller Room, located on the first floor of the historic Bank of Oberlin. The menu changes daily, but owner Gary Anderson says the Southwest Chicken and Lemon Herb Salmon are popular entrees. Among the fortunes inside this old bank are the German chocolate hot fudge ice cream sundae and other tasty desserts. Monday-Saturday 11:30 a.m.-1:30 p.m.; Thursday-Saturday 6-8 p.m. Open for coffee and desserts, Monday-Saturday 9:30 a.m.-5 p.m. Reservations recommended. 785.475.2340.

Oberlin Mercantile Company:

189 S. Penn. Local art, Kansas books and food products, Victorian collectibles, collectible toys, and year-round Christmas items fill the shelves inside this delightful old-fashioned Victorian mercantile. Monday-Saturday 9 a.m.-5:30 p.m.; Thursday-Saturday 6-8 p.m. 785.475.2340.

Decatur County Courthouse:

120 E. Hall. Built in 1927 with orange brick and stone trim, this Modern Eclecticism structure features all marble floors and staircase. Outside the courtroom take note of Barb Beisner's mural of the

last Indian raid and other county depictions. Monday-Friday 8 a.m.-5 p.m. 785.475.8102.

Downtown: The all-weather sidewalk canopies and light fixtures, mounted in 1972, and the red-brick streets combine to create a pleasant downtown atmosphere.

The Dresser: 152 S. Penn. Hats off to the more than 100 all-female co-operative investors who keep this fine women's boutique up and running in Oberlin! Monday-Friday 9:30 a.m.-5 p.m.; Saturday 10 a.m.-2 p.m. 785.475.3407.

Old Czech Country Antiques:

301 W. Frontier. Primitives, weathered barn wood, rustic treasures, and more make this a dandy place to scavenge. The hand-painted signs are intriguing too. Most days 9:30 a.m.-5:30 p.m. 785.470.4363. oldczechcountry.com.

Decatur County Last Indian Raid Museum:

258 S. Penn. The events of the 1878 Indian raid in Kansas are told here from both the settler and Indian points of view. The tragedy unfolded on September 30, 1878, when Chiefs Dull Knife and Little Wolf and their Cheyenne warriors killed many settlers during their flight from the Oklahoma reservation to their native homelands in the north. In addition to its artifact and photo collections, the museum complex comprises 15 buildings. April-November, Tuesday-Friday 10 a.m.-12 p.m.

and 1-4 p.m.; year round, Saturday 10 a.m.-2 p.m. Admission charge. 785.475.2712. decaturcountylastindianraid museum.com.

Last Indian Raid Monument:
E. U.S. 36 (Oberlin Cemetery). On the cemetery's north side a memorial commemorates the lives of the 19 settlers killed during the last Indian raid in Kansas in 1878. Their graves were the beginnings of this cemetery. A historical marker at the roadside stop beside the cemetery explains the circumstances of the raid.

WPA Band Shell:
E. Hall and S. Marks. A 1939 WPA band shell and two early limestone pillars are historic highlights in City Park.

Historical Mural:
108 E. Ash. In the lobby of the Good Samaritan senior-living home, a wonderful mural created in 2007 by Jeanette Diederich depicts historic scenes in Decatur County. The mural includes Elephant Rock near Traer, a longtime landmark that weather has destroyed. Daily 8 a.m.-8 p.m.

Sunflower Recreation:
220 N. Penn. How lucky can this town be to have a new bowling alley and cinema! Volunteers run the cinema, and two employees

operate the six-lane bowling alley. Bowling, Thursday-Saturday 5-9 p.m.; movies, Friday-Saturday 7 p.m., Sunday afternoon. 785.470.2200. FB.

Frontier Restaurant:
209 E. Frontier. Homemade food is the mainstay on this frontier. Chicken-fried steak is made the Explorer Way, and the meringue on the coconut cream pie is standing high! Monday-Saturday 6:30 a.m.-8 p.m.; Sunday 7 a.m.-2 p.m. 785.475.3429.

The Re-Load: 133 S. Penn. Gleaming dark wood floors, a high ceiling, a warm environment, and the aromas of spicy pizza greet you here. Lunch on Fridays offers Explorer Way chicken-fried steak, and Rocky Mountain oysters are up for grabs Fridays and Saturdays. Monday-Saturday 11 a.m.-10 p.m. 785.475.2421. FB.

explorer extras... In Oberlin

The small Ferris wheel and other spinning rides are part of the longest-running, home-owned carnival in Kansas, dating to 1973. The rides rest at 706 W. Frontier while waiting for the next fair, starting the first Tuesday of each August. FB.

It's a little known fact but Sappa Park, 2 miles east of Oberlin on U.S. 36, was the first national park in Kansas. In 1935 the National Park Service (NPS) approved construction of the park and lake just east of town on Sappa Creek. The Civilian Conservation Corps built the park and the WPA constructed the lake, both under NPS supervision. Dedicated in 1939, Sappa Park was the first National Park Property in Kansas and was operated by the NPS until presented to the State of Kansas in 1939.

Remote control car racing, a fun pastime, is increasing in

popularity, and kids and adults alike have a great time racing 1/10-scale remote control cars on tracks at E. Maple and N. Garfield (offroad track) and at Sappa Park (oval track). Stop by and watch or bring your cars and race! 785.475.2271. ee

Ellis County

AROUND THE COUNTY

Ellis County Churches:
Visible from miles away, the spires rising through the treetops mark the more than a dozen historic churches that dot the Ellis County landscape. These handsome structures are a testament to the Volga German imprint on this area. A historic churches self-guided tour brochure is available in Hays at the visitor center, 2700 Vine, and at tinyurl.com/elliscohistoricchurches.

CATHARINE

Unincorporated

Immigrants that came from Katharinestadt, Russia, in 1876 established Catharine. A sign on the north edge of town states the name of both cities.

St. Catherine Church:
1681 St. Joseph. Dedicated in 1892, the native limestone church was constructed mainly by parishioners. Trumpeting your arrival, two white angel statues stand atop the entrance pillars. 785.623.6847.

Pioneer Cross: On the St. Catherine grounds, a cross standing within a landscaped ring signifies where settlers gathered to pray when they first arrived in 1876.

Big John's Saloon: 2111 Catharine. The Wednesday night burritos are famous, and customers love the seafood on Friday nights! Tuesday-Saturday, 4 p.m.-2 a.m. 785.621.4700. FB.

ELLIS

Population 2,090

Walter P. Chrysler Boyhood Home (NRHP): 102 W. 10th. The family of Walter Chrysler, founder of the Chrysler automobile, moved to Ellis from Wamego in 1878 when Walter was only three

years old. A short video tells about his life, and the museum is filled with Chrysler's personal and automobile memorabilia, including one of his 1924 cars. March-October, Tuesday-Saturday 9 a.m.-4 p.m.; November-February, Tuesday-Saturday 11 a.m.-3 p.m.; year round, Sunday 1-4 p.m. Admission charge. 785.726.3636. chryslerboyhoodhome.com.

Ellis Railroad Museum: 911 Washington. At home in this two-story, red-brick former city hall, the museum displays artifacts and early photos of Ellis' railroad heritage. You'll see switchman lanterns, a telegraph room, and an elaborate model railroad layout. Outside, a two-and-a-half-mile mini-train

ride takes you past the historic Penokee depot and a Union Pacific caboose. April-October, Tuesday-Saturday 9 a.m.-3 p.m. For train ride schedule, call 785.726.4493.

Memorial Park: 9th and Washington. Memorials come in all shapes and sizes in this shaded little park. Plaques provide the commemorative significance of a fountain, benches, an armillary sphere, a granite memorial to the 1866 settlers from Bukovina, Austria; a drinking fountain with a goose reaching for grapes; and *The Railroader*, a bronze statue by Ellis native Thomas Schlotterback.

Bukovina Society: 103 W. 8th. Located in the former First Congregational Church (NRHP), the Society's headquarters operate a research center, and its museum maintains a collection of artifacts from early Bukovina immigrants. Call ahead, 785.623.7844. bukovinasociety.org.

St. Mary's Church: 703 Monroe. Four roof-top crosses mark this striking 1911 brick and limestone church.

The beautiful interior features statuary, most of which were imported from Munich, Germany. 785.726.4522.

Mount Hope Cemetery: From Washington, ½ mile east on E. 12th. Within the cemetery's 1940 WPA walls are a Pioneer Woman statue dedicated in 1933, a GAR Union soldier statue, and a small Pete Felten limestone sculpture of Ellis' legendary Praying John Horrigan.

Arthur's Pizza & Mexican Foods: 103 W. 9th. Five crusts, 17 toppings, homemade sauces and dough, and daily specials have kept hungry folks happy since 1986. Daily 11 a.m.-8:30 p.m. 785.726.4683. FB.

Lodging: Ellis Lakeside Campground (785.726.4812, ellis.ks.us/camp.htm).

explorer extras... In Ellis

The 1920 Warren pony truss bridge, W. 11th and Dorrance, is closed to traffic but open to pedestrians for a pleasant stroll across Big Creek.

In the downtown area on Washington, look for the big sunflowers painted on the street intersections. These colorful images were added in the 1950s to welcome visitors. Volunteers gather each May to repaint the sunflowers in time for the annual alumni reunion.

The public is invited to golf at the nine-hole, grass-green Ellis Golf Club, 1301 Spruce. A bar and grill awaits you after the last hole. 785.726.4711. ellisgolfclub.com.

The shortest state highway in Kansas is K-247 at Ellis, running a little over 417 feet south from I-70. **ee**

explorer extras...
Near Emmeram

Unincorporated

The 1901 Sacred Heart Church at Emmeram burned down in 1998, and the charred scent is still present. Parts of the limestone walls remain, and even in its ravaged state these ruins retain a sense of beauty. The parish closed in 1967. From Catharine, go 1½ miles east on Catherine, 2 miles north on Codell, then 3 miles east on Emmeram. **ee**

HAYS

Population 21,038

Sternberg Museum of Natural History:

3000 Sternberg. From Vine, ¾ mile east on 27th. Ancient animals come to life inside the Sternberg. Venture into the walk-through diorama depicting life more than 70 million years ago. You'll be amazed by the life-sized, robotic dinosaurs, various plant eaters, and huge flying reptiles in a subtropical environment. Then walk down into the sea that once covered Kansas and discover prehistoric marine animals. The most photographed fossil in the world is on display here—

the Fish-Within-a-Fish— excavated by George F. Sternberg in 1952 in Gove County. Tuesday-Saturday 9 a.m.-6 p.m.; Sunday 1-6 p.m. (October-March, closed Mondays). Admission charge. 785.628.4286. sternberg.fhsu.edu.

Fort Hays State Historic Site (NRHP):

1472 U.S. 183 Alternate. Pete Felten's limestone buffalo at the entrance is your signal that you're about to go back to 1867. The military fort was established in that year to protect travelers on the Smoky Hill Trail and workers building the Kansas Pacific Railway. The original blockhouse, guardhouse, and officers' quarters still stand, and excellent interpretive signs relate the story of military presence in the West. Spend some time examining the storytelling carvings on the guardhouse limestone walls.

Start in the visitor center to gain an understanding of this historic fort. Wednesday-Saturday 9 a.m.-5 p.m. Admission charge. 785.625.6812. kshs.org.

Blue Light Lady: Elizabeth Polly died from cholera in 1867 while helping ailing soldiers in the Fort Hays hospital. She was buried on Sentinel Hill two miles south of the guardhouse. Thirty years later her ghost was first spotted, and it is occasionally still seen today. Some say she appears in a misty blue light,

giving rise to the moniker "Blue Light Lady." A Pete Felten statue of her stands on a stone pedestal in Elizabeth Polly Park at 26th and Indian Trail.

Buffalo Herd: U.S. 183 Alternate (in West Frontier Park across from historic Fort Hays). The small buffalo herd in residence here started in 1953 with a bull named Wild Bill and a cow named Calamity Jane!

Frontier Park: From Main, ½ mile west on U.S. 183 Alternate. Frontier Park is a scenic recreational area complete with walking trails, disc golf, tree stump art, and stone shelters built by the National Youth Administration in 1938 and 1939.

Fort Hays State University: 600 Park. Founded in 1902 on the grounds of an abandoned frontier military post, this campus features many stone structures, including an 1874 schoolhouse, a 1934 pedestrian bridge, and the 1937 WPA Lewis Field football stadium. Art enthusiasts will want to stop at the Moss-Thorns Gallery of Art in Rarick Hall. Also worth noting are the many outdoor sculptures throughout the campus. fhsu.edu.

Ellis County Historical Society and Museum Complex:

100 W. 7th. The museum is at home in a 1926 addition to the 1879 First Presbyterian Church (the oldest church in Hays; NRHP). Inside this stately red-brick structure you are introduced to area personalities such as Buffalo Bill Cody, Wild Bill Hickok, George Custer, and George Grant. Exhibits also focus on locally significant topics including the Dust Bowl, water, and ethnic immigration. The museum complex comprises the 1879 stone church, a Volga German Haus, a reconstructed typical early immigrant home, Younger Harness Shop, and the Hays

Fire Department Museum. Behind the museum is a tall piece of limestone that Buffalo Bill Cody had used for target practice. Tuesday-Saturday 11 a.m.-5 p.m. Admission charge. 785.628.2624.

Stone Gallery: 107 W. 6th. You may run into famous stone sculptor Pete Felten between 10 a.m. and 4 p.m. at his studio and gallery in Shinbone Alley. But if you can't find him you're welcome to explore the outdoor courtyard. The limestone wall filled with carvings of animals, shapes, and arches is Pete's lifelong artistic endeavor. Nearly 30 of his stone sculptures are found throughout Hays and Ellis County. A guided-tour brochure, which provides a map and depictions of his works, is at 2700 Vine and at tinyurl.com/feltenstonetour.

Ellis County Courthouse: 1204 Fort. This native limestone courthouse is a 1942 WPA project. *Justice and Equality: An Evolving Legacy*, a 2002 Kris Kuksi acrylic mural, hangs behind the judge's bench in the courtroom. Near the courthouse a veterans memorial at 13th and Fort honors the Ellis County soldiers who gave their lives while serving our country.

Historic District: 502 and 504 W. 12th. The Justus Bissing Jr. Historic District (NRHP) offers two examples of Bissing's architectural skills. The 1920 two-story, red-brick house, 502 W. 12th, combines Craftsman and Prairie School styles; and the 1932 Tower Service Station, 504 W. 12th, was built in a Queen Anne variation style. A Volga German immigrant, Bissing was a well-known craftsman, designer, and inventor in Hays.

Boot Hill Cemetery: 18th and Fort. The first Kansas cemetery called Boot Hill is in Hays. It is marked by a

dedication plaque and by the Pete Felten sculpture *The Homesteader*. This cemetery served the town between 1867 and 1873 and estimates are that 79 people are buried in this first Boot Hill cemetery west of the Mississippi.

Mount Allen Cemetery: 27th and Vine. It's the only cemetery in the state with not one but two old-time tree swings, but few facts about them are known. Much history is tied to many of the gravestones here. In 1875 Sheriff Alexander Ramsey died in a shootout with a horse thief. His grave marker states he was killed by an outlaw in pursuit of his duty. A poignant statue of a little boy and his dog mark the resting place of five-year-old Jack Downing who died from diphtheria in 1878. The dog was Jack's constant companion as the two roamed about town. tinyurl.com/mountallen.

Chestnut Street Historic District (NRHP): From Vine, ¾ mile west on 13th, then south on Main into historic downtown Hays. A century ago the commercial and social life in Hays centered on Chestnut Street (now Main) where residents gathered to meet friends and shop. During the past 15 years the soul of Hays has been restored, and you can feel the energy in the renovated buildings, new businesses (such as a microbrewery and

trendy restaurants), and works of art. 785.628.8201. chestnutstreetdistrict.com.

Hays Arts Center Gallery: 112 E. 11th. Admire the changing exhibits and shop in the gallery store, which specializes in local Kansas art. Ask here about other area art galleries. Monday-Friday 10 a.m.-4 p.m.; Saturday 10 a.m.-1 p.m. 785.625.7522. haysartscouncil.org.

Green Bean Dumpling Soup Circuit: Grun Bohna und Kneebble Suppe is a traditional recipe handed down through generations and brought to Hays by the Volga Germans. Because so many local restaurants serve this soup, the Kansas Sampler Foundation named Hays the Green Bean Dumpling Soup Capital of Kansas. The restaurants that serve this warm, hearty dish year-round are Augustine's Bakery, Gella's Diner, and Vernies (*see* following entries).

Gella's Diner and Lb. Brewing: 115 E. 11th. Wondering about the name? Both reference the Volga German heritage. Lb. stands for "liquid bread" and is a nod to field-working settlers who drank beer when they couldn't stop for lunch. Gella's means "you know" and is said at the end of a sentence to make sure the listener agrees. Everyone agrees that the handcrafted microbrews and regional cuisine are award winning. Opening in 2005 the innovative architecture spans four storefronts in the heart of the Chestnut

Street Historic District. Kitchen hours, daily 11 a.m.-10 p.m. 785.621.2739. lbbrewing.com.

Augustine's Bakery:

1305 Main. Treat yourself to Volga German favorites such as Kuchen (German coffee cake), Spitzbuben (sugar cookies filled with jam), and Kolaches (sweet yeast dough pastries with fruit or poppy seed fillings). Homemade bierocks and fried noodles with dumplings and white beans are popular items here too. Tuesday-Friday 7 a.m.-3 p.m.; Saturday 7 a.m.-12 p.m. 785.621.2253. augustinesbakery.com.

Vernie's Hamburger House:

527 E. 17th. Since 1969 folks have been pulling into Vernie's for a juicy burger, a legendary milkshake, chili, and more. In keeping with the local German heritage, Vernie's serves Grebble fried bread with a side of syrup. Tuesday-Saturday 10 a.m.-8 p.m. 785.628.1462. vernieshamburgerhouse.com.

Al's Chickenette:

700 Vine. Al's has had near legendary status in these parts since 1949. And although the ownership has changed, the neon sign and recipes remain the same. The seasoning is mixed by hand for the famous fried-chicken dinners. Wednesdays feature the popular chicken pot pie, and every day homemade ice cream tops the made-from-scratch dessert pies.

May-August, daily 11 a.m.-9 p.m; September-April, Monday-Tuesday 11 a.m.-3 p.m. and Wednesday-Sunday 11 a.m.-9 p.m. 785.625.7414. FB.

Soda Shoppe Cafe:

800 Main (enter through Northwest Printers).This 1940s soda fountain is a nostalgic stop in the center of the Chestnut Street Historic District. Fountain treats are accompanied by sandwiches and a hot daily special. Lunch, Monday-Saturday 11 a.m.-2 p.m. 785.625.7323.

Sake 2 Me: 700 Main. Sushi in a Volga German community in Kansas? The environment in this former filling station is vibrant and the menu is outstanding. Sushi chefs are dedicated to their art and are happy to have you watch them roll your order. Try the Kansas Roll and for those who don't like sushi, the Bang Bang Shrimp will become your addiction. Monday-Saturday 11 a.m.-2 p.m. and 5-10 p.m. 785.301.2999. FB.

Defiance Brewing Co.

Taproom: 2050 E. U.S. 40. No food, just great beer! Gutch, Thrasher, Happy Feet, Flannel Pants, and Joe Man Bun are brewed right here. 785.301.2337. Thursday-Saturday 4-8 p.m. defiancebeer.com.

More Good Restaurants:

Gutch's Bar and Grill (111 W. 7th, 785.623.4088, gutchspizza.com); Pheasant Run Pancake House (3201 Vine, 785.628.1044, FB); The Paisley Pear and Cafe (1100 Main, 785.621.4660, paisleypear.net); TRIO Tap House (1106 E. 27th, 785.621.2221, FB). Find more at haysusa.net.

Blue Sky Miniature Horse

Farm: 1710 Canterbury. Set amid the rolling hills and river valleys north of Hays, Blue Sky Farm is the home of miniature show horses. Owners Marion and Donna Schmidt provide a fun group tour where you'll watch their champion horses perform, see a grooming demonstration, view the training area and stables, and, best of all, meet all the beautiful little horses. Cart rides pulled by a miniature team top off the tour! Admission charge. Group tours only. 785.625.6725. blueskyhorses.com.

Lodging: haysusa.net.

explorer extras...
In Hays

North of the library at 1205 Main, a marker relates the importance of the Walker Army Airfield. This WWII base, 12½ miles northwest of Hays, operated from 1942 to 1946 (see p. 19). A Statue of Liberty replica erected in 1950 by the Boy Scouts stands just north of the airfield sign.

Founded in 1867, Rome was the first town in this area, established before the military fort and the railroad were built. Buffalo Bill Cody was a promoter of the new town and constructed its first stone building. From Main, go 1 mile west on 12th to see the tall stone marker that stands near the site of Rome.

The Hangman's Bridge marker tells the story of mob hangings here during the town's early years from 1869 to1870. To find this aged bronze monument, from the Rome stone marker, go 350 feet south on Rome, then ¼ mile east on Old U.S. 40.

Although having a street name, Mission Mount, off Elm between 17th and 19th, is actually a sidewalk between two rows of houses that face each other. A Spanish-style apartment complex brings the sidewalk to an end. These rows of Mission style houses were built in 1921 on the highest point in the city.

The Kansas Merci Boxcar, 13th and Canterbury, is one of 49 boxcars that France sent to each state in 1949 as a thank you for the train loads of food the United States shipped to its ally after WWII. To see the displays inside the boxcar, call 785.625.9681.

If you'd like to see a Super Dual Auroral Radar Network, from Main, go ½ mile west on U.S. 183, 2¾ miles south and west on the unpaved Golf Course Road, then just north on 210. This strange looking matrix of silver towers, poles, and wires is a Doppler radar system that measures the effects of the sun's solar flares on our communication systems. tinyurl.com/ksradar. **ee**

MUNJOR

Unincorporated

St. Francis of Assisi Church: 883 Moscow.
Dedicated in 1890, this impressive native limestone church never replaced its steeple lost after a 1932 fire. A Pete Felten statue of St. Francis of Assisi was added in 1978.

Iron Crosses:
From St. Francis Church, ¼ mile south on Moscow, then ½ mile west and south on Kazan. St. Francis of Assisi Cemetery is dotted with iron crosses. Although early burial markers were simple wooden crosses,

Volga German blacksmiths soon replaced them with sturdy crosses made from wrought iron scrap. The crosses truly are works of art!

PFEIFER

Unincorporated

A drive into the Smoky Hill River Valley takes you to the small town of Pfeifer, settled by Volga Germans in 1876-1878. Notice that the landscape changes quickly as you near the sandy river bottom. From 3rd and Old U.S. 40 in Victoria, go 9 miles south on Pfeifer, then ¾ mile west on Schoenchen.

Holy Cross Church
(8 Wonders of Kansas Architecture): 1606 Sarratov. Even though the parish closed in 1993, the pride and spirit of this beautiful and immaculate church are evident. The exterior alone is extraordinary with its 165-foot center spire flanked by 100-foot corner spires. Inside, the 1918 Romanesque Gothic structure features stunning vaulted ceilings on tall quadrille columns. The stained glass was added in 1962. Built of native limestone, Holy Cross sometimes is referred to as the "two cent" church. Funds to build it were raised when each parish family agreed to be assessed two cents on every bushel of wheat sold. Daily 8 a.m.-6 p.m.

Post Rock: You'll see post rock fence posts everywhere in this part of the county. Most posts weigh between 250 and 400 pounds!

SCHOENCHEN

Population 210

Say "Shen-Chen" and you're close. German old-timers say it means "pretty little place."

St. Antonius Kirche:
The name of this splendid and historic limestone church is written in German above the door. Another stone is ornately inscribed, "O.A.M.D.G," which stands for Omnia Ad Majorem Dei Gloriam, Latin for the Jesuit motto, "All for the Greater Glory of God."

St. Anthony Cemetery:
From St. Antonius Kirche, ½ block south on Church, then ½ mile west on Arapahoe. Artworks abound here in the form of elaborate iron cross grave markers whose delicate scrollwork features ivy leafs, sunbursts, cherubs, angels, stars, and more. They are typical of the handcrafted work by Volga German farmers and blacksmiths.

VICTORIA

Population 1,234

When George Grant came to the United States from England in 1872 he encouraged English and Scottish immigration to this area, which he named Victoria in honor of England's queen. In 1875 Volga Germans from southern Russia immigrated here to flee the Czar's army and founded the village of Herzog. *The British soon found pioneer life too demanding and left the area to the Volga Germans. In 1913 the two towns combined under the name Victoria. A historical marker at W. Main and Old U.S. 40 tells the story of Victoria's unusual beginnings.*

St. Fidelis Church (NRHP; 8 Wonders of Kansas):

900 Cathedral. You can't miss the twin bell towers of St. Fidelis rising majestically above the Plains. With a seating capacity of 1,100, St. Fidelis was the largest church west of the Mississippi when it was completed in 1911. Its beauty and size inspired William Jennings Bryan (visiting the area in 1912 on a presidential campaign) to dub it the "Cathedral of the Plains." The stone for this massive Romanesque structure was

hauled in from a quarry seven miles south, and its granite pillars were shipped in from Vermont. In 2014 it was named a minor basilica, the only one in Kansas. Open daily. 785.735.2777. stfidelischurch.com.

Parish Office and Gift Shop:

601 10th. To purchase a memento of your visit to St. Fidelis or if you have questions, visit the office and gift shop across the street from St. Fidelis. Monday-Thursday 8:30 a.m.-4:30 p.m.; Friday 8:30 a.m.-12 p.m. 785.735.2777.

Limestone Statues:

Sculptures of a Volga German family and of a Capuchin Franciscan priest, both near the church, are the work of Pete Felten. The statues are a tribute to the first 23 Volga German families who arrived here in 1876 to establish Herzog.

St. Fidelis Cemetery:

15th and Cathedral. You'll find German inscriptions on the gravestones and on many iron crosses—the cross represents religion and the iron symbolizes strength.

White Cross:

Across from St. Fidelis Cemetery. The white cross marks the site of the community's first Roman Catholic cemetery.

Railroad Workers Memorial:

From 10th, ¾ mile south on Cathedral, then 300 feet southwest on 3rd to the driveway. In this small cemetery, a plaque on a large granite base states that in 1867 Cheyennes killed six railroad laborers who were working near here. An old piece of limestone was the original and only memorial to these workers until it suddenly went missing. Eventually found under a veil of mystery, it was rededicated in 2003 and now rests in a plexiglass-covered box above the granite base.

George Grant Grave and Marker:

From Old U.S. 40, 430 feet south on E. Main, then 500 feet west on 1st to

St. George Cemetery. A plaque on the large limestone marker tells us that Grant (1823-1879) founded Victoria. A small statue of an Aberdeen Angus stands atop the marker.

Stone Bridge:

From Victoria, 1 mile north on Cathedral, then 2 miles west on Victoria. A stone five-arch bridge built by the WPA in 1940 lies just east of the Victoria and 320 junction. Keep your eyes open for Big Creek, then look for the bridge arches beneath the road.

The Library Bar and Grill:

1102 3rd. Put down your cell phone, order a cold one and pick up a book from the shelves while waiting for your hot-off-the-grill food. Tuesday-Saturday 10 a.m.-8 p.m. 785.735.2839.

VINCENT

Unincorporated

George Grant Villa (NRHP):

From Old U.S. 40 in Victoria, 5¼ miles south on Pfeifer, then 1¾ miles east on Grants Villa. A marker explaining the George Grant villa is on the driveway of a working farm, but you're welcome to drive up to the sign. The Grant villa was home of this country's first Aberdeen Angus cattle, shipped from Scotland in 1873.

WALKER

Unincorporated

Walker Army Airfield:

From Walker, 1 mile west on Old U.S. 40, 1¼ curving miles north on 370 (becomes Victoria), then 2 miles north on Vincent. One of the nation's first B-29 Superfortress bomber training air bases, the WWII airfield, now abandoned, leaves only tall brick chimneys, a water tower, remains of hangars and other structures, and huge "No Trespassing" signs. You can drive along the edge of the field and picture the almost 6,000 military and civilian personnel who were stationed here from 1942 to 1946. At that time the base comprised three runways, five hangars, a hospital, recreational centers, and more.

Fort Fletcher Stone Arch Bridge (NRHP): From I-70 exit 172, 4½ miles south on Walker. After crossing Big Creek, pull over and look under the road to see the four-arch bridge. It was completed by the WPA in 1936 and renovated by the county in 2003. The short-lived Fort Fletcher was established in 1865 just west of the bridge. It was moved in 1866 and renamed Fort Hays.

Gove County

Monument Rocks
(8 Wonders of Kansas):
For directions, see next entry. These massive vertical sentinels appear suddenly on the broad,

flat plains. Monument Rocks, also known as Chalk Pyramids, stand along the old Butterfield Overland Despatch route (Smoky Hill Trail) on private property. These rock formations, buried under water for millions of years, are part of the amazing

geological diversity of Kansas. Look for the natural "doors" and "windows" formed in these rock pyramids. Climbing, camping, and fossil hunting are prohibited but you are welcome to walk up to them. Please read visitors' guidelines on the sign. FB.

Gove to Monument Rocks Scenic Back Road: High Plains vegetation, shortgrass prairie, and small chalk formations are a pleasing prelude to your arrival at Monument Rocks. Starting at Gove, go 11½ miles west on 4th (becomes S). Here you'll pass remnants of the early town of Orion (*see* next entry). From S, continue 7 miles south on 22, 4 miles west on L, 4 miles south on 14, 1 mile east on unnamed road, then ½ mile south on 16 to Monument Rocks. For a blacktop route, *see* p. 24.

Orion: From Gove, 11½ miles west on 4th (becomes S) to 22. An abandoned general store on the northwest corner is nearly all that remains of Orion, named for a beloved 1890s teacher Justin Orion McBurney. A tornado, failure of the railroad to come through, and a nearby WWII aerial gunnery range combined to seal the fate of this small town. Gaeland Cemetery lies just east of Orion, its name spelled out in hand-cut tin letters on the entrance gate.

Monument Rocks to Keystone Gallery Scenic Back Road: If the roads are dry, take this subtly spectacular less-traveled route from Monument Rocks to U.S. 83 or to Keystone Gallery (*see* p. 25). Along the way you'll view chalk bluffs in a hilly pasture and pass the Pyramid View Cemetery. From the Chalk Pyramids, go 2½ miles south on 16, 4 miles west on E, 1 mile south on 450, then 1¾ miles west on Dakota to U.S. 83. Keystone Gallery is just west of the highway.

Population 82

Gove City Yarns: 319 Broad. Merlyn and Betty McDonald refurbished a deteriorating building in downtown Gove and gave it new life. Since 2003 it's been home to a neat little shop with room after room displaying

a dizzying array of natural yarns, specialty yarns, buttons, knitting books, and antiques. Monday-Friday 10 a.m.-5 p.m.; Saturday, call 785.938.2255. FB.

Gove County Courthouse: 420 Broad. The smallest county seat in the state, Gove's two-story red-brick courthouse originally was the Benson boardinghouse. It was converted to a courthouse in 1885. Monday-Friday 8 a.m.-5 p.m. 785.938.2300.

Gove County Historical Museum: 505 Washington. Inside a 1920 brick high school, this museum is preserving the legacies of Castle Rock, Monument Rocks (Chalk Pyramids), and also features artifacts and information about county ghost towns. Mid-April to mid-October, Wednesday 10 a.m.-5 p.m. 785.938.2385.

Gove Country Store: 203 Broad. Stop and buy. Visit with Megan about how hard, but rewarding, it is to keep a grocery store open in a town of 80. Fresh salads are sold at noon. Monday-Friday 7:30 a.m.-6 p.m.; Saturday 8 a.m.-2 p.m. 785.938.4434.

Gove Country Kitchen:
203 Broad. Farmers, ranchers, and small-towners are the regulars for hand-pattied burgers made with meat from Grinnell Locker. Monday-Friday 11 a.m.-2 p.m.; Wednesday 5-8 p.m. 785.938.4455.

GRAINFIELD

Population 280

Grainfield Opera House (NRHP): Main and 3rd. This elegant opera house, built in 1887 with local brick and limestone, was renovated in 2012. The embellished iron facade, fabricated by the Mesker Brothers, is one of the earliest and most impressive in Kansas,

and is one of two opera houses remaining in the state whose exterior incorporates the distinctive fleur de lis pattern and opulent detail. Call 785.673.5585.

Harvest Market: 289 Main. Harvest Market and Harvest Spirit adjoin here—groceries on one side, liquor on the other. The community definitely comes together at Harvest. Monday-Saturday 9 a.m.-6 p.m. 785.673.5501.

Main Street Dugout:
223 Main. Homemade pizza is the draw, and if you want to

cheer for a sports team, turn on one of the TVs. Monday-Saturday 11 a.m.-8 p.m. 785.673.4810.

Lodging: Tail Feather Inn Bed and Breakfast (KBBA, 785.673.3170, tailfeatherinn.net).

GRINNELL

Population 264

Hometown Grocery:
102 Adams. Selling homemade breakfast burritos and sandwiches helps support this community-owned store. Monday-Friday 8 a.m.-6 p.m.; Saturday 8 a.m.-12 p.m. 785.824.3260.

Grinnell Farm and Home Center: 109 S. Adams. If you have a hankering for hardware stores, especially those small-but-packed with all things hardware, you'll want to stop at this one. Monday-Friday 8 a.m.-5 p.m.; Saturday 9 a.m.-12 p.m. 785.824.3383. grinnellhardware.com.

Grinnell Locker:
108 S. Adams. Bring a cooler and stock up on fresh, hand-cut and ground meats. Monday-Friday 8 a.m.-6 p.m.; Saturday 8 a.m.-12 p.m. 785.824.3400. FB.

Cow Paddy Golf Course:
N. 3rd. Built in an old cow pasture, this par-3, grass-green course is open to the public and is a self-pay operation. Despite its name, there are no cow paddy hazards. 785.824.3909.

Grinnell-Angelus Area Heritage Center: 110 S. Adams. Housed in the old township building, the museum

is grateful to volunteers for gathering a wide variety of artifacts from Grinnell, Angelus, Orion, Campus, Orange, and the surrounding rural areas. May-October, Tuesday, Thursday 2-4 p.m. 785.824.3458. FB.

**explorer extras...
In Park**

Population 129

Sacred Heart Catholic Church is a landmark recognized by many I-70 travelers because its magnificent single-spire steeple can be seen for miles. Unpaved streets in Park lead you to this 1921 brick church at 202 Cottonwood. Use the south entrance to step inside and see the beautiful stained glass that features various saints. 785.673.4684.

Great Western Cattle Trail: A sign in the green space on 2nd explains that originally (1879) the town of Park was named Buffalo Park.

For a brief time it was on the Great Western Cattle Trail, and in 1880 alone more than 165,000 Texas longhorns came through the town. By 1882 the trail had moved farther west, and in 1895 the town's name was changed to Park. **ee**

QUINTER

Population 955

Castle Rock (8 Wonders of Kansas): From I-70 exit 107, 15 miles south on Castle Rock, 4 miles east on K to the Castle Rock sign, ½ mile north on 80, cross a cattle guard, continue ½ mile north, and take the north fork. Once much larger, Castle Rock has been whittled away by wind and rain erosion and by vandals. During the late 1860s it was a landmark on the Butterfield Overland Despatch route (Smoky Hill Trail), and travelers once passed by here on their way to the Colorado gold fields. From

Castle Rock continue slowly northward along the rutted road to the "badlands." Note that some ruts may force you to turn back. You'll see piles of chalk residue resulting from the deterioration and the ever-changing

nature of these prairie sentinels. Climbing is not advisable as the rock formations are very soft and will break off easily. And please do not quarry any rock; the weather is hard enough on these natural monoliths. Private property.

Ray's Pharmacy: 414 Main. Choose any one of the 13 shiny stools with red leather seats at the 1904 30-foot bar. It provides plenty of room for all who want to order from this old-fashioned soda fountain. Monday-Saturday 9 a.m.-6 p.m. 785.754.3312.

Lodging: Cobblestone Inn (785.754.3600, staycobblestone.com/ks/quinter).

explorer extras...
In Quinter

With an elevation of 2,665, Quinter is the half-mile-high city.

For fresh sandwiches, stop by the deli in the back of Family Market, the successful and well-supported grocery at 231 Main. 785.754.3791. **ee**

Graham County

AROUND THE COUNTY

Placed by the Solomon Valley Heritage Alliance, the blue-roofed kiosks in Bogue, Hill City, Morland, Nicodemus, and Penokee provide helpful information about those towns.

HILL CITY

Population 1,468

Two Main Streets: Main and Pomeroy. Land speculator W.R. Hill, for whom the town was named in 1876, and business partner James P. Pomeroy became embroiled in a vicious feud as the town developed. The quarrel eventually led to the designation of two main streets, each representing one of the men and his followers— Main Street (for W.R. Hill) and Pomeroy Street. The competition was so fierce that when a business opened up on one main street a corresponding business opened up on the other. The two main streets are still evident today (but the feuding has ended!).

Controversial Post Office: Main and Pomeroy. The story goes that an attempt to heal the north-south (Pomeroy-Hill) feud happened in 1917 when a new post office was built at Pomeroy and Main. But bad feelings surfaced when it could not be agreed upon on which side to put the door. In the end, the post office had two doors and these words were inscribed on the sidewalk: "Where we meet and part forever." The maxim can still be read on the sidewalk at Pomeroy and Main in front of what is now a one-door post office.

Ogallala Quartzite: Unique to this area, the green-gray rock is a tightly cemented sandstone from the Ogallala Formation. It can be seen in several buildings including Longfellow Middle School, 203 N. 2nd, constructed in 1920 as Memorial High School. The home at 621 N. Pomeroy also was built with the quartzite along with other stones.

City Hall: 205 N. Pomeroy. Besides having the unique green quartzite on its exterior, this 1938 WPA city hall also has an unusual feature inside—the floors in the hallway and one of the rooms were made from marble chips of different colors. Each color is from a different state. Monday-Friday 9 a.m.- 5 p.m. 785.421.3437.

City Park: Elm and West. Plaques indicate that the gazebo, fireplace, tables, benches, and retaining wall are part of a 1937 WPA project and a 1939 National Youth Administration project. The unusual green quartzite used to build many of the structures makes this park a stand-out and lovely during any season of the year.

Penokee Stone Man: 414 N. West. The best place to unravel the mystery of the Penokee Man is at the Graham County Public Library. An exhibit includes an aerial view and information about this phenomenon. Monday-Friday 9:30 a.m.-5:30 p.m.; Saturday 9:30 a.m.-2:30 p.m. 785.421.2722. On the library's front lawn is a 1984 Pete Felten sculpture of a young girl and her book.

Oil Museum: 801 W. Main (U.S. 24). The museum is in a little tan building beneath the oil derrick. Besides enjoying the scientific information and oil equipment exhibits, you may feel some nostalgia viewing photos of old-time gas stations and looking at all the oil cans of brands long gone. The adjoining Chamber of Commerce will open the

museum for you or will request a key from the nearby Western Hills Motel. 785.421.5621.

Graham County Historical Museum: 103 E. Cherry. Within this well-kept museum are a variety of interesting

Graham County artifacts including a Pony Express saddlebag, early baseball gloves and bats used at Nicodemus, and a genuine 1950s poodle skirt. Monday, Friday 1-4 p.m. 785.421.5421.

Frontier Stage Movie Theater: 305 E. Main. Sit back, relax, and watch a first-run movie for a reasonable price at this community-owned theater operated by volunteers. Friday-Sunday evenings. 785.421.3344. hillcitymovie.com.

Buck's Bar & Grill: 222 N. Pomeroy. Home-style cooking is available all day long. Monday-Saturday 6:30 a.m.-10 p.m.; Sunday 7 a.m.-2 p.m. 785.421.2249. gotbucks.com.

Lodging: Spring Creek Guest House (KBBA, 785.421.4125, kbba.com); additional lodging (785.421.5621, tinyurl.com/grahamcolodging).

Comic Book Collection: 511 W. Main. Within Citizen's State Bank you'll find The Lone Ranger and Tonto, Lassie, Roy Rogers and Trigger, and Tarzan. They are the real riches inside this bank—some 164 western and adventure comic books, framed and displayed on the bank walls. Floyd Riggs' collection of these 1950s comics also include illustrated Zane Grey classics. Monday-Friday 9 a.m.-3:30 p.m. 785.627.3165.

Bas-Relief Sculpture: 511 W. Main (on Citizen's State Bank). This bas-relief mural by Jack Curran depicts the Minium Fossil Quarry and the woman, Charlotte Keith, who helped a young 4-H boy with the excavation of a jaw bone, a critical find that led to further discoveries.

Morland Mercantile: 502 W. Main. The Morland Community Foundation owns the grocery for this town of 155, but by shopping here we can all be supporters. Monday-Friday 9 a.m.-6 p.m.; Saturday 9 a.m.- 2 p.m. 785.627.4040. FB.

Prairie Junction Restaurant: 512 W. Main. A determined and dedicated group of people work hard to keep this quality restaurant operating in Morland. Steaks in the evening; good food and homemade ice cream, always. Monday-Friday 10 a.m.-2 p.m.; Friday-Saturday 5-8 p.m. 785.627.5355.

Anvil: From 5th, the cemetery is 3 blocks east on Main, then ½ mile south on 2nd (becomes 1st). Catching your eye at Morland Cemetery are the anvil and pliers set between two gravestones. They mark the resting places of blacksmith J.E. Prout and his wife, Lena.

Scenic Back Road for Cuspers:

From 5th, 13 miles east on Main (becomes River Road). Paralleling the South Fork of the Solomon River, this route follows the cusp of the Smoky Hills and High Plains physiographic regions. Contrasting landscapes are obvious to the discerning explorer's eye. Follow this mostly sand road until you come to just south of Hill City.

Antelope Lake Park (NRHP):

From K-85, 2¼ miles west on U.S. 24, then 1 mile north on 125. Built in the 1930s as a WPA project, this fishing lake is a popular walking spot among townsfolk. A WPA Pratt truss bridge with a wood plank floor crosses the spring-fed Antelope Creek on the west side of the lake. All stone outhouses and shelters, built as part of the National Youth Administration program, are constructed from a green rock unique to this county.

NICODEMUS

Unincorporated

Nicodemus, a national historic site since 1996, is the oldest surviving town west of the Mississippi established by African Americans following the Civil War.

Nicodemus National Historic Site (NRHP):

304 Washington. Start your visit to this national park in the limestone Township Hall, a 1939 WPA project. A video and large interpretive signs relate the beginnings of this historic town and the people who lived here. Originally founded in 1877, Nicodemus soon was home to 300 black settlers. By the mid-1880s it was a prosperous town, but good times were short-lived. More than 130 years ago the town boasted two newspapers, three

general stores, three churches, some small hotels, a school, literary society, ice cream parlor, bank, livery, and many homes. Memorial Day-Labor Day, Monday-Sunday 9 a.m.-4:30 p.m.; Winter, Monday-Saturday 9 a.m.-4:30 p.m. 785.839.4233. nps.gov/nico.

Walking Tour Brochure:

Available at Township Hall, the brochure describes the 1878 St. Francis Hotel, the 1907 First Baptist Church, the 1907 A.M.E. Church, and the 1918 school district building. All are still standing in this historic town.

Nicodemus Historical Museum:

611 5th. At the end of a dirt road, a single-family home has been converted into the depository for the collections of the town's rich past. Photos, personal belongings, documents, and changing exhibits tell the story, and volunteers bring it to life with their own oral histories and anecdotes. Hours irregular. Call ahead, 785.839.4280.

Ernestine's:

U.S. 24 and 1st. Angela Bates clearly inherited the barbecue genes and recipes from her aunt Ernestine DuVall whose legendary barbecue restaurant (closed in 1985) was known far and wide. Now Angela is getting rave reviews for her ribs, brisket, barbecue sauce, potato salad,

barbecue beans, and sweet potato pie, served in Ernestine's home. Buy a jar of Ernestine's Bar-B-Q Sauce at the gift shop. Friday-Saturday 12-8 p.m. Call ahead, 785.839.8200.

Nicodemus Cemetery:

From Nicodemus, ¾ mile east on U.S. 24, then 1 mile north on 400. Early settlers, veterans of the Civil War and WWII, and Ernestine Van Duvall, longtime owner of the original Ernestine's Bar-B-Q, are buried here. Heed the warning sign at the cemetery to "Please keep gate closed to keep cows out."

Stone Dugout (NRHP):

From Nicodemus, 16 miles east on U.S. 24. The stone dugout is visible on the north side as you round the curve nearing Stockton. When settlers traveled to Stockton for supplies they needed a place to stay overnight on the way home. Local laws prevented blacks from staying in public hotels, so this stone dugout, built in the side of an embankment, accommodated them. Privately owned. View from the highway only.

Logan County

AROUND THE COUNTY

Monument Rocks

(8 Wonders of Kansas):
From Oakley, 20 miles south on U.S. 83, 4 miles east on Jayhawk, 3½ miles south and east on 14, 1 mile east on unnamed road, then ½ mile south on 16 (*see* p. 20). Dry weather roads.

Keystone Gallery:
401 U.S. 83. From Oakley, 26 miles south on U.S. 83. Barbara Shelton and Chuck Bonner can answer just about any geological or historical question you have about the area. Inside their historic 1917 limestone building are over 30 fossil specimens on display including a large xiphactinus fossil fish, a seven-foot pteranodon wing, and a 21-foot mosasaur. Chuck's artwork portrays area landscapes, often in abstract or whimsical application. Summer, daily 9 a.m.-6:30 p.m.; winter, daily 9 a.m.-5 p.m. 620.872.2762. keystonegallery.com.

Monument to Lake Scott Scenic Back Road:
Countless chalk formations, abandoned stone structures, and High Plains vegetation highlight this compelling 36-mile, one-way route. Ready? Here we go. From the west side of Monument, go 15 miles south on unpaved 350 to the Smoky Valley Ranch trailhead (*see* later entry). Continue 5 miles south on 350, 2½ miles east on Indian, then stairstep 3 miles south and east on 380. To the north is the dramatic Little Jerusalem formation (*see* later entry). Continue 7 miles south and east on 390 (becomes N. Kansas). At the fork just north of Lake Scott (*see* p. 443) go either way around the lake to K-95, which will connect you to U.S. 83, 30 miles south of Oakley.

Bertrand Home:
From Monument, 6 miles south on 350, then ½ mile east on Wagon. With cropland surrounding it, this three-story house, home to the Bertrand family for more than 20 years, stands like a monument to an earlier time. The window glass is long gone and tin has replaced the shingles, but you can still see the second-story porch on the south side where the five kids slept. This limestone-block house, built in the early 1920s, was abandoned in the late 1940s.

Smoky Valley Ranch Trailhead:
From Monument, 15 miles south on 350. Look for a parking area and kiosk on the east side of the road. Two trail loops begin here, one is five-and-a-half miles long and the other is one mile. The trails are difficult to discern, but it's a beautiful walk. In this area, owned by the Nature Conservancy, the main features are the chalk bluffs and shortgrass prairie. Keep your eyes open for swift foxes, pronghorns, rattlesnakes, and other wildlife. nature.org/kansas.

Little Jerusalem:
From Oakley, 23 miles south on U.S. 83, 4½ miles west on Gold, then 1 mile north on 390. Great news! Little Jerusalem, 220 acres of awe-inspiring badlands, was acquired by the Nature Conservancy in 2016. For years one has had to stay about a half mile away from the largest Niobrara Chalk Formation in Kansas. There are plans to open

Little Jerusalem to the public sometime in 2017. Opening updates are available at nature.org/kansas. In the meantime, please enjoy this dramatic photo from Bruce L. Hogle.

Western Vistas Historic Byway:
This 100-mile drive from Lake Scott on U.S. 83 to Oakley and then west to Sharon Springs on U.S. 40 takes you through chalk formations, buttes, and valleys—all buried under the sea 80 million years ago. Buffalo, American Indians, pioneers, early military, Wild West characters, and paleontologists were deeply connected to this prodigious and legendary land. 785.671.1000. travelks.com/ksbyways.com.

OAKLEY
Population 2,082

Buffalo Bill Sculpture
(8 Wonders of Kansas Art):
U.S. 83 and 2nd. Just as Buffalo Bill Cody seemed larger than life, this Charlie Norton sculpture is a double-life-sized bronze of this famous western scout, hunter, and showman. The magnificent bronze depicts Cody on his horse Brigham pursuing a buffalo bull at top speed. Legend has it that in 1868 Cody hunted buffalo to feed the Kansas Pacific Railway construction crews. Ironically, Fort Wallace had commissioned army scout Bill Comstock to

do the same thing. A contest between the two men (both nicknamed "Buffalo Bill") was staged near today's town of Monument to see which one could shoot the most buffalo in one day. Cody won, 69 to 46. On that spring day in 1868 the legend of Buffalo Bill Cody was born. The Cody statue is illuminated at night and can be visited anytime of the year.

Buffalo Bill Cultural Center: 3083 U.S. 83. Inside this impressive visitor center you'll find colorful paintings and displays that tell the story of the Wild West, Buffalo Bill Cody, and the region. Awaiting you too is a gift shop, hot coffee, and a bowl of fresh water for your pets. Monday-Friday 9 a.m.-5 p.m.; Saturday 11 a.m.-5 p.m. 785.671.1000. buffalobilloakley.org.

Fick Fossil and History Museum: 700 W. 3rd. Fossils are the main feature here, even as an art form! During the 1960s-1970s Ernest and Vi Fick collected thousands of fossils and shark teeth in Logan County. Using fossils, fossil pieces, oyster shells, fish vertebrae, and snails, Vi created her own art form, an art so unique it was featured in *Ripley's Believe it or Not!* The museum also presents some of George F. Sternberg's fossil finds, the oldest documented

mosasaur, a sod house, artifacts, excellent historical photos, and the story of the 1874 German family massacre. Monday-Friday 9 a.m.-5 p.m.; Saturday 9 a.m.-3 p.m. 785.671.4839. FB.

Oakley High School Stadium (NRHP): 118 W. 7th. A 1939 WPA project, this stadium was built with locally quarried limestone and with the help of area farmers needing work. Handmade tools used to cut the stone and construct the stadium are displayed at the Fick Fossil and History Museum.

Doughboy Statue:
209 Hudson. *The Spirit of the American Doughboy* statue by E.M. Viquesney was installed in 1923 and stands in front of the Oakley city office.

Coyote Sculpture:
710 W. 2nd. In 1963 the county seat moved from Russell Springs to Oakley. Dedicated in 1987, *Survivor of the Plains*, a Charlie Norton bronze sculpture of a coyote, accents the courthouse grounds.

Oakley Livestock Commission:
208 S. Freeman. Wednesdays are sale days, and the auction usually starts after lunch. The sale barn cafe opens around 9 a.m. and stays open till the last critter is sold. 785.672.4100.

Memorial Garden:
700 W. 3rd. Veterans are honored here among these beautifully landscaped gardens. Also remembered is Stan Clark, a 10-year state senator who died in a 2004 dust storm on I-70. Stan was a photographer and created a mailbox covering to look like a camera. It stands next to his memorial.

Palace Community Theater: 101 Center. Since 2003 members of Oakley High School's senior class have run the local theater. This unusual, but effective arrangement has proved successful for both students and community. 785.672.3115. FB.

Don's Drive-In: 3448 U.S. 40. Since 1982 Don's carhops have been delivering hamburgers, burgers, and fries to happy customers. Monday-Saturday 11 a.m.-9 p.m. 785.672.3965.

More Good Restaurants:
The Colonial Steakhouse (464 U.S. 83, 785.672.4720); Cap'n Jacks Pub (462 U.S. 83, 785.672.4444); and Buffalo Bill's Bar and Grill (207 Center, 785.671.1287).

Lodging:
tinyurl.com/oakleylodging.

RUSSELL SPRINGS

Population 30

BOD Markers:
In the 1960s octogenarian Howard Raynesford of Ellis erected 138 limestone markers along the Butterfield Overland Despatch (BOD) route from Fort Harker to the Colorado state line. The markers are placed at most public road crossings and at stage station sites. A notch at the top of the marker indicates the direction of the trail. Russell Springs can claim two BOD markers, one at K-25 (Armstrong) and Vine, and the second on the east side of town, just south from Broadway on 270.

Butterfield Trail Historical Museum: 515 Hilts. You'll find the museum inside the former Logan County courthouse (NRHP), an 1887 two-story limestone

and brick structure. The last county seat change in Kansas happened here in 1963 when the county government moved from Russell Springs to Oakley and abandoned this courthouse. Today you can wander through this revitalized building and learn about the Butterfield Overland Despatch, the Messamore Fossil Collection, and area history. The courtroom retains original furnishings and fixtures, and you can almost hear the gavel fall. Memorial Day-Labor Day, Tuesday-Saturday 9 a.m.-12 p.m. and 1-5 p.m.; Sunday 1-5 p.m. 785.751.4242. butterfieldtrailmuseum.org.

Lodging: The Logan House (785.751.4247, theloganhouse.com).

Norton County

AROUND THE COUNTY

Sebelius Lake and Prairie Dog State Park: From U.S. 283, 4 miles west on U.S. 36. At the Pete Felten sculpted prairie dog, go 1¼ miles south on K-261 past the park office and over the railroad gorge to arrive at the prairie dog colony. Here black-tailed prairie dogs,

named for their black-tipped tails and dog-like bark, scurry amid their dirt mounds from which they watch for predators. State park entrance charge. Cabins available, reservations required. 785.877.2953. ksoutdoors.com.

Adobe House: Prairie Dog State Park (south of the park office). When the park was developed (completed in 1966) this adobe home, built by the John Spencer family around 1894, was scheduled for demolition. Local citizens protested its demise, renovated it, and donated period furniture for its interior. It is the last surviving adobe house in Kansas in its original location.

ALMENA

Population 401

Windmills and More: From Main, just west on Brockton. Reminiscent of old-time water resources and farming are the two wooden windmills and the 30 or so mounted windmill heads. A 1916 Case steam engine and other farm equipment also are exhibited here thanks to the Sunflower Pioneer Power Association. 785.669.2221.

Almena Market: 517 Main. Providing groceries and a lunch special in this small town, the market will appreciate your visit and purchases. Monday-Saturday 7 a.m.-6 p.m. 785.669.2512. FB.

Historic Photos: 415 Main. Almena's past is captured in pictures displayed inside the new community center. The center shares a building with the city hall and the library, and when they are open, the community center is too! Hours irregular. 785.669.2425.

Historic Jail: Walnut and Benton. The shady Bantam Park is home to a jail built in the 1920s.

DENSMORE

Unincorporated

St Mary's Catholic Church: From K-173, 1 block east on Z. Amid the deteriorating buildings in this almost-ghost town, this church stands out as it's about the only building in fairly good condition. Built in 1948 from native stone quarried in nearby Edmond, its design is modified Colonial. It served as a church until the 1990s.

Mount Calvary Cemetery: From Densmore, ½ mile north on E8. A handmade iron fence surrounds this cemetery, whose

gravestones tell interesting stories. Henry John Lohmeyer was a Bronze Star Medal WWII veteran. Joseph C. Riemann, a WWI veteran, served in the 12th Balloon Company Air Service (balloons functioned as high flying observation platforms to gather intelligence). The anvil on top of Timothy Daniel O'Connor's gravestone signifies he was a blacksmith.

LENORA

Population 245

Country Corner: 110 S. Main. You'll find a tidy grocery and deli inside this old former gas station. Monday-Friday 8 a.m.-6 p.m.; Saturday 9 a.m.-3 p.m.; Sunday 11 a.m.-3 p.m. 785.567.4482.

Barbeau House (NRHP): 210 E. Washington. Settling in the area in the 1880s, French-Canadian Joseph Barbeau became an early founder and influential businessman of Lenora. He built this frame Queen Anne style home in 1902. It still serves as a private residence.

NEW ALMELO

Unincorporated

St. Joseph Catholic Church: 28035 St. Joseph.

As you come from the northeast on K-9, the

church steeple beckons and urges you to stop. Before you reach the front step, look up. On the tower's southeast corner you'll see a cross that appears to be barely hanging on. But it has done just that since the 1970s when a construction project accidentally led to this precarious looking situation. To go inside, move the bundled weight that keeps the door closed. Be sure to put it back when you leave!

NORTON

Population 2,880

"They Also Ran" Gallery:

105 W. Main. Where losers are not forgotten! On the mezzanine of the First State Bank, the gallery of "also-rans" exhibits portraits of unsuccessful presidential candidates dating to Thomas Jefferson. In case you didn't know, Jefferson lost to John Adams in the race of 1796! You'll find Kansas' own Bob Dole pictured on the wall between George H.W. Bush and Al Gore. Monday-Friday 9 a.m.-3 p.m. 785.877.3341. theyalsoran.com.

Washington Street Park:

S. State and Washington. After two buildings burned in 2006, their lots were donated, volunteers went to work, and art pieces were added to make this a desirable downtown green space. The pergola vines and leaves and the ornamental iron fencing were created by the local Rawhide Iron Works.

Historic Conoco Station (NRHP): 106 S. 1st.

Pull into this 1925 service station and fill up on nostalgia. Larry Urban's restored station and gas pumps produce memories dating from the 1920s to the 1960s.

Historic Sinclair Station (NRHP): 119 S. 1st.

This 1940s filling station has a 1974 Dino the Dinosaur (Sinclair's logo) on top, and an original gas pump out front. Renovated in 2014 by Mick and Colette Miller, the former station currently houses a title company.

Historic Kent Station (NRHP): 205 S. State.

One of the businesses inside this 1934 Spanish Revival filling station, renovated by Mick and Colette Miller, is the Norton Visitor Center. You're welcome to stop here for local information. Monday-Friday 8 a.m.-5 p.m. 785.877.2501.

Norton County Courthouse (NRHP): 101 S. Kansas.

This 1929 Modern Eclecticism structure stands out in brown brick and contrasting light stone trim. Inside, sunflower medallions surround the historic courtroom beneath its barrel vaulted ceiling. A *Justice Enthroned* mural hangs behind the judge's bench. Monday-Friday 8 a.m.-5 p.m. 785.877.5710.

Heaton Building: 107 S. State.

Inside this renovated 1906 building, notice the historic light fixtures that combine to create a unique chandelier. Beyond the chandelier is the Gloria A. Nelson Cultural Arts Center, two clothing boutiques, and a coffee shop. Monday-Friday 7 a.m.-5 p.m. 785.874.5106.

Norton Theatre:

215 E. Main. Sure to catch your eye is this theatre's smooth pink stucco exterior and its original green marquee. Built in 1906 in the Streamline Moderne style, the auditorium was converted to a theatre in 1948. Volunteers keep everything running smoothly. 785.877.2075. nortontheatre.com.

Norton Downtown Historic District (NRHP):

In 2011 44 properties were approved and designated as the Norton Downtown Historic District, including the nearly six miles of brick streets laid in 1919-1920. One of the premier properties is the restored Dr. L.E. Lyons home, 212 S. Kansas, circa 1893. 785.874.4816.

Norton County Historical Society Museum:

105 E. Lincoln. The rich history of Norton County is told inside this structure, built in 1938 by the WPA as a public library. May-October, Wednesday, Saturday 2-4 p.m. 785.877.5107. FB.

Stage Coach Station Number 15: U.S. 36.

In 1859 William Russell and John Jones operated the Leavenworth and Pike's Peak Express stagecoach line from Leavenworth to Denver. This replica of Station Number 15, a log cabin, has a viewing window through which you can see furnishings of that era. Russell later partnered with Alexander Majors and William Waddell on another venture— the Pony Express.

Destination Kitchen:

115 W. Main. You'll want to make this a recurring destination after you see what's inside this historic red-brick building. In the front, you'll find top-of-the-line kitchen and housewares, gourmet food items, and tasty desserts. In the back, lunch (11 a.m.-2 p.m.) offers sandwiches, soups and salads, and pizza from the brick oven. Monday-Friday 9 a.m.-5:30 p.m.; Saturday 9 a.m.-3 p.m. 785.877.2911. destinationkitchenks.com.

Los Canteras:

203 W. Washington. Enter this bright, lively setting and you'll be ready for a delicious, authentic Mexican meal and an icy margarita. Daily 11 a.m.-9:30 p.m. 785.874.4074. FB.

Lodging: thenortonlocal.com.

explorer extras... In Norton

Rawhide Iron Works of Norton did the 25 Norton scenes that you see as metal banners on the light poles throughout town. Thanks go to the Norton County Community Foundation for this nice touch. rawhideironworks.com. **ee**

Phillips County

Population 258

Grocery Store: 315 Main. New People's Store is a community-owned grocery where you can pick up all your explorer and travel needs. Monday-Friday 7 a.m.-6 p.m.; Saturday 8 a.m.-2 p.m. 785.638.2228.

Agra Lake and Park (NRHP):

From Main, ½ mile west on Kansas. Recent restoration efforts have the five 1937 WPA structures looking good. See them around the Civilian Conservation Corps

dam and spillway. A rare old-time trap shooting court with concrete walkways is found at the west shelter house.

Population 95

Triple C: 471 Central. Every burger shape is different because each one is hand formed. Really hungry customers go for the the Triple C Burger—a juicy tier of two half-pound burgers and all the fixings. You might have to undo your belt a notch or two before you leave! Monday-Saturday 11 a.m.-2 p.m. 785.543.6257.

Population 165

Kirwin Lake and National Wildlife Refuge:

From Kirwin, 4 miles west on K-9, then 1 mile south on E. 700. The first national wildlife refuge in Kansas, it was established in 1954 as an overlay project on a Bureau of Reclamation irrigation and flood control reservoir. Its primary purpose is to provide nesting cover, food, and shelter for songbirds, waterfowl, upland game birds, and mammals. 785.543.6673. tinyurl.com/kirwinlakenwr.

Refuge Overlook:

From Kirwin, 4 miles west on K-9, then ½ mile south on E. 700. A refuge information kiosk and an observation deck with telescope provide a superb view of the lake, ecosystem, and wildlife.

Kirwin Wildlife Visitor Center:

From Kirwin, 4 miles west on K-9, then 1 mile south on E. 700. Pick up maps showing

hiking trails, including the interpretive nature trail, and the Prairie Dog Town. Monday-Friday 7:30 a.m.-4 p.m. 785.543.6673.

Kirwin Cemetery:

From Kirwin, 1 mile west on K-9, then ¼ mile south on N. Kirwin Lake. This cemetery on a small rise provides excellent views of the lake. A simple gravestone is all you'll find for Henry W. Landes, so here's the story. A veteran of the Civil War, Landes re-enlisted in the marines and was assigned to guard the body of John Wilkes Booth. Landes also was a guard at the White House on the day of Lincoln's funeral, and later he guarded Booth's accomplice prior to his hanging. Landes later came to Kansas. To find his gravestone, turn east at the first intersection and go six rows east. His is the fourth marker.

City Hall (NRHP):

1st and Main. This red-brick building was erected on the town square in 1916 as a city hall and fire department (you can still see "F.D." above the door), and today it houses the city office

and library. If you're a book or library aficionado, ask to see the upstairs library. You'll like its original wood floors, old-time book shelves, and the many vintage books. Monday-Thursday 9 a.m.-4 p.m.; Friday 9 a.m.-12 p.m. 785.543.6652.

Little Free Library: In front of the city office/library. Take a book, leave a book!

Fort Kirwan and Camp Kirwin: A 1938 DAR marker on the southeast corner of the town square tells the story of Fort Kirwan (not Kirwin), which once stood 1 mile west and a ½ mile south. Lieutenant Colonel John S. Kirwan established the camp in July 1865 when his troops came west to escort a survey party. Used as a summer bivouac, Fort Kirwan was abandoned in September that same year. The DAR plaque also notes Kirwin Stockade, three blocks east of the square, created for settlers' protection. The stockade, also known as Camp Kirwin, was the first permanent settlement in Phillips County.

Historical Marker: A wooden kiosk on the north-west corner of the town square denotes Station Number 13, a stagecoach stop for the 1859 Leavenworth and Pike's Peak Express.

Solid Rock Cafe: 161 Deer. Eclectic decor fills the spacious interior of this rustic and remodeled barn. Scrumptious bison burgers, hot roast beef sandwiches, homemade Mexican, and other delicious fare are rock solid favorites. Monday-Tuesday 11 a.m.-1:30 p.m.; Wednesday-Sunday 11 a.m.-7:30 p.m. 785.259.0098.

LOGAN

Population 575

Dane G. Hansen Museum: 110 W. Main. A beautifully landscaped Memorial Plaza surrounds the museum of the Dane G. Hansen Foundation, which has brought new cultural and social experiences to Kansans since 1972. You're introduced to entrepreneur Hansen through exhibits about

his life and his family's immigration from Denmark. The facility is well known for its diverse and high-quality art from around the world. One of the most popular permanent exhibits is Syl Sijan, the security guard! You can find out why when you come in and meet Syl and visit the excellent displays under his watchful eye. Monday-Saturday 9 a.m-4 p.m.; Saturday 9 a.m.-5 p.m.; Sunday 1-5 p.m. 785.689.4846. hansenmuseum.org.

Walking or Driving Tour: An architectural and historical tour brochure leads you to 24 sites, including the Victorian House of Seven Gables (201 N. Washington) and the small 1890 limestone Episcopal Church of the Transfiguration (NRHP; 210 N. Washington). The brochure is available at the Dane G. Hansen Museum.

Logan Area Historical Museum: 219 W. Main. Housed inside the 1905 historic Dye Building, this is the place to experience the area's history. Friday-Saturday 1-4 p.m. 785.689.4374.

Center Parking: Logan is another town with parking in the middle of its broad street. According to local newspaper editor John Sullivan, Main Street once had angle parking in the center and at the curbs, but cars backing into each other prompted the change in the 1950s to parallel parking.

Main Street Pizza: 221 W. Main. The secret recipe for extra good pizza has made this business a big success. Wednesday-Sunday 11 a.m.-9 p.m. 785.689.7510. FB.

PHILLIPSBURG

Population 2,541

Phillips County Courthouse: 301 State. Completed in 1913, this Modern Eclecticism limestone structure stands on the town square. Seth Thomas clock works are on display on the first floor, and a stained-glass skylight highlights the second floor. On the south-west corner of the courthouse grounds, a steel beam from the World Trade Center forms a memorial to 911.

The Shepherd's Mill: 839 3rd. The only fiber-processing mill in the state, Shepherd's creates exquisite natural yarns and fabrics from the finest llama, alpaca, sheep, and yak wool. For sale is a line of woven natural fiber items, yarns, and weaving looms. Monday-Friday 9 a.m.-5 p.m.; Saturday 9 a.m.-3 p.m. For tours, call 785.543.3128. kansasfiber.com.

The Rollin' J: 747 3rd. You'll find this cool boutique inside a turn-of-the-century building with pressed-tin ceiling and repurposed furniture. Peruse and purchase current fashions for women and children, accessories, home decor, and gifts. Tuesday-Friday 10:30 a.m.-5:00 p.m.; Saturday 10 a.m.-2 p.m. 785.302.1688. therollinj.com.

Scott-McCoppin Bookstore and Hometown Grounds Coffee and Gifts: 767 3rd. Books, office and party supplies, gifts, cards, and Kansas souvenirs are available at this java stop. Monday-Friday 7 a.m.-6 p.m.; Saturday 7 a.m.-2 p.m. 785.543.6521. FB.

Majestic Theatre: 724 4th. Originally built as an opera house in 1905, this structure was converted into a motion picture house in 1925 and has been showing movies ever since. Saved from destruction by a community effort in 2000, the theatre is smoothly run by volunteers. Friday-Monday 7:30 p.m. 785.543.2724. FB.

C&R Railroad: 860 Park (Huck Boyd Center). The late Bill Clarke's incredible O-scale train layout of more than 1,200 feet of track winds through a multilevel landscape of small towns and farmland. The trains' many colors and the fine details of this miniature world create a visual delight. Equipment from Clarke's Photography Studio dating to 1947 is also on display. Monday-Friday 8 a.m.-5 p.m. For your whistle stop, call ahead 785.543.5415.

WPA Projects: Still standing are these 1930s structures. The former high school, now Phillipsburg Middle School (547 7th); the old Panthers Stadium (650 5th); the community building (425 F); Fairview Cemetery rock wall (U.S. 183 and Park); and two stone arch bridges at City Park (Fort Bissell Ave.).

Fort Bissell: 501 Fort Bissell. The original fort was built not for military use but to protect settlers who homesteaded here in the 1870s. The fort was demolished in 1878 but re-created on this site in 1961 to tell its history. Start your tour at the fort visitor center which features county displays, then follow the boardwalk through the replica stockade, an 1885 general mercantile store, 1872 log cabins, an 1887 school-house, a sod house built by students—and stocks used

for punishment! Memorial Day-Labor Day, Tuesday-Friday 9 a.m.-4 p.m.; Saturday 9 a.m.-2 p.m. 785.543.6212. fortbissellmuseum.org.

Water Tanks: U.S. 36 and 10th. Two vertical blue tanks that hold 30,000 gallons each and are identified by the local school colors and mascot contain recycled water from the nearby ethanol plant. The water is used to irrigate the Phillipsburg Golf Club's greens and tee boxes! Come play a round. Scheduled tee times not required. FB.

Third Street Bakery: 729 3rd. The Doissant (half donut and half croissant) and other baked goods glazed to perfection will make you drool and leave your sweet tooth satisfied. Know in advance that ordering the Honker is a noisy experience. Daily specials are made from scratch. Monday-Friday 6 a.m.-3 p.m.; Saturday 6 a.m.-2 p.m. 785.543.6340.

The Chubby Pickle: 603 State. Inside a 1960 former Phillips 66 station, you can fill up on Chubby subs, dogs, and BLTs, all served with a Chubby Pickle. Monday-Friday 11 a.m.-8 p.m.; Saturday 11 a.m.-7 p.m. 785.543.6474. thechubbypickleusa.com.

Shelly Ann's: 210 State. It's the place for a classic diner experience for breakfast and lunch. Monday-Saturday 6 a.m.-1:30 p.m. 785.543.5386.

explorer extras...
In Prairie View

Population 132

Around town are reminders of the Holland immigrants who came to Kansas in 1879.

Many who still live in this small community have roots to Holland and several display Dutch mementos outside their homes. As the sign beside the tiny Dutch windmill at the city limits reads, you are Welkom in Prairie View. Although now closed, the 1907 Reformed Church is another tribute to the Dutch heritage. **ee**

SPEED

Population 36

Hot Wheels: In 2008 Hot Wheels chose Speed as one of its stops and event hosts for the Hot Wheels 40th Anniversary Cross-Country Road Trip.

Speed's water tower still sports a Hot Wheels ribbon, and the city limits sign confirms that Speed is recognized by Hot Wheels as the "Birthplace of America's Need for Speed."

Memorial: 200 block of Main. A stone memorial honors PFC Kenneth W. Miller, a Speed native and a casualty of the Vietnam War.

Sundowner Bar and Grill: 135 W. 500. Slow down and enjoy the burgers at Sundowner Bar and Grill but hurry up and get there early on Fridays and Saturdays for steak night. Monday-Saturday 5-9 p.m. 785.302.8058.

explorer extras...
In Stuttgart

Unincorporated

The town was established in 1888 by German immigrants, many originally from Stuttgart, Germany.

At Main and Kansas, the large hand-painted yellow lettering on the faded red 1880s shop is a reminder that G.E. "Ed" Woodard was once the blacksmith here. The building was moved to this site from elsewhere in the county in the early 1900s. This icon of Stuttgart provides a great photo opportunity. **ee**

Rawlins County

ATWOOD

Population 1,225

Atwood Lake: From U.S. 36, 1 block north on K-25, then ¼ mile east on Lake. Enjoy the drive around this 43-acre lake that dates to 1926. Take the cottonwood-lined lane along the south side or walk through the pedestrian covered bridge, which is part of a one-mile lighted walking path around the lake. The quarter-mile Hayden Nature Trail is in the West Lake area and leads to a wooden stilt house observation tower. If you're a disc golf player check out the 18-hole course at the lake. 785.626.3640.

Atwood Country Club: 561 Lake. Just north of Atwood Lake you'll find this beautiful nine-hole, grass-green golf course built in the early 1950s and open to the public. Greens fee. 785.626.9542.

The Ol' Depot: 99 N. Lake. Find a delightful assortment of antiques, collectibles, crafts, and gifts inside this historic red depot. An added attraction is the caboose outside. Friday-Sunday 12-5 p.m. 785.626.0012.

Rawlins County
Historical Museum:

308 State. Rawlins County native Rudolph Wendelin created the stunning and masterful 20x10-foot mural that captures the area's story and greets you as you step into the museum. You'll also find exhibits about Atwood native and Kansas governor Mike Hayden and re-created pioneer rooms. Monday-Friday 10 a.m.-5 p.m.; Saturday 1-4 p.m. 785.626.3885.

Rawlins County Courthouse: 607 Main. At the front of this red-brick 1907 Romanesque Revival courthouse, the impressive Pete Felten stone buffalo sculpture is sure to attract your attention. Inside, it's the Christmas Cactus that attracts attention. In the 1930s a couple was married in the courthouse and gave this Christmas Cactus as a thank you. Courthouse staff have nurtured the plant all these years and it's thriving beside the district court clerk's office. Ask for Sierra and she'll show it to you! Monday-Friday 9 a.m.-5 p.m. 785.626.3465.

Jayhawk Theatre: 420 Main. Movies are still showing at the renovated Jayhawk Theatre, built in the 1920s. Two smiling jayhawks adorn the historic and colorful marquee. FB.

Kelley Park: The new swimming pool in Kelley Park built in 2011 has many fun features. But it's the thank-you garden for pool donors that will capture your heart. The large flowers are made from rusted metal and old road signs, and almost 700 "water droplets" hold the names of those who helped with the pool project.

Mojo's Espresso: 113 S. 4th. Find your mojo with a good cuppa joe, breakfasts, or daily specials! Monday-Saturday 7 a.m.-2 p.m. 785-626-9011.

Mulligan's on Main: 503 Main. Inside the historic Shirley Opera House (NRHP) is a pub—and a boutique! Drinks and pub food always help your shopping decisions. The boutique is in the 1940s addition that once housed a meat locker. Thursday-Saturday 3-10 p.m. 785.626.9470. FB.

Park Hill Restaurant: 116 S. 4th. The meat and cheese sopapillas give Park Hill its excellent reputation. All the food is homemade including the green and red chili, salsa, chips, and guacamole. Tuesday-Saturday 11 a.m.-9 p.m. 785.626.8040.

Lodging: Country Corner Bed & Breakfast (785.626.9516); Holste Homestead Bed & Breakfast (785.626.3522); additional lodging (visitrawlinsco.com/lodging).

explorer extras...
In Herndon

Population 133

The limestone football stadium is a 1940 National Youth Administration Work project. Located at Sunfield and Jupiter, it hasn't been used for years but some townspeople have dreams for its brighter future. 785.322.5341.

In City Park, 400 block of Keystone, a tall memorial tells us that Herndon is the "Birthplace and Boyhood Home of Rudolph Wendelin, 1910-2000," the "Caretaker of Smokey Bear" for 30 years.

Local volunteers have worked hard to tell the Herndon story. See what they've accomplished at the Herndon Community Museum, 228 Quincy. Memorial Day-Labor Day, first and third Sundays 1-3 p.m. 785.322.5302.

At Ash Creek Bar & Grill, 335 N. Quincy, the Pat Pizza is topped with Canadian bacon and sauerkraut and is a big favorite. But steak nights on Fridays and Saturdays are equally popular. Tuesday-Saturday 11 a.m.-9 p.m.; Sunday 11 a.m.-2 p.m. 785.322.5000. FB.

A scenic back-road drive to Ludell parallels Beaver Creek and the railroad. From Herndon, go 11 miles east on 179. Enjoy! **ee**

explorer extras...
In Ludell

Unincorporated

An unassuming red-brick building at Main and Goltl was once the place to be on weekends in the 1920s-1940s.

The Samson Dance Hall featured live dance bands of some of the well-known greats including Glenn Miller and the accordion maestro himself, Lawrence Welk.

The stone school, a 1937 WPA project, has new life as the community center, one block east of 982.

In the early 1940s the U.S. Forest Service asked Rudolph Wendelin to supervise the artwork of its forest-fighting campaign, thus making Wendelin the best-known artist of the beloved Smokey Bear. From 1944 to 1973 he served as "caretaker" of the famous bear. The artist was born in 1910 in nearby Herndon and grew up in Ludell.

In Immanuel Cemetery the grave for Rudolph Wendelin, who died in 2000, is in the second row. Also of interest is the elaborate stone marker for the Immanuel Lutheran Church, which operated from 1910 to 1966 in Ludell. From the north end of Ludell, the cemetery is just west, then ¼ mile north on 25. **ee**

MCDONALD

Population 165

McDonald Grocery: 202 Rawlins. Inside this small, red-brick corner store you'll find not only an old-fashioned checkout counter but a lot of

heart, coming straight from owners Brad and Eileen Porubsky. They do a fabulous job providing groceries, daily lunch specials, and authentic Mexican food on South of the Border Wednesdays. Monday-Saturday 8 a.m.-6 p.m. 785.538.2528. FB.

Bison Inn: 132 Rawlins. Across from McDonald Grocery, the two-story 1888 hotel has been renovated for the modern traveler. On the first floor the new restaurant serves bison steak, burgers, and more. Its red-brick interior walls create a handsome backdrop for good eating. 785.855.2344. FB.

Rooks County

AROUND THE COUNTY

Webster Lake and State Park: From Stockton, 8 miles west on U.S. 24. Completed in 1956, the lake is on the South Fork of the Solomon River and offers many recreational opportunities. It covers the original town of Webster. State park entrance charge. Cabins available, reservations required. 785.425.6775. ksoutdoors.com.

Placed by the Solomon Valley Heritage Alliance, the blue-roofed kiosks in Damar, Stockton, and Woodston provide helpful information about those towns.

explorer extras...
In Codell

Unincorporated

Believe it or not, Codell garnered *Ripley's Believe It or Not* fame because it was hit by a tornado on May 20 three years in succession—1916, 1917, and 1918. The last tornado wiped out a large part of town, and it never fully recovered. The marker at Maple and 4th tells Codell's unfortunate story. **ee**

DAMAR

Population 133

The welcome sign to Damar tells us French Canadians settled here in 1888.

St. Joseph's Church: 107 N. Oak. The double bell towers topped with crosses can be seen from miles away and lead you to this beautiful limestone church. The first mass was held here in 1917, but it took decades to complete the church. The copper roof and steeples,

interior decor, and brilliant stained glass were added between 1944 and 1952. Step inside to see one of the most breathtaking church interiors in the state. Always open. 785.839.4343.

Designer Downtown: In 2007 10 women with ties to Damar decided to dress up 10 buildings on Damar's main street. Each of the women chose a design for one of the stand-alone buildings and went to work. Many of the motifs promote the town's French Canadian heritage. Although none of the buildings contains a retail business, all are fun to see and appreciate.

Damar Community Historical Foundation: 208 Main. Named the "French Quarters," the community foundation is housed in an older building nicely renovated in 2014. The foundation is a source for genealogical research and helps promote and preserve the area's French Canadian culture. 785.839.4445.

Lodging: Rose Bed and Breakfast (785.839.4239, damarkansas.com).

PALCO

Population 277

Palco Grocery and Deli: 404 Main. Every dollar spent in these independently owned stores makes a big difference. Stop in for breakfast biscuits and gravy, fresh sandwiches, lunch specials, or some travel supplies. Monday-Friday 7 a.m.-6:30 p.m.; Saturday 7 a.m.-5 p.m. 785.737.5166.

McKenna Youth and Activity Center: 311 Main. Dedicated in 2014, the amazing community center, complete with a movie theater, was built thanks to the generosity of Everett McKenna. Kids ages 5 to 12 can enjoy the new playground equipment next to the activity center. Have fun on the zip line! 785.737.2175.

Golf Course: 2 miles east on K-18. Play a relaxing nine holes at the sand-green Palco Golf Course set amid rolling hills and valleys. Greens fee.

PLAINVILLE

Population 1,902

Pineapple Post: 111 N. Jefferson. Pineapple is a symbol for hospitality, and post refers to a place to shop. And indeed, Pineapple Post is a friendly store filled with gifts and unique wares. Housed in a former car dealership, Pineapple Post provides plenty of space to stock that perfect gift or hard to find item. Monday-Saturday 10 a.m.-5:30 p.m. 785.434.2769. FB.

Dessin Fournir: 308 W. Mill. In French, dessin fournir means design and furnish, and that is what founder and Plainville native Chuck Comeau does so well. His natural design talent and business acumen led to the success of this company that creates luxury furniture, fabrics, and lighting for upscale customers. Design and manufacturing happens here in Plainville and elsewhere in the United States, and showrooms are in the United States, Canada, and Russia. dessinfournir.com.

Rock Features: W. Mill and Section Line. Unusual rock benches and a rock sign promoting Home Oil Co. were placed in City Park after WWII. The benches were part of a rest stop built in 1932 by Home Oil Company just west of its gas station (now gone) at Mill and Broadway. At the rest stop site you can still see curious rock features including the former lily pond, tiny lighthouse, pillars, and bench.

Pilot Memorial: 111 S. Main. Set on a granite base, a bust and engraved monument honors Plainville native Clarence Gilbert. A pioneer of the air mail service, he lost his life in 1924 during a night delivery from Omaha to Chicago.

Civil War Monument: 108 S. Jefferson. A GAR monument stands in front of the former township hall, now the senior center. It is one of several Civil War monuments in the county.

Hospital Art: 1210 N. Washington. From the outside, Rooks County Health Center resembles the countryside around it—it's painted red for barns, green for fertile fields, and sports a silo-looking structure to complete the effect. Inside, the walls are nicely accented with large landscape photographs by local artist Lawrence Pfortmiller. Monday-Friday 7 a.m.-5 p.m. 785.434.4553.

Blue-Roofed Kiosk:
From U.S. 183, ½ mile east on U.S. 24. Learn more about Plainville from the kiosk in the park.

Veterans Memorial:
U.S. 183 and 5th. Dedicated in 2016, this memorial "honoring those who served" features iron cutouts of veterans and a large U.S. flag.

Wild West Saloon & Grill:
1935 U.S. 183. From Plainville, 3½ miles north on U.S. 183 to the Rooks County Golf Course. Whether you're a golfer or not, you'll want to tee up for hearty helpings, like the John Wayne Burger, the menu's signature item. Monday-Saturday 11 a.m.-11 p.m.; Sunday 7 a.m.-2 p.m. 785.688.4181. FB.

Burgers and Beer:
105 Mill. You're greeted with delicious food and friendly service. And don't be surprised if you hear, "Hi, y'all" when you come in the door. Monday-Saturday 11 a.m.-2 p.m. and 5-10 p.m. 785.203.5020.

Lodging:
rookscounty.net/lodging.

STOCKTON
Population 1,327

Baxter Bait and Tackle: 424 Main. All you need for fishing, hunting, and camping is found in this classic setting. Old-time gear and collectibles are displayed around the room. Daily 7 a.m.-8 p.m. 785.425.6321.

Rooks County Courthouse (NRHP): 115 N. Walnut. Completed in 1924, this Modern Eclecticism building has a beautiful third-floor courtroom. Everything is white marble—the jury box, witness stand, judge's bench, and lower portion of the walls. On the second floor, if the commissioners aren't in session, take time to look at the murals of Rooks County scenes painted around 1925 by a prisoner being held in the courthouse jail. If door is locked, ask for assistance at the county clerk's office. Monday-Friday 8 a.m.-5 p.m. 785.425.6881.

Stockton Heritage Walking Tour Brochure:
Pick up one on the first floor of the courthouse. Get to know Stockton with this excellent guide, which introduces you to about 50 sites ranging from the old city power plant and replica log hotel to the first funeral home in northwest Kansas and the limestone WPA grade school.

Carnegie Library (NRHP):
124 N. Cedar. Still serving the town is this 1911 Eclectic Classical Revival public library. The building stands out in red-brick with white trim and a red-tile roof.

Nova Theater: 517 Main. Hats off to the Stockton community for its efforts in re-opening the 1932 art deco Nova Theater. This red-brick structure has been renovated

and now functions as a first-run movie theater and an event center. 785.425.6007. FB.

Rooks County Historical Museum: 921 S. Cedar. A Pete Felten limestone sculpture of a draft horse marks this museum. This outdoor statue and a small display within commemorate one of the most famous and largest horse barns in the state—the 1912 classic Thomas Big Barn (NRHP) near Woodston. The museum also features county and town exhibits, a doll collection, and the musical instruments of Stockton native Lorenzo Fuller, who was a Broadway performer and early television pioneer. Tuesday, Thursday, Saturday 10 a.m.-4 p.m. 785.425.7217.

Rooks County Fairgrounds: 918 S. Elm. The Rooks County Free Fair has been bringing the county together since 1879. The fairgrounds comprise a complex of native limestone buildings—the grandstand, race-track fence, horse barn, and three livestock pavilions—erected in 1936-1937 by the WPA.

Sand Creek Mercantile:
316 Main. From the bakery, step into the mercantile and shop for repurposed furniture, primitive and rustic pieces, tablecloths, linens, and fabrics. Wednesday-Friday 10 a.m.-5 p.m. 785.425.8605. FB.

Carousel Bakery:
318 Main. Satisfy your sweet tooth here! You'll go round and round deciding

which delicious pastry and baked goods to choose. Tuesday-Friday 7 a.m.-2 p.m.; Saturday 7 a.m.-12 p.m. 785.415.2000. FB.

Weston's: 323 Main. Polished wood floors, red-brick walls, and assorted collectibles inside this 1888 building can't help but raise your expectations—and this restaurant meets them with its hand-cut steaks, burgers, sandwiches, and salads. The full bar stocks what you need in liquid refreshment. Monday-Thursday 11:30 a.m.-9:30 p.m.; Friday-Saturday 11:30 a.m.-2 a.m. 785.415.2131.

Webster's Deli: 303 Main. This renovated gas station is brimming with quality deli meats and cheeses of all kinds, a salad bar, barbecue, and desserts to go. Monday-Friday 8 a.m.-5:30 p.m.; Saturday 8 a.m.-3 p.m. 785.425.6317.

Stone Dugout: From Stockton, about 3 miles west on U.S. 24. You can see the remains of a limestone dugout once used by Nicodemus settlers as an overnight stop when returning from Stockton (*see* p. 24).

Lodging: rookscounty.net/lodging.

(*see* p. 24).

WOODSTON

Population 137

Ash Rock Church: From Woodston, 5 miles north on 28, then 1 mile east on D. Built in 1882, this beautiful limestone building is known locally as the "Stone Church." It's the oldest standing church in the county.

Woodston to K-18 Scenic Back Road: From Woodston, 18 miles south on Spruce (becomes 28) to K-18, just east of Plainville. This unpaved road crosses the South Fork of the Solomon Valley River and then takes you past chalky bluffs that dot this Blue Hills region as it follows the Medicine Creek Valley to more level ground.

Sheridan County

AROUND THE COUNTY

Placed by the Solomon Valley Heritage Alliance, the blue-roofed kiosks in Hoxie and Studley provide helpful information about those towns

HOXIE

Population 1,195

Sheridan County Courthouse: 925 9th. The beautiful green wall-tile designs are similar to those in the Smith

---

County courthouse. In Hoxie, this 1918 Classical Eclecticism structure of buff brick occupies a full block square, and a war memorial enhances its front lawn. Monday-Friday 8 a.m.-5 p.m. 785.675.3361.

Soda Fountain: 833 Main. Inside Mahanna Pharmacy, a 1950s soda fountain sports an orange Formica counter top and nine stools. Spin on the stools while you ponder your order. How about a Chocolate Peanut Delight or maybe a Swirley? Monday-Friday 9 a.m.-6 p.m.; Saturday 9 a.m.-12 p.m. 785.675.3461.

Sheridan County Historical Society and Mickey's Museum: 1224 Oak. In 1963 Vernon and Isabelle Mickey built a replica old-time hardware store to house their own hardware displays. County displays and other diverse collections now have found a home here too. Studley's Bee Hive one-room school is part of the museum complex. Tuesday-Friday 8:30 a.m.-12 p.m.; 1-4:30 p.m. 785.675.3501. FB.

Red's: 1641 Oak. Look for the big red-and-white striped building and stop in for some bait, snacks, drinks, or a creamy and delicious soft serve ice cream cone. Monday-Thursday, Sunday 6:30 a.m.-10 p.m.; Friday-Saturday 6:30 a.m.-11 p.m. 785.675.3327.

Oscar's: 845 Main. Remembering Oscar, a lone steer in her herd of Texas longhorns, Michelle Foote memorialized him in her restaurant name and placed his likeness near the entrance.

Inside, modern decor adds to your enjoyment of the espresso, French press coffee, gourmet boards, healthy menu items, and daily specials. Monday-Friday 6:30 a.m.-2 p.m.; Saturday 7 a.m.-12 p.m. 785.675.2022. FB.

Lodging:
tinyurl.com/hoxielodging.

SELDEN

Population 220

Karl's Cash Store:
101 S. Kansas. Buy spices, laundry detergent, canned green beans—and anything else that travels well. Your cash will help Karl's carry on! Monday-Saturday 6:30 a.m.-8 p.m. 785.386.4246.

Paul's Furniture: 105 N. Kansas. It's the exceptional selection and service that has kept folks coming to Paul's for more than 87 years. We hope you come too! Monday-Friday 9 a.m.-5:30 p.m.; Saturday 9 a.m.-4 p.m. 785.386.4310. paulsfurnitureco.com.

Golden Acres Nature Trail: 210 W. 6th. Take a stroll on this Outdoor Wildlife Learning Sites (OWLS) nature trail. It's beautifully landscaped with native plants and trees, and the big metal sunflowers add a cheerful touch.

Midway Cafe:
202 N. Nebraska. This little place may not look like much, but there's nothing middling about its home cooking! Some Kansas Explorers say the Midway has the best chicken-fried steak in the state. Could be because it's made with an extra crunchy corn-flake breading. Monday-Friday 7 a.m.-7 p.m.; Saturday 7 a.m.-2 p.m. 785.386.4545.

STUDLEY

Unincorporated

Cottonwood Ranch State Historic Site (NRHP): 14432 E. U.S. 24. John Fenton Pratt came to this area in the late 1800s and established a sheep ranch similar to those in his native England. Visitors will first notice the unusual architectural style and coloring of the one-story stone home. The stone blocks are different colors—shades of pink, pale yellow, and gray with an overall golden tone—because they come from various rock formations. The piece that catches everyone's eye is the stone oval surrounding a stained-glass window. When the site is open, Don Rowlison will take you on a tour of this English homestead. Otherwise, storyboards help you tour the ranch. May-September, Thursday-Saturday 9 a.m.-5 p.m. Donation suggested. 785.627.5866. cottonwoodranchks.com.

Sherman County

Sherman County is in Mountain Time Zone (MT).

AROUND THE COUNTY

The Kansas Travel Information Center at I-70 mile marker 7 is a good rest stop and is the place to load up on Kansas information. Daily 9 a.m.-5 p.m. MT. 785.899.6695.

EDSON

Unincorporated

Post Office: 6419 Main. At this quaint little post office inside a former residence, Jan greets you with a smile and is happy to sell you as many stamps as you can afford. We can always use stamps! Monday-Friday 7-11 a.m.; Saturday 7-8:45 a.m. MT. 785.899.5890.

GOODLAND

Population 4,557

Giant Van Gogh Painting:
1998 Cherry. Canadian artist Cameron Cross painted enlarged reproductions of

Van Gogh's seven sunflower paintings and displayed them in seven countries. The site chosen in the United States was Goodland! The 24x32-foot *Three Sunflowers in a Vase*, completed in 2001, rests on an 80-foot easel and weighs 40,000 pounds.

Art in the Park: Inspired by the giant Van Gogh painting, the community has erected easels in three city parks featuring works by high school art classes and local artists. See these bright artistic touches in Chambers (13th and Center), Rosewood (Acacia and Willow), and Gulick (9th and Caldwell) Parks.

Goodland Carnegie Arts Center (NRHP): 120 W. 12th. The art exhibits inside this 1913 former library change regularly and much of it is for sale. The center does a marvelous job supporting local artists, and it operates a great gift shop. Tuesday-Thursday 12-4 p.m.; Saturday 10 a.m.-4 p.m. MT. 785.890.6442.

Post Office Mural (NRHP): 124 E. 11th. *Rural Free Delivery* is the title of this 1937 Section artwork by Kenneth Adams, which depicts a hard-working farm family welcoming the horse-and-buggy mail carrier.

Sherman County Courthouse: 813 Broadway. The art deco tile accents this 1931 blond-brick structure. The interior and courtroom retain much of the original hardware and many lighting and decorative elements. The pioneer statue on the grounds, *They Came to Stay*, was

sculpted by Greg Todd in 1987. Monday-Friday 8 a.m.-5 p.m. MT. 785.899.4806.

Library Art: 812 Broadway. In front of the public library the Greg Todd bronze, *More than Words*, depicts a mother reading to her children. Displayed inside the library is a copy of Jean Francois Millet's *The Gleaners*, painted by an unidentified Polish count residing in Kansas. Also of interest is a striking 1911 stained-glass window of a steam engine. The image was created in memory of a young railroad brakeman who was killed on the job. Monday-Thursday 10 a.m.-7 p.m.; Friday-Saturday 10 a.m.-5 p.m. MT. 785.899.5461.

Opera House Outdoor Mural: 1002 Main. The History of the Opera House stretches 100 feet along a red-brick wall and brightly portrays 90 years (1906-1996) of opera house history, including its varied activities and the stores that later occupied the building. The local group project, headed by building owner Rod Cooper and completed in 2012, resulted in a beautiful work of art. tinyurl.com/operahousemural.

Olde Westport Spice & Trading Company: 1218 Main. This family-owned business has been blending and selling high-quality spices and

dry soup mixes for more than 35 years. They are manufactured in the back and sold in the front. Monday-Friday 8 a.m.-2 p.m. MT. 800.537.6470. FB.

Telephone Building: 1003 Main. The front of this two-story, buff-brick structure is lavishly decorated with red, yellow, and blue terra cotta tiles inspired by Aztec art. The handsome design is the work of architect Charles Shaver.

Historic Building Tours: Stroll the downtown district and look for brass plaques identifying historic buildings. Additionally, a driving-tour brochure will lead you to 13 historic structures in the area including Goodland High School built in 1937 by the WPA. Pick up your brochure at the High Plains Museum or at 1206 Main.

High Plains Museum: 1717 Cherry. The feature exhibit is the full-sized replica of America's first patented helicopter, invented in Goodland by W.J. Purvis and C.A. Wilson in 1909. Push a button and its wings go in motion! A good place to start your exploration of Sherman County, this museum displays local history and present-day agriculture, and tells the story of the Dust Bowl era. Monday, Wednesday-Saturday 9 a.m.-5 p.m. MT. June-August, Sunday 1-5 p.m. MT. 785.890.4595.

Historic White Eagle Station: E. 17th and Clark. In 2011 Rod Cooper moved this 1928 stucco gas station 17 miles from Kanorado to this spot. He then restored it to its present condition.

Ennis-Handy House:
202 W. 13th. The Queen Anne Ennis-Handy House was built in 1906 for widow Mary Ennis after her husband, William, a prominent businessman, died. With gingerbread trim and covered porches, this two-story beauty is worth a stop. Memorial Day-Labor Day, daily 1-5 p.m. (closed Tuesday); winter, Wednesday-Sunday 1-5 p.m. MT. 785.899.6773.

U.S. Weather Service:
920 Armory. Every Kansan should experience how the weather service works, and the Goodland office is happy to offer behind-the-scenes tours for individuals or groups—just call ahead. You'll see how forecasts are researched and observe Doppler radar in action. Weather forecasting will take on a whole new meaning! Monday-Friday 8 a.m.-4 p.m. MT. 785.899.7119, dial "0" for front desk. weather.gov/gld.

Grasshopper Sculpture:
From Main, ¼ mile east on 1st, 1½ miles north on Caldwell, then ¾ mile north on K-27. Farmer Lloyd Harden whiled away the winter hours making fun sculptures from old farm equipment. Although Harden is gone now, you can see one of his pieces, a larger-than-life John Deere green grasshopper, north of town. tinyurl.com/hardenart.

Goodland Cemetery:
630 N. Main. Southeast of the chapel, six stones, each inscribed "Unknown U.S. Soldier," form a memorial to county soldiers killed during WWI. Buried nearby is Sherman County's sole black Civil War veteran W.M Johnson. Brook Berringer, legendary Nebraska Cornhusker quarterback killed in an airplane crash two days before the 1996 NFL draft, is buried beside his father, Warren. Cornhusker fans often leave mementos. A kiosk provides the location of the grave, which is also marked by a Cornhusker flag.

Crazy R's Bar and Grill:
1618 Main. Inside a plain metal building, Crazy R's walls and corners are filled with the antique collections of owner and cook Rod Cooper. Since 1987 dining has been a Crazy enjoyable event!. Monday-Saturday 11 a.m.-8 p.m. MT. 785.890.3430.

Butterfly Cafe: 602 Renner Field. Head for the flagpole at the main airport building. People fly to this cafe to pick up boxes of homemade pies. No kidding! One bite will tell you why. Also made from scratch are the buttermilk pancakes served with warm maple syrup, pan-fried chicken, and tasty rolls. Explorer Way chicken-fried steak is available on Fridays. A display in the airport lobby introduces you to M.J. Renner, the "flying doctor" for whom the airfield was named. Daily 6 a.m.-2 p.m. MT. 785.890.2085.

Kidder Battle: From Main, 8¼ miles east on 8th (becomes 65), then 12 miles north on 28 to 77. Here a historical marker relates the Kidder massacre and its aftermath. One mile east on 77 is the battle site, where in 1867 Lieutenant Lyman Kidder and his 10-man patrol were confronted by Cheyennes. No one in Kidder's company survived. George Custer and an advance party of the Seventh U.S. Cavalry found the soldiers' mutilated bodies. The tragedy is further told at the High Plains Museum in Goodland (*see* p. 38) and at the Fort Wallace Museum (*see* p. 45).

Lodging: Prairie Castle Guest House Bed and Breakfast (NRHP, KBBA, 785.899.5306, kuhrtranch.com); additional lodging (visitgoodland.com).

(*see* p. 38) and at the Fort Wallace Museum (*see* p. 45).

NW

explorer extras...
In Goodland

The red-brick streets have quite the story. They were laid in 1921 by Jim Brown, an American Indian, who could lay 150 bricks per minute or "as fast as five men could bring him the bricks." He could lay 36,000 bricks in a day and do it so accurately that no adjustment was needed!

Goodland, with an elevation of 3,965 feet, is the highest county seat in the state. A national geodetic marker is found under the small easel in Chambers Park, 13th and Center.

Since 1926, and many changes later, movies are still showing on the big screen in the Sherman Theatre, 1203 Main. The most recent remodel uncovered four illustrious 1928 panels of the peacocks and roses design, and, by the same artist, an elaborate framed 1928 mural. 785.899.6103. FB. **ee**

KANORADO

Population 157

The town name is a portmanteau of Kansas and Colorado.

Kings Cafe: 206 Main. Kings is the first Kansas cafe to greet you if you're coming from Colorado on I-70. Named for original owner Darrell King, the cafe is now owned by Robin and Donald Valdez, a hard-working pair who open it after they've completed their day jobs. The locals really appreciate this, both the effort and the food! Monday-Friday 6-9 p.m.; Saturday 7 a.m.-2 p.m. and 5-9 p.m. MT. 785.821.3044.

Highest Elevation in Kansas: To reach the highest point, from Main, go ½ mile east on Front, 22 miles south on 3, 1 mile west, cross a cattle guard, then ½ mile north on a pasture driveway to Mount Sunflower (see p. 45).

Thomas County

BREWSTER

Population 303

Brewster Grocery: 325 Kansas. The locals support this great little store, and explorers/travelers are encouraged to stock up here too! Monday-Friday 8 a.m.-7 p.m.; Saturday 9 a.m.-12 p.m. 785.694.2824.

Northwest Kansas Heritage Center: 401 Kansas. Exhibits and collections inside this handsome corner bank building preserve the story of local schools and area history. Monday, Wednesday 1-4 p.m.; Saturday 9-11 a.m. 785.694.2891.

Chelle's Bar & Grill: 402 Kansas. You'll agree with Chelle's claim of the "Juiciest burgers– hottest fries– coldest beer in town!" And locals appreciate this homey place to gather in their small town. Monday-Saturday 11 a.m.-2 p.m.; Wednesday-Friday 5-8 p.m. 785.694.2727. FB.

COLBY

Population 5,416

Visitor Center: I-70 exit 53. Shaped like a grain bin, this is one unique and eye-catching center! It offers area and state-wide information, restrooms, free coffee, and a seven-foot-tall panorama of 1907 Colby that wraps around the interior. Monday-Saturday 9 a.m.-5 p.m.; Sunday 1-5 p.m. 785.460.0076.

Prairie Museum of Art and History: 1905 S. Franklin (I-70 exit 53). Joe and Nellie Kuska gathered artifacts from all over the world, and their quality collections of glass, furniture, ceramics, toys, dolls, jewelry, and more are artfully displayed inside a unique building designed by their son George. In addition, the museum features excellent exhibits about western Kansas. The outdoor complex includes the Cooper Barn, a 1930s furnished farmhouse, a pioneer sod house, a one-room school, and an old country church. Interpretive signs tell the story of

each structure. Monday-Friday 9 a.m.-5 p.m.; Saturday-Sunday 1-5 p.m.; November-March, closed Monday. Admission charge. 785.460.4590. prairiemuseum.org.

Cooper Barn (8 Wonders of Kansas Architecture): 1905 S. Franklin. Part of the Prairie Museum of Art and History complex, the largest publicly accessible barn in Kansas was built in 1936 to house Hereford show cattle. The barn, including the massive

loft, is open for your inspection. Signage shares information about Foster Farms, the original owner of the barn. For hours, see Prairie Museum of Art and History.

WPA Projects (NRHP): The 1935 Colby Community High School (750 W. 3rd) is an Eclectic Mediterranean Revival style structure with art deco influences. Colby City Hall (585 N. Franklin), built in 1936 of native limestone, features a minimal art deco style. The former St. Thomas Hospital (210 S. Range), a 1941 project, was constructed of red brick in the 19th-century Georgian Revival style.

Statue of Liberty: W. 8th and N. Franklin. Fike Park hosts one of 200 Statue of Liberty replicas placed throughout the country as part of the Boy Scouts of America's 40th Anniversary in 1950.

Thomas County Courthouse (NRHP): 300 N. Court. *Spirit of the Prairie*, a 1985 Charlie Norton bronze of a prairie woman and her

baby, welcomes you to this impressive 1906 Romanesque Revival courthouse.

Wheat Sculpture: 375 W. 4th. Italian sculptor Giorgio Spadaro created the copper and fiberglass sculpture that stands in the fountain at Pioneer Memorial Library. Created in 1966, the sculpture is designed to resemble a wheat head.

Title Office Mural: 160 E. 4th. What do you do when your building has an ugly exterior wall? Paint a mural on it! That's what Quality Title and Abstract did. With the help of Rebel Mahieu and her Colby Community College art club, four artistic storefronts relating to titles and abstracts, including the Titewad Bank, now decorate the wall.

Masonic Lodge Mural: 215 N. Franklin. The colorful mural at St. Thomas Lodge hall depicts Masonic brother George Washington laying the cornerstone at the Capitol in Washington, D.C. Credit goes to Colby Community College art teacher Rebel Mahieu and her students for painting the image.

Colby Aquatic Park: 1610 S. Franklin. Splash, cool off, and have fun with a Lazy River, water obstacle course, slides, and spray and play fountains. The half-mile Frahm Family Trail sidewalk starts at this park. 785.460.4429.

J & B Meat Market: 1996 S. Range. For years I-70 travelers have detoured to the big red letters promoting burgers and shakes. If you're really hungry, try this popular J & B trio: hand-pattied bacon cheeseburger, sweet potato fries with marshmallow sauce, and a creamy shake. Monday-Friday 10 a.m.-7 p.m.; Saturday 10 a.m.-4 p.m. 785.460.0414. FB.

Beyond the Mug: 365 N. Franklin. Beyond your favorite coffee, you'll find this family-run business uses fresh ingredients for its daily specials (try the ravioli or chicken madeira). The bread, brioche, and cinnamon rolls are made from scratch, and the homemade ice cream takes the whole meal past normal expectations. Monday-Friday 7 a.m.-2 p.m. 785.460.0202. FB.

 **The "B" Hive Bar & Grill:** 170 W. 4th. Kenny Bieber's son chose the "B" Hive name when they opened this tavern in 1980. Kenny's grandson runs the place now, and his fresh meat, hand-formed burgers are as popular as ever. Monday-Saturday 11 a.m.-10 p.m.; Sunday 12-10 p.m. 785.460.8813.

City Limits: 2227 S. Range (at the Comfort Inn). You'll have to loosen your belt for a little comfort after you've eaten the one-pound Explorer Way chicken-fried steak! You'll also like the salads, steaks, and the decor. Monday-Saturday 5-10 p.m. 785.462.6565. colbycitylimits.com.

Lodging:
Historic Philip Houston House Bed & Breakfast (NRHP, KBBA, 785.687.2565, tinyurl.com/rexfordbb); additional lodging (tinyurl.com/staycolby).

explorer extras...
In Mingo

Unincorporated

World's Oldest Geocache: This geocache was the seventh cache ever placed, although the first in Kansas, and it's now the oldest currently active site in the world. The Kansas Stasher hid the cache on May 11, 2000, at N39° 16.677 W100° 56.621. More than 6,966 geocachers have logged visits at this site.

Trego County

AROUND THE COUNTY

Smoky Valley Scenic Byway: From WaKeeney, 26 miles south on U.S. 283, 9 miles east on K-4, then 25 miles north on K-147. This 60-mile official state scenic byway through the Smoky Hill River Valley and High Plains shortgrass prairie introduces you to beautiful wildflowers, rock outcroppings, and cropland, and to the Wilcox School (NRHP) and the Swedish Lutheran Emanuel Church (*see* next entries). The picturesque Cedar Bluff Lake is the landscape highlight of this drive. 800.684.6966. travelks.com/ksbyways.

Wilcox School (NRHP):
From WaKeeney, 15 miles south on U.S. 283 to X. Built in 1886 and closed for classes in 1947, this native limestone structure is one of the few remaining rural schoolhouses in the county.

Swedish Lutheran Emanuel Church:
From I-70 exit 135, 7½ miles south on K-147. A nearby quarry supplied the native limestone for this church established by Swedish settlers in 1902. A small congregation still meets here. 785.743.6629.

Cedar Bluff Lake and State Park:
From I-70 exit 135, 13 miles south on K-147. On the south side of the lake you'll find the cedar-lined, 100-foot-tall limestone bluffs for which the reservoir is named. A sign south of the lake on K-147 directs you to the scenic overlook. The reservoir, completed in 1951, is nationally recognized for its black bass. A giant fishing pole complete with reel, bobber, and hook was created in 2014 by state park employees. It stands at a small pond near the state park office. State park entrance charge. Cabins available, reservations required. 785.726.3212. ksoutdoors.com.

Threshing Machine Canyon:
From I-70 exit 135, 10½ miles south on K-147, 1 mile west on U, then 2½ miles south on 330. In 1867 American Indians attacked and killed freighters transporting a threshing machine along the Butterfield Overland Despatch route. The machine was set on fire and left in this canyon for many years. The names of late 1800s travelers are carved in the canyon bluffs. It's recommended to stop at the park office and ask for directions. 785.726.3212.

Snappin' Minnow:
35003 310 (south side of lake). If the fish aren't biting (or even if they are) stop here and Angie Lutters will whip you up a hearty meal. Fridays are catfish nights, and the Saturday night headliner is hand-cut ribeye steaks on the grill. Some say Angie's homemade cheesecakes are better than fishin'! November-April 15, Wednesday-Saturday 8 a.m.-8 p.m.; Summer, Sunday-Monday 8 a.m.-3 p.m., Wednesday-Saturday 8 a.m.-8 p.m. 785.481.2332. FB.

Shiloh Winery:
16079 M. Kirk and Treva Johnston brought wine making to western Kansas in 2008 and transformed a chicken house into a charming wine-tasting venue. They'd love for you to stop by, try one of their exquisite wines, and tour the vineyard. You might even see a cute goat or two! Call ahead, 785.743.2152. shilohvineyard.com.

Lodging:
Butterfield Trail Bunkhouse (KBBA, 785.743.2322, butterfieldtrailbunkhouse.com); Saline River Hunting Lodge (KBBA, 785.743.5878, salinelodge.com); additional lodging (wakeeney.org/lodging).

COLLYER

Population 109

St. Michael's School and Convent (NRHP):
700 and 704 Ainslie. Collyer was founded as an Irish railroad settlement but later was populated by Volga German immigrants. Between the limestone St. Michael's Church and the 1918 red-brick school stands the restored red-brick convent, built in 1925 and now a private residence. The school and convent closed in 1968.

Water Tower (NRHP):
From Ainslie, ½ block west on 4th, then north into the alley. Here you can view this rather unusual 1931 brick and wood water

tower. It served several homes and businesses before a modern water system was installed.

Pontiac Bar and Car: 322 Ainslie. The fellow who owned the former Pontiac Bar and Grill is no longer living, but his half-a-car building accessory is alive and well. The early 1950s Pontiac stuck high into the exterior wall is a fun surprise for all Collyer visitors.

WAKEENEY

Population 1,846

WaKeeney is known as the "Christmas City of the High Plains." Since 1950s volunteers have decorated a four-block area of downtown during the holidays. A beautiful spectacle is created with thousands of lights, miles of electrical wiring, fresh greenery and garland, and the centerpiece—a 35-foot-tall tree of fresh pine. All year round colorful Christmas tree sculptures dot main street, celebrating the town's claim to fame and immense source of community pride.

Gibson Health Mart:
125 N. Main. A drugstore opened in this building in 1892 and has not been without a soda fountain since. The present one is a sweet little nine-stool job. Come by for a spin, a cold drink, or a cup of coffee for just five cents. Monday-Friday 9 a.m.-6 p.m.; Saturday 9 a.m.-12 p.m. 785.743.5753.

Trego County Courthouse: 216 N. Main. It was built of native limestone in 1889, and when the cupolas and bell tower were removed in 1952 it gained the title "the courthouse that lost its top." In 2012 the gable, reminiscent of the original, was revived with some of the original limestone. The courthouse's claim to fame may have come in June 1974 when several scenes from *Paper Moon* were filmed in the county treasurer's office. If you have horseshoes, bring them and play a game on the courthouse grounds. Monday-Friday 8 a.m.-5 p.m. 785.743.2148.

The Studio and Kansas Art Gallery: 128 N. Main. Stop here for a souvenir ornament from the town that celebrates Christmas year round. Monday-Friday 10:30 a.m.-6 p.m. 785.814.7170. FB.

City Hall: 408 Russell. With assistance from the WPA, the city built the limestone art deco style city hall in 1937. Its auditorium once hosted a variety of events, from ball games to dances.

Trego County Museum: 128 N. 13th. The story of Trego County is told through artifacts and exhibit vignettes. Also displayed is a small piece of the threshing machine from Threshing Machine Canyon (*see* p. 42). A new addition hosts a fossil collection; a large mural depicting early county history; and a saddle, bit, and spur collection. Sunday, Wednesday-Thursday 1-4 p.m.; Tuesday, Friday-Saturday 10 a.m.-4 p.m. 785.743.6651. FB.

State Veterans Cemetery: 403 S. 13th. Dedicated in 2004, this cemetery

is a dignified final resting place for many Kansas veterans.

Western Kansas Saloon and Grill: 121 N. Main. Built in 1925 as a hardware store, this narrow building with its original pressed-tin ceiling and wood interior is enhanced with

historical memorabilia decor. It's a great place to settle in and fill up on burgers, steaks, pasta, seafood, and salads. Tuesday-Saturday 11 a.m.-2 p.m. and 5-9 p.m.; Sunday 5-9 p.m. 785.743.2050. FB.

Jake and Chet's Cafe: 233 S. 1st. Comfort food such as hot roast beef sandwiches, liver and onions, and other daily specials make for a comfortable experience inside this A-frame building. Breakfast is served all day. Monday-Sunday 6 a.m.-10 p.m.

WaKeeney Livestock Commission: 24088 G Terr. Sherry Kuntz runs the WaKeeney Sale Barn Cafe, and folks recommend her made-from-scratch lunches and pies. Eat your fill then find a spot on the bleachers and take in the sale.

Tuesdays are sale days, starting at noon. Cafe hours 11 a.m.-9 p.m. 785.743.2691.

explorer extras... In WaKeeney

The Lustron home (NRHP) at 409 N. 13th was constructed in 1950 by Dreiling Implements of Hays. Following WWII approximately 100 of these prefabricated metal homes were built in Kansas. Around 91 exist today.

Entering the fairgrounds at 13th and Russell, you'll pass through the elegant limestone gate pillars constructed in 1939 as a National Youth Administration project. On the grounds you'll see the 1916 Trego County Fair Exhibit Building (NRHP), one of the few of this structure type still standing.

A beautifully landscaped area greets you at the Main Street Nature Trail, S. Main and N. Railroad. Benches and a gazebo accent a short walkway, and the restored antique wooden windmill is a delightful highlight.

Looking for fun and recreation? You'll find plenty of both at the WaKeeney Water Park and Pool (716 N. 6th); the Frisbee Golf Course (Scout Park, 900 E. Russell); and the Big Creek Golf Course (24073 J).

You might notice the street signs are a vibrant purple and gold, the colors of Trego Community High School. **ee**

Wallace County

Wallace County is in Mountain Time Zone (MT).

AROUND THE COUNTY

Western Vistas Historic Byway: A 100-mile route from Lake Scott north on U.S. 83 to Oakley, then west on U.S. 40 to Sharon Springs takes you through chalk formations, buttes, and valley remains of a sea that flowed here 80 million years ago. Buffalo, American Indians, pioneers, early military, Wild West characters, and paleontologists knew this land well. 785.671.1000. travelks.com/ksbyways.com.

SHARON SPRINGS

Population 788

Wallace County Courthouse: 313 N. Main. A buff-brick and limestone structure, this stately Modern Eclecticism courthouse was built in 1915. Monday-Friday 8 a.m.-5 p.m. MT. 785.852.4282.

The General Store: 212 N. Main. Judi Selzer has been selling bulk food products, fabric, sewing supplies, candles, and gifts since 1991. Monday-Friday 9:30 a.m.-5:30 p.m. MT. 785.852.4256.

Rhea Reed Organ Museum: 117 N. Main. For years Dick and Bernice Rhea

traveled throughout the Midwest buying reed (pump) organs (dating from 1848 to 1918) and restoring them to amass this one-of-a-kind collection. Call ahead, 785.852.4951. rhea-antique-pump-organs.com.

Home-Owned Carnival: From 4th, ½ mile south on Main, west into the park, and take the first right. In 1976 the locals heard about carnival rides in Colorado that were scheduled to be scrapped due to flood damage. The rides were brought to Sharon Springs, overhauled, and made ready for the next county fair. The Wallace County Amusement Association offers 13 rides and 11 games at the annual fair. You can see the "skeletons" of these rides resting at the fairgrounds year round. FB.

Stephens' Restaurant: 200 E. 40. Home cooking is on the menu here. Come hungry! Monday-Saturday 6 a.m.- 8 p.m.; Sunday 8 a.m.-2 p.m. MT. 785.852.4182. FB.

Lodging: Mount Sunflower Bed and Breakfast (KBBA, 785.852.4935, mtsunflower-bandb.com); additional lodging (wallacecounty.net/business).

WALLACE

Population 58

Fort Wallace: Established in 1865, Fort Wallace originally was named Camp Pond Creek and was founded to protect travelers on the Smoky Hill Trail and workers on the Kansas Pacific Railway. The name was changed in 1866 to honor W.H.L. Wallace, a Union general. The fort was abandoned in 1888, and settlers carried away its remains to use as building materials.

Fort Wallace Museum:
2655 U.S. 40 (just east of Wallace). A big makeover is making this a destination museum. You'll see first-class exhibits about area paleontology; the American Indian connection; and how Wild Bill Hickok, George Custer, and Buffalo Bill Cody put their stamps on the fort's history. A second gallery displays an impressive collection of American Indian and military artifacts amid the striking artwork of western and wildlife artist Jerry Thomas. Visitors can also stroll down a three-quarter scale street facade of the fort and early Wallace. The museum complex includes the 1865 Pond Creek stagecoach station (NRHP), the Weskan depot, a pioneer and agricultural equipment shed, and the 1888 Bethany Lutheran Church. Monday-Saturday 9 a.m.- 5 p.m.; Sunday 1-5 p.m. MT. 785.891.3564.

Barbed Wire Buffalo:
It took artist Ernie Poe 240 hours and two miles of barbed wire to create the impressive life-sized buffalo that stands outside Fort Wallace Museum. More Poe creations are found inside.

Fort Wallace Cemetery:
From the museum, ½ mile east on U.S. 40, ¾ mile south on 27,

then ¾ mile east on E-O. The post cemetery, surrounded by a stone wall, is at the back of the larger city cemetery. A marker beside the flagpole provides a timeline and layout of the fort. Although the soldiers' remains were removed to Fort Leavenworth after Fort Wallace was abandoned, those of early civilians and scouts remain. You'll see gravestones for two 1868 scouts and for the massacred German family. A tall stone cenotaph (inside an open-faced shed) was erected by members of the Seventh U.S. Cavalry in memory of comrades lost during the Indian battles of 1867.

Section House: From 2nd and Main, take the driveway south. Described as the finest superintendent's residence on the railroad, this splendid 1879 stone building is one of only two remaining original Kansas Pacific Railway structures.

Clark-Robidoux House (NRHP): Madigan and 4th. This 1880 frame house was built in the Gothic Revival style by Peter Robidoux, an early and influential Wallace businessman. Drive by only.

WESKAN

Unincorporated

Mount Sunflower:
From Weskan, 3 miles west on U.S. 40, 10¾ miles north on N3, 1 mile west, cross a cattle guard, then ½ mile north on a pasture driveway. When you arrive at the sunflower sculpture made of railroad spikes you'll be higher than anyone else in Kansas. Congratulations! The site was surveyed in 1961 and designated by the U.S. Geological Survey as the highest elevation point in Kansas—4,039 feet above sea level. In the late 1970s Ed Harold commemorated this site, homesteaded by his grandparents in 1906, with his unique welded sunflower sculpture. From this vantage point you may see cattle (after all, you are in their pasture) grazing on buffalo grass. And keep your eyes open for jackrabbits, coyotes, antelope, deer, pocket gophers, and foxes. If you time it right, you can look toward Colorado and watch a sunset explode into rich colors in the western sky. 785.943.5444.

North Central Kansas

Counties: Clay, Cloud, Dickinson, Ellsworth, Jewell, Lincoln, Mitchell, Osborne, Ottawa, Republic, Russell, Salina, Smith, Washington

Architecture: House Contest, Burr Oak

Art: Miller's Park, Lucas

Commerce: Fifth Avenue Antique Auto Parts, Clay Center

Cuisine: Renaissance Cafe, Assaria

Customs: World's Largest Czech Egg, Wilson

Geography: Eisenhower Park and Rose Garden, Abilene

History: Home on the Range Cabin, Athol

People: National Orphan Train Complex, Concordia

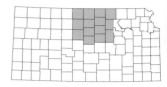

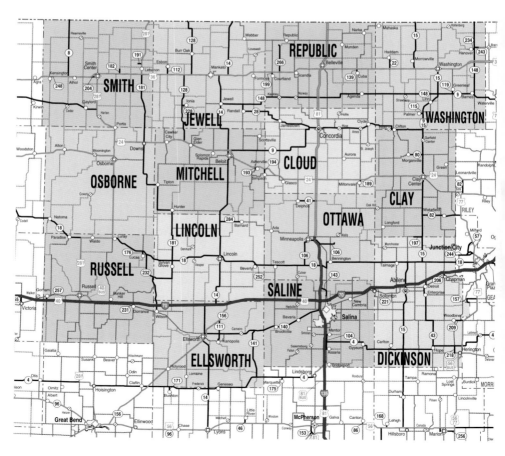

Clay County

Potato Hill Scenic Back Road: For a dare-to-do-dirt back-road drive, from Burr Oak in Oak Hill, ½ mile east on 9, 3 miles north on Cherokee, 1 mile east on 12, 1 mile north on Deer Trail, 1 mile east on 13, then 200 yards south on Elk. You've reached Potato Hill, elevation 1,450 feet.

Indian John: From U.S. 24 in Clay Center, 9 miles north on K-15, then 3 miles east on 27. One of the few gravestones at Idylwild Cemetery is that of John Derringer, 1832-1924. Known as Indian John, he was a legendary herbal medicine healer, a Mormon, and a nurse in the Civil War.

Population 4,239

Utility Park: 4th and Pomeroy. During the Great Depression customers of the city-owned power plant who couldn't pay their utility bills were given the opportunity to work off their debt. Their work resulted in the creation of Utility Park.

The park's stone walls are a tribute to the workers, and stone used for steps, footbridges, and to line the bed of a small creek offer a nice accent to the lilac hedges, flower gardens, and flowering trees. In 1934 *Better Homes and Gardens* awarded the park its highest community honor with a More Beautiful America Achievement Award.

A bronze plaque commemorating the award is on a large red glacial rock in the center of the park.

Clay County Courthouse (NRHP): 724 5th. A working clock tower stands atop this 1901 Romanesque Revival structure built of Manhattan limestone. Throughout this James Holland designed courthouse you'll find Lincrusta Walton wainscoting and brass Victorian door knobs. Monday-Friday 8 a.m.-5 p.m. 785.632.2552.

Courthouse Grounds: The courthouse occupies a full block and is surrounded by the business district. A 1911 GAR Civil War statue stands among the trees on this nicely landscaped square, and an impressive eagle sculpture, added in 1998, honors Clay County war veterans.

Carnegie Library (NRHP): 706 6th. The 1912 blond-brick library stands on the east side of the courthouse square. "Carnegie Library" is boldly written above the front door, which is framed by large columns. Monday-Friday 10 a.m-6 p.m.; Saturday 10 a.m-2 p.m.

Fifth Avenue Antique Auto Parts: 415 Court. Randy Rundle became famous for his six-volt alternator and for his work on the Queen Mum's 1951 Royal Cadillac and the pre-WWII Great Race cars.

Although he sells antique auto parts online, a visit to his Fifth Avenue shop is a rewarding trip down memory lane of all things related to automobiles. Monday-Friday 9 a.m.-5 p.m. 785.632.3450. fifthaveinternetgarage.com.

Ginger's Uptown: 721 5th. Ginger's offers contemporary women's clothing, accessories, home decor, a kitchen store— and a handbag bar! Monday-Saturday 9:30 a.m.-5 p.m. 785.632.2922. gingersuptown.com.

Downtown: Old-fashioned street lights augment the pleasing presentation of shops around the square. In addition to several antique shops are a family clothing store, a coffee and light lunch shop, boutiques, a jeweler, and gift and specialty shops.

Tasty Pastry Bakery: 531 Court. The signature item, the Nut Roll, is legendary and known far and wide. But don't overlook other tasty items including strawberry squares and cinnamon sugar and maple sticks. Monday-Friday 5:30 a.m.-5 p.m.; Saturday 6 a.m.-2 p.m. 785.632.2335.

Lodging: Life's Finer Moments Event Lodge and Cabins (785.447.1678, lifesfinermoments.com).

explorer extras... In Clay Center

In Dexter Park, K-15 and Grant, you'll find a restored 1934 band shell constructed with Public Works Administration funds.

A picturesque concrete walking bridge built in 1916 is one of the entrances (at Dexter and A) to Huntress Park, named for early prominent settlers. It is home to the popular aquatic park, a nine-hole disc golf course.

The Clay Center Tigers football team plays its games at the Otto D. Unruh football stadium, 1630 9th, built by the WPA in 1940.

The Clay County Historical Museum is planning a move to the former furniture store at 518 Lincoln. **ee**

GREEN

Population 130

Governor's Bell:
503 Batey. While serving as Kansas governor, Nehemiah Green offered to buy a bell for a Methodist church established in a Kansas town named for him. In 1881 a town was established in northeast Clay County, and remembering the former governor's offer, the founders named their town Green. You can still see the governor's bell atop the United Methodist Church.

Historic Park:
Utah and 22nd (north of Green). The sign on the limestone entrance pillars states that the city park was a 1938 WPA project. Although vegetation hides most of the stone structures, including a

stone walking bridge across a little creek, one can still imagine the picnics and walks that must have taken place here.

Green Outdoor Mural:
1st and Dixon. A colorful mural by artist Jim Fisher tells you that you're definitely in Green!

LONGFORD

Population 78

Coachlight Restaurant:
114 Weda. One well traveled customer boasts that Amy Wayman's fried chicken is the best in the world—and people come from all over to try it. But

they also clamor for the Explorer Way chicken-fried steak and other tasty made-from-scratch entries. Homemade pies are a tempting finale! Tuesday 8 a.m.-2 p.m.; Wednesday-Saturday 8 a.m.-8 p.m.; Sunday 11 a.m.-2 p.m. 785.388.2437.

Longford Water Company:
108 Main. The Kiowa aquifer naturally filters the area water giving it an inherent sweetness, softness, and quality. You can buy bottled Kiowata water here or at the Coachlight Restaurant. Tours are available too! Usually open Monday-Friday 8 a.m.-12 p.m. Call ahead, 785.388.2233. longfordwater.com.

Longford Spray Park:
108 N. Main. During the hot days of summer, cool off with a blast! Turn on the water with the hand activator at the side of the public restrooms and get ready for a refreshing spray from four water features or 14 water jets guaranteed to beat the heat.

explorer extras... In Longford

On an exterior tile wall in this one-block downtown district, Clarissa Kramer painted a mural of a train coming into Longford's 1888 depot. Great job for her first mural!

Buy your stamps at the post office, 115 Weda. Every dollar helps keep these small post offices open. Monday-Friday 8-10 a.m.; Saturday 8-8:45 a.m.

The Stone Buffalo sculpture stands in Ottawa County (*see* p. 75) at Limestone and 280. But to find it from Longford, start at the rodeo grounds, go 1 mile south on Cherokee, 4 miles west on 3rd (becomes Nugget), then 2 miles south on 280. **ee**

MORGANVILLE

Population 189

Amphitheater:
From Allen, just south on Main. Movies and dances once were presented at this sunken, outdoor amphitheater built in 1939 by the WPA. Local volunteers hope to repair the concrete walls, stage, and eight levels of seats and steps.

WAKEFIELD

Population 976

Glebe: From Wakefield, 3 miles west on K-82. A glebe is a small tract of land traditionally given to English clergy to farm and help provide a living for the family. This 15-acre glebe is across the road to the east from St. John Cemetery and is the only glebe

remaining west of the Mississippi. The land is leased to a local farmer but is still owned by the Episcopal Diocese of Kansas. St. John Episcopal Church originally was located here (now at 5th and Birch in Wakefield).

Wakefield Museum:

604 6th. Learn more about the glebe here, see an exhibit on former governor William Avery, find an eye-popping and glittering collection of brooches, admire Charles Smith's fishing tackle and rod and reel collection, view an original 13-colony flag, and discover more about Wakefield. Wednesday-Sunday 1-4 p.m. Donation welcome. 785.461.5516.

St. John and St. George Episcopal Church:

5th and Birch. The 1876 St. John church originally stood west of Wakefield on K-82. In 1930 it was moved into town and attached to the larger St. George church, built in 1886. The exquisite wood interior of St. George is unusual in that each individual piece for the wall was cut on a pump-treadle jigsaw (by Fred Dodson) before putting it into place. To see inside these churches, contact the Wakefield Museum. 785.561.5516.

Wakefield Public Library:

205 3rd. Inside this 24x40-foot limestone building constructed by the WPA in 1937 you'll find a "living room" filled with books—that's what it feels like! This pleasing library has a stone fireplace, windows with home-made valances and curtains, a floor lamp, comfortable chairs—and librarians. Monday, Wednesday 1-7 p.m.; Friday-Saturday 10 a.m.-4:30 p.m. 785.461.5510.

Old Main Street:

On the original Main Street, most businesses, including the grain elevator, were razed in 1964 for construction of Milford Lake. Where businesses once stood are now vast grassy areas and a ballpark. During the flood of 1993, water was over the top of the concession stand you now see in the park.

Kansas Landscape Arboretum:

From 6th, ½ mile south on Dogwood. More than1,000 species of native and exotic woody plants are represented at this arboretum founded in 1972. At the Meadow Willow Trail trailhead walk across the one-plank bridge with branch railings. In the southeast end of the arboretum, a bronze plaque on a rock pays tribute to early settlers. 785.461.5760.

Auld Barn (NRHP):

255 Utah. From Wakefield, 1 mile west on K-82 to the grain elevator, 4 miles south on Sunflower, follow the curve (becomes 3rd) 2 miles east, then ¼ mile south on Utah. This magnificent 30x180-foot barn with eight arches was built in 1910 for breeding and raising draft horses. The bottom half of the barn is limestone and the top half is metal panels that imitate stone. Three gabled dormers line the south-facing elevation. Park at the roadside sign or in the driveway to view the barn.

Lodging:

RV campsites at Clay County Park (201 2nd, 785.447.1547, claycountypark.com).

Cloud County

AROUND THE COUNTY

Boston Corbett Dugout Site:

From Concordia, 7 miles south on U.S. 81, then 3½ miles east on Key. Boston Corbett, the man who allegedly shot John Wilkes Booth, Lincoln's assassin, homesteaded here. Stone steps lead you through a gate to an informative plaque on a stone pillar. To see the slight indention that remains from his dugout, pass through another turnstile.

NC

Sunset Viewing Area:

1664 N. 70. From Concordia, 7½ miles west on 11th (becomes Rock), then 1 mile south and east on 70. We can thank Susie Haver, Kansas Explorer #27, for creating this public place to watch the sun setting over the river valley amid the lovely Smoky Hills.

Fairview Cemetery:

From Concordia, 2¼ miles west on K-9 (4th/Rust), then 4 miles northwest on K-28. A more-than-fair view, a sundial, sidewalks that date to the early 1900s, a stepping stone into family sections, and many French (surname) gravestones make this an interesting stop. William J. French deeded the tract of land for the cemetery in 1879.

AURORA

Population 59

Broken Arrow Saloon:
240 Main. Fans of Explorer Way chicken-fried steak, pan-fried chicken (Thursdays), or pork chops done to perfection in a cast-iron skillet (Fridays), this is the place for you. Tuesday-Saturday 10 a.m.-9 p.m. 785.464.3014.

Historic Jail: 2nd and Main.
Worth seeing is this restored jail.

CLYDE

Population 692

How did the town get its name? David Turner, one of the town founders, lived near the River Clyde in Scotland as a boy.

Reflections Park:
Just west of the library, 107 S. Green. The beautification committee created this restful flower garden spot in 2007.

Seifert Jewelry:
316 Washington. One of the few jewelry shops remaining in towns under 1,000 inhabitants, Seifert Jewelry has been in Clyde since 1902. In addition to jewelry, it sells watches, crystal, and baby jewelry and offers full-service watch, clock, and jewelry repair. Scott and Dawn Seifert are fourth-generation owners. Monday-Friday 9 a.m.-5 p.m. 785.446.3731.

Clyde Historical Museum Square: Green and Campbell.
On your own you may tour the outdoor complex, which includes a limestone jail and historic schoolhouse. 785.446.2844.

Clyde Arboretum:
204 Campbell. Home to more than 50 deciduous and evergreen species of trees (labeled), the arboretum is complemented by a small but charming park. A "grandfatherly" bur oak highlights this pleasing natural setting.

Clyde School (NRHP):
620 Broadway. Completed in 1924, the school was designed by Wichita-based architect Lorentz Schmidt. Schmidt, who was born and raised in Clyde, became widely known for public school design.

CONCORDIA

Population 5,261

Cloud County Tourism:
130 6th. Stop here for county tourism information, help from friendly staff, and clean restrooms. Monday-Friday 9 a.m.-12 p.m. and 1-5 p.m.; Saturday 10 a.m.-1 p.m. 785.243.4303. cloudcountytourism.com.

***Whole Wall* Mural:** 130 6th. WWII German POWs, orphan train riders, coal miners, and beehive kilns are just a few of the 24 Cloud County historical scenes carved into 6,400 bricks by artists Catharine Magel and Mara Smith. Installed in 2009, it is the longest sculpted mural in the nation. The Travel Information Center parking lot, U.S. 81 and 6th, offers a close-up view of the 140-foot-long mural.

National Orphan Train Complex: 300 Washington.
From 1854 to 1929 more than 250,000 orphaned, abandoned, and homeless children traveled west on orphan trains to relocate from overcrowded cities in the East. Your journey through this incredible experience begins at the Morgan-Dowell Research Center, then to a full-sized railcar representing an orphan train, and onto the adjacent 1917 Union Pacific depot (NRHP). Here the story is told through compelling photos, interpretive signage, and outstanding artifacts including a ledger with names of actual riders. Tuesday-Saturday 10 a.m.-12 p.m. and 1-4 p.m. Admission charge. 785.243.4471. orphantraindepot.org.

Orphan Train Rider Statues:
Each year additional statues of orphan train riders are being added in various downtown locations near the initial statue standing at Broadway and 6th.

Camp Concordia WWII Guardhouse:
From Concordia, 2 miles north on U.S. 81, then 1 mile east on Union. The most complete remnant of the POW camp is the restored limestone guardhouse. The base of the camp water tower is visible in the field to the north, and just east of the guardhouse are the camp's stone entrance pillars and wall. The small white house north of the entrance was the main gate guard post.

WWII German Prisoner of War Camp Museum:
From Concordia, 2 miles north on U.S. 81, then 1 mile east on Union. Inside the tin-clad former camp warehouse you'll learn about the 304 buildings that once stood here, including housing for 4,000 German POWs, a hospital, and the administration buildings for 880 American soldiers. Photos, exhibits, and accounts reveal the camp's history and the experiences of those stationed or incarcerated here. Operating from May 1943 to November 1945, it was the largest of the 16 POW camps in Kansas and has the most remaining evidence. Call ahead, 785.243.4303. powcampconcordia.org/museum.php.

Brown Grand Theatre

(NRHP): 310 W. 6th. Restored to its 1907 glory, this 650-seat theatre features gold decorative molding and lights around the proscenium arch, brass rails in front of the box seats, and forest green curtains behind them. Self-guided and guided tours present an entirely new view of this Carl Boller designed theatre. The stage curtain, with its immense painting of French emperor Napoleon Bonaparte, was a gift to theater owner Napoleon Bonaparte Brown from his son Earl V.D. Brown. Tuesday-Friday 10 a.m.-4 p.m. Admission charge. 785.243.2553. browngrand.org.

Brownstone Hall: W. 6th.

Drive by this 23-room Victorian home built in 1883 for Colonel Napoleon Bonaparte Brown, original owner of the Brown Grand Theatre. On W. 6th between 2nd and 1st you can see the sign on the roof that reads, "Brownstone Hall."

Frank Carlson Library:

702 Broadway. A room in the public library honors Frank Carlson, former Kansas governor, U.S. congressman, and U.S. senator. Political cartoons, mementos, and information provide a snapshot of Carlson's life during the 1950s and 1960s, and his elephant collection is a reminder of his Republican Party affiliation. Monday-Thursday 9 a.m.-8 p.m.; Friday-Saturday 9-5 p.m. 785.243.2250.

Nazareth Motherhouse

(NRHP): 1300 Washington. A drive by this mammoth 1903 Gothic style motherhouse is indeed awe inspiring. Although their numbers are dwindling since arriving in Concordia in 1884, the Sisters of St. Joseph still use the facility as a retirement home. Tours are offered of portions of the motherhouse, including of the chapel, which features impressive stained-glass windows and hand-

carved statuary. Monday-Friday 2-4 p.m. Donation welcome. Call ahead, 785.243.2113.

Lourdes Park and Grotto:

Nazareth Motherhouse, 1300 Washington. Next to the mother-house a tranquil park features an intriguing grotto that replicates the historic religious site in Lourdes, France. Built of petrified vegetable material, the grotto's entrance is an imitation of the Abbey Moyne ruins in Ireland. Ask at the motherhouse office for permission to visit the grotto. 785.243.2113.

Cloud County Historical

Museum: 635 Broadway. A 1928 Lincoln-Page biplane, a Boston Corbett exhibit, a replica letter from Martha Washington, agricultural displays, and WWII POW camp memorabilia, are just a few reasons to visit this museum housed in a 1908 Carnegie library. Tuesday-Friday 1-5 p.m.; Saturday 11 a.m.-5 p.m. 785.243.2866.

Pleasant Hill Cemetery:

W. 18th and Cedar. The arched memorial to the Brown family of Brown Grand Theatre fame stands at the south end of the cemetery. Note the unusual epitaphs. Also of interest is the elk statue (in view from the Brown family arch) with "Elks Rest" etched in the stone. The flat stones nearby mark Elks lodge members' graves, buried in proximity to show fraternal unity.

Downtown: You'll find wonderful shopping opportunities plus buildings featuring various architectural styles. Me & Ma's Bakery (134 W. 6th, 785.818.5055); Rod's Food Store (307 W. 6th); Britt's Fountain & Gifts (118 W.

6th, 785.243.4755); Jitter's Coffee House and Deli (221 W. 6th, 785.243.4630); and several antique stores are just a few of the places not to miss.

Marla's Joy: 512 State. With Chef G's Italian background and Marla's joy in creating a classy dining experience, every menu item will make you happy. Linen tablecloths, fresh flowers, and raspberry tea enhance your enjoyment of homemade everything, from dressings and pastas to the carrot sheet cake and Snicker's cheesecake. Tuesday-Saturday 11 a.m.-3 p.m.; Friday-Saturday 5-8 p.m. 785.262.4294. marlasjoy.net.

Kristy's: 101 W. 6th. Home-style breakfasts are served all day at this local cafe. Monday-Wednesday 5 a.m.-4 p.m.; Thursday-Friday 5 a.m.-9 p.m.; Saturday-Sunday 5 a.m.-2 p.m. 785.243.4653.

More Good Restaurants:

Heavy's Steakhouse & BBQ (103 W. 7th, 785.262.4132, FB); Easy G's Sports Grill (107 W. 6th, 785.262.4099, FB).

Lodging: Kansas Creek Inn Bed and Breakfast (KBBA, 785.243.9988, kansascreekinn.com); additional lodging including RV (cloudcountytourism.com).

**explorer extras...
In Concordia**

A dog park, an 18-hole disc golf course, and an RV park are found at Airport Park on south U.S. 81. The National Youth Administration (NYA) built the shelter and entrance columns in 1939. Can you find the initials NYA on the shelter house?

In City Park near the parking lot at 11th and Washington, a 1949 bronze statue by William Wallace Rosenbauer of a shirtless young man in belted jeans and boots is inscribed, "To the young men of Cloud County who have fought the nation's battles."

Now the Stonehouse Event Center, Elmhurst and 11th, the building was once the bishop's house. Sunset Home, a nursing home and rehabilitation center at 620 2nd, was formerly the old hospital.

On most Saturdays an estate sale is happening at Kearn Auction, 220 W. 5th. If a box is on a seat, that seat is saved! 785.614.2082. kearnauction.com.

The Concordia Flour Mill at 410 Cedar was erected in 1912 at a

cost of $75,000. In recent years the grain elevator and mill were painted pink, but no one seems to know when or by whom. The prevailing opinion is that it was a marketing ploy. Currently the complex is used by a construction company.

Jets of water help keep the giant eyeball, an 1,800-pound granite sphere, afloat and spinning in the fountain in front of the courthouse at 8th and Washington.

A splash pad, public restrooms, and a place for outdoor entertainment opened in 2016 as Broadway Plaza at Broadway and 6th. **ee**

GLASCO

Population 484

Solomon Valley/Highway 24 Heritage Alliance:
Glasco is the eastern end of the Solomon Valley Heritage Alliance, which promotes the Solomon River Valley and 24 towns along U.S. 24 between Glasco and Hoxie. This scenic route takes you through the Smoky Hills and into the High Plains, and along the cusp of both regions. You'll come across 16 national register sites, five county seats, two state lakes, one state historic site, and one giant ball of twine. In or around each of the 24 towns along the route, a blue-roofed kiosk provides information about the Solomon Valley and the nearby town. The Glasco kiosk is found near a former gas station on U.S. 24.

Hodge Podge: 113 E. Main. A potpourri of things happen here, but the main event is ordering an ice cream treat at the 1927 soda fountain. Monday-Friday 9 a.m.-5 p.m.; Saturday 9 a.m.-12 p.m. 785.568.2542.

Stained-Glass Tour:
A colorful way to enjoy the town is through the stained-glass windows in Glasco's four churches. The St. Mary's Catholic Church windows date to 1912, St. Paul's Lutheran Church has contemporary stained glass with biblical references for each, and the United Methodist and Christian churches both have rare Woman's Christian Temperance Union windows. For a guide and to ensure the churches are open for viewing, call ahead. 785.568.0120.

Downtown Historic District (NRHP):
Twenty-five buildings are included as significant contributors to the historic district. Despite a 1911 fire that destroyed many structures, downtown is a fine example of a turn-of-the-century commercial district.

The Corner Store (NRHP):
129 E. Main. A former grocery, the Corner Store still nurtures the community. Exhibited art reflects area history, and sales support local artists. A Farmers Market is also on hand. Tuesday 10 a.m.-4 p.m.

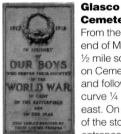

Glasco Cemetery:
From the east end of Main, ½ mile south on Cemetery, and follow the curve ¼ mile east. On one of the stone entrance pillars, a 1917-1918 plaque reads, "In Memory of Our Boys who served their country in the World War in camp on the battlefield and on the seas." At the fourth driveway east of the pillar entrance, turn south into the cemetery. Look for two iron cutouts created by Kevin Williamson as memorials to his brothers Michael and Joe.

Potts Ford Historic Bridge (NRHP):
From Main, ½ mile west on Crest, ¾ mile south on N. 40, and at the curve 100 yards southwest on Camp. Here a one-lane 1884 iron truss bridge built by the Wrought Iron Bridge Company crosses the Solomon River.

JAMESTOWN

Population 277

Jamestown Wildlife Area:
From Jamestown, 1½ miles north on N. 40, 2 miles west on Vale, then north on N. 20 to reach the

southeastern point of the refuge. This wetlands/uplands region contains numerous different shallow-water salt marshes, which present an ideal place for thousands of migrating water-fowl and shorebirds. The best viewing seasons are mid-February into May, and late August through November. Look for the helpful kiosks. 785.439.6243. tinyurl.com/jamestownmarsh.

MILTONVALE

Population 523

Tootle Park: E. 1st. Milton Tootle owned the land designated for the townsite, thus the name of the town, park, and festival (Tootlefest). Among the amenities in this picturesque park is the pedestrian stone bridge with three arches. The band shell, park entrances, and creek were built as 1936 WPA projects and have been recently restored. One of the entrance posts at E. 1st contains a WPA plaque, and in the other post is etched, "Tootle Park." In 2002, as a community project, the townspeople built a park playground and named it Tootleville.

DK's Bar and Grill: 121 S. Starr. On Wednesdays come for chicken-fried steak made the Explorer Way on the grill. Tuesday-Saturday 11 a.m.-9 p.m.; Sunday 12-7 p.m. 785.427.2282.

Kountry Kafe: 210 N. Starr. Daily specials and homemade pies are only a few of the good eats that make this place popular with the locals. Pan-fried chicken is part of the Sunday buffet. Monday-Saturday 5 a.m.-8 p.m.; Sunday 9 a.m.-2 p.m. 785.427.2662.

Grassland Gardens: 1739 Camp. Trish Remley sells drought-tolerant plants, native plants, pollinators for butterflies, and 60 varieties of ornamental grasses. 785.427.2438. grasslandgardens.com.

Lodging: RV campground at the city park (785.427.3380).

explorer extras... In Miltonvale

The Miltonvale Lumber Company, 21 E. Spruce, is part of the longest-running business in town, starting in the late 1800s. Although the old building is used for storage, the lumber-yard is still going strong and is operated by the Graham family's fourth-generation.

The buildings of Miltonvale Wesleyan College, a two-year college from 1909 to 1972, are now the home of Miltonvale High School at 619 W. Tootle. The school, like the town, is named for town founder Milton Tootle. **ee**

explorer extras... In Rice

Unincorporated

You can cross the Republican River on an 1893 Pegram iron truss bridge by going 1 mile west of Rice (or about 4 miles east of Concordia) on K-9, then 1½ miles north on 190. Constructed for the Junction City and Fort Kearney Railroad, the bridge was utilized for the county road system after the railroad ceased operation. North of this bridge is yet another abandoned railroad bridge.

To see an 1899 J.B. Tremblay stone single-arch bridge, go 5 miles east of Concordia on K-9 to unincorporated Rice, north 1 block into Rice, then east to the river. Ray Doyen restored the bridge almost 100 years after it was built. In 2015 a large section of a cottonwood tree fell and broke the bridge's wooden guard rail making it impossible to use the stone steps to see underneath the bridge. An interpretive sign at the bridge tells the story. **ee**

SIMPSON

Population 86

Trapper Joe's: 304 Elkhorn. Owner young Nick Jensen takes pride in every plate of food he creates. He buys the meat locally for his famous grilled-in-butter chicken-fried steak and serves it up with a mound of made-from-scratch mashed potatoes and cream gravy. Wednesday-Saturday 11 a.m.-8 p.m.; Sunday 11 a.m.-2 p.m. 785.593.6678.

Blue-Roofed Kiosk: Learn more about Simpson at the Solomon Valley Heritage Alliance kiosk across from Trapper Joe's.

explorer extras... In St. Joseph

Unincorporated

The beautifully designed twin towers of the historic red-brick Catholic Church guide you to the tiny town of St. Joseph, originally a French Canadian settlement. The first church, a wooden structure built in 1873, was destroyed by fire in 1910, and the current church was erected that same year. Although the church is closed, viewing its exterior is worth your drive. In the nearby cemetery, the gravestones inscribed in French are also of interest. ee

Dickinson County

As you drive the county roads, notice that no road name has more than five letters. It was a financial decision—more than five letters increased the price! North-south roads are alphabetical from west to east. East-west roads are numerical, starting with 100 Ave. in the southern end of the county and increasing by 100 each mile.

ABILENE

Population 6,456

Visitor Information Center (NRHP):
201 NW 2nd. Begin your visit here and stock up with Abilene and area brochures. The visitor center (Civic Center) is in Abilene's 1928 Union Pacific depot, built in the Mission style with terra cotta design. Monday-Saturday 9 a.m.-4 p.m.; Sunday 11 a.m.-4 p.m. 785.263.2231.

Eisenhower Museum Campus (8 Wonders of Kansas):
200 SE 4th. The museum campus comprises several buildings, so we recommend a start at the visitor center (daily 9 a.m.-4:45 p.m., 877.746.4453, eisenhower. archives.gov). Other stops in the Eisenhower campus include the Eisenhower Museum (*see next entry*), Ike's boyhood home (NRHP; tours every 15 minutes on the hour 9 a.m.-4:30 p.m), special exhibits in the research library, the 11-foot statue of Eisenhower as a WWII general, and the Place of Meditation, and the final resting place of the president, his wife, Mamie, and infant son Doud.

Eisenhower Museum:
200 SE 4th. The lobby murals are a wonderful beginning to this journey through Dwight Eisenhower's life. The military gallery presents a moving tribute to his role as supreme Allied commander during WWII, and the presidential gallery summarizes his political accomplishments. You'll learn about Eisenhower's

progressive highway system, the first lady, and such little gems as Ike being the first television president. Daily 9 a.m.-4:45 p.m. Admission charge. 877.746.4453. eisenhower.archives.gov.

Heritage Center of Dickinson County:
412 S. Campbell. The area's colorful past is preserved in the museum and several outbuildings. The museum depicts life on the Plains during the American pioneer movement and includes exhibits about

cowboy life on the Chisholm Trail, Joseph McCoy, the amazing evolution of the telephone, and the story of Abilene entrepreneur C.L. Brown, whose 1899 start-up company is known today as Sprint. In a separate facility, climb aboard one of 24 original carved ponies or four chariots for a musical ride on the restored 1901 C.W. Parker carousel (NRHP; 8 Wonders of Kansas Customs). Monday-Friday 9 a.m.-3 p.m.; Saturday 10 a.m.-5 p.m.; Sunday 1-5 p.m. Admission charge. 785.263.2681. heritagecenterdk.com.

Seelye Mansion (NRHP; 8 Wonders of Kansas Architecture):
1105 N. Buckeye. In 1905 A.B. Seelye, famous patent medicine inventor, completed this grand 25-room Georgian style mansion with massive portico at a cost of $55,000. Guided tours highlight the original furniture, Edison light fixtures, a ballroom, and a bowling alley—this mansion is an example of opulent living! Monday-Saturday 10 a.m.-4 p.m.; Sunday 1-4 p.m.

Admission charge (pay at the Seelye Patent Medicine Museum east of the mansion). 785.263.1084. seelyemansion.org.

Seelye Patent Medicine Museum:
1105 N. Buckeye. A.B. Seelye created more than 100 organic home remedies for humans, horses, and chickens. Here you'll see a collection of original cans, bottles, jars, and pharmacy equipment used in Seelye's patent medicine enterprise. Monday-Saturday 10 a.m.-4 p.m.; Sunday 1-4 p.m.

Lebold Mansion (NRHP; 8 Wonders of Kansas Architecture):
106 N. Vine. An early founder of Abilene, Conrad Lebold built this 1880 Italianate Tuscan Villa mansion primarily with Kansas limestone. Drive by only.

Jeffcoat Photography Studio Museum:
321 N. Broadway. Since 1921 three generations of the Jeffcoat family have chronicled in photographs the people, places, and events in and around Abilene. The large collection of historic cameras and photo equipment is impressive. Thursday-Saturday 9:30 a.m.-5:30 p.m. 785.263.9882. jeffcoatstudio.com.

Greyhound Hall of Fame:
407 S. Buckeye. Two sweet greyhounds are here to greet you and say, "Pet me, please." The story of early race tracks and the mechanical rabbit, plus racing videos are found inside this impressive museum. The Hall of Fame honors champion dogs and their owners and trainers. Daily 9 a.m.-4:45 p.m. 800.932.7881. greyhoundhalloffame.com.

Great Plains Theatre:
401 Cottage. Known for professional theatre, Great Plains Theatre has now added concerts, comedians, magicians, and state-of-the-art cinema to its offerings. 785.263.4574. greatplainstheatre.com

Abilene and Smoky Valley Railroad:
200 SE 5th. Board the train at the 1887 Rock Island depot at Old Abilene Town. Enjoy a two-hour, 10-mile, round-trip ride in a 100-year-old coach or in an open-air observation car. A 1945 diesel-electric locomotive powers this conveyance through the lovely Smoky Valley between Abilene and Enterprise. Memorial Day-Labor Day, Wednesday-Saturday 10 a.m. and 2 p.m.; Sunday 2 p.m. Admission charge. Reservations recommended.

785.263.1077. asvrr.org. The website provides additional dates and options including a dinner train, a steam locomotive, a Silver Flyer Railbus tour, and a historic homes and barns bus tour.

Eisenhower Park and Rose Garden (NRHP):
500 NW Pine. Plan to visit in the spring and summer when the flower garden is an explosion of color and textures. The rose garden, pergola, concrete paths, landscaping layout, and park buildings, including the swimming pool and bath house, were built by the WPA in 1938. Come and smell the roses! 785.263.7266. FB.

Abilene Stadium (NRHP):
Pine between NW 4th and NW 8th (at the fairgrounds). At this 1938 WPA limestone stadium on June 6, 1952, General Dwight D. Eisenhower announced his candidacy for president.

World's Largest Spur:
From Pine and NW 4th (Eisenhower Park entrance), ¼ mile north on Pine. The gigantic spur stands at the north entrance of the rodeo arena. Created by Larry Houston, his one-ton steel production measures 20x28 feet!

Abilene Public Library:
209 NW 4th. The interior dome of this 1907 Carnegie library

was refurbished to its original grandeur in 2010. Monday-Thursday 9 a.m.-6 p.m.; Friday-Saturday 9 a.m.-4 p.m. A tasteful accessory to the library's front lawn is a statue of Benjamin Franklin seated on a bench and reading. 785.263.3082.

NC

Union Pacific Depot (NRHP):
10 N. Cedar. The decorative detailing and red clay tile of this exquisite Spanish Colonial Revival building, circa1928, is punctuated with cornucopias overflowing with red, green, blue, yellow, and orange flowers and fruits flanking the red and blue Union Pacific shield. It is now home to Geske Interiors.

Abilene Cemetery:
NW 14th. David and Ida Eisenhower, C.W. Parker, A.B. Seelye, Alva Duckwall, 1870 marshal Thomas J. Smith, and rodeo legend

Gerald Roberts are only a few of the famous people buried in this intriguing cemetery. Another point of interest is the gravestone for Marlin and Melinda Fitzwater, neither of whom have died as of 2016. She had worked in the Reagan White House and he for Presidents Reagan and Bush. Find the Fitzwater stone in the northwest corner.

Brown's Park and Memorial Home:
1974 Hawk. From Abilene, 1½ miles south on K-15, east on 2000 (first paved road south of river bridge), and follow the signs. C.L. Brown, founder of what is now Sprint, built this still-operating retirement facility in 1928 as a memorial to his parents. You are welcome to stop at this historic home and ask for a tour. During daylight hours you may drive through this serene area

even beyond the "private property" sign. Along the park's curving roads you'll see the stone buildings used as a backdrop for the Easter Sunrise Pageant that started in 1946, a Boy Scout camp, disc golf course, and nature trails.

Brookville Hotel

(8 Wonders of Kansas Cuisine): 105 E. Lafayette. From I-70 Abilene exit 275, ¼ mile north on K-15. This famous dining experience dates to 1915 and to the small town of Brookville west of Salina. Since 2000 the legacy continues in

this Abilene facility, re-created just as it was in Brookville's historic hotel and bank. And the celebrated family-style fried chicken meal is as delicious as ever! Wednesday-Friday 5-8 p.m.; Saturday 11:30 a.m.-8 p.m.; Sunday 11:30 a.m.-7 p.m. Reservations recommended. 785.263.2244. brookvillehotel.com.

Mr. K's Farmhouse:

407 S. Van Buren. From downtown, 1½ miles west on NW 3rd, then ½ mile south on Van Buren (Old U.S. 40). Formerly famous as Lena's, this hilltop restaurant (still in the original white farmhouse) has hosted such satisfied customers as President Eisenhower. Lena used to paddle guests on their birthdays, and even Eisenhower wasn't immune for his 75th! The paddle, signed by Eisenhower, still hangs on the wall. Lunch is lighter fare; dinner includes steaks, chicken, seafood, and evening specials. Tuesday-Saturday 11a.m.-2 p.m. and 5-9 p.m.; Sunday 11 a.m.-2 p.m. 785.263.7995. mrksfarmhouse.com.

Amanda's Bakery & Bistro:

302 N. Broadway. Enjoy Amanda's culinary skills inside this historic

building (complete with pressed-tin ceiling and old wooden tables). The chicken salad is homemade as are the bagels, English muffins, and desserts. Tuesday-Friday 8:30 a.m.-4 p.m.; Saturday 9 a.m.-3 p.m. 785.200.6622. FB.

Restaurant Three One One: 311 Spruce. Chef

John Shaft and his wife, Helen Darrington, moved back from Florida and brought Cuban style cuisine with them. The Mahi taco, cornitas, and hand-pattied burgers are a few favorites to go along with the craft beer, wine, and fun cocktails. This vegetarian-friendly place is quickly becoming known as the Key West of the Midwest. Monday-Saturday 11 a.m.-8:30 p.m. FB.

Local Cafes: For home-town atmosphere tie up your buggy at the Hitching Post (100 SE 5th, 785.263.1868) or at Joe Snuffy's (209 W. 1st, 785.263.7802).

Lodging: Abilene's Victorian Inn (KBBA, 785.263.7774, abilenesvictorianinn.com); Engle House Bed and Breakfast (785.263.0453, englehouse.com); additional lodging (800.658.4667, abilenekansas.org).

explorer extras... In Abilene

Installed in 1999, the *Little Ike* statue by artist John Forsythe accents the corner of NW 3rd and Spruce. On the plaque at the feet of young Eisenhower is Ike's quotation, "The proudest thing I can claim is that I am from Abilene."

A renovated 1920s soda fountain is nestled in the back of Auburn Pharmacy, 304 N. Broadway—great stop for a cold treat. Monday-Friday 8:30 a.m.-6 p.m. 785.263.4330.

Look for the plaque on the boulder in front of the post office, 217 N. Buckeye, to find the northern terminus of the

Texas Cattle Trail (1867-1871), also known as the Chisholm Trail.

Architectural driving or walking tours highlight some of Abilene's finest historic structures on N. Buckeye, NW 3rd, and N. Vine. A tour of historical markers guides you to 28 historic points including the site of Abilene's late-1800s cattle yards. Self-guided tour brochures are available at the Visitor Information Center, 201 NW 2nd.

From I-70 Abilene exit 275, ¼ mile north on K-15, look west to see two sets of four red-brick gate pillars, turn west at the south set of pillars, and follow a narrow grassy driveway to the southwest corner of the property. Along with the Dakota sandstone grotto surrounded by vegetation, all that remains are the driveway entrance pillars and an abandoned rectory. **ee**

CARLTON

Population 41

Nothing Sign: From K-4, ¼ mile north on Deer, and follow the curve east. In 1986 residents Virgil and Faith Meyer erected a sign that read, "Nothing Happened Here in 1986." In the past several years members of the Model A Club of Wichita have come to Carlton and put up their own signs to refute the claim.

Grain Elevator Barn:

Just south of the "Nothing" sign is a magnificent barn that was moved in from the country and retrofitted as part of Carlton's grain elevator. The barn was built by the Cornell family who founded Cornell University in Ithaca, New York, and was part of a large Shorthorn cattle ranch near Carlton.

NC

CHAPMAN

Population 1,252

Astronaut Outdoor Mural:
Marshall and Old U.S. 40.
A large mural recognizing
Chapman native Joe Engle

hangs on the north side of the
1917 concrete grain elevator. At
age 32, Engle was the youngest
pilot ever to qualify as an astronaut, and he commanded three
space shuttle flights—the *Enterprise*, the *Columbia*, and the
Discovery. Drive by his boyhood
home at 534 W. 6th.

Concrete Grain Elevators
and Scale House: Marshall
and Old U.S. 40. Like the grain
elevator with the astronaut
mural, the small unassuming
concrete scale house next to it,
also was built in 1917. A third
structure, the westernmost
elevator, is the oldest in the
complex. Erected in 1911 it
is one of the earliest concrete
grain elevators in Kansas.

Londeen's Hardware
Store: 445 N. Marshall.
Located on Chapman's
red-brick main street, Londeen's
Hardware has been selling
"everything under the sun"
since 1938. Paint, gardening
equipment, recliners, appliances,
home decor, and all the little
things in between are found
here. Monday-Friday 8 a.m.-
5:30 p.m.; Saturday 8 a.m.-
4 p.m. 785.922.6550.

Butterfield Overland
**Despatch Wagon Ruts
(NRHP):** From Marshall,
¾ mile west on 5th to Indian Hill

Cemetery. Inside the cemetery,
signage leads you to the ruts,
which are west of the cemetery
and enclosed by chain-link
ropes. The ruts are best viewed
from inside the cemetery.
Sharing a segment of the Smoky
Hill Trail, the Butterfield Overland
Despatch operated a relay
station along Chapman Creek.

St. Patrick's Cemetery:
From K-206 north edge of
Chapman, ¾ mile east on 2650.
Many gravestones record Irish
birthplaces such as County
Limerick, Tipperary, County
Kerry, and County Cork.

St. Patrick's Mission
Church (NRHP): West of
St. Patrick's Cemetery. Built
as a Catholic mission for Irish
Settlers and American Indians,
the simple 1861 stone building
was destroyed by a tornado in
2008. Using stones from the old
mission, four corner pillars were
reconstructed to their original
dimensions and now anchor
this open-air structure/memorial.
Note the bend in the handrails,
a result of the tornado.

Kansas Auto Racing
Museum: 1205 Manor. Learn
about our state's contribution
to the world of racing—the first
NASCAR event (1949) and the
first NHRA event (1955; held in
Great Bend) were both won by
Kansans! Plus, the museum's
collection of jalopies, dragsters,
midgets, and modified cars is an
impressive one. Monday-Saturday
9 a.m.-5 p.m. 785.922.6642.
kansasautoracingmusem.org.

Southern Comfort:
114 E. 4th. Daily specials are
homemade and include schnitzel,
catfish, lasagna, and meatloaf.
Biscuits from scratch with pan
gravy is the top breakfast item

and confirms that comfort food
can't get any better than this.
Tuesday-Saturday 6 a.m.-
7:30 p.m. 785.922.7176. FB.

Windmill Inn Bed
and Breakfast: 1787 Rain.
This 1917 Prairie School style,
four-square with egg-and-dart
trim is home to Deb and Tim
Sanders, a quiet place in the
country for a gourmet meal for
groups of 8 to 24. If weather
permits, the wraparound porch
is a perfect place to begin your
evening. Reservations required.
785.263.8755.
windmillinnbb.com.

Prospect Park Farm
(NRHP): 2178 2000. From
Old U.S. 40, 6 miles south on
Rain, then 2 miles east on 2000.
Just before Trail, above the tree
line, you'll see the cupola of the
1884 Italianate Villa style stone
home. The original stone home,
built in 1876, is now the kitchen
wing of the larger house. Nearby
are two large stone barns, built
in 1876 and 1882. Drive by only.
For tours (tour charge), call
785.922.6600.

Longview (NRHP):
2250 2100. From Old U.S. 40,
5 miles south on Rain, then 2½
miles east on 2100. The Second
Empire style farmhouse, built
in 1880 by Joseph S. Hollinger,
is rare for a rural residence. It
is characterized by a mansard
roof, central tower, cupola (down
for restoration), quoins (corner
features), eave brackets, and a

decorative one-story side porch. Drive by only. For tours (tour charge), call 785.922.7181.

explorer extras...
In Chapman

Shamrocks on downtown light poles reflect the Irish influence in Chapman.

On 4th between Broadway and Logan, a sign informs us that Chapman had the first county high school (established in 1886) in the world.

An old and weathered Federal Aid Project marker stands along Old U.S. 40 near Logan and 4th. With the increased economic impact of automobiles after WWI, the Federal Aid Highway Project of 1921 was enacted to provide 50–50 matching funds for states to construct and improve roads. **ee**

ENTERPRISE

Population 823

Enterprise is a town perfectly named since enterprising industry (milling and manufacturing) made the town viable and strong. Jacob Ehrsam built a gristmill on the Smoky Hill River in 1869 for his brother-in-law Christian Hoffman. Before long Hoffman's operation included a grain-storage elevator, a corn meal mill, and 33 grain-storage facilities in towns along the railroad.

Gristmill: 1st and Factory. A new venture in 2016, this old-time mill is a nod to the early flour mills in Enterprise. Whether it's grinding flour to sell or simply demonstrating the bygone craft of converting grain to flour, this mill is an interesting stop. Hours likely to change; a retail store may be added. 785.922.6582.

Carrie Nation: Historic photos in the public library, 202 S. Factory, document famous temperance leader Carrie Nation smashing

the bar in Enterprise in 1901. 785.263.8351.

America's Park: W. 3rd and S. Grant. The park was named for Catherine America Hoffman, who donated the land for the park in 1917. Mrs. Hoffman, a leader in the Woman Suffrage campaign of 1912, was a strong supporter of Carrie Nation and the Woman's Christian Temperance Union. It was she who invited Carrie to Enterprise and hosted her in her home before Carrie and her followers smashed Schillings Saloon.

Enterprise Ecological Gardens: E. 1st. The gardens can be found in a wooded area two blocks east of downtown. Trails and bridges provide a relaxing stop for a short respite.

Kindergarten: The first public kindergarten in Kansas started in Enterprise in 1903, a fact stated on the sign at the north end of town.

HERINGTON

Population 2,491

M.D. Herington purchased land here in 1880 for his cattle business and eventually built a town around the ranch, naming the town Herington. Seeing that the future was in railroads, he offered the right of way through town to railroad companies. By 1888 Herington was a railroad boom town.

Railroad Yard: You'll have a birdseye view of the yard from the overpass, which includes a pedestrian sidewalk, on W. Main between 3rd and 7th. Observing today's modern activity, it's

interesting to reflect that this is the old railroad yard where more than 100 years ago you would have witnessed quite a different scene, one that included two roundhouses, a freight house, a telegraph office, and a two-story limestone depot.

Post Office Mural (NRHP): 17 E. Main. *Arrival of the First Train in Herington–1885* is the title of this 1937 Section artwork by H. Louis Freund. When Freund consulted Herington citizens about a subject for the mural, they chose the town founding. The mural portrays the arrival of the first Missouri Pacific train with the original town in the background, which includes M.D. Herington's ranch on the right.

Outdoor Murals: The railroad heritage of Herington is featured in Milton Fleming's train mural (Broadway and Day). His Coca Cola mural (1st and Main) replicates the advertisement once depicted on the former drugstore building.

Sunset Hill Cemetery: 930 W. Burns. From Walnut, ½ mile north on 8th, then ¼ mile west on Burns. The WPA stone fence, the GAR cannon presented in 1908 by the Woman's Relief Corps, the 1914 Civil War statue, and the M.D. Herington gravestone (second driveway past the WPA stone house) are only a few of the reasons to visit this cemetery.

Herington Public Library (NRHP): 102 S. Broadway. The Carnegie Foundation and the city funded the construction of this handsome 1915 blond-brick building. Renovated in the early 2000s, the library added

Cathy Mayer's colorful murals to the interior walls. Monday-Thursday 1 a.m.-6 p.m.; Friday-Saturday 9 a.m.-3 p.m.

Tri-County Museum:
800 S. Broadway. Displays capture the story of the tri-county (Dickinson, Marion, and Morris Counties) area, emphasizing its railroad history. Tuesday-Friday 1-5 p.m. 785.258.2842.

Father Padilla Memorial Park:
Broadway and Vine. In the park's southwest corner stands a 1904 memorial to Father Padilla, the first Christian martyr killed in Kansas (in 1542). Note the fascinating tree swing; it looks as if the tree grew support cuffs for the bar that joins them. Additional park attractions are the trail around Memorial Lake, a nine-hole disc golf course, the 1937 WPA swimming pool, and on the park's west side a picturesque area

featuring WPA stone steps and a stone bridge crossing a creek.

Kay's Pharmacy:
2 W. Main. Kids and adults love coming to this 1920s six-stool soda fountain. The brass foot rail, ceramic-tile counter, and the back bar create a nostalgic backdrop for enjoying ice cream sundaes and Green Rivers. Monday-Friday 8:30 a.m.-5:30 p.m.; Saturday 8:30 a.m.-12 p.m. 785.258.3717.

Sweet Creations Bakery:
400 E. Trapp. Pop one of the donut holes into your mouth

and on first bite experience that delicious, sweet fried dough moment. Dawn Melcher lovingly makes every pastry, hoagie bun, and pizza bread, and the breakfast sausage rolls are a favorite. Monday-Friday 6:30 a.m.-4:30 p.m.; Saturday 8 a.m.-12 p.m. 785.258.0458. FB.

The Spot and Dining Car:
304 W. Walnut. Burgers, sandwiches, and cold beer hit the spot at this bar and grill. The decor pays homage to the importance of the area's railroad industry. Breakfast, Friday-Sunday 7:30-9:30 a.m.; lunch, daily 11 a.m.-1:30 p.m.; dinner, Monday-Saturday 5-9 p.m. 785.258.5987. FB.

Lodging:
Herington Inn & Suites (785.258.3300, heringtoninnandsuites.com).

explorer extras... In Herington

A "Freedom is Not Free" plaque, 409 N. Broadway, stands as a memorial to the six local men who died in the Vietnam War.

The picturesque Herington City Lake, 1 mile west of town on 500, is good for walleye fishing, bird watching, or stretching your legs. cityofherington.com. **ee**

HOPE

Population 367

Hope in Kansas:
Stone signs at both ends of town remind us, "There Will Always Be Hope in Kansas."

Gridiron Cafe:
211 N. Main. School and sports decor accents the Gridiron, which offers such winners as the chicken cranberry salad and the Vista Heat Burger, named for the school (Rural Vista) and the mascot (Heat). Monday-Saturday 11 a.m.-1:30 p.m.; Tuesday, Thursday 5:30-7:30 p.m.; Sunday 11:30 a.m.-1:30 p.m. 785.366.7700. FB.

Hope Community Historical Museum:
203 S. Main. Along with local artifacts, an 1860 Civil War revolver and an 1890 Redina disc music box are on exhibit in this small but important museum. May-September, Saturday 1-2 p.m.; Sunday 1:30-4 p.m. 785.366.0487.

NC

SOLOMON

Population 1,062

Downtown:
You might notice something different here—nearly all of the buildings in a one-block area serve as frontage for the operations of the Solomon Corporation. Headquartered downtown, the company sells, repairs, and recycles electrical transformers throughout the United States and internationally. The corporation also thoughtfully transformed the downtown area into a sleek, modern environment with landscaping, streetscaping, and outdoor lounge areas.

Shady Lane Drive:
Old U.S. 40 and 2200. The locals so loved this tunnel of Dutch elm foliage that the road was rebuilt and new trees planted in 1976 in honor of the country's bicentennial. Telling the Shady Lane story is the plaque atop a base built with limestone from the 1885 Solomon depot.

E's Cafe & Pub:
139 W. Main. This place will charm you the minute you step inside. Beautifully renovated, the dark pressed-tin ceiling casts a warm gleam on the original restored brick walls and the tile and wood floors. Explorer Way chicken-fried steak and the breakfast cinnamon rolls keep people coming through the door. Cafe hours, Monday-Saturday 7 a.m.-8 p.m.; Sunday 7 a.m.-2 p.m. 785.655.9003. FB.

explorer extras...
In Talmage

Unincorporated

At home in a former bank building, the Talmage Museum and Library, 2978 Main, is impressively run by an all-volunteer staff. Monday, Wednesday, Friday-Sunday 2-4 p.m. 785.388.2089. talmagekansas.com.

The hitching post in front of the museum and library had its beginnings in the wild cowtown of Abilene. When Abilene modernized and removed the posts, the Bennett family saved this hitching post. After relocating to Talmage, the family donated it to the community. **ee**

WOODBINE

Population 206

Our Store: 8 N. Broadway. If you are Tom and Tamara Blake and own a trucking company, what do you do to answer the town's need for groceries? You put a mini-store in your trucking company office. It's appropriately named Our Store because in a small town it's up to everyone to make it work. You're welcome to shop here too! Monday-Friday 7 a.m.-7 p.m.; Saturday 7 a.m.-12 p.m. 785.257.3239.

Wolf Road/Lyon Creek Road Scenic Drive:
From Woodbine, 1 mile east on K-209, then north on Wolf Road (½ mile west of U.S. 77). The seven-mile drive north on Wolf Road takes you on a scenic winding route. At the five-mile marker, in an area known as Lyona (at the Dickinson and Geary county line), you'll see a lovely stone church. Built in 1871, it was the first church organized (1859) in the United Methodist Kansas West Conference (785.257.3474). In Geary County, Wolf Road

becomes Lyon Creek Road. Follow it north past a stone barn and house to a 1925 Marsh rainbow single-arch bridge. From there, choose any road that meets your fancy. Roads named for creeks are the best bet for a picturesque drive

Ellsworth County

AROUND THE COUNTY

Post Rock Scenic Byway:
This 18-mile drive from Wilson to Lucas, passing Wilson Lake, delivers sweeping vistas of grasslands, rock outcroppings, and long rows of the post rock fences. Wildflowers dot the roadway during their growing seasons. travelks.com/ksbyways.

Kanopolis Lake Legacy Trail Self-Guided Auto Tour: Drive through the Smoky Hills on this 80-mile trail featuring 27 historic sites—from forts and caves to cemeteries and ghost towns. Pick up a brochure at Kanopolis State Park office or the Corps information office. 785.546.2565.

Mushroom Rock State Park (8 Wonders of Kansas Geography)**:**
#11 on the Kanopolis Lake Legacy Trail tour. From K-140, 2 miles south on K-141, then 2 miles west on K. These mushroom-shaped rocks are a geologic phenomenon of sandstone spheres. Two are balanced on a stone "mushroom stem!" They likely served as meeting places and landmarks for American Indians and early pioneers. Cross the footbridge

and to the east find the rock bearing an etching of the U.S. flag.

Faris Caves: #16 on the Kanopolis Lake Legacy Trail tour. From Kanopolis, 3 miles east on L, 1 mile south on 22, ¼ mile left on M, 1 mile south (again) on 22, then west on N to the road's end. Look right toward the bottom of the bluffs and you'll see three distinct openings of the caves. Originally dug by Charles Griffee in the 1880s for a dwelling, they later were used by the Faris family for a spring house, generator room, and school. Annette Thille White uncovered the caves again in the 1980s. If the terrain is dry, you can go inside the caves.

Kanopolis Lake and State Park: From K-4, 3 miles north on K-141. Completed in 1948, Kanopolis is the oldest recreation state park in Kansas. Among its 35 miles of trails, the five-and-a-half-mile Horsethief Canyon Trail is a statewide favorite for hiking, biking, or horseback riding. A beautiful trail, it features canyons, sandstone bluffs, prairie, and low-water crossings. State park entrance charge. Cabins available, reservations required. 785.546.2565. ksoutdoors.com.

I-70 Cross: 888 C. Between the I-70 exits for Vesper (216) and Sylvan Grove (209), on the south side of the highway, interstate travelers have seen a "guiding light" every night since 1976. In that year Gerald Klema and friends erected a 60-foot steel cross lit with 44 bulbs. It stands near the Excelsior Lutheran Church.

ELLSWORTH

Population 3,077

When the railroad built through to Ellsworth in 1872, the Texas cattle drovers followed. It was during these trail driving days that Ellsworth gained its reputation as the "wickedest" cowtown in Kansas.

Historical Plaza Walking Tour: Seventeen interpretive signs around town, marked by silhouettes, feature the history of Ellsworth and help you visualize the Wild West and Ellsworth's cowtown days.

National Drovers Hall of Fame (NRHP): 115 N. Douglas. The ornate, historic Insurance Building will one day be home to the hall of fame dedicated to preserving the heritage of the cattle trailing industry.

1873 Jail: 110 Court. The oldest building in Ellsworth, the limestone jail is a shell of its former self, but it still stands to tell the story of some of the wickedest lawbreakers in the Wild West. A small interpretive sign and iron cutout explains.

1910 Jail: 200 Court. It just might be the fanciest historic jailhouse in Kansas. Constructed in 1910, it held prisoners in the back area until 1981. The front section served as living quarters for the sheriff and his family. Six Ionic columns span the entrance of this three-story Classic Revival structure, which today is privately owned.

Ellsworth County Courthouse (NRHP):
210 N. Kansas. This 1951 structure is an excellent architectural example of the Modern Movement. A Civil War statue stands in front. Monday-Friday 8 a.m.-5 p.m. 785.472.4161.

Ellsworth Area Arts Council
Gallery: 223 N. Douglas. Works by local and regional artists using a variety of mediums are on display and for sale. Monday-Friday 12:30-4:30 p.m. 785.472.5658. FB.

Hodgden House Museum
(NRHP): 104 SW Main. The museum complex is on the two-block site of the original commercial district. It features the 1878 Victorian Hodgden House and the 1886 livery stable—both constructed with Dakota sandstone. Tuesday-Saturday 10 a.m.-4 p.m. 785.472.3059.

Preisker Park: 3rd and Blake. Because it's off the main drag, finding this old-time park is a nice surprise. It includes a 1940 National Youth Administration band shell, a rock-lined creek, and a series of bridges— a nostalgic and lovely place!

Mother Bickerdyke Memorial Cemetery:
From K-156, just north on K-14, ½ mile west on L, then 1 mile north on 14th. Follow the sandy road past the TV towers to a hilltop cemetery where you'll enjoy a great view of Ellsworth. Mother Bickerdyke isn't buried in this cemetery, but you'll find a memorial to her among the graves of 32 of her Civil War nurses and the wives of Civil War veterans.

Ellsworth Antique Mall
(NRHP): 210 N. Douglas. It's known as one of the most unique antique malls in the state! Most antiques are on the main floor, but some are displayed in the former Masonic hall (1898-2003) on the second floor. A coffee and ice cream shop is on the main floor. Tuesday-Friday 10 a.m.-5 p.m.; Saturday 10 a.m.-3 p.m. 785.472.4659.

Pretty Boy Floyd's Steaks & Shine (NRHP):
210 N. Douglas. An alley entrance and descending stone steps create an intriguing welcome to a place named for the notorious 1930s gangster. Josie Roehrman and her late husband, Mark, literally dug out these underground rooms that admitted "men only" back in the 1870s. Now the Dakota sandstone walls and low ceilings block off the outside world while you hole up for some great steaks, "moonshine," and many more delicious offerings. Thursday-Saturday 5-8:30 p.m. 785.472.2183. FB.

HOLYROOD

Population 438

Fire Department Sign:
100 block of S. County. In front of the converted grade school, now a fire department, stands a little shelter with a blond-brick base, a red bell, and a bright  red sign. As a reminder of the fire department's past, the sign reads, "1901 Holyrood F.D. Chemical No. 1."

H&B Communications:
108 N. Main. Originally the Ford Building, in 1985 it became the office of this locally owned telecommunications company. Small glass tiles from the original transoms are now in the chandeliers and front desk, and early telephones are on display. Monday-Friday 8 a.m.-5 p.m. 785.252.4000.

Taxpayer Recognition:
110 S. Main. "Erected by the taxpayers of Holyrood" is etched into the bottom right corner of the 1926 red-brick former city building.

Wide Main Street:
Why is Main wide enough to double park in the middle? Before the automobile age, posts and stone water troughs for tying up and watering horses stood midway from either side of the street. As the story goes, with their horses and buggies parked in the center, folks could sit alongthe sidewalks and visit and not be in danger of being kicked!

Holyrood Depot (NRHP):
N. Main. Constructed in 1886, this structure is an example of the earlier style Santa Fe depots in Kansas. On the exterior you'll see decorative eave brackets, a gabled bay window, and a large overhang that once protected passengers from the weather.

K-jack Bar and Grill:
606 N. Main. Cheeseburgers, steaks, and a full bar bring customers back to K-jack! Grill hours, Wednesday-Saturday 5 -8:30 p.m. 785.252.3577. FB.

KANOPOLIS

Population 482

Kanopolis Drive-In Theater:
804 N. Kansas. Kanopolis preserves one of the few remaining drive-in theaters in Kansas, and folks have been coming here since 1952 to watch movies under the stars. It generally operates from the first weekend of April to mid-September. 785.472.4786. Movie schedule at kanopolisdrivein.com.

Fort Harker Museum (NRHP):
308 W. Ohio. Fort Ellsworth was established in 1864 to protect travelers enroute to Santa Fe or to Denver City. Renamed Fort Harker in 1866, it was moved months later to the present site of Kanopolis and became a major supply post for military campaigns against the Plains Indians. The fort closed in 1872, but four original buildings, all constructed with Dakota sandstone, still stand. A depot has been moved next to the guardhouse and presents the history of Kanopolis and area salt mines. Tuesday-Saturday 10 a.m.-4 p.m.; Sunday 12-4 p.m. (closed Sundays during the winter). Admission charge. 785.472.5733.

Fort Ellsworth Site:
#19 on the Kanopolis Lake Legacy Trail tour. From downtown Kanopolis, ½ mile west on Ohio (becomes L), then 1 mile south on 18th. At M, signage tells us that from 1864 to 1867 Fort Ellsworth, consisting of dugouts in the river bank, guarded supply wagons, stagecoaches, and early settlers.

Orozco's Portales:
117 N. Kansas. Hungry for great Mexican food? The huevos rancheros and homemade biscuits and gravy are breakfast favorites, and the flour tortillas are homemade. Tuesday-Saturday 6:30 a.m.-8 p.m.; Sunday 6:30 a.m-2 p.m. 785.472.4226.

WILSON

Population 763

Kansas Originals Market and Gallery:
233 K-232. From I-70 Wilson exit 206, ¼ mile north on K-232. Food products, books, art, and crafts

of more than 225 Kansans are showcased and for sale here. *Rusty Rojo*, an 8x10-foot chicken by artist John Scott, greets you at the entrance. Monday-Saturday 9 a.m.-6 p.m.; Sunday 11 a.m.-6 p.m. 785.658.2602. kansasoriginals.com.

Czech Capital of Kansas:
Immigrants from Czechoslovakia began settling here in 1874, and 100 years later Wilson rightfully dubbed itself the Czech Capital of Kansas. The Czech Festival celebrates this heritage the last weekend of every July. Signs in Czech welcome you (Vitame Vas na Wilson) to this unique town where even downtown's narrow red-brick street presents a European feel (Kansas style).

World's Largest Czech Egg:
27th and D (Old U.S. 40). Thousands of volunteer hours and countless gallons of paint resulted in a giant colorful egg painted in the traditional kraslice style. Designed by local art teacher Christine Slechta, the fiberglass egg weighs 7,000 pounds and measures 20x15 feet. The egg rests under a stylish gazebo shelter.

Circular Stone Jail

(NRHP): Behind 2528 E in an alley between 25th and 26th. Built as a water tower in 1907, this structure is the only native limestone circular jail in the state. The lower level was a jail until 1963 and held prisoners until they could be transported to the county jail. For tours, ask Virginia or Jerry at Grandma's Soda Shop, 2524 E., 785.658.2200.

Wilson Opera House:

27th and D (Old U.S. 40). Out of the ashes of the 2009 fire will come an open-air pavilion with both outdoor and indoor stages. The salvageable stone from the 1901 limestone opera house will be incorporated into the pavilion. wilsonoperahouse.com.

Soukup and Kyner

Elevators: North and south side of the railroad tracks nearest E. Although no longer in use, the complex of historic grain elevators is a favorite subject for photographers. Built prior to 1900, Soukup Elevators (south side of the tracks) also sold coal and implements, thus the Sunflower Coal mural on the smaller building. Kyner Elevators are on the north side of the tracks.

Historic Water Tower:

615 27th. The unusual two-story wooden structure on the grounds of Simple Haven Bed and Breakfast is a late-1920s water tower (no longer in use).

Lustron Home: 2315 C.

The buttery yellow Lustron home is one of only 91 of the approximately 100 prefabricated steel homes built in Kansas. After WWII, housing needs expedited the building of these low maintenance, highly durable homes.

Wilson Cemetery:

1916 2nd. Not to be missed is the impressive granite Civil War monument featuring a Union soldier statue at its apex. Further adorning the memorial is a metal lion's head out of which water once poured to fill the watering trough for horses. The Czechoslovakian influence is apparent in this cemetery in the names of the interred.

WWI Monument: E and 26th (Legion Park.) An American doughboy statue stands atop this monument dedicated in 1919 "In Honor of our Soldiers Sailors and Marines of the World War."

Historic Midland Railroad Hotel (NRHP): 414 26th.

This 1899 three-story hotel has been restored to its former glory and offers 28 guest rooms appointed with Mission style furniture, all with private baths. The restaurant has a stellar reputation for excellent food including Explorer Way chicken-fried steak. Tuesday-Saturday 11 a.m.-2 p.m. and 5-8 p.m.; Sunday 11 a.m.-8 p.m. Reservations recommended. 785.658.2284. midlandrailroadhotel.com. FB.

Grandma's Soda Shop and Diner: 2524 E. Owners

Virginia and Jerry Florian have put a lot of love into this place. Their secret recipe for pizza crust and sauce along with the handmade kolaches (a traditional Czech pastry filled with fruit) and bierocks keep people coming back for more. A 1950s soda fountain is an added treat. Monday-Saturday 11 a.m.-9 p.m. 785.658.2200. FB.

Made from Scratch:

527 27th (Old U.S. 40). Nearly everything, as the name tells us, is made from scratch—from the jellies to the ice cream. Bierocks, homemade pies, and kolaches are served daily. Come Saturdays for the lunchtime German buffet; Thursdays feature chicken-fried steak made the Explorer Way. Daily 7 a.m.-9 p.m. 785.658.3300. FB.

Lodging: Midland Railroad Hotel (785.658.2284, midlandrailroadhotel.com); Simple Haven Bed and Breakfast (KBBA, 785.658.3814, simplehavenbandb.com).

Jewell County

AROUND THE COUNTY

Mind the stop signs. There are no flashing stop lights in Jewell County!

White Rock Creek Scenic Back Road: From U.S. 36

north of Formoso, go 5 miles north on 280 to the ghost town of Lovewell, 2 miles west on V, 4 miles north on 260, ½ mile west on Z, then ¼ mile north on Lamm into Webber. This 12-mile route on gravel and blacktop is a drive through beautiful Jewell County scenery. First you'll approach a line of hills south of White Rock Creek, then cross the Lower Courtland Canal and find yourself in the former town of Lovewell. As you continue west and north to Lovewell Reservoir, notice more open canals, all part of the Kansas Bostwick Irrigation District. Pass the reservoir and continue north to Webber (*see p. 65*). If you have more endurance in your tank for more back roads, continue west from Webber to K-14, then meander southwest following roads near White Rock Creek to Burr Oak. It's a great tour past fertile cropland and through wooded and hilly terrain. This dare-to-do-dirt drive is a true test of Explorer fortitude. Consult your GPS or *DeLorme Kansas Atlas*.

Canals: The many canals you cross while traveling in Jewell and Republic Counties fall within the Kansas Bostwick Irrigation District Canal and Lateral system. The system is part of a Bureau of Reclamation project that began in 1931 for irrigation development and flood control. Construction finished in 1968.

Lovewell Lake and State Park:
From U.S. 36, 8¼ miles north on K-14. Completed in 1957, the reservoir was developed for flood control and irrigation but is also used for recreational purposes. State park entrance charge. Cabins available, reservations required. 785.753.4971. ksoutdoors.com.

Lovewell Marina and Grill:
2400 250 (Lovewell State Park; permit required). Smoked meats, made-from-scratch pizza, and Becky's bierocks are among the choices here. April-Labor Day, daily 7 a.m.-7 p.m.; after Labor Day-October 2, Friday-Sunday 7 a.m.-7 p.m. 785.753.4351.

BURR OAK

Population 169

Queen Anne Style Home (NRHP):
628 N. Main. Built by farmer O.W. Francis in 1909, this lovely home stands out with its turret tower, wraparound and pillared porch, Palladian windows, and patterned siding and gables. Drive by only.

House Contest: The story goes that an early-1900s coffee shop wager started a contest on who could build the fanciest and biggest house. Locals claim that the winner was the O.W. Francis home, and the 1909 Wellman House, 249 South, was a viable competitor. Although additional contestants are no longer known, other large, decorative turn-of-the-century homes in the area might well have been contenders.

Lumberyard: 230 Main. This huge building was part of the downtown scene as early as 1886, operating as the Chicago Lumber & Coal Company, a chain of lumberyards at that time. Sold to the Burr Oak Lumber Company in 1920, it functioned as a lumberyard until the late 1990s.

J.C. Holland:
Renowned architect for the Kansas State Capitol, Holland designed the Burr Oak School in 1900, now the Burr Oak Museum (NRHP) at 776 Kansas. In 1912 he designed the United Methodist Church (NRHP) at 974 Pennsylvania.

explorer extras...
In Formoso

Population 92

The story of the 1909 Formoso School is told on a sign at Patterson and Spencer. After a fire destroyed the school in 1960, the city and alumni erected this sign to honor the 536 students educated here.

You can't miss the owl-shaped community bulletin board on the door of the city's water building, Main and Patterson. Locals recall that it was made by Joe Brown and Carl Studer with help from Lavernia Peters and Carl's granddaughter Amanda Reynolds. ee

JEWELL

Population 426

Fort Jewell Marker:
Custer and Delaware (southwest corner of Maag Memorial Park). A fort of four-foot-thick, seven-foot-high sod walls was erected near here in 1870 after Indians killed three men along the Solomon River.

Robbery Alarm: 120 N. Washington. Stained-glass pieces form the words "Robbery

Alarm" on this ornate 1930s alarm box (no longer in use) on the side of the Guaranty State Bank. If the trigger, attached to the bank vault, wasn't disarmed before the vault door was opened, the alarm would sound.

Jewell Grocery:
320 Delaware. Your support of this independently owned grocery will be appreciated

and help it stay alive. Look for the old Nesbitt's Orange sign. Monday-Saturday 8 a.m.-7 p.m.; Sunday 10 a.m.- 6 p.m. 785.428.3271.

Lake Emerson and Walking Trail:
From K-14 and Pearl, less than ¼ mile west on Pearl. Enjoy a pleasant walk on the crushed white limestone trail that takes you around the lake.

Lodging: Jewell Inn and RV campground (785.428.3600); The Lofts (785.534.2532, FB).

MANKATO

Population 856

Jewell County Courthouse (NRHP):
307 N. Commercial. Built in part by the WPA in 1937,

this art deco structure designed by architect Joseph Radotinsky features native limestone walls and trim. Note the two 3D limestone medallions on the west side, and a bas-relief of the book and scales of justice—with a corn stalk! Monday-Friday 8:30 a.m.-4:30 p.m. 785.378.4020.

1899 Limestone Jail

(NRHP): Center and Madison. Long after J.C. Holland designed the Kansas State Capitol, he was the architect for the Jewell County jail and sheriff's residence. Created from native limestone with a brown streak, this double-walled jail (in use until 1978) is topped with a striking galvanized metal cupola.

Architecture: You don't see many original YMCA buildings anymore, but you will at 210 N. Commercial. The old First National Bank building (NRHP) at 201 N. Commercial is of the Richardsonian Revival style and completed in 1888.

Downtown: Enjoy shopping at Hidden Treasure Quilt Shop (101 N. Commercial, 785.378.8020); Ost Furniture (106 N. Commercial, 785.378.8133); and Possibilities, a home decor, gift, and clothing shop (121 N. Commercial, 785.378.8484).

Jewell County Museum:

118 N. Commercial. Several structures house the museum's diverse collections, including the Wint Smith building, which features exhibits about Brigadier General Smith. Mid-April to mid-October, Wednesday-Friday 10 a.m.-2 p.m. 785.545.7658.

Sweden Creme: 610 E. South. Named for an ice cream machine, this former grocery/gas station opened in the 1950s as the Sweden Creme Drive-In. Still offering soft-serve ice cream, Sweden Creme also carries employee-developed menu items. Daily 11 a.m.-8 p.m. 785.378.8600. FB.

Buffalo Roam Steak House: 740 U.S. 36. In business for 50 years, the Buffalo Roam is where you go for a fine variety of great food, top-notch service, and a hometown family atmosphere. Customers come from far and wide for the seafood buffet on the first Saturday of every month.

On Tuesday, Friday, and Saturday evenings, you're greeted at the door by Freddie Murphy, a sweet woman whose endearing smile makes you glad you came. Tuesday-Friday 11 a.m.-1:30 p.m.; Tuesday-Saturday 5-9 p.m. 785.378.3971. FB.

Bob's Inn: 119 E. Jefferson. With a loyal local following since 1931, Bob's keeps customers happy with his made-from-scratch food and the beer served from the 1930s New Brunswick beer tap. Tuesday-Friday 11a.m.-1:30 p.m. and Tuesday-Saturday 5-9 p.m. 785.378.3201.

Lodging: Crest-Vue Motel (785.378.3515).

explorer extras...
In Mankato

The American Indian with colorful headdress design forms an impressive historic marquee on the 1905 Ute Theater,

203 N. Commercial. For movie schedule, call 785.378.3141.

Fridays are sale days at the Mankato Livestock barn, 810 N. Commercial, where you can stop by the cafe for lunch and cherry and apple pie. Opening at 10:30 a.m., the cafe stays open until the cows go home (4-11 p.m.). 785.378.3283.

A rare Kansas memorial to Thomas Edison stands at 303 N. West, across from the old high school, now the Rock Hills Elementary School. The inscription reads, in part, "for gratitude for his illustrious inventions and services." **ee**

WEBBER

Population 25

Post Office: 202 Lamm. Inside this old-fashioned post office, even the post boxes date to an earlier era. Stop in and buy your stamps here—more purchases earn the post office points that help keep it open. The city hall shares space with the post office inside a nicely renovated depot. Monday-Friday 7:30-9:30 a.m.; Saturday 7:15-9:30 a.m. 785.753.4495.

Frank Herrmann Park: Lamm and Commercial. As a local newspaper related, when a woman broke a butter mold her little boy said, "Take it to Frank, he can fix it." Beloved by all, blacksmith Frank Herrmann was known as a man who could fix anything but a broken heart. He donated this land to the city for a park for the children of Webber. The anvil that his father brought from Germany in 1908 rests steadfastly next to the limestone park sign.

NC

Lincoln County

AROUND THE COUNTY

Post rock is the "friendly" name for the Greenhorn Limestone rock layer when it is used to make fence posts. When that layer is used for structures, it is referred to as native limestone. Lincoln County is known as the Post Rock Capital of Kansas.

Historic Bridges Scenic Back Road: From Lincoln, go 8 miles south on K-14, curve west and continue 3 miles west on Elk. You'll pass wind farms and rolling hills and arrive at a pony truss bridge (NRHP) on the Spring Creek tributary. From the bridge, go 3 miles north on 150 past an abandoned but beautiful stone home and barn, then 2 miles west on Hawk to the stone single-arch Bullfoot Creek Bridge (NRHP). Four miles north on 130 and 1 mile west on Lark brings you to Vesper.

County Line School: From Beverly, 2 miles east on K-18, then ¼ mile north on N. 310. All alone beside a dirt road, this school stands out in lustrous red brick, a contrast to the typical limestone structures in this post rock countryside. Next to the stairs is a water pump where decades of children quenched their thirst.

Open Range Zoo: Kids will love finding Jim Dickerman's creatures along K-18 between Beverly and Lincoln, around

Lincoln, and at the south end of Lincoln on K-14. The creatures, made from scrap farm equipment, car parts, bones, and feathers, come in all sizes.

explorer extras... In Beverly

Population 158

Plat maps show a native limestone structure at 1st and Otis that served as a livery stable as early as 1901. Although the building is roofless, the original front window casings, double doors with slanted wood design, and iron door handle and lock present a rustic scene to please any photographer. **ee**

DENMARK

Unincorporated

Denmark Evangelical Lutheran Community Church (NRHP): From Lincoln, 7 miles west on K-18, then 3 miles north on 120 via a winding, hilly road. The first indicator that you're near Denmark is the steeple of this 1878 native limestone church. At the church (originally named Dansk Evangelical Lutheran Kirke) you have a great 360-degree view of the Spillman Creek Valley.

Old Denmark: From the Denmark church, ½ mile west on Denmark. Just before reaching the grain elevator, look for a stone single-arch bridge. West of the tracks you'll find the abandoned stone buildings that once housed the bank and other businesses. A sign indicates that the Denmark Hotel formerly occupied a two-story wooden building, now a residence.

LINCOLN

Population 1,253

Lincoln County Courthouse (NRHP): 216 E. Lincoln. This Romanesque Revival courthouse was built in 1900 using native

limestone to achieve a striking result. A 1913 Civil War statue of a soldier at parade rest stands to the southeast of the courthouse. Monday-Friday 8 a.m.-4 p.m. 785.524.4757.

Lincoln Carnegie Library (NRHP): 203 S. 3rd. The beauty of limestone quarried in Lincoln County enhances the facade of this 1914 library.

Marshall-Yohe House (NRHP): 316 S. 2nd. Constructed mainly of wood, this circa 1895 Queen Anne style home stands on massive limestone porch piers. For tours, call 785.524.4744.

Post Rock Scout Museum and Crispin's Drug Store Museum (NRHP): 161 E. Lincoln. Two museums are housed inside the 1881 two-story limestone bank building. One tells the story of scouting in the United States. The second museum resembles an actual old-time drugstore. Product containers, shelving, druggist tools, and a "shock box" are a few exhibits that make this an exceptional stop. Usually open Monday-Saturday 1-5 p.m. Call ahead, 785.524.5383.

Lincoln Art Center: 126 E. Lincoln. Look for the big awning that announces this art center, housed in yet another golden limestone building. Rotating exhibits of unique work from Kansas and other states are displayed in an appealing open space. A gift gallery features products by Kansas artists. Tuesday-Friday 12-4 p.m.; Saturday 9 a.m.-12 p.m. 785.524.3241. lincolnartcenter.org.

Village Lines:
139 W. Lincoln. Here you'll find delightful Kansas products and art as well as gluten-free natural products. Plus, get all the scoop on area attractions and feel the enthusiasm for rural Kansas! Monday-Saturday 10 a.m.- 5:30 p.m. 785.524.5133. FB.

Kyne Museum (NRHP):
216 W. Lincoln. You can't miss the wagon wheels that accent the exterior of the Kyne House. This native limestone museum helps tell the county story and showcases F.A. Cooper's work including an unfinished county map depicting historical events. Tuesday, Thursday 1-4 p.m.; Saturday 10 a.m.-1 p.m. Donation welcome. 785.524.9997.

Lincoln City Park:
E. Elm (east side of town). Go ahead and give the big cottonwood tree a hug! The park has a number of limestone structures made by the National Youth Administration in the 1930s including picnic tables, a shelter, and an amphitheater.

Lincoln Cemetery:
K-18 and E. Lincoln. Take the main cemetery entrance to the second crossroad. Just in front

of the limestone mausoleum stands the gravestone for a Civil War drummer boy. Continue to the end of that driveway, turn west on South, then north at the next crossroad. The first gravestone on the west side is shaped like a suitcase and marks the 1891 grave of a traveling salesman. A fitting epitaph reads, "Here Is Where He Stopped Last."

Lincoln Golf Course:
2058 E. Milo. This is one of the best nine-hole, sand-green courses in the state. Greens fee. 785.531.0940.

Lodging:
livelincolncounty.com/staying.

SYLVAN GROVE

Population 268

Fly Boy Brewery & Eats:
105 N. Main. When you combine a beer-making crop duster,

a chef who propels regular food into something special, and an old hardware store with great atmosphere, you have just the right landing place for a great evening. Try the beer flights or a full pour of Tail Spin IPA, Barnstormer Brown, or Gear Up. Thursday-Saturday 5-10 p.m.; Sunday 11 a.m.- 2 p.m. 785.526.7800. FB.

Hometown Cafe: 116 N. Main. Ronda serves up hand-pattied burgers and home-cooked daily specials, and her pan-fried chicken is a delicious staple on Sundays. Tuesday-Sunday 7 a.m.-2 p.m. 785.526.7376.

Evangelical Lutheran School (NRHP): 308 N. Indiana. Built in Prairie School style, this 1913 school served many of the area's German Lutheran immigrants. It was

closed during WWI due to anti-German hysteria. The school later re-opened but closed permanently in 1981. 785.524.6034.

Vonada Post Rock Quarry Tour (8 Wonders of Kansas Commerce):
You can watch the extraction of post rock using the feathers and wedges method at Vonada quarry north of Sylvan Grove. Admission charge. Group tours only. 785.658.7889.

South Fork Spillman Creek Bridge (NRHP):
From K-18, 8 miles north on K-181. Pull into the driveway just north of the new bridge to view the 1908 stone double-arch bridge and to read its story on the historical marker. From here, backtrack 3/4 mile south on K-181, then 1/8 mile east on Sage to find a stone single-arch bridge.

Mitchell County

AROUND THE COUNTY

Learn more about Asherville, Beloit, Cawker City, and Glen Elder at the blue-roofed kiosks placed near these towns by the Solomon Valley Heritage Alliance.

Bell-Bogardus Cemetery:
From 8th in Beloit, 5½ miles southeast on U.S. 24, 1¼ miles east on Asherville (K), then north onto a gravel road. Just 600 feet north you'll find the small cemetery nestled among the trees along West Asher Creek. It is enclosed by a small limestone wall with a wrought iron gate. At the cemetery's center, a granite marker states that Benjamin and Mary Bell and David Bogardus were killed by Indians in 1868.

Sunflower: From Beloit, 7 miles south on K-14, 2 miles west on P, 2 miles south on 280, then ½ mile west on R. On the south side of the road a limestone

NC

marker informs us that the small community of Sunflower was founded on this spot in 1890, flourished for a short time, and faded away by the 1940s.

BELOIT

Population 3,846

Mitchell County Courthouse (NRHP):

111 S. Hersey. With its limestone walls and sandstone trim, this beautiful structure was designed in Romanesque Revival style by J.C. Holland, architect for the Kansas State Capitol. It is the only courthouse in the state with screen-door entrances. Of interest are the ornate fireplaces in some offices. Monday-Friday 8:30 a.m.-5 p.m. 785.738.3652.

St. John the Baptist Catholic Church (NRHP):

701 E. Court. This double-tower church built in 1904 is thought to be the first church in the United States constructed with flying buttresses and a ceiling made entirely from stone. The exquisite frescos in the nave were painted by renowned church artist Gonippo Raggi and his brother Palamedo. Open daily. 785.738.2851. stjohnsbeloit.org.

Mitchell County Museum:

402 W. 8th. A Williamsburg brick structure, it was built in 1929 as a home for nurses at the community hospital. Inside the museum, each town in the county has its own exhibit room. Be sure to look for the milk cooling trough outside. Monday, Tuesday, Thursday 10 a.m.-4 p.m. 785.738.5355. FB.

Abram Click Farmstead:

K-14 and U.S. 24. Park in the driveway and walk around this circa 1880s limestone Gothic Revival farmhouse, barn, and water tower and the 1890s wash house and granary.

Chautauqua Park:

From downtown, ¼ mile south on Hersey (becomes Roosevelt) to Chautauqua. Of interest are the footbridge across the Solomon River and the swimming pool and shelter house built as 1930s WPA projects. 785.738.2270.

Gray Drug and Fountain:

100 S. Mill. A colorful giant sundae greets you as you enter this appealing pharmacy, gift shop, and old-fashioned soda fountain. The turn of the century meets the 1950s with the turquoise-and-black counter and impressive 1909 back bar. Monday-Friday 8 a.m.-6 p.m.; Saturday 9 a.m.-1 p.m. 785.534.1200. FB.

Kettle: 204 S. Mill. A group of hawks is called a kettle and that's the name B (a Kansas Jayhawk fan) and Mandy (an Iowa Hawkeye fan) settled on for their trendy and comfortable coffee shop and wine bar. Relax as you enjoy coffee, wine, craft beer, eats, and live music. Menu items are familiar, using many locally sourced products, yet they are handmade with a twist. A must try is the Biscuit and Gravy Pot Pie. Monday-Thursday 7 a.m.-8 p.m.; Friday-Saturday 8 a.m.-10 p.m. 785.534.1971. kettlebeloit.com.

Plum Creek Restaurant:

118 E. Court. Brett Wichers was 19 when he opened Plum Creek in 2001 and he continues to run this popular local eatery. Noon specials served 11 a.m.-1 p.m. are made from scratch. Monday-Saturday 11 a.m.-9 p.m. 785.738.3893. plumcreekbeloit.com.

Lodging: beloitks.org/visiting.

explorer extras...
In Beloit

Historic homes grace the residential areas. Find any brick street and follow it! NRHP homes are at 304 E. Main and 422 W. 8th.

An original little red schoolhouse on U.S. 24 is a reminder of the old one-room school days. **ee**

CAWKER CITY

Population 461

In 1871 it was decided that the winner of a rousing game of poker would have the privilege of naming the newly formed town. Holding the winning hand was E. Harrison Cawker. In 1914, in honor of her father, Lenora Cawker presented the town with a drinking fountain. The fountain and a large water trough are on the west side of City Park on Lake.

Ball of Twine: U.S. 24 (Wisconsin) and Lake. The world's largest ball of sisal twine is found downtown under a canopy. Started in 1953 on a farm, the ball's twine is now more than 1,531 miles in length, more than 45 feet in circumference, and weighs over 10 tons! Farmer Frank Stoeber started this ball in an effort to save twine scraps, and caretaker Linda Clover keeps it growing. If she sees you at the ball she'll drive over with a trunk full of twine so you can add to the legendary ball. Call ahead, 785.781.4470.

Ball of Twine Art:
Yellow twine painted on the sidewalks leads you up and down Wisconsin (U.S. 24) past store windows featuring art masterpieces with one common denominator—twine! Artist Cher Heller Olson's spoofs are worth seeing. For example, the Mona Lisa is holding a ball of twine, as is the woman in Olson's version of *An American Gothic*. More than 20 "twine" paintings cheerily decorate downtown.

Old Cawker City Library (NRHP):
7th and Lake. A bright red roof and dainty architectural touches to this 1885 limestone structure mark the current home of the Cawker City Hesperian Historical Society Museum. The building is being painstakingly restored inside as well. 785.781.4961.

Lakeshore Tailgaters Bar & Grill:
804 Oak. Satisfy your hunger with quality burgers, steaks, and more. Monday-

Saturday 5-11 p.m. 785.781.4400. lakeshoretailgaters.com.

Waconda Lake and Glen Elder State Park:
From Cawker City, 3 miles east on U.S. 24. Glen Elder Dam and Waconda Lake were completed in 1968 for flood control and recreational purposes. Having a 100-mile shoreline, it is one of the largest lakes in Kansas. State park entrance charge. 785.545.3345. ksoutdoors.com.

Legend of Waconda:
From Cawker City, 2½ miles east on U.S. 24. The legend has many versions, although all are similar. Essentially it tells of Waconda, the beautiful daughter of an Indian chief, who fell in love with a warrior from an enemy tribe. When he asked the girl's father for her hand in marriage, a battle ensued. An arrow mortally wounded the warrior, and he fell into the springs as he died. Heartbroken, Waconda dived in after him and never resurfaced. Waconda Spring, also called Great Spirit Spring, is now under the waters of Waconda Lake. A historical marker stands just south of U.S. 24.

Lodging:
Old Station Inn (785.545.6877, FB); Waconda Springs Guest House (785.545.6877, FB).

GLEN ELDER

Population 443

Historic Norris Station (NRHP):
100 S. Market. Here a striking limestone building calls out as a reminder of bygone days. Built in 1926 with an addition in 1929, the service station resembles a little castle.

Wayne's Sporting Goods:
129 S. Mill. Camping, boating, and fishing supplies are available here along with groceries, snacks, antiques, and gifts. Monday-Saturday 9 a.m.-5:30 p.m.; Sunday 1-5 p.m. 785.545.3333. waynessportinggoods.com.

Glen Elder Dam:
From Market, ½ mile west on Main. Completed in 1968, the dam is 15,200 feet long and stands 115 feet above the Solomon River. glenelder.com.

HeBrew's Cafe:
120 S. Market. Enjoy daily specials at this community-oriented cafe. Tuesday-Saturday 7 a.m.-2 p.m. 785.545.3663. FB.

Lodging:
RV campground and lodges (glenelder.com/businesses).

HUNTER

Population 57

Hunter Cafe:
109 E. 1st. What does this community-owned cafe have that so many bigger restaurants want? Someone who cooks from scratch. And that would be Kay Heller, who has been baking her famous cinnamon rolls and homemade pies here since 1993. The mashed potatoes and biscuits and gravy are "real" too. Fridays at noon offer chicken-fried steak made the Explorer Way. Monday-Friday 7:30 a.m.-3 p.m.; Saturday 7:30 a.m.-2 p.m. 785.529.3325.

TIPTON

Population 211

Tipton Grocery:
601 Main. Some of the best sausage in the state is made here. Owners Fred and Vali Smith are big Tipton boosters, which makes it feel even better to spend money at their grocery. Walls are adorned with Tipton memorabilia, including Great Uncle Leo's band uniform. Monday-Friday 8 a.m.-6 p.m.;

NC

Saturday 8 a.m.-2 p.m.
785.373.4125. FB.

Hake Hardware:
608 State. This old-fashioned hardware store is in the third generation of family ownership.

The nails forming numbers in the floor were used in the old days to measure rope. Monday-Friday 8 a.m.-12 p.m. and 1-5 p.m.; Saturday 8:30 a.m.-12 p.m. 785.373.4165.

St. Boniface Catholic Church:
310 Gambrinus.The present church was built in 1954 but the grotto dates to the 1930s.

Tipton Catholic High School:
301 State. The 1919 red-brick school is home to the smallest high school in the state with an enrollment of 15 students in the 2015-2016 school year.

Tipton Heritage Museum:
602 Main. Local history displays are found in the oldest (but remodeled) building in Tipton. Friday 1-4 p.m. To visit the museum on other days, call 785.373.4800 or see Vali at Tipton Grocery (601 Main) or Kim at Old School Seals (600 N. Main).

The Cafe:
504 Main. Home-made daily lunch specials are always good, and evenings offer chicken-fried steak finished in a cast iron skillet. Tuesdays are pot roast days. Tuesday-Friday 7 a.m.-2 p.m.; Friday-Saturday 5-9 p.m. 785.373.7111.

Ringneck Ranch:
655 Solomon. Stay overnight or come for the day to fish, bicycle, hike, or hunt. 785.373.4835. ringneckranch.net.

Osborne County

AROUND THE COUNTY

The Solomon Valley Heritage Alliance has placed blue-roofed kiosks in Alton, Bloomington, Downs, Osborne, and Portis to inform you about each town.

B-24 Bomber Memorial:
From Osborne, 17 miles south on U.S. 281, 4 miles west on 412, 1½ miles north on S. 150 and follow the curve ¼ mile west, then 1 mile north on S. 152. Near this spot 11 servicemen lost their lives when their WWII B-24-D bomber plane crashed on September 22, 1943. In 2004 local citizens erected a memorial at this road-side pull over. The crash occurred about ¼ mile to the west of the marker. 866.346.2670.

ALTON

Population 103

Historical Marker:
704 Mill. Erected in front of the post office (originally the 1882 Bull City Bank), the marker explains the unusual naming of the town and how founder General Bull died of a gore wound from his pet elk.

Founder Marker:
Mill and Nicholas. Under the limestone Alton sign, a granite marker commemorates town founders Hiram C. Bull and Lyman T. Earl. In 1870 these men flipped a coin to determine if the town would be named Bull City or Earlsville. Bull won the flip but after he died, the town name was changed to Alton in 1885.

Memorial Park:
Mill and Nicholas. An entrance gate of sturdy steel and historical accoutrements invites you down the brick paver path to an impressive life-sized bronze sculpture of a bull elk and an awning-covered sign listing area veterans.

General Hiram Bull:
From Alton, ¾ mile east on U.S. 24, then ½ mile north on 240.

In Sumner Cemetery, the gravestone topped with a large marble ball is that of Hiram Bull. Among other things, his marker states, "Killed by Pet Elk." The elk horns are displayed in the Osborne County courthouse (*see* p. 71).

explorer extras...
In Alton

Alton's claim to fame is that candy magnate Russell Stover was born 11 miles south of town in 1888. Follow a series of stair-step turns south on 657 to find the sign marking his birthplace.

The Bohemian Cultural Hall, 602 Mill, was moved 16 miles into town to help tell the local Bohemian culture. The hall's tin-clad building also houses the Bull City Cafe. Monday-Saturday 7 a.m.-2 p.m. 785.984.2221. **ee**

DOWNS

Population 886

Sod and Stubble Monument:
From K-181, just east on U.S. 24 in the rest area. Shaped like the front of a one-room school, this monument stands as a worthy tribute to *Sod and Stubble*, the story of the Ise family who lived near here from 1873 to 1909. Son John wrote this compelling work

in 1936 detailing his parents' struggles as they sought to make it on a prairie farm.

Pioneers, O Pioneers Monument:
From K-181, ½ mile west on U.S. 24. This seven-ton granite monument

was erected in 1969 by the children of Henry and Rosa Ise (their son John authored the popular book *Sod and Stubble*). The monument memorializes the indomitable families who settled this area before the railroad arrived in 1879.

Missouri Pacific Depot (NRHP):
710 Railroad. This red-brick 1917 depot with a mansard roof has been beautifully restored. It stands as a testament to the town being established in 1879 specifically due to the railroad. A Missouri Pacific engine and a replica gazebo are in the adjoining Railroad Park.

Carnegie Library (NRHP):
504 S. Morgan. This 1905 structure is one of the two smallest Carnegie libraries in Kansas. It hosts formal teas every so often, and as you enter note the large collection of tea cups and pots. Monday-Wednesday, Friday-Saturday 1-5 p.m. 785.454.3821.

Schoen's Bridal World:
818 Morgan. In business for more than 40 years, the newest owner, Eve Albert, offers her expertise and excellent customer service to everyone who walks in the door. Monday-Saturday 9 a.m.-5 p.m. 785.454.6292.

Shoes Etc. and Stonz Jewelry:
818 Morgan. Women travel miles to this stylish boutique to buy trendy casual apparel, shoes, accessories, and jewelry made by owner Joni Heiland. Monday-Friday 9 a.m.-5:30 p.m.; Saturday 9 a.m.-5 p.m. 785.454.6272. FB.

Howell House (NRHP, KBBA):
701 Blunt. Lumber baron George Howell built this stately Italianate house in 1883. Steve and Joan Heide restored the exterior and made the home a desirable bed and breakfast. Fans of the 1885 Muchnic House and Art Gallery in Atchison (*see* p. 97) will be interested to know that Howell built that beautiful house too.

Lodging:
Howell House (785.454.3888, howellhousebandb.com).

explorer extras... In Downs

Downs is the home of the Kansas Storytelling Festival held the last weekend of April. kansasstorytelling.com.

Dedicated in 1923, Memorial Hall, 501 S. Morgan, is the only monument in Osborne County honoring WWI veterans. **ee**

(*see* p. 97)

NATOMA
Population 330

Historic Church (NRHP):
408 N. 3rd. The 1898 Presbyterian church is of the unusual Carpenter Gothic architectural

style, rendering it a unique structure to examine from outside. Evident from inside is the no-sag, self-supported roof style, invented by Natoma native Louis Beisner. For interior viewing, call 785.885.4442.

Stan Herd Mural:
702 N. 2nd. Plains Indians are overlooking buffalo in a valley in this 1985 mural in the Southwind Bank lobby. Monday-Friday 9 a.m.-4 p.m.

Shop on the Corner:
435 Elm. Antiques and vintage or repurposed items are waiting for you here. Wednesday-Friday 10 a.m.-5 p.m. 785.623.2011.

Natoma Heritage Museum:
416 Elm. Housed in the historic limestone Pohlman Building, this museum was created by the hard-working Natoma Heritage Seekers. Friday 1-4 p.m. 785.885.4214.

NC

OSBORNE
Population 1,416

Osborne County Courthouse (NRHP):
423 W. Main. This limestone Romanesque Revival structure was completed in 1908. Of particular interest are the stylized sunflowers engraved on the exterior, a stone lion's head

and Medusa at the entrance, the displayed elk horns that gored to death legislator Hiram Bull, and the five green-tile fireplaces. Of peculiar interest is the tale of the so-called "sidewalk superintendent," John Wineland, who was such a nuisance when the courthouse was being built that the construction crew engraved his face on the clock tower! See it on the south side. Monday-Friday 8:30 a.m.-5 p.m. 785.346.2431.

Settlers Memorial:
Main and 4th (northeast section of the courthouse square). A pedestal topped with a round sphere was erected in 1929 "To the memory of those early settlers, of Osborne Co., who made possible our homes of today." The words Adventure, Home, Pioneers, and Freedom are engraved on each side of the pedestal base.

Carnegie Research Library (NRHP):
307 W. Main. Built in 1912, the red-brick library is now the center for Osborne County genealogical and historical research. It's a good place to ask Explorer questions. Friday-Saturday 10 a.m.-4 p.m. 785.346.9437.

Geodetic Center Marker (NRHP):
U.S. 281 and U.S. 24. The historical marker at this roadside park explains that a site near here (18 miles southeast) is the Geodetic Center of North America. As the sign reads, "What Greenwich is to the longitude of the world, a Kansas pasture is to the lines and boundaries of this continent." Below the sign an inscribed granite marker incorporates a bronze replica of the geodetic marker.

Blue Hills Bikes:
107 S. 1st. Inside this white quonset hut is the place to buy bicycles and accessories or have your bike repaired. John McClure, owner and passionate cyclist, will be glad to share information about local trails and bike events. Monday-Saturday 10 a.m.- 6 p.m. 785.346.6156. FB.

Shady Bend Recreation Area:
From N. 1st, 1¼ miles west on Main (becomes W. 90). At the road's end you'll find the Shady Bend Walking/ Biking Trail along the banks of the South Fork Solomon River and the 1936 Osborne Dam. Unfortunately you can't go inside the limestone scout cabin built by the WPA in 1938.

The Hideout Coffeehouse:
130 W. Main. The aroma and flavors of house-roasted blends are anything but hidden inside this turn-of-the-century building with exposed limestone walls and original pressed-tin ceiling. Monday-Friday 7 a.m.-4 p.m.; Saturday 8 a.m.-1 p.m. 785.345.4020. FB.

Circle Inn Truck Stop and Restaurant:
1106 W. U.S. 24. The Mexican food is popular here, and the pork and green-chili smothered burritos are a favorite. The chicken-fried steak is made the Explorer Way! Tuesday-Saturday 6:30 a.m.- 8 p.m.; Sunday 6:30 a.m.-2 p.m. 785.346.9444.

explorer extras... In Osborne
Tee off at two public nine-hole golf courses. Shady Bend grass-green course (920 S. 123, 785.346.2024) is on the banks of the South Fork Solomon River. The sand-green course at the Osborne County Country Club (1 mile north of Osborne on U.S. 281, 785.346.2361) is well known for its challenging terrain. Greens fee. ee

explorer extras... In Portis
Population 103

A limestone marker at Market and 5th recognizes Portis native Tubby Millar, animator for *Looney Tunes* Porky Pig cartoons and assistant to Porky Pig creator Friz Freleng.

The hard-to-read Walronds Stockade sign is 1 mile south of town on the east side of U.S. 281. Z.T. Walrond was just 23 years old when he and two friends came to Kansas from Kentucky in 1870. They constructed the stockade as protection from Indians and lived there until 1873. ee

Ottawa County

AROUND THE COUNTY

Stone Arch:
East of U.S. 81 between Rifle and Sunset. As you travel on U.S. 81, you may notice a stone arch to the east that seems out of place. And that's just the case. In 1975 Ron Parks and his family built this arch for no particular reason other than perhaps for wonderment. Constructed with field stones, the arch stands at the crest of the hill in a pasture and is clearly visible from the highway.

ADA
Unincorporated

Luke Park:
Main and Wood. Climb the steps to the stone stage and belt out a song. The folks at the nearby co-op probably won't mind. An inscribed stone on the stage front tells you it was built by the WPA in 1936.

BENNINGTON
Population 660

The Linger Longer:
119 N. Nelson. From its striped awnings to its pressed-tin ceiling and wood floor, this soda fountain, restored by Sharolyn and Jay Wagner, has the original 1912 solid oak back bar and a1920s counter. Sitting amid the world's third largest Dr. Pepper

NC

collection, you'll want to order a hand-mixed fountain drink, a Green River, or an ice cream treat. April-October, Monday-Friday 3-7 p.m.; Saturday 3-9 p.m. 855.378.7632. thelingerlonger.com.

Kansas Troubles Quilters:
103 N. Nelson. Shop for sewing supplies, fabric, quilt patterns, notions, and Kansas Troubles products designed by Lynne Hagmeier. As a bonus, just ask and they'll show you the one-of-a-kind quilting retreat center on the second floor. Tuesday-Friday 10 a.m.-5 p.m.; Saturday 10 a.m.-3 p.m. 785.488.2120. ktquilts.com.

Westside Ventures:
113 N. Nelson. Grab a bite to eat, have a cup of coffee, and pick up a few deli items along with convenience and grocery store products. Monday-Friday 7 a.m.-7 p.m.; Saturday 8 a.m.-8 p.m. 785.488.3700. FB.

Kansas Figure Drawing:
200 N. Nelson (at Three Rivers Studio). Learn, draw, and have fun with the Kansas Figure Drawing Group. You're welcome to join Deb Wagner and company any Thursday. 6-9 p.m. 785.488.8182.

Prairie Lavender Farm:
69 Alpine Ridge. From Bennington, 1 mile west on K-18, 4 miles south on N. 170, 1 mile west on Aspen, then ¼ mile south on Alpine Ridge. You might not see the lavender in bloom (June into October) but you can see the lavender fields and buy made-in-house products such as lavender

lotion, body butter, soap, and wreaths. June-September, Tuesday-Saturday 9 a.m.-12 p.m.; October-December and April-May, Thursday-Saturday 9 a.m.-12 p.m. 785.488.3371. prairielavenderfarm.com.

Old, Old U.S. 81:
The original highway ran north-south through town. To find the best evidence of the old, narrow concrete road, go 1 mile north of Bennington on N. 180, then west on Granite (the original 81). The road is rough but still in use. About ¾ mile west, watch closely, and on the north side you'll see a Kansas Federal Aid Project marker stating that the road was built in 1922. The old beaten highway continues 8½ miles north and west in stair-step fashion to K-106 south of Minneapolis.

DELPHOS

Population 353

Lincoln's Little Correspondent: E. 5th and
N. Custer (downtown square). On the square's northwest

corner, a granite monument and bronze plaque memorialize the letter from Lincoln's Little Correspondent, Grace Bedell Billings. When Grace was 11 years old and living in Westfield, New York, she wrote to Abraham Lincoln suggesting that if he grew a beard her brothers would vote for him for president. Lincoln took the girl's advice and

was duly elected in 1860. The monument also incorporates Lincoln's reply. Grace moved to Delphos as an adult.

Delphos Cemetery:
From Main, 1 mile east on K-41. A gravestone for Douglas Eames posts a thought-provoking proverb: "All things have an end, except a sausage... which has two." The inscribed stone stands about 200 feet south of the main entrance and about three rows west of the main driveway. A few more rows to the west, look for the gravestone with an etching of a covered wagon.

Milburn Stone: In 1925,
years before he became famous as Doc Adams in the television series Gunsmoke, actor Milburn Stone met local woman Nellie Morrison while he was performing in Delphos. They were married in the Presbyterian church at 307 N. Main.

Pike's Monument:
From Main, 3½ miles west on 5th (becomes Volunteer), ½ mile south on N. 52, 1 mile west on Victory which veers south and becomes N. 42, continue 500 feet and turn west onto a circular drive. The monument is at the end of the drive. Captain Zebulon Pike came through this area on his 1806 expedition. From this point he continued northwest to present Republic County near what is now Pawnee Indian Village State Historic Site. This hilltop provides a great view of the Solomon River Valley.

MINNEAPOLIS

Population 2,017

Rock City (8 Wonders of Kansas Geography):

1051 Ivy. From W. 1st, 3 miles west and south on K-106, then ½ mile west on Ivy. In this flat,

fertile Solomon River Valley it's surprising to find 200 ancient and giant rocks—the best natural playground in the state! Nowhere else in the world are this many enormous sandstone concretions concentrated in one location. Designated a National Natural Landmark in 1976, the rocks are accessible year round. Small admission charge. Memorial Day-Labor Day, daily 9 a.m.-5 p.m. 785.392.2092.

George Washington Carver Marker:

From 2nd, ½ block north on Sheridan. Minneapolis is one of the boyhood homes of famous black agricultural scientist George Washington Carver (8 Wonders of Kansas People). A marker shows the site where Carver attended school from 1880 to 1884.

Ottawa County Museum:

110 S. Concord. A major section of this museum is devoted to George Washington Carver, who lived in Minneapolis for several years during his youth. Tuesday-Saturday 10 a.m.-12 p.m. and 1-5 p.m. 785.392.3621. ottawacountyksmuseum.com.

Historic Bank Building:

313 W. 2nd. The 1887 former Minneapolis National Bank with balcony, marble pillars, bright yellow sunflower highlights,

and colorful cornucopia is pure eye candy.

Hometown Hardware:

317 W. 2nd. Soft-serve ice cream is sold at the hardware store window—you don't even have to go inside. But if you do you'll like the old-fashioned ambience, complete with creaky wood floors. Monday-Friday 8 a.m.-7 p.m.; Saturday 8 a.m.-5 p.m.; Sunday 1-5 p.m. 785.392.2692.

Town Founder:

From W. 1st, just south on Mill. As you cross the Solomon River on Mill (becomes K-106), notice the dam and waterfall to the west. This is where town founder Israel Markley first built a dam and mill in 1864. The city park 1/8 mile south is built on land donated by the Markley estate in 1911 and aptly named Markley Grove. A large memorial with water fountains honors the Markleys.

Highland Cemetery:

From 1st, ½ mile east on K-106. A veterans memorial (white crosses and a flag) graces the northeast corner of the cemetery. To the south stand more than two dozen gravestones encircling an 1861 GAR memorial. Elsewhere in the cemetery, the stone shaped like a huge football is a must see for every gravestone aficionado.

Blue Store Emporium:

307 W. 2nd. The locals say the store dates to 1884, originally sold goods, and always was called the Blue Store. Its exterior Dakota sandstone wall has long been the perfect spot for the store's advertising billboard.

Blue Moon Restaurant:

307 W. 2nd. Enter through the back alley (behind the historic Blue Store) into this basement restaurant accented with little white lights sparkling against the Dakota sandstone walls. Octogenarian owner Kermit will be in the alley grilling steaks while his wife, Kathleen, spreads good cheer among the customers. Kansas Explorer #2 and many others proclaim the salmon the best in the state. Cocktails are available in this speak-easy-like setting. Friday 6-9 p.m. Reservations required. 785.392.3491. FB.

Lodging: Mill Street Inn
(785.392.7232, millstreetinn.net); additional lodging (minneapolis-ks.com).

explorer extras... In Tescott

Population 312

Tescott is named for 1865 settler T.E. Scott, and a mural in the 100 Block of S. Main features him in an early street scene. The mural also serves as a backdrop for Hal's Hangout Park, a sweet flower garden

rest stop containing a couple of large sandstone concretions.

The sandstone band shell, a 1936 WPA project, stands at the back of the park at W. 1st and N. Nebraska.

Housed in a former school, the Tescott Museum, 3rd and Minnesota, is open by appointment only, but the landscape around it is lovely to drive by. 785.283.4388.ee

Unincorporated

Sunset Spiritualist Church Camp:
The unusual structures you see in Wells are those of the Sunset Spiritualist camp meetings held here since 1934. Covered with tin to preserve them, the row of white cabins were moved here from the Delphos Spiritualist camp in 1934. Note the seance building (1958), the Dakota sandstone church (1966), and the medicine/prayer wheel. sunsetcamp.org.

Stone Buffalo Sculpture Scenic Back Road:
From Piper (in Wells), ½ mile south on N. 203, 5½ miles east on Limestone, 1 mile south on N. 260, then 3 miles east on Kiowa. In the last mile on Kiowa look for the graffiti carved into the Dakota sandstone road cut. From Kiowa, turn north on 290. Who will be first to spy the Stone Buffalo on the hilltop!

Stone Buffalo Sculpture:
This 50-ton, 23x15-foot behemoth can't hide! Made of concrete, rocks, and stones, it was the brainchild of rancher Ray O. Smith who, with his brother Chester, built it in 1978. Ray died in 1999 and he and his wife, Maude, are buried on the hill beside the buffalo. Drive around the section to view the statue from every angle, and keep your eyes open for live buffalo and a couple of zebras in the pasture!

Republic County

For hundreds of years much of present Kansas and Nebraska was home to the powerful Pawnee Nation. In the late 1700s this area of northern Kansas was inhabited by the Kitkehahki (Republican) band of Pawnees.

Population 66

The town of Agenda is open when the businesses of entrepreneur Glenda Trecek are open. Wednesday-Saturday 10 a.m.-5 p.m. 785.732.6595.

The Cedar Porch:
413 Railroad. Glenda's entrepreneurial endeavors began with this building, which she renovated into a destination shopping experience. The original pressed-tin ceiling and wood floor complement the quality merchandise and make this off-the-beaten-track store a real find. Choose from clothing, jewelry, crafts, home decor, skin care items, and more.

Glenda's Downtown:
Eventually Glenda purchased every building in this one-block downtown and renovated them all. Her amazing efforts and intent to do something good for the community were aided by her husband, Millard, and friends. Although pats on the back are in order, Glenda and team would really rather have visitors! Stroll the block and enjoy an old-fashioned soda fountain, shop for home and garden decor and antique furniture, and peruse the museum and library. There's even a place for small group events. For groups, call 785.732.6595.

Garden Stop:
A paved walkway between the Cedar Porch and Hope Floats will lead

you to an enchanting space complete with gurgling water, a serene mural by Glen Lojka, and seating areas surrounded by charming flower gardens and rock landscaping.

Shoe Pole Art:
K-148 and 230. Dale Cherney of rural Agenda saw a picture in a farm magazine some 30 years ago of shoes nailed to a post. He liked the idea, so he and his son Chris erected a post and nailed some family shoes to it.

Population 1,924

Incorporated in 1878, Belleville was named for founder A.B. Tutton's wife, Arabelle.

Republic County Courthouse (NRHP):
1815 M. Built as a 1939 Public Works Administration project, a New Deal economic recovery program, this structure is said to be the best example of courthouse art deco architecture in the state. It has a marble interior with staircase rails of brass and stainless steel.

Monday-Friday 8 a.m-5 p.m. 785.527.7238.

Post Office Mural (NRHP):

1119 18th. *Kansas Stream* is the title of this 1939 Section artwork by Birger Sandzen. The mural depicts a Republican River scene near Scandia. The Public Works Administration provided part of the funding to construct the 1937 post office and pay the artist. Monday-Friday 8 a.m.-4 p.m.; Saturday 8:30-10:30 a.m. 785.527.2421.

Boyer Gallery of Animated Carvings:

1205 M. Mastermind folk artist Paul Boyer has created motion machines for the past 75 years. One must stand

and stare to fully appreciate Paul's attention to detail and to catch his humor in these clever animated carvings, motion displays, and mechanical marvels. See hillbillies hammer, horses kick, goats bump heads, and ball bearings jump from one drum to the next in perfect rhythm. May-September, Wednesday-Saturday 1-5 p.m. 785.527.5884.

Belleville High Banks:

7th and O. Although the track had its beginnings in 1880 as a race venue for horses, it was transformed for auto racing in 1910. In 1937 the WPA built the limestone grandstand and converted the flat track to a high-banked oval. Belleville High Banks is known as the fastest half-mile dirt track in the world.

Belleville High Banks Hall of Fame and National Midget Auto Racing Museum:

1204 H (off U.S. 81). Jeff Gordon, Tony Stewart, and Clint Bowyer are just a few who got their start on the High Banks dirt track. The history of the track, the racers, and the cars is preserved in this hall of fame and museum. Even if you aren't a race fan, these streamlined racing cars will impress you. May-September, Tuesday-Sunday 10 a.m-5 p.m.; October-April, Tuesday-Saturday 11 a.m.-4 p.m. 785.527.2488. highbanks-museum.org.

Blair Theatre: 1310 19th. After the theatre closed in the late 1990s, its Spanish Colonial facade was restored, the interior renovated, and the 1928 theatre reopened in 2008 as a state-of-the-art movie theatre. Tuesday-Sunday 7:30 p.m. 785.527.8080. theblairtheater.com.

Belleville Public Library:

1327 19th. During the Great Depression people were urged to create handicrafts and be paid for them through the WPA. Now on permanent display are some results of that work: costume dolls wearing international or period clothing, images of Kansas landmarks, paintings of Kansas wildflowers, and intricate wooden models of American industry. Monday-Friday 10 a.m.-5 p.m.; Saturday 10 a.m.-3 p.m. 785.527.5305.

WPA in the Park: 8th and M. City Park features several WPA projects including the art

deco band shell and swimming pool bathhouse, tennis courts, and other structures. The band shell, completed in 1937, was constructed of monolithic concrete (a building style first used by Thomas Edison).

Republic County Historical Museum:

615 28th. In addition to the county displays inside, outside you'll find an antique farm implements building, blacksmith shop, country school, church, log cabin, barn, caboose, and round limestone smokehouse. April-November, Monday-Friday 1-5 p.m. and Sunday 1:30-4:30 p.m; December-March, Monday- Friday 12:30-4:30 p.m. Admission charge. 785.527.5971.

Fisher Rock:

2003 E. Frontage. From M, ½ mile east on 20th, then just north on Frontage. Limestone rocks, quarried near Cottonwood Falls, come in all shapes and sizes designed with collegiate logos, popular sayings, flags, and more. Monday-Friday 8 a.m.-5 p.m. 785.527.8236. fisherrocks.com.

The Feathered Nest:

1914 M. Destination shopping at its best! The "nest" is a preserved historic building and it's "feathered" with a modern chic interior that presents unique shopping experiences. Featured are home decor, personal care specialities, garden acces-sories, and a coffee lounge offering beverages, fruit smoothies, and baked goods. Monday-Friday 8 a.m.-6 p.m.; Saturday 8:30 a.m.-5 p.m. 785.527.7200. featherednestshopping.com.

Dinner Bell Restaurant:

1301 18th. You don't need a dinner bell to come running for this homemade food, especially the daily specials and the Explorer Way chicken-fried steak on Wednesdays. Monday

6:30 a.m.-2 p.m.; Tuesday-Saturday 6:30 a.m.- 8 p.m.; Sunday 8 a.m.-2 p.m. 785.527.5171.

Lodging: bellevilleks.org.

explorer extras... In Belleville

Successful dry goods merchant S.T. Stevenson mail ordered the design for his 1894 house

(NRHP) from George F. Barber and Company. Located at 2012 N, it is an exquisite example of a high-style Queen Anne structure with a tower, delicate spindle work, and a variety of exterior wall textures.

In 2008 artist Cindy Chinn painted a fun outdoor mural that looks like something has crashed into the Belleville Farm & Home store! See the crash at 1825 N.

Around the courthouse square, four historical information kiosks relate the stories of Belleville beginnings, transportation, the WPA, and agriculture. **ee**

Population 273

Depot Market:
1101 30 (U.S. 36 and K-199). Find this family-owned roadside market at the refurbished Santa Fe depot. The orchard out back makes you feel connected to the land as does the fresh seasonal produce from the family's gardens. Food specialty products are also sold here. Mid-June to Halloween,

Monday-Saturday 9 a.m-5:30 p.m.; Sunday 1-5 p.m. 785.374.4255. depotmarket.net.

Art Center Arch: 421 Main. Around 1890 Swedish immigrant John Sederlin built a limestone barn with a unique arch. A few

years ago his descendants donated the arch (and additional limestone) for the archway and the wall around the nicely manicured garden adjoining Courtland Art Center.

The Cantina and Jensen Tire and Service: 225 Main.
In front of the tire service, the Cantina is an expanded convenience store carrying gifts and home decor items. Thanks go to Cindy and Gary Jensen for bringing groceries to a small town. Monday-Saturday 7 a.m.-6 p.m. 785.374.4315.

AnTeaQues: 415 Main. You get a two-fer—lunch and antiques—at this rustic store. Enjoy homemade specials and a search through a large variety of antiques. Lunch, Tuesday-Friday 11 a.m.-1 p.m.; store hours, Tuesday-Saturday 9 a.m.-5 p.m. 785.374.9292.

Pinky's Bar and Grill: 428 Main. Beer signs bedeck the log-cabin look of Pinky's, now owned by siblings Betty

and Wayne and named for the original owner. Lunch includes fried chicken on Wednesdays and Explorer Way chicken-fried steak on Thursdays. Steaks are on the evening menu. Monday-Saturday 11 a.m.-9 p.m. 785.374.4200.

Clock Tower Bridge:
From Courtland, 6½ miles south on 30, 1 mile west on Xavier, ¼ mile north on a private drive.

Jim Elliot built this picturesque 20x80-foot covered bridge and clock tower from Western Red Cedar. A covered walkway with windows provides a view of the quiet landscape. Jim is happy to show you the bridge, and he enjoys explaining how he built the arches and clock tower. For tours, call 620.245.7774. The Elliotts also own the nearby Snow Goose Lodge on a salt marsh overlooking the Jamestown Wildlife Refuge.

Lodging: Snow Goose Lodge (KBBA, 620.245.7774, retreat-logcabin.com/snow-goose-lodge).

Population 149

Czech Us Out: So says the town's entrance sign!

Cuba Cash Store:
301 Baird. Walt and Cheri Cardi are the new owners of this store, which has been so important to Cuba. Tell them thanks for stepping up to help their small town. You can help too by buying a few things—such as the made-on-site Czech ring bologna! Monday-Saturday 8 a.m.-6 p.m.; Sunday 8-12 p.m. 785.729.3632.

NC

Two Doors Down:
305 Baird. You guessed it, it's two doors down from the Cuba Cash Store. Homemade kolaches are among the many tasty edibles at this local restaurant. Monday-Saturday 9 a.m.-2 p.m.; Wednesday-Saturday 5-9 p.m.; Sunday 8 a.m.-1 p.m. 785.729.3633.

Cuba Community Hall:
200 block of Baird. Each March community boosters host a week-long Rock-a-Thon at Cuba's 1930 auditorium, Ceska-Narodin-Sin (Bohemian Hall). Two rocking chairs are kept rocking 24 hours a day for an entire week. You pay to rock, and proceeds go to community projects. This hall is the heart of the community.

Glen Lojka Sculpture:
313 Baird. Standing in front of Cuba City Hall, this 8,000-pound limestone sculpture was a gift from artist Glen Lojka to his hometown. Dedicated in 2005, *Czech Immigrants* depicts a typical Czech family arriving on the prairie in the late 1800s.

Historic Bank Vault:
400 block of Baird. What looks like a limestone jail with a fancy door is really a bank vault. The stone walls are part of the

vault that once stood inside the First Commercial Bank. When the bank was razed, the vault survived!

Blacksmith Shop (NRHP):
From Baird, ½ block west on Lynn. Union veteran John Davidson came to Cuba in 1884 and built a native limestone blacksmith shop, which he operated until 1892.

Closed in 1970, the shop has been restored and is open for demonstrations. 785.729.3861.

Downtown: Worth visiting are these small-town venues. The one-room country school was moved into town thanks to Rock-a-Thon dollars. Closed since 1981, the office of "Doc" McClaskey remains on main street as a tribute to this doctor's 52 years of service. Treasures await at the Cuba Antique store, Friday-Saturday 12-5 p.m.

National Bohemian Cemetery (formerly Narodni Hrbitov):
From Lynn, 1 block south on Baird, ¾ mile east on Linden, 1 mile south on 270, then ¼ mile east on Queen. Inscribed names such as Kopsa, Lesovsky, and Huncovsky leave no doubt that you're in Bohemian country. At one time Czechs were denied burial in some cemeteries, so they created their own where any Czech could be buried without regard to religion.

explorer extras...
In Narka

Population 91

Located north of Cuba at 280 and Diamond, Narka was named in 1887 for the daughter of a railroad employee. Little remains of this town, which is tucked away in the northeast part of the county. Its claim to fame is the water tower. Or, is it an alien spaceship? See for yourself, and try to find the geocache hidden there. **ee**

Unincorporated

Trip to Norway: No cruise ship needed. Enjoy a nice drive to Norway from Scandia through the Republican River Valley. From Scandia, go 1 mile south on Kansas (becomes 90) and follow the curve, continue 1 mile east on Limestone Trail, 5½ miles south on 100, then ½ mile west on K-148. You've arrived in Norway! The bluffs and trees along the river beyond the fertile cropland make this a beautiful winding drive.

Ethnic Heritage: Norwegians settled this small community in 1870. You'll find Scandinavian names on the stained-glass windows of the Lutheran church on K-18 and in Norway Cemetery just east of town.

Norway Flag:
K-148 and Nelson. The flag on a monolith provides the town's founding date, stating in part, "Norway 1869."

Ada Lutheran Church:
442 Valley. From Norway, 4½ miles west on K-148, 1 mile north on 50, then ½ mile west on Valley. This limestone country church is one you come upon unexpectedly and is a pleasant find. In the church cemetery an anchor marks the grave of merchant marine S.A. Haggman (1842-1930).

REPUBLIC

Population 113

Pawnee Indian Village State Historic Site

(NRHP): 480 Pawnee Trail. From U.S. 36, 8 miles north on K-266. On this site an early-1800s Pawnee village once comprised 40 earth lodges and 2,000 inhabitants. A museum, which encloses the excavated

floor of the largest lodge, features panoramic exhibits and, of special interest, a rare Pawnee sacred bundle. This is the only site in the state dedicated to one of the indigenous tribes and is of major archeological signif-icance. Wednesday-Saturday 9 a.m-5 p.m. Admission charge. 785.361.2255. kshs.org.

SCANDIA

Population 362

The Scandinavian Agricultural Society of Chicago formed a colony here in 1868. Its original name, New Scandinavia, was soon shortened to Scandia. The Colony House stood 200 feet west of the historical marker on U.S. 36 that describes this immigration. Most of the early settlers were Swedish, Danish, and Norwegian.

Downtown: The Scandia Antique Mall will quench your vintage thirst (309 4th, 785.335.3303). The Rusty Wheel carries repurposed items, fashion accessories, home decor, and more (304 4th, 785.547.6499).

Scandia Museum: 409 4th. A miniature scene (built with 8,557 hard-carved pieces by Allen Larson) of a wagon train attack is one of the museum's highlights. Memorial Day-Labor Day, Monday-Saturday 2-4 p.m. 785.335.2561.

Tile Mural: 402 4th. Made with colorful tiles, a mural depicting bridges and roads can be seen above the entrance of Reece Construction Company. The mural reflects the company's business—building bridges and roads.

T.A.G.'s Grill & Bar:

319 Cloud. Terry and Carol Garmin choose the best ingred-ients and come up with winners. Favorites are the barbeque, daily specials, all-day breakfasts, a self-service ice cream bar— and the green beans! The restaurant's name? The Garmin kids' initials. Monday-Saturday 6:30 a.m.-10 p.m.; Sunday 7 a.m.-3 p.m. 785.335.2020.

Russell County

AROUND THE COUNTY

A constant roadside companion in this county is the post rock fence post. Much respect should be given to these time-honored posts, which average 350 to 500 pounds each, are five to six feet in length, and 8 to 12 inches thick. Each one is a remarkable tribute to the early settlers who solved their fencing problems by quarrying rock from the surface of the earth.

Post Rock Scenic Byway:

From Wilson, north on K-232 to K-18, then ½ mile west on K-18 to Lucas. The 18 miles of post rock fence posts and limestone structures, some abandoned, will give you a glimpse into the natural resource of the area. Breathtaking scenery will hit a zenith about 2 miles north of Wilson Lake. A Scenic Byway kiosk at the west end of Wilson Lake Dam provides information. travelks.com/ksbyways.

NC

Wilson Lake and State Park:

From I-70, 5 miles north on K-232. Surrounded by the grasslands of post rock country, this clear lake provides a variety of recreational opportunities. The two-and-a-half-mile hiking loop at the Rocktown Natural Area features diverse prairie grasses, plants, and Dakota sandstone formations in a secluded cove. As the Conard *Kansas Trail Guide* states, the 21-mile Switchgrass Trail is a Kansas mountain biker's dream. Shorter trails are also worthy of your time. The dam and lake became operational in 1965 as a flood control measure. State park entrance charge. Cabins available, reservations required. 785.658.2465. ksoutdoors.com.

Faces in Stone: Post Rock Scenic Byway on K-232

between Wilson Lake Dam and Lucas. A sharp eye will spot four limestone fence posts carved with faces. As a tribute to the area, artist Fred Whitman chose local folks for his subjects. Seven more "face posts" can be found in Lucas. For a list, stop by the Grassroots Art Center in Lucas (*see* p. 81).

BUNKER HILL

Population 95

Rock Sculpture:

From Washington, just east on 2nd. According to a local historian, an early settler made this one-of-a-kind pillar/sculpture from limestone, Dakota sandstone, bricks, and septarian (veiny) rocks, all of which are melded together with mortar. If you look closely you can see remnants of colored glass that were once another prominent feature. Scheduled to be destroyed, Alvin Baral saved it and moved it from a nearby church to his yard.

Historic Jail: Elm and 6th. The first jail in Russell County still stands in City Park. No longer in use, it's still a reminder that miscreants once landed in this sturdy slammer.

Bunker Hill Museum:

331 Kansas. Housed in an 1872 limestone Lutheran church, the museum preserves and exhibits the community's history. Outside, markers tell the story of Mother Bickerdyke, a Civil War nurse who died in Bunker Hill in 1901. Memorial Day-Labor Day, Sunday 1-4 p.m. 785.445.8098.

Bunker Hill Cemetery:

From 1st, ½ mile north on Winthrop

(193), then 1 mile east on Balta. Pawnee Chief Spotted Horse, the first person to be buried in this cemetery, died of pneumonia at Bunker Hill in 1874 as he and his tribe were being escorted from Nebraska to Oklahoma. His father requested that his son be buried in the "White Man's Burial Ground." To see his grave, turn east at the first intersection from the cemetery entrance. The gray granite monument is on the right.

Bunker Hill Cafe: 609 Elm. You'll satisfy your appetite with made-from-scratch goodness served inside this rustic 1916 limestone building, formerly a drug store. Specialties include steak, king crab, green shrimp, and catfish. Fresh salads and honey-raisin, home-baked bread are as famous as the

homemade jellies. And the chicken-fried steak is made the Explorer Way! Owners Tom and Janet Taggart and daughter Lacy ensure it's all good. Thursday-Saturday 5-10 p.m. Reservations recommended. 785.483.6544.

Wilson Lake Scenic Drive:

From 1st, go ½ mile north on Winthrop (193), 1 mile east on Balta, 3 miles winding northeast on Anspaugh, then 12 miles east on Shoreline to K-232 on the east edge of the lake. The Smoky Hill scenery stands out against Wilson Lake on this beautiful 24-mile drive.

DORRANCE

Population 181

Reiff Building/Dorrance Historical Society Museum (NRHP): 513 Main.

Once a social hall, the 1911 limestone Reiff Building is now home to the Dorrance Historical Society Museum. 785.420.0819.

School Monument:

Jellison and Taylor. Built with remains of the 1917 local high school, this monument pays tribute to the school, lost to fire in 1982. Perched on top, a ceramic cardinal (school mascot) safeguards the marker.

Old 40 Bar & Grill:

525 Main. Kerry and Chrissy Andrews serve warm welcomes and juicy, thick burgers and hand-cut fries. A frosty mug awaits those wanting a cold one. Leave your name on the ceiling or on any open space. Wednesday-Friday 11 a.m.-2 p.m.; Wednesday 5:30-8 p.m. 785.666.4398.

FAIRPORT

Unincorporated

Find Fairport by going 1 mile west of Gorham on Balta (Old U.S. 40), 11 miles north on 177 (becomes Gorham Fairport), then 1½ miles west on Fairport.

Carrie Oswald No. 1:

From Fairport, 1½ miles east on Fairport, 2 miles south on Gorham Fairport, then ½ mile west on Beatty to 176. Here a plaque on a limestone base announces that you've arrived at the Oswald No. 1. Ed and Carrie Oswald and the Lucky Seven struck oil on this site in November 1923 making it the first oil discovery well in the Fairport oil field. By 1933 production was down to two barrels. Luckily, that same year a new process (pumping acid under pressure into the casing) was performed for the first time in the nation on the Oswald No. 1. It proved a huge success and production increased to 108 barrels a day. It was a game changer that affected all future oil production.

A Fairport Knight: 200 Main. You have the opportunity to spend a night in Fairport in an 1886 two-story limestone house outfitted for your every convenience. Fairport Mills was a flour mill on the Saline River, and this house was built by one of its owners, William Knight. Current owner Charlotte Oswald David is the granddaughter of Carrie Oswald (of oil well fame). 785.998.4388. FB.

LUCAS

Population 390

Lucas is the Grassroots Art Capital of Kansas (8 Wonders of Kansas Art). Even the bright mosaic entrance sign on E. K-18 is grassroots art. This art style is fashioned by people who haven't formally studied art, and it has no inhibiting rules. Stop in Lucas to see the world from a grassroots artist perspective.

Note that the hours are irregular for many businesses. If you are coming from a distance, call to confirm hours. Everyone is happy to accommodate if you call ahead.

Garden of Eden (NRHP): 305 E. 2nd. A sight full of character, the Garden of Eden is the epitome of grassroots art. S.P. Dinsmoor built his 11-room limestone and concrete log cabin home and Garden of Eden

sculptures from 1907 to 1929 using 113 tons of cement and goodness knows how many tons of limestone! The sculptures are Dinsmoor's interpretation of the Bible, Populist politics, and modern civilization. He built the 40-foot-tall limestone mausoleum for himself and his first wife, and he is laid to rest in a handmade, glass-topped concrete coffin. Folks in Lucas tried to run Dinsmoor out of town, but in time his work became the area's main attraction, and still is today. March-April, daily 1-4 p.m.; May-October, daily 10 a.m.- 5 p.m.; November-February, Saturday-Sunday 1-4 p.m. Admission charge. 785.525.6395. garden-of-eden-lucas-kansas.com.

Miller's Park: Just east of the Garden of Eden. Roy and Clara Miller collected rocks and shells during their 1930s-1960s travels and transformed them into miniature Lucas buildings. The stand-alone towers they made from slag glass and barite roses. Visitors stopped often to see this roadside attraction, but after Roy's and Clara's deaths the miniatures were moved to Hays in 1969. Thanks to passionate efforts, these works of art came home to Lucas in 2013. In a park-like setting, the miniatures can be admired from behind the fence. lucaskansas.com.

Grassroots Art Center: 213 S. Main. Permanent grassroot art exhibits include Inez Marshall's colorful limestone sculptures and Ed Root's concrete and glass-embedded creations. You'll see Herman Divers' life-sized motorcycle made so sturdily from pop-can tabs that you could sit on it!

NC

This art center also has an endless flow of tickle-your-fancy temporary exhibits. The outdoor Post Rock Courtyard displays elements of distinctive native limestone architecture and its artistry. May-September,

Monday-Saturday 10 a.m.- 5 p.m. and Sunday 1-5 p.m.; April and October, Thursday-Monday 1-4 p.m.; March and November, Thursday-Saturday 1-4 p.m. Admission charge. 785.525.6118. grassrootsart.net.

Florence Deeble's Sculpture Rock Garden and the Deeble House: 126 Fairview. From 1942 to 1995 this schoolteacher used colored concrete and rocks to design "postcards" in her backyard of her favorite vacation sites. Deeble's house has become an interior art gallery for artist Mri-Pilar. The walls and ceilings are wrapped in silver insulation, and every inch is filled with Pilar's sculptures of recycled products including not-so-usual paper dolls. For hours, see Grassroots Art Center. Admission charge. For tours, ask at the Grassroots Art Center. 785.525.6118. grassrootsart.net.

Bowl Plaza: 100 block of S. Main. Mosaics of colorful tiles and glass, toy cars, dominoes, badges, wine corks, and more

adorn the walls for your viewing pleasure while you're "resting" at this artistic public restroom. If you arrive after hours you can still sit on the outdoor toilet seat bench and admire the mosaic toilet lid that arches over the bathroom entrances. A large concrete roll of toilet paper unravels into a sidewalk. Mri-Pilar and Eric Abraham led a local effort to create this plaza. For hours, see Grassroots Art Center.

Brant's Meat Market

(8 Wonders of Kansas Commerce): 125 S. Main. One step inside the door and you'll think you've stepped back in time at least 50 years. You'll see fresh meats in window coolers, a Czech mural on the wall, and a few grocery staples. While you're pondering your purchase from a variety of specialty and homemade sausages, cheeses, and bologna, rest your foot on the counter's brass rail and chat with owner Doug Brant. This shop has been in his family since 1922. Monday-Saturday 8 a.m.-5:30 p.m. 785.525.6464.

Erika Nelson Home Base:

226 Kansas. *The World's Largest Collection of the World's Smallest Versions of the World's Largest Things* are housed in various areas in Erika's back yard. Two circus wagons house the Kansas Collection and Fabulous Food-stuffs displays. Outdoor displays are open during daylight hours. worldslargestthings.com.

World's Largest Souvenir Travel Plate:

From K-18 Cafe, just east on K-18. In 2006 Erika Nelson cooked up a visually pleasing spread of Lucas's story on this giant satellite dish.

Da Da Muse'Um Art Gallery:

104 N. Main. If you're lucky enough to find Alan Vopat's gallery open you'll see alphabet letters used as you've never seen them before. Clusters of them form faces, bodies, objects, and much more. Not limited to "letter art," Vopat's creativity knows no bounds. Hours irregular. Call ahead, 785.404.2637.

Aunt Gertie's:

304 E. 2nd. Cleverness is on display. As Aunt Gertie says, the art and antiques are repurposed, restyled, and reimagined! Hours irregular. 620.213.1026. FB.

Lodging:

Garden View Lodge (785.658.6607, airbnb.com); Set in Stone Cabins & RV Park (785.525.7742, set-in-stone.net).

explorer extras... In Lucas

• A group of locals led by Mri-Pilar created 15 colorful fork sculptures of varying designs, thus producing American Fork Art! See them in Fork Art Park next to the Bowl Plaza.

• In a 2011 mural covering the entire wall south of Brant's, artist Erika Nelson has cleverly illustrated the early uses of Dakota sandstone by Czech immigrants to this area.

• Look in on the 1902 limestone jail in the 100 block of W. 2nd.

• K-18 Cafe, 5495 K-18, is the local eating stop for daily specials. Daily 6 a.m.-10 p.m. 785.525.6262.

• Look for the "Open" flag outside, and enjoy good food inside at Backstreet Bakery, 208 S. Main. Tuesday-Saturday 11 a.m.-9 p.m. 785.525.6351.

• Bluestem Stoneworks and Bohemian Bluestem Gallery have repurposed the old Lucas lumberyard (115 W. 2nd) for their stone and architectural salvage businesses. Hours irregular. 785.525.6494.

• Possumbilities, 123 S. Main, hosts a coffee and antique shop and an art gallery in part of Eric Abraham's Flying Pig Studio. **ee**

explorer extras... In Luray

Population 190

An early log cabin stands in the rest area on K-18 across from Main. It was built by Civil War veteran Jonathan Wesley Van Scoyoc during the winter of 1870-71.

Designed by volunteers, Luray's 18-hole, sand-green golf course is a unique one. It actually is a nine-hole course but the second time through, three holes have a second green and the other six have a different tee box. Located 1 mile east of Luray off K-18 at 5824 195. Greens fee. 785.698.2272. **ee**

PARADISE

Population 49

In the 1880s when James Mead entered the wooded valley with a creek flowing into the Saline River, he exclaimed to his hunting companions, "Boys, we have got into paradise at last!" The hunters' paradise was home to elk, black-tailed deer, buffalo, beavers, otters, and wolves. The valley, the creek, and the town are all named Paradise.

Water Tower (NRHP):

Waldo and Main. Beside the 1938 WPA stone water tower, a limestone sign reads, "Welcome to Paradise." Take a picture; it may be your only opportunity to be photographed in paradise!

RUSSELL

Population 4,475

Bob Dole: Born in Russell in 1923, Dole served from 1968 to 1996 in the U.S. Senate and was the Republican nominee for president in 1996 against incumbent Bill Clinton. You can see Senator Dole's home at 1035 N. Maple, a limestone carving of him in the beautifully restored courthouse at 401 N. Main, and a large limestone marker with a plaque dedicated to the senator at the entrance of the VFW building at 248 N. Memorial (Bob Dole Dr.).

Post Office Mural (NRHP):

135 W. 6th. *Wheat Workers* is the title of this 1940 Section artwork by Martyl Schweig. The scene of farm laborers and oil derricks reflects the area's economy of the 1930s.

Art in the Park:

325 N. Grant (Bickerdyke Park). A 12-foot sculpture of an angel, made from the steel of oil-field and farm materials, was created by art educator Trudy Furney in 1988. The angel blows a trumpet in anticipation of better times ahead. The park also contains a replica of the Statue of Liberty and a 1987

Roustabouts sculpture by Richard Bergen.

Deines Cultural Center:

820 N. Main. Featured are rotating and permanent exhibits of E. Hubert Deines' art, including his wood engravings. Traveling art exhibits and displays of regional artists' works change on a regular basis. Tuesday-Friday 12-5 p.m.; Saturday-Sunday 1-5 p.m. 785.483.3742.

Outdoor Mural:

8th and Main. Artist Rick Rupp incorporated 35 black-and-white images on the 30x100-foot building wall to tell the story of Russell, beginning in the 1870s.

Dream Theatre (NRHP):

629 N. Main. Volunteers keep the dream alive and the movies running in this beloved theatre. Originally built in 1923 and, after a fire, rebuilt in art deco style in 1949, the theatre is owned by the Russell Arts Council. 785.445.1949. dreamtheater.org.

D. Palma & Co. Mercantile:

604 N. Main. Friendly and knowledgeable service puts a shine on the quality antiques, vintage items, and art deco artifacts. Have a relaxed time shopping for everything from glassware to furniture. Monday-Saturday 10 a.m.-5 p.m.; Sunday 12-5 p.m. 785.483.2177. dpalmaco.com.

Encore Antiques & Collectables and Veez Unlimited:

590 S. Fossil. The owners say everything deserves an encore, and all sorts of items get second chances here. Also featured are Kansas food products and works by Kansas artists. Tuesday-Saturday 10 a.m.-6 p.m.; Sunday 1-5 p.m. FB.

Fossil Station Museum (NRHP):

331 N. Kansas. Originally named Fossil Station, this castle-like building was built in 1907 to house Russell's jail and sheriff's residence. Now a museum, it includes displays

on extracting post rock; Russell's own Mother Bickerdyke, Bob Dole, and Arlen Specter; and "The Tooth Story." Memorial Day-Labor Day, Monday-Saturday 11 a.m.-5 p.m. and Sunday 1-5 p.m.; September-May, Saturday 11 a.m.-5 p.m. and Sunday 1-5 p.m. Donation suggested. 785.483.3637.

Oil Patch Museum:

1430 S. Fossil. Russell flourished in the oil-boom days of the 1920s and 1930s, and the story of the people and events surrounding these times is told here. Outside the museum, see oil-field equipment and three limestone sculptures by artist Gary Christy. Memorial Day-Labor Day, daily 4-8 p.m. Donation welcome. 785.483.6640.

1872 Gernon House (NRHP):

818 N. Kansas. Built by Russell's first blacksmith, Nicholas Gernon, this home is the town's oldest house still standing. For tours, ask at the Fossil Station Museum. Call ahead, 785.483.3637.

Heym-Oliver House:

503 N. Kansas. In 1981 Mary Lynn Beech Oliver, daughter of Wichita aviation leaders Walter and Olive Ann Beech, purchased and restored this 1879 limestone home built by John Heym. She later donated it to the Russell County Historical Society. For tours, ask at the Fossil Station Museum. Call ahead, 785.483.3637.

Waudby's Sports Bar & Grill (NRHP): 719 N. Main.

Half the fun of eating and having a cold one in Waudby's is stepping inside the 1886 building with wood floors and wainscoting. In 1926 Alfred Waudby converted it into a pool hall for oil workers, and billiard benches still line both sides of the long open room. Also of interest are the two murals, painted in 1939 by a transient named Gesser and restored in 2004 by Rick Rupp. Monday-Tuesday 4 p.m.-2 a.m.; Wednesday-Saturday 11 a.m.- 2 a.m. 785. 483.2532.

Meridy's: 1220 S. Fossil. Locals rave about the steaks. Breakfast is served all day. Daily 7 a.m.-10 p.m. 785.483.4300.

LaSada Inn Restaurant:

3721 183. From Russell, 3½ miles south on U.S. 281, 2 miles west on Pioneer West, then just south on 183. The country gourmet meals range from simple to elegant and everything is homemade. Individual dining, Thursday-Saturday from 6 p.m. Reservations required. 785.483.3758.

Lodging: LaSada's Black Swan Inn (785.483.3758, lasada.com); additional lodging (russellchamber.com, russellcoks.org).

explorer extras... In Russell

The boyhood home of Pennsylvania U.S. senator Arlen Specter is at 115 N. Elm.

The Ruppenthal Middle School, 400 N. Elm, is a 1938 WPA project.

Fun is in store at Memorial Park, 1056 E. 4th, with its playground, swimming pool, horseshoe pits, lighted skateboard park, and frisbee golf.

Local war veterans are honored at the impressive Russell County Veterans Memorial, 1142 E. Wichita (E. U.S. 40 Business) in Memorial Park.

In Russell City Cemetery, 1600 E. Wichita (E. U.S. 40 Business), a memorial to two railroad workers killed in 1869 by Cheyennes stands northwest of the center circle containing the soldiers monument. ee

explorer extras... In Waldo

Population 30

Where's Waldo? It's been here since 1888 and was established by the Union Pacific Railroad as an agriculture shipping and receiving point until the railroad abandoned the line in 1993. Take your picture with the Waldo water tower as a backdrop so you can let everyone know you've finally found Waldo.

At U.S. 281 and Main you'll see an old wooden filling station that dates to the 1930s. Closed in the 1960s, it's still hanging on but leans a little bit more each year. ee

Saline County

AROUND THE COUNTY

Rolling Hills Wildlife Adventure: 625 N. Hedville.

From Salina, 6 miles west on I-70 to Hedville exit 244, then 2 miles south on Hedville. This quality zoo in a country setting is an adventure indeed! Whether you take the narrated tram ride or walk the grounds at your own pace, you'll be enthralled with the natural-as-possible habitats for the 100-plus species living here among pleasing landscapes. Through animatronics and robotics, the Rolling Hills Wildlife Museum presents faraway wildlife cultures—the Great

Wall of China, a Hindu temple, a rainforest, and an African watering hole are only a few of the stops on this fascinating exploration. Daily 9 a.m.-4 p.m. Admission charge. 785.827.9488. rollinghillswildlife.com.

County Cemetery and Poor House: From I-135 at

Salina, 3½ miles west on K-140, then 1¼ miles south on Lightville. It's a rare sight to see a sign announcing a county cemetery. No longer in use, the cemetery once belonged to what was called the county farm and asylum for the poor. Each grave for the 62 burials between 1873 and 1927 is marked with a simple white cross, and names of the interred are listed on a plaque. The three-story, red-brick former county poor house is now St. Francis Community Services and can be seen northwest of the cemetery. A historical marker at the cemetery tells the story.

ASSARIA

Population 414

Renaissance Cafe:

210 N. Center. The restaurant is housed in a former 1919 Assaria High School, but school

cafeteria food definitely is not served here! You're seated at tables around the balcony above a sunken gym to enjoy exceptional cuisine prepared by chef Shana Everhart. She offers a creative medley of pasta, chicken, fish, pork, and beef dishes along with salads, soups, antipasti, and divine desserts. Thursday-Saturday 5-9 p.m. Reservations recommended. 785.667.5535. renaissancecafeassaria.com.

BROOKVILLE

Population 260

Old Brookville Hotel:

204 N. Perry. The 1870 Brookville Hotel still stands, but the restaurant famous for family-style chicken dinners moved some years back. The hotel is in private ownership and is undergoing renovations.

Sandstone Saloon:

102 E. Anderson. Saunter in for a cool one at this distinctive 1879 sandstone building renovated in 2013 by owner Mike Haug and his son Michael. Decor favors Brookville's cowtown heritage and school history. A small grill menu and an outdoor patio are also on hand. Friday-Saturday 5 p.m.-2 a.m.; Sunday 3-10 p.m. 785.225.6715. sandstonesaloon.com.

explorer extras... In Gypsum

Population 399

A sign outside of Gypsum proclaims there are 13 exits into this small town. But if you go to 512 Maple you'll find yourself at Exit 14 Restaurant. Pan-fried chicken is served the first Sunday of the month. Tuesday-Saturday 11 a.m.-2 p.m.; Thursday-Saturday 5-9 p.m. 785.577.8921.

A water-fountain pavilion with red-brick pillars and a red-tile roof stands at 6th and Maple. The 1927 pavilion originally sheltered a fire cistern (water storage for fire fighting). **ee**

explorer extras... In Mentor

Unincorporated

Jump in the car for a road trip to see Rex's Antique Car Museum, 856 E. Mentor. From Schilling in Salina, go 3 miles south on I-135, then 1 mile east on E. Mentor. Rex Russell is passionate about cars and it shows in his collection, which includes steam cars and other rare vehicles. If Rex isn't there a neighbor will come over and show you around. Call ahead, 785.452.3089. **ee**

SALEMSBORG

Unincorporated

Salemsborg Church:

From Smolan, 3 miles south on S. Burma. Head for the twin steeples and you'll find the Salemsborg church and cemetery. This 1926 church has two entrance doors, both inscribed "Salemsborg Lutheran EV Church," but one inscription is in English and the other in

Swedish. Near the cemetery Swedish artist Anton Pearson erected an outdoor sandstone

pulpit. It's at the exact spot where the pulpit stood inside the first sod church.

Pioneer White Cross:

From the Salemsborg church, 2 miles south on S. Burma to W. Hedberg. In 1941 Carl Linholm set whitewashed Dakota sandstone into the hillside in the shape of a cross to honor Swedish pioneers of the Smoky Valley. Youth from the Salemsborg church still whitewash the cross as needed. The service control center for a Nike missile base (never completed) existed nearby in the 1960s.

SALINA

Population 47,846

Smoky Hill Museum

(NRHP): 211 W. Iron. Housed in a 1938 art deco post office, the museum brings Salina and the surrounding Smoky Hills region to life in beautifully designed exhibits. It's a museum that's fun for all ages! *Land and Communication,* the Section art bas-reliefs on the building's front exterior, are by artists Carl Mose and Jon Johnson. Tuesday-Friday 12-6 p.m.; Saturday 10 a.m.- 5 p.m. Donation welcome. 785.309.5776. smokyhillmuseum.org.

H.D. Lee: Wear your Lee jeans in Salina! H.D. Lee founded Salina's first garment factory, the HD Lee Mercantile Company, in 1911 which eventually led to the invention of the popular denim Lee jeans. While in Salina, the entrepreneur lived with the Flanders family from 1889 to 1916 at the current Flanders-Lee House (NRHP), 200 S. 7th.

Trails and Historical Walking Tours

Experience historic Salina on foot via self-guided tours of downtown (Lee District), Lee employee homes, and Gypsum Hill Cemetery, which includes Lee's resting place and those of many other famous (and infamous) Salina citizens. Available too are 24 miles of maintained trails. Information and maps are at walksalina.com.

SculptureTour Salina:
A walk through the Lee District in downtown Salina leads you to an amazing outdoor exhibit of more than 20 unique and juried sculptures by national artists. The sculptures change each spring. sculpturetoursalina.com.

Architecture:

• Terra Cotta Capital:
Salina is the Terra Cotta Capital of Kansas, a city rich in the art deco architectural style. Look for examples along Santa Fe (and blocks on either side) between Mulberry and Ash. The 1929 United Life Insurance Building (Salina's "skyscraper") at 7th and Iron is one not to miss.

• Roosevelt-Lincoln Junior High School (NRHP):
210 W. Mulberry. On this property occupying almost a full city block, Lincoln School, on the north end, was completed in 1917, and Roosevelt School, to the south, was completed in 1925. Lincoln School's Prairie School style architecture

features beautiful bas-relief figures and shapes on the central tower and pilasters. Both buildings have been renovated for senior housing.

• Salina Masonic Center:
336 S. Santa Fe. Completed in 1927, the row of famed copper gargoyles along the roof line is a subtle accent to the building's monumental Ionic columns.

• Marymount College Administration Building:
2035 E. Iron. Opened in 1922 as a women's college, Marymount closed its doors in 1989. The grand 1922 Tudor Gothic style Administration Building, on the circle drive, is being converted to luxury condominiums.

• Country Club Heights:
Marymount and Crestview. A long-standing stone kiosk with slate roof welcomes you to Country Club Heights where old brick streets wind you past lovely homes that date to the 1920s. "The Hill," as the area was known, was first populated by the city's elite, and early homes were built to the owner's taste by architect Charles Shaver.

• Voting Station: 216 W.
Crawford. Using limestone and Dakota sandstone, the National Youth Administration built this beautiful precinct voting station and Boy Scout meeting place in 1940. The building currently serves as the Shelter Insurance office.

Downtown: Enjoy shopping at Prairieland Market, featuring organic and local foods (305 E. Walnut, 785.827.5877); Connected–a Fair Trade Store, carrying home decor, gifts, and more (117 S. Santa Fe, 785.829.0237); and Sweet on You, specializing in fine chocolates (157 N. 7th, 785.577.7238). A host of other downtown stores sell antiques, yarn, music, repurposed items, and more. salinadowntown.org.

Salina Art Center:
242 S. Santa Fe. Enjoy visual art experiences for all ages through fine exhibitions.

Wednesday-Sunday 1-5 p.m. 785.827.1431. salinaartcenter.org.

Salina Art Center Cinema:
150 S. Santa Fe. For something different in movie going, enjoy films of thought-provoking, imaginative, and artistic genres shown here. 785.452.9868. salinaartcenter.org/cinema.

Stiefel Theatre (NRHP):
151 S. Santa Fe. The colorful marquee announces this 1931 theatre built in art deco style. Renovated in 2003, the theatre is enhanced with gold-leaf decor, a grand staircase, and gleaming chandeliers. 785.827.1998. Performance schedule at stiefeltheatre.org.

Yesteryear Museum (formerly Kansas Central Flywheels): 1100 W. Diamond (Diamond intersects with 9th just north of I-70). This large museum houses just about anything from bygone days. Antique farm equipment forms the museum's main collection. Tuesday-Saturday 9 a.m-5 p.m. 785.825.8473. yesteryearmuseum.org.

Oakdale Park: 730 Oakdale. Completed in 1918, the Spanish-American War and GAR memorial gateway greets you at the park's north entrance. Bronze statues of a Spanish-American War soldier and a Civil War soldier stand atop the two impressive granite pillars. Inside this lovely 50-acre park, important features include the 1885 fountain, a 1935 WPA comfort station (restroom), a 1950 Statue of Liberty replica, and an outdoor Sound Garden sporting musical instruments of varying sorts for kids of all ages to play.

Ad Astra Books and Coffeehouse: 141 N. Santa Fe. As the name implies, you'll reach the stars through good coffee, good eats, good books, and good music, all within a cool, laid-back atmosphere. Monday-Saturday 8 a.m.-10 p.m.; Sunday 10 a.m.-5 p.m. 785.833.2235. adastrabooksandcoffee.com.

Cozy Inn (8 Wonders of Kansas Cuisine): 108 N. 7th. Same burger, same location since 1922. And folks love it! With only a six-stool counter and standing room, indeed it gets real cozy inside. The recipe for the famous sliders is simple: smash the fresh ground beef on the grill, pile on the onions, and steam the buns. The result is mouth watering. And, as the nostalgic sign reads, customers "Buy 'em by the sack." Daily 11 a.m.-8 p.m. 785.825.2699.

Blue Skye Brewery and Eats: 116 N. Santa Fe. Specializing in in-house crafted beer, wood-fired pizza, and more, the Blue Skye provides first-class food and fun. Kitchen hours, Tuesday-Sunday 11 a.m.-9 p.m. 785.404.2159. blueskyebrewery.com.

Martinelli's Little Italy: 158 S. Santa Fe. Generous portions of traditional Italian

entrees, homemade sauces, wine and cocktails, and classic crooners in the background make this a popular local restaurant. Daily 11 a.m.-9 p.m. 785.826.9190. FB.

Seoul USA Korean Restaurant: 750 S. Broadway. Enjoying Japchae, Beef Bulgogi, and Hot Stone Pot Bibimbab and meeting owner Joomi Bobbett are just a few of the excellent reasons to come to Seoul USA. Tuesday-Saturday 11 a.m.-8 p.m.; Sunday 11 a.m.-2 p.m. 785.404.2114.

Gourmet to Go: 1402 E. Iron. You must drive through to pick up your gourmet selections, but be prepared for awesome—it's definitely not your typical drive-through place. Tuesday-Friday 7-10 a.m. and 11 a.m.-2:30 p.m. 785.820.8888. FB.

More Good Restaurants: Gutierrez, specializing in unique Mexican and vegetarian (640 Westport, 785.825.1649); Heart of Dixie, offering cajun, creole, and Southern (109 N. Santa Fe, 785.404.6007); Hickory Hut, featuring barbeque (1617 W. Crawford, 785.825.1588); and The Scheme, serving homemade pizza and sauce (123 N. 7th, 785.823.5125). More restaurants at salinakansas.org.

Bar and Grills: Maggie Mae's, a longtime favorite for one-pound burgers and cold beer (409 S. Broadway, 785.825.9829, FB); Chuck's, providing in-house smoked wings, tasty burgers, and a roomy environment for watching sports on TV (600 N. Santa Fe, 785.404.3225, FB).

Lodging: C&W Ranch Bed and Breakfast (KBBA, 785.227.5363, cwranch.com); End Iron Inn Bed and Breakfast (785.577.1979, endironinn.com); additional lodging (salinakansas.org).

SMOLAN

Population 215

Camp Phillips: 1 mile south on S. Burma, then 2½ miles west on McReynolds. A tall concrete water tower is the only evidence remaining of this WWII army training and POW camp. The water tower is now a private residence. Drive by only.

Ammunition Storage Facilities: 1 mile north on S. Burma, 3 miles west on W. Farrelly, then ¼ mile north on S. Hohneck. Old concrete ammo storage structures used when Camp Phillips was in operation can be seen on the east side of S. Hohneck between W. Water Well and W. Farrelly.

Smith County

ATHOL

Population 42

ATHOL WEATHER STATION

WET ROCK	RAIN
DRY ROCK	FAIR
WHITE ROCK	SNOW
SWINGING ROCK	WINDY
INVISIBLE ROCK	FOG

Weather Station: Main and Kansas. In City Park a rock on a chain hangs from a sign that serves as the Athol Weather Station. Very scientific—a wet rock indicates rain, a swinging rock wind, an invisible rock fog, and so forth.

Home on the Range Cabin (NRHP): 7032 90. From Athol, ¾ mile west on U.S. 36, 8 miles north on K-8, then 1 mile west

on 90. Follow the mile-long, narrow driveway to the 1872 cabin and former home of Brewster Higley. Standing in this peaceful setting beside the woods and Beaver Creek, it's easy to see how Higley was inspired to write the poem "My Western Home," known today as "Home on the Range." Inside, the cabin contains simple furnishings, photos of the renovation process, and other mementos. On an outside wall the words and music to "Home on the Range" are engraved in stone, with credits to Dan Kelly for the music. Kansans (and Kansans at heart) might enjoy standing here and singing the song named the Kansas state song in 1947. 785.476.5216. thehomeontherange.com.

CEDAR

Population 14

Missouri Pacific Depot: Main and Center. Extremely well preserved, this 1879 depot is at home in City Park. On the building's exterior a chalkboard provides town announcements, and inside, the depot doubles as the town museum and contains railroad memorabilia. This classic little structure has been renovated, painted a welcoming yellow, and is well kept by volunteers.

GAYLORD

Population 110

Park Entrance: 5th and Gilman. A Wrought Iron Company bridge remnant has been repurposed as an archway entrance to City Park. When the bridge was removed from south of Gaylord, a local welder and artist saved several pieces to create the entrance.

Statue of Liberty: From K-9, 1 mile south on U.S. 281. A Statue of Liberty replica, erected by the Boy Scouts in the 1950s, stands at a roadside park surrounded by a first-rate, 360-degree view of cropland, river valley, and open sky.

HARLAN

Unincorporated

Gould College: From K-9 at Harlan, ¼ mile north on Q (becomes Commercial). In 1880 the United Brethren conference established Gould College near Harlan to provide education for students in western Kansas. It was named for railroad mogul Jay Gould with the hope that he would be a benefactor for the new college. Gould's fortunes were never bestowed. Harlan Church, north of town on Commercial, is all that remains of the college. A plaque describing the college location is found on a rock monument just north of the church.

KENSINGTON

Population 451

Established in 1887, Kensington bills itself as "The Biggest Little Town of its Size in the State of Kansas!"

Kensington Community Store: 128 S. Main. Since 2002 the community-owned grocery has been providing healthy food choices for Kensington and the area. Monday-Friday 8 a.m.- 6 p.m.; Saturday 8 a.m.-5 p.m. 785.476.2852.

Rusty Tractor: 410 N. Main. In 2014 Pro Ag Marketing, a local business, built this new log cabin restaurant for the

community and region to enjoy. Its hand-cut steaks, weekly specials, full bar, and friendly service are all you need to feel fully satisfied. Monday-Saturday 11 a.m.- 9 p.m.; Sunday 11 a.m.-2 p.m. 785.476.2500.

LEBANON

Population 206

Geographic Center of the United States: From Lebanon, 1 mile north on U.S. 281, then 1 hilly mile west on K-191. Get centered at the geographic center of the 48 contiguous states. In a small park, a limestone pedestal with a plaque and flagpole mark the exact point. Thanks go to the Lebanon Hub Club for erecting the marker in 1940. Notice the nearby abandoned motel behind the park. Built pre I-70, the motel succumbed to new traffic patterns created by the interstate in the 1960s. Like many businesses along this route, a dream became an abandoned relic.

Ladow's Supermarket: 403 Main. Supermarket means super effort at Ladow's. Filling many community needs, it provides hardware, variety store items, grocery goods, and a lunch cafe offering cook's choice. Store hours, Monday-Friday 7:30 a.m.-5:30 p.m.; Saturday 7:30 a.m.-4 p.m. 785.389.3261.

SMITH CENTER

Population 1,610

Smith County Courthouse:
218 S. Grant. Start in this 1920 limestone courthouse to explore Smith Center and the area. In the lobby outside the courtroom, you'll find information about the Old Dutch Mill, a mural documenting the mill's construction, and a Nelson Chubb painting of Brewster Higley sitting beside his cabin. The bright green and pink floral pattern tile running throughout the courthouse adds a classic touch. Inspirational poems highlight the outdoor veterans memorial. Monday-Friday 8 a.m.-5 p.m.

Old Dutch Mill:
200 E. 3rd (Wagner Park). Much of this mill is a replica of the original octagonal structure built by native German Charles Schwarz near Reamsville in 1879-1882. It used wind power to grind corn and wheat until a kerosene engine was installed in 1913. A rare structure on the Kansas landscape, the mill was moved to Smith Center in 1938 as part of a National Youth Adminis-tration project. Imagine sailcloth on the mill's 60-foot fan blades! That must have been quite a sight around the turn of the century. The mill caught fire in 1955 and everything on the inside burned. 785.282.3249.

Old First National Bank Building (NRHP):
100 S. Main. In 1889 J.R. Burrow built this lavish red-brick structure complete with granite pillars, circular steps to a corner entrance, limestone-accented arched windows, and a turret. Over the years the former bank fell into major disrepair, but thanks to local effort, a restoration was completed in 2015.

Forks of Beaver Creek Indian Fight Historical Marker:
From Smith Center, 3¼ miles west on U.S. 36, then ¾ mile south on M. One of the largest battles among Plains Indians happened in this area in July 1853. Known as the Forks of Beaver Creek Indian Fight, the clash engaged 1,000 Cheyennes and their allies (Arapahoes, Sioux, Kiowas, Comanches, and Crows) in a revenge attack against some 800 Pawnees and their allies (Otoes and Potawatomis). The Pawnees' success was due in part to the timely assistance of the Potawatomis and their rifles. The old Pawnee Trail from the Pawnees' earth lodge villages (*see* p. 79) to their hunting grounds passed through here.

Jiffy Burger:
815 E. U.S. 36. This is one of those throwback places where you just walk up to the window and order. The interior, brightly decorated in 1950s style, offers plenty of seating for an eat-in option. The slushes, malts, and cyclones are perfect on a hot day. Daily 11 a.m.-9 p.m. 785.282.6435.

More Good Restaurants:
Las Canteras (233 S. Main, 785.686.3074, FB); Paul's Cafe (114 E. U.S. 36, 785.282.6271); Lyon Saloon (113 N. Madison, 785.686.4000); and Pooches Bar & Grill (106 E. Kansas, 785.686.4195).

Lodging:
Ingleboro Mansion Bed and Breakfast (785.282.3798, ingleboromansion.com);

Home on the Range RV Park & Campsite (785.620.7771, FB); additional lodging (smithcenterks.com).

explorer extras... In Smith Center

Relihan Row (also known as Millionaire Row) were homes for the wealthier folks in early Smith Center—four generations of Relihans! Still used as residences, the homes are at 102, 108, 112, 114, 118, 120, and 204 E. 3rd. ee

Washington County

AROUND THE COUNTY

Pony Express Mural and Historical Marker:
U.S. 36 and K-148. This 10x20-foot bas-relief mural created by Ina Fike of Endicott Brick depicts a Pony Express rider galloping toward Hollenberg station. The historical marker provides an excellent history of this short-lived mail service. Go north on K-148 to visit Hollenberg station.

Pony Express Grave:
From U.S. 36, 3 miles south on K-148, then ¼ mile east on 16. In Pine Hill Cemetery lies one of the oldest riders of the Pony Express, Ezra Perkins. His grave-stone, the first on the left, tells us that he died in 1906, and a small bronze plaque states that he was an express rider. More information about Perkins can be found at Hollenberg station.

BARNES

Population 155

Sunflower Mercantile of Barnes:
15 N. Center. Primitives, furniture, architectural salvage, and items to repurpose that you didn't know you needed are found in this 1905 hardware store. Monday-Saturday 10 a.m.-5 p.m.; Sunday 1-5 p.m. 785.763.4052. FB.

Always Christmas Shoppe:
107 W. Railroad. It's all Christmas all year round in the historic 1911 Barnes State Bank Museum. Daily 12-4 p.m. 785.747.8757.

I.O.O.F. Park:
1st and Center. The band shell, the smallest in the state, was built by the WPA in 1940 in the International Order of Odd Fellows (I.O.O.F.) Park. In 2003 local volunteers cleaned and put back into use a rock fountain and lily pond that had been filled with dirt in the 1930s. Local gardeners make this a lovely spot in Barnes.

Hometown Cafe:
11 N. Center. On Wednesdays customers pack this cafe (community-owned since 1994) for the pan-fried chicken. It also offers daily noon specials, homemade pies, and great breakfasts. The pork tenderloin is a crowd favorite. Monday-Saturday 7 a.m.-7 p.m.; Sunday 10 a.m.-3 p.m. 785.763.4560.

CLIFTON AND VINING

Populations 537 and 45

One of the curiosities about Clifton and Vining is that both towns (about a block apart) are in two counties. Parallel, both towns' main street, runs on the county line making the north sides of Clifton and Vining in Washington County, and the south sides in Clay County. A sign at Berner Park explains that these two small towns ended up so close to each other because of a disagreement between two railroad companies.

T's Grocery:
100 W. Parallel, Clifton. So named for owner Randy Tiemeyer, T's Grocery is a store you'll want to support. In addition to groceries, it offers a separate section that sells antiques, crafts, and home decor. Monday-Friday 8 a.m.-7 p.m.; Saturday 8 a.m.-5 p.m. 785.455.3317. FB.

Veterans Memorial:
500 block of W. Parallel (Berner Park, Clifton). Three distinctively different vertical monuments honor veterans from WWI through the Vietnam War.

Miss Marie's Diner:
101 W. Parallel, Clifton. Miss Marie's Diner was named for the owner's daughter Avery Marie. Pan-fried chicken with homemade mashed potatoes and gravy is served on Sundays. Daily 6 a.m.-2 p.m. 785.455.2010.

Tailgater's Steakhouse:
410 E. Parallel, Vining. Steaks, burgers, and nightly specials, plus a full-service bar make Tailgater's a popular place for good food and good times. Grill hours, Monday-Saturday 5-9 p.m. 785.455.3438.

Strawberry:
From Clifton, 10 miles north on Eagle, then 1 mile east on K-148 to Fox. A gray stone marks the site of Strawberry. The settlement, named for the wild strawberries that grew here, existed from 1868 to 1951.

LCL Buffalo Ranch and Museum:
431 1st. From Clifton, 1 mile north and 1 mile west on K-9 (1st). Casey Amerin will take you in his pasture-seasoned pickup into the buffalo herd if you call ahead and make arrangements. He can answer any questions you have about our state animal. We have this educational and enjoyable opportunity thanks to Lester Lawrence, who established the Lawrence Foundation for the Preservation of Buffalo and Agricultural Heritage. Back at the ranch, a shed showcases old-time farm equipment that Lester had collected. Donation ($20) suggested. Call ahead, 785.455.3707. Bring a cooler and buy buffalo meat to take home!

HADDAM

Population 101

Historic Jail:
From Main, 1 block south on Taylor. Haddam's 1901 election produced an all-woman city council along with female mayor, city clerk, and police judge, even though women were not given the right to vote until 1912. One of the council's first acts was to commission building a limestone jail "for containment of Haddam's unruly men."

Haddam Cafe:
417 Main. Stop in for a home-cooked meal in this city-owned cafe. JoAnna Novak keeps things running smoothly and does most of the cooking. The popular Fried Fish Dinner takes place the second Wednesday of the month (5-9 p.m.). Monday-Friday 8:30 a.m.-2:30 p.m. 785.778.3135. FB.

explorer extras...
In Greenleaf

Population 318

It's not every community that has its own clubhouse. "Community Club-House" is etched on the limestone building at 308 N. 4th, and it is still used today as a community meeting place. It and the jail next door are 1939 WPA projects.

Look for a long one-story, dark-brown brick building that doesn't quite seem to fit in a rural town. Here's the story. A 1973 tornado destroyed 17 businesses and 42 residences in Greenleaf. With the help of federal money, a mall was built in 1975 to house businesses, including the grocery store (Greenleaf General Store, 406 Commercial). Monday-Friday 8:30-5:30; Saturday 8:30 a.m.-3 p.m. 785.747.2843. **ee**

HANOVER

Population 668

Hollenberg Pony Express Station State Historic Site (NRHP): 2889 23rd.

From U.S. 36, 4 miles north on K-148, then 1 mile east on K-243. The only Pony Express station remaining on its original site, Hollenberg station reflects a colorful but brief time in our nation's history. The Pony Express operated only 18 months (1860-1861) but its legacy has endured. The visitor center's interpretive signs, artifacts, and colorful Charles Goslin mural set the stage before you walk across the field to the 1858 station. Gerat and Sophia Hollenberg built this wood structure as a general store and tavern for Oregon-California Trail travelers. However, it became better known as a stopover for Pony Express riders to change horses. May-October, Wednesday-Saturday 10 a.m.-5 p.m. Admission charge. 785.337.2635. kshs.org.

St. John the Baptist Church: 114 S. Church. Built

by parishioners in 1880, it is the oldest church in the Salina diocese. The church still has its original fixtures and steeple, which stands 110 feet.The impressive interior is open to visitors. 785.337.2207.

Rock Creations:

309 S. Hanover. You'll do a double take when you see these unusual rock creations, which include a small castle-like structure with turrets, parapets, and windows; a rock birdbath perched precariously on stones; large petrified wood pieces; and a tall slender stone containing petroglyphs. The mystery is that no one knows when or why they were built. One theory is that a local man had always promised his wife he would build her a castle. However, he couldn't afford a real one so he settled for this little creation. It was possibly built around 1920.

You're welcome to look and photograph; please don't touch.

City Hall: 205 S. Jackson.

Hanover founder Gerat Hollenberg donated the land for the town square, which doubles as a park and the site of the city hall. Still functioning as the city hall, the art deco building was a WPA project built in 1939.

NC

Pony Express Plaque:

E. Washington and S. Hanover (City Park). Look for the 1934 circular plaque on a Glacial Hills rock in front of the wooden bandstand. Phimister Proctor sculpted the plaque's lone Pony Express rider and horse.

Historic Brewery: From

S. Hollenberg, just east on Washington. The two-story, red-brick building was built in 1870 to house the Western Brewery and Malt House.

German Society Hall:

Hollenberg and Jaedicke. One look at this red-brick and limestone structure tells you something is a bit different, especially when you see the stone plaque that's engraved with German text and two clasping hands. Translated, the words mean German Society Hall / Unity is strength. Built in 1874, it was an important haven where the German community gathered to host athletic games and social functions.

August Jaedicke Home:
106 S. Hollenberg. August Jaedicke emigrated from Prussia and was one of the first settlers in Hanover, becoming a successful merchant and banker. It is not known if Jaedicke or his son August Jr. built this distinguished 1890 home, but it certainly is worth driving by.

Historic Buildings: South of downtown on Hollenberg, Washington, and Jaedicke. The masonry of many European immigrants who were part of the building boom starting in the 1870s can be seen in many historic buildings. Enjoy a drive around town to see them.

Hollenberg Memorial:
From North, 1 mile south on East (becomes Shady). Gerat Hollenberg died and was buried at sea during an 1874 voyage to visit his native Germany. In 1878 the town erected a white marble monument in Hanover City Cemetery honoring Hollenberg as Hanover's founder.

Ricky's Cafe: 323 W. North. Kermit Rickenberg has owned this cafe for more than 50 years, and every day he's in the kitchen cooking. The cafe is famous in these parts for good food, especially the fresh-cut ribeyes. Monday 7:30 a.m.-2 p.m.; Tuesday-Saturday 7:30 a.m.-9 p.m.; Sunday 9 a.m.-2 p.m. 785.337.8903.

LINN

Population 395

Jack's Food Market:
303 5th. Find sausage products, jerky, knip, smoked turkeys, home-cured hams, ground buffalo, and other specialties in addition to Wolverine and LaCrosse boots. Monday-Saturday 8 a.m.-6 p.m. 785.348.5411.

MAHASKA

Population 81

1856 Surveyor's Monument (NRHP): From Mahaska, ½ mile west on 29, then 1 mile north on Meridian. The Initial Point for all land surveys in Kansas, Nebraska, much of Colorado and Wyoming, and a small part of South Dakota was marked on this site in 1856. The survey, which created the Sixth Principal Meridian (40th Parallel), resulted from the congressional decision on May 30, 1854, to establish and

survey Kansas and Nebraska Territories. From this Initial Point more than 200 million miles of land were surveyed. Today the survey point is marked with a plate (manhole cover) in the middle of the road. Nearby, monuments and an informational marker tell the intriguing story surrounding the survey.

**explorer extras...
In Mahaska**

The red-brick 1921 bank building is now the town post office at 212 N. Main. Monday-Friday 8 a.m.-12 p.m. 785.245.3258.

The J-shaped, red-brick 1927 Mahaska Rural High School

(NRHP) was constructed during the Progressive Era, a time that included reforming urban and rural school programs.

The big, bold 1940 WPA water tower rises over Mahaska City Park at Main and Henry.

You'll find the historic city jail at the north end of Main. **ee**

MORROWVILLE

Population 151

First Bulldozer: Morrowville is credited as the home of the world's first bulldozer. A crude oak blade mounted on a Fordson tractor, the dozer was built by local draftsman J. Earl McLeod and farmer Jim Cummings in 1925. A replica of the original is displayed in Cummings Park at S. Main and Oak.

PALMER

Population 108

Palmer Store: 105 E. 2nd. Owner Randy Tiemeyer makes the Palmer grocery possible. By also owning the grocery in Clifton, he can order for two stores and meet the weekly required minimum volume. Your purchases will help both stores keep going! Monday-Friday 9 a.m.-6 p.m.; Saturday 8 a.m.-2 p.m. 785.692.4323.

Peat's Creek Trading Company: 200 E. 2nd. Repurposed items and locally made crafts make this a great stop in Palmer. Monday-Friday 9 a.m.-5 p.m.; Saturday 8-12 p.m. 785.692.4536.

Stone Cave: 2nd and Nadeau. In the early 1900s a hotel stood in front of this stone cave/cellar.

The consensus is that the cave was used to store the hotel's produce and canned goods.

Historic Jail: A rare 1920s white frame jail is located east of the post office (101 E. 2nd). A commode remains in the corner.

Palmer Cafe: 203 N. Indiana. It's not community owned but locals treat it like it's their own. They even hold an annual auction to support it. Although advertising says it has the coldest beer and best food in Palmer, all would agree that as the only restaurant in town it does serve terrific food, and yes, the beer is cold! Monday-Saturday 8 a.m.-2 p.m.; Thursday-Friday 6-9 p.m. 785.692.4354.

Population 1,095

Washington County Courthouse (NRHP):
214 C. Built in art deco style, this 1933 limestone courthouse is impressive regardless of a few structural alterations. In the courtroom floral designs are embossed on the elaborate German nickel cornice. Monday-Friday 8 a.m.-5 p.m. 785.325.2974. A Statue of Liberty replica stands in the southwest corner of the courthouse square.

Herrs Car and Truck Museum: 1745 Prospect. Lawrence Herrs has collected and restored more than 100 vintage cars, tractors, trucks, and engines. His interesting stories about vehicles, such as the 1907 IHC Mogul tractor

and the 1930 Model A roadster, make this museum a memorable adventure. Monday-Friday 8 a.m.-5 p.m. Admission charge. Call ahead, 785.541.0650. herrsmachine.com.

Washington County Museum: 208 Ballard. Local history is exhibited inside this former American Legion building. Of special interest is the Luebs Camera Collection displaying more than 600 cameras from every era. Tuesday-Friday 10 a.m.-3 p.m. Donation welcome. 785.325.2198. wchistoricalsociety.org.

Historic Jail (NRHP):
23 C. This two-story limestone 1889 jail housed the Washington County sheriff's office until 1996. The architect was J.C. Holland, who designed the Kansas State Capitol.

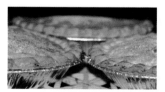

MarCon Pies (8 Wonders of Kansas Commerce):
124 W. 8th. Nearly 30 years ago Marilyn and Connie started this business—thus the name MarCon! The crusts are hand crimped and the women who make them can always identify their own. Your local grocery may carry MarCon pies, but a delicious assortment is always available right here where they're made. Monday-Friday 8 a.m.-5 p.m. For tours, call 785.325.2439. marconpies.com.

Architecture: The native limestone buildings at the Washington County Fairgrounds are 1930s WPA projects (from U.S. 36, ¼ mile south on E). Art deco features accent the old city hall building (114 N. C).

Mayor of Munchkinland House: 6th and E. Charlie Becker, the German American actor who played the mayor of Munchkinland in the film *The Wizard of Oz*, and his wife, a Mahaska native, retired to this house in Washington in the 1960s. Drive by only.

Munchkinland Playground:
From U.S. 36, 2 blocks south on D. This impressive Oz-themed playground was built in 2010 with $90,000, 42,000 screws, 6 miles of lumber, and 14,000 volunteer hours!

Downtown: Smoky Hills Boots (315 C) and Miss Donna's Doll House (313 C) are the places to find cowboy boots and western wear for the whole family, plus jewelry and one-of-a-kind clothing. Hours irregular. 785.510.6018. FB.

Kansas Territory Brewing Company:
310 C. Summer Breeze Lemon Shandy, Wind Wagon I.P.A., Aeroplane Pale Ale, and Horse Power Red Ale are just four of the nine beers brewed here. The beers are cold, and the tap room, with exposed iron girders and original brick, is one cool place to bring your friends. Pizza is served too. Thursday-Saturday 5:30 p.m.-12 a.m. For tours, call 785.325.3300. kansasterritorybrewingco.com.

Mayberry's:
307 C. The traditional menu (steaks, fried chicken, and much more) offers big taste for a big appetite. Monday-Friday 8 a.m.-9 p.m.; Saturday 5 p.m.-10 p.m. 785.325.2778.

Northeast Kansas

Counties: Atchison, Brown, Doniphan, Douglas, Franklin, Geary, Jackson, Jefferson, Johnson, Leavenworth, Marshall, Miami, Morris, Nemaha, Osage, Pottawatomie, Riley, Shawnee, Wabaunsee, Wyandotte

EXPLORER ELEMENT EXAMPLES

Architecture: Dutch Mill, Wamego

Art: Joe Tinker Outdoor Mural, Muscotah

Commerce: Dodson International World Headquarters, Rantoul

Cuisine: Mad Jack's Fresh Fish, Kansas City

Customs: Pelican Pete's, Junction City

Geography: Echo Cliff, Dover

History: William J. Marra Museum (Deaf Cultural Center), Olathe

People: Robert J. Dole Institute of Politics, Lawrence

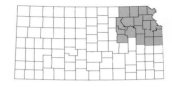

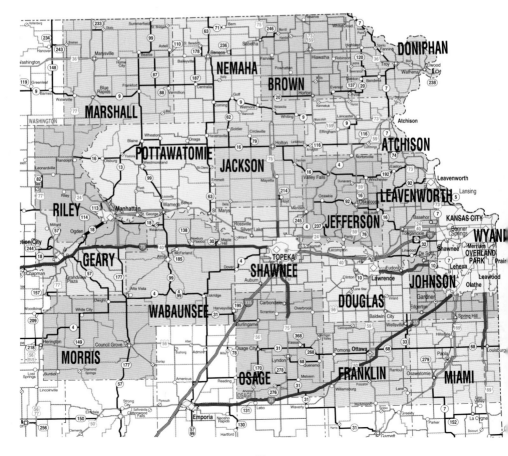

Atchison County

AROUND THE COUNTY

Glacial Hills Scenic Byway:
Running from the Kansas-Nebraska line to the K-7 and K-92 junction in Leavenworth, this 63-mile route takes you through the beautiful and rolling Glacial Hills region. You'll often see bluffs along one side of the road and the river or cropland in the flood plain bordering the other. A glacial deposit left the large red rocks (quartzite). Towns along this byway are some of the oldest in Kansas, and the architecture and historic sites are evidence of our state's early days. You'll also learn about major historic events including the Lewis and Clark Expedition and the Pony Express. travelks.com/ksbyways.

ATCHISON

Population 10,925

Visitor Information Center:
200 S. 10th. Visitor guides; self-guided tours of historic homes, art, and downtown; hiking maps; trolley information; restrooms; a gift shop; and a museum are found inside this former Santa Fe depot (NRHP). This 1880 limestone building is the last standing structure of the Santa Fe railway in Atchison. Monday-Saturday 10 a.m.-4 p.m.; Sunday 12-4 p.m. January-February, closed Sunday. 800.234.1854. visitatchison.com.

Atchison County Historical Society Museum and Rail Museum (NRHP):
200 S. 10th. Start your explorations here to learn about Atchison's early history. Lewis and Clark came through the area in 1804, and some 50 years later Atchison became a busy commercial center for steamboats, wagon trains, and eventually railroads. Exhibits about Amelia Earhart; Deafy Boular, the bricklayer; and David Atchison, the one-day president, are featured. Train enthusiasts can view an outdoor collection of rail cars year round. Miniature railroad rides are available on weekends June to October. Memorial Day-October, Monday-Saturday 10 a.m.-4 p.m.; Sunday 12-4 p.m. January-February, closed Sunday. Donation welcome. 913.367.6238. FB.

Railroad Workers Sculpture:
200 S. 10th. Near the Visitor Information Center entrance a bronze sculpture by Kwan Wu honors the "Working Men of the Railroads" whose labors helped open the West.

Historical Marker:
S. 10th and U.S. 59. South of a covered pedestrian bridge crossing a small creek, a DAR plaque explains that Lewis and Clark camped near here on Independence Day and named it "4th of July 1804 Creek."

Atchison Trolley:
200 S. 10th. Trolley tours provide a close-up perspective of the architecture, history, commerce, and scenic views of Atchison and its environs. Spooky tours of the most haunted town in Kansas are also offered. April-October. For tours, ask at the Visitor Information Center. Tour charge. 800.234.1854. visitatchison.com.

Atchison County Courthouse (NRHP):
423 N 5th. George Washburn designed this grand 1897 limestone Romanesque Revival structure, which features a seven-story clock tower. A plaque on a rock in front of the courthouse states that Abraham Lincoln spoke near here on

December 2, 1859, during his campaign visit to Kansas.

Historic Homes:
Because Atchison is one of the oldest towns (established in 1855) in Kansas and once supported many wealthy residents, it has one of the most impressive collections of historic homes of any town in the state. The architectural styles of these grand and lovely houses range from Gothic to Italianate. The greatest concentration of well-preserved residences is north of downtown along 3rd, 4th, and 5th. Dozens of other homes also can be found throughout this town, which boasts more than 30 properties

NE

on the national register. Self-guided tour brochures are available at the Visitor Information Center, 200 S. 10th.

Bridge Tender House:
Main and S. 2nd. This gingerbread style house looks out of place in a railroad yard, but it's been there since 1875. It's the former home of the bridge tender, the person who rotated the bridge for boat traffic. Learn more at the Atchison County Museum. Drive by only.

Deafy Boular Statue:

From Main, 1 block north on 5th. The plaque on this Aleda Haug sculpture tells the story of William "Deafy" Boular (1869-1953), a deaf man who had lost both his legs in a train accident when he was 10 years old. Overcoming adversity, Boular wore custom-designed boots on his stumps and became a champion brick-layer, once laying 46,000 paving bricks in less than eight hours. His boots are preserved in the Atchison County Society Museum.

Lewis and Clark:

Meriwether Lewis and William Clark led the Corps of Discovery, commissioned by President Thomas Jefferson, into what is now the western portion of the United States. An exploration for scientific and commercial purposes, the journey spanned from May 1804 to September 1806, and 14 of those days were spent in Kansas. For the Lewis and Clark Bicentennial in 2004, many historical markers were established to recognize this expedition.

Lewis and Clark Pavilion:

119 Commercial (Riverfront Park). An interpretive open-air pavilion commemorates the Lewis and Clark Expedition stopping here on the banks of the Missouri on July 4, 1804. Adjoining the pavilion is an impressive Veterans Memorial Park with multiple plaques and memorials and a relic display from the battleship *Arizona*, sunk at Pearl Harbor in 1941.

Independence Creek Hike/ Bike Trail:

119 Commercial. A 10-mile round-trip hiking and bicycle trail along the Missouri River leads you to and over Independence Creek (named by Lewis and Clark) and through the area where members of the Lewis and Clark Expedition camped. The Kanza lodge (*see* next entry) is at the trailhead.

Kanza Lodge:

From Main, 3 ¾ miles north on 2nd (becomes Sedgewick), then 1 mile east on 314. Prior to white settlement the Kanza tribe controlled much of what would become Kansas. Their main colony was in this area of Independence Creek (8 Wonders of Kansas History). A lodge using the same available building materials and design that the Kanzas would have used has been re-created on this site. The interior can be viewed through a gated doorway, and interpretive signage tells you the story of the Kanza nation and the Lewis and Clark Expedition in this region.

Amelia Earhart Birthplace Museum (NRHP, 8 Wonders of Kansas People):

223 N. Terrace. Amelia was born in the home of her grandparents, Judge Alfred and Amelia Otis, and spent much time here during her first 12 years. The frame house, built about 1860, has been well restored, and excellent photographs and interpretive signage help you get to know the daring and record-setting aviatrix. Amelia Earhart and her navigator Fred Noonan disap-peared in the *Electra* on July 2, 1937, during their attempted flight around the world. A model *Electra* hangs inside the museum. Monday-Saturday 10 a.m.-4 p.m.; Sunday 1-4 p.m. Admission charge. 913.367.4217. ameliaearhartmuseum.org.

African American Structures:

The Campbell Chapel A.M.E. Church (NRHP; 715 Atchison) was the first black church in Atchison. It was built in 1878 but was stuccoed and painted white in 1919. Lincoln School (NRHP; 801 Division) was built in 1921 for African American students. In 1955 schools in Atchison were integrated.

Mount St. Scholastica Academy:

801 S. 8th. Seven Benedictine sisters founded the academy in 1863 as a school for girls. Sixty years later, in 1923, it became Mount St. Scholastica College. Perhaps the most impressive structure on the campus is the 1901 red-brick monastery (NRHP), built in Renaissance design. Gothic touches are evident in its tall square tower and in the flying buttresses of its north wing chapel.

Benedictine College (NRHP):

N. 2nd. This college was founded in 1971 through the merger of Mount St. Scholastica College for women and St. Benedict's College for men. You'll enjoy a drive around the hillside campus just to admire the architecture. Reminiscent of Germany's Rhineland churches is St. Benedict's Church on the corner of the campus at 2nd and Division. The doors of this beautiful edifice are open inviting you to come inside to see its vaulted ceiling, stained-glass windows, and fresco. The church was completed in 1906.

St. Benedict's Abbey:

1020 2nd. From Main, ¾ mile north on 2nd. Benedictine monks established this abbey in the late 1850s, and about 32 monks reside here today. Barry Byrne, a student of Frank Lloyd Wright, completed the present abbey church in 1957. A brochure in the lobby explains this structure, the organ, choir stalls, the fresco, and the crypt.

Monks gather here four times a day for common prayer. Daily 8 a.m.-8 p.m. 913.367.7853. kansasmonks.org.

Evah Cray Historical Home Museum (NRHP):

805 N. 5th. A three-story, castle-like tower of white-painted brick identifies this 25-room mansion. Ornate fireplaces and beautifully carved woodwork are the dominant features inside this grand 1882 home. May-October, Monday, Wednesday-Saturday 10 a.m.-4 p.m.; Sunday 1-4 p.m. Admission charge. 913.367.3046. visitatchison.com.

Muchnic Art Gallery

(NRHP): 704 N. 4th. Parquet floors, embossed leather paneling, and leaded-glass conservatory windows with flower design are just some of the finery in this 1885

three-story, red-brick home built by lumber merchant George Howell. Especially curious are the faces of the family carved into the newel posts on the first floor. H.E. Muchnic purchased this Victorian mansion in 1922. Its second floor now features rotating art exhibits. Wednesday, Saturday-Sunday 1-5 p.m. 913.367.4278; atchisonart.org.

Mount Vernon Cemetery:

6920 Rawlins. Senator John J. Ingalls; Governors John A. Martin, Willis J. Bailey, and George W. Glick; and both sets of Amelia Earhart's grandparents (Alfred and Amelia Otis and David and Mary Earhart) are buried here. A number of tall obelisks create a stately charm to this final resting place.

International Forest of Friendship:

178620 274 (Warnock Lake). Amelia Earhart, in the form of a life-sized bronze statue, welcomes you to the Forest of Friendship, filled with trees from all 50 states and more than 35 countries. In this beautiful park, founded by the Ninety Nines, an international organization of women pilots, plaques are embedded in the sidewalks each year to honor those involved in aviation and space exploration.

Amelia Earhart Earthwork:

178620 274. A viewing deck at Warnock Lake offers the best perspective of the one-acre earthwork portrait of Amelia Earhart created by Stan Herd in 1997 with plantings, stone, and other natural materials.

Providence Hill Farm:

8096 Pratt. On this 1898 family farmstead, you can meet the Nubian goats and buy products they "helped" create—soaps, lotions, and cheese. Christy Harris will explain. She also is happy to teach small groups how to make artisan bread and cheese and to demonstrate candle and soap making. 913.367.9622. tinyurl.com/providencehillfarm.

Van Dyke Grocery:

401 N. 4th. This small neighborhood grocery has been owned and operated by the same family for more than 100 years. Locals really appreciate the fresh meat and deli counter. Stop in and experience this longtime Atchison icon. Monday-Saturday 8 a.m.-5 p.m. 913.367.3485.

Gateway to Kansas:

504 Commercial. We're told the chocolate soda is everyone's favorite at this perky drug store soda fountain. But we think you should take a seat on the red stools at the red-and-white tile counter and taste it for yourself! Monday-Saturday 10 a.m.-3 p.m. 913.367.1533. FB.

Jerry's Again: 125 N. 5th. The original Jerry's Restaurant opened in 1964 and closed in 1995. Now the next generation has opened Jerry's Again! Along with other menu items, homemade chicken and noodles are served every Monday, pan-fried chicken every Thursday, and Virginia's famous homemade pies every day. Monday-Friday 11 a.m.-3 p.m. 913.367.0577. FB.

The Snowball: 111 N. 8th. Oh sure, you can order soup, sandwiches, fresh pies, coffee, or an ice cream cone, but the best thing, and you should get one, is the five-pound banana split! 913.367.7632. Monday-Saturday 8 a.m.-9 p.m.; Sunday 9 a.m.-9 p.m. FB.

NE

Willie's: 701 Commercial. Named for "Willie" the K-State Wildcat mascot, this family sports bar has a broad menu, good service, and a clean, dark wood, modern interior. Monday-Saturday 11 a.m.-11 p.m.; Sunday 11 a.m.-9 p.m. 913.367.2900. FB.

Paolucci's Restaurant: 115 S. 3rd. Paolucci's Grocery opened in 1894, and more than 100 years later Paolucci's Restaurant is still serving the flavor of Italy. The Paolucci family continues to operate the restaurant and uses those wonderful family recipes handed down through generations. Within Paolucci's walls, bedecked with historic Atchison photos, be ready for a delicious taste of tradition. Monday-Saturday 7 a.m.-9 p.m.; Sunday 7 a.m-1 p.m. 913.367.6105. paoluccibegley.com.

Chuck and Hank's River Shack: 102 E. Atchison. It's all about the view and the 'cue—barbecue, that is. Watch the swirling Missouri River go by while you chow down pulled pork and slow smoked ribs. Monday-Saturday 11 a.m.-9 p.m.; Sunday 11 a.m.-7 p.m. 913.367.4837. FB.

Cedar Ridge Restaurant: 17028 318. A five-mile drive from Atchison over gravel roads leads you to this inviting farm for pan-fried chicken on Fridays, homemade chicken and noodles on Saturdays, and a sumptuous brunch on Sundays. Everything is served family style, so come hungry! Friday-Saturday 5-9 p.m.; Sunday 9:30 a.m.-1 p.m. 913.367.4357. cedar-ridge-restaurant.com.

Mr. G's: 1710 Main. If you're craving Cedar Ridge Restaurant's homemade chicken and noodles on days other than Saturday (see previous entry), you'll find it here. Ask about Mr. G's cupcake of the day. Monday-Friday 11 a.m.-3 p.m. 913.426.4674. FB.

Daisy House Atlantic: 832½ Commercial. Owner Daisy Henson has decorated this local hang-out in an eclectic style, and she makes homemade meals with zest and farm-fresh ingredients. Her Kansas Chicken Salad is chock full of fruit, nuts, and cheese. Coffee and baked goods are on hand too! Tuesday-Friday 6:30 a.m.-7 p.m.; Saturday-Sunday 10 a.m.-5 p.m. 913.370.0323. FB.

Lodging: Tuck U Inn at Glick Mansion (NRHP, KBBA, 913.367.9110, glickmansion.com); The Inn on Oak Street (KBBA, 913.367.1515, kbba.com); additional lodging (visitatchison.com).

explorer extras... In Atchison

Each night color-changing fiber-optic lighting outlines the Amelia Earhart Memorial Bridge, which connects Kansas and Missouri via U.S. 59. In 2012 this four-lane bridge replaced the two-lane bridge erected in 1938 as a WPA project.

Standing between the railroad tracks and the Farmers Market Plaza (on Main between 4th and 6th), 22 large concrete panels

covered with 75,000 colorful glass tiles in mosaic patterns create an impressive sight. New York artist and mosaic expert Susan Jablon assisted the local arts organization with this project and donated much of the glass tile.

Atchison has developed a reputation for being one of the most haunted towns in Kansas. Find out for yourself by taking a tour of the infamous Sallie House, one of the most well-documented haunted homes in America. If that's a little intense for you, other tours and haunted activities are offered including a guided cemetery walk and murder mystery theatre. 800.234.1854. visitatchison.com.

A Pony Express memorial plaque can be found on a granite rock at 3rd and Main (in the parking lot). It's on the site of the Massasoit House, a Pony Express station division headquarters.

The prominent corner tower with a conical top is a stand-out feature on the 1894 Romanesque Revival limestone post office (NRHP) at 621 Kansas. **ee**

EFFINGHAM

Population 538

Post Office: 407 Main. The employees here really enjoy out-of-towners, especially if they (you!) buy some stamps and help keep this post office in operation. Monday-Friday 8 a.m.-3:30 p.m.; Saturday 10 a.m.-11:30 p.m.

Art Deco School: 306 Main. With just six votes to spare, a bond passed in 1938 to build Effingham Grade School. This art deco style school now houses Unified School District 377 offices.

Slippery Pigs BBQ and Pub: 409 Main. Owner Shaylen Kearney knows a good cook, and her name is Mom. Mom whips up all the yummy sides—hand-cut fries, cole slaw, smoked beans, and more—from scratch. They go perfectly with any of the smoked meats that Shaylen prepares. Monday-Saturday 6 a.m.-10 p.m. 913.833.2021. FB.

MUSCOTAH

Population 176

Joe Tinker: A sign at the town entrance announces that Muscotah is the home of Joe Tinker, the shortstop in the Chicago Cubs famous double play combination "Tinker to Evers to Chance." Playing from 1902 to 1916, Tinker was the Cubs' shortstop when the team won the World Series in 1908. He was elected to the National Baseball Hall of Fame in 1946.

Largest Baseball in Kansas: U.S. 159 and E. 1st. In 2012 when the city razed the old water tower, resident Jeff Hanson thought that the tower's round top, which resembled a baseball, could serve as a memorial to Joe Tinker. With Jeff's leadership and stellar out-of-town and community volunteers, the water tank became a 20-foot diameter baseball. Red-painted rebar served as stitching. The largest baseball site includes metal cutouts representing the famed double play trio (*see* previous entry), Joe Tinker, Johnny Evers, and Frank Chance, on a miniature infield. Complete your experience by stepping inside the large steel ball and singing, "Take Me Out to the Ball Game."

Town Monument: 6th and Kansas. A large limestone marker at the City Park entrance bears the town name; a colored flag and two bats and a ball inset in stone; and a bronze plaque paying tribute to Joe Tinker.

Joe Tinker Outdoor Mural: From U.S. 159, ¼ mile north on Kansas. Baseball fans, especially Chicago Cubs fans, will admire this mural that wraps around City Park's cinder-block concession stand. Kansas artists Erika Nelson and Matthew Farley spent several months in 2013 researching, designing, and painting this elaborate and colorful mural.

Muscotah Mercantile: 110 E. 1st. C.J. Hanson's dream was having a place where locals and visitors could gather for a cup of coffee or a bite to eat, buy a few groceries, and take home a gift item or two (many made by C.J. and friends). In 2016, after operating for several years in a small house, the mercantile moved into a new red metal building on U.S. 159. It's a warm, friendly spot, and C.J. and friends will be glad to see you when you stop by. Tuesday-Friday 7 a.m.-4 p.m.; Saturday 7 a.m.-3 p.m. 785.872.5000. FB.

POTTER

Unincorporated

Potter Country Store & Bakery: 18345 K-74. The community is happy to have the convenience of this store in their small village. If you're traveling through, this is a nice little stop

to pick up some groceries, savor the tasty homemade pastries, or sit down for a meal. Monday-Saturday 10 a.m.-8 p.m.; Sunday 8 a.m.-6 p.m. 913.773.5657. FB.

Brown County

The Kickapoo Nation Indian Reservation is the second largest reservation in the state. With more than 1,600 members of the Kickapoo tribe in Kansas, half still live on the reservation assigned to them in the treaty of 1854. The Sac and Fox tribe and the Iowa tribe also have reservations in Brown County.

NE

EVEREST

Population 282

Mom & I's Candy: 521 Main. If you have a sweet tooth you'll either want to avoid the temptation (if you can!) or run as fast as you can to Mom & I's. We recommend the latter so you can savor the fudge, peanut clusters, pretzel rods with different toppings, dipped licorice, and so much more. Tuesday-Friday 10 a.m.-5 p.m. Call ahead, 785.548.7550.

City Park: 628 N. 2nd. In the well-groomed park you'll find a founder's plaque secured to a large red glacial rock beside an old Missouri Pacific caboose. Next to it is a bench with an attached silver plaque heralding the beginnings of this small hamlet when the railroad was established in 1882.

Everest Cafe: 533 Main. This cafe has been here since the 1950s, and for the past 17 years owner Rita Hill has been rising early each day to make breakfast for her customers, bake the coconut meringue pies, and hand patty the burgers for the lunch crowd. Meat loaf and other comfort foods are on the menu too. Monday-Friday 7 a.m.-2 p.m.; Sunday 11 a.m.-1:30 p.m. 785.548.7433.

Norwegian Cemetery:
From S. 5th, ½ mile west on Main, then 3½ miles north on Prairie. Zion Lutheran Church and Cemetery were established in 1895 by Norwegian immigrants. Stroll through the cemetery and on almost every gravestone you'll find evidence of Norwegian ancestry in such names as Torkelson, Thorson, Knudson, and Gigstad.

FAIRVIEW

Population 258

A sign on the west side of town announces that Fairview was the home of General Bernard Rogers, retired U.S. Army general and NATO commander.

Railroad Collection:
211 Commercial. You have permission to drive through Elvon and Cleo Van Dalsem's yard to see their outdoor collection that includes a Santa Fe caboose, railroad signals, a maintenance motor car, and several Federal Express baggage cars.

Cozy Cafe:
428 W. Commercial. Linda Lehmkuhl is only the second owner since this hometown cafe opened in 1954. She's carried on the tradition of serving roast beef every day, one daily special each day (noted on the chalkboard), and pan-fried chicken on Tuesdays. Everything is made from scratch including the mashed

potatoes, bread, and pie shells. The cole slaw dressing recipe is the same one used by the original owners. It's homey and comfortable inside, so pull up a chair, loosen your belt, and dig in. Tuesday-Friday 11 a.m.-1:30 p.m. 785.467.3465.

HIAWATHA

Population 3,178

Hiawatha, settled in 1857, is named for the American Indian in Longfellow's poem The Song of Hiawatha. *Oregon is the name of the main street, so called because the Oregon Trail passed just southwest of town. Parallel streets north of Oregon are named for Indian tribes that lived north of the trail. Streets to the south carry the names of tribes that resided south of the trail.*

City of Beautiful Maples:
In 1918, when T.H. Korthanke and his wife moved to their home at 200 Miami, a stately maple tree stood on the property. Korthanke was inspired to plant seeds from this tree, and as the seedlings grew he shared them with anyone who agreed to care for them. As a result, mature maples grow all around town and give Hiawatha a beautiful red-maple glow in the fall.

Koranthke Fountain:
411 Oregon (just west of the fire department). In appreciation of T.H. Korthanke's gift of maple trees to the city, H. Bernerd and Ruth Garvey Fink honored his memory with this water fountain in 1973.

Davis Memorial (NRHP):
From U.S. 73, ½ mile east on Iowa to Mount Hope Cemetery. It's rather startling to find this incredible memorial so casually situated within a town cemetery. John Davis erected it for his wife, Sarah, who died in 1930. By 1934 the memorial contained 11 life-sized statues made of Italian marble and covered by a marble canopy. The statues depict stages of John and Sarah's lives. One shows him without his left hand, which he had lost due to infection. Another life stage includes a "vacant chair," indicating Sarah's death. The detail of the faces and features was excellent at one time, but weather and vandals have taken a toll. Controversy remains about why Davis built the memorial. Some think he did it to spite his wife's heirs (spending all the money that they would have inherited). Others believe Davis should have donated the money to build a hospital during the hard days of the Great Depression. In any case, it remains one of the most remarkable cemetery memorials in the country. And Davis apparently was pleased with the creation—during his later years he would come to the cemetery to watch tourists view it. A nearby pavilion tells the story of the memorial. tinyurl.com/davismem.

Brown County Poor Farm:

1260 220. From Oregon, ¼ mile south on U.S. 36, 1¼ miles south on Kestrel, then ½ mile west on 220. John Davis, who died in 1947, lived the last year of his life here, although it was a nursing home and not a poor farm at the time. The three-story, red-brick building was built by the WPA as the new "poor farm" residence building in 1936.

Brown County Agriculture Museum: 301 E. Iowa.

Forty-two fascinating windmills line a lane running south from the museum complex that depicts an early 1900s farm. Explore the farmhouse, a milk barn housing farm implements, a blacksmith shop, hen house, and more. One building contains a display of horse-drawn equipment. May-October, Tuesday-Friday 10 a.m.-4 p.m.; Saturday 10 a.m.-2 p.m. Admission charge. 785.742.3702. bckshistory.com.

Brown County Historical Museum (NRHP): 611 Utah.

Memorial Auditorium was built in the Classical Revival style in 1920 to honor soldiers of WWI. The auditorium is now home to the county museum and preserves local and military history. May-October, Tuesday-Friday 10 a.m.-4 p.m.; Saturday 10 a.m.-2 p.m. Admission charge. 785.742.3330.

Brown County Courthouse:

601 Oregon. Built in 1926, this Modern Eclecticism courthouse features limestone walls and exterior carvings. The interior

is equally impressive with its highly ornamented decor and marble floors, walls, and staircase. Monday-Friday 8 a.m.-5 p.m.

Clock Tower Building (NRHP): 701 Oregon. The

unique clock tower was built in 1891 as part of the First National Bank. The two-story, red-brick building with limestone trim and arched windows is a beautiful example of Richardson Romanesque architecture.

Having fallen to disrepair, the structure was restored in 2010 to become the Frances Sewell Plamann History Center. City hall now occupies the first floor, and featured on the second floor along with temporary art exhibits is the colorful 1963 Ron Allerton mural depicting the history of Brown County. Monday-Friday 8 a.m.-5 p.m. 785.742.7417.

Hiawatha Armory: 108 1st.

In front of the armory, built in 1938 by the WPA, stands a row of trees and in front of each tree a granite marker recognizes a member of the "130th Regiment Who Rose to the Rank of General Officer."

First Street Bar & Grill:

602 N. 1st. The mushroom Swiss burger, as well as other burger specialties, is first rate. Ask about the home-cooked daily specials. You'll be glad you did! Monday-Friday 11 a.m.-9 p.m.; Sunday 12-8 p.m. 785.742.3692. FB.

Gus' Restaurant:

606 Oregon. Take the whole family to this longtime local favorite, whose good basic menu will satisfy you and the kids. Tuesday-Saturday 11 a.m.-8 p.m.; Sunday 11 a.m.-2 p.m. 785.742.4533. FB.

Daily Perk: 402 Oregon.

Specialty coffees, full breakfasts, and Panini sandwiches keep people coming in the door for their daily perk-me-up. 785.740.7375. FB.

Country Cabin Restaurant and Cabins: 2534 Kestrel.

From Oregon (west end of town), 2 miles north on Kestrel. This culinary destination in an appealing country setting is known for its steaks, but you might want to try the Bourbon Glazed Salmon or the prime rib and baby back ribs served on Fridays and Saturdays. A full bar is available. You may make reservations to stay in cabins that overlook the lake and are within a short walking distance of the restaurant. Tuesday-Saturday 5-9 p.m. 785.742.4320. FB.

Klinefelter Farm:

1774 230. Six miles of mowed trails are available on this beautiful 480-acre property. The farm was a gift to Highland Community College from John M. Klinefelter whose family had owned the land for 130 years. The site and the restored barn host many activities and events to benefit the northeast Kansas community. Monday-Friday 8 a.m.-5 p.m. 785.741.2829. FB.

Crossdale Barn: 2529 U.S.

73. From Oregon, 1½ miles north on U.S. 73. Look closely

NE

at the white prairie style barn on Wayne Starr's farm and notice the interesting painting under the hay hood. In researching the property's origin, Wayne learned that in 1855 President Franklin Pierce gave Abigail Crossdale this section of land as recompense for her husband's death in the War of 1812. Because she lived in the East, Abigail sold the land, never having seen it. When Wayne purchased it in the 1950s, he honored the farm's original owner by creating a Crossdale coat of arms and painting it on the barn.

Lodging: cityofhiawatha.org/visitors/where-to-stay.

HORTON

Population 1,772

First Power Pole: 5th and E. 15th. The first rural electric power pole in Kansas was erected here on November 10, 1937, for the Brown-Atchison Electric Cooperative. A historical marker notes that it was the first rural electric project to energize Kansas and was financed with a loan from the Rural Electrification Administration.

Post Office Murals (NRHP): 825 1st. Kenneth Evett was the artist of two pieces of Section artwork: *Picnic In Kansas*, installed in 1938, and *Changing of Horses for the Pony Express*, installed in 1939.

WPA Projects: The WPA built the Bureau of Indian Affairs Agency building (908 1st) in 1942 and the Horton Free

Public Library (809 1st) in 1938. Interestingly, the library houses a collection of 24 pairs of WPA dolls. The Horton Civic Center (125 W. 7th) is also a WPA project and originally was used as a county fair building.

Electric City Emporium: 140 E. 8th. Owner Tom Reed moved his huge inventory into a restored historic building to make shopping there an epic experience. Items range from variety and flea market to antiques and hardware. Tuesday-Friday 10 a.m.-5:30 p.m.; Saturday 9 a.m.-5 p.m. 785.548.6224. FB.

English Leather Shop: 119 W. 8th. In 2003 Lawrence English turned his longtime business over to young Luke Pollock, a sharp Horton businessman who had perfected the age-old craft of shoe repair and general leatherwork. Bring in your leather items for expert repair or buy Luke's finished products such as belts, wallets, cell phone cases, knife cases, or horse tack. Tuesday-Friday 10 a.m.-5 p.m.; Saturday 10 a.m.-12 p.m. 785.741.0128.

Werner Wagon Works: 1705 Yates (just east of Mission Lake). Don Werner makes and restores horse-drawn vehicles and is reputed to be one of the best in this field in the Midwest. Don is one of about six non-Amish craftsmen in the United States who works full time as a wainwright and wheelwright, and his wagons, buggies, carriages, and other conveyances are

beautiful works of art. For a tour of this family operation, call Connie. 785.548.5500. wernerwagonworks.com.

Lodging: Werner Guest House (wernerwagonworks.com); RV camping (tinyurl.com/missionlakerv).

explorer extras... In Horton

A plaque on a red glacial rock marks the site of the Kickapoo Presbyterian Mission established in 1856. Its purpose was to educate and Christianize school-age children of the Kickapoo tribe that dwelled in this area. The mission continued as a day school for the tribe from 1860 to 1871. From 1st, ½ mile east on 5th, then ¼ mile south on 7th. **ee**

MORRILL

Population 226

Historic Bank Building: Roxanna and Fanning. Standing stately, but empty, this red-brick structure was built in 1901 as the Farmers Bank of Morrill. The thick, double-arch entryways trimmed in limestone and the intricately carved detail on the facade are evidence of the building's Richardson Romanesque architecture.

City Hall: 612 Roxanna. From the outside, this building has little personality. But step through two antique doors (a wood-frame screen door and a polished wood door with oval window and brass handle) to find a different story. The ornate bank vault and the original counter with its iron barred teller window are thought to have been installed by an early insurance company that occupied this building. Explore the mystery with City Clerk Linda Hill. If she's not too busy she'll be glad to show you around. Monday-Friday 7 a.m.-12 p.m. and 1-4 p.m. 785.459.2231.

**explorer extras...
In Kennekuk**

Unincorporated

Kennekuk, established in 1858, was once the home of a Pony Express relay station, two stagecoach lines, and a military road. Today it is only a spot in the road (Atchison County) with a few houses, but a Pony Express marker at 330 and Chautauqua preserves the legacy of this historic site. From Horton, ½ mile south on K-159, 1¾ miles east on 330, then just south on Chautauqua. **ee**

**explorer extras...
In Powhattan**

Population 78

The public school was abandoned due to declining enrollment and was given to the Kickapoo community in 1981. Now the Kickapoo Nation School, 400 W. 1st, it is the only tribal school in Kansas. 785.474.3550. **ee**

**explorer extras...
In Reserve**

Population 85

Especially of interest to American Indian enthusiasts,

the Sac and Fox Nation of Missouri Tribal Museum, 305 N. Main, exhibits a fine but small collection of authentic tribal costumes, native clothing, historic daily wear, and ceremonial beadwork. Monday-Thursday 8 a.m.-5 p.m. 785.742.0053. **ee**

ROBINSON

Population 230

Robinson Community Store: 115 Parsons. Cans of soup, peas, and peaches and bags of pasta, chips, and candy would love to jump off the shelves and into your shopping cart! Stock up for your exploring journey at this all-volunteer, nonprofit business. Hours irregular. 785.544.6506.

Historic Stone Barn: From Railroad, ¾ mile south on Parsons (becomes Temple), then 2¾ miles east on 205. Two-foot-thick walls and arched window heads and entryway are features of this durable 1861 barn, likely the oldest extant structure in the county. It was built to house horses and mules on the first floor, grain and hay on the second, and seed on the third. It is now owned by the Dennis Tietjens family, who invites you to come in and take a look.

Doniphan County

Founded in 1855, Doniphan was the first named county in the state. Bearing the surname of Alexander Doniphan, a colonel in the Mexican War, the county thrived in those early days thanks to prevalent steamboat travel on the Missouri River. Immigrants from Switzerland, France, and Germany settled the area, and due to the landscape of hills and valleys, it earned the nickname Little Switzerland.

NE

AROUND THE COUNTY

Glacial Hills Scenic Byway: From the Kansas-Nebraska line in Doniphan County to the intersection of K-7 and K-92 in Leavenworth, this 63-mile route takes you through the scenic and rolling Glacial Hills region. Often bluffs parallel the road on one side and the river or cropland in the flood plain borders the other. Notice the large red rocks, or quartzite, remnants of glacial deposits. This byway leads you to some of the oldest towns in Kansas, treats you to early architecture and historic sites, and presents accounts of major events including the Lewis and Clark Expedition and the Pony Express. travelks.com/ksbyways.

California Trail Markers: Settlers and fortune seekers heading west traveled through parts of Doniphan County from the early 1840s through 1865. In 2014 59 signs were installed to mark the California Trail through the county. To find the first trail marker, from S. 3rd in Wathena, go ¼ mile east and south on U.S. 36, just east on Saint Joseph, then north on Treece. Proceed to subsequent markers by following the arrows. You will end up east of Fanning at

K-7 and 230.
nps.gov/cali/index.htm.

Historic Barn Tour:

Six barns in the county are featured on this self-guided tour, several of which are on the national register. Signs at each barn provide information. You are welcome to take photos, but due to the barns' fragile condition, visitors are asked not to enter the buildings. Tour brochures are available on the first floor of the county courthouse at 120 E. Chestnut in Troy. 785.985.2235.

BENDENA

Unincorporated

Bendena State Bank:

933 Friendship. From Main, ¼ mile north on Friendship. Take the long driveway to the 1925 barn remodeled into a bank in 1985. Stop in and say hello to the cashiers and see a historic photo of the original barn. Monday-Friday 8 a.m.-4 p.m. 785.988.4453.

Weiland's Grocery:

210 Commercial. Stop by this downtown grocery and stock up on goods that will travel well as you explore the area. Monday-Saturday 8 a.m.-6 p.m.

explorer extras...
In Denton

Population 185

The Denton post office is a classic, and it will continue to operate as long as enough stamps are purchased here! Make your transaction over the brass plate covering the counter. Monday-Friday 12-4 p.m.

Don't run into the old water pump in the middle of town! A flagpole stands guard near the red pump, which is surrounded by a little flower garden. **ee**

DONIPHAN

Ghost town

Finding Doniphan:

From E. Walnut in Troy, go ¼ mile south on Main, ¼ mile east on Lower State, then 10 miles south on Mineral Point. A few ghostly buildings let you know you've arrived at Doniphan.

Missouri River: The river once flowed at the foot of the bluffs near Doniphan, creating steamboat trade for the settlement and making it one of the largest towns on the upper Missouri in the 1850s. The river bank originally was the southern edge of town, but with each flood, especially during the spring of 1892, lots, blocks, and streets were swept away. Now the river lies more than a mile east of Doniphan.

Doniphan Cemetery: From 95, ¾ mile north on Mineral Point, ½ mile east on 100, then ¼ mile south on Moon Light. The view from the cemetery of the Missouri River, bluffs, valley, and the ghost town of Doniphan is magnificent! The largest and most elaborate monuments in the cemetery are those of

brothers Jacob and Adam Brenner, whose vineyards were a major part of the area economy from the 1860s to 1912. Another noteworthy person, Samuel T. Carpenter, is also buried here. He was a member of the honor guard that escorted President Lincoln's body from Washington, D.C., to Springfield, Illinois. Carpenter's gravestone (a black stone standing southwest of Adam Brenner's marker) provides a short commentary on this event.

St. John the Baptist Church:

From Mineral Point, ½ mile west and south on 95. Part of the Brenner Vineyards Historic District (NRHP), this red-brick church was built in 1867 on land donated by Adam Brenner. Adam and Jacob Brenner came to the area in 1857 and 1860 and established prosperous vineyards and wineries. The historic district reflects the Brenners' agrarian farmsteads and remnants of the winery.

ELWOOD

Population 1,197

Fort Luxembourg Visitor Center:

203 Roseport (U.S. 36). The country of Luxembourg was so taken by the devastation that occurred in Elwood after the flood of 1993 that its residents sent relief money. The result is this log cabin visitor center named for its benefactor. County and state brochures are available here. Monday-Friday 8:30 a.m.-4:30 p.m. 913.365.5561.

Historical Markers:

203 Roseport (U.S. 36). A Kansas Historical Marker relates that in 1856 Elwood (first called Roseport) prospered with steamboat and ferryboat trade. But floods are part of this community's story, and eventually the river washed away much of the old town. Near the marker an inscribed Glacial

Hills granite stone serves as a monument to the Pony Express.

HIGHLAND

Population 1,008

Highland Community College:
606 W. Main. The college, established in 1858, is the oldest institution of higher education in Kansas. The red-brick Irvin Hall (NRHP) is the first college building constructed in Kansas and is named for Samuel Irvin, a Presbyterian missionary who established the Iowa and Sac & Fox Mission in this area in 1827.

Boone Statue: 606 W. Main
(in front of Irvin Hall). The large bronze of Dr. William Boone (1860-1936), physician, community leader, educator, and Highland College trustee, was sculpted by his granddaughter Carey Boone Nelson.

Rubeti Memorial:
Ives and Main (in front of Ben Allen Fieldhouse). The brick wall bearing the Highland College name stands as a memorial to Sophie Rubeti, a young Sac of the Iowa and Sac & Fox Mission. A plaque tells Sophie's story and why, following her death around 1861 at age 18, a lodge for Indian girls was built in her honor. When the lodge was razed in 1978, the hand-hewn bricks from its fireplace were used to build the memorial wall.

St. Martha's A.M.E. Church (NRHP): 101 S.
Canada. It is believed that African Americans settled in Doniphan County around 1860. This simple frame church, built around 1882, was named for Martha Hubbard, a former slave who escaped to Kansas from Missouri via the Underground Railroad. She made a living as

a cook and worked with great devotion to help establish the "little church" in Highland.

Highland Presbyterian Church (NRHP): 101 South.
This church has the earliest formed Presbyterian congregation in the state, dating to 1843. After the 1888 church burned down, the new church, constructed around 1914, was designed with a flat roof and without a steeple, which was highly unusual for that time period and location in a rural community.

Iowa and Sac & Fox Mission State Historic Site (NRHP): 1737 Elgin.
From Kansas, 2 miles east on Main, just north on Elgin, then west into the driveway. The 1845 Presbyterian Mission was originally built to educate the Iowa and the Sac & Fox children. Although the mission is no longer open to the public, exterior interpretive signage tells the story of the American Indian tribes that were relocated to this area. The exhibits have been moved to Shawnee Indian Mission State Historic Site (*see* p. 134). kshs.org.

A.L. Wynkoop Home (NRHP): 307 W. Pennsylvania.
In 1912 local carpenter and contractor Ely Saunders interpreted the popular Prairie School and Craftsman architectural styles to design a distinctive home for wealthy merchant A.L. Wynkoop. The Shingle style exterior is an unusual feature of this two-story house with third-story dormers.

Highland Christian Church (NRHP): 102 E. Main. When
completed in 1904, the church was deemed the "handsomest in Highland." The architecture is significant because the Shingle style exterior is rare on a church building. Ely Saunders, designer of the Wynkoop home (*see* previous entry), oversaw the construction. The building's red-brick veneer accented by the buff-brick quoins make this church quite a beauty!

Kansas-Is-Not-Flat Scenic Drive: From Main, go 2¼ miles
north on Kansas (becomes Coronado), ½ mile east on 265, 1 mile north on Denmark, ¾ mile east on 275, then 1½ miles north on Dove Creek to Iowa Point. This six-mile route takes you on winding roads through hills and valleys and wooded landscapes, along little creeks, and past old wooden barns. From Iowa Point, continue 4½ miles north on K-7 to White Cloud.

NE

explorer extras... In Highland

Smithton Lodge, 306 W. Main, is the oldest Masonic lodge in Kansas, dating to 1854. Across the street, a plaque in the flower-filled Degginger Park commemorates this fact.

In front of Irvin Hall on the Highland Community College campus, 606 W. Main, you'll find a round cement sundial on a concrete table. Both were made

by Richard Schuman when he was in an art class at Highland in 1969. What do the circles mean on the side? The tops of plastic cups were used as indentations for decoration.

Emmett Cole started farming on a 1947 SC Case, a tractor his dad told him he should always keep. Emmett did just that, and today the restored Case stands with about 90 other historic tractors that Emmett has collected. Find his Midwest Classics museum at 602 Colorado. Monday-Friday 8 a.m.-3 p.m. **ee**

explorer extras... In Purcell

Unincorporated

From a distance, the 112-foot steeple guides you to St. Mary's Church (NRHP) at K-20 and K-137. Built in the Late Gothic Revival style, this 1896 red-brick building is the only remaining structure of a religious complex that once stood here. **ee**

explorer extras... In Sparks

Unincorporated

Some of the largest flea markets you'll ever encounter happen in Sparks, White Cloud, and Troy every Labor Day weekend and the first weekend of May. Expect huge crowds! FB. **ee**

TROY

Population 994

Historic Markers:
From Locust, 1 mile east on U.S. 36. Acquaint yourself with Troy by reading the historical marker at this roadside pull over.

A nearby granite marker tells about a Pony Express station that operated for a few months near here.

Doniphan County Courthouse (NRHP):
120 E. Chestnut. Revered Kansas architect George Washburn designed this Romanesque Revival building completed in 1906. Historic pictures and display cases line the hallway inside this picturesque red-brick structure with limestone trim. Monday-Friday 8 a.m.-5 p.m.

Tall Oak: 120 E. Chestnut (courthouse grounds). A citizen of Troy met Hungarian artist Peter Toth while he was sculpting outside of Kansas. Toth told him that his goal was to sculpt an Indian monument in each state. Thus, the artist was invited to Troy and in 1978 created the 27-foot sculpture of an Indian chief with headdress. Sculpted from a bur oak log and christened *Tall Oak*, the monument is a striking landmark in Troy.

Courthouse Grounds:
120 E. Chestnut. Gracing these environs are a replica Statue of Liberty, a plaque to a sheriff and an undersheriff who drowned in 1943, veteran memorials, a plaque recognizing the patent holder of the Burgundy Belle maple tree, and a Pony Express marker.

Courthouse Square Historic District (NRHP):
Highlights of the 18-site, self-guided walking tour include the 1900 opera house (106 E. Walnut); the 1900 former Hotel Avon (122 E. Walnut); and the 1870 Sol Miller Building (101 S. Main). The 100 block of Chestnut is home to several historic houses and businesses. Brochures are available on the first floor of the courthouse, 120 E. Chestnut.

Lincoln Memorial:
138 E. Walnut. It is said that on December 1, 1859, when Abraham Lincoln delivered a campaign speech in Troy, he stopped at the Sidney Tennant home on E. Walnut. A memorial to Lincoln's visit is erected just west of the house, now the Nelson Rogers home, which is the first and oldest residence remaining in Troy.

Boder-Strong Mansion:
433 W. State. A conical roof, rounded tower, wraparound porch, and ornate keystones are just a few of the features that make this 1895 red-brick Queen Anne home a handsome structure.

Feed Store Cafe: 103 S. Main. The three sisters who run this neat little cafe learned well from their mother, a school cook, and now pass on her skill for serving an excellent meal with lots of smiles. Known for its colorful bandana napkins and terrific feed, Feed Store offerings include hearty break-fasts, the Trojan Horse (a half-pound burger stuffed with onions and cheese), and butter-scotch pie. Monday-Friday 6 a.m.-2 p.m.; Saturday 6 a.m.-12 p.m. 785.985.3777.

Lodging: Troy Bed & Breakfast (785.985.2314).

WATHENA

Population 1,352

Fruit Growers' Building (NRHP):
104 3rd. An estimated 25,000 acres of apple orchards in Troy, Blair, and Wathena made Doniphan County a major shipping point for local fruit growers during the 1920s and 1930s. From 1909 to 1945 fruit growers met in the sizable Wathena Fruit Growers' Association Building to work for fair market pricing.

City Hall: 206 Saint Joseph. City Hall is in an impressive 1942 WPA stone structure.

Civil War Monument: From U.S. 36, ¾ mile north on N. 9th. In Bellemont Cemetery, a 1915 bronze statue of a soldier standing atop an engraved granite base honors those who gave their lives during the Civil War.

WHITE CLOUD

Population 175

Lewis and Clark Pavilion: Main and K-7. In a small park by the river, a pavilion, marked by a metal sunflower, commemorates the Lewis and Clark Expedition that came through this area on July 10,

1804. Interpretive signage provides background of this historic event.

Four-State Lookout
(8 Wonders of Kansas Geography): From Main, ¼ mile north and west on 3rd, and at the fork take either turn up the hill. A viewing platform offers a panorama of the broad Missouri River Valley, as well as of Kansas, Nebraska, Missouri, and Iowa.

Wilbur Chapman Monument:
202 Main. In front of the Christian church, a bronze plaque set in a unique stone pedestal pays tribute to Wilbur Chapman and relates a most unusual story of this 10-year-old boy and his pig, Pete. In 1913 Wilbur sold his prized pig to raise money for a leper colony. This news of one boy's generosity captured the public's fancy, and soon school children throughout the world began collecting money for this worthy cause. They saved their coins in, what else, little iron banks shaped like a black pig—created in memory of Pete. The 1880 brick home, 308 Chestnut, where Wilbur grew up is sometimes referred to as the Gingerbread House.

White Cloud Historic District (NRHP):
This small historic river town comprises 67 buildings that represent the development of the town since 1850. The historic district is roughly bordered by Poplar, 6th, Chestnut, and K-7. tinyurl.com/wcnrhp.

Poulet House (NRHP):
205 Poplar. Alexis Poulet, a prominent businessman in White Cloud, built this Italianate home in 1880. The wrought iron balconies on the back of the house reveal Poulet's French background.

White Cloud School (NRHP):
103 S. 5th. The 1872 two-story, Italianate building was designed by Kansas architect Erasmus T. Carr. Today it houses the Ma-Hush-Kah Museum. Hours irregular. FB.

Sol Miller Building:
213 Main. Sol Miller, who founded the *Kansas Chief* newspaper in 1857, constructed the eastern section of this Italianate building in 1866 for his newspaper office. The remainder of the structure was added in 1868. Miller abandoned the building in 1872 when he moved his paper to Troy.

White Cloud Barber Shop (NRHP):
210 Main. This 1864 clapboard frame building was a barbershop for much of its days beginning in 1875. Currently the structure is unoccupied.

Nuzum's Opera House:
114 Main. A dry goods business was the original occupant of this 1869 structure. By 1893 a general store and a bank had opened on the first floor, and an opera house operated on the second. By 1930 the second floor had been vacated and has been empty ever since.

40th Parallel Marker:
From Main, 2½ miles northwest on K-7. Stop here to read the

NE

historical marker that relates the story of the Public Land Surveys of the Sixth Principal Meridian. From here, another 120 yards north on K-7 a little footbridge leads to a path that takes you 150 feet to the top of the bluff (handrails help navigate the steep grade). At this hilltop you'll see the cast iron monument erected in May 1855 by U.S. Deputy Surveyor Charles Manners to mark the beginning point of the 40th Parallel—the border between the future states of Nebraska and Kansas.

Douglas County

AROUND THE COUNTY

Clinton Lake and State Park:
From I-70 exit 197, 3¾ miles south on E. K-10 to Clinton Lake exit, then just west. Created in 1977 by damming the Wakarusa River, the reservoir was built for flood control, recreation, and water supply. One of the best boating lakes in the state, it is surrounded by more than 60 miles of trails for hiking, biking, and horseback riding. All recreational opportunities are available. State park entrance charge. Cabins available, reservations required. 785.842.8562. ksoutdoors.com.

BALDWIN CITY

Population 4,540

Black Jack Park:
184 E. 2000. From 8th, 3½ miles southeast on U.S. 56. This roadside park features a DAR Santa Fe Trail marker, a second historical marker telling the story of the nearby Battle of Black Jack, and a replica log cabin. Cross the footbridge to the Ivan Boyd Memorial Prairie Preserve, a serene landscape of native flowers, plants, and grasses—and history including evidence of Santa Fe Trail wagon ruts (NRHP). tinyurl.com/ivanboyd.

Black Jack Battlefield (NRHP) and Nature Park:
163 E. 2000. From 8th, 3¼ miles southeast on U.S. 56, then ¼ mile south on E. 2000. In this wooded area the Battle of Black Jack occurred on June 2, 1856, when abolitionist John Brown led a group of free-state men into battle against proslavery militia leader Henry Clay Pate. This clash was the first recorded battle between two organized military forces in what evolved into the Civil War. Signage and markers along a nature trail relate the story. Adjoining the battlefield site, now a National Historic Landmark, is the restored homestead of Robert Hall Pearson. Although Pearson fought alongside John Brown this house wasn't built until 1890. blackjackbattlefield.org.

Baker University:
618 8th. Founded in 1858, Baker is the oldest four-year college in the state. The campus is beautiful with its sculptures, lovely gardens, and a grape arbor adding color amid the historic buildings. More than 110 species of trees make for a beautiful campus arboretum. bakeru.edu.

Parmenter Hall (NRHP):

8th and Dearborn (Baker campus). Abraham Lincoln donated $100 for construction of this striking three-story stone building that housed Baker University starting in 1871. A flagpole atop the tower is the exclamation mark.

Clarice Osborne Memorial Chapel:
515 6th (Baker campus). Built in 1864 in Sproxton, England, this quaint little Methodist chapel was moved to the Baker campus stone by stone in 1995. Lady Margaret Thatcher, former prime minister of Great Britain, visited Baker in 1996 to dedicate the chapel. Monday-Friday 8 a.m.-5:30 p.m. Call ahead, 785.594.4553. bakeru.edu/chapel.

Quayle Bible Collection:
518 8th (Collins Library, Baker campus). Housed inside a replica late-17th-century English country manor room, this revered collection was a 1925 gift from the estate of Bishop Quayle (*see* next entry). It includes such rare pieces as cuneiform tablets dating to 2000 B.C., a leaf from the Gutenberg Bible, early biblical manuscripts, early English Bibles, and a collection of Bibles containing presidential signatures from Harry Truman to the present. Saturday-Sunday 1-4 p.m. Call ahead, 785.594.8393. bakeru.edu/quayle-bible-collection.

William A. Quayle House (NRHP):
210 N. 6th. Known as Dream Haven, the house was the retirement home of Bishop Quayle, president of Baker University from 1890 to

1894. The 1913 bungalow with a 1921 Colonial Revival addition was nominated for the national register because of Quayle's significance in the community and Midwest and for the structure's architectural features. Drive by only.

Old Castle Museum (NRHP):

511 5th. The original home of Baker University, this three-story native stone building was erected in 1857. Today it houses collections of early Kansas, Methodist, and Baker history. The small white frame structure nearby served as an early post office and as a grocery store for travelers on the Santa Fe Trail. Also adjacent is a replica of the Kibbee cabin, a log house where Methodist ministers met to form Baker University. Saturday-Sunday 1-4 p.m. Call ahead, 785.594.8380. bakeru.edu/old-castle-museum.

Case Library (NRHP):

800 Grove (Baker campus). Seed money for the start of the library was given by Judge Nelson Case and the remaining money for construction and purchase of books was provided by Andrew Carnegie. This stately Neoclassical limestone building opened in 1907.

Lumberyard Arts Center:

718 High. The renovated 1914 Ives-Hartley Lumber Company building is a work of art in itself. Thanks to dedicated community members this red-brick landmark is now a charming art center offering classes, art exhibits, theater presentations, and events. Tuesday-Friday 1-4 p.m.; Saturday 9 a.m.-12 p.m. 785.594.3186. lumberyardartscenter.org.

Midland Railway:

1515 High. All aboard! Buy your tickets at the 1906 Santa Fe depot (NRHP) for a countryside ride on the Midland Railway. This excursion train travels the line originally constructed in 1867 and offers an 11-mile round trip to Norwood or a 20-miler to Ottawa and back. You'll pass through farmland and woods and cross a 200-foot trestle. May-October, Saturday 11 a.m. and 2 p.m.; Sunday 1:30 p.m.; Thursday 10:30 a.m. Tour charge. 913.721.1211 or 785.594.6982. midlandrailway.org.

Kansas Belle Dinner Train:

1515 High. The 1940s era is re-created for your enjoyment when you board the dinner train. Choose from formal or casual dinners, a murder mystery, or a music show. The train boards at the Santa Fe depot (NRHP) but is a separate enterprise from Midland Railway. May-October, Saturday evening and Sunday afternoon; year round, Saturday evening. Reservations required. 785.594.8505. kansasbelle.com.

Wooden Spoke: 203 1st. This is the quintessential neighborhood restaurant and bar, always good for lunch and dinner. Locals give high marks to the steaks, prime rib, burgers, salads, and more. Monday 5-9 p.m.; Tuesday-Saturday 11 a.m.-2 p.m. and 5-9 p.m. 785.594.2222. FB.

El Patron: 711 8th. Pan-fried chicken tacos, fajitas, and the habanero salsa are favorites at this popular local restaurant as are the sangria-flavored margaritas! Daily 11 a.m.-9 p.m. (closed Wednesday). 785.594.2711. heckestates.com.

Moose's Backwoods BBQ:

522 Ames. Beef brisket piled high on an egg bread bun makes for a lip-smacking sandwich. The many good choices and the homemade

barbecue sauce keep customers coming back to Backwoods. Monday-Saturday 10 a.m.-9 p.m.; Sunday 10 a.m.-7 p.m. 785.594.7427. moosesbackwoodsbbq.net.

Lodging: Three Sisters Inn Bed & Breakfast (785.594.3244, threesistersinn.com); The Lodge (785.594.3900, baldwincitylodge.com).

explorer extras... In Baldwin City

In 1890 Mayor Lucy Sweet Sullivan and an all-woman city council were tired of their skirts getting dirty on the path to the depot. To solve the problem a Women's Bridge, 11th and High, was constructed. It was just one of the town clean-up projects initiated by the female council. From West Park, take the sidewalk to view the stone single-arch bridge from under the road. A plaque tells more of this intriguing history.

Plaques paying tribute to local boys Kenny Shultz and Travis Franklin, both of whom died in 1989 while still in high school, are found inside this memorial shelter in West Park, 11th and High.

Oneida Indian Jim Garfield Brown could lay bricks faster than eight men could bring them to him. He completed laying bricks for High Street and around Baker University in 1926.

A new fountain dedicated in 2007 at 8th and High commemorates Baker University's 150th anniversary. The adjoining Tom Swan Park Demonstration Garden, cared for by the Douglas County Master Gardeners, includes a monarch butterfly garden and little library.

A historical marker recounts Baldwin City's 1850s origin and its involvement with the Santa Fe Trail, Baker University, and the free-state/proslavery conflict. From 8th, 1½ miles east and south on U.S. 56.

A 1932 metal sign and a 1907 DAR stone marker (NRHP) with an illustrated marble plaque designate the site of the old Santa Fe Trail Park (NRHP) formed in 1907. From U.S. 56, ¾ mile north on N. 6th.

Platted in 1854, Palmyra was an important stop on the Santa Fe Trail. In this little town travelers filled their water barrels, purchased supplies, washed their laundry, sent and received letters, and repaired their wagons and harness. Within a few years, the growth of the adjacent Baldwin City ended Palmyra's existence. A metal plaque and a DAR marker tell the story. From U.S. 56, 2 blocks north on 6th, 3 blocks east on Quayle, then 1 block north on Eisenhower. See the original Palmyra well at 400 Washington.

Today you have to go out of your way to find Willow Springs, but luckily it was easier for the wagon trains on the Santa Fe Trail to locate this watering hole. It was also the site of one of the earliest post offices on the trail. You'll have to hunt a little to find the plaque and marker that tell the Willow Springs story. From U.S. 59, 1½ miles west on U.S. 56, 2½ miles north on E. 1100 to N. 550. The markers are on the west side of E. 1100 under a tree.

From atop Santa Fe Ridge gaze across the picturesque Vinland Valley below. A plaque on this site states that in 1856 settlers hung lanterns in Signal Oak (an oak tree now long gone) to warn settlers at Blue Mound (10 miles to the north) that proslavery guerrillas were approaching. From U.S. 56, 1 mile north on 6th, ¼ mile east on State Lake, then ¾ mile north on E. 1750.

Frequently boots are seen on fence posts around the state, but the rocks tied on posts

along N. 700 between E. 2200 and E. 2100 are quite another matter! In the 1970s Wesley Schendel placed them on the posts just for fun. Although some of the stones are now gone, this fence line is still remarkable to see. **ee**

CLINTON

Unincorporated

Clinton Store: 598 N. 1190. A store has existed on this spot since 1908, and new owner Loren Baldwin (local farmer, rancher, and gardener) wants the tradition to continue. Locals and visitors can buy supplies, ice, beer, pop, and bait here. Loren also sells the pork and beef that he raises and serves it in the store's pub and grill on weekends. His sausage gravy is a great complement to the homemade biscuits. Store hours, May-September, daily 7 a.m.-7 p.m; pub and grill hours, year round, Friday-Saturday 5-9 p.m., Sunday 11 a.m.-5 p.m. 785.748.0713. FB.

Wakarusa River Valley Heritage Museum: Bloomington Park East. From E. 596, 1¼ miles east on N. 1190. The museum is housed in a renovated 1930s milk shed with a 2014 addition. Its two main exhibits focus on the area's Underground Railroad and on the early history of the Clinton Lake communities affected by the lake's development. May-September,

Saturday-Sunday 1-5 p.m. 785.783.4420. wakarusamuseum.org.

Freedom Rings: Bloomington Park East (next to Wakarusa River Valley Heritage Museum; *see* previous entry). Large gold hoops stand at odd angles and appear about to fall. Aside from being an interesting art installation that surround a historic windmill, the hoops represent the ten Wakarusa River Valley communities and their relationship to the Underground Railroad. A plaque at the site tells more about these Stephen Johnson sculptures. wakarusamuseum.org.

EUDORA

Population 6,211

Eudora Sculpture: 9th and Main. To celebrate its 150th anniversary in 2007, the city erected a Jim Brothers sculpture of Shawnee tribal leader Paschal Fish and his daughter Eudora.

Eudora Community Museum: 720 Main. The Eudora Community Museum is a small-town treasure housed in an 1870s tin shop, one of the town's oldest and most historic buildings. Recent restorations to the structure and excellent displays about Eudora's fascinating past make this an enjoyable and informative experience. Tuesday-Saturday 11 a.m.-5 p.m. 785.690.7900. tinyurl.com/eudoramuse.

Historic Buildings: Thirteen bronze plaques tell the story of downtown's business lineage and offer interesting side notes. Three buildings, at 707, 720, and 722 Main, are on the national register.

Charles Pilla House (NRHP): 615 Elm. This magnificent 1894 Victorian mansion overlooking the town square was built by Charles Pilla, a German-born community leader who owned a large general merchandise store, helped organize the Eudora State Bank, and had other business interests.

Tile Grain Elevators:

6th and Main. Thanks to the Eudora Community Museum, we know that the stand-out red-tile elevator and silos north of downtown were built in 1918 by local farmers. Tiles were used because they were less combustible than wood. Today the structures are used for storage.

Quilting Bits & Pieces:

736 Main. Known for its appliques, fat quarters fabric, and its in-house pattern line "Of One Mind," this shop also features 1880s and 1930s fabric reproductions, a huge selection of batiks, and much more. Quilters will enjoy every bit (and piece) of this unique store. Monday-Saturday 9:30 a.m.-4 p.m. 785.542.2080. eudoraquiltshop.com.

Jasmin Restaurant:

719 Main. No, you're not seeing double. This small family-owned restaurant of 17 years serves both Chinese and Mexican cuisine. Even the interior is decorated to reflect each ethnicity. Owners J and Maria Ramirez use Maria's family recipes, and J learned Chinese cooking in a previous job. Order an appetizer of steamed dumplings and nachos and a meal of Carne Asada or Moo Shu Chicken. Whatever you order, you'll be pleased with both the food and the service. The restaurant is named for the Ramirez' youngest child, Jasmin. Monday-Saturday 10:30 a.m.-9 p.m. 785.542.1111. jasmineudora.com.

Beni Israel Cemetery (NRHP):

1301 E. 2100. From N. 1400 (Old K-10), 1 mile south on 2011. German Jewish immigrants established this small cemetery in 1858. You'll frequently see piles of pebbles and stones on top of and around the gravestones. One meaning of these pebbles is a sign that someone has visited the grave.

Southwest City Cemetery:

Sycamore and Cedar. From W. 12th, ½ mile south on Cedar. This long strip of grass with a row of trees is the location of Eudora's first cemetery, founded in 1857. Ten years later a new cemetery was established elsewhere and the original became a burial ground for the town's black citizens. A simple sign in a stone base marks the cemetery. The gravestones are small and modest so look carefully to find them. Information about Eudora's immigrant and black history can be found at the Eudora Community Museum.

Delaware Cemetery:

10635 222. From E. 10th, 1½ miles north on Main (becomes 222). The cemetery on the north side of the Kansas River is the resting place for Delaware Indians who lived in this area from 1829 to 1867. A German family deeded the land in the 1870s so members of the tribe would have a burial place. A few Delawares buried here had married German settlers.

Davenport Orchards and Winery:

From Eudora, 3 miles west on K-10, then ½ mile north on E. 1900. Owners Greg Shipe and Charlee Glinka take pride that all their grapes are Kansas grown. Moreover, they are grown on 24 acres once owned by Greg's grandparents, C.W. and and Mary Davenport. Wine bottle labels are designed by Kansas artists. Monday, Wednesday, Friday 4-7 p.m.; Saturday-Sunday 1-5 p.m. Call ahead, 785.542.2278. davenportwinery.com.

BlueJacket Crossing Vineyard & Winery:

1969 N. 1250. From K-10, 1 mile south on E. 2200, 2 miles west on N. 1200, ½ mile north on E. 2000, then ¼ mile west on N. 1250. This family-owned vineyard was named for the nearby Bluejacket Crossing, an 1850s Oregon Trail ferry crossing on the Wakarusa River. Award-winning wines include the sweet red Betty's Blush and the off-dry white vignoles. Wednesday-Sunday 12-5 p.m. 785.542.1764. bluejacketwinery.com.

LAWRENCE

Population 90,811

Lawrence Visitor Center:

402 N. 2nd. Inside this renovated 1889 Union Pacific depot you'll find area brochures about Quantrill's raid on Lawrence, early architecture, historic cemeteries, the KU campus, hiking and biking maps, and other city attractions. Monday-Saturday 9 a.m-5 p.m.; Sunday 1-5 p.m. 785.856.3040. explorelawrence.com.

Robert J. Dole Institute of Politics:

2350 Petefish (KU west campus). As you approach the building you'll see the world's largest stained-glass American flag, and on a sunny day it's a magnificent

sight. Inside, a massive display of black-and-white photos of Kansas World War II veterans forms the Memory Wall, and on the adjoining wall is a stained-glass depiction of Dole's boy-hood town of Russell. State-of-the-art visual and audio displays relate Dole's achievements as a KU student, a World War II soldier, and a politician. Regard-less of your political leanings, you'll be moved by this beautiful facility and its exhibits. Monday-Saturday 9 a.m.-5 p.m.; Sunday 12-5 p.m. 785.864.4900. doleinstitute.org.

Booth Family Hall
of Athletics: 1651 Naismith (KU campus). Enter on the north or east side of Allen Fieldhouse. Honoring KU's athletic programs, coaches (including the vener-able James Naismith and Phog Allen), and athletes, the Booth Family Hall exhibits an outstand-ing collection of history and tradition. Uniforms, equipment, trophies, photos and much

more tell a story every sports fan will enjoy. You can even view the famed Allen Fieldhouse court. Adjoining is the DeBruce Center where Naismith's original rules of "Basket Ball" are on display. Monday-Saturday 10 a.m.-5 p.m. (limited schedule on game days). 785.864.7050. kuathletics.com/boothhall.

James Naismith: In 1891 Naismith developed the game of basketball in Springfield, Massachusetts. Today his handwritten original rules are on display at KU's DeBruce Center, and exhibits at the Booth Family Hall of Athletics (*see* previous entry) credit him for starting the basketball program at KU. A bronze plaque on a concrete base at 8th and Kentucky marks the spot where the first official KU basketball game was played in 1899. Sports fans may want to touch the granite cenotaph erected in Naismith's honor at Memorial Park Cemetery, 1 mile east of Massachusetts on 15th, where he is buried.

Forrest "Phog" Allen:
This longtime KU coach is known as the father of basket-ball coaching. A bronze statue on the east side of Allen Field-house, which is named for him, provides a brief biography. More can be learned at the Booth Family Hall of Athletics. Allen is buried in Oak Hill Cemetery (*see* p.114) along the northeast drive in section 13. People routinely leave pennies on his gravestone. In 1936 Allen had started a penny campaign to help fund James Naismith's trip to Berlin so the man who invented basketball could be part of the basketball debut in the Olympics.

Freedom's Frontier National Heritage Area: 200 W. 9th.
Enter on the east side. From some perspectives the violent border conflict between Kansas and Missouri led to the Civil War.

Freedom's Frontier, at home in a 1904 former Carnegie library (NRHP), bridges the border by offering many viewpoints of freedom's story that occurred in the 41 counties in eastern

Kansas and western Missouri. Monday-Friday 8:30 a.m.-4:30 p.m. 785.856.5300. freedomsfrontier.org.

Watkins Museum of History (NRHP):
1047 Massachusetts. Built as a Romanesque style bank in 1888, this splendid building now preserves the fascinating history of Lawrence and Douglas County. Exhibits explore Civil War history, Quantrill's 1863 raid and burning of Lawrence, the story of civil rights from the 1960s through the 1990s, and more. Tuesday-Saturday 10 a.m.-4 p.m. 785.841.4109. watkinsmuseum.org.

Natural History Museum
(NRHP): 1345 Jayhawk (KU campus). Much of the rich ornamentation on the building's exterior suggests the study of plants and animals. Four floors of exhibits present ancient and modern animals, from fossil dinosaurs to grizzly bears. The horse Comanche, draped in his army blanket, is displayed on the fourth floor. Comanche was the only living member of Custer's Seventh U.S. Cavalry found on the battlefield

following the 1876 Battle of the Little Bighorn. Tuesday-Saturday 9 a.m.-5 p.m.; Sunday 12-4 p.m. Donation suggested. 785.864.4450. nhm.ku.edu.

Spencer Museum of Art:
1301 Mississippi (KU campus). Presenting quality exhibitions and programs, this university art museum is revered as one of the best in the country. Its culturally diverse collection comprises 40,000 art objects. Tuesday, Friday-Saturday 10 a.m.-4 p.m.; Wednesday-Thursday 10 a.m.-8 p.m.; Sunday 12-4 p.m. 785.864.4710. spencerart.ku.edu.

Memorial Campanile:
1450 Memorial (KU campus). One of the most striking features on campus is this towering memorial to World War II veterans. The Campanile carillon bells resound across the valley it overlooks and strike on the quarter hour during the academic year. The tall bronze doors, designed by Bernard "Poco" Frazier, contain symbolic themes of early Kansas. If you're wondering, campanile means free-standing bell tower. carillon.ku.edu.

Downtown:
Historic Massachusetts Street is the hub of the most thriving downtown district in the state. You're bound to feel good just being here for the diverse shopping, art, entertainment, people watching, and the selection of restaurants, coffee shops, and pubs. downtownlawrence.com.

Mass Street Soda:
1103 Massachusetts. Matt Baysinger and Luke Thompson started this craft soda shop in 2014 and now have more soda varieties than any like store in the world! Find 1,300 brands from all over the world including Howdy, Jac Jic, Bedford's, Capt'n Eli's, Always Ask for Avery, and Cheerwine. It's so fun! Daily 11 a.m.-8 p.m. 785.409.1767. massstreetsoda.com.

Raven Book Store:
6 E. 7th. Serving the area since 1987 is this independently owned bookstore—an intimate setting where you'll enjoy perusing and purchasing! Monday-Saturday 9 a.m.-8 p;m; Sunday 12-5 p.m. 785.749.3300. ravenbookstore.com.

Lawrence Arts Center:
940 New Hampshire. Three galleries and the hallway showcase the work of area and nationally known artists. 785.843.2787. Daily 9 a.m.-9 p.m. lawrenceartscenter.org.

Liberty Hall:
644 Massachusetts. Abraham Lincoln once called Lawrence "the cradle of Liberty," thus the original hall (now gone) received its name in 1870. The current structure, christened Bowersock Opera House in 1912, has had many name changes and uses. Today historic Liberty Hall is a main venue for live performances and independent films. The renovated interior features a 37-foot grand vaulted ceiling accented with original chandeliers. Daily 12-10 p.m. 785.749.1972. libertyhall.net.

Lawrence Library:
707 Vermont. One look at the architecture tells you it's unique. But in case you didn't know, the library was designed to be a source of hope bringing light to the community. Each elevation was engineered to engage with daylight. Wonderful resources await you inside. Monday-Thursday 9 a.m.-9 p.m.; Friday-Saturday 9 a.m.-6 p.m.; Sunday 12-6 p.m. 785.843.3833. lawrence.lib.ks.us.

Douglas County Courthouse (NRHP):
111 E. 11th. John Haskell and Frederick Gunn were associate architects for this 1904 limestone Romanesque structure with its impressive clock tower. Inside, the stained-glass dome is visible from the lobby. A balcony is one of the unique features in the historic courtroom. Monday-Friday 8 a.m.-5 p.m. 785.832.5167.

NE

Haskell Cultural Center and Museum:
2411 Barker (Haskell campus). You will be intrigued with the history preserved at this center. Photos and information are well exhibited and provide gripping accounts of the American Indian children who attended the school during its early days, the achievements of students and alumni, daily life at Haskell, and how the school evolved. Monday-Friday 9 a.m.-3:30 p.m. 785.832.6686. haskell.edu/cultural-center.

Haskell Stadium and Arch (NRHP):
2412 Barker (Haskell campus). Dedicated in 1926, the stadium, primarily funded with donations from American Indians, was built in response to Haskell's nationally recognized football team. The impressive arch was dedicated to the 415 Haskell students who served in World War I.

Haskell Cemetery:
From Barker, ¼ mile east on Indian, ¼ mile south on E. Perimeter, then just east on Kiowa. Neatly lined in rows, the simple gravestones provide the anglicized names, birth and death dates,

and tribal affiliation (37 tribes represented) of the children buried here. Half of these children died within the first five years of Haskell's existence. The last burial was in 1943.

Baker Wetlands and Discovery Center: 1365 N. 1250. Before walking the trails of this ancient wetlands, see the Discovery Center's displays and photographs about many of the 278 bird species, 98 vertebrate species, and 487 plant species identified in this area. The trails (open dawn to dusk) include a boardwalk section through the wetlands. Monday-Saturday 9 a.m.-3 p.m.; Sunday 1-3 p.m. bakeru.edu/wetlands.

Oak Hill Cemetery: From Massachusetts, ¾ mile east on 13th, then ¼ mile southeast on Oak Hill. Pick up a cemetery brochure from the Lawrence Visitor Center, 402 N. 2nd, so you won't miss finding the grave-stones of Governors Charles Robinson and Wilson Shannon and of President Lincoln's Secretary of the Interior John P. Usher. The cemetery's winding and shaded roadways encom-pass many more interesting memorials, including a monument to victims of Quantrill's raid.

Robinson Park:
4 W. 6th. Make a stop at this little park named for Charles Robinson, the first governor of Kansas, to see the tall red Glacial Hills boulder known as Founder's Rock. The Kanza tribe considered this rock

sacred and not to be moved from where it came to rest at the junction of Shunganunga Creek and the Kansas River near Tecumseh. Regardless, some thought it should be relocated to the state capitol lawn, but a group from Lawrence moved it to its present location in 1929. A large plaque on the rock honors the pioneers of Kansas and the 1854 founders of Lawrence.

Pioneer Cemetery:
Constant and Irving Hill (KU west campus). A tall white obelisk marks the cemetery's first gravestone, that of Ohio immigrant Thomas Barber who was killed by proslavery supporters in 1855. Civil War soldiers, victims of Quantrill's 1863 raid, and former KU leaders are buried in this small and historic cemetery.

Merc Co-op: 901 Iowa. Eat in, get something to go, or buy groceries at this stylish consumer-owned cooperative. Many temptations are deli-ciously available! Those who think and eat healthy will love shopping at this natural foods store, known to its friends as The Merc. Daily 7 a.m.-10 p.m. 785.843.8544. themerc.coop.

Pendleton's Kaw Valley Country Market:
1446 E.1850. Pendleton's is a diversified family farm growing vegetables, flowers, bedding plants, herbs, and commodity crops. It's a very in-touch-with-nature experience to bring the family and pick your own seasonal produce. The country store is fun for shopping too. Hours seasonal. 785.843.1409. pendletons.com.

Crescent Moon Winery:
15930 246. From N. 3rd, 6 miles northeast on U.S. 24/40, ¼ mile northeast on 243, ¼ mile west on Stillwell, then 1½ miles north on 246. Situated between Law-rence and Tonganoxie, you'll find Crescent Moon a picturesque

spot to try wines made by Keith and Cheryl Hand. All the grapes are grown in Kansas, most of them on site. Kansans will love the labels for the Chardonel and the Noiret. Saturday-Sunday 1-5 p.m. 785.550.5353. moonandwine.com.

Restaurants: Lawrence offers almost every sort of eatery your heart desires from classic coffee shops and sports bars to ethnic restaurants and fine dining. Here is a sampling:

Free State Brewery
(8 Wonders of Kansas Cuisine): 636 Massachusetts. The Free State Brewing Company opened in 1989 as the first legal brewery in Kansas in more than 100 years. Its interior stone walls create a fantastic atmosphere for enjoying in-house brews, such as Wheat State Golden, and excellent cuisine. Grill hours, Monday-Saturday 11 a.m.-10 p.m.; Sunday 12-10 p.m. 785.843.4555. freestatebrewing.com.

Wheatfields Bakery and Cafe (8 Wonders of Kansas Cuisine):
904 Vermont. A large selection of artisan breads are the first wonders you'll see when you step inside. Line up for mouthwatering homemade menu selections that include sandwiches, salads, soups, and quiches. Or try one of the many fresh-baked pastries and specialty coffees. Monday-Friday 6:30 a.m.-8 p.m.;

Saturday 6:30 a.m.-6:30 p.m.; Sunday 7:30 a.m.-4 p.m. 785.841.5553. wheatfieldsbakery.com.

23rd Street Brewery:

3512 Clinton Pkwy. Small batch beers brewed in a 15-barrel system result in fresh beers such as Crimson Phog (Irish style red ale), Wave the Wheat (wheat ale), and Bitter Professor (IPA). Winning foods include 23rd Street Meatloaf (bison and beef), Danny Manning Marsala Chicken, and London Phog Fish and Chips. Daily 11 a.m.-10 p.m. 785.356.2337. brew23.com.

The Roost: 920 Massachusetts. Something magical happens here every day—breakfast, lunch, and Bloody Marys. The breakfast cocktails are fantastic, and the coffee bar is equally as good. Everything is made from scratch with locally sourced ingredients, and favorites include "life-changing" carrot cake, the house-made corned beef hash, and the mushroom, leek, and goat cheese omelet. Daily 7 a.m.-3 p.m. 785.843.1110. 920mass.com.

Limestone: 814 Massachusetts. Organic flour and yeast form just the right dough at this one-of-a-kind pizza place. Everything is made in-house from the mozzarella cheese and sausage to the sweet garlic chili sauce. Sandwiches, salads, bar bites, and other menu items are as tiptop as the pizza. Monday-Saturday 11 a.m.-10 p.m.;

Sunday 12-8 p.m. 785.856.2825. limestonepkb.com.

Terrebonne: 805 Vermont. Tucked away on a downtown side street is the place where locals go for Cajun and Creole fare. Eight different po' boy sandwiches will stir your taste buds as will the homemade gumbo, jambalaya, and red beans and rice. For something with a twist, try the Cajun corndog. Monday-Saturday 11 a.m.-9 p.m. 785.856.3287. FB.

715: 715 Massachusetts. Named simply for the address, this European-style bistro serves more-than-simply-delicious cuisine, and ingredients are locally sourced. Salads, soups, steaks, and more earn top marks. Excellent cocktails come with seasonal concoctions. Monday-Friday 11 a.m.-10:30 p.m.; Saturday-Sunday 9 a.m.-10:30 p.m. 785.856.7150. 715mass.com.

Hank Charcuterie:

1900 Massachusetts. Step inside this former 1927 gas station to try a charcuterie board, a sampling of meats and house-made summer sausage accompanied by pickled vegetables and bread. Everything is locally sourced. Tuesday-Friday 11 a.m.-9 p.m.; Saturday 9 a.m.-9 p.m.; Sunday 9 a.m.-2 p.m. 785.832.8688. hankmeats.com.

Levee Cafe: 239 Elm. Right off the Kansas River levee hike-bike trail is a new neighborhood cafe. Breakfast features old favorites and new, such as the apple crisp French toast stuffed with apples, cinnamon, and streusel and topped with fresh whipped cream. Healthy and international options are also served. Tuesday-Sunday 6:30 a.m.-3 p.m. 785.856.3671. FB.

Alchemy Coffee and Bake House:

1901 Massachusetts. Owners Ben Farmer and Joni Alexander have the right chemistry for this hipster

coffee shop and bakery. Ben creates the cold press and nitrogen-infused coffee, and Joni stirs up tasty morsels, all of which produce enchanting results. Daily 8 a.m.-6 p.m. 785.865.6046. alchemyks.com.

La Tropicana: 434 Locust. Since 1962 four generations of the Del Campo family have been serving homemade Mexican fare, daily specials, fresh guacamole, and margaritas that are well known and well loved around town. In warm weather you can enjoy dining on the outdoor patio. Monday-Friday 11 a.m.-2 p.m. and 5-10 p.m.; Saturday 11 a.m.-9:30 p.m. 785.749.3550. FB.

More Good Restaurants:

Wonderful varieties in eating also await you at Aladdin Cafe, Auntie Em's Deli, Basil Leaf, Bourgeois Pig, Burger Stand at the Casbah, La Prima Tassa, Leeway Franks, Mad Greek, Sylas and Maddy's Homemade Ice Cream, Ramen Bowls, Scone Lady's Coffee Shop, Zen Zero, and more. tinyurl.com/eatlawrence.

Lodging: Circle S Ranch (785.843.4124, circlesranch. com); Eldridge Hotel (NRHP, 785.749.5011, eldridgehotel. com); Halcyon House Bed & Breakfast (888.441.0314, halcyonhouseks.com); Victorian Veranda Country Inn (785.841.1265, vcountryinn.com); RV, cabins, and tent campgrounds (kansascityjellystone.com); additional lodging (tinyurl.com/lawrencestay).

explorer extras...
In Lawrence

Lawrence has a thriving arts community, and many of the murals and sculptures are found outdoors. Among the many colorful Dave Loewenstein works are *Guardians of the Arts* (722 Massachusetts) and *East Lawrence Waltz* (11th

NE

and Delaware). Lin Emery's sculpture, *The Flame* (6th and Massachusetts), symbolizes Lawrence's rebirth after Quantrill's 1863 raid. Many more await you, and brochures at the Lawrence Visitor Center (402 N. 2nd) help guide you on your art hunt.

A colorful butterfly and pollinator garden at Foley Hall, 2021 Constant (KU west campus), was created by the Douglas County Master Gardeners. Some days more than 20 species of butterflies fill the air. Dawn to dusk. 785.864.4441. monarchwatch.org.

A sensory garden next to Audio-Reader Center, 1120 W. 11th, has raised beds to make it easier for those in wheelchairs to touch. Textured plants become an open book for blind visitors, fragrant herbs are olfactory delights, wind chimes supply sounds, and mint furnishes taste. 785.864.4634. reader.ku.edu/sensory-garden.

Many walking and biking trails meander throughout Lawrence in its environs. The 10-mile Riverfront Park Trail runs along the top of the Kansas River levee. You can most easily access it at N. 2nd and Elm. The Kaw River Trail is a National Recreation Trail and extends 4 miles north from the U.S. 24/40/59 intersection. Find more trails at tinyurl.com/hikebikelawrence.

The top of Wells Overlook observation tower provides a wonderful view of Lawrence and the surrounding valley. From 31st, 3 miles south on Iowa

(becomes U.S. 59), ¾ mile east on N. 1000, then south up the winding drive to the overlook park. William Wells generously donated this land to the county in 1971.

Bowersock Mills and Power Company at 546 Massachusetts is the only operating hydroelectric plant in Kansas. It has been continuously producing clean, renewable energy since 1874. 785.843.1385. bowersockpower.com.

Built in the 1920s and named Indian Village, the roadside attraction of tipis once provided a gas station, tourist cabins, a restaurant, and more. Much of this landmark, known in recent years as Te-Pee Junction, is now gone, but the main concrete tipi and a building with smaller tipis on either end remain. From N. 3rd, ¼ mile east on U.S. 24/40.

In the early 2000s when Corbet Collins' sore knees prevented him from bowling, he placed his bowling balls on the fence posts at his vegetable garden. It's likely that 15 bowling balls on posts will draw your attention as you drive by. From N. 3rd, 1 mile east on U.S. 24/40. ee

LECOMPTON

Population 631

Constitution Hall State Historic Site (NRHP; National Historic Landmark): 319 Elmore.
The origin of the Civil War can be traced to Lecompton and

the events that occurred inside this two-story frame building during the Kansas territorial period of the 1850s. A Kansas constitution supporting slavery was written here in 1857 but was voted down at the national level. One can almost feel the

tension these walls and beams witnessed more than 150 years ago. The territorial story is interpreted vividly with signage and exhibits. Wednesday-Saturday 9 a.m.-5 p.m.; Sunday 1-5 p.m. Admission charge. 785.887.6520. kshs.org.

Territorial Capital Museum (NRHP): 640 E.
Woodson (behind the red-brick school). In 1855 President James Buchanan approved federal money and appointed officials to establish government offices in Lecompton. Before this structure became Lane University, it was intended to be the first capitol of Kansas. Construction stopped in 1857 when it became clear that the proslavery Lecompton Constitution would not be passed. Finally, in 1882 Lane University (named for James Lane, a controversial free-state supporter) was constructed, using the capitol ruins. A museum now tells the story of the plans for the territorial capitol, the history of Lane University (including the fact that Dwight Eisenhower's parents met here as students), and other area history. Ask for a Visit Lecompton packet. Wednesday-Saturday 11 a.m.-4 p.m.; Sunday 1-5 p.m. 785.887.6148. lecomptonkansas.com.

Democratic Headquarters:
From Elmore, 1 block east on 3rd, ¼ mile north on Haldeman, then ¼ mile east on 2nd. The small renovated stone building served as Kansas Territory's first Democratic headquarters, operating from 1854 to 1861. During this time Lecompton was known as the birthplace of the Kansas Democratic Party.

Historical Markers: Colorful red, orange, and white markers are found throughout town explaining Lecompton's important role during Kansas' pre-statehood era, 1854-1861.

Historic Jail: Moved to 315 Elmore in 2014, the 1892 limestone jail looks picturesque on its new site.

Sheriff Samuel Jones:
North of Constitution Hall. A colorful sign marks the original gravestone of proslavery supporter Sam Jones. Jones was appointed county sheriff in 1855, began building Constitution Hall in 1856, and that same year led the attack on and sacking of Lawrence. His controversial political and financial activities caused him to quickly leave for New Mexico in 1857. He died there in 1883, but in 1935 his body was moved to a new location and his grave marked with a new headstone. Lecompton was granted the original gravestone, which can be seen on this spot.

Post Office Mural: 525 E. Woodson. An Ellen Duncan mural inside the post office portrays Elmore Street as it was in 1916 before a fire destroyed many buildings. Two dozen historic photos of Lecompton also are displayed here. Daily 5:30 a.m.-9 p.m. 785.887.6494.

Kroeger's Country Meats:
505 Eisenhower. Kroeger's is an old-fashioned meat market, convenience store, deli, and gas station. The Kroeger family—Gary, Linda, and Robin—can build a whopping sandwich from fresh ingredients or grill a hamburger using their fresh ground chuck. You might want to bring a cooler to take home hand-cut steaks, sausages, brats, and more. It's a must stop on your exploring adventures. Monday-Saturday 11 a.m.-5 p.m. 785.887.6091. FB.

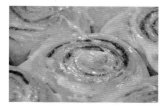

Aunt Netters Cafe:
336 Elmore. Red Velvet, Strawberry Champagne, and Coconut Cream Pie are only a few the gourmet cupcakes. And Honey Crunch Pumpkin, Key Lime, and Turtle are just a sampling of the gourmet pies. Not all varieties are available every day. Oh yeah, breakfast and lunch are served too and come highly recommended. Daily 6 a.m.-2 p.m. and Friday 6 a.m.-7 p.m. 785.503.6004. auntnetterscafe.com.

**explorer extras...
In Lecompton**

An impressive granite marker lists veterans from the Lecompton, Stull, Big Springs, and Kanwaka areas who served in the military beginning in 1861. It stands at the base of the sidewalk to Constitution Hall, 319 Elmore.

Elmore Street was once called the Wall Street of the West because of the large amount of money exchanged at local businesses, particularly at the Kansas Territorial Land Office in today's Constitution Hall.

Lecompton streets bear the names of early territorial officials and town founders. Shannon Ave. is named for the second territorial governor Wilson Shannon. Boone Street is named for Albert Boone, Daniel Boone's grandson and a Lecompton founder.

The unusual limestone curbs on Elmore and Woodson were placed there in 1888.

Lecompton was originally called Bald Eagle because of the bald eagles that nested on the nearby Kansas River. Eagles still make the river their home and can be spotted from time to time.

In 1858 the town of Denver, Colorado (then at the western edge of Kansas Territory), was platted here in the Rowena Hotel by a group of Lecompton men. Denver is named for Kansas territorial governor James Denver. **ee**

**explorer extras...
In Vinland**

Unincorporated

To reach Vinland take the scenic route by starting at Baldwin City and going 4 miles north on E. 1700.

Members of the Coal Creek Library Association (founded in 1859) built the Coal Creek Library (NRHP), 698 E. 1719, in 1900. The library still resides here today and is operated by dedicated volunteers. April-October, Sunday 1-4 p.m.

The quaint 1879 Presbyterian church (NRHP), 697 E. 1725, is now a private residence and its exterior has been restored to its Gothic Revival splendor. James Naismith, inventor of basketball, pastored here in 1919-1920 while employed as a chaplain and physical education professor at KU.

NE

The stone Grange Hall (NRHP) at Oak and Main dates to 1884.

A marker in the northwest corner of town recognizes Delbert Chanay who started the Vinland Valley Aerodrome in 1969. Small planes utilize this country airport, 696 E. 1700. **ee**

Franklin County

AROUND THE COUNTY

Franklin County Quilt Block Tour: Almost 40 large wooden quilt blocks are exhibited on barns, sheds, and silos across the county. To learn about the quilt project and to pick up a map, stop at the visitor center at 2011 E. Logan in Ottawa. tinyurl.com/frankquilts.

Prairie Spirit Trail: Trailhead at the Old Depot Museum, 135 W. Tecumseh in Ottawa. Attention all bikers or hikers! You can now travel 52 miles from Ottawa to Iola on the hard-packed surface trail built on an old railroad grade. This trail takes the traveler through scenic prairies and woodlands, past lakes, and over bridges. Prairie Spirit, the state's first linear state park, connects with the nine-mile Southwind Rail Trail between Iola and Humboldt. Permit required for those over 16. 785.448.6767. bikeprairiespirit.com.

explorer extras... In Lane

Population 258

You can almost feel the ghosts of history in this town. At 5th and Kansas a historical marker identifies the tragic and bloody Pottawatomie Massacre that took place just north of town on Pottawatomie Creek in late May 1856. John Brown and a band of abolitionists massacred a number of proslavery men in retaliation for the raid on Lawrence that had occurred days earlier.

Judge James Hanway was an integral part of Kansas Territory and early state government. He and his two sons built their home, the native limestone Hanway House (NRHP), in circa 1858. A log cabin that once stood on this property housed John Brown on visits to the area and sheltered slaves on the Underground Railroad. From Lane, ½ mile south on Kansas (becomes Virginia), then ½ mile west on Clark.
Drive by only. **ee**

OTTAWA

Population 12,031

Franklin County Visitor Center: 2011 E. Logan. From Main, 1½ miles east on K-68. You've never seen a visitor center in Kansas like this one! It has the look of a Victorian home yet is designed to accommodate the visitor. Pick up area and statewide brochures, including those for four

self-guided historical driving tours of the county, and the quilt block tour. Monday-Saturday 9 a.m.-4 p.m.; Sunday 12-4 p.m. 785.242.1411. explorefranklincountyks.com.

Old Depot Museum (NRHP): 135 W. Tecumseh. County history is well displayed inside this restored 1888 two-story limestone Santa Fe depot. Learn about Silkville, Bleeding Kansas, the early chautauquas at historic Forest Park, and the 1951 flood. A favorite and humorous exhibit is of Ottawa photographer William "Dad" Martin whose trick photography portrays larger-than-life scenes by superimposing images of people, produce, and animals. Tuesday-Saturday 10 a.m-4 pm.; Sunday 1-4 p.m. Admission charge. 785.242.1250. olddepotmuseum.org.

George P. Washburn: One of the most famous architects in Kansas, Washburn had an office in Ottawa for 60 years. He made his mark during the boom days of the 1880s and 1890s when the "look" of Ottawa was established. His signature structure in Ottawa is the Franklin County courthouse, built in 1891-1893. Washburn-designed homes can be seen at 410 S. Elm, 312 E. 11th, 320 E. 11th, 534 S.

Cedar, and 507 S. Cherry. An amazingly talented architect, he designed 13 courthouses across Kansas and innumerable public buildings. He is buried at Highland Cemetery on E. 15th (from Main, ¾ mile east on 15th) in the Washburn mausoleum.

Franklin County Courthouse (NRHP):

315 S. Main. This beautifully restored courthouse, designed by George Washburn, was completed in 1893. The Roman-esque Revival structure has the distinction of being the oldest Washburn-designed courthouse in Kansas still standing. Inside you'll find historical exhibits on the first floor and a polished oak staircase leading to the historic courtroom on the second floor. Outside, *Lady Justice* stands atop the courthouse between its two square towers. Gracing the grounds are the Charlie

Norton *Buffalo Woman* bronze, sculptures of George Washburn and Tauy Jones, and a veterans memorial. Monday-Friday 8 a.m.-4 p.m.

Forest Park:

N. Locust and K-68. One of the early sites for the National Chautauqua Assembly in Kansas, Forest Park hosted these educational and entertaining events (chautau-quas) for hundreds of eager area folks from 1883 to 1914. George Washburn's son Clarence designed the park's entrance pillars. A brass plaque honors a Kansas company that served in the Spanish-American War.

Carnegie Cultural Center (NRHP):

501 S. Main. One of the most beautiful Carnegie libraries in Kansas

now functions as the Cultural Center. Dedicated in 1903, the library was designed by the renowned George Washburn. Inside, local and regional art is displayed. Monday-Saturday 10 a.m.-6 p.m. 785.242.8478. ottawaartscouncil.org.

Chris's Corner and Brenda's Machine Quilting:

3593 N. U.S. 59. Chris loves talking about and showing fabric, and Brenda keeps busy on her machine quilter in this full-line quilting store. Along with quilts and quilters notions, Franklin County Quilt Block self-guided tour brochures are available. Monday-Friday 9:30 a.m.-5 p.m.; Saturday 9:30 a.m.-3 p.m. 785.242.1922.

Downtown:

Antiques, gift shops, and interactive kiosks abound in Ottawa's Victorian downtown. Eight kiosks that explain the story of Ottawa have been placed from the Old Depot Museum to the Dietrich Cabin in City Park. More than 100 buildings are contributors to the Historic Ottawa Central Business District (NRHP).

Wray's Bulk Food Store:

221 S. Main. Candy, spices, noodles, nuts, and much more are sold here in bulk. Also available are meat from the local Bauman's Butcher Block, fresh brown eggs, cheese—and kitchen items! Order soup and sandwiches from the deli but come early to find a seat at one of two tables. This family operation also includes a showroom for its woodworking products. Monday-Saturday 9 a.m.-5 p.m. 785.242.3663.

Plaza Movie Memorabilia Museum:

209 S. Main. Enjoy a movie in the oldest operating cinema house in the world (dating to 1905) and then visit the movie memorabilia museum, or come just for the museum. If you're a movie

buff you'll recognize countless costumes, props, posters, and photographs from old and recent movies. Tuesday-Sunday 1-7 p.m. 785.242.5555. plazacinemaottawa.com.

NE

Haley Park:

205 S. Main. Take time to enjoy the historic murals and gazebo. Two of the murals provide a visual of Forest Park at its heyday.

Tauy Jones Hall (NRHP):

From Main, ¼ mile east on 9th (Ottawa University campus). In 1833, when the Ottawa tribe was removed to a reservation in present Franklin County, the Reverend John Tecumseh "Tauy" Jones, a half Chippewa, assisted the Indians in estab-lishing their new home. To provide a college setting for the Ottawas, Jones helped found Ottawa University in 1865, but before the school opened, the Ottawa tribe was removed to Oklahoma. The limestone and oldest campus building dates to 1869 and is named for Jones.

Ottawa Baptist Mission and Burial Ground:

From Main, 2½ miles east on K-68, ½ mile north on Nebraska Terrace, then ¾ mile east on Osborne Terrace. On one of the stone entrance pillars a plaque reads, "Jotham Meeker, first printer and publisher in Indian Territory." From the pillars, walk about ¼ mile to the burial ground where the first gravestones you'll see

are those for Ottawa chiefs Comchau and Notino. This spot is also the site of Meeker's 1837 Ottawa Baptist Mission. No buildings remain but a curious open space among the gravestones is where a log church once stood. Meeker and his wife are buried to the north of the church site, and the grave of Tauy Jones is to the south.

Tauy Jones House

(NRHP): 3801 Nebraska. From K-68, 2¼ north on N. Main (Old U.S. 59), 3 miles east on Sand Creek, 1½ north on Nevada Terrace, then ¾ mile southwest on Nebraska. Jones' 1860s two-story stone house sits back off the unpaved road. Drive by only. Jones' first dwelling, an overnight stop for travelers between Lawrence and Fort Scott, was burned in 1856 by proslavery forces. The stone for the extant house was hauled by oxen from Fort Scott. An abandoned 1895 Warren truss bridge (NRHP) is 100 feet south of the house on Tauy Creek.

Hope Cemetery: From Main, 1 mile west on 2nd. Among the many gravestones and mausoleums, a large upright stone marks the grave of newspaper editor and publisher Etta

Semple (1855-1914). A plaque on the unhewn stone contains an inscription describing this beloved woman as a freethinker, radical, socialist, feminist, sanitarium founder, and champion of the downtrodden. The Semple stone stands in the middle section of the west side.

Mug Shot Coffee:

110 S. Main. Enter from the alley between Main and Walnut. Old photography equipment on the interior brick and rock walls is your backdrop for enjoying a good mug of coffee. Monday-Saturday 6:30 a.m.-6 p.m.; Sunday 8 a.m.-7 p.m. 785.229.0481. FB.

Luigi's Italian Restaurant:

127 S. Main. Like his sister's restaurant (see p. 146) in Leavenworth, John Marino serves excellent Italian cuisine. Regulars recommend the Shrimp Champagne, Chicken Piccata, Chef's Special, or pizza. Limoncello Cake or Cannoli's for dessert are delizioso! Tuesday-Sunday 11 a.m.- 8 p.m. 785.242.2988. FB.

Smoked Creations BBQ:

222 E. Logan. The owners pride themselves in unique culinary creations including the mac-n-cheese burger and the barbecue burrito. It's all smokin' good. Daily 11 a.m.-8 p.m. 785.242.4227. smokedcreationsbbq.com.

Riverside Diner: 212 N. Main. On the banks above the Marais des Cygnes, this new diner offers homey and comfort (both in atmosphere and food!) along with friendly service. Monday-Saturday 7 a.m.-8 p.m.; Sunday 7 a.m.-4 p.m. 785.242.3463. FB.

Lodging: explorefranklincountyks.com.

explorer extras...
In Ottawa

When the Flint Hills Nature Trail for hiking, biking, and equestrians is finished, it will be 117 miles long between Osawatomie and Herington. Although most of the trail is under development, the 20-mile stretch between Ottawa and Quenemo is complete. The iron railroad bridge that crosses the Marais des Cygnes River, about 1½ miles west of Ottawa, is a scenic spot and within reach with a moderate walk. The trailhead is at E. 7th and Mason. kanzatrails.org.

The former Ottawa High School (NRHP) and Junior High School (NRHP), 526 and 506 N. Main, respectively, are examples of the Collegiate Gothic Revival style. The 1917 high school was designed by George P. Washburn & Son and the 1927 junior high by Washburn and Stookey.

Clarence, son of George P. Washburn, designed the house (NRHP) at 306 S. Elm in 1899 when he was only 17.

The historic Dietrich Cabin (NRHP) was originally built in 1859 and was moved to City Park, 500 block of S. Main, in 1960.

When the Marais des Cygnes River rose to 32 feet in May 2015, massive flood gates were rolled into place and successfully averted disaster. Because of the town's flooding history, the flood control project was completed in 1962. From 1st, ½ block north on Main.

Just south of the flood gates, large iron cutouts represent Victorian buildings that once graced downtown.

The Franklin County Veterans Memorial, 315 S. Main, was dedicated in November of 1999.

If your dog needs a stretch, take it to Bark Park in the northeast corner of Forest Park, N. Locust and W. K-68. FB. **ee**

POMONA

Population 952

Appanoose Area Museum:
600 Shawnee. From K-68, 6 miles north on Colorado, then ½ mile west on Shawnee. The history of surrounding small towns, a covered wagon replica, a 1920 farm kitchen, and more are found at the museum housed in the former 1934 Appanoose High School. June-August, Sunday 2-4 p.m. 785.665.7576.

Woodland Cemetery:
From Madison, ¾ mile west on K-68. The 36-foot-tall granite obelisk marks the resting place of Dr. Henry and Agnes Johnson. Their marker's inspiring inscription begins, "Broad active minds ever seeking truth . . . ."

Buzzard's Pizza:
410 E. Franklin. Folks flock in for the pizza, known for its fresh and heaping toppings. Daily 11 a.m.-9 p.m. 785.566.8383.

LeRoy's BBQ:
203 E. Franklin. Smoked ham, pork brisket, or pork sausage are perfect with the sunny-side up eggs or in an omelet. LeRoy's is also well known for hand-pattied burgers topped with a variety of smoked meats and lip-smackin', finger-lickin' good barbeque sauce. Tuesday-Friday, Sunday 7 a.m.-2 p.m.; Saturday 7 a.m.-7 p.m. 785.566.3833. leroysbbq.net.

PRINCETON

Population 271

Prairie Spirit Trail:
From U.S. 59, ½ mile west on High, then just north on Galveston. The trailhead here is 9½ miles south of the trailhead in Ottawa (*see* p. 120), perfect for a hike or bike ride. bikeprairiespirit.com.

Brand'N Iron Bar & Grill:
1457 U.S. 59 (behind the liquor store and gas station). What a find! The Roecker family has created a great dining atmosphere and a place to serve beef and pork raised by the family and other Franklin County farmers. The brand here is happy people serving delicious food, from appetizers to desserts. Wednesday-Thursday 4-9 p.m.; Friday-Saturday 11 a.m.-10 p.m. 785.937.2225. thebrandniron.com.

RANTOUL

Population 183

Dodson International World Headquarters:
2155 Vermont. From Main, ¾ mile south on McGinnis (becomes Vermont). It appears to be an airplane graveyard but it's actually one of the world's largest aviation parts suppliers. Should you need any assurance that you've found the place,

look for the Jetstar plane on the pedestal. Since 1984 the company has disassembled more than 3,500 aircraft of nearly every shape, size, and model, and it has more than five million parts in stock available to aviation customers globally. Drive by only. dodson.com.

WELLSVILLE

Population 1,595

Grandma Layton:
Wellsville's own Elizabeth "Grandma" Layton has left a remarkable legacy nationwide. Experiencing severe depression during the 1940s, she battled her illness with art. This talented and amazing woman took her first art class when she was 68. Her compelling self-portraits address a wide variety of social issues including AIDS, censorship, the right to die, aging, and loneliness. Some of her originals are displayed in the Wellsville Public Library, 115 W. 6th. Monday-Wednesday, Friday 8 a.m.-5:30 p.m.; Saturday 8:30 a.m.-12:30 p.m. 785.883.2870.

Wellsville Historical Museum:
517 Main. Preserved here is the community's heritage, which includes items once belonging to the town's famous citizen, artist Grandma Layton. Displayed are her original artworks, art supplies, desk, and wedding dress. Saturday 9 a.m.-3 p.m. 785.883.4255. wellsvillehistoricalsociety.org.

Wellsville Bank Building (NRHP):
418 Main. Constructed circa 1885, this structure is one of only a few remaining commercial buildings from the 1880-1890 era.

Rock Creek School:
W. 231 and Pressonville (Miami County). From K-33, 2½ miles east on Stafford (becomes 231). This picturesque little red-brick rural schoolhouse educated students from 1910 to 1966. In 1974 community volunteers purchased the building for $1 and it is now a sweet setting for community suppers, reunions, weddings, and other events.

Chely Wright:
From E. 10th, just north on Poplar. A sign at the city entrance proclaims

NE

that Wellsville is home to Chely Wright, award-winning country music singer.

Smokey's BBQ and Cafe:
510 Main. Along with the barbeque meats, be sure to sample the smoky flavored beans, creamy homemade cole slaw, and the honey apple cornbread. Monday-Saturday 7 a.m.-8 p.m.; Sunday 8 a.m.-2 p.m. 785.883.4119. FB.

Lodging: The Orchard House (785.418.9957, dunnslanding.com).

WILLIAMSBURG

Population 370

Williamsburg Community Museum:
309 S. East. Historic school items, mining artifacts, and veterans' memorabilia help tell the community story. June-August, second and fourth Sunday, 2-4 p.m. 785.746.8830.

Guy & Mae's Tavern
(8 Wonders of Kansas Cuisine): 119 W. William. Customers from across the nation continue to find their way to downtown Williamsburg for the "world's best ribs" at Guy and Mae's. This popular place sells 900 to 1,000 slabs of ribs a week, which equates to 65 tons a year! They're not only good, they're a tradition! Tuesday-Saturday 11 a.m.-12 a.m. 785.746.8830. tinyurl.com/guyandmaes.

Pome on the Range Orchards and Winery:
2050 Idaho. From I-35 exit 176, ¼ mile south on Idaho. Come out to the Range and pick seasonal produce or buy products in the country store. Don't miss tasting or taking home some apple and apple-blended Pome on the Range wine. Monday-Saturday 10 a.m.-5 p.m.; Sunday 12-5 p.m. 785.746.5492. pomeontherange.com.

Geary County

AROUND THE COUNTY

Creek Road Adventures:
If you're driving I-70 in Riley, Geary, or Wabaunsee Counties, a back-road change of pace is only an exit away. Any exit named for a creek (Clarks Creek, Humboldt Creek, McDowell Creek, Deep Creek) is a scenic route, winding and twisting through woods and pasture-land, past old barns, and over bridges. Start by heading south from the interstate then follow your nose.

Geary State Fishing Lake
Waterfalls: From I-70 exit 295, 6½ miles south on U.S. 77, then ½ mile west on State Lake. Keith Stokes, Kansas Explorer #4392, says that after a rain the 35-foot drop creates one of the most beautiful waterfalls in the state. From the parking lot near the northeast side of the dam, walk across the dam, and at the far end, look for a steep path to the north and listen for gurgling water. tinyurl.com/kswaterfalls.

Indian Monument:
From I-70 exit 299, 4 miles south and west on J Hill, then just southeast on Skiddy. Stay on the alert to see the Indian statue standing on a pasture hilltop on the east side of the road. In 1920 landowner Robert Henderson asked artist D.C. Smith to create this concrete statue, which memo-rializes Coronado's legendary visit through the area and honors the Quivira Indians who inhabited this land. Over the years it has deteriorated due to weather and vandalism, but it is still a reminder of this region's rich history.

Old Katy Bridge (NRHP):
From I-70 exit 299, 6½ miles south on J Hill (becomes Lyons Creek), then ½ mile south on Otter Creek. Converted from rail to vehicle use in 1974, this Pratt truss bridge was built in 1895 over Lyons Creek for use by the railroad.

Conroe Bridge (NRHP):
From I-70 exit 303, ½ mile south on Clarks Creek, then ¾ mile east on Ascher. This pony single-arch bridge was completed on Christmas Eve 1925. It was designed by James Marsh, a pioneer in steel and concrete bridge construc-tion, whose bridges are often referred to as rainbow arch.

FORT RILEY

For security purposes, visitors must stop at the Visitor Control Center before entering the fort. From I-70 exit 301, ¼ mile northwest on Henry. All visitors over age 16 must present a valid driver's license. Those from Minnesota, Missouri, and Washington must also provide an additional form of identifica-tion. To move through security more quickly, prior to your visit contact the control center. 785.239.2982. tinyurl.com/fortrileysecurity.

Fort History:
Fort Riley (NRHP; 8 Wonders of Kansas History) was named for Major General Bennett C. Riley who led the first military escort on the Santa Fe Trail in 1829. Built in 1853, the fort was one of a series of military posts founded to protect settlers and traders crossing Kansas to the West. It played a vital peacekeeping role during the 1850s Kansas territorial period, and after the Civil War it became a staging area for troops. The fort has served as a training center during all major wars of the 20th and 21st centuries. A drive through the historic post takes you along curving lanes and shaded environs past the many limestone homes, halls, monuments, and much more. tinyurl.com/fortrileytour.

Custer House: 24 Sheridan. A white picket fence surrounds the only double set of officers' quarters remaining from the fort's early history. The rooms contain period furniture from the late-19th century and offer a glimpse of, what one officer's wife described as the "glittering misery" of army life. Memorial Day-Labor Day, Monday-Saturday 10 a.m.-4 p.m.; Sunday 1-4 p.m. 785.239.2737.

First Infantry Division Museum: Bldg. 207, Custer. Known as the Big Red One, the First Infantry Division was created in 1917 by General John J. Pershing. Its very storied history is told through exhibits that take you through the many wars in which First Division soldiers have participated, from WWI through present operations in the Middle East. Monday-Saturday 10 a.m.-4 p.m.; Sunday 1-4 p.m. 785.239.2737.

Fort Riley Regimental Museum: Bldg. 207, Custer. Chronicling the history of units assigned to Fort Riley and the U.S. Constabulary, exhibits focus on the training and combat operations of Fort Riley units. Monday-Saturday 10 a.m.-4 p.m.; Sunday 1-4 p.m. 785.239.2737.

U.S. Cavalry Museum: Bldg. 205, Henry. This excellent facility showcases the colorful history of the American horse soldier, from the Revolutionary War to 1950. The 1855 limestone building with a clock tower has housed the museum since 1957. Monday-Saturday 9 a.m.-4:30 p.m.; Sunday 12-4:30 p.m. 785.239.2737.

***Duty* Statue:** Henry and Custer. The 2003 sculpture by James Nathan Muir pays tribute to all cavalrymen and their mounts. The impressive statue depicts horse and soldier in 1920s-1930s tack and attire.

Civil War Horse and Mule Memorial: Sheridan and Henry. This poignant sculpture by artist Tessa Pullan of a noble and weary war horse was erected in 1997 "In memory of the one and one half million horses and mules of the Union and Confederate armies who were killed or wounded or died from disease in the Civil War." This one will tug at your heartstrings.

Old Trooper Monument and Chief's Grave: Sheridan and Forsyth (cavalry parade field). Tall and stately, the sculpture of horse and rider memorializes Fort Riley's horse cavalry. In front of the statue is the gravesite of Chief, the last cavalry mount registered on government payroll. Born in 1932, Chief arrived at Fort Riley in 1941 and was retired in 1949. He died at the fort in 1968 and was buried with full military honors. A special casket allowed Chief to be buried standing up.

Great War Memorial: Huebner and E. This vicinity was home to Camp Funston, a vast training facility where more than 50,000 men prepared to serve in WWI. The memorial, erected immediately after Armistice Day in 1918, honors those "who trained at Camp Funston for the Great War 1917-1919."

More Monuments: Among the fort's many memorials is the obelisk (Sheridan and Henry) dedicated to those who died supporting the global war on terrorism. A plaque (Sheridan and Henry) recognizes the

Ninth Armored Division's feat during WWII. The 1923 Ogden monument (Brick Row and Huebner) pays tribute to Major E.A. Ogden, the "Father of Fort Riley." The memorial (Sheridan and Huebner) to the cavalrymen who died at the 1890 Wounded Knee massacre was erected by soldiers who had survived the tragedy.

Post Cemetery: 191 Huebner. Simple white crosses leave powerful messages in this nearly full cemetery. Markers noting the mass graves of those who died in the 1855 and 1867 cholera epidemics stand in the cemetery's southeast corner. Graves in the oldest section include those of Confederate soldiers from the Civil War. German and Italian World War II prisoners of war are buried near the soldiers who were killed at the battle of Wounded Knee.

Mounted Color Guard Stable: Bldg. 275, Henry. Teaching cavalry tactics and maintaining horses played integral roles in army life when Fort Riley became the site of the U.S. Cavalry School in 1887. As wars modernized, however, horses' use diminished and finally ended in 1949. Horses returned to the fort in 1992 with the founding of the Commanding General's Mounted Color Guard. This unit, outfitted in Civil War period gear, honors the horse and horse soldier with demonstrations at events and official ceremonies. An 1889 limestone stable houses the color guard mounts. You may walk its old

NE

cobblestone hallway to see the horses and their dates of service posted at each stall. Monday-Friday 10 a.m. to 3 p.m.

St. Mary's Chapel: 3 Barry. This small chapel behind the 1897 Main Post Chapel is recognized as the first stone chapel erected in Kansas.

First Territorial Capitol State Historic Site

(NRHP): 693 Huebner. Interpretive exhibits inside the limestone structure explain the building's many uses during the past century and a half. Originally used as a warehouse, it was hardly completed when it served as the first territorial capitol of Kansas and briefly housed the 1855 "bogus" legislature. April-October, Saturday 10 a.m.-5 p.m.; Sunday 12-5 p.m. Admission charge. 785.784.5535. kshs.org.

GRANDVIEW PLAZA

Population 1,717

When the First Division moved to Fort Riley from Fort Polk, Louisiana, in 1955 it created a need for more housing. This housing area, primarily for the military, was incorporated as Grandview Plaza in 1963.

Stacy's Restaurant: 118 W. Flint Hills (I-70 exit 299). This sweet little Valentine Diner has been a mainstay for local folks and travelers since 1954. The home cooking and the coconut cream and two-crust raisin pie keep the parking lot packed. Monday-Saturday 5 a.m.-3 p.m.; Sunday 7 a.m.-2 p.m. 785.238.3039. FB.

JUNCTION CITY

Population 25,388

Heritage Park and Civil War Memorial Arch: 6th

and Washington. Enter the park through the striking 1898

GAR Civil War Memorial arch. Enhancing the green space are numerous and moving memorials to the military and law enforcement as well as a historic bandstand and working fountain. 785.238.2885.

Buffalo Soldier Memorial: 18th and Buffalo Soldier. A nine-foot bronze statue of a buffalo soldier and his horse is dedicated to the Ninth and Tenth Cavalry regiments, black units that held the epithet "buffalo soldiers." Plaques in the courtyard tell their intriguing story. The nearby

houses, designated for buffalo soldiers in the 1940s, are the last remaining quarters built for these soldiers and their families during segregation. 785.238.2885. tinyurl.com/9thcavalry.

Geary County Courthouse: 138 E. 8th. Architect J.C. Holland designed this grand 1900 limestone structure in the Romanesque Revival style. Drive by only.

C.L. Hoover Opera House

(NRHP): 135 W. 7th. The beautiful 1882 red-brick and limestone opera house with a four-face working clock tower

experienced many renovations until it finally closed (as a movie theater) in 1982. With a restoration completed in 2008, this structure once again serves as a state-of-the-art performing and visual arts and civic center. Colorful murals in the lobby feature characters, history, and buildings in early Junction City. 785.238.3906. jcoperahouse.org.

Rathert Stadium: 900 W. 13th. Built in 1938 by the WPA, this stone stadium with old-time wooden bleacher seats and roof was renovated in 2005. Known as one of the most historic stadiums in the Midwest, it is now home to the summer league collegiate baseball team, the Junction City Generals. junctioncitygenerals.com.

Geary County Historical Museum (NRHP): 530 N.

Adams. Fred Bramlage bought this 1904 Junction City high school and donated it to the historical society in 1982. Today this three-story limestone building preserves the county's past. Exhibits include those on the Kansa, Osage, Pawnee, and Wichita tribes and on the history of Fort Riley. April-October, Tuesday-Sunday 1-4 p.m.; November-March, Tuesday-Saturday 1-4 p.m. Donation welcomed. 785.238.1666. gchsweb.org.

Pelican Pete's: 103 S. Washington. At first you might think this is someone's house with a yard full of kitschy nautical lawn art. But Pete's is a business, and a Junction City institution, selling shaved ice in millions of flavors. Try

something different, like a watermelon-lime-peach combo. June-October, daily 12-11 p.m. 785.238.7947.

Pusan Diner: 1634 N. Washington. For 30 years locals, soldiers, and visitors have been extolling the virtues of this unpretentious diner. Served in carry-out containers, the food is some of the best Korean in the state. Pusan is known for its bulgogi-marinated beef, chicken wings, and kimchee, and the owner and staff are glad to help explain the menu. Tuesday-Saturday 11 a.m.-7 p.m. 785.238.8848.

Seoul Oriental Restaurant and Market: 204 Grant. The large menu features beef, chicken, pork, and seafood dishes along with stews, rice, and noodles. A buffet weekdays at noon and Friday and Saturday evenings is your opportunity to try new dishes. At the market next door pick up ingredients to make your own Korean edibles. Monday-Saturday 11 a.m.-8 p.m.; Sunday 1:00-8 p.m. 785.238.3387. seouloriental restaurant.com.

Bella Italian: 605 N. Washington. A family-owned business, it uses recipes

handed down through generations. Choose from chicken parmesan, stuffed mushrooms, homemade bread, and much more in this historic downtown setting. Daily 11 a.m.-10 p.m. 785.762.1772.

Cox Bros. BBQ: 812 E. Chestnut (I-70 exit 298). Like all barbecue masters, brothers Bud and Bobby Cox spent thousands of hours perfecting their culinary craft. From the ribs to the pulled pork it's all finger-lickin' good! Daily 11 a.m.-9 p.m. 785.579.6606. coxbbq.com.

La Fiesta: 503 E. Chestnut. It's all tasty and authentic Mexican at La Fiesta. Watch out, the salsa is addictive! Monday-Thursday 11 a.m.-10 p.m.; Friday-Saturday 11 a.m.-11 p.m.; Sunday 11 a.m.-9 p.m. 785.579.4002.

Negril Caribbean Restaurant: 127 W. 7th. Owner Alan White, originally from Jamaica and later a Fort Riley soldier, opened this little place named for a Jamaican town. The flavors of Jamaica add a perfect touch to the chicken and shrimp curry, jerk chicken, escovitch fish (fried and marinated with a peppery vinaigrette), and curried goat. Monday-Saturday 11 a.m.-9 p.m. 785.238.1086.

Hildebrand Farms Dairy: 5210 W. Rucker. From Washington, 4¼ miles west on 8th (becomes K-18), 1 mile north on Gfeller, then ¾ mile west on Rucker. At this dairy farm you can buy glass-bottled milk right where it is produced. Also available in the retail store are flavored milk, soft-serve ice cream, meats, and other Kansas products. The dairy cows, milking barn, and processing plant are nearby. Monday-Friday 9 a.m.-6 p.m.; Saturday 9 a.m.-3 p.m. 785.762.6455. hildebrandfarmsdairy.com.

Freedom Park: From I-70 exit 301, 100 yards south on Kennel to a parking lot. Follow a short path to a steep zigzagging stairway that takes you past military equipment as you make your assent. At the top, atomic cannon "Atomic Annie"—and a great view of the city—await you. The cannon is remarkable—42-feet in length, 42,500 pounds in weight, and can travel 35 miles per hour. The big gun was activated in 1952 and deactivated in 1963.

Spring Valley Heritage Site: From U.S. 77, ½ mile west on K-18, then just south on Spring Valley. This site comprises a collection of historic structures including a restored 19th-century schoolhouse; a pony barn; and a one-room log cabin. Also moved onto the site is the 1857 Wetzel Log Cabin (NRHP). A stone marker designates the cabin's original location. From I-70 exit 300, 2¾ miles east and south on K-57, then 1½ miles south on Clarks Creek. 785.238.1666.

Lodging: junctioncity.org.

NE

explorer extras... In Junction City

The Kansas River runs 174 miles from Junction City to Kansas City, and the Kansas River Trail allows you to explore that area's natural beauty from a new perspective—from the river itself. The Kansas River Trail is the second in the nation to be designated a National Water Trail. The nearest access point is from N. Washington, 2¼ miles northeast on Grant. ksrivertrail.com.

Between 7th and 9th on Washington, downtown offers a stretch of restored limestone and brick buildings (NRHP), many designed with wide transoms and outstanding cornices. Limestone churches, the handsome firehouse, and the municipal building are but a few of the town's bevy of vintage structures. Kiosks in each block provide photos and histories of these buildings.

An obelisk at Washington and Ash recognizes Francisco Vazquez de Coronado's 1541 expedition that is thought to have come through this area during his search for Quivira.

J Hill, I-70 exit 299, is so named for the large stone J lying on the hillside to the south of I-70. It was first placed there around 1928, and for years it was the high school seniors' job to keep the stones painted white. **ee**

MILFORD

Population 598

In 1961 the citizens of Milford voted to relocate the community to accommodate the scheduled construction of Milford Dam. In 1965 the original townsite of Milford was bulldozed and now lies under the waters of Milford Lake.

Milford Museum: 101 11th. Exhibits tell the incredible story of Dr. John R. Brinkley, the "goat gland doctor" who became famous during the 1920s for surgically implanting goat glands in humans to treat male impotence. The flamboyant Brinkley started Kansas' first radio station, KFKB, which helped spread his fame nationwide. Other museum displays examine old Milford and the town's "moving" experience. Call ahead, 785.463.5490.

Milford Lake and State Park: From Milford, 4¾ miles south on U.S. 77, 1 mile west on K-57, then west on State Park. The Fishing Capital of Kansas, Milford is the largest man-made lake in the state. Dedicated in 1968, it was authorized by the Flood Control Act of 1954 and was designed for flood control,

water supply, and recreation/wildlife. State park entrance charge. 785.238.3014. ksdoutdoors.com.

Milford Nature Center: 3415 Hatchery. From Milford, 4¾ miles south on U.S. 77, 3¼ miles southwest on K-57, then ¼ mile north on Hatchery. Inside are nature exhibits, and outside is a Kansas-themed playground complete with an oversized "eagle's nest" (one you can roost in!). A short nature trail leads you by the lake and through a tunnel of branches. During the season, butterflies will tickle your nose in the butterfly garden. Year round, Monday-Friday 9 a.m.-4:30 p.m.; April-September, Saturday-Sunday 1-5 p.m. 785.238.5323. tinyurl.com/milnature.

Lake Rentals: Rent a kayak, canoe, pontoon, or stand-up board and have tons of fun on Milford Lake. acornsresortkansas.com; flagstoprvpark.com.

Milford Tropics Restaurant: 103 11th. Dining and spirits, as the sign says, are mainstays in the Tropics. Island apparel will match the tropical decor, but dress as you wish to enjoy drinks, crab legs, pizza, wings, and more. Daily 11 a.m.-12 a.m. 785.463.5551.

The Cove Bar and Grill: 3710 Farnum Creek. From I-70 exit 295, 11¼ miles north on U.S. 77, ¼ mile west into the Farnum Creek area, then ½ mile north on the service road. Also accessible by boat. This roomy, family-oriented restaurant offers a classy environment and a spectacular view of Milford Lake. Dining (inside or out) at sunset is a winning plan. Choose from steaks, burgers, tacos, salads, and more. A full bar is available. Daily 11 a.m.-10 p.m. 785.463.4000. acornsresortkansas.com.

Lodging: Acorns Resort (785.463.4000, acornsresortkansas.com); Flagstop Resort and RV Park (785.463.5537, flagstoprvpark.com).

Jackson County

AROUND THE COUNTY

Battle of the Spurs Historical Marker: From 4th in Holton, 7½ miles north on U.S. 75 to 286. With 11 liberated slaves from Missouri, abolitionist John Brown reached an Underground Railroad stop just south of this marker in January 1859. When a federal posse attempted to block Brown's passage, he crossed the high-water creek and charged toward his would-be assailants. The posse spurred their horses and fled from this bloodless battle.

CIRCLEVILLE

Population 169

Circleville Cemetery Hitching Rails: From Lincoln, ½ mile west on Mill (becomes 254), then ½ mile south on J. The historic hitching rails standing on either side of the cemetery entrance are recognized as the longest ones remaining in the state.

**explorer extras...
In Delia**

Population 168

The son of an air force pilot, Thomas Abernathy has turned his keen interest in aircraft into

an eye-catching hobby. He collects airplane parts, paints them in colorful fashion, and places them on top of his garage at 327 Nora. You're welcome to look and enjoy his folk art from the street or alley. **ee**

HOLTON

Population 3,278

Jackson County Courthouse:
400 New York. Built in the Modern Eclecticism style, the tan-brick structure with limestone trim features interior marble walls, staircases and original tile floors. At the district court office ask to see the oil paintings by a prisoner held in the courthouse jail in 1938. Monday-Friday 9 a.m.-5 p.m.

Courthouse Grounds:
Features include the Fallen Soldier Memorial to Sergeant Bernie Deghand killed in action in 2006. A brick walkway leading to the memorial honors those from the community who died in wars from the Civil War to the present. In a separate area a cannon dedicated to the soldiers and sailors of the Civil War stands beside a delightful water garden pool filled with goldfish and lilies. Elsewhere on the grounds is an 1880 horse watering trough accompanied by a historic hand pump.

Downtown:
Heritage Walk through downtown, initiated by George Gantz in the early

1990s, includes benches, landscaping, and old-fashioned street lamps along the red-brick sidewalks that lead to many historic buildings. Surrounding the courthouse square are many great shopping options including the Golden Fleece (413 New York); Heart to Home (105 W. 4th); and Jayhawk TV & Appliance (435 New York). 785.364.3963.

The Gossip:
118 E. 5th. Owner Carolyn McKee will tell you that "rumors are of an eclectic style here." Enter through the classy recessed entrance of the 1924 Gossip Printery building to find antiques, repurposed and vintage items, furniture, and local art—and good Holton energy. Wednesday-Friday 9 a.m.-5 p.m.; Saturday 10 a.m.-2 p.m. 785.305.0605. thegossipholton.com.

Quilting on the Square:
400 Pennsylvania. Brightly colored quilt blocks adorn the green facade of this red-brick, turn-of-the-century building.

Fabrics line the walls of the renovated historic interior where you'll enjoy shopping and sharing quilt talk. Monday-Friday 10 a.m.-7 p.m.; Saturday 10 a.m.-5 p.m. 785.364.4050. quiltingonthesquare.com.

More Than Lemons:
424 Pennsylvania. April Lemon has lovingly brought back the shine to the original wood floors, cabinets, and pressed-tin ceiling inside this 1889 building to create a quality shop displaying and selling local artwork. She operates her glass-blowing studio in the back, and on Saturdays (if you call ahead) she'll teach you to blow glass. On Thursdays and Saturdays you are welcome in the studio to watch her work. Monday, Thursday-Saturday 10 a.m.-7 p.m. 785.383.2849. FB.

Koger Variety:
415 New York. This five-and-dime throwback has it all including a working 1920s soda fountain. Monday-Saturday 9 a.m.-4:30 p.m.; Sunday 12-3:30 p.m. 785.364.3321.

Penny's:
409 New York. This 1938 J.C. Penney building is now a tasty spot serving specialty coffees and drinks plus a variety of baked goods. If owner Erin Lassey isn't busy, ask to see how she has converted the rest of the old store into an event center. Monday-Thursday 7 a.m.-5 p.m.; Friday 7 a.m.-2 p.m.; Saturday 8 a.m.-12 p.m. 785.362.6043. FB.

Historic Bank Building (NRHP):
101 W. 4th. The attractive two-story, tan-brick building with red sandstone

NE

trim was built in 1906 as the State Bank of Holton. Now home to Kellerman Insurance, it has retained original interior features including the wooden and marble counter and the iron radiator embossed with the likeness of a child's face. You're welcome to go and take a look. Monday-Friday 8 a.m.-5 p.m. 785.364.2921.

Jackson County Museum: 327 New York. Home to a tin shop when it opened in 1904, this building still has its original pressed-tin ceiling. Artifacts date to 1854 and tell the county story, from its territorial days to education development including the opening of Campbell College in 1882. A collection of WPA dolls also are displayed. May-October, Friday 10 a.m.-4 p.m. Donation welcome. 785.364.2087.

Roebke House Memorial: 216 New York. Fine collections of Victorian-era clothing and wedding gowns are on display inside this 1875 home. A Victorian lace room and an exhibit of children's toys and clothing are special features. Admission charge. By appointment. 785.364.4991.

Big Oak: 7th and Oak. The Searles bur oak is so broad (its crown spreads more than 93 feet) you may wonder how it holds itself up! Experts think this tree was planted between 1792 and 1817.

Holton Bathhouse and Swimming Pool (NRHP): 711 Nebraska. A plaque at the swimming pool states that the first pool and bathhouse in Holton were built in 1936 as WPA projects. The original bathhouse is still used but the swimming pool has been modernized.

Linscott Park: 4th and Iowa (K-16). The handsome park sign depicts a handsome horse representing Otto (1886-1909),

a favorite horse of Holton banker Shepard Keene Linscott. Otto's final resting place is at the south end of the park beside the cement feed trough and is marked with a flat stone.

Dead Ringer: From U.S. 75, ½ mile west on 4th to Holton Cemetery. Because no one else would, Lyle Campbell placed a plaque by his gravestone that offers explanations of several grave expressions—"dead ringer," "saved by the bell," and "graveyard shift." His black granite gravestone at the west end of the cemetery is topped by a "Dead Ringer" silver bell.

Banner Creek Lake: 10975 K-16. From U.S. 75, 1¾ miles west on K-16, then just south to the park office. A fairly new reservoir, it was completed in 1997 as a water supply and for flood control. Bird watching, camping, and recreational opportunities are available, including a 13½-mile hiking and biking trail. Park entrance charge. 785.364.4236. jacksoncountyks.com.

Banner Creek Science Center & Observatory: 22275 N. From U.S. 75, 2½ miles west on K-16, ¾ mile south on N, then west into a driveway. Science and astronomy education come alive with hands-on activities for the youth. Stargazing opportunities will dazzle all ages. Observation activities are on Saturdays beginning at 8 p.m. 785.364.2641. bcscience.myevent.com.

5th Street Sandwich Shoppe: 126 W. 5th. Gourmet chef Adam Van Donge knows how to make a fantastic sandwich. Each month he presents five new specialty sandwiches (for example, sweet ham with sweet potato puree), and each week features a new soup and salad. Enjoy them all to the background tunes of Frank Sinatra or other Rat Pack crooners. Monday-Friday 11 a.m.-3 p.m. 785.362.7045. Go to 5thstreetsandwichshoppe.com to learn about scheduling a reservations-only, seven-course meal in the Drum Room.

Trails Cafe: 601 Arizona (U.S. 75). Broasted chicken, chicken Parmesan, Southern-fried catfish, homemade bread pudding, steaks, and Ooooey Goooey brownies ala mode make the trail to this cafe well traveled! Daily 10:30 a.m.-9 p.m. 785.364.2786. trails-cafe.com.

Boomers' Steakhouse and Grill: 401 Colorado. Pete and Gloria Stavropoulos are baby boomers, thus the name of their restaurant. They also are doing a booming business and are known for their ribeye steaks, fish and chips, strawberry pie—and friendly service. Daily 11 a.m.-9 p.m. 785.364.2468. boomerssteakhouse.com.

Off the Square Bar and Grill: 325 New York. Bring family and friends for great bar food. Where? Just off the square! Grill hours, Monday-Saturday 11 a.m.-2 p.m. and 5-8 p.m. 785.364.3400.

Lodging: Hotel Josephine (785.364.3151, hoteljosephine.com).

explorer extras... In Holton

The concrete-block house at 4th and Kansas was ordered from the 1908 Sears, Roebuck & Co.

catalog. The blocks were made on site with a concrete-block machine also ordered via the catalog. Drive by only.

The McFadden House (NRHP), 315 W. 5th, is one of Kansas' Lustron homes, pre-fabri-cated, all-steel residences built following World War II to help solve the nation's severe housing shortage.

A bronze plaque mounted on a glacial stone at 416 Ohio states that this spot is the birthplace of the city of Holton. The marker further notes the location of the 1856 Jim Lane fort, named to honor free-state supporter James Lane.

Dan Harris welcomes you to take a seat on the wooden bleachers of the Holton Livestock Exchange sale barn at 13788 K-16, east of town. Sale days are Tuesdays starting at noon. The sale barn cafe opens early for breakfast and serves lunch too. 785.364.7137. holtonlivestock.com. **ee**

HOYT

Population 658

City Park: Look closely at the restroom building—the "bricks" are painted on, and likewise is the picturesque scene. Volunteers, with help from students, are credited for this park's beauty. From 4th, ¼ mile north on Highland, then just northwest on Park.

Historic Jail: 6th and Highland (Robinson Park). Dating to 1911, the tiny jail is the oldest building in town. Note the jail's barn-like rounded concrete roof.

Bailey's: 113 E. 4th. Home cooking is the business of this family-owned restaurant. A full breakfast menu includes made-from-scratch cinnamon rolls. Lunch, dinner, and daily specials are equally popular. Evenings feature terrific steaks and all the trimmings. Wednesday 6:30 a.m.-1 p.m.; Thursday-Saturday 6:30 a.m.-9 p.m. 785.986.6165. FB.

MAYETTA

Population 331

Prairie Band of the Potawatomi Nation:
The Potawatomi tribe arrived in this area in 1846. At that time their reservation covered 900 square miles and was promised by treaty to be the Potawatomis' home for all time. However, by the end of the 1860s the reservation had been reduced to only 121 square miles. The National Indian Gaming Act of 1988, which provided for gaming casinos, has helped the tribe improve the infra-structure of the reservation and create job opportunities for tribal and nontribal individuals. 785.966.4005. pbpdindiantribe.com.

Tribal Government Center:
16281 Q. From 1st, ¾ mile west on 162, then ¼ mile north on Q. The Tribal Council is the elected government of the Potawatomi Nation and is responsible for all programs and operations including roads and bridges, Tribal Court, early childhood services, and buffalo stocking. This new center was built in 1999 with Potawatomi Nation resources largely drawn from gaming revenue. Drive by only. 785.966.4000.

Prairie People's Park:
From U.S. 75, 5 miles west on 158, then ½ mile south on M. The striking arched entrance, a Merriell Wahwasuck replica of

the Potawatomi Nation's tribal seal, leads you to the powwow grounds, the centerpiece of this impressive complex. Veterans memorials are a moving testament to tribal members who have served their country.

K-Road Community Complex:
From U.S. 75, 6¾ miles east on 158, then ½ mile south on K. Revenue from the casino is making a positive impact on the lives of those on the Potawatomi Reservation and in surrounding areas. This community center comprises the Elder Center, Boys and Girls Club, early childhood programs, a language program, and community health programs. It also supports an orchard, numerous housing develop-ments, and a fire department.

NETAWAKA

Population 144

Netawaka is the Kickapoo word for "high view." You'll find one of the highest points in the vicinity northwest of Netawaka at U.S. 75 and K-9.

Petersen Memorial Highway:
In 1990 the Kansas legislature designated the 10-mile stretch of U.S. 75 from Holton to Netawaka the Danny J. Petersen Memorial Highway. The road pays tribute to Specialist Fourth Class Petersen, the only Kansan awarded the Congressional Medal of Honor for service in the Vietnam War. Petersen's final resting place is in Netawaka Cemetery, ½ mile east of U.S. 75 on K-9. His grave is in the

NE

cemetery's northeast quadrant and is marked by a simple white military stone.

Whiteway Street: This street is one of only a few remaining references to the Great White Way marketing plan that originated in 1914 to promote businesses along what was then a gravel route. Because it was before the days of billboards and advertising signs, the promoters painted every other telephone pole white from Chicago to Colorado Springs, 1,161 miles, to draw attention to the highway. The current K-9 highway was the Kansas portion of the Great White Way.

SOLDIER

Population 140

Roller Coaster Hills: For good reason the locals call the hills on K-62 going north from K-16 the "roller coaster hills." Take the drive—guaranteed you'll feel the thrill!

Post Office: The double-arch entrance of the current post office (a former bank) matches those on the brick buildings in Goff and Corning (Nemaha County). While you're here, buy some stamps to help keep this beautiful post office operating. Monday-Friday 8 a.m.-12 p.m.; Saturday 8-10 a.m.

Historic Hand Pump: A little white structure protects the historic hand pump at 1st and Jackson (K-62 and 270). The local Extension Homemakers Unit

erected a plaque in the 1970s that tells us this was the site of the original town well in 1877.

Lodging: Red Rock Guest Ranch (785.834.2552, redrockguestranch.com).

WHITING

Population 186

Post Office: Spend some money for stamps and give the revenue a boost in this historic bank building turned post office. Monday-Friday 7:30-11:30 a.m.; Saturday 8-8:45 a.m. 785.873.3241.

Historic Whiting Station (NRHP): 204 Whiting. This iconic former service station, resembling a small home with a canopy, served motorists traveling on K-9 from 1928 to 1966. This style of architecture was popular in Kansas and said to appeal to early-day motorists by conveying the feeling of comfort, safety, and reliability.

Schlaegel's Home-Grown Popcorn: 31030 V. From K-9, 2 miles north on V. Gary and Marian Schlaegel dedicate 20 acres to growing popcorn. They sell it unpopped or popped in more than 20 flavors. One of the most popular is the chocolate drizzled! It's all scrumptious at Schlaegel's. Monday-Friday 8 a.m.-12 p.m. and 1-4 p.m. 800.844.7495. popcorngifts.net.

Whiting Cafe: 308 Whiting. This little white building sits right off the street all by itself, but you won't be alone inside! It's a cozy

joint with a horseshoe counter that seats 11, and the entire cafe has a total capacity of 25. Tell Rosa, the owner/cook, that you're exploring Kansas and she'll make you feel right at home. The setting is classic and so is the food—the mashed potatoes are "real" and the homemade pies have Crisco crusts. An exterior mural designed by Jim Stukey exclaims the food here is "so great, you'll scrape your plate." Pick up a whole pie (made fresh daily) and some of Rosa's yummy homemade chocolates. Monday-Thursday, Saturday 6 a.m.-2 p.m.; Friday 6 a.m.-8 p.m. 785.873.3125. FB.

Jefferson County

AROUND THE COUNTY

Perry Lake and State Park: From Meriden, 7 miles east and south on K-237. This lake and park offer the usual recreational opportunities. Serious hikers will enjoy the 30-mile Perry Lake Trail (Old Military Trail) along the east shore. State park entrance charge. Cabins available, reservations required. 785.246.3449. ksoutdoors.com.

MCLOUTH

Population 858

Rock in the Road: If you're on Granite between Cynthia and Lucy, watch out! There's no warning sign, no caution light, just a big glacial boulder parked in the middle of the street.

It's the darndest sight. You're welcome to stand on it, kiss it, take pictures of it! Apparently the rock was there long before the town, and when time came to build the street, the stubborn boulder simply couldn't be moved. The asphalt around it has built up over the years making the rock look much smaller than it really is.

JL Fabric: 218 S. Union. Your dollars will be well invested inside this 1882 former bank when you purchase any of JL's quilt fabrics and notions. Tuesday-Friday 10 a.m.-3 p.m.; Saturday 9:30 a.m.-1 p.m. 913.796.6287.

Historic Jail: North of JL Fabric. City Park hosts numerous memorials plus a concrete jail thought to have been built in the 1880s. Although seldom used in the old days, it was utilized in the 1920s to teach a lesson to some young boys for throwing hedge apples at the Methodist church.

Rose Park: 109 W. Gertrude. Rose Balao, longtime resident and community leader, donated the land for the park. Locals and visitors alike enjoy the challenging frisbee disc golf course, playground, and walking trail.

Population 1,084

Old Jefferson Town:
701 Walnut. Stroll through this preserved little village of yesterday. The showpiece is the 1900 boyhood home of artist John Steuart Curry (*see*

next entry), which contains an original Curry painting, family photos, his paintbrushes, copies of books that he illustrated, and more. Old Jefferson Town also comprises a chapel, bandstand, blacksmith shop, an 1875 bowstring truss bridge (NRHP), a sculpture of Samuel Peppard's famous wind wagon, plus other vintage structures. If the buildings are closed

you can still walk around the complex. May-September, Saturday-Sunday 1:30-5 p.m. 785.863.2070.

John Steuart Curry:
Born in the nearby community of Dunavant in 1897, Curry was one of the great Regionalist artists of the 1930s-1940s. Unfortunately Kansas state legislators didn't value his style, and a frustrated Curry refused to sign the state capitol murals that he'd been commissioned to paint. His most famous statehouse mural is *Tragic Prelude*, depicting John Brown.

Jefferson County Memorial Park: From K-92, ½ mile north on U.S. 59, then turn into the Jefferson County Law Enforcement Center and continue ¼ mile south to the park parking lot. Stretch your legs along this half-mile sidewalk trail through the horticultural park that honors those who served in the armed forces. Interpretive signs describe the well-established grasses, wildflowers, and forbs.

Country Corner Variety:
321 Jefferson. Enjoy floats, sodas, and malts at this nine-stool 1950s soda fountain

inside a modern variety store. Monday-Saturday 9 a.m.-5 p.m. 785.863.2200. FB.

Union Block (NRHP):
303 Jefferson. "Bank" is inscribed above one of the entrances and "1892" and "Union Block" above the other of this two-story, red-brick structure. The limestone arched entrance and window heads are particularly attractive. The building was designed to house four businesses including the State Bank of Oskaloosa which operated here until 1960.

Lodging: tinyurl.com/jfcolodge.

Population 634

Founded in 1855 and originally named Osawkee for a Sauk Indian chief, Ozawkie was the county's first county seat, a status it lost to Oskaloosa in 1858. In 1964 the town was forced to rebuild on higher ground a mile west of its original site due to the Perry Dam Project. the reservoir now surrounds the town on the north, east, and south.

Crooked Post Winery:
7397 K-92. From Kansa, 1 mile west on K-92. The winery was established in 2006 with six acres of French-American hybrid grapes. These have resulted in delicious wines such as Delaware River Red and Perry Sunset. Call ahead to order handmade pizza from a brick-fired oven to complement your wine tasting. Friday-Sunday 12-6 p.m. 785.876.9990. crookedpostvineyard.com.

PERRY

Population 899

Mitchell Memorial:

From Front, just south across tracks, then look 200 yards east into a field. The 32-foot marble obelisk stands in the middle of cropland and bears the inscription, "Given in loving memory of Amanda M. Mitchell by her son David Garrett Mitchell 1930." In his will David instructed that a park surround the memorial, but due to one thing and another the park never happened. The Mitchell family continues to own the farmland.

Historic Mural: 115 N. Elm.

A colorful 2012 mural featuring the Mitchell memorial, a storied tree, and a historic bridge is the backdrop for the annual town photo. For the last several years at the Perry Fall Festival, community members gather in front of the mural for a photograph which is framed and displayed at Community Hall, 506 E. Front.

Tree of Knowledge:

Elm and Front. The tree depicted in the mural (*see* previous entry) has been part of the town's history since 1895. An American elm sapling grew near the town well where retired men would gather to sit and talk. This spot acquired the name "Bum's Park," and the tree became known as "The Tree of Knowledge" owing to the men being "such a repository of wisdom." The tree eventually died from Dutch elm disease but an oak tree stands in its place.

Historic Bridge (NRHP):

From Main, ½ mile west on Bridge. This Parker truss bridge, built in 1926, spans the Delaware River. It is no longer open to vehicular or pedestrian traffic.

Willkomm Trail:

Main and Front. An arrow on a post rock sign points south toward the Kansas River to the trailhead. Taking you to the confluence of the Delaware and Kansas Rivers, the trail was established in 2014 and is named for longtime community leader and former mayor Mathew Willkomm.

Perry-Lecompton Community Library:

609 Cedar (in the Thriftway Store). When the grocery store closed its video department it donated the space to the community for a library. Volunteers, donations, and help from high school students make it work. It's a win-win for the community! Tuesday, Thursday 9 a.m.-12 p.m. and 4-7 p.m.; Saturday 11 a.m.-2 p.m. 785.597.5031.

American Legion Building:

191 Elm. The Perry Post 142 building was dedicated on Armistice Day, November 11, 1949. Used until a new structure was erected elsewhere in 1976, the beautiful rock building stands on the north side of City Hall. It is now a private residence.

Perry Bar and Grill:

215 E. Front. A colorful fish-and-flag mural on the front and a Harley riders mural on the east, both painted by Cesar DuBois, mark this popular watering hole. Motorcycle enthusiasts, locals, and visitors gather here for cold beers and pub food. Regulars swear by the hand-breaded pork tenders and fried pickle chips. Monday-Friday 11 a.m.-2 p.m. and 5-10 p.m.; Saturday-Sunday 11 a.m.-10 p.m. 785.597.5295. FB.

Lodging: Spirit Lake Lodge (785.597.5889, spiritlakekansas.com).

VALLEY FALLS

Population 1,159

Delaware River Composite Truss Bridge (NRHP):

From Broadway, ¼ mile north on Maple, then ¼ mile east and north on Mill. A rare example of a combination bridge, this 1936 steel structure (358 feet in length) is formed with a Parker truss centerpiece and flanked on both ends with Warren trusses. Regardless of the structural jargon, it's simply a striking bridge!

Valley Falls (Rosehill/Farrar) Cemetery:

From Walnut, ¼ mile west on Broadway, then ¾ mile south on Frazier. Mausoleum styles can vary dramatically. In this cemetery the white Piazzek mausoleum with a heavy stepped parapet and curved vault is an example of Exotic Revival architecture. The

neighboring Crosby family mausoleum was built in the Classical Revival style.

Old Water Tower Site:

900 block of Frazier (beside the water tower). Stones forming a large circle mark the site of an early wooden water tower. At the center, an 1888 concrete and stone marker inscribed "U.S. W. E. & P.C." recognizes the U.S. Wind Engine & Pump Company of Batavia, Illinois, that built the town's waterworks

system. This location was for the reserve water tank.

City Hall: 421 5th. The two-story historic structure, painted a rust red, is nicely accented with arched limestone window hoods. Inside, the exposed stone walls, wood floors, historical photos, and friendly staff are great reasons to go in, look around, and have a chat. Monday-Friday 8:30 a.m.-4:30 p.m. 785.945.6612. valleyfalls.org.

Valley Falls Historical Society Museum: 310 Broadway. Artifacts and photos preserve the history and the memories of Valley Falls and its residents. Saturday 10 a.m.-2 p.m. 785.945.3354.

Earliest Lutheran Congregation: A sign at St. Paul's Lutheran Church, 701 Frazier, states that St. Paul's formed the earliest Lutheran congregation in Kansas, dating to 1857. The first church building, moved from its original site at 901 Elm, stands today at 314 Broadway. Now known as Historical Shrine Church, it is recognized as the first permanent Lutheran church built on Kansas soil. 785.945.3354.

Jefferson Hill Vineyards: 12381 Washington. Savor the flavors of six wines lovingly produced by Don and Maxine Bryant. From their vineyards grown in the glacial moraine soils of Jefferson County come Harvest Moon, Jefferson Red, and more. Available to groups by reservation are lunch and dinner at Cafe de Vine where. Maxine's made-from-scratch dishes never disappoint. Tasting room hours, Saturday-Sunday 12-6 p.m. 913.796.6822. jeffersonhillvineyard.com.

Lodging: The Barn Bed and Breakfast Inn (KBBA, 785.945.3225, thebarnbb.com);

Jefferson Hill Vineyards and Guest House (913.796.6822, jeffersonhillvineyard.com).

explorer extras...
In Williamstown

Unincorporated

Buck Creek School (NRHP), a handsome native limestone schoolhouse, operated from 1878 to 1952. A wooden entry tower with original school bell was added around 1890. A rural township mill levy, fundraisers, and volunteers helped restore this revered building. Privately owned, it is used as the Rural Township Hall Community Center, 15456 13. From 3rd, ¼ mile north on Oak, 1¾ miles east on U.S. 24, then ¼ mile east on 13.

An unusual feature of the 1880 Sunnyside School, 1121 Republic, is the separate entrances flanking a set of arched windows. From 3rd, just north on Oak, 2 miles east on U.S. 24, 2½ miles east on 13, then ¼ mile south on Republic.

The Chrisman Memorial, a tall granite pillar at U.S. 59 and 54th, stands on a small rise near the highway overlooking Bill C. Chrisman's beloved farm. The memorial, erected by Bill's family, is in part inscribed, "The farm was our father's retreat." From 3rd, ¼ mile north on Oak, 5¼ miles north on U.S. 59, west into gravel drive, then walk about 100 yards south. **ee**

Population 540

Curry Grave: 308 Delaware. You'll find the grave of famed artist John Steuart Curry (1897- 1946) in the Reformed Presbyterian Church Cemetery off K-192. The Curry family's large upright glacial stone stands about 500 feet north of the entrance. Following the controversy over the state capitol murals (*see* p. 185), Curry returned to his home in Wisconsin where he died a few years later, purportedly of a broken heart.

NE

Winchester Public Library: 203 4th. Six works by John Steuart Curry hang in this handsome library. Monday-Friday 12-5 p.m.; Saturday 10 a.m.-12 p.m. 913.774.4967. winchesterlibrary.org.

Battle of Hickory Point Historical Marker: From K-192, 2 miles south. The story of an 1856 skirmish between proslavery forces and free-state militia is told on this marker, which stands about a half mile east of the Hickory Point battle site.

Jae's Place: 204 3rd. Breakfast is served all day! If you're partial to pancakes, they're made from scratch and as big as a dinner plate. Not in the breakfast mood? Grilled chicken salads are also popular and so is Friday night fried chicken. Come hungry! Monday 7 a.m.-3 p.m.; Tuesday-Saturday 6 a.m.-8 p.m. 913.774.2045.

Johnson County

Organized in 1855, the county is named for the Reverend Thomas Johnson, a Virginia slave owner who came to Kansas in 1829 to establish the Shawnee Methodist Mission. Johnson operated the mission until 1858.

Find a county hiking and biking trail guide at tinyurl.com/jocohikebike.

DESOTO

Population 5,911

City Hall: 32905 W. 84th. The city did a superb job renovating the former junior high/high school into a multipurpose community building. It houses the city offices, chamber of commerce, arts center, and community gymnasium and wellness center.

Riverfest Park: 33440 W. 79th. Bring your canoe and enter the Kansas River here, park your RV and stay awhile, or walk the trails. You can also enter the river, or let your dog take a run, at Kill Creek Streamway, 33460 W. 95th.

Wanda's Roadside Cafe: 33080 W. 83rd. Set in a low-key, no-frills atmosphere, Wanda's

is known far and wide for excellent homemade edibles, and breakfasts might just be the best. If buttermilk pie is on the menu, don't pass it up. Wednesday-Sunday 7 a.m.-2 p.m. 913.486.9236. FB.

Sunflower Village Historic District (NRHP): 36000 103. This planned housing development is a living reminder of the quick response to housing needs for workers at the Sunflower Ordnance Works munition plant during WW II. The Sunflower Army Ammunition Plant, as it was later known, was the world's largest producer of smokeless gunpowder and of propellants for small arms, cannons, and rockets. The plant sprawled over 10,000 acres of former farmland, comprised 3,000 buildings, and employed 12,000 people. Although it closed in 1992, remnants of the plant are yet visible.

Lodging: tinyurl.com/desotolodge.

EDGERTON

Population 1,700

Public Library: 319 E. Nelson. Across the front of the red-brick Edgerton Public Library, located in a 1906 former bank, is written the appropriate descriptor, "Bank of Knowledge."

Edgerton Community Museum: 406 E. Nelson. Since 2013 the history of Edgerton has been housed in a small clapboard home near downtown. Wednesday 1-3 p.m.; Saturday 12-2 p.m. 913.893.6270.

Lanesfield School (NRHP): 18745 S. Dillie. From 1st, ½ mile east on U.S. 56, ¾ mile north on Sunflower, ½ mile east on 191, then ½ mile north on Dillie. The stone schoolhouse, restored to its 1904 appearance, sits

in a quiet rural setting on the townsite of Lanesfield, named for territorial firebrand James Lane. Start in the visitor center (separate building) brimming with informative exhibits about early schools. A costumed tour guide makes a visit here a special experience for all ages. Friday-Saturday 1-5 p.m. 913.893.6645. jocomuseum.org.

Santa Fe Trail Marker: Lanesfield School grounds. The famous trail is marked by an engraved red granite boulder placed by the Daughters of the American Revolution in 1906. This area is near the Battle of Bull Creek, an 1856 battle that cemented James Lane's reputation as a hero when he and a small militia defeated a large group of proslavery forces.

White Tail Run Winery: 2327 N. 400. From U.S. 56, 2 miles north on Edgerton, then 2¼ miles west on 400. Dan Fuller started a vineyard and winery as a retirement project, but things have gone so well that the whole family has become involved in making the flavorful white, red, and fruit wines. Friday-Saturday 12-5 p.m.; Sunday 12-4 p.m. whitetailrunwinery.com.

FAIRWAY

Population 3,963

Shawnee Indian Mission State Historic Site (NRHP): 3403 W. 53rd. From 1839 to 1862 Shawnees, Delawares, and other Indian tribal members attended the manual training school on this site. The buildings were also used as an early territorial capitol, a supply point on the Santa Fe and the Oregon Trails, and a camp for Union soldiers. A National Historic Landmark, the site comprises three original brick buildings spaced throughout a tranquil natural setting. Admission charge. Wednesday-Saturday 10 a.m.-5 p.m. 913.262.0867. kshs.org.

Shawnee Methodist Mission Cemetery:

3201 Shawnee Mission Pkwy. (between Canterbury and Chadwick).The Reverend Thomas Johnson, founder of the Shawnee Methodist Mission and for whom Johnson County was named, is buried here with members of his family. A proslavery supporter, Johnson was killed in 1865, purportedly by Southern sympathizers, after he swore allegiance to the Union cause. 913.262.0867.

Population 19,944

Spinning Earth Pottery:

102 S. Elm. Danny and Diana Meisinger have transformed this 20th-century bank building into a beautiful gallery to display Danny's art. An accomplished ceramic artist, he specializes in functional pottery as well as impeccable fine art. Tuesday-Friday 12-5 p.m.; Saturday 10 a.m.-4 p.m. 913.626.6028. spinningearthpottery.net.

Gardner Historical

Museum: 204 W. Main. The first floor of this 1893 Victorian home is decorated in period furnishings. Exhibits include histories of the Santa Fe and the Oregon Trails; pieces from the 1940s and 1950s; and a collection of Dr. A. S. Reece, a local doctor and builder of the first hospital in Johnson County. Saturday-Tuesday 1-4 p.m.; Friday 4-7 p.m. 913.856.4447. gardnerhistoricalmuseum.com.

Gardner Pharmacy Soda

Fountain: 131 E. Main. Hop on a seat at the old-fashioned soda fountain and order a Green River, cherry phosphate,

or banana split. Seasonal concoctions are also popular. Try a pumpkin pie milkshake in the fall and a peach shake to cool off in the summer. And don't miss the gift shopping opportunities here. Monday-Friday 9 a.m-6 p.m.; Saturday 9 a.m.-1 p.m. 913.856.8106. FB.

Groundhouse Coffee:

103 S. Elm. This 1907 red-brick building retains its historic ambience to provide a delightful gathering place for enjoying pastries made in-house and specialty coffees, espresso, and teas. On weekends customers scramble for the sweet and savory crepes. Monday-Saturday 6 a.m.-9 p.m.; Sunday 8 a.m.-6 p.m. 913.856.5711. groundhousecoffee.com.

Blazers Restaurant:

131 N. Center. Open since 1976, this Gardner icon is famous for shakes and fresh, hand-pattied burgers—as well as for its support of school and community activities. Soft-serve and hard-scoop ice cream are sold here too. Daily 11 a.m.-8 p.m. 913.856.6565. FB.

Junction Park: From Center, 2 miles west on Main (U.S. 56). The Oregon-California and the Santa Fe Trails divided at this point as they continued westward across Kansas. It is estimated that 500,000 travelers including traders, trappers, missionaries, land seekers, and gold rushers passed through

this one spot on their way west during the early 19th century. Learn more about this historic juncture at the interpretive kiosk, then walk the paved nature trail landscaped with the types of plants that early travelers would have encountered.

Population 32,991

NE

Rye: 10551 Mission. Megan and Colby Garrelts, owners and award-winning chefs, serve comfort food in a swanky, repurposed, rustic environment. It's traditional fare taken to the next level. For example, their famous fried chicken takes 48 hours to prepare and is served with homemade pickles and ham gravy. The menu contains many offerings made with locally sourced meats and fish served with fresh seasonal vegetables. And did we mention the pies? Daily 11 a.m.-10 p.m. 913.642.5800. ryekc.com.

Population 50,344

Sar-Ko-Par Trails Park:

87th and Lackman. Home of the annual Lenexa Spinach Festival, this park hosts a lovely paved walking trail around Rose's Pond. Fifteen large stones take you to the pond island and the *Serpent*—a large welded steel piece created by J. Derek Arnold in 1993. The park was named for a Creek Indian who assisted the U.S. military.

Legler Barn Museum:
14907 W. 87th. Adam Legler built the stone barn in 1864 on a nearby site on the Santa Fe Trail. In 1983 it was moved to Sar-Ko-Par Park, reconstructed, and now contains exhibits telling the story of early Lenexa. Within the park you'll also find a 1912 Frisco train depot, a Northern Pacific caboose, and the Strang Line waiting station. Wednesday, Saturday 10 a.m.-4 p.m. 913.492.0038.

Pak Halal International Market: 12259 W. 87th. Next door to the Holy Land Cafe you'll find a grocery filled with everything you'll need to create your own Middle Eastern dishes at home. The bakery makes pocket breads, sesame breads, cheese and meat pies, baklava, and other favorite traditional baked goods. Monday-Saturday 11 a.m.-8 p.m.; Sunday 11 a.m-6 p.m. 913.599.0700. pakhalalinternational.com.

Holy Land Cafe:
12275 W. 87th. This strip mall cafe is where the locals go for fresh and flavorful Middle Eastern food. The hummus is smooth and creamy with a hint of heat and is served with pillowy, warm pita bread. Frank Thompson, Kansas Explorer #3128, recommends the chicken schwarma. Monday-Saturday 11 a.m.-9 p.m.; Sunday 12-8 p.m. 913.310.9911. holylandcafe.com.

MERRIAM

Population 11,281

Waterfall Park:
5191 Merriam. From Johnson, ¾ mile north on Merriam. Find this wonderful little green spot on the east side of the street. It features a small waterfall in Turkey Creek and an access point to a four-mile paved walking trail.

Georgetown Pharmacy's Old Time Soda Fountain & Espresso Shop:
5605 Merriam. Old-time drinks such as an egg cream or a Green River are served here as are root beer in a frosted mug, limeades, and any kind of ice cream treat. Monday-Friday 9 a.m.-6 p.m.; Saturday 9 a.m.-1 p.m. 913.362.0313.

Lodging: exploremerriam.com.

MISSION

Population 9,516

Werner's Fine Sausages:
5736 Johnson. A good pastrami sandwich is hard to find but this is the place to find it, along with schnitzel, liverwurst, BLTs made with Werner's hand-rubbed hickory smoked bacon, and many other choices. Dave and Judy Miller bought this place from Werner Wohler in 1995 and have continued the tradition of serving great lunches and carrying a line of sausages, German specialty cuts including gelbwurst and leberkas, and other quality meats.

MISSION HILLS

Population 3,582

In 1912 urban planner J.C. Nichols began developing Mission Hills into America's premier garden community. Wooded hills, winding streams, and pleasant valleys provide a natural backdrop to the many fountains, statues, and sculptures that accent the traffic islands and roadsides. Beautiful and graceful homes add a crowning touch to make a drive through Mission Hills a wonderful tour. April is especially breathtaking when the dogwoods and azaleas are in bloom.

Fountains: From the Goddess of the Spring (Mission and W. 55th) to the Swan Fountain in Verona Columns Park (Ensley and Overhill), at least ten handsome fountains accent the intersections in Mission Hills. tinyurl.com/mhfountains.

Wolcott House (NRHP):
5701 Oakwood. From the Belinder Court Fountain, ¼ mile north on Belinder, ¼ mile northeast on Overhill, then ½ mile north on Oakwood. This 1928 stone Tudor Revival and French Eclectic former residence of J.J. Wolcott, a prominent Kansas City grain dealer, is magnificent. And finding it gives you a reason to drive through the winding streets lined with other gorgeous homes.

OLATHE

Population 105,274

City of Governors:
100 W. Santa Fe. A plaque on the outside of city hall recognizes Olathe as the City of Governors—three men from Olathe have held Kansas' highest office (John P. St. John, George Hodges, and John Anderson) and two became governors of other states. In

the city hall courtyard a vertical Phil Epp and Terry Corbett tile sculpture brings gorgeous blue skies to Olathe every day. Arlie Regier and Dave Regier stainless steel sculptures also add to the landscape.

Mahaffie Stagecoach Stop and Farm Historic Site (NRHP): 1100 Kansas

City. From E. Santa Fe, 1 mile northeast on Kansas City. Mahaffie is the last remaining stagecoach stop on the Santa Fe Trail open to the public, and a visit here will transport you back to the days of the western trails. Start your journey with the excellent displays at the Heritage Center then proceed down the steps to the stone dining hall and kitchen. Here Lucinda Mahaffie and her help served more than 50 meals a day to stagecoach passengers and other travelers during the 1860s. The impressive Mahaffie home, built of two-foot-thick native limestone walls, is the centerpiece of this historic farm, which encompasses a stone icehouse, timber frame barn, blacksmith shop, and period

garden. If the buildings are closed, you're welcome to tour the grounds. Monday-Saturday 10 a.m.- 4 p.m.; Sunday 12-4 p.m. Admission charge. 913.971.5111. mahaffie.org.

William J. Marra Museum:

455 E. Park. Inside the Deaf Cultural Center you'll find one of the most interesting museums in the state. Fascinating exhibits explain every part of deaf cul-

ture from early schools and equipment to its impact on sports and families. You might even learn some sign language while you're here. Wednesday-Saturday 10 a.m.- 4 p.m.; Sunday 12-5 p.m. 913.324.5348. deafculturalcenter.org.

Johnson County Courthouse: 100 N. Kansas.

The new courthouse built in 1952 replaced the 1891 structure designed by revered architect George Washburn. The last addition to the 1952 courthouse was finished in 1976. Many historical area photos are displayed just inside the south doors. Security makes it prohibitive to go farther inside. Monday-Friday 8 a.m.-5 p.m.

Courthouse Grounds:

111 S. Cherry. This pleasant green space features a 1907 Santa Fe Trail plaque and marker and a joyful Kwan Wu sculpture of children playing with their dog. The sculpture is in memory of every child lost along the Santa Fe Trail.

FDR Whistle-Stop Tour:

300 block of W. Santa Fe. During his 1936 western campaign trip Franklin Roosevelt stopped in Olathe where he addressed a crowd of 10,000 eager to hear about the New Deal, which promised relief from the Great Depression. Near the railroad tracks where Roosevelt made his stop, a marker tells more about the historic visit.

Park Street Historic Homes (NRHP): Three

stately residences representing progress and wealth in late-19th-century Olathe are the area's few remaining homes from this era. They are the 1869 Isaac O. Pickering House (507 W. Park), the 1901 Frank Lanter House (562 W. Park), and the 1880 Martin Van Buren Parker House (631 W. Park).

Olathe Memorial Cemetery: 738 N. Chestnut.

Highlights include the 1937 limestone chapel, the John Paulding WW I statue and veterans gravestones, and the Civil War statue and circle of grave markers. Elsewhere are the burial sites of President Barack Obama's great-great-great grandfather Robert Wolfley and Kansas governors George Hodges and John P. St. John. A large single stone marks the graves of employees of Olathe's historic Hyer Boot Company. Information booklets are available at the chapel. Monday-Friday 8 a.m.-5 p.m. 913.971.5226.

Bricklaying Contest:

E. Kansas City and E. Poplar. Had you been traveling muddy roads for years in your Model T you might have joined the 10,000 who celebrated the paving of Kansas City Road on the Westport route of the Santa Fe Trail. The highlight was a bricklaying competition between James Garfield "Indian Jim" Brown and Frank Hoffman. On a drizzly September day in 1925, Brown won the contest by laying 46,664 bricks in seven hours and 48 minutes. He received $200 for his effort in addition to his $2 an hour wage. A marker in a landscaped area of the intersection tells this remarkable story.

Downtown Diner: 409 E.

Santa Fe. At this homey downtown spot, Rich Caines runs the kitchen and prides himself on making everything from scratch. His wife, Sue, tends the front and makes you feel at home. For breakfast try Rich's homemade biscuits and gravy, French toast, or a cinnamon roll pancake. The burger specialties and smoked meats are also popular with the regulars. Wednesday-Saturday 6 a.m.- 9 p.m.; Sunday-Tuesday 6 a.m.-2:30 p.m. 913.764.1002. FB.

NE

Lone Elm Park: 21151 W. 167. Beginning in 1821 travelers on the Santa Fe Trail, and later on the Oregon-California Trail, used this spot as a camp-ground and rendezvous point. It's been transformed into a beautiful park with a shelter house, interpretive kiosks, a natural prairie, walking trail, and soccer and softball complexes.

Historic Ensor Park and Museum (NRHP): 18995 W. 183. From E. Old 56, 5 miles south on K-7, then 1 mile east on 183. The home of Marshall Ensor, an Olathe teacher and pioneer in amateur radio, and his sister Loretta, this 1892 farmhouse invites you to see its antique furniture, domestic displays, and ham radio equipment, and to learn about the Ensors extraordinary work in the radio field. A barn from the same period constructed with rough-sawn lumber and wood-peg beams is also open to visitors. May, June, September, October, Saturday-Sunday 1-5 p.m. 913.592.4141. ensorparkandmuseum.org.

Stone Pillar Vineyard & Winery: 11000 S. Woodlawn. A wonderful variety of award-winning wines are produced in a lovely setting. Stop in for a wine tasting or check into the winery's concerts and events. Wednesday-Sunday 12-6 p.m. 913.839.2185. stonepillarvineyard.com.

KC Wine Co.: 13875 S. Gardner. From K-7, 5 miles west on Santa Fe, then ½ mile south on Gardner. This winery produces six different vari-etals—a wine to please every palate—from its seven acres of grapes. Schedule a wine-tasting party or group event. February-December, Friday 3-8 p.m.; Saturday-Sunday 12-6 p.m. 913.915.4297. kcwineco.com.

Ernie Miller Nature Center: 909 N. K-7. With displays and various animals, the oldest nature center in Johnson County offers opportunities for all ages for understanding and admiring nature in its many forms. Lush foliage and creeks make the center's three trails popular walking spots. Nature Center hours, March-October, Monday-Saturday 9 a.m.-5 p.m; trails hours, daily dawn to dusk. 913.764.7759. erniemiller.com.

Lodging: tinyurl.com/olathelodging.

OVERLAND PARK

Population 181,260

Museum at Prairiefire: 5801 W. 135. Dichroic glass (ultra-thin layers of different metals set in a vacuum) creates the colorful and exotic exterior. Collaboration with the American Museum of Natural History provides rare changing exhibits inside that are amazing for all ages. Exhibitions in the Great Hall are free and include the Big Fish Story, the first discovery of the Tyrannosaurus rex, and a rotating photo gallery. Children will love touching and playing with everything in the Discovery Room where ages 3 to 12 are given a wonderful dose of natural history and science. Monday-Saturday 10 a.m.-5 p.m.; Sunday 12-5 p.m. Admission charge. 913.333.3500. museumatpf.org.

Overland Park Arboretum and Botanical Gardens: 8909 W. 179. From College, 8½ miles south on U.S. 69, then ¾ mile west on 179. Several miles south of the hustle and bustle of the city, a serene

waterfall in the Erickson water garden guides you to a collec-tion of aquatic and bog plants. Thematic gardens and colorful flowers expand throughout the arboretum and lead to miles of lush woodland trails. Thirty

amazing sculptures placed throughout the gardens provide sumptuous sparks of amusement and speculation, and a quality visitor center enhances the entire experience. April-September, daily 8 a.m.-7:30 p.m.; October-March, daily 8 a.m.-5 p.m. Admission charge. 913.685.3604. tinyurl.com/oparb.

New Theatre Restaurant: 9229 Foster. Open since 1992, this lovely facility has been recognized as "the best dinner theatre in the country." It invites you to experience a quality dining experience as you watch stage, film, and TV stars perform Broadway comedies and musicals. Reservations required. 913.649.7469. newtheatre.com.

Deanna Rose Children's Farmstead: 13800 Switzer. Farm animals, a petting zoo, birds of prey, vegetable and flower gardens, replicas of farm outbuildings, a pond, and endless stimulation for kids make this a family paradise. The farmstead was named in honor of Deanna Rose, an Overland Park police officer killed in the line of duty. April-October,

Deanna Rose Children's Farmstead

daily 9 a.m.-5 p.m. Admission charge. 913.897.2360. tinyurl.com/opdeannarose.

Johnson County Museum:

8788 Metcalf. Many great finds are inside, but the center-piece is the fascinating 1950s All-Electric House (see next entry). A permanent display, Becoming Johnson County, tells the story of the area's transformation from its earliest times to the landscape of today. The popular KidScape features historical hands-on play in rural, urban, and suburban settings. Monday-Saturday 10 a.m.-4:30 p.m. 913.715.2550. jocomuseum.org.

1950s All-Electric House:

8788 Metcalf (inside Johnson County Museum). Why would electrical outlets be placed waist high? So high-heeled home-makers wouldn't have to bend too far to plug in the vacuum! Learn about all sorts of domestic innovations at the first 1950s all-electric house in the United States open for public tour. You'll get a kick out of the futuristic innovations that KCP&L installed when the company built the house as a showcase home in 1954. Gimmicks include a bedside remote control for the coffeemaker, moonglow lighting near the floor, a hanging wall picture that moves back and the TV appears, and more! It's all-electric and all-amazing fun. For hours and phone, see Johnson County Museum. jocomuseum.org.

Revocup Coffee Roastery:

11030 Quivira. It's one of the friendliest coffeehouses you'll encounter in the metro area. This warm, inviting environment is reflected in the single-source coffee that owners Habte Mesfin and TG Ambachew buy directly from their native Ethiopia. From every cup of coffee sold, a portion of the proceeds goes to the grower. Monday-Friday 6 a.m.-7 p.m.; Saturday-Sunday 8 a.m.-5 p.m. 913.663.3695. FB.

John's Space Age Donuts:

8124 Floyd. The donuts have been "out of this world since 1967," and the regulars know to come early for their favorite donut—raised, glazed, or otherwise—hot out of the fryer. Take a seat on a swivel stool at the counter and savor every sweet bite. Tuesday-Saturday 6 a.m.-2 p.m. 913.381.0980. FB.

ABC Cafe: 10001 W. 87th. The success at this Asian restaurant is as simple as ABC. A) It's a small place with an easy to remember name; B) the fresh cuisine is beau-tifully presented; and C) the service is excellent. Most of the customers are Asian, so that's a clue that the food is authentic. Try something new like the satay shrimp ball noodle or the fish ball and lettuce soup. If it's really busy, you might have to share a communal table. Monday, Thursday-Sunday, 12-10:30 p.m. 913.859.0089. abccafeop.com.

Lodging:

visitoverlandpark.com.

Population 21,892

Prairie Village Gateway:

Tomahawk and Mission. Enhancing the city entrance is a stone fountain and *Pioneer Family*, a concrete and stone sculpture by Annabella Campbell. The 1951 statue was relocated to this spot from the Prairie Village Shopping Center in 2002.

Kentucky Derby Winner:

59 Le Mans Ct. From Mission, ¼ mile west and south on 80th (becomes Le Mans Ct.). Two streets are named Le Mans Ct., but the western one has a surprise at the end of the cul-de-sac. Here you'll find a memorial and a large granite stone marking the grave of Larwin (1935-1955), the only Kansas horse to win the Kentucky Derby (1938). A wrought iron fence surrounds the small manicured garden where Lawrin and his sire, Insco, are buried side by side. Owned by Herbert Woolf, Lawrin is laid to rest on the site of Woolford Farms, which today is a resi-dential area of Prairie Village.

NE

Population 64,323

The town is named for the Shawnee Indian tribe, relocated to this area during the late 1820s.

Pioneer Crossing Park:

10401 Shawnee Mission Pkwy. Enter the park's parking lot from the eastbound lane. Because this enjoyable park is on a busy highway, it'smeasy to pass by and miss discovering its stories of the area's frontier trails. A sidewalk accompanies your journey to interpretive signs and to a closer examination

of the truly magnificent bronze and limestone Charles Goslin sculptures of a wagon train and a wagon master.

Bluejacket Sculpture:
Johnson and Cody (in Herman Laird Park). Charles Goslin created the larger-than-life sculpture of Shawnee Chief Charles Bluejacket reading to two children. A minister, farmer, and tribal leader, Bluejacket lived in this area during the mid-1800s.

Shawnee Indian Cemetery:
10905 59th Terrace. It may appear that you've come to an empty lot, but a sign confirms you're in the right place. Few gravestones stand upright in this nearly hidden cemetery established in 1854. A flat stone marks the grave of Julia Ann Daugherty, wife of Chief Bluejacket, who died in 1870 and is the cemetery's last known burial. Seemingly unrelated are the many gravestone pieces from an unidentified Quaker cemetery that have been embedded into a flat concrete slab.

Shawnee Town 1929:
11501 W. 57th (in Herman Laird Park). Old Shawnee Town interprets its unique role in 20th-century farming, namely truck farms. A number of outbuildings compose the agricultural complex, and a barber shop, schoolhouse, icehouse, and grocery store represent Shawnee in 1929. It's a delightful place to bring the family to learn about this remarkable time in Shawnee's history. Museum grounds hours, March-October, Tuesday-Saturday 10 a.m.-4:30 p.m.;

visitor center hours, year round, Monday-Friday 9 a.m.-5 p.m. Admission charge. 913.248.2360. shawneetown.org.

Renee Kelly's Harvest (RHKP): 12401 Johnson.
Chef Renee uses locally sourced ingredients in her farm-to-table restaurant and changes her menu with each season so every bite is fresh. Nutritious cuisine served inside a 1907

castle-like home combine for a royal dining experience. Wednesday-Friday 11 a.m.-2 p.m. and 5-10 p.m.; Saturday 5-10 p.m.; Sunday 10 a.m.-2 p.m. 913.631.4100. reneekellysharvest.com.

Lodging: visitshawneeks.com

SPRING HILL

Population 5,730

Spring Hill Outdoor Mural:
107 S. Main (opposite the police station). A colorful mural depicts the faces and places of Spring Hill's history. A joint effort by the community and artist Julie Macey has resulted in telling the town's story in creative style.

Spring Hill Cemetery:
799 W. Lawrence. The inscription on the grand stone entrance wall, sponsored in 1923 by the Woman's Relief Corps, reads, "In honor of the veterans of the Civil War 1861-1865, the Spanish-American War 1898, our country's defenders in the World War 1917-1918, and the loyal women of Springhill and the community."

Red Crow Brewing Company:
20561 S. Lone Elm. From 199, ¾ mile south on U.S. 169, then just east on S. Lone

Elm. Meet the Red Crow "ladies": Isabelle (Belgium Blonde), Donna (American Wheat), Frances (Pale Ale), Elaine (Rye Porter), and more. Local food trucks provide a variety of eating options to accompany these fine craft beers. Eating or drinking, you'll enjoy the atmosphere at this festive family-operated brewery. Wednesday-Thursday 4:30-10 p.m.; Friday 3-10 p.m.; Saturday 12-10 p.m.; Sunday 12-7 p.m. 913.247.3641. redcrowbrew.com.

K&M Bar-B-Q: 603 N. Webster.
K&M is well known for its barbecue, but the catfish on Tuesday nights is mighty tasty too! You can't go wrong at this family-owned barbecue serving the best for more than 20 years. Tuesday-Saturday 11 a.m.-8 p.m.; Sunday 11 a.m.-6 p.m. 913.592.5145. kandmbbq.com.

STILWELL

Unincorporated

Quantrill's Raids and the Military Road Historical Marker:
6500 block of W. 199th. Close to the Kansas-Missouri state line, this area was a crossing point for raiders during the Civil War. Quantrill passed through here at least twice when leading attacks in and around Stilwell in 1862. Just a half mile west from this sign is Metcalf Ave., originally the military road connecting Fort Leavenworth and Fort Scott. Union troops often camped along the road while pursuing raiders.

WESTWOOD HILLS

Population 362

Pretty Little City:
Rainbow and 49th Terrace. The city entrance sign claims it's "The Most Beautiful Little City in Kansas," and who can argue? The J.C. Nichols Company platted the Westwood Hills subdivision in 1923, and in 1949

it became an incorporated city. It was the first subdivision that Nichols developed in Kansas using his residential design concepts. The Westwood Hill Historic District (NRHP) is bounded by State Line, Rainbow, 48th Terrace, and 50th Terrace.

Leavenworth County

AROUND THE COUNTY

Frontier Military Scenic Byway: From Fort Leavenworth, follow K-5 south along the Missouri River. Fort Leavenworth is the starting point and northern end of this hilly, winding, and tree-lined byway. Among other highlights, you'll pass the national cemetery and the Lansing Correctional Facility. The byway continues from K-5 to I-435 around the Kansas City metro area to U.S. 69 and south to the Oklahoma border.

Glacial Hills Scenic Byway: From the Kansas-Nebraska line to the K-7 and K-92 junction in Leavenworth, this 63-mile drive takes you through the beautiful and rolling Glacial Hills region. Bluffs often border one side of the road while the river or cropland in the flood plain line the other. A glacial deposit left the large red rocks (quartzite). Towns you'll pass are some of the oldest in Kansas, and the architecture and historic sites are evidence of our state's early days. Historic routes through the area include that of Lewis and Clark and the Pony Express. travelks.com/ksbyways.

Little Stranger Creek Church (NRHP): Tonganoxie and Stranger. From N. Main in Lansing, 3¾ miles west on Eisenhower, then 1½ miles south on Tonganoxie. On a small hill stands what is considered to be the oldest wood frame church in Kansas. Erected in 1868, the church has served as a place of worship, a community center, and a cultural landmark. It currently is being restored.

BASEHOR

Population 4,898

Basehor Museum:
2812 N. 155th. The town and the museum are named for brothers Ephraim and Reuben Basehor, who came to the area from Pennsylvania in 1854 and founded this town in 1889. The small but active museum is proud of its heritage and eager to share it with visitors. Thursday 1-4 p.m.; Saturday 9 a.m.-2 p.m. 913.724.4022. FB.

Holy-Field Vineyard & Winery:
18807 158th (U.S. 24/40 and 158th). The Holy-Field name derives from Holyfield Road, now known as 158th. The winery's excellent gift shop and tasting room is next to the 14-acre vineyard of American and French hybrid varieties. Your only chance to buy chocolates made with wine is during the winter, but we recommend a visit to Holy-Field any time! Monday-Friday 10 a.m.-6 p.m.; Saturday 9:30 a.m.-6 p.m.; Sunday 12-6 p.m. 913.724.9463. holyfieldwinery.com.

explorer extras...
In Easton

Population 253

In the back of Hilltop Market, 21315 Easton, is a little gem of a cafe and bakery with a loyal following. Customers rave about the home-cooked meals, especially the pork tenderloin sandwiches, homemade soups, and amazing pies. Monday-Saturday 6 a.m.-9 p.m.; Sunday 7 a.m.-6 p.m. 913.773.5710. FB. **ee**

NE

FORT LEAVENWORTH

Before entering the fort, visitors must stop at the Visitor Control Center at 4th and Metropolitan to receive a temporary pass. Vehicle drivers must have a valid driver's license plus current registration and proof of insurance. Passengers 16 and over must also show a driver's license or other form of photo identification. Daily 6:30 a.m.-4:30 p.m. 913.684.1724.

Fort History (NRHP; 8 Wonders of Kansas History): Colonel Henry Leavenworth established Fort Leavenworth on May 8, 1827. The small cantonment was founded to protect the western frontier, keep peace among

Indian tribes resettled to this area, and provide escort on the newly opened Santa Fe Trail. Today the fort is an active military post, home of the U.S. Army Combined Arms Center and the U.S. Army Command and General Staff College. Designated a National Historic Landmark, Fort Leavenworth is the longest continuously active post west of the Appalachians.

Buffalo Soldier Monument (8 Wonders of Kansas People): Grant and Stimson. General Colin Powell initiated this sculpture project to honor African American soldiers of the Ninth and Tenth Cavalry regiments. The result is a larger-than-life, 13-foot bronze monument of a buffalo soldier astride his horse. Within the monument area also are several busts of soldiers. Inscriptions explain each one's relevance to black military history.

Berlin Wall Monument: Grant and Stimson. From the Buffalo Soldier Monument, follow the sidewalk around the lake to the south to see three sections of the wall that once separated West and East Berlin.

Frontier Army Museum: 100 Reynolds. This fine museum preserves and interprets the story of the frontier army from 1804 to 1917 and of

Fort Leavenworth from 1827 to the present. It houses one of the finest collections of 19th-century military artifacts in the country. Included is a large selection of horse-drawn military vehicles, a wagon in which Abraham Lincoln rode in 1859, and Henry Leavenworth's 1832 general officer's coat. Monday-Friday 9 a.m.-4 p.m.; Saturday 12-4 p.m. 913.684.3191. FB.

Wayside Tour: A self-guided tour features informational markers at 16 points of interest throughout the fort. Pick up a brochure at the Frontier Army Museum or the Leavenworth Convention & Visitors Bureau, 100 N. 5th. tinyurl.com/fortwayside.

Historic Homes: The oldest continuously occupied residence in Kansas, known as the Rookery, was built in 1832 and stands at the northeast corner of the parade ground. Not far away are two Syracuse Houses, constructed in 1855 as officers' quarters. Drive around the parade field to see many more beautiful homes of red brick with white pillars and white front steps. Many have signs stating the year the house was built.

Grant, Sherman, and Sheridan Halls: Scott and Augur. Named for Generals Ulysses Grant, William Sherman, and Philip Sheridan, the halls reflect how deeply Fort Leavenworth is steeped in rich military history. Sherman and Sheridan Halls were built in 1859 as ordnance storehouses. Later they served as the first Command and General Staff

College. The 1908 domed clock tower (repaired in 2010) and Grant Hall unite Sherman and Sheridan Halls.

Grant Memorial: Grant and Kearny. The impressive bronze statue of Civil War general Ulysses S. Grant was dedicated in 1889.

Old U.S. Disciplinary Barracks: 310 McPherson. The barracks, built by prisoners, opened in 1921. After the facility closed in 2002, most of "the Castle" (as it was known) was dismantled except for the outside walls, guard towers, and a section that is now home to the 12th Brick Grille, open for lunch during the week. As you explore the area, interpretive signs provide the story of the barracks.

Lewis and Clark Center: 100 Stimson. Inside the U.S. Army Command and General Staff College, the Fort Leavenworth Hall of Fame displays photos and biographies of officers from the Union and the Confederate armies, the International Officer Hall of Fame recognizes international officer graduates who have made significant contributions, and the Lewis and Clark area exhibits artifacts of military history. Stop at the security desk for a self-guided tour brochure. Monday-Friday 8 a.m.-4:30 p.m. 913.684.2420.

Fort Leavenworth National Cemetery (NRHP): 395 Biddle. A vast and impressive cemetery, it

was among the first 12 national cemeteries established by Abraham Lincoln in 1862. Soldiers serving in every war since the War of 1812 are buried here. The most famous of the 23,000 interred is Colonel Henry Leavenworth. His large gray cylindrical monument is topped with an eagle. 913.758.4105.

Oregon and Santa Fe Trails Ruts: From Grant and Kearny, ¼ mile east and south on Riverside. The wagon ruts date to the fort's earliest days when fur traders made their way north and to the 1840s when settlers and freighting caravans traversed the Oregon and the Santa Fe Trails, which branched off from this point. The ruts run from the old boat landing on the river to the fort's parade ground.

LANSING

Population 11,642

Angel Falls Park:
900 Ida. In 2015 the city dedicated this beautiful park and half-mile walking trail that runs between Ida and Mary. The wide concrete sidewalk is perfect for walking, jogging, and bicycling. A trail highlight is a bridge with a view of picturesque Angel Falls, a small waterfall on Seven Falls Creek. Public parking is available.

Lansing Historical Museum:
115 E. Kansas. The history of Lansing, the railroad, and the Kansas State Penitentiary are told inside this 1887 Santa Fe depot museum.

You'll enjoy the exhibit of prison escape tools and a prisoner's illustrations of penitentiary life. The museum is on the prison grounds, and if you continue east on Kansas you'll drive past the Lansing Correctional Facility. Call ahead, 913.250.0203. FB.

Kansas State Penitentiary:
301 E. Kansas. Now named Lansing Correctional Facility, it is the state's first maximum-security prison and houses more than 2,000 inmates. Those once incarcerated here include Emmett Dalton, captured during the 1892 Dalton Gang raid; Topeka's Alvin "Creepy" Karpis, FBI Public Enemy Number 1 in 1936; and Richard Hickock and Perry Smith, who committed the Clutter murders in 1959.

Delaware Cemetery:
26199 K-5. From U.S. 73, ½ mile east on Eisenhower, then 1¾ miles south on K-5 (Wolcott). The burials here date from between the 1820s and the early 1960s. One flat gray granite stone is inscribed, "All the souls of African Descent Buried Here." The grave of Beatrice Payne who died in 1933 shares that stone. Lansing Correctional Facility inmates maintain the cemetery.

Mount Muncie Cemetery:
From K-7 (S. 4th), ¾ mile east and south on K-5 (Muncie). Situated on the Leavenworth-Lansing line, Mount Muncie is the final resting place for many prominent and infamous individuals. 913.727.1935.

• Fred Harvey (1853-1901).
Founder of the famous Harvey House, Harvey is buried alongside his wife, two infant sons, and two grown daughters and their spouses. His flat grave marker is behind the large Harvey family stone. From the cemetery entrance, take the first right. The Harvey stone is the third standing monument on the left.

• Levan Dadiani (1897-1963).
A marker declares that Dadiani was the Prince of Mingrelia. Born in Zubeda, Georgia, Russia, he later married Eleanor Anthony, granddaughter of D.R. Anthony (*see* later entry). The prince and princess are buried in an above-ground tomb. Take a right at the main entrance, and at the Stillings monument follow the roadway. You'll find the Dadiani tomb before you reach a large mausoleum.

• Thomas Carney (1824-1888).
Carney was the second governor of Kansas, serving from 1863 to 1864. As you enter the cemetery, go toward the flagpole and bear right (as opposed to a hard right). Northeast of the next intersection you'll see the Carney monument, a tall obelisk.

• D.R. Anthony (1824-1904).
Newspaper editor and Susan B. Anthony's brother, D.R. Anthony is buried east of the Thomas Carney obelisk, on the south side of the road. A bronze plaque on his gravestone notes that he published the *Daily Times* and states, "He was no hypocrite."

• Helen Fritsche Cronkite (1892-1993).
Helen Cronkite, mother of the former CBS news anchor Walter Cronkite, is buried just east of the D.R. Anthony grave. Look for a flat marker near the Edward and Linda Fritsche stone.

• Richard Hickock and Perry Smith.
Richard Hickock and Perry Smith's murder of the Clutter family of Holcomb was chronicled in Truman Capote's *In Cold Blood*. The two men are buried two rows in front of a spruce tree in potter's field (all stones are flat). Hickock and Smith were executed at the Kansas State Penitentiary in Lansing in 1965.

NE

LEAVENWORTH

Population 35,891

The first thing you need to know about Leavenworth, besides its wonderful history, is that it has a tricky street numbering system. The numbered avenues become numbered streets as they proceed west across Spruce. For instance, 5th Avenue becomes 7th Street north of Spruce. Keep this in mind as you explore!

Wayside Tour: Leavenworth has erected 21 Wayside stops, or interactive displays, that offer a colorful and broad perspective of Leavenworth and Fort Leavenworth. At 19 locations around the city and the fort, you can push a button and hear about a range of subjects, from Lincoln's speech at the Planter's Hotel to the story of the fort. Tour brochures are available at the Riverfront Community Center, 123 S. Esplanade. 913.758.2948. tinyurl.com/leavwayside.

C.W. Parker Carousel Museum: 320 S. Esplanade. C.W. Parker was once the world's largest producer of amusement rides and carousels, and his largest factory was in Leavenworth. The museum showcases three carousels: the oldest operating Flying Horse carousel (1850-1865) in the world; a 1950 Paul Parker (C.W.'s son) aluminum

carousel; and the feature, a C.W. Parker 1913 carousel (8 Wonders of Kansas Customs). It is not only a beauty to behold with its 24 horses, three ponies, a rabbit, chariot, and a lover's cup, but you can ride on it! A 1920 band organ plays carousel music as you go round and round. Thursday-Saturday 11 a.m.-5 p.m.; Sunday 1-5 p.m. Closed January. No museum admission charge, but charge for tour or carousel ride. 913.682.1331. firstcitymuseums.org.

Leavenworth Landing Park: 2 Cherokee (behind Riverfront Community Center). Historical sculptures, interpretive signs, benches, and old-fashioned street lights blend well with the landscape along the quarter-mile riverfront walk. This scenic area commemorates the riverboats, railroad, wagon escorts, outfitters, trails west, and military roads that made Leavenworth an important transportation hub.

Riverfront Community Center: 123 S. Esplanade. Beautifully repurposed, this former 1888 Union Pacific depot retains vestiges of its historic role. Most interesting are the arched doorway windows lettered "Women" and "Men" indicating where each should wait—in separate rooms—for the trains. Monday-Saturday 9 a.m.-5 p.m.; Sunday 1-5 p.m. 913.651.2132.

Carroll Mansion (NRHP): 1128 5th Ave. All the original furniture has been replaced because in 1964, Ella Carroll, the last Carroll to live in this home, announced at church that she was leaving the

mansion and people could come get anything from the house they wanted. After the last item was removed, Ella gave the key and the house deed to the Leavenworth Historical Society. The home is one of the finest mansions in the state open for tours and is a pristine example of an elite lifestyle. Completed in 1882, it features finery at every turn, from the parquet floor pattern to the carved woodwork. It's also fun to look for its subtle dog theme (ask about it when you visit). Images from the famous Everhard photo collection are a tasteful addition throughout the home. Tuesday-Saturday 10:30 a.m.-4:30 p.m. Admission charge. 913.682.7759. leavenworthhistory.org.

Heroic Dog: Carroll Mansion grounds. You can't help but notice the life-sized statue of a large black dog wearing a red collar and standing in front of the mansion. The story goes that in 1865 a dog gave his life when he chased down a runaway carriage with a young girl inside. The dog threw himself under the horses to stop them, saving the girl. To honor the brave canine, the girl's family purchased the statue and placed it in front of their home. When that house was torn down in 1967, the statue was donated to the Leavenworth Historical Society and moved to the Carroll Mansion. Due to vandalism of the original, a replica statue was made in 1975 and has been greeting visitors ever since.

Lincoln Steps: Carroll Mansion grounds. Place your feet on the very steps that

President Lincoln stood on when he delivered a campaign speech in 1859. At that time these steps were in front of the downtown Planter's Hotel.

First City Museum:

743 Delaware. View early frontier displays, jail and prison exhibits, and a diverse collection of artifacts about Leavenworth—the First City of Kansas. Thursday 1-5 p.m. 913.682.1866. firstcitymuseums.org.

Richard Allen Cultural Center:

412 Kiowa. Exhibits include compelling images of early Leavenworth from the famous Everhard photo collection, uniforms once belonging to General Colin Powell, and displays focusing on the buffalo soldier, Leavenworth's impressive black heritage, and the nation's African American history. On the lawn is a bronze bust memorial to Cathay Williams, the only female buffalo soldier. Monday-Friday 11 a.m.-4 p.m. Donation suggested. 913.682.8772. richardallenculturalcenter.info.

Leavenworth Downtown Historic District (NRHP):

Enjoy the variety of shopping experiences in this historic downtown. Among the shaded environs you'll find restaurants, coffee shops, a bicycle shop, antiques, art, gifts, and a kitchen accessories store. 913.682.3924. leavenworthmainstreet.com.

Historic Districts:

Because nine historic districts in Leavenworth are on the National Register of Historic Places you can drive in almost any direction and discover beautiful homes and buildings. Homes designed by William and Myron Feth can be found in the 1000 and 1100 blocks of 3rd Ave., the 200 and 500 blocks of N. Broadway, the 200 block of Arch, the 300 block of Pine, and the 800 to 1000 blocks of S. Esplanade. tinyurl.com/leavnrhp.

Fred Harvey Home (NRHP):

624 Olive. Fred Harvey established the first restaurant chain in the United States, tying it to the Atchison, Topeka and Santa Fe Railway. His first restaurant opened in the Santa Fe depot in Topeka in 1876, and in 1883 the Harvey Girls became part of the Harvey House system. Fred and his family moved into this home in 1883, and although Fred died in 1901, the family remained until 1944. firstcitymuseums.org.

Carnegie Library (NRHP):

601 S. 5th. One of two oldest Carnegie libraries in the state, this brick and limestone Neoclassical structure opened in 1902 and served as the Leavenworth Public Library until 1987. In recent years the building was renovated into apartments.

Leavenworth County Courthouse (NRHP):

300 Walnut. The 1913 limestone courthouse features a central rotunda stained-glass dome and scagliola columns inside. Colorful murals by artists Ernst Ulmer (Bleeding Kansas) and Michael Young (Struggle for Freedom) were added in 2006. Outside, a tall veterans memorial "To the memory of our boys who made the supreme sacrifice in the World War" and a WWI charging doughboy statue grace the grounds of this Modern Eclecticism structure. Monday-Friday 8 a.m.-4 p.m. 913.684.0700.

U.S. Penitentiary:

1300 Metropolitan. Many have commented that the "Pen" resembles the U.S. Capitol when it's lit up at night. It has a wide block of front steps and a silver dome, but the similarities end with the razor wire and guardhouses. Prisoners from the U.S. Disciplinary Barracks at Fort Leavenworth helped with the first phase of construction in 1903. The penitentiary was completed in the mid-1920s, and although it was once one of the largest maximum-security prisons in the country it is now a medium-security federal prison to 1,800 inmates. Incarcerated here were such well-knowns as the "Birdman of Alcatraz" Robert Stroud, George "Machine Gun" Kelly, George "Bugs" Moran, boxer Rocky Graziano, and drug trafficker Manuel Noriega. Visitors are not allowed on the grounds.

Dwight Eisenhower VA Medical Center Campus:

4101 S. 4th St. Trfy. Drive slowly through the campus to view the many elegant structures originally part of the Old Soldiers Home built in the mid-1880s. Responding to a 1999 plan to downsize the campus, combined preservation efforts resulted in saving 38 historic buildings from demolition. Today they are being privately renovated for various uses while the VA center continues to offer medical services.

Leavenworth National Cemetery:

150 Muncie. Established in 1886, this national cemetery has interments of more than 40,000 veterans, from the Indian Wars to the present, and their eligible dependents. Six Medal of Honor recepients are buried here. A memorial spire overlooks the Missouri River Valley from the highest point of this awe-inspiring cemetery.

NE

Chapel of the Veterans:
4101 S. 4th St. Trfy. (VA campus). The 1893 red-brick and limestone church shares a chapel and stained-glass window for two denominations—Protestant is upstairs; Catholic is on the lower level—and in 1921 the chapel was listed in *Ripley's Believe It or Not* because it conducted two services simultaneously. The ornate stained-glass windows feature both religious and patriotic themes, and W.B.N.H.D.V.S. engraved in one window stands for Western Branch National Home of Disabled Volunteer Soldiers. The gargoyles on the outside Gothic tower were designed to frighten away evil spirits. The church no longer provides services but is open to visitors. Daily 8 a.m.-5 p.m.

Mount Zion Cemetery:
From N. 4th, 3¼ miles west on Metropolitan, then ¼ mile southwest on 172. The entrance gate to this Jewish cemetery bears the inscription, "Society Sons of Truth, Organized June 10, 1858." The oldest grave is marked 1860 and the latest burial was in 2000. Of interest are the many gravestones written in Hebrew and the 1931 Salinger mausoleum.

Mama Mia's: 402 S. 20th. During warm weather you'll want to take advantage of the outdoor garden and dine beside the babbling brook. Since 1991 Mama Mia's has been serving some of the best steaks (hand cut) and Italian food in the area. A full bar is available. Tuesday-Friday 11 a.m.-1:30 p.m.; Tuesday-Saturday 4-8:30 p.m. 913.682.2131. FB.

Metropolitan Steak House:
1501 Metropolitan. Good taste is locked up at the Metropolitan, which stands just across from the U.S. Penitentiary. Locals rave about the filet mignon! Daily 11 a.m.-9 p.m. 913.651.6624. FB.

Luigi's: 418 Cherokee. "We'll always have Luigi's" say many who have eaten here and bonded over the delicious food and wine. A robust menu features mussels and Spaghetti "Aglio e Olioa" e Peperoncino to steaks and wood-fired pizza, plus your favorite traditional Italian fare. A full bar is available with an excellent cocktail and wine selection. Desserts change daily but if Limoncello Cake is offered, get it! Daily 11 a.m.-10 p.m. 913.675.7200. luigisitalian.us.

Baan Thai: 301 S. 4th. The freshest ingredients go into mouth-watering dishes so good you can't wait to go back and try more. Daily 11 a.m.-8 p.m. 913.682.6999. baanthaikansas.com.

Marfield's Irish Pub
& Grill: 312 N. 2nd. Owner Dave Spangler named his bar for his mother-in-law! Inside this 1903 former carriage house you'll find Guinness on tap, and on the menu Dublin Coddle and Bangers and Mash, to name a few. It's clear you've come across a traditional Irish pub. Daily 11 a.m.-9 p.m. 913.651.4401. marfieldspub.com.

First Taste Cafe:
424 Cherokee. A unique and locally owned business, First Taste Olive Oils operates in a historic building complete with original floors, pressed-tin ceiling, and brick walls. It's a perfect setting to sample infused olive oils and vinegar such as Black Truffle Olive Oil, Persian Lime Olive Oil, Blueberry Balsamic Vinegar, and Champagne Balsamic Vinegar. The olive oils and vinegars are also some of the ingredients in lunch, dinner, and desserts served in the cafe. Top off your experience with an olive oil ice cream and Tahini brownie! Store hours, Monday-Saturday 10 a.m.-6 p.m.; cafe hours, Monday-Saturday 11 a.m.-2:30 p.m. and Friday-Saturday 5-9 p.m. 913.744.5138. firsttasteoliveoil.com.

Towne Pub: 1001 Ottawa. Thick, fresh, hand-pattied burgers have been sizzling here for more than 27 years—and they are memorable! Monday-Saturday 11 a.m.-2 p.m.; Tuesday-Saturday 4-8:45 p.m. 913.682.5456. FB.

Homer's: 1320 S. 4th. Car hops and friendly waitresses have provided excellent service at Homer's since 1931. Expect fresh burgers, old-fashioned shakes and malts, and classic breakfasts at this classic drive-in/diner. Monday-Sunday 6:30 a.m.-8 p.m. 913.651.3500.

Santa Fe Depot Diner
(NRHP): 781 Shawnee. Breakfast is served all day at this elaborate 1887 stone depot. Its turrets and interior woodwork are reminiscent of the early days of railroad travel. Daily 6 a.m.-2 p.m. 913.297.0361.

Pullman Place Family Restaurant: 230 Cherokee. Breakfasts, luncheon specials, and burgers taste great inside this old brick building filled with railroad memorabilia. Daily 7 a.m.-8 p.m. 913.682.0200. FB.

More Good Restaurants: Abe's Place (5101 10th, 913.727.2661); Grinder's High Noon (602 Choctaw, 913.651.1000); Harbor Lights Coffeehouse & Cafe (316 Shawnee, 913.682.2303).

Lodging: 913.758.2948, visitleavenworthks.com.

explorer extras... In Leavenworth

A Statue of Liberty replica stands in front of City Hall at 5th and Shawnee.

To celebrate the 150th anniversary of Lincoln's speech in Leavenworth and the 200th anniversary of his birth, the city commissioned artist Martin Leo Pyle to create a full-sized statue of our 16th president. Dedicated in 2009, the statue, at 100 N. 5th, is a few blocks from where Lincoln spoke at the now-demolished Stockton Hall.

Michael Young painted the mural at 5th and Delaware commemorating Leavenworth as the first (1854) incorporated city in Kansas. Another of his murals, in sepia tones of historic Leavenworth, graces the west side of First City Photos and Frames, 406 Shawnee.

The Performing Arts Center, in the 1938 art deco theatre (NRHP) at 500 Delaware, is home to the River City Community Players. 913.651.0027. rccplv.com.

Rock singer and songwriter Melissa Etheridge is from Leavenworth. Her childhood home is at 1902 Miami.

explorer extras... In Linwood

Population 375

The two-story frame William A. Harris House (NRHP) was erected in 1883. Known as the country's authority on Shorthorn cattle, Harris also served as a U.S. congressman and senator. From Main, ¼ mile west on K-32.

Look closely in the corner lot at 3rd and Ash and you'll find the few scattered gravestones of Congregational Cemetery founded on this spot in 1870. **ee**

TONGANOXIE

Population 5,165

Outdoor Book Mural: 4th and Delaware. Are those books real? No, but they look like it! This colorful mural of giant books depicts titles, people, and places that formed the cultural heritage of this small town. Artfully painted by muralist Kelly Poling, the book titles incorporate themes submitted by town residents. A central figure in the image is beloved local doctor "Doc Stevens," and this unique mural adorns the side wall of his former office.

People of Tonganoxie Outdoor Mural: 4th and Delaware. In the same pocket park as the book mural (*see* previous entry) artist Kelly Poling has painted vignettes of past and present Tonganoxie including Chief Tonganoxie's lodge; Magdalena Bury, who platted the town; Danielle Boatwright, 1996 Miss Kansas and winner of TV reality show

Survivor: Guatemala; and Kirby McRill, known around 1900 to have walked from Tonganoxie to Chicago in just over seven days!

Drayman Outdoor Mural: E. 4th and Bury. In 1980 Steve Murill painted an early-1920s depiction of Bill Ridgeway, the last of the town's horse-drawn draymen. Bill delivered freight from the railroad depot to town merchants.

Tonganoxie Museum: 201 W. Washington. The Tonganoxie Community Historical Society is on what was once the largest dairy farm in Kansas. Museum exhibits telling the area's story are inside the 1929 Fairchild/Knox dairy barn. Also on this pleasant site is a 1916 one-room school, a 1936 fire pumper truck, a red-brick silo, working windmill, and the 1918 Reno Methodist Church. In 1989 the church was used in the filming of the Michael Landon movie Where Pigeons Go to Die. Sunday, Wednesday 1-4 p.m.; Tuesday 9 a.m.-4 p.m. 913.845.2960. FB.

Magnatech Park: Tonganoxie and Pleasant. Pull into the small parking lot, tie up your laces, and enjoy a walk through this garden oasis, lovingly cared for by the local Master Gardeners. A walking path north takes you to Chieftan Park and trails totaling just over a mile.

It's A Sweet Treat Day Bakery: 528 E. 4th. Treat your sweet tooth to a cupcake—

NE

16 flavors to choose from—or any of the other mouth-watering goodies. Cinnamon rolls for breakfast, gourmet coffee anytime, and the "Blue Plate Special" box lunch on Wednesdays are as pleasing as they are popular. Tuesday-Friday 6:30 a.m.- 6 p.m.; Saturday 7:30 a.m.-12 p.m. 913.284.9074. FB.

Myers Hotel Bar:

220 S. Main. Built in 1879, the hotel stands on the old Kansas City to Denver stage route. Molly Myers ran it from 1889 to the 1930s as a hotel and later a bus stop. It was here that Kansas playwright William Inge was inspired to write the Broadway play *Bus Stop*. Now, in its new life, Myers has become the hip place to sip signature cocktails, beer, and wine in a historic atmosphere. "Barchitec" (bartender and architect) Kate Brubacher makes everyone feel welcome and loves building creative drink concoctions. It's strictly a bar business but occasionally food trucks are on hand Friday or Saturday nights. Thursday-Saturday 5 p.m.-12 a.m.; Sunday 12 p.m.-5 p.m. 785.840.6764. FB.

Flashbacks: 630 E. 4th.

Rub elbows with the locals as you enjoy a home-cooked breakfast (served all day) or bite into a thick hand-pattied burger for lunch. Decorated with area memorabilia, Flashbacks offers interesting flashbacks to the past. Daily 6 a.m.-1 p.m. 913.845.2224. FB.

Grandpa's Burger Box:

106 W. 2nd. It's touted as serving one of the best burgers in the state. They are huge, cooked to order, and worth the wait. The hot dogs get a thumbs up too. A bright and colorful mural is a fun addition to this well-loved drive-in. Tuesday-Friday 11 a.m.-7 p.m.; Saturday 11 a.m.-3 p.m. 913.369.8994.

Marshall County

AROUND THE COUNTY

Blue River Rail Trail:

An 82-mile trail on a retired railroad bed connects Marysville through Oketo to Lincoln, Nebraska. Twelve miles of the crushed stone trail meander along the Big Blue River and lead you through scenic woods and cropland and across bridges to create a pleasant bike ride or hike. Trailheads are at Oketo on Mill (from Center, 2 blocks south on State, then ¼ mile north on Mill) and in Marysville on Jayhawk (from Alston, ¾ mile north on 8th, then ½ mile west and north on Jayhawk). blueriverrailtrail.org.

The following places are all within a few miles of each other southwest of Frankfort. Go from one to the next to the next.

• Oregon Trail Marker:

From 2nd in Frankfort, 3½ miles south on K-99, 2½ miles west and south on Yonder, then 2 miles west and south on Yeoman. The marker indicates the location of the Vermillion River lower crossing that wagons on the Oregon Trail used.

• Bigelow: From the Oregon

Trail marker, ¼ mile west on Yoeman, then ⅛ mile south and west on Zenith. On the south side of the road is the site of the former town of Bigelow, founded in 1881. Once famous for its limestone quarry industry, the town met its demise in the 1960s when it was razed for construction of Tuttle Creek Lake. Only a large marker in a small park remains to tell the Bigelow story. Register your visit in a notebook at the mailbox.

• Bicycle on a Pillar: From

the Bigelow site, 1¼ mile west on Zenith to the bridge crossing

the Black Vermillion River. Down river to the south two railroad pillars still stand in the water. Look closely to see the bicycle on top of one of them. For more than 20 years it has stood there, but no one knows how it got there or what happened to the rider.

• Antioch Cemetery:

From the bicycle on a pillar, ¼ mile west on Zenith, then ½ mile north on 15 Terr. The cemetery was spared from the Tuttle Creek Lake project, and more than 800 former residents of Bigelow still rest peacefully there.

AXTELL

Population 401

WWI Doughboy Statue: 5th and Maple. A plaque dedicates this statue to the "Axtell boys who served in the World War 1914-18."

Historic Home: 107 State. The large white frame house was built in the early 1900s and was converted to a city hospital in 1929. In 1958 the hospital was deactivated, and the house was sold to become a private residence once again.

St. Michael's Catholic Church: 504 6th. The tall spire leads you to this 1905 red-brick church whose beautiful vaulted ceilings and walls with detailed stenciling are worth seeing. 785.736.2220.

St. Bridget Catholic Church (NRHP): From Elm, 6½ miles north on 30. This handsome red-brick church stands proudly (although with no steeple) on the rolling hills. When construction was completed in 1909, no money remained to add a steeple. Inside you'll find a magnificent vaulted ceiling and beautiful stained-glass windows, eight of which were moved here from an earlier church. The archdiocese of Kansas City closed St. Bridget in 1967, but the St. Bridget Historical Society saved the church from demolition. A bronze plaque on a glacial stone tells the church's story. 785.736.2910.

Pony Express Marker: From Elm, 1¾ miles north on 30. Standing on the west side of the road, an old and weathered limestone marker preserves the 1861 site of David Smith's Pony Express and Stage Station.

ACE'S (Axtell Community Effort) Restaurant: 402 Maple. Everything is cooking on all cylinders at this former community-owned cafe, now owned by Wynn Buessing. The

daily special is posted outside on a sidewalk board. Monday-Saturday 11 a.m.-1:30 p.m.; 5-8 p.m. 785.736.2218.

BEATTIE

Population 198

Historic Homes: The limestone FitzGerald house (305 Smith) was built by town founder James FitzGerald in 1875. The circa 1900 Hawk house (611 Whiting), constructed by an early businessman, is a four-story limestone home with decorative features.

Hitching Posts: An attractive feature throughout downtown are the black hitching posts with the horse heads and tie rings.

Beattie Heritage Museum: 716 Main. To go inside and see artifacts from Guittard Station (a stop on the Pony Express route) and other local displays, pick up a museum key from Coleen at Coleen's Mop Shop, 717 Main. 785.556.0461.

Limestone Kiln: From Center, ½ mile west on Elm (Ironstone). Nearly the size of a small room and visible from the county road, the kiln stands on the south side of Ironstone, just west of 21. Constructed in the 1860s by James FitzGerald, the kiln produced mortar used in constructing area stone buildings.

Pony Express Marker: From Elm (Ironstone), 3¼ miles north on 21. Surrounded by concrete bridge railings, a pony and rider plaque on a red stone notes that the site of Guittard Station, a Pony Express stop, is just to the east.

Beattie Cafe: 713 Main. A small town needs a cafe! After being "cafe-less" for two years, a small group fixed up the old cafe. Now a happy community once again has a place for breakfast and lunch. The locals are happy to see visitors here too.

BLUE RAPIDS

Population 997

NE

Alcove Spring (NRHP; 8 Wonders of Kansas Geography): 1780 E. River. From Main, 2½ miles east and north on U.S. 77, 1¼ miles west on Tumbleweed, ½ mile south on 8, then 3¾ miles north on E. River. Roughly paralleling the sandy river bed of the Big Blue River, E. River Road was part of the Oregon Trail beginning in 1843. As it does today, it led to Alcove Spring, a well-known campsite for trail travelers. From the Alcove Spring parking lot, signage will guide you along the eighth-mile walk to the spring. Water from a wet-weather creek flows (usually during April and May) over a rocky outcrop and falls 10 feet into a pool. The spring below and to the right of the waterfall never dries up and is presumed to be the spring for which the site was named. You're in peaceful environs here and surrounded by the presence of history. Across the road from the parking lot in an area known as Emigrant  Campground you'll find additional signage and a memorial to Sarah Keyes. The 70-year-old Keyes, a member of the Donner-Reed party, died here in 1846. tinyurl.com/alcovespring2.

Prospect Hill Cemetery:
From Main, 2½ miles east and north on U.S. 77, 1¼ miles west on Tumbleweed, then mile south on 8. Once you arrive at the cemetery, proceed to the back. There the view of the confluence of the Big and Little Blue Rivers is beautiful, and the sunsets are breathtaking.

Round Square (8 Wonders of Kansas Customs):
4 Public Square. From U.S. 77, 1 block south on Main. Blue Rapids holds the distinction of having the only round town square in the state. Dating to 1870 when Taylor Holbrook platted the town, the round square acts as the town hub with streets projecting from it like wheel spokes. Within the square you'll find Fountain Park, complete with picturesque fountain and an ornate stone veterans memorial. Among the memorial's several plaques, a unique bronze plate placed in 1920 honors the "Blue Rapids Boys in the Service 1914-18." tinyurl.com/roundbr.

Monument to the Ice Age:
On the square. The oldest rocks in Kansas are found in this region, thus this Monument to the Ice Age. In an open exhibit area, you'll find several billion-year-old red rocks, plus signage that provides the fascinating history of the rocks' formation in Minnesota and South Dakota and the glaciation that carried

them to northeast Kansas about 600,000 years ago.

Blue Rapids Museum:
36 Public Square. A special exhibit area changes every few months while permanent displays tell the story of this charming community. You'll be delighted by the history preserved here in exhibit and archival form, which includes such topics as prehistory, trails, the gypsum industry, and early floods. Saturday 9 a.m.-12 p.m. 785.363.7949. FB.

Holm Cabin and Mural:
South side of the square. The log cabin was built in 1876 by Swedish emigrants using oak and walnut from a homestead south of town. It was occupied until approximately 1981 and some years later moved to this site. On the building next to the cabin a large mural by Kenny Winkenwader depicts an early settlers scene.

Oldest Library (NRHP):
14 Public Square. A two-story limestone structure built in 1876, the Blue Rapids Public Library is the oldest library in the state in continuous operation in the same building. 785.363.7709.

Blue Rapids Mercantile:
401 E. 5th. Antiques, collectibles, and a myriad of other great finds await your discovery. Monday-Saturday 10 a.m.-5 p.m. 785.363.7900. FB.

Historic Baseball Game:
From Main, ½ mile west on U.S. 77. Metal silhouettes of baseball players flank a sign that recounts the story of a historic game played here between barnstorming major leaguers in October 1913. Several

participants later became Hall of Famers: Christy Mathewson, Jim Thorpe, and John McGraw. Earl Woods, father of golfer Tiger Woods, played for a Blue Rapids team here in the 1950s.

American Woman's League Chapter House:
513 Lincoln. This 1911 one-story Arts and Crafts stucco house is evidence of a nation-wide organization founded in 1907 by magazine publisher Edward Gardner Lewis. He formed the League in an effort to increase subscriptions to his women's publications. By 1912 the League folded and a second organization, more concerned with women's rights, became the surviving entity.

Round Barn: From Main, 1½ miles east on U.S. 77, then 1¼ miles east on K-9. Benton Steele built this unusual round barn in 1913 for John Drennan and his Hereford cattle. It measures 92 feet in diameter and is approximately 60 feet tall with a large cupola on top. Dave Stump and family now own the barn. They are happy to show it to you, but would appreciate a call before you stop in. 785.556.0124.

East Side Cafe: 505 E. 5th. The locals rave about the "really good eatin'" here. Daily specials might include ham loaf, beans and cornbread, and roast beef. But there's no "might" about the always-special homemade pies! Tuesday-Saturday 8 a.m.-8 p.m.; Sunday 8 a.m.-2 p.m. 785.562.7008. FB.

Lodging: RV Park (785.363.7991).

**explorer extras...
In Blue Rapids**

On the east side of the State Bank of Blue Rapids, 21 Public Square, you'll find a very unusual robbery alarm. A sculpted, no-nonsense bulldog stands guard above the inscription, "Always on the Job." Manufactured by Bankers Electric Protection Company of Minneapolis, Minnesota, the alarm would sound outside when someone inside pushed a button. Painted red and blue, the old-time alarm was permanently turned off in the 1980s. 785.363.7721.

Enjoy a ride on historic tracks in an open-air passenger car (see p. 154) from Blue Rapids across the Big Blue River. April-October. Admission charge. Reservations required. 785.799.4294. centralbranchrailroad.com.

The area once boasted four gypsum mines, but the Georgia-Pacific north of town on U.S. 77 is one of only two mines remaining in the state. In 1858 Frank Marshall, for whom the county is named, recognized the rock as gypsum. He burned it and produced plaster from the powder, which he used to build his house.

At 703 East, Jesse Axtell built his "cement veneer" house, as he called it, in 100 days in 1909. He made his own hollow cement blocks, but during the same period, others ordered concrete blocks for home exteriors from catalogs such as Sears, Roebuck & Co.

A magazine article inspired Carol Johnston to create a fence displaying bowling balls, plus two bowling ball totem poles. Carol and her mother, along with donations from friends and family, collected 98 of the heavy orbs and placed them atop fence posts along K-9 near Carol's home. She is always looking for more balls, so if you have any to donate simply leave them at the

driveway entrance. To see the odd-ball fence, from U.S. 77, go 2¼ miles east on K-9 to 1281 K-9. **ee**

FRANKFORT

Population 709

Elsie Grace's Gift Shoppe and Fudge Factory:

123 N. Kansas. An 1867 red-brick corner bank building is now the place to buy gift items and Elsie's dry food, pie, soup, and pancake mixes, and her Drunken Chicken rubs. And you were just expecting fudge! It's here too. Monday-Friday 9 a.m.-5 p.m.; Saturday 9 a.m.-3 p.m. 785.292.4438. FB.

Memorials and Markers:

2nd and Elm. In the south-central area of City Park you'll find a stone memorial to those who lost their lives on the *USS Maine* in 1898 and a DAR marker inscribed "Pike's Peak Trail 1842." A veterans memorial rests in the park's southeast corner.

Historic Jail: The restored

1890 stone jail (NRHP) stands at its original location at E.1st and Locust. It ceased being a lockup in the early 1950s.

Frankfort Grade School

(NRHP): 400 Locust. This 1902 Renaissance style former school is a stunning building in disrepair. But volunteers are bringing this gray/brown-brick structure back to life! Built at a 45-degree angle, the broad porch with

wooden columns sits under a central tower whose limestone arch windows match those on the front of the first floor. FB.

2nd Street: 200 N. Kansas. Smoked meats, fresh burgers, made-from-scratch meals, and homemade pies make this restaurant a top choice for good food. Fridays and Saturdays feature grilled ribeye and KC strip steaks. Tuesday-Friday 11 a.m.-2 p.m. and 5-8 p.m.; Saturday 5-9 p.m. 785.292.6064. FB.

Lodging: Banker's Inn Bed and Breakfast (785.292.4225; thebankersinn.com).

HOME CITY

Unincorporated

Family Home Treasures:

302 3rd. In this restored church-turned-gift shop, owner Kelly Schroedl has made shopping a heavenly experience. Decor created from recycled church items, plus unique treasures for sale make this a beautiful place to visit. Tuesday-Friday 10 a.m.-5:30 p.m.; Saturday 10 a.m.-4 p.m. 785.799.3418. FB.

Little Hap's Bar & Grill:

211 2nd. This locally owned co-op restaurant has been making taste buds happy since 2008. Find all the comfort foods

NE

here including meatloaf and made-from-scratch daily specials. Monday-Saturday 9 a.m.- 8:30 p.m. 785.799.9920.

MARYSVILLE

Population 3,295

Visitor Information
Center: 101 N. 10th. Stop here for local and area tourist information. Kenny Winkenwader painted the mural portraying Marysville history. Monday-Friday 8 a.m.-5 p.m.; Saturday 9 a.m.-3 p.m. visitmarysvilleks.org.

Pony Express Rider
Sculpture: 700 Broadway. This 1985 Richard Bergen bronze sculpture portrays the first Pony Express rider, Jack Kectley, to carry the mail west from Marysville, which he did on April 3, 1860, on the initial run to Sacramento, California. The plaque recounts that the Pony Express lasted 18 months and in the 650,000 miles that riders traveled during that time, only one rider was killed, one rider lost, and only one schedule not completed.

Outdoor Murals:
700 Broadway (Pony Express Plaza). Three Lifetiles murals depicting local historical scenes "move" along with you. They appear as fixed images but as you walk by they seem to come to life. Quite the moving experience! Opposite these murals are four colorful wooden quilt murals by local artists.

Post Office Art: 109 S. 9th. In front of the post office a bronze plaque relates the Pony Express story. Inside, a framed mural depicts a horse and rider galloping off from the Marysville station in 1860. 785.562.3236.

Historic Trails Park:
From Broadway, ¾ mile south on U.S. 77 (10th), 1½ miles east then north then west (under U.S. 77, across railroad tracks), continue north, then before going under an overpass, turn west into the park. Eight historic trails crossed Marshall County (Oregon Trail, Overland Trail, Pony Express route, Military Trail, Mormon Trail, Otoe-Missouria Trail, St. Joseph-California Trail, and Pike's Peak-California Trail). Excellent plaques and interpretive signs explain each one, and a map shows each route. A replica rope ferry shows what trail travelers used to cross the Big Blue River.

Koester House Museum
and Gardens (NRHP):
919 Broadway. Coming from Germany to Marysville in 1860, Charles F. Koester became one of the first bankers in town. In 1876 he built his family home—a showplace surrounded by trees, shrubs, and flower gardens. Cast iron lions and dogs still guard the Koester gates, and a dozen white bronze (zinc) statues (significant works of art made between 1880 and 1910) still adorn the front yard. Guided tours of the house, summer kitchen, icehouse, and carriage house provide the story of the

entire Koester Block (NRHP). April-October, Monday-Saturday 10 a.m.-4:30 p.m.; Sunday 1-4 p.m. 785.562.2417. FB.

City Cemetery: From U.S. 36, ½ mile north on 15th, then 1 mile east on North. The cemetery entrances, chapel, and privy are 1939 WPA projects. A Civil War monument stands at the center of the cemetery, and the Koester family plot is to the south and a bit east of this monument, across two driveways. The Koester plot is a crowded grouping of varied gravestones, including a concrete tub. The Helverings, related to the Koesters, are buried to the north of the Koester plot.

Historic Courthouse
Museum (NRHP):
1207 Broadway. The Marshall County Historical Society is housed inside the former 1891 brick-faced Romanesque style courthouse. Its columns are polished red granite, and the word "Justice" stands out in terra cotta in the cornices above the second-floor windows. Visit the historic courtroom and the more than 20 display rooms that

present the history of area schools, the military, industry, agriculture, trails, and more. April-October, Monday Friday 10 a.m.-4 p.m.; Saturday-Sunday 1-4 p.m.; November-March, Monday-Friday 1-4 p.m. 785.562.5012. FB.

Pony Express Home Station No. 1 (NRHP):

106 S. 8th. For 18 months courageous young Pony Express riders carried the mail across the West between Missouri and California. A home station was available every 40 to 50 miles along the 1,966-mile route where riders changed horses or were relieved by other riders. This 1859 stone barn in Marysville is the only original Pony Express home station remaining on its original site. To understand this colorful time in history, watch the introductory video then visit the horse stalls and blacksmith shop. You'll also see a replica mochilla (a large four-pouch leather mail bag that fit over the saddle) and a painting illustrating the first ride by Johnny Fry on April 3, 1860. The museum also exhibits additional Marshall County history. May-October, Monday-Saturday 9 a.m.-5 p.m.; Sunday 12-4 p.m. Admission charge. 785.562.3825.

Pusch-Randell House (NRHP):

1000 Elm. This 1904 Queen Anne two-and-a-half-story brick home was built with many angles plus an octagonal tower and wooden porch. What a beauty!

Union Pacific Depot (NRHP):

400 Hedrix. As volunteers restore this 1929 Spanish Revival style depot for use as an event center and trailhead, the east side will always be stunning. Several panels feature the Union Pacific Overland System logo within a terra cotta ornamentation floral background. The gold of the stucco and the red barrel-tile roof make

this a captivating structure no matter its stage of repair.

City Park:

S. U.S. 77 (S. 10th). After the Union Pacific converted to diesel power, a massive steam locomotive found a home in City Park along with a depot, sod house, and a little red schoolhouse.

Black Squirrel City:

Keep an eye out for the black squirrels scurrying about in City Park. The story goes that a pair of black squirrels came to town with a carnival in 1912, and a boy opened their cage and turned them loose. Over the years the numbers have increased through inbreeding and breeding with the eastern gray squirrels. The black squirrel is the official mascot of Marysville, and these little guys are given the right of way all over town.

Black Squirrels on Parade:

As you drive around town you can't help but notice the many creatively decorated five-foot-tall fiberglass black squirrels. Professional and amateur artists were invited to embellish 21 of them to pay homage to the town mascot and tell the story of this beloved creature.

Recreation:

Included are the playground and swimming pool at City Park (S. 10th, 785.562.2859); Landoll Lanes bowling alley (2005 Center, 785.619.6111); and the Astro 3 Theatre (820 Center, 785.562.3715).

Las Cabanas Restaurant:

908 Elm. This limestone house built by the Koester family in 1906 is now home to Las Cabanas. The home's grandeur is still obvious, and

although you won't find typical Mexican decor, any reason to enjoy excellent cuisine while surrounded by a wraparound porch, leaded-glass windows, and beautiful woodwork is a good one. Monday-Saturday 11 a.m.-9 p.m.; Sunday 11 a.m.-3 p.m. 785.562.5003.

Wagon Wheel:

703 Broadway. Biscuits and gravy for breakfast, a whiskey burger for lunch, smoked pork chops, coconut cream pie, and cherry cream cheesecake are five good reasons to roll into the Wagon Wheel. Monday-Saturday 6 a.m.-9 p.m. 785.562.3784. FB.

Toledo Coffee and Deli:

723 Broadway. Nourish yourself with soups, salads, sandwiches, and coffees. Spoil yourself with pies, cinnamon rolls, cheesecakes, and scones! Everything is homemade. Tuesday-Friday 7 a.m.-3 p.m.; Saturday 7 a.m.-2 p.m. 785.562.3354. FB.

Big Blue River Scenic Back Road:

From 10th, 1 mile west on U.S. 36, 4¾ miles south on W. River, then ¾ mile west on Osage. This narrow, winding road follows the river, drifts into bottomland, and takes you past farmsteads tucked into wooded areas. When you turn west, head for the microwave tower to find the 1914 Lewis Rowe round barn, the only barn in the state known to come from a Sears, Roebuck & Co. catalog kit. Drive by only.

Lodging: visitmarysvilleks.org/lodging.html.

explorer extras...
In Marysville

When you drive over the brick streets, think about this. During a recent effort to redo the streets, each brick (originally laid in 1920) was removed, cement was laid, and each brick was replaced. It took six weeks to do each block!

NE

The 1934 WPA retaining wall, N. 9th and Carolina, is locally known as "the wall" and is quite a work of art. It's several stories high, and the stairs lead to a school.

The 1937 football stadium and the 1939 art deco high school at 1011 Walnut were constructed by the WPA. The 1963 junior high school also contributes to this complex being on the national register.

In Lions Park, 16th and North, a fun winding sidewalk leads you to the top of a small grassy mound where you can take a seat and enjoy the pleasant environs. A playground is nearby as are a gazebo, benches, and a picnic area. **ee**

OKETO

Population 84

Oketo Community Museum (NRHP):
100 Center. The 1884 Moore General Store was Oketo's first commercial structure, built with stone from a local quarry. It now houses a museum whose exhibits include the original advertising stage curtains from the opera house, farm machinery, elements of the original general store, and the history and artifacts of the Otoe Indians whose reservation was just north of town. Call ahead. 785.744.3497.

Oketo Cutoff Markers:
From 12th (State), 1 mile west on K-233, and from K-233 (Cherokee), ¾ mile south on 12. Stone markers at each of

these two spots indicate portions of the short-lived Oketo Cutoff, a shorter stagecoach route for the Central Overland California and Pikes Peak Express from 1862 to 1863.

explorer extras... In Oketo

The importance of local stone is apparent at the historic jail (1½ blocks west and south of the community museum) built between 1889 and 1895; and at the stone bank (1 block east of the museum) built in 1889. **ee**

SUMMERFIELD

Population 154

Summerfield's north city limits is the Nebraska state line. From Bethel, follow Main 3 blocks into Nebraska. When you return, take your picture beside the "Welcome to Kansas" sign!

Transue Brothers Blacksmith & Wagon Shop (NRHP):
309 Main. James and George Transue built this limestone and brick building in 1898 for shoeing horses and repairing wagons. Eventually they converted the shop to an auto repair garage. Today it's a blacksmith museum but is rarely open. 402.520.0644. transueblacksmith.org.

Holy Family Church:
600 Main. Step inside this 1919 brick church to admire its beautiful stained-glass windows and stations. 785.736.2220.

Historic Jail: From Main,
½ block east on Bethel, then

south into the alley. That's where the old limestone jail, complete with brick chimney, sits empty— in the alley.

Border Bar & Grill:
306 Main. Every board, every window, every inch of this place was put together by local volunteers and paid for by donations. From home-cooking (including Judy's pies) to a sense of community, you'll find it here. Tuesday-Saturday 11 a.m.- 8 p.m. 785.244.6230. FB.

WATERVILLE

Population 666

Central Branch Railroad:
The Marshall County Railroad Historical Society has saved 12 miles of historic Central Branch/ Missouri Pacific tracks. You may ride in an open-air passenger car pulled by a gang-car on one

of three routes ranging from 45 minutes to two hours. The thrill is going over the trestle bridge 85 feet above the Big Blue River. April-October. Admission charge. Reservations required. 785.799.4294. centralbranchrailroad.com.

Waterville Railroad Depot Museum: 101 Kansas. At this
1907 Missouri Pacific depot you can find out what turkeys and the railroad have in common.

You also will see several Kenny Winkenwader murals dedicated to area railroad

history, plus county and railroad exhibits and an 1850 U.S. map. 785.799.4294.

Caboose Museum: Across from the opera house (200 E. Front). The Marshall County Railroad Historical Society preserves county railroad history. Among its historic assets is this 1925 Union Pacific caboose, which serves as a museum complete with potbelly stove, icebox, and bunk beds. 785.799.4294.

Waterville Opera House (NRHP): 200 E. Front. Audiences of 300 can enjoy theatrical productions and other community events inside this restored 1903 two-story limestone building. 785.363.2515. FB.

Victorian Homes: William Fitzgerald is credited with building 85 percent of Waterville's homes before 1935, including the 1895 Samuel Powell House (NRHP) at 108 W. Commercial. The three Victorian houses in the 200 block of E. Hazelwood were built for early bankers between the late 1880s and 1903 and were dubbed Banker's Row.

Waterville Golf Course: 600 K-9. From Kansas, 1 mile east on U.S. 77/K-9. Built and

maintained by volunteers, this nine-hole, grass-green course provides five frog ponds and several red glacial rocks as obstacles. Greens fee. 785.363.2224.

Weaver Hotel (NRHP): 126 S. Kansas. Waterville's anchor building is this striking three-story railroad hotel built in 1905 and restored in 2009. The facade of the long, narrow exterior is made with precast concrete blocks, and mounted over the curved corner entrance is an ornate pediment accented in green, orange, and yellow. You're welcome to stay

overnight in one of the beautifully furnished rooms, or just stop by the gift shop. Monday-Friday 9 a.m.-4 p.m.; Saturday 9 a.m.-12 p.m. 785.363.2515. weaverhotel.com.

Lodging: Vintage Charm Bed and Breakfast/Guesthouse (785.363.2327, vintagecharmbandb.com); Weaver Hotel (785.363.2515, weaverhotel.com).

**explorer extras...
In Waterville**

The stone shelter house at Lake Idlewild was built by the National Youth Administration in 1940. From K-9, ¼ mile north on Colorado, 1 block west on Elm, 1 mile north on Division (becomes 4), then ½ mile east on Temple to the lake.

For special occasions, Anntie M's Attic, 101 E. Commercial, presents a program on women's fashions and women's history from 1850 to 1990 followed

by a Victorian tea or a 1950s malt shop ice cream special. Reservations required. Call ahead, 785.799.4294. FB. **ee**

Miami County

AROUND THE COUNTY

Hillsdale Lake and State Park: 26001 W. 255. From Main in Hillsdale, 1¾ miles west on 255, ½ mile southeast on Lake. Authorized in 1954 as part of a flood-control plan and completed in 1982, this is one of the newest Kansas reservoirs and is a good one for recreational opportunities. There are several hiking, biking, or equestrian trails. Cabins available, reservations required. 913.783.4507. ksoutdoors.com.

KC Watersports: 25825 Edgemore. From K-68, 3 miles north on U.S. 169, just east on 255, then ½ mile south on Edgemore. At this boat-less ski and wakeboard lake, a series of cables propels riders through the water. The Midwest's only cable lake, it also offers an obstacle course for inflatables. June-August, daily 12-8 p.m.; April, May, September, Saturday-Sunday 12-6 p.m. 913.783.4300. kcwatersports.com.

Lodging: Netherfield Natural Farm Bed & Breakfast, Fontana (202.487.6742, netherfieldnaturalfarm.com).

LOUISBURG

Population 4,299

Louisburg Cider Mill & Country Store: 14730 K-68. From U.S. 69 exit 121, 3 miles west on K-68. Tom and Shelly Schierman made their first jug of Louisburg Cider Mill apple

cider in 1977 in their restored hay barn. A country store was soon added to accommodate their growing product line and growing number of satisfied customers. Along with the cider, the most popular items include Lost Trail Root Beer and sarsaparilla, preserves and butters, and apple cider doughnuts. The old-fashioned store is filled with Cider Mill delights plus other Kansas products and seasonal produce. Monday-Saturday 8 a.m.-6 p.m.; Sunday 9 a.m.-6 p.m. The cider mill press operates September-January, Monday-Friday 8 a.m.-6 p.m. For tours, call 913.837.5202. louisburgcidermill.com.

Simply Selah: 5 S. Peoria. Selah (pronounced Say-lah), a Hebrew word, means to consider or think about. You'll find plenty of vintage and new treasures to consider buying as you roam the 12,000 square feet of antique heaven. Surprises around every corner include mint condition retro furniture, home decor, gift items—and it's all wrapped up with great service. Tuesday-Saturday 10 a.m.-5 p.m.; Sunday 1-5 p.m. 913.837.3110. FB.

Cedar Cove Feline Conservation Park: 3783 K-68. From U.S. 69 exit 121, 4 miles east on K-68. Cedar Cove is the culmination of William Pottorff's long-held vision to educate the public about the large cats of the world and the need to protect the many species endangered in the wild. Siberian and Bengal tigers, African spotted leopards, African lions, mountain lions, and other felines and mammals claim residence in the park. April-October, Saturday 10 a.m.-5 p.m. and Sunday 10 a.m.-3 p.m.; November-March, Saturday-Sunday 11 a.m.-3 p.m. 913.837.5515.

Powell Observatory: 26500 Melrose. From N. Metcalf, 1 mile west on N.16, then 1 mile north and west on Jingo (becomes Melrose). Here's your chance to take a long look through one of the largest telescopes in the five-state area! Programs here include an astronomy talk, observatory tour, and (if skies are clear) viewing of the moon, planets, and stars. May-October, Saturday 30 minutes after dusk. Please dim your headlights when approaching and leaving the observatory. Donation recommended. 913.438.3825. askc.org.

Miss B's: 1006 S. Metcalf. Let the enticing aroma of fried chicken lead you inside Miss B's. Although fried chicken is served only on Thursdays, there is plenty of good home cookin' and bakin' during the rest of the week. Breakfast is served all day. Monday, Wednesday-Saturday 6 a.m.-2 p.m.; Sunday 7 a.m.-2 p.m. 913.837.5974. missbscafe.com.

Timbercreek Bar and Grill: 14 E. Amity. Like the big horse rearing up outside this bar and grill, hungry customers are reared up for the barbecue, steaks, daily specials, and Sunday brunch. Monday-Saturday 11 a.m.-11 p.m.; Sunday 9 a.m.-9 p.m. 913.837.2600. timbercreeklouisburg.com.

Lucille's Diner: 1286 W. Amity. Located in a strip mall, Lucille's might be small but it's big on taste. This diner is known for huge pork tenderloins, burgers, hand-cut fries, homemade pies, and ice cream. What more could you want? Tuesday-Saturday 7 a.m.-8 p.m.; Sunday 7 a.m.-3 p.m. 913.837.5330. FB.

Lodging: Rutlader Outpost RV Park (913.377.2722, rutladeroutpost.com).

OSAWATOMIE

Population 4,385

John Brown Park: 10th and Main. The Battle of Osawatomie was fought on this site on August 30, 1856, a tragic day when abolitionist John Brown and his men tried to defend Osawatomie against proslavery Border Ruffians. The antislavery forces were unsuccessful and the town was burned. A life-sized statue of John Brown, sculpted by George Fite Waters, stands near the entrance to the park, which was dedicated in 1910 by President Theodore Roosevelt. The park later was designated a national historic site. The "Pledge of Allegiance" is etched in stone below the flagpole, and the "Gettysburg Address" appears on a plaque on the pergola's outside wall.

John Brown State Historic Site and Adair Cabin (NRHP): 10th and Main (John Brown Park).

Until he was hanged on December 2, 1859, for raiding a federal arsenal at Harpers Ferry, John Brown was one of the most notorious figures during the period leading up to the Civil War. His crusading life is interpreted inside this log cabin that belonged to Brown's half sister, Florella, and her husband, the Reverend Samuel Adair. Brown lived here with them for a time. The cabin originally stood a mile west of town but was moved to this location in 1912. It is complete with family furnishings

and belongings and Civil War weapons. A limestone pergola was built over the cabin in 1928 to help preserve it. Tuesday-Saturday 10 a.m.-5 p.m. 913.755.4384. kshs.org.

Old Stone Church (NRHP): 315 6th.
This landmark church was built in 1861 by the Reverend Samuel Adair, who, with the help of his sons, hauled in the native stone from the surrounding hills. It stands today, complete with original pews and altar, as the third oldest Congregational church in Kansas.

Soldiers Monument (NRHP): 9th and Main.
Five town defenders killed during the Battle of Osawatomie, including John Brown's son Frederick, are buried near this monument that was dedicated in 1877.

Territorial Land Office: 6th and Lincoln.
The original 1854 building was the area's first land office. A plaque here recounts Osawatomie's significance on the Trail of Death—an 1838 forced march of Potawatomis from their Indiana homeland to eastern Kansas.

Charles Adair House: 1926 Parker.
The two-story clapboard home was built for John Brown's nephew, Charles Adair and his wife, Mary, in 1904. The original site of the Samuel Adair cabin, moved to John Brown Park in 1912, was north of Charles's cabin. A large stone marker near the highway memorializes Frederick Brown, son of John, who died near this spot during the Battle of Osawatomie on August 30, 1856.

Osawatomie Museum: 628 Main.
A reconstructed Missouri Pacific depot is a handsome addition to this local museum. Inside the depot, artifacts preserve the area's railroad history, and a Hall of Honor recognizes county police and fire officials and local residents who served in the military. Displays in the main museum provide background about John Brown, the early history of Osawatomie, and the beginning of Osawatomie State Hospital, the first mental health facility in the state. Tuesday-Saturday 1-4 p.m. 913.755.6781.

Whistle Stop Cafe: 901 S. 6th.
Ride the rails to Dixie's excellent home cooking at the Whistle Stop! River rock and ceramic tile form a track design across the floor, and, upon request, a model train runs around a track suspended from the ceiling.

Dixie's husband, Steve, was a railroad engineer for 33 years. Monday-Tuesday, Thursday, Saturday-Sunday 5:30 a.m.-2 p.m.; Wednesday, Friday 5:30 a.m.-8 p.m. 913.256.4110.

Chris' Cafe: 537 Main.
The daily specials, sandwiches, wraps, soups, and salads are really good here but, oh my, the desserts—they are fabulous! Monday-Saturday 7 a.m.-2:30 p.m. 913.256.6012. FB.

explorer extras...
In Osawatomie

Creamery Bridge (NRHP), spanning the Marais de Cygnes River on N. 8th, is a Marsh triple-arch bridge built in 1930. The largest of its rainbow arches is 140 feet at its zenith. For those stopping to observe or take pictures, a parking lot is on the north side of the bridge. From Brown, ½ mile north on 8th.

A sister bridge, Pottawatomie Creek Bridge (NRHP) on S. 6th is also a Marsh triple-arch structure but was built in 1932. From Brown, 1 mile south on 6th.

Simple white wooden signs around town claim "firsts" and other historic events that happened in Osawatomie. One Main Street sign states that Horace Greeley formed the Republican Party here in 1859. Another explains the origin of the term "jayhawk."

The 1902 Mills House (NRHP), 212 N. 1st, was the dream home of oilman William Mills. He located the Norman No.1 well in Neodesha which effectively opened up the Mid-continent oil fields for drilling. Rock face detailing on the gables is a stand-out on this grand Queen Anne home.

Eighteen holes is a rarity for a small-town course, but that's what you'll find at the Osawatomie Municipal Golf Course, 32942 W. Lakeside. The first nine were built in 1941, the back nine in 1972. Greens fee. 913.755.4769. tinyurl.com/golfosa. **ee**

PAOLA

Population 5,630

Pick up brochures about area wineries and Miami County wine tours at the visitor center, 6 W. Peoria. Monday-Friday 8:30 a.m.-4:30 p.m. 913.294.4335.

Park Square: Peoria and Pearl. Baptiste Peoria gave this plot of land to the Paola Town Company in 1858 with the proviso that no buildings be constructed on it. A bust of Peoria and his wife, Mary Ann, is accompanied by a plaque that describes their contribution to the development of Paola. The first gazebo and fountain were built in the late 1800s, but in 1912 George Washburn created the present Park Square design. Trees and gardens, old-fashioned street lamps, a soldiers monument and statue, benches, and sidewalks leading to the fountain make this a lovely green space for all to enjoy. A storyboard plaque includes inform-

ation about the removal of the Potawatomis from Indiana to Kansas in 1838. They camped here during the forced march, often referred to as the Trail of Death.

Miami County Courthouse (NRHP): 120 S. Pearl. Designed by George Washburn, this red-brick with limestone trim Romanesque Revival structure was completed in 1898. The restored courtroom is the interior highlight with its high ceiling and beautiful oak woodwork. Throughout, the stained glass, ornate wood, and stonework accent one of the best renovated courthouses in the state. Enter on the east side through security (no cell phones allowed). Monday-Friday 8:30 a.m.-4 p.m. 913.294.3326.

Miami County Swan River Museum: 12 E. Peoria. The museum's new addition thoughtfully displays the story of American Indian relocation to this region. Other exhibits provide insight into prehistoric times, the slavery struggle, the Ursuline Sisters, early settlement, and more. Look for the iron cutouts depicting county history that adorn the museum's exterior. Monday-Friday 10 a.m.-4 p.m. 913.294.4940. thinkmiamicountyhistory.com.

City Hall and Bell (RHKP): 19 E. Peoria. A product of yet another George Washburn design, the two-story, red-brick City Hall was completed in 1909. As in the early days, the building is still home to city government and to the police and fire departments. The 400-pound bell that now stands on the grounds once occupied City Hall's cupola. When a fire

was reported, the bell rang a certain number of times to designate in which district the fire was located. 913.259.3600.

Mid-Way Drive-In Theater: 29591 W. 327. From Old Kansas City Road, 2 miles west on 327. Operating since 1952, this classic drive-in still hosts satisfied moviegoers at its original location—midway between Osawatomie and Paola. June-August. Admission charge. 913.755.2325. FB.

Paola Cemetery: From the courthouse, 6 blocks west on Miami, just south on West, then west on the fourth driveway into the cemetery. The graves of early Indians and descendants of Baptiste Peoria are found on the north side of the drive in the Oak Grove addition. The gravestone for Alex Young is one row west of Peoria's descendants. Young's epitaph tells us that he built the steamship Lady Elgin that sank in Lake Michigan in 1860. All 400 passengers on board drowned.

Beethoven's #9: 2 W. Piankishaw. The draw here is the made-from-scratch German food. Quality ingredients go into every dish including the exceptional cabbage rolls, rouladen, schnitzels, weisswurst, and frikadellen (German-style meatloaf). Beethoven's also features hand-cut steaks, Italian entrees, and homemade breads and desserts—an entire symphony of fine cuisine! Local wines and German beer are available. Thursday-Saturday 11 a.m.-8 p.m. 913.294.3000. beethovens9.com.

Grandstand Burger: 812 S. Silver. Jason Camis, Kansas Explorer #3479, gives two thumbs up for the burgers here made fresh and pattied into a thick juicy disc. You'll like the race-car theme inside this Grandstand, and gear up to have your picture taken in front of an authentic sprint race car. Daily 11 a.m.-8 p.m. 913.594.4258. FB.

We B Smokin':

32580 Airport. From Baptiste, 3¼ miles south on Pearl (becomes Silver, then Old Kansas City Road), then 1½ miles west on 327 to the Miami County Airport. Lots of folks say we b flyin' to We B Smokin' for the superb barbecue, hand-breaded tenderloins, and home- made breakfasts. Fly in or drive, but get there anyway you can! Tuesday-Friday 11 a.m.-8 p.m.; Saturday 7 a.m.-8 p.m.; Sunday 7 a.m.-1 p.m. 913.256.6802. websmokin.com.

Jackson Hotel Coffee and Wine Bar: 139 W. Peoria.

George Washburn designed this 1921 red-brick hotel (NRHP) with a handsome full-length porch. After sitting vacant since 1992, the hotel was renovated in 2006 and now serves coffees, wines, salads, soups, sandwiches, and appetizers. Wednesday-Friday 11 a.m.- 2 p.m.;Wednesday, Friday 5-9 p.m.; Saturday-Sunday 9 a.m.-1 p.m. 913.207.8686. thejacksonhotel.com.

New Lancaster General Store (NRHP)and Winery:

36688 New Lancaster. From Pearl, 2 miles southeast on Baptiste, 4 miles east on 311, 4 miles south on Somerset, 2 miles east on 343, then 3 miles south on New Lancaster. This 1903 building has been lovingly restored and is once again a commercial and social gathering place—and the official tasting room for Middlecreek Winery (middlecreekwinery.com). Kansas art, foods, crafts, gifts, antiques, and Middlecreek wine mingle appealingly with the ambience of the store's original shelving, pressed-tin ceiling, and wood floors. Once home to the Kansas Anti-Horse Thief Association, the general store is now the destination place for good times. Friday, Sunday 12-5 p.m., Saturday 10 a.m.- 5:30 p.m. 913.377.4689. newlancastergeneralstore.com.

Grange Hall (NRHP):

12655 W. 367. The New Lancaster Grange bought the 1885 Baptist church in 1901 and used it for its home base until 2005. Today the building functions as a community center.

Somerset Ridge Vineyard and Winery: 29725 Somerset.

From Pearl, 2 miles south-east on Baptiste, 4¼ miles east on 311, then 1¾ miles north on Somerset. Food and music often accompany your opportunity to taste and buy wine in this beautiful setting Wednesday-Saturday 11 a.m.-5p.m.; Sunday 12-5 p.m. 913.491.0038. somersetridge.com.

Nighthawk Vineyard and Winery: 16381 W. 343. From

Pearl, 2 miles southeast on Baptiste, 4¼ miles west on 311, 4 miles south on Somerset, then ¼ mile east on 343. Another beautiful stop in the countryside for wine tasting, listening to music, munching on cheese and crackers, and perusing the gift shop. Friday-Saturday 11 a.m.-5 p.m.; Sunday 12-5 p..m. 913.849.3415. nighthawkwines.com.

Miami County Wine Tour:

You don't need directions if you choose to ride the Miami County Trolley to three area wineries. The main pick-up point for this popular tour is the Jackson Hotel, 139 W. Peoria. Trolley charge and tasting charge at each winery. March-November, Saturday 11 a.m.; Sunday 11:45 a.m. Reservations required. 913.306.3388. miamicountytrolley.com.

Lodging: Canaan Oaks Bed and Breakfast (KBBA, 913.557.5378, canaanoaks. com); Casa Somerset Bed and Breakfast (KBBA, 913.557.9288, casasomerset.com); Hoot Owl Hill (913.271.7451, hootowl-gardens.com); additional lodging (tinyurl.com/paolalodging).

NE

explorer extras...
In Paola

The striking Paola Free Library (NRHP), 101 E. Peoria, with its limestone arched entrance, was designed by George Washburn and completed in 1905. Monday-Thursday 9 a.m.-8:30 p.m.; Friday-Saturday 10 a.m.-4 p.m. 913.259.3655. paolalibrary.org.

In a landscaped circle at 2100 Baptiste (south of Miami County Medical Center), look for a large stone with bronze plaques. One depicts a likeness of Baptiste Peoria and honors this chief of the confederated tribes in the Miami County area. A second plaque commemorates the area's American Indian heritage.

At Baptiste and Hospital stop to see the impressive Miami County Veterans Memorial wall that serves as an honor roll of the men and women who have served in the military. From Pearl, ¾ mile southeast on Baptiste to Hospital.

The Ursuline Sisters of Paola trace their roots back to Brescia, Italy, in 1535. Their rich history travels from there through France and Germany, to Kentucky in 1858, and then to Paola in 1895. Upon settling here they established a boarding school that grew and prospered until it closed in 1971. The Sisters have moved to Kentucky, and their convent, 901 E. Miami, is now used as a community center. Drive by only.

The first successful oil well west of the Mississippi was drilled at Paola in 1860.

In 1886 Paola became the first town west of the Mississippi to use gas commercially. **ee**

Morris County

The tribal names Kanza and Kaw are interchangeable. They are among the many name variations given by early French traders to American Indians residing in what would become the state named for this tribe.

AROUND THE COUNTY

Flint Hills National Scenic Byway: K-177. Forty-seven
miles of curving roadway take you through the heart of the beautiful Flint Hills past engaging vistas of the tallgrass prairie. The byway follows K-177 south from Council Grove through Morris County to the Tallgrass Prairie National Preserve in Chase County and ends at Cassoday in Butler County. travelks.com/ksbyways.

Allegawaho Memorial Heritage Park (NRHP):
From Main in Council Grove, 2 blocks south on 5th, 2 blocks east on Walnut, 3½ miles southeast on Dunlap, ½ mile east on X, then ¼ mile north on 525. Once owned by the

Kaw (Kanza) Nation, this area was part of the original Council Grove Kaw Reservation. The Kaws were forcibly removed from Kansas in 1873 to a new reservation in Oklahoma. Chief Allegawaho, who became the head of the Kaw tribe in 1867 (and was succeeded in 1875 by Chief Washunga), made an eloquent protest against his people being forced from their beloved homeland. The Kanza Heritage Trail (*see* next entry) explains key sites in the park.

Kanza Heritage Trail:
In Allegawaho Memorial Heritage Park. A self-guided, two-mile trail loops through the prairie and riparian valley and past the former Kaw Agency building, stone hut ruins, and a replica earth lodge. Designs reflecting Kanza culture are seen in two large concrete circles on the path. A bronze plaque of the Kaw Tribal Seal is at the center of one circle, and a prayer is on the outer rim. On the other circle's rim are the names of each of the clans in the Kaw tribe. Colorful Kanza patterns are embedded in cast stone sections. An important feature visible from the trail is the Monument to the Unknown Kanza Warrior, a 35-foot-high limestone obelisk erected in 1925 by local citizens as a tribute to the Kanzas native to this area. Discovery of a Kanza's remains in a nearby area prompted the creation of

the monument. The remains have been reinterred in the monument's base. The Kaw Nation asks that you honor him by maintaining a respectful distance.

Flint Hills Nature Trail:
From the Neosho Riverwalk (*see* p. 161) in Council Grove, ½ mile east on Main, 2 blocks south on 5th, then 2 blocks east on Walnut to the trailhead. The old Missouri Pacific railroad bed has been converted into a trail for hiking and biking. It takes you just over three miles to the Allegawaho Memorial Heritage Park and then 95 miles on to Osawatomie. The trail is in stages of development and in several years it will extend west to Herington.

Council Grove Lake:
From Main in Council Grove, ¼ mile north on K-177, then just west to the dam. The Pioneer Nature Trail here is just over a mile long and features buffalo wallows created in the 1800s. ksoutdoors.com.

**explorer extras...
In Burdick**

Unincorporated

The sign at the city limits reads, "Friendly town—population growing." We know it's friendly, and we hope it's growing.

To find the Burdick Meat Locker on south Main at 416 2750, look for the big Pepsi sign above the door and the Rainbo Bread screen door. Bring your ice chest and buy frozen meats processed here, everything from steaks to summer sausage. Monday-Friday 8 a.m.-12 p.m. and 1-5 p.m.; Saturday 8-11 a.m. 785.983.4818.

Photographers will want to find the old wooden grain elevator and red-tile silo hiding behind the trees at the south end of main.

In the small Swedish Mission Cemetery is a steeple from the Swedish Evangelical Mission Church and a granite marker dedicated to the founders of the church, organized in 1894. From Smith, 2½ miles west on BB, then just south on 3000.

In Burdick United Methodist Cemetery, flat stones are stacked carefully around two graves, and another such formation encases a plaque honoring the "Pioneers of Morris County Since 1878." From Smith, 1½ miles west on BB. **ee**

COUNCIL GROVE

Population 2,275

A treaty signed in 1825 with the Great Osage and the Little Osage Nations allowed for overland wagon traffic through this area on the Santa Fe Trail. The council took place under the Council Oak, thus the town's name. Council Grove (8 Wonders of Kansas History) was the pre-eminent rendez-vous point for wagon trains proceeding west from 1829 to the early 1860s.

Santa Fe Trail Sites:
A self-guided tour brochure features more than 25 historic sites around town. Most of these sites form the Council Grove National Historic Landmark District. Pick up the brochure at many of the businesses or at the Council Grove Chamber office, 207 W. Main. councilgrove.com/historicsites.

Neosho Riverwalk:
Main and Union. The Neosho River crossing was one of the crossings on the Santa Fe

Trail, which is explained in a wayside exhibit on the east side of the riverwalk. To honor this heritage, a beautifully landscaped and lighted walkway was completed in 1997. *Guardian of the Grove*, an impressive bronze sculpture of a Kanza warrior by Mark Sampsel serves as the anchor at Main and Union. The north end of the riverwalk connects to the Kaw Mission.

Madonna of the Trail:
Main and Union. In 1928 the DAR dedicated this memorial to pioneer women, symbolizing their courage and strength.

Sculpted by Auguste Leimbach, the monument stands in a small park that was part of an early wagon train campsite.

Seth Hays Home (NRHP):
201 Wood. Seth M. Hays, the great-grandson of Daniel Boone, was a trader, rancher, and founder of and first settler in Council Grove. Hays built this brick house in 1867 and lived here with his adopted daughter Kittie and his servant, Sarah Taylor, who everyone called "Aunt Sally." Outside the home are bronze statues of an Indian girl and of Seth and Kittie.

Last Chance Store (NRHP):
Main and Chautauqua. Built in 1857, this store, for a brief time, provided the last opportunity for trade wagons bound for Santa Fe to pick up supplies. It is the oldest remaining commercial building in Council Grove.

Hermit's Cave on Belfry Hill (NRHP):
Hays and N. Belfry. Belfry Hill was a prominent landmark overlooking the community and a Santa Fe Trail campsite. Italian priest Giovanni Maria Augustini lived in the rock cave on the hill for five months in 1863.

Council Oak:
3rd and Main. Before a windstorm destroyed this tree in 1958, it was 70 feet high and 16 feet around. On August 10, 1825, represen-tatives from the Great Osage and the Little Osage tribes and three U.S. commissioners met

NE

under this tree and signed a treaty giving Americans and Mexicans passage through Osage territory in exchange for $800. The tree stump has been preserved beneath a canopy.

Post Office Oak and Museum: 22 E. Main.

Although this 270-year-old bur oak died in 1990, the mighty tree is where Santa Fe Trail travelers left messages for each other about trail conditions. Today a canopy stands over the oak's remains. The adjacent museum was originally a stone home built in 1864 that housed a commercial brewery. Inside, early medical equipment, railroad memorabilia, and a stickpin collection is displayed. Call ahead, 620.767.5413.

Kaw Mission State Historic Site (NRHP):

500 N. Mission. Thirty Kaw Indian boys lived and studied in this historic stone mission from 1851 to 1854. Exhibits help us understand the intersection of white and American Indian cultures and how this area was the longtime home of the Kaws. May-October, Wednesday-Saturday 10 a.m.-5 p.m. Admission charge. 620.767.5410. kawmission.org.

Post Office and Mural

(NRHP): 103 W. Main. *Autumn Colors* is the title of this 1941 Section artwork by Charles B. Rogers. A poppy seed oil on canvas, it depicts a late fall scene of a Flint Hills farmstead.

Farmers and Drovers Bank (NRHP): 201 W. Main.

Still used as a bank, this 1892 two-story red-brick building with stone trim is well preserved. Its architectural design, incorporating Romanesque arches, a Byzantine dome, and minarets, reflects the prosperity of its era.

Cottage House Hotel

(NRHP): 25 N. Neosho. The white-brick curved exterior and the 1900 double gazebos at either end of the graceful front porch create an appealing first impression of this restored prairie Victorian hotel. Guests have been staying here since 1870 and soon it may again be open.

Carnegie Library (NRHP):

303 W. Main. Now home to the Morris County Historical Society, the 1918 library building was constructed using a grant from industrialist Andrew Carnegie. The original interior has been retained. Wednesday 1-4 p.m. 620.767.7388. FB.

Aldrich Apothecary: 115 W.

Main. The drug store has been in continuous operation since 1892. Six swivel stools, working chrome spigots, and a tile and marble counter make this 1920s soda fountain one of the nicest anywhere. Enjoy shopping for art, crafts, and Flint Hills-made products. Monday-Saturday 10 a.m.-5 p.m. 620.767.6731. FB.

Alexander ArtWorks:

204 W. Main. Bob and Christy Alexander's historic building is filled with their beautiful plasma cut steel artistry and customized stained glass. Creativity at its finest! Thursday-Saturday 10 a.m.-5 p.m. 620.767.6698. FB.

Greenwood Cemetery:

Main and Madison. A tall white stone marks the grave of Seth Hays. At his insistence, his servant (a former slave), Sarah Taylor, was buried in his lot rather than in the segregated section for blacks. To find the Hays marker, from the small building inside the cemetery entrance, go east (right) at the next crossroads.

Hays House (8 Wonders of Kansas Cuisine):

112 W. Main. Built by Seth Hays, this restaurant was opened circa 1857. Santa Fe Trail travelers appreciated the accommodations then, and today's travelers are happy to find its doors are still open. You'll feel a sense of the past inside the rustic dining room, which features large wooden beams and a grand stone fireplace. But the cuisine is far better than you could have rustled up on the trail. The chicken-fried steak is made the Explorer Way, and the skillet-fried chicken ranks high as another house specialty. The most popular lunch item is the Crunchy Chicken Salad. In season, the strawberry and peach pies are the best—and there is always homemade ice cream! Monday-Saturday 6 a.m.-8 p.m.; Sunday 7 a.m.-4 p.m. 620.767.5911. hayshouse.com.

Trail Days Cafe and Museum: 803 W. Main. For

several years this 1861 stone house was the last house that wagons passed before heading

west for Santa Fe. Purchased by William Riley Terwilliger in 1870, it has now been restored by the Historic Preservation Corporation, and cafe proceeds go toward developing the adjoining Maple Camp Historic Site. The food is made from scratch and reflects the area's American Indian past and ethnic settler groups. Dishes include roast buffalo, roast elk, Swedish meatballs, German schnitzel, and Irish bangers. Antiques, pictures, and artifacts augment the historic atmosphere highlighted by an Indian pictograph etched on a door casing. The historic site complex comprises eight buildings, including a 1902 country school, 1858 log house, and a 1930 tourist cabin. Monday-Saturday 11 a.m.-8 p.m. 620.767.7986. traildayscafeandmuseum.org.

Station: 219 W. Main. Inside this long, narrow, cozy lunch and dinner spot, start at the counter to order your sandwich, salad, taco, or soup. Then settle into one of the rustic booths along an original brick wall decorated with railroad memorabilia. Monday-Saturday 11 a.m.-7:30 p.m. 620.767.5619.

Saddlerock Cafe: 15 S. 6th. Looking for the locals? You'll find farmers and ranchers here chowing down on home cooking. Homemade cinnamon rolls are a must to start your day off right. Daily 6 a.m.-2 p.m.; Thursday-Saturday 5-7:30 p.m. 620.767.9000. FB.

Lodging: Bradford Guest House (785.466.6588, bradfordguesthouse.com); Prairie Lodge Motel (785.466.6588, prairielodgemotel.com); The Lodge, a prairie bed and breakfast (785.499.5634); Young Guest House (785.767.6103, groveoccasions.com); Heritage House (620.767.5923, canningcreek.com); Cottage House Bed and Breakfast (620.767.6828, cottagehousehotel.com); additional lodging (council-grove.com/diningandlodging).

explorer extras...
In Council Grove

You don't see this everyday—parrots in a laundromat. Sylvia Kieffer's Conuer parrots come to work with her. Maddie Rose, Baby, Casey, and Joey are people- and laundry-loving birds. Find them at Clothesline Laundrymat, 217 E Main. Daily 8 a.m.-5:30 p.m. 620.767.7376.

The 1913 First Baptist Church (NRHP) at 325 W. Main has been renovated into the Bowers Center for community events. Public restrooms are available here April-November, daily 8 a.m.-6 p.m.

The McKinley/Old Bell Monument bell was once an alarm and a school bell before it was retired in 1901 to the top of the monument at Belfry and Columbia. The stone monument honors President William McKinley, who was assassinated in 1901.

The high school football stadium and stone wall at Chick and Wood were built by the National Youth Administration program in 1940.

A rare Missouri-Kansas-Texas (KATY) depot standing on its original site is this 1894 depot at Main and 6th. Nearby is the 1900 privately owned Sylvan Park depot relocated here from the KATY line northwest of Council Grove.

Seth Hays built the Big John limestone bank barn (NRHP) in 1871, now known locally as the old stone barn. The Morris County Poor Farm used the barn from 1889 to 1945. From K-177, 2¼ miles east on U.S. 56, turn into the highway department drive and follow it west, then ¼ mile north.

A Speed Slide, Open Flume, four spray features, one- and three-meter diving boards, and a toddler area are just a few of the fun features at the Council Grove Aquatic Center, 500 Swimming Pool Lane. 620.767.6516. FB. **ee**

explorer extras...
In Dunlap

Population 29

In 1878 Benjamin "Pap" Singleton helped form a black colony in the Dunlap area in eastern Morris County. The colony comprised former slaves (who became known as Exodusters) migrating from the South.

Because of its black population, Dunlap created two cemeteries. From Broadway, the integrated Dunlap City Cemetery is ½ mile east on 1st. Dunlap African American Cemetery is ½ mile farther north on 100. **ee**

PARKERVILLE

Population 59

C.G. Parker started his little town in 1870 and challenged Council Grove for the location of the county seat. He even set aside a town square as the site for the future courthouse. But in an 1871 vote, Council Grove won the honor. The space once reserved for the courthouse is now a large town park between Grape and Olive. There you

NE

will find a footbridge, gazebo, vintage playground equipment, and a large sign that tells the Parkerville story.

Bank Building: 301 Main. The Peoples State Bank opened in 1909 but failed in 1932 during the Great Depression. Now used as the city hall, it retains its striking appearance—red-brick exterior with arched windows and a corner entrance.

Parker-Highland Cemetery: J and 1800. From Main, ¼ mile north and west on Plum. Town founder C.G. Parker is buried here beside the second of his three wives. He had no children or relatives in the area, and although a number of Parkers are buried here, they are not related to C.G. Upon his death in 1909, C.G. left everything to his housekeeper, Rose Rennolds.

WHITE CITY

Population 596

KATY Park: Main and MacKenzie. Among the finds here are a veterans memorial, the one-room Baxter schoolhouse containing local school displays and artifacts, and the Boxcar Museum, filled with area history and exhibits about the Missouri-Kansas-Texas (KATY) railroad. Second Saturday of each month 11 a.m.-3 p.m. 785.349.2318.

KU Tree: Adolph and Goodnow. A plaque beside a tree tells us the tree was planted in 1941 by Douglas Lee to commemorate the 75th anniversary of the University of Kansas. The tree is beside the old library building near the water tower.

Historic Jail: Adolph and Goodnow. Beside the water tower you'll find the old concrete jail built around the turn of the 20th century.

Pioneer Cemetery: 6th and MacKenzie. Thomas MacKenzie, a White City founder,

and a few others were buried here before a permanent cemetery was established elsewhere.

Lodging: The Flint Hill Inn (NRHP, 785.349.2929, theflinthill.com).

Nemaha County

BAILEYVILLE

Unincorporated

Marion Hall (NRHP): Main and First. Monroe Bailey, father of our state's 16th governor, Willis J. Bailey, founded the town, and in 1895 Willis had this meeting hall built for community purposes. The building features a double-slope roof, and the exterior walls incorporate distinctive lines, textures, and curved parapets on either side of the tower entrance.

**explorer extras...
In Bancroft**

Unincorporated

The Bancroft Depot Museum at Bancroft and 2nd is housed in one of only two surviving depots that served the Kansas City, Wyandotte and Northwestern Railroad from 1887 to 1919. Moved about a block to this location, the depot includes railroad memorabilia, but its primary exhibits relate to the Bancroft community. Memorial Day-September, Sunday 2-4 p.m. 785.866.5288. **ee**

BERN

Population 166

Swiss settlers came to this area in 1888 and named their community for Bern, Switzerland. Into this town of only 166, more than 200 workers come every day for their jobs.

Bern Meat Plant: 411 Main. Since 1961 clientele have been stocking up on fresh meats processed by owners Terry and Nancy Miller. Load your ice chest with quality, natural beef and pork cuts, which include the popular brats, dried beef sticks, and jerky. Monday-Friday 8 a.m.-5 p.m.; Saturday 8 a.m.-12 p.m. 785.336.2165. bernmeatplant.com.

Shirley's Place: 406 Main. This community-owned building is leased to Richard and Shawna Dietrich whose cafe succeeds with made-from-scratch meals. Popular fare includes the prime rib sourdough sandwich and the coconut cream pie. Customers come from far and wide to eat at Shirley's. Daily 6 a.m.-1:30 p.m. 785.336.0042. FB.

**explorer extras...
In Centralia**

Population 510

A colorful sign celebrating Centralia "Spirit... Pride... Heart" stands at 4th and Main beside the remaining cell of a long-gone jail. If you're waiting for someone, a bench conveniently sits nearby.

When you drive over the bridge crossing the Black Vermillion River, note the concrete guardrails with historic streetlights at either end. A block to the west, and crossing the same river, is a wood-planked pedestrian bridge with steel guardrails from an earlier bridge.

John Riggins Avenue is named for the Centralia native who earned fame as football running back at the University of Kansas and later with the New York Jets and the Washington Redskins. Riggins was named Most Valuable Player of Super Bowl XVII. His boyhood home is at 512 John Riggins. ee

CORNING

Population 157

New Deal Projects:
The museum building at 7th and Atlantic (City Park) was originally the shop facility for Corning Rural High School, constructed in 1939 by the National Youth Administration. Behind the museum a memorial contains a picture of the old school. The limestone structure in the 6500 block of Main is a WPA project, built in 1938. Now the city hall, it originally was the school gymnasium.

Double-Arch Entrance:
6501 Main. This red-brick corner building, now the First Heritage Bank, features the same double-arch entrance design as found on the bank in Goff and on the post office in Soldier (Jackson County).

Corning General Store and Corn Crib Restaurant:
6730 K-63. Travelers can find supplies and groceries in the general store. And if you're hungry, sit down at the Corn Crib for breakfast or lunch. Store hours, Tuesday-Friday 7:30 a.m.-4:30 p.m.; Saturday 7:30 a.m.-12 p.m.; cafe hours, Tuesday-Friday 7:30 a.m.-1 p.m. 785.868.2460.

explorer extras... In Goff

Population 126

More than 2,000 toy tractors, trucks, and cars are on display at Skeezix's Toy Museum, ½ mile west of Goff on K-9. Gerald takes great delight in showing the collection of his late brother, Melvin, known by the family as Skeezix. The collection's oldest toy tractor was made in 1920 in Bulgaria. Call ahead, 785.305.1553. FB.

The Goff Bank, along K-9 at 5200 Stahl, has the same double-arch entrance design as the bank in Corning and the post office in Soldier (Jackson County).

Across from the Goff Bank (5200 Stahl) is a 1930 green-and-white drinking fountain covered with a little green-and-white kiosk. ee

explorer extras... In Kelly

Unincorporated

A single spire acts as a magnet drawing you to St. Bede's Church at 7344 Drought. St. Bede's stands on the highest point in the area and is surrounded by cropland and a small cluster of buildings. It's worth going out of your way to see the interior of this 1915 Gothic church, built of brick with limestone trim. The stained-glass windows from Munich, Germany, are fine examples of 19th-century art, and the painted ceiling is breathtaking. Notice the sounding board (looks like an umbrella) above the ambo. Open daily. ee

SABETHA

Population 2,568

Sabetha's Name:
1001 Main. How did the only city in the world named Sabetha come to have that name? A plaque on the north side of a

building shares the theory that a Greek scholar-turned-gold-seeker was in this area when one of his two oxen died on the Sabbath. Unable to go farther, he pitched a tent, performed last rites for his faithful ox, and named the site Sabetha in honor of the day his ox died.

Mary Cotton Public Library:
915 Virginia. Built by the WPA, the library has unique art deco features on its exterior, but don't stop there—go inside. The silver light fixtures are intricate and decorative, and the painting of Queen Louise of Prussia is by Robert Stroud, more infamously known as the "Birdman of Alcatraz." Monday-Friday 9:30 a.m.-5:30 p.m.; Saturday 10 a.m.-4 p.m. 785.284.3160.

Tile Murals:
935 Main. Look closely! The tiles on the United Bank and Trust exterior are each only about an inch square and are assembled into six murals depicting area history. They include a farmer and horse plowing, a cornfield,

NE

a farm tractor, dairy cows, a factory, and a steer. The artist is unknown, but the project occurred in 1965 when the bank was forced to remodel due to water leakage.

Post Office Mural (NRHP):
122 S. 9th. *The Hare and the Tortoise* is the title of this 1937 Section artwork by Albert T. Reid. This oil on canvas depicts a Pony Express rider galloping past an overland stagecoach.

Veterans Memorial:
8th and Main. Standing on the sidewalk just west of City Hall are a series of large handsome plaques listing Sabetha area veterans from each war.

Historic Bank: 907 Main.
The oriel window against the blond brick is striking as is the scrollwork beneath it. Look closely in the entablature above the window to see the word "bank" and "1886." On the wall you'll also see an "Always on the Job" robbery alarm complete with bulldog design.

Sabetha Healthmart
Pharmacy: 934 Main. Take a seat and order a treat at the soda fountain with old-fashioned spigots. Monday-Friday 8 a.m.-5 p.m.; Saturday 8:30 a.m-1 p.m. 785.284.3414. FB.

Buzz Cafe: 820 Main.
The buzz is that locals come here for the hot roast beef sandwich, fresh salad bar with homemade dressings, and the daily specials. Monday-Saturday 6 a.m.-1:15 p.m.; Sunday 11 a.m.- 1:30 p.m. 785.284.3177.

El Canelo: 1777 Frontage.
Attached to a filling station, you can fill up on tasty carnitas, enchiladas, fajita salads, and margaritas. Free chips and salsa—and fast, friendly service. Daily 11 a.m.-9 p.m. 785.284.3283.

Southside Grill: 1112 S.
Old U.S. 75. They come for the burgers and smoked pork chops all the time, and for the whole catfish and prime rib on Fridays and Saturdays. Homemade desserts are the cherry on top. Wednesday-Saturday 4-9 p.m.; Sunday 11 a.m.-2 p.m. 785.300.3333. FB.

Hearthside Country Store:
2494 200. From Main, 1¾ miles north on 6th (becomes X4), then ½ mile east on 200. For bulk foods, snack foods, or kitchenware, Hearthside is shopper heaven. Monday-Saturday 8 a.m.-5:30 p.m. 785.284.0303. hearthsidecountrystore.com.

Albany Historical
Museum: From Main, 2¼ miles north on 6th (becomes X4). The Albany townsite was laid out in 1859, and although the town never incorporated, it was a thriving trade center between Seneca and Hiawatha. It was also known as a stop on the Underground Railroad, and it was here that John Brown spent his last night in Kansas. Today the museum complex comprises 15 buildings including the two-story Old Albany Schoolhouse (NRHP), which houses a collection of artifacts. Memorial Day-Labor Day, Saturday-Sunday 2-5 p.m. 785.285.0349.

Sycamore Springs:
3126 Bittersweet. From 6th, ½ mile east on Main, ¾ mile north on Acorn, 2 miles east on K-246, then 3¼ miles north on Bittersweet (Brown County). This resort dates to 1886 when people began coming here to take advantage of the natural

healing springs. As you drive through this shaded, historic property you'll see the 1917 stone hotel and the 1936 roller skating rink, and across the wooden plank bridge you'll find

two of the historic springs, one under a gazebo. Recreation facilities (including the roller rink) are available, and you may RV or tent camp here, rent a cabin, or book a room in the historic hotel. May-October, 9 a.m.-9 p.m. 785.284.3088. ssresort.com.

Lodging:
tinyurl.com/sablodging.

explorer extras... In Sabetha

If you have ballplayers in your family, you'll want to stop at the new Somerset Park at N. 6th and 192, one of the best ballparks in the state. Across town at 740 Blue Jay you'll find an aquatic park complete with spray features.

Lane Trail, named for free-state leader James Lane, was established to bypass proslavery strongholds and provide a safe route for free-state settlers and slaves. A historical marker explains that the rock piles marking the way were known as "Lane's chimneys." From Main, 1¾ mile north on U.S. 75 to a pull over on the west side of the road. **ee**

ST. BENEDICT

Unincorporated

St. Mary's Church (NRHP; 8 Wonders of Kansas Art):
Built of native limestone in 1894, St. Mary's has become famous for having one of the most

beautiful interiors of any church in the state. A principal feature in the award-winning interior is the symbolic art painted in 1901 by G.F. Satory, which includes beautifully colored patterns, bands, and friezes on the walls, ceiling, and columns. Adding to the church's lavish adornment are six large oil murals, exquisite statuary, and leaded-glass windows. Daily dawn to dusk. 785.336.3174. stmarystbenedict.org.

Grotto at St. Mary's Church:
North of the church. The 1936 rock and stone grotto was inspired by the Grotto of our Lady of Lourdes, France.

SENECA

Population 2,004

Nemaha County Veterans Memorial Wall:
U.S. 36 and K-63. One of the most moving veterans memorials in the state, this 340-foot-long wall lists 2,000 names of area veterans of the Civil War to the present. A special section pays tribute to those killed in action (KIA). The 45 individual KIA plaques provide military details including how each person died. For example, in the 1942 Bataan Death March, in 1944 on Normandy beach, lost at sea in a submarine. The wall was dedicated in 2009. 785.231.9721.

Post Office Mural (NRHP):
607 Main. *Men and Wheat* is the title of this 1940 Section artwork, an oil on canvas by Joe Jones that portrays two farmers harvesting wheat. A sign outside the post office tells an interesting backstory—after the mural was installed the local International Harvester dealer complained that the green equipment was an advertise-ment for John Deere. So the artist repainted the combine International red, and on the green tractor he painted his own name as the logo.

Seneca Free Library (NRHP):
606 Main. This 1867 Old Stone Universalist Church was the first of its denomination in the state. In 1928, with the congregation gone, it became the home for the library. An addition built in 1997 now houses the library, and the church is used as a meeting space. Monday-Friday 10 a.m.-5 p.m.; Saturday 10 a.m.-2 p.m. 785.336.2377. FB.

Nemaha County Museum (NRHP):
113 N. 6th Built in 1879, this two-story brick structure was once the jail and residence of the county sheriff. Today 20 rooms are filled with county artifacts and memora-bilia. Tuesday 10 a.m.-4 p.m. 785.556.4094. nemahacounty-historicalsociety.com.

Masonic Temple Museum (NRHP):
33 N. 6th. In addition to the County Museum, the Nemaha County Historical Society operates this museum in the former Masonic hall. Here military displays cover 150 years

of county veteran history by showcasing uniforms, photos, artifacts, and documents. 785.556.4094. nemahacounty-historicalsociety.com.

Seneca Main Street Historic District (NRHP):
Forty-two buildings and the brick streets on Main between 3rd and 6th (laid in 1919) are part of the historic district. Interpretive signage on Main provides the buildings' histories as does a brochure for self-guided walking tours. Brochures are available at the 4th and Main kiosk mailbox.

Painted Ladies:
A painted lady is a Victorian building painted with three or more colors to enhance the architec-tural detail. Beautiful "ladies" are the Emery Mansion at 7th and Walnut and several south of Main between 4th and 8th.

Historic Theatre:
301 Main. Around 1885 an opera house was built on this site. In 1927 the red-brick building, remodeled in art deco style, became a movie house, first named the Royal Theater and today the Seneca Twin. 785.336.2512. FB.

Historic Fire Truck:
6th and Main. Stop at the city hall, 531 Main, and ask to see the 1922 Stutz fire engine, restored to pristine condition. Other early-1900s fire depart-ment artifacts are also displayed. 785.336.2747.

Pony Express Museum:

327 Main. Seneca had the first Pony Express home station west of St. Joseph, Missouri. Although the station is long gone, artifacts and information about the famous mail service are preserved in this former general mercantile. June-Labor Day, Wednesday-Saturday 10 a.m.-3 p.m. 785.336.1739.

Pony Express Monument:

4th and Main. A red glacial stone holds a plaque that describes the Seneca connection to the Pony Express.

Hand-Dug Well (NRHP):

301 N. 11th (City Park). Dug in 1895, the well is 34 feet wide and 65 feet deep, the second largest extant hand-dug well in the state. It's a visible reminder of the town's original water system. The well is covered, so contact the Nemaha County Historical Society if you'd like to see it. 785.336.6366.

Horse Watering Fountain:

301 N. 11th (City Park). A gray granite 1910 fountain stands as a testament to an early Seneca mayor who persuaded Hermon Lee Ensign, founder of the National Humane Alliance, to donate one of his fountains to the town. Between 1906 and 1911 Ensign donated 125 fountains nationwide to provide drinking water for horses and other animals. One of the few remaining in the country, the Seneca fountain originally stood at 3rd and Main.

Seneca City Cemetery:

From U.S. 36, ½ mile north on 11th. You'll be drawn to the unusual red-brick arched memorial that is the gravestone for Aaron and Olive Shaul. Little is known about it except that the Shauls' son George was an architect who built Carnegie libraries, Masonic halls, and courthouses, and possibly this memorial for his parents. Drive carefully through the cemetery as gravestones closely border the driveway.

Lake Nemaha Dam Guardrails (NRHP):

From U.S. 36, 5 miles south on K-63. Lake Nemaha was built in the 1930s by the Civilian Conservation Corps, which finished the job with artistic guardrails stretching across the spillway. More than 200 posts of quarried stone were placed seven feet apart along the west side. A continuous stone wall with stone posts every 17 feet gave the east side a slightly different look.

Spring Creek Golf Course:

1800 Spring Creek. Spring into action at this first-class, par 71, 18-hole public course. In the northeast section of the course you'll see an oversized golf ball and tee made from a tree stump! Greens fee. 785.336.3568. springcreek-seneca.com.

The Willows Restaurant & Bar:

1921 North. With the golf course in sight, you'll feel like you've hit a hole in one with such options as crab cakes with chipotle cream sauce, homemade onion rings, caramelized mashed potatoes, smoked pork chops, and filet mignons. Monday-Saturday 5-9 p.m. 785.336.0201. FB.

Cornerstone Coffee Haus:

431 Main. A double-horseshoe counter is a fun place to imbibe treats at this old-fashioned soda fountain. Coffee specialties, breakfast, and lunch are also on the bill of fare. Monday-Friday 7 a.m.-5 p.m.; Saturday 8:30 a.m.-2 p.m. 785.334.4287. FB.

WETMORE

Population 361

Shoe Tree: From Kansas, 1 mile west on K-9, 5¼ miles north on W, then 1 mile west on 80. In the 1980s John Kissel read a magazine article about a shoe tree that inspired him to start one too! Although John has passed away, son Jerry takes care of the tree and monitors the notebook of shoe donors. By now the cottonwood at 80 and V is decorated with many a shoe and has been the site of many a tradition—including a marriage proposal. Although the tree has been diminished by weather, its fame has grown. A can of nails and a hammer beside the tree invite you to add your shoe to the mix. 785.866.4381. tinyurl.com/theshoetree.

Spring Creek Classic Car and Truck Museum:

315 2nd. Bob Carson's 30 or so restored cars and trucks are a visual treat as are the vintage

gas pump and mechanic equipment inside this restored 1925 Texaco station. The station is home to the 1957 Ford Skyliner and the 1946 Chevy pickup that Bob used when dating his wife, June. Most of the cars are in the old Chrysler/Plymouth dealership next door. Call ahead, 785.250.8484. springcreekclassics.com.

Rock and Critter Garden:
From Kansas, 1¼ miles east on 2nd (becomes 36), then 2 miles north on N (becomes Acorn). Retired farmer and welder Paul Fritz has positioned his handmade metal "critters" among strategically placed rocks, flowers, trees, and shrubs. Drive by and see if you can spot the ladybug, spiders, dinosaur, giraffe, and grasshopper. To stroll around the garden, call ahead, 785.866.5685.

Wetmore Cemetery:
7th and Nebraska. An etching of a galloping horse and rider adorns the granite gravestone of Pony Express rider Don Clarence Rising (1844-1909), aka Johnny Granada. His grave is at the south end of the cemetery about eight stones north on the first row of the east side.

Wetmore Calaboose:
2nd and Nebraska. This 1883 jail has stood empty since its last occupant left in 1942.

Dinner Bell: 404 2nd. Daily specials are made from scratch and the pies are homemade. Fried chicken is what's for dinner on Sundays. Monday-Saturday 7 a.m.-2 p.m.; Thursday-Saturday 5-8 p.m.; Sunday 11 a.m.-2 p.m. 785.866.2233. dbcafewetmore.com.

Osage County

AROUND THE COUNTY

Melvern Lake and Eisenhower State Park:
U.S. 75 and K-31. In response to the devastating 1951 flood, Congress authorized construction of this reservoir in 1954. Recreational opportunities abound at the lake and park. Just for fun, go to Outlet Park and walk over Long Creek bridge, a replica of a historic suspension bridge once located outside Melvern. State park entrance charge. Cabins available, reservations required. 785.528.4102. ksoutdoors.com.

Pomona Lake and State Park:
From K-268, 1 mile north on K-368. Built in 1963 for flood control, the lake and park offer a wide array of water recreations plus camping, hiking, and nature experiences. State park entrance charge. Cabins available, reservations required. 785.453.2201. ksoutdoors.com.

ARVONIA

Unincorporated

In 1869 many Welsh immigrants came to the area for mining and farming. Today little remains of the community except a school, a church, an unusually shaped wooden township hall (NRHP), and an immaculate homestead. When the railroad failed to come through Arvonia, the population quickly declined.

Arvonia School (NRHP):
From I-35 exit 148, 3½ miles north on Hoch, ¼ mile west

on 325, then north on Arvonia. Designed by the first state architect, John Haskell, the 1872 native stone school sits atop a grassy knoll. Why the three front doors? The middle door opened to a staircase to the second floor (second floor was removed in circa 1900). And the other doors? One was an entrance for boys and the other an entrance for girls.

The bell tower and the tall, narrow masonry window and door openings create a stately and picturesque building. 620.794.3917.

Welsh Calvinistic Methodist Church (NRHP):
Northeast of Arvonia School. In 1883 this wooden church was built by the Calvinistic Methodist congregation. Through a series of transitions, in 1922 the Methodists joined the Presbyterian denomination, which occupied the building until the congregation disbanded in 1968. 620.794.3917.

Arvonia Cemetery:
From Arvonia, 1¼ miles west on 325, then ½ mile north on Docking. Due to this community's Welsh ties it is not surprising to see inscriptions in Welsh on many gravestones.

BURLINGAME

Population 916

Santa Fe Trail: Today's Santa Fe Avenue follows the old trail, which roughly parallels K-31 heading west over the hill and out of town. Santa Fe Trail evidence is visible west of Burlingame on K-31—a sign

NE

marks wagon ruts along the south side, just east of the ruts are remnants of Havana Stage Station (*see* next entry), and a DAR marker stands on the north side of the highway.

Havana Stage Station:

From Dacotah, 4¼ miles west on Santa Fe (becomes K-31). A large sign on the south side of the road tells the story of the stone stage station built here around 1858 and abandoned by 1869. At one time a hotel and store were part of the small town of Havana that provided a stop for travelers on the Santa Fe Trail. The crumbling stone walls of the stage station are all that remain.

Samuel Hunt Grave (NRHP):

From Dacotah, 4¾ miles west on Santa Fe (becomes K-31) (north side of the highway maintenance pullout). Surrounded by a pipe fence, a weathered headstone marks the earliest known grave of a soldier on the Santa Fe Trail. Samuel Hunt, a private in the U.S. Dragoons, was on Colonel Henry Dodge's Rocky Mountain expedition in 1835 when he died of "inflammation of the bowels" during the regiment's return to Fort Leavenworth.

Wide Street:

Settled in 1858, Burlingame immediately took advantage of freight wagon traffic traveling the Santa Fe Trail. The road through town was made wide enough for oxen teams to circle the wagons for camping, restocking supplies, or making repairs. In 1922 brick and concrete replaced the dusty road, but businesses had already been established

along either side, so the street's great width (94 feet from curb to curb) remained. Today's Santa Fe Avenue is so wide that cars park down the middle!

Schuyler Museum:

117 S. Dacotah. Named for an early settler who moved to this area in 1854, the 1902 Schuyler Grade School (NRHP) is now home to the museum. Featured are exhibits about area history, coal mining, the railroad, and the Santa Fe Trail. Wednesday, Friday, Sunday 1-4 p.m.; Saturday 10 a.m-4 p.m. 785.654.3170.

Earl W. Sutherland Jr.:

Burlingame native Earl Sutherland won the Nobel Prize in Physiology or Medicine in 1971 "for his discoveries concerning the mechanisms of the action of hormones." An exhibit about his life is in the Schuyler Museum. An army captain in World War II, Sutherland died at the age of 58 and is buried in Burlingame City Cemetery (from Santa Fe, 1 mile south on U.S. 56). His grave, which notes the Nobel Prize, is in the cemetery's southeastern-most corner.

Aunt B's: 113 W. Santa Fe. The famous rolls (caramel pecan, peanut butter, and cinnamon) are tasty reasons to come to B's. But so are the daily made-from-scratch specials and the sandwiches on homemade bread. Tuesday-Saturday 7:30 a.m.-2 p.m. 785.654.3108. FB.

explorer extras...
In Burlingame

Burlingame's slogan "Where Rails Cross Trails" denotes that

the Santa Fe Trail and the Santa Fe railroad first intersected in 1869 at the east edge of town, today's junction of U.S. 56 and the railroad.

A marker at Santa Fe and Dacotah honors Fannie Geiger Thompson, who led DAR efforts to mark the Santa Fe Trail in 1906. **ee**

LYNDON

Population 1,039

Carnegie Library (NRHP):

127 E. 6th. When this one-story brick and limestone library was built in 1910 it became the smallest one (30x48 feet) in the state—and still is. Monday-Thursday 9 a.m.-12:30 p.m. and 2-6 p.m.; Friday 1-4 p.m.; Saturday 9 a.m.-12 p.m. 785.828.4520. lyndonlibrary.org.

Osage County Courthouse and Jail (NRHP):

717 Topeka. Several war memorials grace the grounds of this 1923 Modern Eclecticism courthouse. But something behind it (northeast side) is perhaps more interesting. The structure here appears to be a mini-courthouse (same design and materials) but it has a smokestack—and bars on the windows.It was a combination jail and heating plant, designed to prevent escapes and fires.

Osage County Museum:

631 Topeka. It's a great place for genealogical research, and it features local history displays. April-October,

Wednesday-Saturday 1-5 p.m. 785.828.3477. osagechs.org.

Wild Bill and Miss Ellie's EZ Rock Cafe: 1304 Topeka. You'll "meet" Elvis, Marilyn Monroe, and James Dean inside this brightly colored and chrome-filled 1950s-themed cafe. The burgers are terrific, so find a seat amid the guitars, records, and the rear of a pink Cadillac! Tuesday-Saturday 11 a.m.-9 p.m. 785.828.4612. FB.

Buzzard's Pizza: 708 Topeka. The local faithful travel quite a ways to eat at Buzzard's, which makes a crispy, flavorful crust and is generous with the toppings and cheese. Monday-Saturday 11 a.m.-9 p.m. 785.828.4870.

Lodging: Crossroads and Camps RV Park (785.221.5482, crossroadsrvpark.com).

**explorer extras...
In Lyndon**

Shoe shop owner John Gutsmithl built the house at 428 Topeka in 1902. He liked the design so much he erected a house like it for his daughter at 506 Topeka, but he made it one square foot smaller!

Built in 1928 as an ice plant, the structure at 202 W. 3rd later became a slaughterhouse, locker plant, and ice cream shop. The roof garden was once used as a roller rink where Fourth of July dances were hosted.

A one-and-a-half-story traditional hewn log house (RHKP) built in 1870 by Wells P. Bailey now stands in City Park, 131 W. 11th. Originally it was two miles east of town. ee

MELVERN

Population 377

When the city incorporated on April 17, 1884, its name was to be Malvern, for the Malvern Hills

of Scotland, but the new charter misspelled it Melvern.

Railroad Overpass Bridge (NRHP): From Emporia, 2 blocks south on Pine. High above the present railroad tracks, this 1909 Santa Fe truss bridge is now only open to pedestrians.

Melvern Riverfront Parks and Trails: From Emporia, ½ mile north on Pine. Ten unpaved trails, some primitive and all less than a mile long, provide views of the Marais des Cygnes River.

Danish Cemetery: From Emporia, 4½ miles north on Main (becomes S. Berryton). A front-and-center gravestone announces that you're in Danish Cemetery, and family names—Larsen, Hanson, Peterson, Broderson—bear witness that indeed you are!

Melvern Cemetery: From Main, 1 mile west on Emporia. Within the cemetery you'll find a Civil War monument erected by the Woman's Relief Corps in 1888 as "A tribute to those patriots who sleep in southern graves uncoffined unshrouded and unknown."

Whistle Stop Cafe: 117 S. Main. Breakfast is served all day. Eat your fill (breakfast or lunch) as you fill up on history, provided by the old photos decorating the walls. Monday-Saturday 6:30 a.m.-2 p.m. 785.549.3575.

OSAGE CITY

Population 2,899

Osage County Railroad and Mining Museum (NRHP): 507 Market. By 1871 the coal fields of Osage County had become a prime spot for mining and for employment west of the Mississippi. Inside this museum, housed in a restored 1912 Spanish Mission style Santa Fe depot, exhibits and memorabilia preserve

the stories of coal mining, the railroad, and local history. Call ahead, 785.219.2510.

Ramblin' Rose: 629 Market. Nancy Washburn has created the quintessential gift and flower shop that responds to a community need. Visitors will enjoy the seasonal decorations, gifts, and antiques inside the blue-awning-clad building. Monday-Saturday 10 a.m-5:30 p.m. 785.528.3337.

Veterans Memorial: From Market, 1¼ miles north on K-31 to American Cemetery. Beside the flagpole, this memorial was dedicated in 1925 by the Canby Woman's Relief Corps. Erected to the soldiers, sailors, and marines of the Civil War, Spanish-American War, and World War, the monument reads, "Sleep, with the sunshine of fame on thy slumbers."

NE

Rapp School (NRHP): From Market, 1 mile north on K-31, then 4 miles west on U.S. 56. Built in 1929, the red-brick, one-room, eight-grade schoolhouse finally closed in 1959 when its enrollment was down to five students. 785.528.3445.

Marilynn's Place: 1216 Laing. Homemade pies and daily noon specials keep the locals—and visitors—more than satisfied. Monday-Saturday 6 a.m.-8 p.m. 785.528.3769. FB.

**explorer extras...
In Osage City**

Operating as a White Eagle gas station for five years, this relic of the past at 5th and Holliday was built in 1927. ee

OVERBROOK

Population 1,042

Little Girl Gravestone: From Maple, 2 blocks east on Market, 2 blocks south on Cedar, then ¼ mile east on 1st to Overbrook Cemetery. Vivian

Butel was born in 1914 to local dentist Arthur Butel and his wife, Maud. When Vivian was four years old she accidentally took pills that contained strychnine. She died within hours. The family memorialized its daughter with a stone full-length likeness of her. Emanating much symbolism, the stone shows Vivian with one hand on a gate (gateway to heaven), her other hand on a tree stump (life cut short), and at her feet is a broken bud (premature death). Vivian's stone stands in the south side of the cemetery.

Overbrook Quilt Connection:
500 Maple. It's a well-known quilters' paradise—any quilter would be in heaven among the more than 2,000 bolts of fabric! Tuesday-Saturday 10 a.m.-5 p.m. 785.665.7841. overbrookquilts.com.

Landon Nature Trail:
From Market, 2 blocks south on Shawnee Heights. The nature trail is a 40-mile hike, bike, and equestrian route from Topeka to Pomona Lake on the retired Missouri Pacific railroad bed. The trail is still under development in many places. Find updates and trail conditions at kansastrails.org.

Karnes Stone Barn
(NRHP): 4204 E. 129. From U.S. 56, 3½ miles north on Maple (becomes Shawnee Heights), then 2 miles west on 129. The limestone barn with center gable and cupola was built in 1877 by circus owner George R. Bronson as a place to house his circus animals in the winter. The Karnes family purchased the farm in the 1930s and still owns it today.

Hiram K. Reilly
Monument: From U.S. 56, 3½ miles north on Maple (becomes Shawnee Heights), 2¼ miles west on 129, ½ mile north on Paulen, then ½ west on 125 to Ridgeway Cemetery. In 1912, two years before his death, loner Hiram Reilly had eight marble slabs inscribed with text from *The Magic Staff*, an 1857 autobiography of spiritualist Andrew Jackson Davis. Several slabs were erected upright in a cluster, and three are supported by concrete posts.

Lickskillet School:
125 and Stanley. From 157 (U.S. 56), 4 miles north on Maple (becomes Shawnee Heights), then 1 mile east on 125. Rural schools in this area were known by nicknames: Lickskillet, Apple Pie, Pancake, Spunky Point, and Brown Jug. Local lore ties this school's moniker to a dog who licked a skillet clean. The school, now the meeting place for the Busy Bee Hobby Club, was built circa 1905.

explorer extras... In Overbrook

The outdoor mural on a small building at U.S. 56 and Oak depicts Santa Fe Trail history and reminds everyone, "Don't Overlook Overbrook."

Can you see the faded red barn bedecked with a charming row of colorful birdhouses? From

Walnut, ¼ east on U.S. 56 on the north side of the road.

Fourth Street was the route of the Santa Fe Trail even before Overbrook became a town. **ee**

explorer extras... In Quenemo

Population 382

Oak trees dominate the valley view from Oak Hill Cemetery, ½ mile north of Quenemo on K-68. The cemetery contains many gravestones of Scottish immigrants plus monuments honoring veterans from the Civil War to the Vietnam conflict. **ee**

SCRANTON

Population 697

4 Corners Steakhouse & Lounge:
15745 S. Topeka. From Mercer, 3 miles east on U.S. 56. If the "Duke" were alive he'd enjoy sauntering in to see all the John Wayne memorabilia that adorn the walls. And he'd say, "thank you, ma'am," to Lisa Jolly for serving up good grub. Daily 7 a.m.-9 p.m. 785.793.2800. FB.

VASSAR

Unincorporated

Vassar Mercantile:
310 Main. Behind the doors of Carolyn Totman's 1911 building is a bevy of home decor items ranging from new to repurposed, vintage, and antique. If you plan to visit nearby Pomona Lake, you can pick up camping and biking supplies here. A portion of each sale goes to support the Vassar Community Center. May to mid-December, Wednesday, Friday-Saturday 10 a.m.-5 p.m. 785.219.2559. FB.

Flint Hills Nature Trail:
From Vassar Mercantile, 1 block south on Topeka, then 1 block southwest on Front to the trailhead. Parts of the trail are complete and other areas

are in stages of development. When finished, the trail will run 117 miles from Osawatomie to Herington. kanzatrails.org.

Town Pump: Main and Topeka. In the middle of the intersection is where you'll find the old-fashioned hand pump. It stands as evidence of the town well where people and animals once came for water. The pump is proudly preserved inside a white fence surrounded by flowering shrubs.

Little Red Schoolhouse: Main and Croco. This iconic 1912 red-brick school served students until 1978 and the following year became the community center. 785.828.4188.

Lamont Hill Restaurant: 22975 KS-368. From Main, ¼ mile north on Croco, 1 mile east on 229, just south on K-368. Locals have many good things to say about this eatery. Among their favorites are the melt-in-your-mouth ham on the Sunday buffet (11:30 a.m.-2 p.m.) and the cinnamon rolls and breads made fresh daily. Daily 6 a.m.- 9 p.m. 785.828.3131.

Breck's Green Acres Restaurant: 4961 E. K-268. From Main, ¾ mile south on Croco, 2½ miles east on K-268. Broasted chicken, daily specials, homemade pie, and breakfast served all day are only a few reasons to stop at Breck's. Daily 5:30 a.m.-9 p.m. 785.453.2166.

Pottawatomie County

Named for the Potawatomis who settled on a government reservation around 1850 at present St. Marys, Pottawatomie County is a beautiful area in the Glacial Hills region and teems with scenic drives through hills and valleys.

AROUND THE COUNTY

Vermillion Creek Tributary Stone Arch Bridge (NRHP): From 5th in Emmett, 3¾ miles north on K-63, 6¼ miles west on Aiken Switch, 1¼ miles north on Day to a T, then ½ mile east on Day

to the stone arch bridge sign. In this scenic rural setting you'll find a sidewalk leading to the overlook of the 1870 single-arch bridge. A sign tells about the construction of the bridge and its history.

BELVUE

Population 202

Fulmer's Kansas Premium Meats & Eatery: 22580 U.S. 24. "The Way Beef Should Taste" is prominently printed on the wall, and you'll confirm that claim when you sink your teeth into a burger made with Fulmer's beef. Other choices include a daily special, bierocks, pulled pork, and hot dogs. The store carries Kansas products, cuts of Angus beef raised by the Fulmer family, and other meats, so bring your cooler and stock up. Eatery hours, Monday-Saturday 10:30 a.m.-3 p.m.; store hours, Monday-Friday 10 a.m.-5 p.m. 785.456.6500. kansaspremiummeats.com.

Kansas River Trail: From U.S. 24, 1 mile south on Mills. See the scenic river from the water itself on the Kansas River Trail, a designated National

Water Trail that runs from Kaw Point in Kansas City to Junction City. The river access ramp near Belvue is 119 of 173 access miles. ksrivertrail.com.

Oregon Trail Nature Park: From Broadway, 1¾ miles east on U.S. 24, ¾ mile north on Schoeman, then ¼ mile west on Oregon Trail Rd. Standing near the entrance, a silo has been painted with three scenes commemorating the Oregon Trail through this area. Thanks go to Cindy Martin for this

colorful art. Hikers may choose from three self-guided trails, which start at the circular garden. One includes a section so steep that a rope has been installed to help climbers. A great view rewards you when you reach the summit. Grasses and forbs along the trails are the same varieties as those experienced by Oregon Trail travelers. tinyurl.com/otnaturepark.

Louis Vieux Cemetery (NRHP): From Oregon Trail Nature Park, 5¾ miles west on Oregon Trail Rd. The cemetery's namesake was a Potawatomi leader who operated a nearby

NE

ferry over Vermillion Creek as well as a blacksmith shop and other enterprises that assisted travelers on the Oregon Trail. Lying several hundred yards east of the creek, the historic burial ground holds the graves of Vieux and some of his family members. Vandals desecrated 24 of the 30 stones in this cemetery, but they were caught, paid restitution, and were supervised in reconstructing the stones.

Cholera Cemetery: ¼ mile west of Louis Vieux Cemetery on Oregon Trail Rd. Perils were common on the Oregon Trail, and in 1849 tragedy struck when emigrants camped at the nearby Vermillion Creek Crossing (*see* next entry) died from a cholera outbreak. They were buried on the creek bank, where, over the years others who died on the trail also were interred. While as many as 50 graves were marked at one time, only three stones are evident today. An interpretive sign on the cemetery fence recounts this story.

Vermillion Creek Crossing (NRHP): Just west of the cholera cemetery on Oregon Trail Rd. An illustrated sign tells the story of the nearby Oregon Trail crossing over Vermillion Creek. Commonly known as Vieux Crossing (named for Louis Vieux), it also accommodated the military road from Fort Leavenworth to Fort Riley.

explorer extras... In Blaine

Unincorporated

The tall steeple of the lovely St. Columbkille Church leads you to Blaine. Against a deep blue sky, this red-brick church and

rising steeple is picture perfect. St. Columbkille (or Columba), born in 521, is Scotland's most revered saint and is credited with taking Christianity to Scotland. Colum means "dove" and "cille" means church, which combine to form "dove of the church."

Ernest White was the artist, welder, and sculptor of the entrance arch and angels at Mount Calvary Cemetery, 1 mile south of Blaine on K-99.

The five miles between Blaine and Wheaton on K-16 deliver some of the best tummy-tickling downhill dips in the state. **ee**

explorer extras... In Flush

Unincorporated

The high-rising steeple of St. Joseph Church guides you into the once flourishing agricultural settlement of Flush. Just south of town a hilltop overlooking the Rock Creek Valley offers a spectacular view, especially in the fall. Little remains of Flush, only the abandoned school and gym. But still, almost 1,000 people annually attend the Flush Picnic at the end of July. From Wamego, 6½ miles west on U.S. 24, then 6½ miles north on Flush.

A rock sign on K-16 just south of St. Joseph Church relates the story of the German immigrants who established Flush in 1854. **ee**

HAVENSVILLE

Population 142

Why does the town have streets named Barbara and Mabel? Barbara was the wife of Richard Croy, one of the early town founders. Mabel was the wife of R.C. Coverdale, who later built an addition to the town.

With empty bell tower and broken windows, the 1880 two-story brick grade school stands sadly abandoned at Barbara and Pottawatomie. It was condemned in the early 1960s.

Linnemann Memorial: From Commercial, ¼ mile west on North to Havensville Cemetery. It's easy to see that John Linnemann loved playing baseball. When he died in 2014, John's best friend, Harold Huntsman, made sure his bats, balls, and cleats remained with him. Look for the red case and the bright yellow baseballs.

Charlies: 321 Commercial. Operating in an early red-brick post office, Charlies (named for the owner's dog) ensures good times, cold beer, and made-from-scratch good food—from burgers to the daily special. Monday-Tuesday and Sunday 11 a.m.-2 p.m.; Wednesday-Friday 11 a.m.-8 p.m.; Saturday 8 a.m.-4 p.m. 785.948.3000. FB.

OLSBURG

Population 226

Olsburg Cemetery: From 1st, ¼ mile west on K-16 (south side). This Swedish cemetery was relocated here in 1959 due to construction of Tuttle Creek Lake. Gravestone inscriptions reveal that some of the interred were born in Sweden. Red glacial stones form solid entrance pillars topped with upright and sharply pointed rocks. These present a decora-

tive touch and prevent anything (man, beast, or bird) from sitting on them!

Mariadahl Orphan Home and Cemetery:
Across from Olsburg Cemetery (north side of K-16). A large concrete and granite marker relates the story of the orphan home, established in 1879 in the original Mariadahl settlement. Named for Maria Johnson, the first Swedish pioneer to die in this new settlement, the home cared for 620 children from 1880 to 1959. Closed due to the construction of Tuttle Creek Lake, the home was buried under lake waters, but the graves were moved to this location.

Loberg Grocery:
400 2nd. For a small-town grocery experience step inside the screen door onto the wood floor of this nifty little store and restaurant. Order a full meal or a deli sandwich at the meat counter or buy potato sausage, a Swedish delicacy made here.

Stock up on groceries too! Wednesday-Thursday 8:30 a.m.-8:30 p.m.; Friday-Saturday 8:30 a.m.-2 p.m. 785.468.3511. FB.

Carnahan Creek Scenic Drive:
From 2nd, ½ mile east on K-16, 6¼ miles south on Carnahan, then ¾ mile southwest on Park. From the plains to hilly wooded areas and river valleys of the upper Flint Hills, this scenic route is especially lovely in autumn. When you come to the Carnahan Park entrance, bear left to find Carnahan-Garrison Cemetery. This beautiful old cemetery filled with tulip beds rests on a bluff overlooking Tuttle Creek Lake. Many of the graves were moved to this location when the reservoir was built during the 1950s. From this hilltop cemetery you'll not only see the lake, but also stone building foundations in the valley. Note the old schoolhouse just before the cemetery entrance.

ONAGA
Population 706

WWI Soldier Statue:
4th and Leonard. A bronze charging doughboy, made famous by artist Ernest Moore Viquesney, was dedicated in 1920 as a memorial to the veterans of the Great War and the sacrifices they made.

Pottawatomie County Fair Pavilion (NRHP):
901 High. In its original location at the fairgrounds, this 1921 octagonal barn was first used to showcase county fair exhibits, and later it served as a livestock sale barn. The building was restored by a group of dedicated citizens. 785.889.4456.

Onaga Historical Society Museum:
311 E. 2nd. The complex includes an original homestead cabin, a historic one-room schoolhouse, and a Union Pacific caboose. 785.889.4456.

Cool Springs Golf Course:
20770 Kelley Creek. Northwest of town you'll find this challenging nine-hole course that includes three sets of tee boxes, a putting green, chipping green, and driving range. 785.889.7128. coolspringsgc.com.

The Cattlemens Grille:
106 W. 2nd. Come in, sit down, relax, and order a daily special or one of the delicious steak dinners. And it's not only cattlemen who love the homemade desserts. Monday-Thursday 6 a.m.-2 p.m. and 5-7 p.m.; Friday-Sunday 7 a.m.-1 p.m. 785.889.0170. FB.

Buffalo's Grill & Pizzaria:
324 Leonard. Can't decide between a hot, juicy burger and a hot, tasty pizza? Here you can have both and homemade soups (seasonal), chili cheese dogs, and ice cream. Gluten-free buns and pizza crusts are available. Daily 11 a.m.-9 p.m. 785.889.4776. FB.

NE

ST. GEORGE
Population 712

Dalton Elevator:
From 1st, 1 block south on Lincoln. The tall concrete elevator was built in 1915 by William Dalton. Adjacent, the two eight-sided wooden silos constructed in the 1920s to store grain are the last standing wooden silos of this type in the state. All three structures have long since been abandoned.

Champion Tree:
From 1st and Grant, 1 block south. Beside the giant tree a sign reports that this bur oak is 88 feet tall, its circumference

is 19 feet 11 inches, and its crown spreads 82 feet. The big granddaddy of a tree turns 274 years old in 2017.

Historic Springs: 3rd and Lincoln. A concrete tank, dedicated to the early settlers of St. George, still catches water from the ever-running Black Jack Springs. The springs were a well-known rest stop for travelers on the old military road between Fort Leavenworth and Fort Riley and for those on the Smoky Hill Trail. An overland stage station stood near the springs prior to the coming of the railroad.

Outdoor Mural: 1st and Lincoln. Depicting the area's settlement, the refurbished mural on the side of the 1861 general store was first painted in 1976 by local high school students.

Boggs Landing/Kansas River Trail: From 1st, ¼ mile south on Lincoln, across the railroad tracks to the river. The Kansas River Trail, a designated National Water Trail, runs from Kaw Point in Kansas City to Junction City. The Boggs Landing access ramp in St. George is at river mile 137 of 173. ksrivertrail.com.

Double T's Snack Shack & Canoe Rentals: 202 1st. Your starting point for fun on the river is in this former 1920s service station. Rent a kayak or a canoe or pick up snacks or a hot pizza to go. Double T's owner Tim Calmes will transport you and your rented boat to a

river access point in Manhattan so you can float down river back to St. George. Rental reservations recommended. Tuesday-Sunday 11 a.m.-7 p.m. 785.494.8081. FB.

ST. MARYS

Population 2,677

In 1848 Jesuit priest Father Hoecken established St. Mary's Mission to educate area Pota- watomis. For about 10 years (1848-1858) the mission was the last point of civilization on the Oregon Trail before wagons reached Salt Lake City.

St. Mary's Academy & College: 200 E. Mission. The present institution has evolved from the Indian mission (1848-1869), to an early Catholic college (1869-1931), to a Jesuit seminary (1931-1967). The educational complex then sat empty until 1978 when the Society of St. Pius X acquired the college, restored the buildings, and established St. Mary's Academy for grades K-12 and re-established St. Mary's College. Today students from around the world attend this facility. smac.edu.

WWI Memorial Victory Arch: 200 E. Mission (St. Mary's campus). This elegant Beaux Arts style arch, dedicated in 1923, honors the men of St. Mary's College who served during the World War.

Presence of Three: Between 6th and 7th on E. Bertrand (Railroad Park). A sculpture of interlocking stones represents three important aspects of St. Marys history: the Potawatomi Indians, St. Mary's Mission, and the Oregon Trail.

Indian Pay Station (NRHP): 111 E. Mission. Potawatomi Indians came to this building from 1857 to 1870 to collect the meager allotments they were promised when settling on the reserva- tion. The station is one of the oldest buildings in the state. Displays inside two nearby structures interpret the history of St. Marys, from the founding of the mission through the early settlement period. Memorial Day-Labor Day, daily 1-4 p.m. 785.437.6387.

Florence Adams: 529 W. Bertrand. This unique boutique began with the original owner's trip to Poland and her return with lovely Polish pottery. Although the store now focuses on apparel and accessories, it also carries housewares and handmade pottery. Inside a restored 1907 building, Florence Adams is named for the first owner's beloved grandmother. Monday-Saturday 10 a.m.-6 p.m. 888.977.3110. florenceadams.com.

MJ's Coffee House: 512 W. Bertrand. Specialty coffees, Italian sodas, chais, flavored lemonades, bagels, and muffins are among the morning starters or afternoon pick-me-ups in this cozy, laid-back coffee shop. Monday-Friday 6:30 a.m.-6 p.m.; Saturday 7 a.m.-4 p.m. 785.437.6577. FB.

WAMEGO

Population 4,603

Columbian Theatre, Museum & Art Center:

521 Lincoln. Like many Kansans and those from around the world, Wamego resident J.C. Rogers attended the 1893 World's Columbian Exposition in Chicago, which celebrated the 400th anniversary of Columbus' discovery of the New World. At the close of the event, Rogers bought exposition paintings and artifacts to adorn this theatre, which he opened in 1895 and duly named the Columbian. The silver iron eagle above the exterior entrance is a replica of a 13-foot iron eagle that he bought at the expo-sition. Rogers also obtained eight 11x17-foot murals. In 1929 the theatre became a movie house, then closed in 1950. The building sat empty for 40 years until community leaders decided to showcase it once again. They found and refurbished six of the murals that now are featured master-pieces. The decor throughout is

elegant, combining rich colors with beautiful woodwork, large mirrors, and chandeliers. Step inside to see the art gallery and retail area and ask for a tour. Tuesday-Friday 10 a.m.-5 p.m.; Saturday 10 a.m-3 p.m. 785.456.2029. columbiantheatre.com.

City Park: 406 E. 4th. In addition to the historical museum complex (see previous entry), this 1901 picturesque park features two statues (the Goddess of Science and the Goddess of Art) purchased by J.C. Rogers at the 1893 World's Columbian Exposition. Additionally, this setting includes the Ernie White crane sculpture atop a 100-year-old glacial stone fountain, and the colorful Children's Train, which offers rides through the 12-acre park. Train hours, April 15-October 15, Thursday, Saturday 10 a.m.-12 p.m. and Sunday 2-4 p.m. 785.456.2040. visitwamego.com.

Dutch Mill (NRHP):

406 E. 4th (City Park). The 40-foot-tall Schonhoff Mill with a base diameter of 25 feet was built of native limestone by a Dutch immigrant in 1879. In 1924 members of the park board took the mill apart stone by stone and moved it 12 miles to its present site where the public

can admire it. All parts of this impressive mill were moved by horse-drawn wagons.

NE

Wamego Historical Society Museum: 406 E. 4th (City Park). The museum's appealing facade welcomes you in to see pictures, artifacts and displays of the park, the Columbian Theatre, Wamego's historic homes, the Dutch Mill, and more. Outside, along a sidewalk and under the trees, enjoy strolling past the historic buildings in Prairie Town Village. April-October, Monday-Saturday 10-4 p.m. and Sunday 1-4 p.m.; November-March, Tuesday-Sunday 1-4 p.m. Admission charge. 785.456.2040. wamegohistoricalmuseum.org.

Duty Called: 405 6th. Sculpted by Charlie and Carson Norton, this beautifully detailed, larger-than-life bronze portrays a WWII soldier posed in tribute before a traditional battlefield cross. *Duty Called* is a main feature at the new and impres-sive Wamego Area Veterans Memorial. Granite bricks honor more than 700 veterans, and the names of the area's 91 fallen soldiers are inscribed on the black granite wall. wamegoveteransmemorial.org.

Oz Museum (8 Wonders of Kansas Customs):
511 Lincoln. In 2003 "the yellow brick road" found its way here when a Wamego native loaned

his large collection of Oz memorabilia to the town. From that the Oz Museum was born. You'll meet the Cowardly Lion and the Tin Man, but you'll also find artifacts and information

about the film, the original Oz books, and the toys and games that spawned from this classic tale. The gift shop is a treasure trove for Oz

fans. Memorial Day-Labor Day, Monday-Saturday 10 a.m.-6 p.m. and Sunday 12-6 p.m; September-May, Monday-Saturday 10 a.m.-5 p.m. and Sunday 12-5 p.m. Admission charge. 785.458.8686. ozmuseum.com.

Oz Winery: 417 Lincoln. A fine tasting area and retail shop make for an appealing stop. Wines named Blue Gingham Dress, Poppy Fields, Angry Trees, Surrender, and Squished Witch let you know there's no place like Oz Winery. 785.456.7417. ozwinerykansas.com.

Downtown: Follow the "yellow brick road," which starts north of Vanderbilt's, 510 Lincoln, and continues east to the Friendship House, 507 Ash. Planters and old-fashioned street lamps make the downtown sidewalks pleasant paths to specialty gift shops and antique stores.

John's Shoe and Saddle

Repair: 404 Lincoln. John's place might look a bit rickety on the outside, but that makes it an intriguing explorer stop. John has been making and repairing saddles, tack, and leather goods for more than 30 years.

It's a step back into Wamego's early days. Monday-Friday 8 a.m.-5 p.m.; Saturday 8 a.m.-12 p.m. 785.456.2872.

Paramour Coffee:

810 4th. Jim Hovind is passionate about the artisan roasted coffee process and sharing the best blends in his family-owned shop. Try his coffee with a homemade peach cobbler muffin or breakfast sandwich and you'll fall in love with Paramour. Monday-Friday 6-11 a.m.; Saturday-Sunday 7 a.m.-2 p.m. 785.458.5282. paramourcoffee.com.

Friendship House: 507 Ash. Soups, sandwiches, and weekly specials are scrumptious as are the fresh-baked delights, all made from scratch. Order at the counter then find a seat inside this lovely old home, or eat outside on the porch. Wherever you sit, you'll enjoy a wealth of good taste, and the friendship is always free. Monday-Saturday 6:30 a.m.-3 p.m.; Sunday 8 a.m.-2 p.m. 785.456.9616. friendshiphouse.biz.

Friendly Cooker:

520 Lincoln. Locals love the daily specials, the homemade desserts and cinnamon rolls, and especially the hot roast beef sandwich. Breakfast is served anytime. Daily 7 a.m.-2 p.m.; Thursday-Friday 5-8 p.m. 785.456.8460.

Toto's Tacoz: 515 Lincoln. A cheery place where it's fun to order tacos and other Mexican edibles with Oz-themed names—Bust my Buttons burrito, Auntie Em's nachos, and a Dorothy quesadilla. Order at the counter for fast and friendly service. Tuesday-Saturday 11 a.m.-8 p.m. 785.456.8090. FB.

Barleycorn's Downtown

Deli: 410 Lincoln. Inside this historic building with native limestone walls, take a seat in a high-backed wooden booth and choose from a wide selection of sandwiches, wraps, salads, appetizers, and daily specials. A full bar is available. Daily 11 a.m.-9 p.m. 785.456.7421. FB.

Lodging:
visitwamego.com/stay.

explorer extras...
In Wamego

Drive by to see the beautiful Trout House (NRHP), an 1896 Queen Anne style home at 615 Elm. Asymmetrical arrangement, multiple roof planes, a three-story rounded tower with a conical roof, fish scale shingles, and spindlework make it a captivating sight.

With its 14 gables, the 1890 Ditto/Leach House, 910 5th, appears like a grand Sicilian villa. At one time an underground tunnel connected this house with the 1882 Leach Opera House at 901 5th. Drive by only.

The Victory Highway movement began in 1921 to commemorate WWI veterans. A bronze sculpture of an eagle on a nest

with her eaglets was chosen as the highway symbol. In 1925 the U.S. highway system began its numbering system, and Victory Highway and parts of other roads became U.S. 40. A stone Victory Highway marker with a bronze plaque and eagle sculpture stand at 4th and Ash.

From K-99, the Kansas River Trail access ramp is 1 block west on Valley then 1 block south on Elm. Bring your kayak or canoe for an up-close river experience. The Kansas River Trail is a designated National Water Trail that runs from Kaw Point in Kansas City to Junction City. The access point in Wamego is river mile 128 of 173. **ee**

WESTMORELAND

Population 788

Scott Springs Oregon Trail Park: From Main, ¾ mile south on K-99. In commemoration of this significant site on the Oregon-California Trail, Ernest White sculpted the bronze oxen team hitched to a covered wagon that you'll see in this park. Between 1842 and 1870 more than 300,000 pioneers

stopped at this campground, famous for its springs, on their way west. Interpretive signs provide the area's historic background, and you can walk by Rock Creek to see where wagons forded. A sidewalk trail leads you to the graves of emigrants who lost their lives here to cholera.

Hand-Dug Well: From Main, ¼ mile north on K-99 (Dechairo Park). Built in 1914, this well is reputedly one of the largest remaining hand-dug wells in the United States. It's 29 feet in diameter and 38 feet deep. The park is a wonderful place to stretch your legs and learn about this historic well.

Pottawatomie County Courthouse: 106 Main. Constructed of native limestone and built in 1884, it is the second oldest Kansas courthouse in continuous use. On the grounds are a large stone county map and an impressive veterans memorial. Monday-Friday 8 a.m.-4:30 p.m. 785.457.3392.

Rock Creek Historical Society Museum: 507 Burkman. A collection of artifacts and documents interpret the story of the Oregon-California Trail and early area settlement. You'll also see an exhibit on Westmoreland native Wayne Dunafon, better known as the Marlboro Man.

The Wiziarde Novelty Circus family (the son became Whizzo the Clown) was also from Westmoreland, and photos and costumes here portray

the family's circus lifestyle. Restored Model T and Model A Fords also are displayed. April-November, Tuesday-Sunday 1-4 p.m. 785.457.0100. westmorelandkshistory.org.

Westmoreland City Cemetery: From Main, ½ mile south on Pine. Situated on the southwest side of town, the cemetery overlooks the lovely Rock Creek Valley. A glacial stone wall and landscaping surround a GAR memorial dedicated in 1905.

Downtown: Enjoy shopping at Rock House Antiques (321 Main, 785.456.5230); The Tin Station (209 Main); and the Westy Country Market (314 Main, 785.457.3776).

The West Pharm: 402 Main. The old favorites—shakes, malts, sodas, sundaes, and friendly service—are offered at this 1950s soda fountain with eight stools and a Formica counter. Monday-Friday 8 a.m.-6 p.m.; Saturday 8 a.m.-12 p.m. 785.457.3611.

South 40 Cafe: 401 S. K-99. Lunch specials and hearty, made-from-scratch food make the South 40 a favorite meal stop for the locals. Chicken and handmade noodles are served on Thursdays, and during the cold months you can warm up with homemade soups. Daily 6 a.m.-2 p.m.; Wednesday, Friday 4-8 p.m. 785.457.3307. FB.

Lodging: Oregon Trail RV Park (785.457.3361).

NE

explorer extras...
In Westmoreland

A nine-hole disc golf course in DeChairo Park, 613 Campbell, features elevation changes in a lightly wooded area north of town. 785.457.3361.

The building at 202 Main was originally the pump house for the hand-dug well (*see* earlier entry). The structure was dismantled, every stone was marked, and it was resurrected at this location as the city office, which it is today.

The Little Dog Lost Walking Trail starts at the Oregon Trail Park, winds its way to the Rock Creek Historical Society Museum, and ends at the swimming pool, 613 Campbell. A marker south of the K-99 bridge (where a little dog waited daily for her family to return) tells the heartwarming story about a little dog that was accidentally left by travelers but was befriended and adopted by the community. **ee**

WHEATON

Population 99

American Gas Pump:
318 Front. Through several discussions, many locals think that this little red pump probably was the first gasoline dispenser for the Kufahl Hardware store (and John Deere dealer). Later it was used to pump white gas and then kerosene. Drive by and see if you can add more to the story of this American Oil Pump and Tank Company icon.

Historical Structures:
From Wheaton, ½ mile south on Wheaton, then 1¾ miles east on Possum Hollow. The striking 1886 limestone horse barn, known as the Henneberg Barn, is at 18745 Possum Hollow. Continue ¼ mile east on Possum Hollow, 2 miles north on Fremont, 2 miles east on Golden Belt, then 1 mile south on Major

Jenkins to the Teske Farmstead (NRHP). Here you'll see a circa 1870 stone farmhouse, spring house, and the 1907 gable-roof barn. If you're looking for reasons to tour the countryside, these structures are good ones! Drive by only.

Riley County

AROUND THE COUNTY

Konza Prairie (8 Wonders of Kansas Geography):
From I-70 exit 307, 5 miles north and east on McDowell Creek. The Konza Prairie is a biological research station, but three hiking trails (three, five, and seven miles in length) provide an opportunity to enjoy the pristine tallgrass prairie. Creeks, woods, rustic bridges, and colorful wildflowers are found along the routes. Trail hours, daily dawn to dusk. 785.587.0381. kpbs.konza.k-state.edu.

Konza Prairie Scenic Overlook:
From 3rd in Manhattan, 3¾ miles south on Pierre (becomes K-177). Plan to stop for an expansive view of the gorgeous Flint Hills and the tallgrass prairie. During the spring the endless grassy hills resemble green velvet. During the summer the big bluestem grass can grow as tall as 10 feet, depending on moisture.

Pillsbury Crossing
(8 Wonders of Kansas Geography): From 3rd in Manhattan, 2¼ mile south on Pierre (becomes K-177), 3¾ miles south and east on Deep Creek, then 2¼ miles east on Pillsbury Crossing. Deep Creek flows over a limestone ledge

forming a four-foot waterfall at Pillsbury Crossing. You might see cars or people on the stone creek bottom. College kids and families all enjoy this natural ford that has been a landmark and a fun place to hang out for generations. tinyurl.com/pillscross.

Rocky Ford Outdoor Recreation Area:
From Marlatt in Manhattan, 1 mile north on U.S. 24 (Tuttle Creek Blvd.), ¾ mile east and northwest on Rocky Ford, then just east on Mill. Because of the natural flat rock bottom, pioneers and the military could ford the Big Blue River here. It's a scenic area with a 1908 gristmill dam creating a waterfall, and it is a river access point for canoes and kayaks. tinyurl.com/rockyfordrec.

Tuttle Creek Lake and State Park:
From U.S. 24 (north of Manhattan), 1¾ mile east on K-13 across the dam, then 1 mile south (circling back north) on River Pond Rd. to the state park. Congress first recommended the construction of the lake in 1938 as a flood control measure. This need was debated for years, but the great floods of 1951 sealed its approval. Construction started in 1952 and operation began 10 years later. Tuttle is the state's second largest reservoir and offers 100 miles of rugged, wooded shoreline. The park contains the usual recreational opportunities including excellent hiking, biking, and equestrian trails. State park entrance charge. Cabins available, reservations required. 785.539.7941. ksoutdoors.com.

Bala Stone Bridge and Park:
From Riley, 5 miles west on U.S. 77, ¼ mile north on K-82, 1 mile west on Bala, just south on Lasita, then south and west on a driveway and follow the sign to Bala Park. Enter the park through a rustic gateway

and walk under the tall trees past playground and picnic areas, and suddenly there it is—a grand stone single-arch bridge with a 30-foot span! Built in 1887 as a rail line trestle, the rail line is now abandoned, but the bridge survives and is aging gracefully among the trees and the creek flowing beneath it. The area is one of the top explorer stops in the state, and everyone respectful of this privately owned property is welcome to enjoy it. 785.762.3335.

LEONARDVILLE

Population 458

Nelson's Landing:
107 N. Erpelding. KSU and Green Bay Packer fans will feel the presence of football star Jordy Nelson when entering this restaurant owned by Kim Nelson, Jordy's mom. Especially popular is the famously large chicken-fried steak covered in country gravy, which fills up football fans and food fans alike. Save room for homemade

pie, especially for the one with Reese's Peanut Butter Cup. Monday-Thursday 11 a.m.-10 p.m; Friday-Saturday 11 a.m.-11 p.m.; Sunday 11 a.m.-3 p.m. 785.293.5661. nelsonslandingks.com.

MANHATTAN

Population 56,143

Flint Hills Discovery Center:
315 S. 3rd. Enhance your adventure in the Flint Hills by starting here and discovering the fascinating geology, history, and culture of the precious tallgrass prairie. Displays and a video help you understand the nuances of the grasses, wildflowers, prairie burning, the cattle, the cowboys, and much more. Monday-Friday 10 a.m.-5 p.m.; Saturday 12-5 p.m. Admission charge. 785.587.2726. flinthillsdiscovery.org.

KSU Campus Drive:
View historic Kansas State University with a drive through campus where shaded lanes lead you past vintage limestone halls of learning. Beginning as an agricultural college, KSU is the nation's oldest land grant university, dating to 1863. Stroll the campus and absorb its tradition.

Hale Library:
1117 Mid-Campus (KSU campus). Romanesque Revival architecture renders this library, dedicated in 1997, an impressive sight. If you're a Harry Potter fan, you'll want to see room 304, said to resemble Hogwarts Castle Great Hall! On the library's third floor, the Great Room (part of the original 1927 library) is stunning. It features dark wood-work, tall windows, ceiling timbers, and four 11x14 foot murals by David Hicks Overmyer that were a 1934 Public Works of Art Project. Monday-Friday 8 a.m.-6 p.m.; Saturday-Sunday 1-5 p.m. 785.532.3014.

The Gardens:
1500 Denison (KSU campus). The gardens simple beginning dates to 1871, and through several transitions, they are today a beautiful horticulture educational resource and laboratory. The 1933 limestone dairy barn provides a historic focus to this botanical landscape and the 1907 Victorian style conservatory. A fountain, gazebo, and sculptures are charming backdrops for an explosion of colors, espe-

cially in the Daylily, the Iris, and the Rose Collections. The Insect Zoo (inside the barn), containing live insects, helps us learn to appreciate bugs!

Seasonal gardens hours, daily dawn to dusk; Insect Zoo hours, Tuesday-Saturday 1-6 p.m., admission charge; Quinlan Visitor Center (inside the barn) hours, March-November, Monday-Friday 10 a.m.-4 p.m. 785.532.3271. ksu.edu/gardens.

Call Hall Dairy Bar:
144 Call Hall (KSU campus). Students and the public have been making the call for ice cream at this dairy bar since 1964. Thirty flavors are available at any one time, including a blueberry ice cream called Purple Pride. Products (all made on campus) for sale include milk, cheese, butter, eggs, and meat. August-May,

NE

Monday-Friday 8 a.m.-6 p.m.; Saturday 8 a.m.-4 p.m.; summer, irregular hours. 785.532.1292. ksu.edu/asi/dairybar.

Beach Museum of Art:
701 Beach (KSU campus). The permanent collection includes worldwide art, and the Kansas Art Collection is the largest and most diverse assemblage of its kind in the state. Tuesday-Saturday 11 a.m.-4 p.m.; Thursday 10 a.m.-8 p.m. 785.532.7718.

Aggieville:
N. Manhattan and Bluemont. Aggieville, a student village south of the KSU campus, is the oldest shopping district of its kind in Kansas, dating to 1889. As late as 1912 the streets were still dirt. Things have changed over the years, and today more than 110 shops of all sorts and varieties converge here. By day it's a great place to shop and lunch, and by evening the tones of night life emerge. aggieville.org.

Downtown:
Shoppers love the many downtown businesses including Connected–a Fair Trade Store (327 Poyntz, 785.212.1801); Yee Haw Country Outfitters (431 Poyntz, 785.320.2570); Claflin Books (103 N. 4th, 785.776.3771); and Hazel Hill Chocolate Traditions (106 S. 4th, 785.320.6313). downtownmanhattanks.com.

Strecker-Nelson Gallery:
406½ Poyntz. The clever, colorful, and contrasting works by regional artists fill the oldest continuously operating commercial art gallery in the state. Open since 1979, the gallery comprises paintings, ceramics, glasswork, sculpture, photography, lithographs, and printmakers. All are tastefully displayed on the second floor of this historic building in the heart of downtown. Monday-Saturday 10 a.m.-6 p.m. 785.537.2099. strecker-nelsongallery.com.

Downtown Manhattan Historic District (NRHP):
Sixty-one buildings are part of the district from 3rd to 5th on Poyntz and mostly between Humboldt and Pierre. Give yourself some time to study the exquisite exterior detail on the 1906 Riley County Courthouse (500 Poyntz); the Carnegie library building (510 Poyntz); and the Wareham Hotel and Theatre (412, 418 Poyntz).

Sunset Zoo:
2333 Oak. At this small and beautifully landscaped zoo, you'll enjoy an engaging, pleasant, and up-close visit with animals from Kansas and places around the world including Africa, Australia, and Asia. Butterfly, hummingbird and sensory gardens add to your experience. November-March, daily 12-5 p.m.; April-October, daily 9:30 a.m.-5 p.m. Admission charge. 785.587.2737. sunsetzoo.com.

Union Pacific Depot (RHKP):
120 Fort Riley Blvd. (K-18). Theodore Roosevelt stopped here on a whistle-stop campaign tour in 1903, a year after this eye-catching depot was built. In 1990 the city renovated the depot to its current grandeur, restoring the tower based on original architectural plans. It now functions as an event center.

Riley County Historical Museum:
2309 Claflin. With its quality exhibits, the museum preserves the history of Riley County from 1855 to the present and the story of Kansas State University. Behind the museum is the unique Hartford House, an 1855 prefabricated home brought to Manhattan by early settlers on the steamboat *Hartford*. Ask for a brochure of the self-guided architectural and historical driving tour. Tuesday-Friday 8:30 a.m.-5 p.m.; Saturday-Sunday 2-5 p.m. 785.565.6490.

Goodnow House State Historic Site (NRHP):
2301 Claflin (across from the Riley County Historical Museum). Pioneer educator Isaac Goodnow and his wife, Ellen, built this limestone farmhouse in 1860-1861. Isaac was one of the founders of Manhattan and also established Bluemont College, a forerunner of Kansas State University. The Goodnows' lives unfold inside this home, where interpretive exhibits offer a slice of Kansas during its early years of statehood. For tours, ask at the Riley County Historical Museum.

Wolf House Museum:
630 Fremont. Serving from 1870 to the 1930s as a German boardinghouse, this two-story limestone structure is interpreted as an 1880s home. It is named for Lucile Wolf, who owned the house from 1941 to 1982. Saturday-Sunday 2-5 p.m. 785.565.6490. rileychs.com.

Bluemont Youth Cabin (NRHP):
5th and Bertrand (Goodnow Park). Nestled at the base of Bluemont Hill, a series of tiered steps lead to the secluded and intriguing limestone cabin. The National Youth Administration program helped construct it in 1938. A narrow concrete trail to the west leads to the stone letters that spell "Manhattan" on top of Bluemont Hill.

Sunset Cemetery:
2000 Leavenworth. Along the shaded lanes you'll find a section of white crosses placed by Gold Star Mothers, the eerie Fortune

mausoleum, a monument built "In Memory of Our Union Soldiers 1861-1865," and many intriguing gravestones. The impressive limestone arched entrance and the stone wall around the cemetery was a 1935 WPA project. Tiger Woods' father, Earl, is buried here but has no gravestone.

Wildwood Outdoor Adventure Park:

375 Johnson. Up to seven zip lines, with hiking trails between each line, are available for your enjoyment. It's a high-flying way to experience the hills and ravines of the Flint Hills. March-December, Friday-Sunday 9 a.m.-4 p.m. Admission charge. Reservations required. 785.477.9543. wildwoodzip.com.

Liquid Art Winery and Estate:

1745 Wildcat Creek. David Tegtmeier has been growing grapevines since he was 15, and now you can enjoy the fruits of his labor. At their newly opened winery, David and his wife, Danielle, offer seven wines ready to be sampled in the tasting room. Hard cider is also available. Friday-Saturday 12-8 p.m.; Sunday 12-6 p.m. 785.370.8025. liquidartwinery.com.

Little Apple Brewing Company:

1110 Westloop Plaza. A mainstay in Manhattan, this award-winning restaurant uses locally sourced ingredients as much as possible and is especially known for the Angus beef steaks. The names of the handcrafted ales—Wildcat Wheat, Prairie Pale, and Riley's Red—affirm the Little Apple's local flavor! Daily 11 a.m.-10 p.m. 785.539.5500. littleapplebrewery.com.

Tallgrass Tap House:

320 Poyntz. The public face of the Tallgrass Brewing Company, this downtown brewpub serves burgers, sandwiches, and appetizers, and is the place to try the more than 15 different Tallgrass craft beers and specialty brews. Daily 11 a.m.-10 p.m. 785.320.2933. tallgrasstaphouse.com.

Varsity Donuts:

704 N. Manhattan. Open since 2011, Varsity is already a local institution for food and fun. With such a large selection of donuts and sprinkles, tough choices must be made at this hipster, interactive shop. Take a seat at the marble counter or, if you're so inclined, at the piano and play a tune. Daily 6 a.m.-10 p.m. 785.539.7654. FB.

Radina's Bakehouse:

227 Blue Earth Place. Baguettes, ciabatta, cinnamon raisin, or whole clove roasted garlic are only some of Radina's traditionally made breads. The classically trained bakers here use only fresh and real ingredients, and most of the grains and flour are grown and milled in Kansas. You can buy bread by the loaf or order a sandwich that, of course, uses only Bakehouse breads. Salads are available too, but, really? Monday-Friday 6:30 a.m.-11 p.m.; Saturday-Sunday 8 a.m.-11 p.m. 785.537.2345. radinascoffee.com.

The Chef:

111 S. 4th. This little downtown breakfast place started in 1943 but closed its doors in 1986. To the delight of many, it's back again! Since 2008 the Chef offers traditional home cooking both in its tasty lunches and in a wide array of breakfast choices—from the classic breakfast to biscuits and gravy, Florentine frittata, and every kind of amped-up entree you can imagine. Look for the original neon Chef sign outside. Monday-Friday 6 a.m.-2 p.m.; Saturday-Sunday 7 a.m.-3 p.m. 785.537.6843. thechefcafe.com.

Bourbon and Baker:

312 Poyntz. Most dishes on the menu are offered tapas style (small portions) so you can try combinations of midwestern and southern cooking. Popular choices include chicken and waffles, figs in a blanket, Kobe slider, and stuffed piquillo peppers. The ingredients are by no means ordinary! The bakery offers some wonderfully sweet choices, and for the bourbon lover, you can select from more than 70 varieties! Monday-Saturday 11 a.m.-10 p.m. 785.320.4959. bourbonandbakermanhattan.com.

Keltic Star: 1215 Moro. Perry and Shirley McCall and their son Darren have created a menu of family recipes with authentic Welsh, Scottish, and Irish origins. Order the Pub Platter to experience bangers and mash, fish and chips, shepherd's pie, and a Cornish pasty. Tuesday-Saturday 11 a.m.-9 p.m. 785.320.7456. kelticstarmanhattanks.com.

NE

Taco Lucha: 1130 Moro. This is Mexican street food taken to the next level. Some top choices are the pork tinga slider (slow roasted pork, tinga sauce, and spicy slaw on a mini-slider bun) and carnitas (braised chopped pork in adobo, pineapple salsa, and queso fresco on a corn tortilla). The margaritas and sangrias are legend. Tuesday-Sunday 11 a.m.-9 p.m. 785.320.5255. tacoluchamanhattan.com.

Harry's: 418 Poyntz. Dining in the 1926 historic Wareham Hotel is always a treat whether it's for lunch or dinner. Inside this downtown classic you'll enjoy fine wines, hand-cut steaks, fresh seafood, daily specials, and the pastry chef's seasonal desserts. Monday-Friday 11 a.m.-2 p.m.; Monday-Saturday 5-9 p.m. 785.537.1300. harrysmanhattan.com.

Little Grill: 6625 Dyer. From Casement, 1 mile north on Dyer. Looking for island atmosphere? Head to Little Grill where you'll find Jamaican inspired food with a twist of Americana. The jerk chicken with red beans or gumbo pair nicely with the Jamaican rum punch or pina coladas. When owners Kenrick and Cathy Waite opened in 2002 they cooked all the food on a little grill, thus the restaurant's name! Live music sometime is performed by Jamaica native Kenrick. 785.323.0112.

More Good Restaurants:
AJ's New York Pizzeria (301 Poyntz, 785.587.0700); Coco Bolos (1227 Bluemont, 785.537.4700); Della Voce (405 Poyntz, 785.532.9000). manhattancvb.org.

Lodging:
Anderson House (KBBA, 785.539.4994, andersonbnb.com); Bed and Buggy Inn (KBBA, 785.494.8232, bedandbuggyinn.com); Lazy T Ranch (KBBA, 785.537.9727, lazytranchadventures.com); Moore House Bed and Breakfast (KBBA, 785.776.5603, moorehouse-bnb.com); Prairiewood Retreat & Preserve (785.537.9999, prairiewood.com); Scenic Valley Inn Bed & Breakfast and Event Center (KBBA, 785. 776.6831, scenicvalleyinn.com); additional lodging (manhattancvb.org).

explorer extras... In Manhattan

Johnny Kaw, a fictitious and larger-than-life pioneer farmer who dug the Kaw River Valley, planted wheat, invented sunflowers, grew giant potatoes, and controlled the weather, was created by KSU professor George Filinger in 1955 as the Kansas answer to Paul Bunyan. In 1966 a 30-foot-tall steel structure of Johnny Kaw was erected in City Park at 11th and Poyntz. There he stands with giant scythe in hand, gazing out at all who pass by.

Linear Park provides nine miles of trails (crushed limestone to sidewalks) that take you from riverside corridors into town. One trailhead is just south of the junction of Fort Riley Blvd. and S. Manhattan. 785.587.2757.

Customers have been enjoying fine fruits, fresh veggies,

and fast, friendly service at the Eastside (219 E. Poyntz) and Westside (521 Richards) Markets since 1976. Stop in for your helping of fine, fresh, fast, and friendly. 785.776.8111. eastsideandwestside-markets.com.

"Community House" is etched above the door on this three-story brick building (NRHP) at 120 N. 4th. Built in 1917, it was designed to provide a place for soldiers to relax and be entertained during the two World Wars. A brochure for a self-guided driving tour that includes more historical buildings is available at the Riley County Historical Museum, 2309 Claflin. tinyurl.com/archtourman.

explorer extras... In Randolph

Population 171

The mile-long stringer bridge, completed in 1960, carries vehicles across the Big Blue River/Tuttle Creek Lake. It's the longest bridge in Kansas. From Randolph, 1 mile east on K-16.

explorer extras... In Zeandale

Unincorporated

The stone 1896 Christian Church, complete with bell tower and bell, is a picturesque

site in this small village. It's now home to the Zeandale Community Church. From K-177, 7 miles east on K-18 to Zeandale. **ee**

Shawnee County

AROUND THE COUNTY

Rees Fruit Farm:

2476 K-4 (U.S. 24 and K-4). Home of the original Apple Cider Slush, Rees is the oldest commercial fruit farm in the state. Established in 1901, it has been owned and operated by the Rees family ever since. Inside the retail store, complete with pot-bellied stove, you can purchase sandwiches, food products, and fruit grown in the nearby orchards. Monday-Saturday 9 a.m.-6 p.m.; Sunday 11 a.m.-5 p.m. 785.246.3257 reesfruitfarm.com.

DOVER

Unincorporated

Dover is the east end of the Native Stone Scenic Byway (see p.192), which provides 48 miles of winding roads past native limestone structures and fences in the lovely Flint Hills. travelks.com/ksbyways.com.

Historic 66 Station:

K-4 and SW Douglas. In the late 1920s this little corner Phillips 66 station (later a Sinclair station) was built to take advantage of its prime location on K-4.

Sage Inn (NRHP):

13553 SW K-4. Alfred Sage built this two-story limestone home in 1878 for his residence but also made it available as a hotel for 20 years during the late 1800s. In more recent times it has operated as a bed and breakfast.

Sommerset Hall: 5701 SW

Douglas. Alfred Sage built this long, narrow wooden structure in the late 1890s, and it remains

the pulse of this tiny town. The lower floor carries a few grocery items and shares most of the space with the cafe. The menu includes the standard breakfast

and lunch favorites and some of the best pie in the state. It is a legendary stop for travelers, by car or bicycle. Monday-Thursday, Saturday 7 a.m.-4 p.m.; Friday 7 a.m.-8 p.m. 785.256.6223. FB.

Iron Truss Bridge: From

Douglas, ½ mile west on K-4, then ½ mile south on Carlson. On your way to Echo Cliff (*see* next entry), take this half-mile detour to drive across the 1910 truss bridge over Mission Creek.

Echo Cliff: From Douglas,

1½ miles west on K-4, 1 mile south on Echo Cliff, and before the truss bridge, east onto the driveway. Prior to seeing the cliffs you'll pass some round concrete and metal picnic tables and stools handmade by Earl Hepworth. The sandstone cliff appears to be at least 70 feet high, and Mission Creek's shallow stream flows at their base. Shout into the cliff and you'll hear why it's called Echo Cliff.

explorer extras...
In Rossville

Population 1,140

Parts of an old iron truss bridge now form a sturdy pedestrian bridge over Cross Creek at the corner of Pottawatomie and Pine.

Joe Campbell Stadium, 301 U.S. 24, is one of the few remaining all-wood grandstands in the country. Built in 1924, it is home to the Rossville Rattlers, a collegiate summer league baseball team. **ee**

SILVER LAKE

Population 1,437

Agency House: 9545 NW

U.S. 24. From Lake, 1¼ miles south and east on U.S. 24. Strong evidence suggests that this is the oldest standing house in Kansas, built in 1827 from native stone. It was constructed as the winter quarters for a U.S. Army survey party while it surveyed Indian lands following the treaty of 1825. Private residence, drive by only.

TOPEKA

Population 127,679

Kansas State Capitol

(NRHP, 8 Wonders of Kansas Architecture):

300 SW 10th. It took 37 years (1866-1903) to build this stately Neoclassical Renaissance structure, and 13 years (2001-2014) to complete a recent

NE

renovation. Enter on the north and stop at a visitor center desk to pick up a self-guided tour brochure or learn about guided tours and dome tours (up the 296 steps to the dome). Of major interest in one of the nation's most beautiful state capitols are the stunning murals by John Steuart Curry (see p. 131; 8 Wonders of Kansas Art), Lumen Martin Winter, and David Overmyer. The most famous is Curry's *Tragic Prelude* featuring a fierce John Brown holding a Bible in one hand and a rifle in the other. Among other impressive features are the Pete Felten stone sculptures of four famous Kansans in the second-floor rotunda, the majestic stained-glass dome, the marble walls and floors, and the brass and copper staircases. If the legislative chambers are not

occupied, step inside to admire the ornamentation that dates to the late 1880s. Standing atop the capitol dome is Richard Bergen's 22-foot-tall bronze sculpture of a Kaw Indian pointing his drawn bow toward the North Star. Monday-Friday, 8 a.m.- 5 p.m.; Saturday 8 a.m.-1 p.m. For tours (reservations recommended), call 785.296.3966. kshs.org.

Statehouse Grounds:

On the south lawn is the Robert Merrell Gage sculpture of a seated pioneer woman holding an infant, with a young boy and a dog at her feet. A second Gage sculpture, east of the capitol, is of a seated Abraham Lincoln. Numerous other plaques and a Statue of Liberty replica also adorn the grounds.

Kansas Museum of History (8 Wonders of Kansas History): 6425

SW 6th. This award-winning museum features excellent exhibits that tell the many fascinating stories of our state. The centerpiece is an 1880 locomotive, one of the first to run on the newly completed Santa Fe railway. Nearby, a biplane of A.K. Longren, the first Kansan to build an aircraft that flew successfully, hangs from the ceiling. You'll see artifacts of famous Kansans such as Dwight Eisenhower, Carry Nation, and John Brown, and a collage from the 1940s, 50s, and 60s will tickle the fancy of many. A fine gift shop is filled with Kansas books, art, and many specialty items. *The Great White Buffalo* sculpture stands near the museum entrance. Tuesday-Saturday 9 a.m.-5 p.m.; Sunday 1-5 p.m. Admission charge. 785.272.8681. kshs.org. A nature trail meanders a little

more than two miles through the prairie and woodland surrounding the Kansas History Center. 785.272.8681. kshs.org/museum.

Brown v. Board of Education National Historic Site: 1515 SE

Monroe. The story of the landmark Supreme Court case *Brown v. Board of Education of Topeka* is interpreted inside Monroe Elementary School (NRHP), one of four black schools in Topeka at the time of the ruling. The Court's decision on May 17, 1954, legally ended segregation in public schools. The museum here offers visitors an experiential journey into the struggles of blacks before and during the Brown v. Board era, the Civil Rights movement of the 1960s, and today. Daily 9 a.m.-5 p.m. 785.354.4273. nps.gov/brvb.

Historic Ritchie House:

1116 SE Madison. Topeka's oldest standing house was built in 1856 by ardent abolitionist John Ritchie. Ritchie, involved in bringing Kansas into the Union as a free state, was also a Topeka founder. He and his wife, Mary, supported women's rights, managed an Underground Railroad station, and created the first housing and schooling for area blacks. The brick and limestone home has been renovated and offers a hands-on history experience. Monday, Wednesday, 10 a.m. and 2 p.m. 785.234.6097. tinyurl.com/ritchiehouse.

Constitution Hall:

429 S. Kansas. The Topeka Constitutional Convention met here in 1855 and drafted the first state constitution. This constitution, however, which would have prohibited slavery in Kansas once statehood was attained, was not accepted by Congress. The building, now undergoing restoration, also served as the first

Kansas statehouse, 1864-1869. Interpretive panels in a pocket park to the south of the hall relate the 1850s political struggle and that of the 1954 *Brown v. Board of Education* case. The federal trial for Brown v. Board was held in the courthouse across the street. 785.250.8228. oldkansascapitol.org.

Old Prairie Town at Ward-Meade Historic Site:

124 NW Fillmore. Anthony Ward's family established a homestead and an Oregon Trail stop here in 1854. The Ward-Meade house (NRHP), built in 1870, was the first Victorian mansion in Topeka. The beautiful home is now a backdrop for lovely botanical gardens and a turn-of-the-century prairie town complete with church, depot, schoolhouse, and a working soda fountain in Potwin Drug. The Mulvane General Store operates as the park's gift shop and visitor center. Monday-Saturday 10 a.m.-4 p.m.; Sunday 12-4 p.m. 785.251.2989. FB.

Charles Curtis House Museum (NRHP): 1101 SW

Topeka. Future Topeka mayor J.C. Wilson built this Italianate style residence in 1878, and later a Topeka architect added the Moorish domes and terra cotta carvings. The house was Charles Curtis' official Topeka residence during the years he served as U.S. Senate majority leader (1925-1929) and as U.S. vice president (1929-1933). Curtis, a Topeka native, is the only American Indian to have held the office of vice president. Saturday 11 a.m.-5 p.m. 785.357.1371. charlescurtismuseum.com.

Potwin Place Historic District (NRHP): SW 4th

and SW Greenwood. From 1888 to 1899 Potwin Place was a separate city from Topeka, but today it's a lovely Victorian historic district noted for its Queen Anne homes and circular park intersections. The city's premier Prairie School style residence, built in 1917, is at 400 SW Greenwood.

Topeka High School (NRHP): 800 SW 10th.

The 165-foot tower, reminiscent of a spire at England's Oxford University, highlights this magnificent Gothic structure built in 1931. The library is modeled after Henry VIII's Great Hall at Hampton Court Palace and now exhibits new Mark Flickinger murals. An English classroom resembles an Elizabethan withdrawing room, and the cafeteria has a wood-beamed ceiling and wainscoting. Tour charge. Reservations required. 785.295.3200. thsweb.org/alumni2.

Cedar Crest Mansion (NRHP): 1 SW Cedar Crest.

Built in 1928 by publisher Frank MacLennan, this French architecture estate was later donated to the State of Kansas by MacLennan's widow. In 1961 it became the official residence of the governor, the smallest in the country but on the largest acreage. Notice the iron sunflower art on the entrance gate. Tours, Monday 1:30-3:30 p.m. Reservations required. Parking is west of the mansion. 785.296.3636. kshs.org.

Combat Air Museum:

7016 SE Forbes (Forbes Field). The museum, inside an air force hangar, features a collection of more than 30 military aircraft that span WWI to the present. Along with a re-creation of a field kitchen and a German POW barracks, you'll see an aviation art gallery and extensive military aviation artifacts. January-February, daily 12-4:30 p.m.; March-December, Monday-Saturday 9 a.m.-4:30 p.m. and Sunday 12-4:30 p.m. Admission charge. 785.862.3303. combatairmuseum.org.

Museum of the Kansas National Guard: 125 SE

Airport (Forbes Field). The story of the Kansas National Guard dating to the Civil War is told through indoor exhibits, military artwork, and an outdoor display of large military equipment. The Kansas National Guard Hall of Fame is also housed here. Monday-Saturday 10 a.m.-4 p.m. 785.862.1020.

Historic Harley-Davidson and the Evel Knievel Museum: 2047 SW Topeka.

Inside Historic Harley-Davidson, Yesterday's Museum exhibits a collection of photos, clothing, cycle parts, collectibles, and 30 antique motorcycles. Opening in 2017 the Evel Knievel Museum comprises the world's largest collection of Knievel's performance leathers, jump bikes, and memorabilia. These museums will rev the engines of any motorcycle enthusiast. Tuesday-Friday 10 a.m.-6 p.m.; Saturday 9 a.m.-5 p.m. 785.234.6174. historicharley.com.

Truckhenge: 4124 NE Brier.

Grassroots artist and avant-garde thinker Ron Lessman will entertain you as you walk by trucks, boats, and a bus stuck vertically in the earth like arrows. Beer-bottle sculptures and chain-sawed-stump faces are arranged in mind-boggling juxtapositions. It may not be Stonehenge, but bring your camera! Call ahead, 785.234.3486. FB.

Warehouse 414: 414 SE 2nd. The huge array of vintage fashionable furnishings, home decor accessories, art, glassware, and fun doodads are stylishly displayed in this former 1889 power station for electric trolleys. Industrial and architectural salvage is also on hand. John and Chris Grandmontagne's excellent eye for interior design brings you the best. Tuesday, Thursday-Saturday 11 a.m.-5:30 p.m. 785.232.8008. warehouse414.com.

SouthWind Art Gallery: 3074 SW 29th. Owner Gary Blitsch provides a spacious and inviting atmosphere to showcase original works by artists with roots in Kansas and the Midwest. The landscape art alone is reason enough to come, peruse, and buy! Tuesday-Friday 10 a.m.-6 p.m.; Saturday 10 a.m.-2 p.m. 785.273.5994. southwindartgallery.com.

Great Mural Wall of Topeka: SW 20th and SW Western. Vibrant colors and clever depictions of people, places, and issues in the Chesney Park neighborhood make this mural wall an enchanting stop that requires some study to fully appreciate it.

Grant Cushinberry, a beloved neighborhood leader and mentor, is featured in the first of 12 panels, created in 2007. Lead artist Dave Loewenstein works with many artists and the neighborhood to produce these meaningful murals. FB.

Aaron Douglas Celebration Mural Wall: SW 12th and SW Lane. Artists Dave Loewenstein and Stan Herd mentored a large group of Topekans in creating this mural that honors leading black artist Aaron Douglas. A Topeka native, Douglas graduated from Topeka High School and is considered the leader of Harlem Renaissance art of the early 1930s.

Topeka Art Guild and Gallery: 5331 SW 22nd Pl. (Fairlawn Plaza). The beautiful gallery provides a forum for local artists to display and sell their art. A multitude of mediums are exhibited including paintings, textiles, pottery, jewelry, and much more. Wednesday-Saturday 11 a.m.-5 p.m. 785.263.7646. topekaartguild.org.

Tiffany Windows: 817 SW Harrison (First Presbyterian Church). Ten stunningly beautiful Louis Comfort Tiffany

windows were installed in the church in 1911. Different from most stained glass, the remarkable iridescent colors of varied hues and shades are within the glass itself. These windows are remarkable! Brochures are available in the church lobby. Monday-Friday 9 a.m.-3:30 p.m. 785.233.9601.

Topeka Civic Theatre: 3028 SW 8th. Dinner theatre or performances sans dinner are presented for your enjoyment inside the 1929 former Gage Elementary School. This award-winning community theatre, founded in 1936, is the longest-running community dinner theatre in the country. 785.357.5211. topekacivictheatre.com.

Topeka Performing Arts Center: 214 SE 8th. Touring Broadway shows, dance companies, symphonies, popular singers, and entertainers offer stirring performances inside this historic municipal building. 785.234.4545. tpactix.org.

Mariachi Sculpture: 214 SE 8th. On the west side of the Topeka Performing Arts Center an eight-foot bronze statue of a female mariachi player honors Mariachi Estrella de Topeka. The troupe of seven women formed the first all-female mariachi group in Kansas. Tragically four members were killed when the walkway at the Hyatt Regency in Kansas City collapsed in 1981.

Mr. Ichabod: SW 17th and SW Jewell (Washburn campus). Washburn University was named for its benefactor Ichabod Washburn. A bronze *Mr. Ichabod*, the jaunty college mascot, can be found in the garden behind Thompson Alumni Center. Sculptor Mark Lundeen depicts the beloved character tipping his hat as his long coattails fly behind him.

Mulvane Art Museum:

1700 SW College (Washburn campus). Built of Bedford Limestone in the Florentine Renaissance style, this 1922 building is probably the first free-standing art museum in Kansas and is considered a work of art itself. The museum's collection of more than 4,000 objects includes paintings, prints, drawings, sculptures, photographs, and decorative arts. Don't miss the very entertaining ArtLab, a huge studio with activity stations where kids and adults are encouraged to get their hands messy. Tuesday-Friday 10 a.m.-5 p.m.; Saturday 1-4 p.m. 785.670.1124. FB.

Topeka and Shawnee County Library: 1515 SW

10th. Even if you don't have a library card, come inside this warm and wonderful place to visit the Sabatini art gallery, the heritage room and museum, the gift shop, and the cafe. In the kids library, walk under the dinosaur legs and look for books in the bus. Monday-Saturday 9 a.m.-6 p.m.; Sunday 12-6 p.m. 785.580.4400. tscpl.org.

Gage Park: 635 SW Gage. The park was once the Gage family farm, but in 1899 it was donated to be developed into a park. The Topeka Zoological Park, a mini-train with a mile-long track, an operating 1908 carousel complete with 1900 Wurlitzer band organ, the Gage

Park War Memorial, and the beautiful Reinisch Rose Garden are special highlights within the park. The rose garden, established in 1930, features more than 350 varieties of roses and blooms June through October. Admission charges for zoo, mini-train, and carousel. 785.273.6108. visittopeka.com.

Kansas Children's Discovery Center:

4400 SW 10th. Be ready to explore, create, discover, and learn through play! A variety of stations invite children to do everything from working on a car to creating art projects and learning about bugs. Outside, trek in the woods, play in the shallow brook, ride tricycles, or play musical instruments. The opportunities are endless, and kids won't want to leave. Tuesday-Friday 9 a.m.-3 p.m.; Saturday 10 a.m.-5 p.m.; Sunday 1-5 p.m. Admission charge. 785.783.8300. kansasdiscovery.org.

Historic Topeka Cemetery (NRHP)): 1601 SE 10th. The

hillside mausoleums and the 1895 Civil War memorial are impressive landmarks in this cemetery. Noteworthy individuals interred here include Vice

President Charles Curtis, Santa Fe railway founder Cyrus K. Holliday, five Kansas territorial or state governors, three U.S. senators from Kansas, and three veterans of the War of 1812. A kiosk lists gravesites of persons of note. 785.233.4132. topekacemetery.org.

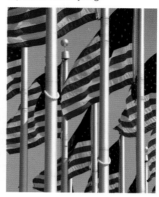

NE

Great Overland Station:

701 N. Kansas. Known as one of the finest on the line, this grand 1927 Union Pacific passenger station was built in Neoclassical design with ornate glazed terra cotta ornamentation. It's a striking backdrop for learning the history of Topeka and its railroads. Connecting the station to an impressive All Veterans Memorial, the Corridor of Flags flies 50 historical American flags above those from the 50 states. Plaques are inscribed with facts about each state. Tuesday-Saturday 10 a.m.-3 p.m. Admission charge. 785.232.5533. greatoverlandstation.com.

NOTO Arts District:

800-900 blocks of N. Kansas. The pulse of the art community has been aglow in North Topeka (NOTO) since 1995. The NOTO Art Gallery, located in a former brick post office, is the anchor for more than two dozen unique art studios, galleries, outdoor art, antique shops, and eateries. The developing sculpture park (Redbud Gardens), across from the NOTO Art Gallery,

will celebrate the rock band KANSAS. This area is close to the band's early recording studio. Wednesday-Saturday 11 a.m.-5 p.m. 785.408.8996. notoshopping.com. The Topeka and NOTO art scene sparkles during the First Friday Artwalk. artsconnecttopeka.org.

RagaZagar Mural:
905 N. Kansas. Led by visiting renowned mural artist Isaiah Zagar, the community completed an 80x10-foot mosaic mural that features cement blobs of various found objects. Tile and pieces of mirrors were added to create the amazing designs.

Bradley's Corner Cafe:
844 N. Kansas. You know the pie is good when it's ordered for breakfast—and you'll have more

than 20 choices! The regulars at this NOTO corner cafe swear by the coconut meringue, strawberry-rhubarb, and choc-olate-peanut butter homemade goodness. Everything is made from scratch, including the Explorer Way chicken-fried steak. Tuesday-Saturday 6 a.m.-8 p.m.; Sunday-Monday 8 a.m.-2 p.m. 785.235.0086.

Norsemen Brewing Company: 830 N. Kansas. With a nod to the mascot of a former North Topeka school, the Norsemen serves craft beers with such appropriate names as Odin's One-EyePA, Shield

Maiden Wheat, and Attempted Conspiracy. Tuesday-Thursday 4-9 p.m.; Friday 4-11 p.m.; Saturday 11 a.m.-11 p.m. norsemenbrewingco.com.

Wheel Barrel: 925 N. Kansas. Craft beer and grilled cheese are the ingredients for a masterpiece here, and every sandwich is made with a delicious cheesy touch. Set in the NOTO district, the shop with its original wood floors and brick walls fits well into the artist community. Tuesday-Thursday 11 a.m.-9 p.m.; Friday-Saturday 11-12 a.m.; Sunday 10 a.m.-3 p.m. 785.289.6767. thewheelbarrel.com.

Blind Tiger Brewery & Restaurant: 417 SW 37th. This 14-barrel, award-winning brewhouse has at least six flagship beers on tap at all times. Among the many menu selections are the popular prime rib dinners on Fridays and Saturdays. Restaurant hours, daily 11 a.m.-9 p.m. 785.267.2739. blindtiger.com.

Happy Basset Brewing Company: 6044 SW 29th. The Happy Basset is named for the two basset hounds that supported the owners (with silent approval and much tail wagging) through the process of opening this trendy micro-brewery. Sporting a slick industrial decor and a laid-back vibe, it's a happy spot to try such craft beers as Irish Red, Raspberry Wheat, and Bourbon Stout. Sunday 12-8 p.m.; Monday-Thursday 4-10 p.m.; Friday-Saturday 12 p.m.-12 a.m. 785.783.3688. happybasset-brewingco.com.

Bobo's Drive In (8 Wonders of Kansas Cuisine): 2300 SW 10th. At this 1953 diner with carhop service and die-hard fans, the burgers, homemade onion rings, and apple pie are packed with old-fash-ioned flavor. Inside, a little horseshoe counter with stools

and a few booths perfect the step-back-in-time experience. Monday-Saturday 11 a.m.-8 p.m. 785.234.4511. FB.

Cafe Holliday: 800 SW 12th. A quaint little spot, this corner cafe is on the first floor of Devon Apartments (NRHP) in the historic Holliday Park neighbor-hood. It is run by passionate people whose deli sandwiches, soups, salads, Mexican specials, and Saturday breakfasts make it a Holliday to enjoy. Tuesday-Thursday 11:30 a.m.-2:30 p.m.; Friday 11:30 a.m.-8 p.m.; Saturday 7:30 a.m.-2:30 p.m. 785.232.2188. cafeholliday.com. Take a walk in Holliday Park to the south to see the bronze plaque paying tribute to Topeka founder Cyrus K. Holliday.

C.W. Porubsky Grocery and Meats: 508 NE Sardou. From SW 1st, ¾ mile north on NW Topeka, ¾ mile east on Morse (becomes Sardou), then ¼ mile north on NE Porubsky. Important folks and regular joes frequent this small combo grocery/lunchroom/neighborhood tavern in "Little Russia" (original residents of this area migrated from Russia to work for the railroad). Since 1947 customers have eagerly squeezed in for Porubsky's famous very hot chili, hot (hot) pickles, and the cold plate (bread, meat, and cheese piled on a little plastic plate—you assemble). Monday-Saturday 11 a.m.-2 p.m.; chili season, September-April, Monday-Thursday. 785.234.5788.

Chez Yasu: 2701 SW 17th. Lovely table settings, crisp tablecloths, Lenox dinnerware, and fresh flowers add to the luster of this French restaurant. Delightful options include coquilles St. Jacques meunière (sea scallop and mushroom in lemon butter sauce) and carré d'agneau (roasted rack of lamb). Fine wine and cocktails are also available. Bon appétit! Monday-Friday 11 a.m.-2 p.m. and 5-8:30 p.m.; Saturday 5-9 p.m. 785.357.1003. chezyasufrenchrestaurant.com.

Monsoon Grille:

2040 SW Wanamaker. Among the authentic and fresh Indian cuisine entrees are curries, kebabs, and delicious naans (breads). Try the buffet or order from the menu. Vegetarians will love this Grille. Daily 11:30 a.m.-2:30 p.m. and 5:30-9:30 p.m. 785.783.7776. monsoonindiangrill.com.

RowHouse Restaurant:

515 SW Van Buren. Inside a restored row house just steps from the capitol, this restaurant offers a changing menu of world-class cuisine. A set price includes a "tasting" of a five-course meal with all platings exquisitely prepared by owner and chef Greg Fox. Multiple levels for dining add to the intimate atmosphere. Thursday-Saturday, seatings at 5:30 and 8:30 p.m. Reservations required. 785.235.1700. rowhouserestaurant.net.

Tuptim Thai Restaurant:

220 SW 29th. The local owners are natives of Thailand and have brought the foods, spices, and elegance of the Far East to Topeka. Try the Pad Thai or the spring rolls with peanut sauce. Monday-Friday 11 a.m.-2:30 p.m. and 5-9 p.m.; Saturday 12-9 p.m.; Sunday 1-8 p.m. 785.266.2299. tuptimthaitopeka.com.

More Good Restaurants:

Banjo's Cafe (5824 SW Topeka, 785.862.1406); El Centenario (1306 S. Kansas, 785.783.8968); Hanover Pancake House (1034 S. Kansas, 785.232.1111); Lonnie Q's (3150 SE 21st,

785.233.4227); The Burger Stand at College Hill (1601 SW Lane, 785.783.8900). visittopeka.com.

Lodging:

Ravenwood Lodge (785.256.6444, ravenwoodlodge.com); The Woodward Inn on Fillmore (785.354.7111, thewoodward.com); Keene Road Country Estate with Rustic Barn (785.272.3086, vrbocom/429285); additional lodging (visittopeka.com/hotels).

explorer extras... In Topeka

Mount Hope Cemetery, 4700 SW 17th, is home to the first singing tower in a U.S. cemetery. The carillon in this stone castle-like tower was first played in 1931.

A Carnegie library (NRHP), erected in 1903, stands on the Washburn University campus at SW 17th and SW Jewell.

A giant wren sculpture sits at the triangular-shaped Huntoon Park at the intersection of Huntoon, 12th, and SW Topeka. For five decades the wren's former nest was atop the WREN radio building on SW 10th. The bird was sculpted in the 1930s by an artist whose name today is unknown.

Enjoy a one-mile walking trail just south of Cedar Crest, the governor's mansion. Ponds and beautiful demonstration gardens highlight the walk. From SW Wanamaker, ¾ mile east on 6th, then just north on Governors Lake.

Kaw River State Park, the newest state park, provides hiking and biking trails (trailhead at 300 SW Wanamaker). An access ramp to the Kansas River Trail, a designated

National Water Trail, is from SW Wanamaker, ½ mile east on 6th, then ¾ mile north. It's a great location for canoes and kayaks to enter the Kaw. 785.273.6740. ksoutdoors.com.

Rent paddleboats and enjoy all the recreational amenities within the 1,100-acre park at Lake Shawnee, 3137 SE 29th. 785.267.2211. visittopeka.com.

Flowers bloom between April and October in the Ted Ensley Gardens on the west side of Lake Shawnee at 3650 SE West Edge. With the lake in the background, the 20 acres of botanical gardens provide a beautiful respite. **ee**

WAKARUSA

Unincorporated

Glaciers Edge Winery & Vineyard:

1636 SE 85th. From SW Topeka, 1¾ miles east on 85. Situated on the edge of a glacial moraine, this winery produces fine grape and fruit wines that range from dry to sweet. Mike and Lisa Steinert support local sustainable agriculture and have a passion for educating the public about wines and the winemaking process. Enjoy free tastings while relaxing on the porch or patio in a country setting. Wednesday-Sunday 12-5 p.m. 785.862.5421. glaciersedgewine.com.

WILLARD

Population 92

Uniontown and Uniontown Cemetery

(NRHP): From Carlson, ½ mile east on 2nd, then ½ mile south on Gilkerson (becomes Douglas). Uniontown was a short-lived but significant community founded in the 1840s on the area's Potawatomi reservation. Joseph Napoleon Bourassa, a prominent Potawatomi, was instrumental in establishing the settlement, which for a time thrived as a ferry crossing and supply post for Oregon Trail travelers. But in 1849 and 1850 cholera outbreaks devastated the community. After the second outbreak, the inhabitants burned the settlement (60 buildings) and abandoned it. The exact site of the town is unknown. The only remaining evidence is the small cemetery comprising three separate marked burial areas, each enclosed by a native stone wall: (1) the circle of stones around the tree marks the mass grave of the cholera victims; (2) a rectangular wall surrounds the graves of the Joseph Bourassa family, but Joseph likely is not buried here; (3) and to the south are graves of the Green family who bought this property in the 1870s. Additional gravestones can also be found throughout this grassy area. Today Uniontown Cemetery is owned by the Citizen Potawatomi Nation, which allows respectful visitors to view the cemetery.

Green Wildlife Area:
Across from Uniontown Cemetery. The 83-acre site of diverse eco-systems offers two maintained trails for hiking and wildlife viewing. Among the lush flora, a creek, and steep hills, interpretive markers note historical and natural points of interest. This area was part of the 1840s Uniontown settlement and later was owned by the Green family. Oregon Trail ruts are visible in the vicinity.

Wabaunsee County

AROUND THE COUNTY

Native Stone Scenic Byway:
The route comprises 48 miles of winding, stair-stepping roads past stone fences and buildings and undulating Flint Hills pastures. The west

end begins at I-70 exit 328 and proceeds 4 miles south on K-99 through Alma, continues 9 miles south to the K-4 intersection, then 35 miles east on K-4 through Eskridge and Dover in Shawnee County, ending at Glick southwest of Topeka. 800.684.6966. ksoutdoors.com/ksbyways.

Native Stone Fences:
When the federal government abolished the open range in 1867, it paid farmers 40 cents per rod (16½ feet) to build and maintain 4½-foot-tall fences of stone. Many miles of these original fences can be seen around the county.

Skyline-Mill Creek Scenic Back Road:
From Alta Vista, go north on Logan to start this 17-mile narrow, winding route past Volland to Alma following the west branch of Mill Creek on Old K-10. Stone buildings, wall remnants, and the wooded areas along the creek are enchanting. At Alma, go 1¼ miles south on K-99, 11½ miles generally east on Skyline (mostly gravel), then 10½ miles northerly on Snokomo (mostly gravel) into Paxico. Two stone schools are about the only

structures that will distract you from the incredible Flint Hills vistas as you go north.

Clapboard Ravine Scenic Back Road:
From Ohio in Alma, 2 miles east on 11th (becomes Clapboard Ravine). About ¾ mile into your drive you'll cross Mill Creek, and within the next mile you'll see a natural spring that has been flowing for hundreds of years through this scenic valley. You can keep going through more scenic environs or turn around and come back to Alma.

Lake Wabaunsee:
From Eskridge, 4¼ miles west on K-99/K-4. Just to the south, see a picturesque lake that has quite a history. It was completed in 1939 in a joint effort with the Civilian Conservation Corps (CCC) and the WPA. The CCC also built structures for its housing, which later was used as barracks for troop training here during WWII. In 1942 the area became a POW camp. None of the camp buildings remain. Two lovely 1938 WPA stone triple-arch bridges (NRHP) can be seen on your drive around the lake.

The Lodge at Lake Wabaunsee:
1 W. Flint Hills. Formerly an officers' quarters during the POW camp days, the Lodge is now a popular restaurant serving homemade pizza, barbecue ribs, and prime rib specials. Monday-Saturday 5-9 p.m. 785.449.2424. FB.

Settlers' Graves:
From the Lake Wabaunsee entrance, less than ½ mile west on K-99/K-4 (south side). Four settlers' graves are surrounded by a native stone wall constructed by the WPA. If you can't spot this little cemetery from the highway, backtrack and turn into the lake entrance, then proceed ¼ mile west on W. Flint Hills toward the dam. Park just before reaching the dam and walk northwest on a path leading to the cemetery.

Wabaunsee Pines Pinecone:
From K-99/K-4 at Lake Wabaunsee, 2¼ miles south and east on E. Flint Hills along the southeast side of the lake. You are looking for a pine cone. A big one. Made from shovel heads. Resting on a large native stone base, it was a project of the Lady Lakers and master welder Doug Clark. The pine cone greets those who play golf on the nine-hole course at Wabaunsee Pines Golf Course. 785.633.5002. FB.

Plumlee Buffalo Ranch:
29300 SW 99 Frontage. From I-70 exit 328, ¾ mile west on Frontage. Enjoy sixty minutes in the Flint Hills on a pasture drive to see and learn about buffalo—up close! Tour charge. Reservations required. 785.776.1271. plumleeranch.com.

Mount Mitchell Heritage Prairie Preserve:
From I-70 exit 328, 5¾ miles north on K-99, then ½ mile east on Mitchell Prairie. Rising out of the Flint Hills, Mount Mitchell is a 45-acre prairie hilltop and public park. Interpretive panels in the parking lot explain that American Indians, explorers, immigrants, and slaves seeking freedom on the Underground Railroad passed through this area. In season, wildflowers and grasses surround you as you hike the quarter-mile grassy path to the summit. Captain

William Mitchell, for whom the hill was named, came to this area with the Beecher Bible and Rifle Colony in 1856 (see p. 198). Near the top of the hill a bronze plaque commemorates Mitchell and the Beecher colony. A second plaque, on a red

glacial rock, pays tribute to a Mitchell relative Captain George T. "Dodge" Fielding. To the north you can see the privately owned Mitchell homestead, which comprises original structures that once sheltered escaping slaves. mountmitchellprairie.org.

Shamrock Cafe:
36207 Tallgrass. From I-70 exit 324, 2½ miles north on Wabaunsee, then 1 mile west on Pavillion. When you see the three-leaf clover "Shamrock Cafe" sign you'll have found this open-air "cafe." The sign says "Always Open," but if someone gets there before you, you may have to wait. It seats two. Naming it the Shamrock Cafe in good fun, the Crenshaws, owners of the nearby Shamrock Farm, have provided seating by securing two vintage metal chairs into cement on top of large slabs of flint. Although you have to bring your own food and drink and bus your own table (such as it is), the Flint Hills view is priceless. Be sure to leave a note and a token in the geocache box chained to the leg of the table.

Grandma Hoerner's:
31862 Thompson (I-70 exit 324). Grandma Hoerner was born in the late 1800s but her recipes

made such an impression on grandson Duane McCoy that he started a production facility to re-create her old-fashioned tastes. While you shop for the famous Big Slice Kettle Cooked

Apples, organic reduced sugar preserves, pie fillings, jams, and more, you can also look through windows to view the products being made. Monday-Friday 9 a.m.-5 p.m.; Saturday 10 a.m.-4 p.m. 785.765.2300. grandmahoerners.com.

Guard of the Plains Sculpture:
I-70 rest area, mile marker 336 (3¾ miles east of Paxico). Eastbound travelers can easily spot the tall abstract work created by James Johnson in 1970 standing on the hilltop near the eastbound rest area. But to walk to the sculpture, you must start at the westbound rest area (you can drive to the westbound side via a connector road between the

two rest areas). Just west of the parking lot, a quarter-mile wooded trail leads to the sculpture. The path is narrow and a little steep but it's worth the climb to see the *Guard of the Plains* and a splendid view of the Flint Hills.

Kansas Flint Hills Quilt Trail:
Wabaunsee is one of the counties included in this project, which leads you to large wooden quilt blocks on

barns, sheds, and houses. Find these colorful pieces and learn about the project and the patterns from the Quilt Trail map at ksflinthillsquilttrail.com.

ALMA

Population 824

City of Native Stone:
The many historic Cottonwood Limestone buildings have earned Alma the designation City of Native Stone. The Downtown Historic District (NRHP), on Missouri between 2nd and 5th, comprises 21 buildings of architectural significance built between 1880 and 1936. Self-guided tour brochures are available at the newspaper office (323 Missouri), the Wabaunsee County Museum (227 Missouri), and the Antique Emporium (322 Missouri).

Brandt Hotel (NRHP):
400 Missouri. This landmark building first served as a hotel when it opened in 1887. Note the smooth limestone facing on the angled entrance and the ornate balcony above the doorway. Currently the building is vacant.

Antique Emporium:
322 Missouri. Inside an 1880s native stone building, nine rooms are filled with antiques and collectibles. You're bound to find just what you want (or didn't know you wanted). Monday-Saturday 10 a.m.-6 p.m.; Sunday 12-6 p.m. 785.765.3332. FB.

Wabaunsee County Historical Museum:
227 Missouri. Photo and artifact displays provide excellent information of the area's many historic sites such as the POW camp at Lake Wabaunsee (*see* p. 192) and the Beecher Bible and Rifle Church (*see* p. 197) at Wabaunsee. *Freedom's Frontier: Stories from the Western Border* is an excellent timeline exhibit that brings to life the local stories of American Indians, early explorers, abolitionists, and emigrants. March-November, Tuesday-Saturday 10 a.m.-4 p.m.; December-February, Tuesday-Wednesday 10 a.m.-4 p.m. 785.765.2200. wabaunseecomuseum.org.

Railroad Park:
Missouri and K-99. This small park contains an 1880s log cabin and a millinery shop, both relocated here from their original sites. The stone building, constructed in 1930, encloses one of the wells that once provided water for the town. All buildings are for outside viewing only.

Wabaunsee County Courthouse (NRHP):
215 Kansas. You'll appreciate the marble stairways, handrails, and corridor walls inside this Modern Eclecticism courthouse completed in 1932. On the second level, a county map is incorporated into the terrazzo floor. Several memorials and historical markers highlight the courthouse grounds. Monday-Friday 8 a.m.-4 p.m. 785.765.2401.

Historic High School:
912 Missouri. Still in use today, the native stone two-story school with a red-tile roof was built in 1936 by the PWA. The auditorium retains the original lighting, stage, wooden seats, and arched ceiling tiled in art deco style. Open during the school year; to see the auditorium, ask at the school office. 785.765.3315.

Alma Creamery:
509 E. 3rd. Alma has been famous for its cheese for more than five decades. All natural and handmade, the cheeses of many flavors come from only the finest ingredients. Cheese lovers especially will want to stock up! Other Kansas products are also available. Monday-Friday 8 a.m.-5 p.m.; Saturday 9 a.m.-3 p.m. 785.765.3522. FB.

Alma Bakery and Sweet Shoppe:
118 W. 3rd. Jeanette's homemade cinnamon and caramel pecan rolls, cookies, turnovers, and toffee are big sellers, and one bite will tell you why! A lunch special is served daily, and bierocks are available in the freezer case. Monday-Friday 6 a.m.-4 p.m.; Saturday 6 a.m.-2 p.m. 785.765.2235. FB.

Farmacy:
327 Missouri. The eclectic, shabby-chic decor and unique lighting create a delightful first impression. The menu presents a satisfying variety of sandwiches, full meals, salads, a daily special, and homemade pies. Tuesday-Friday 7 a.m.-2 p.m.; Thursday-Friday 5-7:30 p.m.; Saturday 7:30 a.m.-7:30 p.m. 785.765.2366. FB.

ALTA VISTA

Population 439

Ag Heritage Park:
103 S. Main. Everett Zimmerman was struck by the collecting

bug after he semi-retired from farming. The result is an extraordinary display of horse-drawn equipment, early tractors and implements, and pioneer history. A log cabin, one-room school, 1880s house, brooder house, and even an outhouse are part of the complex. Everett has passed on, but his wife, Hazel, enjoys sharing their passion with the public. Call ahead, 785.482.3865. agheritagepark.com.

Alta Vista Market: 615 Main. Alta Vista was without a grocery store for three years until Shane and Morgan Tiffany stepped up to open one. Thanks to them, the town can now enjoy a store with grocery items, fresh deli sandwiches, hot pizza, and other diverse items. Monday-Saturday 7 a.m.-8 p.m.; Sunday 1-4 p.m. 785.499.6333. FB.

Antique Stores:
Mill Creek Peddlers (519 Main, 785.565.2547) and Anne's Attic (504 Main, 785.317.1184) have irregular hours but they are worth a phone call to find them open.

Folk Art: 37419 K-4. From Main, 2 miles east on K-4. Who says pigs can't fly! On the north side of K-4, keep your eyes peeled for a flying pink pig. This little guy is the work of Larry Frese, who uses a chainsaw to carve assorted animal characters. He places his brightly painted creations on fence posts to bring smiles to passing travelers. You can buy one if you'd like. 785.499.6359. tinyurl.com/larryfrese.

Rock Island Bridge:
From Main, ¼ mile west on Sea. Going west out of town you'll find yourself driving up a small hill on a gravel road and onto a 1911 one-lane wooden bridge with raised wooden planks. It's open to vehicles, so cross if you dare!

Barnyard Cafe: 605 Main. All-you-can-eat fried chicken on Friday nights and chicken-fried steak made the Explorer Way keep this Barnyard busy! Monday-Friday 6 a.m.-2 p.m.; Wednesday-Friday 6-8 p.m.; Saturday 6 a.m.-3 p.m. 785.499.5595. FB.

ESKRIDGE

Population 527

Waugh Building (NRHP):
123 S. Main. A double-arch corner entrance with marble columns welcomes you to this historic bank building. In the Waugh family since 1904, it is now home to the law practice of father and son Charles and John Waugh. The big screen door opens to a massive bank teller's cage, tile floor, clocks, original pressed-tin ceiling, bank vault, book shelves, and stained-glass windows, all of which take you to a different era, as does the Moorish dome atop the building. The Waughs are pleased to have you stop in and will gladly show you around. 785.449.2452.

City Park: In the early 1900s Mayor J.Y. Waugh, a prominent banker and supporter of community improvements, championed this park. A 1908 octagonal wooden gazebo (RHKP), veterans memorial, picnic shelter, tennis courts, and a round stone restroom building are also located here.

Alpacas at Wildcat Hollow: 23224 Wildcat Hollow. From Main, 6 miles east and north on K-4, 1 mile east on Nighthawk, then ¼ mile north on Wildcat Hollow. Ed and Marta Howe's country setting is a delightful place to visit the quirky-looking, soft-coated alpacas and the big white

NE

Maremma guardian dogs. The Last Stall retail store is inside the alpaca barn (in its own nicely styled spot) and offers a selection of alpaca-related products, some made on site. 785.449.2206. alpacasofwildcathollow.com.

HESSDALE

Unincorporated

You know you've arrived in the historic Hessdale area when you see a road sign citing three different roads (Hessdale, Halifax, and Maby) with four different directions. This is Hessdale.

Peter Thoes Barn (NRHP):
25709 Hessdale. From 3rd in Alma, 1½ miles south on K-99, ¾ mile east on Skyline, then 2 miles south on Hessdale. Peter Thoes built this barn in 1875 using native stone and wood from the Mill Creek Valley. Note the stone fence near the barn.

Historic Marker: From Peter Thoes Barn, 5 miles south on Hessdale. A brown metal sign provides a brief background of Hessdale and the Hessdale Stockyards, which once served as a major shipping point for cattle brought from Texas to graze on the rich Flint Hills grass.

MCFARLAND

Population 256

City Hall and Heritage Center:
518 Rock Island. McFarland artifacts and railroad memorabilia are exhibited inside this former Rock Island depot that doubles as the city hall. The wood building was moved from Peck to McFarland in 1954 to function as a depot. Monday-Friday 1-3:30 p.m. 785.765.2265. mcfarlandks.com.

**explorer extras...
In Newbury**

Unincorporated

Built of tapestry brick with limestone trim, the 1922 Sacred Heart Church is also known as the Cathedral of the Flint Hills. Its two tall towers with golden crosses are dominant landmarks in the western end of the Mill Creek Valley and draw people from a distance. One mile north of Paxico at 22283 Newbury. **ee**

MAPLE HILL

Population 621

Old Stone Church:
From I-70 exit 341, 1¼ miles north on K-30, then ¼ mile west on Old Stone Church. For eastbound travelers on the interstate, the hillside church and cemetery form a picturesque setting. In 1991 the church was struck by a tornado and sustained heavy damage. Locals raised funds and rebuilt it as it originally appeared in 1882. Regular services were held here until 1905. It is one of the only churches in the state surrounded on three sides by a cemetery. From the driveway just north of the church, look east to find the gravestone of Sarah Oliver. The printing on the stone is inverted, likely due to a printing plate error. 785.256.4506.

Mill Creek Pratt Truss Bridge:
From Main, 1 mile east on Maple Hill (becomes Willard). A beautiful setting entices you to park, get out of your car, and step onto this 1935 bridge (open to vehicles) with a length of more than 200 feet. From the bridge you can see the nearby railroad bridge to the south.

PAXICO

Population 220

If you like antiques, you'll love Paxico. This charming small town offers several antique stores within a short three-block area. Almost a ghost town in the late 1970s, Paxico started coming back to life as the historic buildings strategically reopened as antique stores. The town's original look returned when the tin awnings and old signs were resurrected. In season, flowers hang from the awnings, and benches in the shade welcome you to "sit a spell" if you're waiting for the obsessive antique shopper. Antiques of all kinds are found here, from pot-bellied stoves and jewelry to primitives, western items, magazines, glassware, books, furniture, and much more. You can come to Paxico just about any day of the year between 10 a.m.-5 p.m. and find at least a couple of the stores open. During winter months, weekends are best.

Mill Creek Antiques:
109 Newbury. You'll feel cozy just stepping into this historic building filled with gleaming antiques and magnificent old wood stoves, beautifully restored by owner Bud Hund. Specializing in the restoration of vintage wood and gas heating stoves and cook stoves, Bud has customers from across the nation. In addition to the stoves, an assortment of antiques in connected showrooms bear witness to Bud's 40-plus years of collecting. Monday-Saturday 9 a.m.-5 p.m; Sunday 11 a.m.-4 p.m. 785.636.5520. millcreekantiques.com.

Hidden Treasures:
109 Newbury. Inside Mill Creek Antiques you'll find Rex Fiddler's store containing his antiques and collectibles. He's a longtime Paxico antique dealer and an all-around nice guy. Monday-Saturday 9 a.m.-5 p.m; Sunday 11 a.m.-4 p.m. 785.224.0300.

Fowl Territory:
206 Main. This place is wild... with wildlife, that is. If you need elk antlers, wooden duck decoys, a giant metal catfish, or stuffed animals, you'll find them here. The Territory also includes many rarities in furniture, knickknacks, wall decor, and more. Thursday-Saturday 10 a.m.-5 p.m.; Sunday 12-5 p.m. 785.636.5308. fowlterritoryllc.com.

Old Woodman Antiques:

218 Main. Owner Mike Holper calls himself a steward of America's past, and you will see that in his early country furniture and tools collected throughout the Midwest. Mike also hand-crafts custom tables in the 1850s style. Friday-Saturday 10 a.m.-5 p.m.; Sunday 11:30 a.m.-4:30 p.m. 785.608.4646. oldwoodmanantiques.com.

European Antiques and Upholstery:

211 N. Main. The stunning furniture comes from various countries, and the tapestries, glassware, tools, home decor, and wide variety of collectibles are top quality. The shop owner's upholstery talents are highly coveted and appre-ciated by her many customers. Saturday-Sunday 10 a.m.-4 p.m. 785.466.0198. europeanantiques-andupholstery.com.

Longbranch Bar and Grill:

123 Newbury. Good eating inside the Longbranch includes pulled pork sandwiches, burgers, and homemade specials. Tuesday-Thursday 4:30-9 p.m.; Friday-Saturday 11 a.m.-9 p.m. 785.636.5599.

Prairie Fire Winery:

20250 Hudson Ranch. From I-70 exit 335 (south side), 1 mile east on Hudson Ranch. Enjoy a Flint Hills view with samples or a glass of handcrafted wine made from grapes grown on the prairie. Owners and growers Bob and Julie DesRuisseaux invite you to visit the tasting room and try the more than 17 labels including the first and only methode

champenoise sparkling wine made in the state. Take a hike around the grapevines or enjoy playing petanque—a French ball game. Monday-Saturday 10 a.m.- 5 p.m.; Sunday 12-5 p.m. 785.636.5533. prairiefirewinery.com.

Lodging:

Mill Creek Campground and RV Park (785.636.5321, millcreekcampground.com).

VOLLAND

Unincorporated

Volland is about half way between Alta Vista and Alma on Old K-10. Look for a small sign that leads you south into the Volland village. It was once a shipping point for cattle headed to Kansas City. For a back-road drive into the Flint Hills, go south past the Volland Store, across the tracks, and into the hills.

The Volland Store:

24098 Volland. It stands out, this 1913 red-brick two-story building. As the Kratzer Brothers Mercantile, it was once the hub of the town. Then it fell into disrepair and abandonment. Patty and Jerry Reece saw the good bones, felt the small-town spirit, and renovated the iconic building to once again bring people together. Today the exposed red-brick walls, two-story open space with window lighting, and gleaming wood floors make it ideal for art exhibitions and memorable gatherings. Saturday-Sunday 12-5 p.m. (unless reserved for private use). 620.271.2953. thevollandstore.com.

Lodging: Volland Store Loft (620.271.2953, thevollandstore. com); Mill Creek Lodge at Volland Point (785.764.3300, millcreeklodgevollandpoint.com).

WABAUNSEE

Unincorporated

NE

Beecher Bible and Rifle Church (NRHP):

31624 Chapel. ½ mile south of K-18. During the territorial days New Englanders migrated to Kansas to support the free-state cause. At a meeting in New Haven, Connecticut, the Reverend Henry Ward Beecher announced that his congrega-tion would purchase 25 rifles to send to Kansas if the audience would purchase another 25. The agreement was made, and a shipment of Bibles was sent with the rifles, both placed in crates marked "Bibles" to avoid arousing suspicion. The emigrants became known as the Beecher Bible and Rifle Colony, and that name is etched in concrete near the peak of the church roof. Today's Wabaunsee residents take care of this historic landmark. In summer, flowers and trees around a stone sign add to the beauty of this 1862 limestone building. The doors are closed, but all are welcome to attend the 9:45 Sunday morning service. 785.617.1300.

Historical Marker: K-18 and Main. In a small park on the north side of K-18, a granite marker reads, "In memory of the Beecher Bible and Rifle Colony which settled this area in 1856 and helped make Kansas a free state. May future generations forever pay them tribute."

Wabaunsee Cemetery: From Elm, 1¼ miles east on K-18. The attractive glacial stone gateway is dedicated to the valiant pioneers of the Wabaunsee community and the Beecher Bible and Rifle Colony of 1856. On one pillar a John Greenleaf Whittier poem reads, "They crossed the prairies as of old / Our Fathers crossed the sea / To make the West as they the East / The homestead of the free." Maude Mitchell, daughter of William Mitchell, an Underground Railroad operator, designed the gateway. Sixty Civil War veterans are buried on these cemetery grounds.

Wyandotte County

AROUND THE COUNTY

Wyandotte County Lake Park: 91 and Leavenworth. You will enjoy the tranquil lake, bridges, and shelters (1930s WPA projects) and the nine-mile hiking and equestrian loop through the woods. Of special interest is the Mr. & Mrs. F.L. Schlagle Library and Environmental Learning Center, 4051 West, a year-round interactive library providing many activities focusing on science and nature. 913.573.8327. wycokck.org/parks.

Korean-Vietnam War Memorial: 91 and Leavenworth. The nation's first dual war memorial dedicated to veterans in both conflicts graces the entrance of Wyandotte County Lake. The very moving and impressive marble monument features two exceptional life-sized bronze statues of a soldier from each war.

Grinter House State Historic Site (NRHP): 1420 S. 78. Moses and Annie Grinter, two of Kansas' earliest settlers, established this red-brick home near the site of the first ferry crossing at the Kansas River. When built, this 1857 Georgian vernacular home was on the Delaware Indian Reservation. May-October, Wednesday-Saturday 10 a.m.-5 p.m. Admission charge. 913.299.0373. kshs.org.

BONNER SPRINGS

Population 7,480

National Agricultural Center and Hall of Fame: 630 N. 126. From I-70, ¾ mile north on U.S. 73, ½ mile east on Riverview, then just north on 126. High relief bronze panels depicting farm scenes are a memorial to farmers and a greeting to visitors. A Hall of Fame room features a "who's who in farming," and an art gallery shares the nostalgia of family farms. Harry Truman's plow is here as are farm buildings,

farm equipment, and displays of rural domestic science. April-November, Wednesday-Saturday 10 a.m.-4 p.m.; December-March, Wednesday-Friday 10 a.m.-4 p.m. Admission charge. 913.721.1075. aghalloffame.com.

Wyandotte County Historical Museum: 631 N. 126 (Wyandotte County Park). County history is told through a range of exhibits featuring such topics as early American Indian culture, Kansas City firefighters, the early black settlement at Quindaro, the 1903 flood, and Strawberry Hill prior to I-70 construction. May-September, Monday-Friday 9 a.m.-4 p.m.; Saturday 9 a.m.-12 p.m. October-April, closed on Saturday. 913.573.5002. wycomuseum.org.

Bomber Builders Memorial: In front of the Wyandotte County Museum. An engraved stone monument pays tribute to the employees who built 6,608 B-25 bombers in the Fairfax district factories during WWII.

Sunflower Hills Junior Golf Course: 12200 Riverview (Wyandotte County Park). This course is part of the First Tee program, which provide lessons and classes for young golfers. Adjacent to the Sunflower Hills Golf Course, the junior course features six holes with three sets of tees, a putting green, driving range, and a practice bunker. Greens fee. Call ahead. 913.573.8570. sunflowerhillsgolfcourse.com.

Moon Marble Company
(8 Wonders of Kansas Commerce): 600 E. Front. A long, narrow building is where you'll find frosted cats eyes, the patch and ribbon, and alien swirls—all beautiful, colorful, handcrafted artisan marbles! You can shop here for marble games and retro toys, but the highlight is watching the marbles being made. An amazing art! Tuesday-Saturday 10 a.m.-5 p.m. 913.441.1432. moonmarble.com.

Zip KC: 12829 Loring.
Zip line adventures over the bluffs next to the Kansas River take place day and night! Hike and zip packages are available for all ages. Reservations required. Admission charge. 913.214.9478. zipkc.com.

Red Fortune Chinese Restaurant: 117 Oak.
Slip into a red-leather booth and choose from a large menu. Everything is served hot, fresh, and fast. The shrimp with lobster sauce is popular with the locals. Monday-Saturday 11 a.m.-9 p.m. 913.441.1988. myredfortune.publishpath.com.

Lodging: Back in Thyme
Bed and Breakfast (KBBA, 913.422.5207, backnthyme.com); additional lodging (tinyurl.com/lodgingbs).

KANSAS CITY

Population 148,483

Ethnic Neighborhoods:
Kansas City, Kansas, contains a host of diverse ethnic communities. Murals, architecture, church names, street signs, and neighborhood cafes and bars provide clues to which ethnic group

dominates any particular area. You're an explorer, be curious!

Strawberry Hill: Between
Orville and Armstrong and N. 4th and N. 7th. The heart of Strawberry Hill is home to Croatian, Slovenian, and mixed ethnic immigrant descendants. Around the turn of the century immigrants from eastern Europe's oldest cultures moved to this area to work in the Kansas City stockyards. This very charming little neighborhood, named for the wild strawberries that once

grew here, is characterized by narrow streets and alleys and quaint houses perched among its hills. Numerous signs with strawberry designs welcome you to this well-known ethnic community. Sadly, in 1957 construction of I-70 destroyed one-third of the neighborhood.

Strawberry Hill Museum (RKHP) and Cultural Center: 720 N. 4th. This facility
represents the cultural diversity of those who have lived in Kansas City. Housed in an 1887 Queen Anne home (later used as an orphanage), the museum hosts permanent exhibits representing community cultures of Croatia, Poland, Slovakia, Slovenia, Russia, Lithuania, Ukraine, and the Netherlands. Desserts and teas are served in the museum's tearoom.

Saturday-Sunday 12-5 p.m.; tearoom hours, 1-4 p.m. (most of the year). Admission charge. 913.371.3264. strawberryhillmuseum.org.

Krizman's Sausage:
424 N. 6th. In business since 1939, Krizman's produces more than a dozen kinds of ethnic sausages, but it specializes in Croatian recipes brought to America by the family in 1914. Other tasty surprises include barbecued sausage, homemade sauerkraut, and sour heads of cabbage. Tuesday-Friday 8 a.m.-5 p.m.; Saturday 9 a.m.-3 p.m. 913.371.3185. krizmansausage.com.

Holy Family Church:
274 Orchard. Completed in 1927 to serve the Slovenian immigrant community, this Romanesque Revival structure stands as a stunning landmark.

Old City Hall and Fire Station (NRHP):
805 and 815 N. 6th. The 1911 three-story, stone-trimmed, brick city hall was built in the Renaissance Revival style. No longer functioning as the city hall, the building was converted into loft apartments in 2004. The 1930 fire headquarters still serves as the downtown fire station.

Old Fire Station No. 9 (NRHP):
2 S. 14th. This distinctive three-story former fire station opened in 1911 and served until 1967. On the corners of this terra cotta building are several charming

gargoyles resembling dwarfish firemen, complete with the iconic fireman's hat. Today the building is privately owned.

Polish Hill: Between 7th and
Mill and St. Joseph and St. Benedict. Within the nucleus of this Polish neighborhood, All Saints Catholic Church,

NE

229 S. 8th, stands as a historic landmark. Established in 1887, the parish built its church in 1916 to serve the area's community of Polish immigrants.

Big Eleven Lake: N. 11th and State. In the 1930s the WPA added the beautiful rock work to the lake and park, founded in 1911. At the rock stage over the lake, a plaque on an abstract metal saxophone sculpture honors Charlie "Yardbird" Parker, legendary jazz musician born in Kansas City.

Quindaro Ruins (NRHP) and Overlook: 3507 N. 27th. From the overlook you see an area that once was Quindaro, a short-lived territorial town and black settlement. Due to the river's changing course, only a few sections of the town's rock and brick foundations remain. Now an archeological district (NRHP), Quindaro was also home to Wyandot Indians and abolitionists, and it was an important stop on the Underground Railroad. 913.573.5100.

John Brown Statue: 27th and Sewell. A tall marble statue of abolitionist John Brown stands on the site of the town of Quindaro. The 1911 statue is the only physical evidence remaining of Western University, the earliest school for blacks west of the Mississippi River.

Huron Indian Cemetery (NRHP): 631 Minnesota. Ten large plaques on 7th recount the history of the Wyandotte Nation. The cemetery was established in 1843 after the forced migration of the Wyandot Nation from Ohio. The many who died from typhoid fever and cholera were carried to this point overlooking the Missouri and Kansas Rivers. Although more than 400 Wyandots are buried here, only 120 graves are marked, including those of the Conley sisters (Eliza and Helena). For three years in 1907 the two sisters camped on the cemetery grounds to protest the sale of the cemetery for commercial use. In 1910 Eliza

argued the sisters' case before the U.S. Supreme Court, becoming the first woman of American Indian descent to argue before the Court. Although the Court was sympathetic, she lost the case. Even so, public opinion and community support prevented the sale of the cemetery. In 1913 Senator Charles Curtis from Kansas, himself part Kanza Indian, persuaded Congress to repeal the sale authorization. The wall on 7th was constructed by the WPA in 1935.

Scottish Rite Temple (NRHP): 803 N. 7th. This three-story Tudor Revival building constructed in 1909 was the base for Red Cross and Liberty Loan campaigns during WWI. During the flood of 1951 the temple became the center of relief activities. The building is owned by the Wyandotte Nation of Oklahoma and has been converted into 7th Street Casino.

Wyandotte County Courthouse (NRHP): 701 N. 7th. Completed in 1927, the limestone courthouse is an imposing building of Neoclassical design with six, four-story Doric columns. Security is very tight. Drive by only.

Soldiers and Sailors Memorial Hall (NRHP): 600 N. 7th. Erected in 1924 to commemorate the sacrifice of the men of Wyandotte County during WWI, this stately hall is dedicated to the more than 6,480 who served. Above the six Doric columns and flanked by bald eagle sculptures, an inscription reads, "Dedicated to the heroes who fought and died for their country." Terra cotta ornamentation adds to the majesty. Call ahead, 913.573.5332.

Wyandotte High School (NRHP) 2501 Minnesota. The 1937 school is an architectural masterpiece built at the height of the Great Depression with funding from the PWA. The impressive structure blends several architectural styles including Romanesque and pre-Columbian Indian design. Drive by only.

Westheight Manor Historic District (NRHP): From 22nd, east on Washington to 18th. A beautiful stretch of homes is part of a large planned residential subdivision that began in 1915. The first home to notice is at 2108

Washington, built circa 1916. As you continue east to 18th, note how the planners and architects utilized the rolling terrain of this district to achieve the best effects for each home and style. Several streets off Washington are included in the historic district. tinyurl.com/westheight.

Westheight Apartments Historic District (NRHP):

1601-1637 Washington. This set of apartments constructed between 1947 and 1952 is a rare example of the Modern Movement style that was more commonly seen in commercial buildings. Federal Housing Administration funds were used to build the units.

Sumner Academy of Arts and Science (NRHP):

1610 N. 8th. This art deco beauty was constructed as a PWA project in 1939 to replace the 1905 Sumner County High School. That high school had

the distinction of being the only school in Kansas history legislated to serve black students. In 1978 the name and intent of the school changed to serve all races.

Lewis and Clark Historic Riverfront Park at Kaw Point:

1403 Fairfax Trfy. The Lewis and Clark Expedition arrived at Kaw Point, the confluence of the Kansas and Missouri Rivers, on June 26, 1804. Interpretive signage at the pavilion provides background about this historic expedition. A boardwalk along the river and a trail through the woods enhance the experience. 913.573.8302. Complete driving directions are at lewisandclarkwyco.org.

Kansas River Trail:

A designated National Water Trail, this 173-mile trail invites you to experience the river in your canoe or kayak. Twenty-one river access points are between the easternmost point at Kaw Point (1403 Fairfax Trfy.) and the west end of the trail in Junction City. kansasriver.org.

Riverfront Heritage Trail:

Fifteen miles of bicycle and pedestrian trails take you through some of the oldest and most historic parts of Kansas City, Kansas and Missouri. The trail links communities, parks with unique new venues, historical markers, and public

art. Start at Kaw Point (1403 Fairfax Trfy.) and cross the Kansas River on the Woodswether Bridge (the pedestrian/ bicycle crossing runs under the bridge for vehicles). kcrivertrails.org.

Argentine:

The town had its beginning in 1880 when many workers for the Santa Fe railway and for a silver smelting and refining company moved into this neighborhood. In 1901 the silver company closed, and the devastating floods of 1903 and 1904 hit the town very hard. By 1910 Argentine consolidated and became part of Kansas City. The name Argentine derives from the Latin word for silver.

Argentine Outdoor Mural:

31st through Woodland on Metropolitan. Jesus Ortiz, Joe Faus, and Alisha Gambino spent ten months completing

NE

Anthology of Argentine, an incredible 660x20-foot mural that documents the life and times of Argentine area residents dating to the 1800s.

Argentine Carnegie Library (NRHP):

2800 Metropolitan. Built in 1917, this Neoclassical Revival structure is one of the last of the Carnegie libraries to be constructed. The Carnegie-financed library program discontinued that same year. The building is no longer used as a library. Drive by only.

Argentine Steps:

13th and Ruby. Why is a street sign at the base of these concrete steps? The 169 steps actually are a street (nearly a block long and comprising three or four tiers). When it was built it was the only access to many of the homes along either side, and it is the only street in Kansas made from a series of steps. A sign wisely discourages climbing.

Shawnee Prophet:

3818 Ruby. Tenskwatawa, a religious and political leader of the Shawnee tribe and a brother of the prominent Chief Tecumseh, established a village near here in 1826. Near the place where Tenskwatawa is thought to be buried, a marker pays homage to this man.

Rosedale Memorial Arch (NRHP): 35th and Booth (Mount Marty Park).

The Rosedale Memorial Arch commemorates those from the Rosedale area who served and sacrificed during WWI. Local resident John LeRoy Marshall designed the arch, basing it on the Arc de Triomphe in Paris. Dedicated in 1923, it stands at the crest of a hill and overlooks the Kansas City skyline. In 1993 a large monument was placed under the arch to honor the Rosedale veterans who lost their lives in WWII through Vietnam.

Tribal Boundary Plaque:

7250 State (Kansas City Community College campus). A monument marks the division between Wyandot and Delaware lands and acknowledges the Delawares' generous gift of land to the Wyandots in honor of past acts of friendship.

Jack Wyatt Museum:

4444 Forest. If you're a pianist, piano tuner, or a curious explorer you'll be interested

in the museum of the Piano Technicians Guild Foundation that recognizes the piano tuner! Displayed are technicians' tools and historic pianos including a 1782 Buntebart square piano and a Chickering piano that was on stage the night Lincoln was assassinated at Ford's Theatre. Jack Wyatt collected the majority of the pianos in the collection. Monday-Friday, 9 a.m.-3 p.m. 913.432.9975. tinyurl.com/ptgmuseum.

Boulevard Drive In

Theatre: 1051 Merriam Ln. From Antioch, 3 miles east on Merriam Ln. Beneath the shade trees you'll see the beautiful red and yellow original Boulevard marquee. The theatre opened in 1950, and current owner Wes Neal has been a part of this legendary drive-in since 1954. In 1999 the Boulevard became the first drive-in in the world to

install digital sound. April-September. 913.262.2414. FB. A Swap & Shop is held on the Boulevard grounds year round, Saturday-Sunday 5 a.m.-2 p.m.

Kansas City T-Bones:

1800 Village West. The T-Bones belong to baseball's Northern League and play in the 4,300-seat CommunityAmerica Ballpark. You sit close to the action, the entertainment between innings is great fun, the parking is free, and the tickets and ballpark food are affordable. The T-Bones call it "fun well done!" 913.328.2255. tbonesbaseball.com.

Legends Outlets:

1843 Village West. Shoppers and diners can choose from more than 75 stores and restaurants, but you can also learn a great deal about Kansas without going in a store. In this very beautiful outdoor shopping center, more than 80 Kansas legends are recognized through outdoor murals, statues, medallions, and banners. You'll even see Dwight Eisenhower fishing! Monday-Saturday 10 a.m.-9 p.m.; Sunday 11 a.m.-6 p.m. 913.788.3700. legendsshopping.com.

Schlitterbahn Waterpark:

9400 State. Every kind of water ride is here for all ages!—surf riding, water coasters, tube slides, zip lines, and a heated pool. Or just lounge and relax. You're bound to have a great time. Memorial Day-Labor Day, daily 10 a.m.-6 p.m. 913.312.3110. schlitterbahn.com/kansas-city.

Mad Jack's Fresh Fish:

1318 State. Half fish market, half restaurant, Mad Jack's is one of those not-so-fancy places that the locals love because it's the best place to find fresh fish. And

you will find most everything, from Asian carp and bluegill to shark. The fried catfish, crunchy and flavorful, is made with Mad Jack's special seasoning. Monday-Saturday 10 a.m.-9 p.m.; Sunday 12-6 p.m. 913.371.3384. madjacksfreshfish.com.

Big Grill and More:
501 NE 6th. The character of the Big Grill, where red-and-white oilcloths cover the tables,

is as big as the taste of the barbecue, burgers, peach cobbler, sweet potato pie, and more. The sweet and spicy barbecue sauce is classic! Monday-Friday 7 a.m.-7 p.m. 913.371.0088. FB.

El Camino Real: 903 N. 7th.
Some call it a hole-in-the-wall, but even so, they all sing the praises of the authentic tacos al pastor as well as the burritos, pico de gallo, and more. The tortillas are made fresh. Daily 10 a.m.-10 p.m. 913.342.4333. FB.

Fritz's Railroad Restaurant:
250 N. 18th. All grown-up "kids" from this blue-collar, old Irish Catholic neighborhood have memories of their food being delivered by train at

Fritz's. This 1954 diner features a miniature railroad car that circles the restaurant, stops at your table, and lowers your order on a miniature elevator! Fritz's most famous burger, the Gen-Dare, comes with crunchy hash browns, grilled onions, and melted cheese. Monday-Thursday, 6 a.m.-3 p.m.; Friday-Saturday 6 a.m.-8 p.m. 913.281.2777. fritzskc.com.

Joe's Kansas City Bar-B-Que: 3002 W. 47th.
This giant in the barbecue world started in 1990 when Jeff and Joy Stehney entered a barbecue contest and won. And they kept winning. In 1997 they opened the first of their three restaurants inside a former gas station. As word spread of their remarkably succulent barbecue, lines began forming out the door for the ribs and everything else, and it hasn't stopped since. Monday-Saturday 11 a.m.-10 p.m. 913.722.3366. joeskc.com.

Woodyard Bar-B-Que:
3001 Merriam. It's called the Woodyard because this is where all the barbecue places bought their wood—and you can still buy six kinds of wood here. It's also called one of the best places for barbecue in Kansas City. It's famous for its smokehouse meats, but the chili has a huge following too. Lots of kitschy signs, lots of seating, lots of good barbecue. Monday-Saturday 10:30 a.m.-8 p.m.; Sunday 11 a.m.-3:30 p.m. 913.362.8000. woodyardbbq.com.

More Good Restaurants:
visitkansascityks.com. Find more barbecue at tinyurl.com/kcksbarbecue.

Lodging:
visitkansascityks.com.

explorer extras...
In Kansas City

High water marks from the 1903 and 1951 floods are indicated on plaques at St. John the Evangelist Catholic Church at 2910 Strong, and on a second-floor window sign at L.A. True Value Hardware at 631 Kansas.

Public art brightly celebrates the history and culture of Kansas City and the unique groups and people within the community. High school students helped lead artists Joe Faus and Alisha Gambino portray the powerful stories. Five of the eight murals can be seen on Minnesota between 6th and 10th. 913.321.5800. goo.gl/kcdgpu.

In 1914 Frank Winkler purchased a large street clock from the Seth Thomas Company and placed it in front of his jewelry store to advertise his watch-making and watch repair business. In 1990, after 101 years of operation, Winkler's Jewelry Store closed, but the clock remains, now at standing the bus stop at 7th and Minnesota. **ee**

NE

Enjoy more examples of Kansas Rural Culture Elements

**while we say thanks to our valued partners,
underwriters, and supporters.**

What building materials were used? Who built and designed the structures, in what style, when, and what are the special details? What community significance do they have?

Thank you to **Liz King** and **Bobbie Pray** for helping build this book.
To create this legacy to Kansas we turned to the best graphic designer, Liz King, and editor, Bobbie Pray, that a guidebook could ever have. Bobbie scrutinized every word and questioned every fact to bring you an easy-read about what Kansas is. Liz, Marci's sister, created a first-class backdrop for the content. Her picture placement, page design, and creativity in showcasing the best of Kansas make this a book for the ages.

Rural Culture Element 2: Art

Murals, statues and sculptures, architectural design, fine art and grassroots art, performance venues, music, and dance. Art adds spice and joy!

Kansas Department of Wildlife, Parks and Tourism, thank you for your support, which made it possible for us to be on the road for four years researching this beautiful state. We also are grateful for your work in so artfully letting the world know, "There's no place like Kansas."

travelks.com

Rural Culture Element 3: Commerce

What businesses led to the founding of a town? What are the current businesses and who are the entrepreneurs? What is the economic story of a town?

Monarch Cement Company, not only do we thank you for your contribution to this guidebook, but we also appreciate the more than 100-year contribution you've made to the history and economic stability of your hometown of Humboldt in southeast Kansas.

monarchcement.com

Where do folks eat out? Cafes, restaurants, soda fountains, drive-ins, coffee shops?
Who are the cooks and chefs and what are their treasured recipes and specialty foods?

Come join the family

MCPHERSON · HILLSBORO · HUTCHINSON · NEWTON

We loved driving around the state in ERV (Explorer Research Vehicle) that you, **Midway Motors**
of McPherson, provided for our journey. Thank you. We parked our GMC Terrain in front of hundreds
of local cafes, restaurants, drive-ins, and dives before going inside to do our "tasty research."

midwaymotors.com

The traditions woven into the fabric of a community show themselves in ethnic practices, long-standing community rituals, and in endearing, quirky features.

Kansas Humanities Council, every day you help traditions and history rise to the top, uniting communities. Now you've made it possible for us to tell a big-picture Kansas story including those uniquely singular things that make each town different from the next. Thank you.

kansashumanities.org

Rural Culture Element 6: Geography

Nature and place, they include physiographic regions, vegetation, wildlife,
native grasslands, natural landmarks, and expansive views—all so varied in our state.

Jim and Bonnie Miller, Kansas Explorers #612, thank you for nurturing
the Kansas Sampler Foundation as well as your prairie home and its birds, wildflowers, and grasses.
It's fitting that you've dedicated this page to two people who have done so much
to recognize the soul of the prairie, Mil Penner and Jake Miller.

Rural Culture Element 7: History

Places, events, points of interest, and individual and community efforts preserve the meaningful story of Kansas' past.

Mariah Fund, thank you for supporting this guidebook and for making a difference by promoting tourism and historic preservation in southwest Kansas.

mariahfund.com

Historic figures, present-day characters, prominent and regular folks come from every background to add their personality and talents to our state.

It takes a team to create a book like this. **Sarah Green** and **Shannon Martin** helped us reach the finish line with fact checking, proofing, and special assignments. **Bob Topping** checked every set of directions. **Betty Stevens** proofread every word. **Katrina Ringler, Amanda Loughlin, Leo Oliva, Jim Gray,** and **Rex Buchanan** were the experts we turned to time and again. **Mom (VLee Penner)** fed, helped and cheered us on every day. **Kim Clark, Jan Topping, Nadine Reimer Penner** and the **Kansas Sampler Foundation board** pitched in too. Hundreds of you answered our calls to share information—and the love— of your towns and communities. All of us, as a team, made this book a reality.

Additional guidebook support

With gratitude to each of the following for helping make this guidebook possible:

Ad Astra Sponsors
Blue Beacon International, Inc., Salina
Cloud County Tourism, Concordia
Lon Frahm, Colby
Sally Frame, Kinsley
Kansas Electric Cooperatives, Topeka
Fred and Nancy Kerr, Pratt
Jerry Kissel, Wetmore
Lindsborg Convention and Visitors Bureau and Lindsborg Ad Hoc Roundtable
Gene and Barb Merry, Burlington
Mikesell Family Foundation, Clearwater
Eileen Robertson, Humboldt
Donald and Janet Shepherd, Haysville
"Valley Falls Crew"

Friends of the Road Sponsors
Abilene Convention and Visitors Bureau
Ronnie and Judy Dayhoff, Boulder, CO
Helen L. Graves, Salina
Bruce L. Hogle, Overland Park
Kansas Barn Alliance
Kansas I-70 Association
Tom & Liz King, Park City, UT
Sidney and Carole McKnight, Parker
North Central Kansas Tourism Region
PowerUp Core Team
Glenda Purkis, Abilene
Rock City Park, Minneapolis
"In memory of Bobbi Prinz" from Kansas Explorers
Jim and Kathy Richardson, Lindsborg
Rooks County Economic Development, Stockton
South Central Kansas Tourism Region

Our thanks also to all of you who made this research journey possible by:

• paying for meals along the way,

• providing overnight lodging,

• or adding a little extra to your Kansas Explorer Club membership.

Southeast Kansas

Counties: Allen, Anderson, Bourbon, Chase, Chautauqua, Cherokee, Coffey, Crawford, Elk, Greenwood, Labette, Linn, Lyon, Montgomery, Neosho, Wilson, Woodson

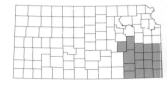

Architecture: Clements Stone Arch Bridge, Clements

Art: Logan Fountain Sculptures, Independence

Commerce: Nelson's Old Riverton Store, Riverton

Cuisine: Radius Brewing Company, Emporia

Customs: Pedestrian Suspension Bridge, Moline

Geography: Teter Rock, Teterville

History: Miners' Memorial, Pittsburg

People: Lowell Milken Center for Unsung Heroes, Fort Scott

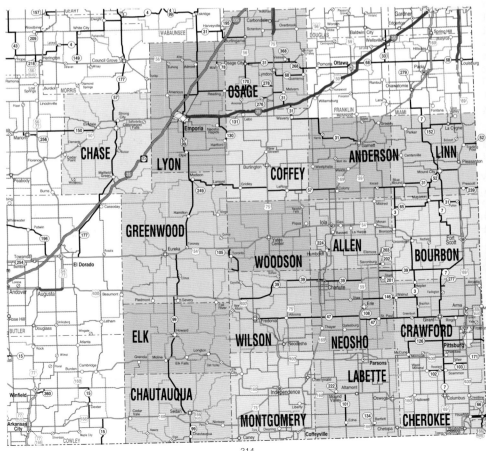

Allen County

explorer extras...
In Bassett

Population 15

Bassett was founded as a company town, created in 1903 by the Iola Portland Cement Company for its 900 employees. The largest cement plant in the nation, it was sold in 1917 to the Lehigh Portland Cement Company, which closed its doors in 1970. The plant is now occupied by other businesses, but from Washington and Portland you can see the vestiges of other remains. The company workers' houses have been removed or demolished, and the plant's quarry is now a lake and recreational center for the Iola Elks Club.

A sign at Elm Creek Park South, Bassett and Wheeler, takes us back to 1923 when this area was a tourist camp. The stone wall remains are from the stone arch entrance to the camp. Today the park is a great place to enjoy a picnic and some good fishing. **ee**

GAS CITY

Population 540

When natural gas was discovered in Elm Township in 1898, E.K. Taylor sold lots on his land to develop a town. He named it Gas City.

Gas Kan: Pine and Osborn. When the water tower was built in the early 1970s, the city council had it painted red with white letters bearing the name of its city and state, making it the largest "Gas Kan" in the world! 620.365.3034.

Woodmen Circle: From Main, ¼ mile east on U.S. 54, then ¾ mile north on 2200 (Gas City Cemetery). Look for a tall stone tree stump engraved "Woodmen Circle" above the name Maggie McKeon. Woodmen Circle was a women's auxiliary of the Woodmen of the World, an 1890s fraternal organization that helped members during financially difficult times. Members carried life insurance policies that provided for these customized and hand-carved gravestones. The tombstone program, which created an obvious identity with the organization, ended in the 1920s, although the Woodmen Circle still exists today.

HUMBOLDT

Population 1,927

Town Square: 100 S. 9th. In September 1861 Confederate forces raided Humboldt and returned in October to burn the town. A Civil War monument on the northwest side of the square includes a mural of marble etchings portraying this traumatic time in Humboldt history. A 1907 bandstand (NRHP) and a veterans memorial also grace the square.

Civil War Markers: Twelve limestone markers placed throughout the town feature etched marble plaques that provide a pictorial history of the 1861 Humboldt raid and burning by Confederate forces. Brochures with tour maps are available in shops around the square and at Johnson's General Store, 218 N. 9th. tinyurl.com/civilwarmarkers.

Neosho River Park: From 9th, ¾ mile west on Bridge. Overlooking the Neosho River dam is a beautiful amphitheater made from large native limestone blocks. In season, flowers bloom in the Osage Prayer Wheel, and tall trees provide shade in this picturesque setting. An open staircase takes you down for a closer look at the river.

Monarch Houses: Monarch Portland Cement Company was founded in 1908 and reorganized in 1913 as Monarch Cement Company. Three homes on S. 8th, across from the plant, are known as the Monarch Houses and were built in 1908 for the Monarch president and two other executives. Today descendants of H.F.G. Wulf, who took over the company in 1913, live in two of these beautiful concrete homes.

SE

Neosho Valley Woodworks: 118 S. 8th. Patrick Haire has one of the most unique working setups in the state—he crafts period-style furniture using a system of pulleys and wheels to power the antique machines. You'll feel you've stepped into another era when you're among the sawdust, belts, and old-time tools. Working with this antique machinery is an art, and Patrick is the masterful artist. Call ahead, 719.293.4177.

Lander's Carriage & Wagon Shop (NRHP):

403 Bridge. At this 1876 two-story stone carriage shop you can almost see the carriages and wagons pulling up outside, waiting their turn to be repaired. To keep up with the times, Charles Lander built the one-story red-brick wagon shop next door in 1910. This rare building is virtually unchanged, and its 19th-century woodworking machines and blacksmith's forge are in working order. Currently Patrick Haire utilizes the building and its original furnishings for his woodworking business. Tour charge. Call ahead, 719.293.4177.

Humboldt Historical Museum:

416 N. 2nd. Housed in the historic 1876 residence of a former wealthy merchant, the museum is where to start your exploration of town history, which includes the Monarch Cement plant and baseball greats Walter Johnson and George Sweatt. The museum complex also includes an early jail, pioneer home, antique farm equipment, a cannon, and Lewis Howland's hand carvings of horse-drawn circus wagons and carriages. June to mid-October, Saturday-Sunday 1:30-4 p.m. 620.473.5055. humboldtksmuseum.com.

Walter Johnson:

A Humboldt native, Johnson was one of the premiere baseball pitchers when he played for the Washington Senators from 1907 to 1927. He was nicknamed "The Big Train" due to the power and speed of his fastball. In 1921

Humboldt named its athletic field at S. 6th and Pine for this pitching legend. The masonry wall around the field was built in 1936 by the WPA. The site of Johnson's birthplace is, from Bridge, 2½ miles north on 9th, then 1 mile west on Iowa. In a corner of a field near Iowa and 900 a plaque on a large native stone marks his birth site. In front of the stone, a home plate is embedded in a concrete base. Displays about Johnson's life are at City Hall, 725 Bridge, and at the Humboldt Historical Museum.

George Sweatt Park:

S. 12th and Wulf. Also a native of Humboldt, George Sweatt was second baseman from 1922 to 1927 for the Kansas City Monarchs and the Chicago American Giants in the Negro National League. The Monarchs won the first World Series of the Negro League in 1924, the same year Walter Johnson won the World Series with the Washington Senators. In the mid-1970s this park was named in honor of Sweatt, and a plaque about him and his career is mounted on a large boulder just beyond left field. Displays about his life are at the Humboldt Historical Museum.

Southwind Rail Trail:

Hawaii and 14th. From this trailhead, all roads lead north along a former Santa Fe rail line. Follow it 6½ miles to Iola's Riverside Park then, if ou wish, continue 51 more miles on the Prairie Spirit Trail (see p. 219) to Ottawa. The crushed-stone surface on this scenic

route is accessible for wheel-chairs, bicycles, and walking. FB.

Stacy Cakes:

804 Bridge. After suffering storm damage in 2016, this business came back to life in 2017 after much hard work. You'll be glad it did when you discover the seven-stool soda fountain inside this 1905 building. Home-baked cakes, pies, cupcakes, cookies, a hearty lunch menu, and ice cream treats await you in this inviting atmosphere. Monday-Friday 8:30 a.m.-5 p.m.; Saturday 8:30 a.m.-1 p.m. 620-473-5035. FB.

Good Local Eateries:

Estrellita Mexican Restaurant (818 N. 9th, 620.473.2654); and H&H Grill (119 N. 8th, 620.473.3332).

Stony Lonesome School:

From Bridge, 3¾ miles north on 8th (becomes 1100). On the west side of the road, partially hidden by trees and vines are the remains of the 1884 Stony Lonesome school where the future military general Frederick Funston (see p. 217) taught after he failed the entrance exam into West Point. A plaque honoring Funston was placed here by the DAR in 1928.

Vegetarian Colony:

From Bridge, 4½ miles south on 9th (becomes 1200). In 1856 60 families, members of the Vegetarian Kansas Emigration Company headed by Henry S. Clubb, moved here to form an Octagon settlement, a type of colony devoted to communal and healthy (vegetarian) living. Severe hardships and illness forced most families to abandon the failing community within a year. A marker on the west side of the road at 1200 and Arizona relates the unusual tale of the Vegetarian Colony. Additional information is at the Allen County Museum in Iola.

Lodging:

tinyurl.com/hunterrv.

explorer extras... In Humboldt

A rare 1932 Marsh rainbow double-arch bridge spanning the Neosho River provides a beautiful entrance to Humboldt from the west.

A drive through the wooded Camp Hunter Park at 1st and Ohio reveals structures of native rock built by the National Youth Administration in 1937. The funding was made possible during the New Deal era of the Great Depression.

If you have the need for speed, head to the Humboldt Speedway, 1663 Georgia, to watch stock car races on its high-banked oval track. 620.473.3694. humboldtspeeway.com. **ee**

IOLA

Population 5,613

Thomas H. Bowlus Fine Arts & Cultural Center:

205 E. Madison. The art deco aluminum accents and geometric shapes beautifully augment both the inside and the tan-brick exterior. Banker Thomas Bowlus' will made it possible to build and furnish this center as a gift to his hometown in 1964. Both a school and community resource, the building features permanent fine arts collections on the lower level and special exhibits in the Mary L. Martin Gallery. The large main auditorium hosts a variety of nationally known performers and local theatre troupes. Monday-Friday 8 a.m.-4 p.m. 620.365.4765. bowluscenter.org.

Courthouse Grounds:

Iola can legitimately claim it is home to the nation's largest

downtown square—two blocks by two blocks. The 1959 Allen County courthouse holds center stage, and surrounding features include a beautiful brick veterans memorial wall and the clock tower preserved from the original 1904 courthouse. Since 1876 locals have been gathering around the old gazebo for band concerts, which are still enjoyed every Thursday evening in June and July. 620.365.5252.

Downtown: Colorful Victorian buildings will capture your attention. The Allen County Museum and Funston home are the downtown anchors, and stores such as Audacious Boutique (511 N. Broadway, 620.380.6366) and Sophisticated Rose (19 S. Jefferson, 620.365.6278) entice you to walk around the square. Signage provide buildings' histories and information about famous Iola citizens.

Allen County Museum:

20 S. Washington. Excellent exhibits about the history of each of Allen County's towns and a well-designed display about famous area people start your tour of this museum. Discover how gas and cement played important roles in early Allen County, and learn about General Frederick Funston before you visit his boyhood home next door (*see* next entry). May-October, Tuesday-Saturday 12:30-4 p.m.; November-April, Tuesday-Saturday 2-4 p.m. 620.365.3051.

Major General Frederick Funston Boyhood Home:

14 S. Washington. Although "Fighting Fred" Funston was a major figure in military history, few recognize his name. At his boyhood home you'll learn about the man who became

a brigadier general at age 35, gained fame during the Spanish-American War, commanded such later military greats as Pershing, Eisenhower, Patton, and MacArthur, and led the response to the 1906 earthquake and fires in San Francisco. Funston's 1860s boyhood home was moved into Iola from the country and is a pleasing site sporting a white picket fence. For hours, see Allen County Museum. 620.365.3051.

Old Allen County Jail (NRHP): 203 N. Jefferson.

Inmate graffiti and jail-house artifacts highlight the tour of this two-story limestone structure. Built in 1869, it was used as a jail until 1958. Call ahead, 620.365.3051.

Iola Cemetery:

From Washington, ½ mile west on Madison (U.S. 54). J.F. Colborn was a member of the town company organized to establish a new town—and he named it for his wife, Iola. The first tall monument along the cemetery's center drive is a tribute to the town's namesake. A Civil War memorial, dedicated in 1909 and standing at the north end of the cemetery, is one of only four white-bronze (cast zinc) statues in the state. Along the main road in block 1, lot 110, you'll find the

SE

gravestone for none other than Cinderella. Well, Cinderella M. Anderson, that is.

Eleanor: While you're in the cemetery, look for the outhouse on the west side near the row of trees. This type of outhouse, built with cement pads, a metal roof, and good ventilation, resulted from a project spearheaded by Eleanor Roosevelt to help fight typhoid fever through better sanitation. The outhouses became a New Deal project, and because of the First Lady's role, they became known as the "Eleanor," and the nickname stuck.

Riverside Park:

From W. Madison, ¼ mile south on State, then just west on Park. Several 1930s WPA buildings (including a bathhouse, shelter houses, and original community building) mix with new buildings to grace the beautifully wooded park near the Neosho River. Vintage playground equipment provides old-time fun, and a mural on the new community building adds color. From the west side of the park it's an easy walk down the embankment for a close-up view of the river, or take a longer walk on the Sunflower Rail Trail.

Trail Connection: Riverside Park. The 51-mile Prairie Spirit Trail (*see* p. 118) connects in Riverside Park to the shorter Southwind Rail Trail, which goes south to Humboldt. The highlight of the latter route is the restored railroad trestle over Elm Creek, less than a mile from Riverside Park. Tree-lined much of the way, the trail also offers views of prime cropland. FB.

Around the Corner:

110 S. Jefferson. Just around the corner from Madison is a spot made for coffee lovers and those who connect easily with others. Log in with free Wi-Fi, order your favorite coffee blend and a homemade pastry, and settle in for the morning. Or stop

for lunch to enjoy freshly made soups, salads, and wraps. Monday-Friday 6:30 a.m.-4 p.m.; Saturday 8 a.m.-2 p.m. 620.380.6595. FB.

King's Sandwich Shop:

321 S. State. The King family has been serving burgers here since 1955, and they grind the meat fresh every day. Monday-Friday 10 a.m.-8 p.m.; Saturday 10 a.m.-7 p.m. 620.365.6271. FB.

Bolling Meat Market and Deli:

201 S. State. For the best sandwich, you need fresh ingredients. That's the belief at Bolling's, which serves fresh only—bread, meat, cheese, and toppings piled high. A special favorite is the French dip with caramelized onion jam. The soups, sides, daily specials, and desserts all deserve gold stars. You can also buy fresh or frozen top-grade meat from the store's coolers. Monday-Saturday 10 a.m.-6 p.m.; Sunday 9 a.m.-5 p.m. 620.380.6328. FB.

El Charro: 19 W. Madison. A Mexican theme blends with rustic and shabby-chic to create a warm, charming interior. You'll even see evidence of the old pressed-tin ceiling from the building's dry goods store origins. A huge menu of authentic cuisine is accompanied with a selection of Mexican beers, cocktails, and a perfect margarita. Daily 11 a.m.-9 p.m. 620.365.7771.

Dudley's Done Right BBQ:

2402 N. State. This crazy-good barbecue joint has a legion of fans. Locals love the famous pit potato and the one-pound barbecue wrap. Take a seat at one of the ultra-cool tables, made from the front ends of old pickup trucks! Tuesday-Saturday 11 a.m-8 p.m. 620.380.6580. FB.

Lodging:

tinyurl.com/iolalodging.

explorer extras...
In Iola

Iola created something magical in the flood plain of Elm Creek. The town removed trees and brush and replaced them with one of the most functional and beautiful community gardens in the state. Birdhouses, antique farm equipment, raised plots, tool sheds, recycle areas, and clever gardening practices make Elm Creek Community Garden, 702 S. 1st, a must stop. 620.365.5577. tinyurl.com/iolacommgard.

The magnificent Queen Anne style Northrup House (NRHP) at 318 East was built in 1895 and expanded in 1905 and 1912. Among its amenities is the large and pleasant porch. Drive by only.

Beautiful, clean modern lines and curves of two art deco schools, designed by architect Lorentz Schmidt, make them worth your while to drive by. Built as New Deal projects in 1939, Jefferson Grade School, 300 S. Jefferson, and Lincoln Grade School, 700 N. Jefferson, still operate as schools.

An impressive 1937 WPA flood control project is the mile-long, stone-lined Coon Creek channel. It starts at 803 N. Cottonwood and winds through town to the Neosho River.

In the center of Highland Cemetery the towering, white marble obelisk (a miniature Washington Monument) was erected by the American Legion to honor soldiers who died during WWI and whose bodies were not brought home. The memorial is inscribed, "In memory of those whose final resting place is known to God alone." From Madison, 1¼ mile north on Cottonwood.

Candy magnate Russell Stover was born near tiny Alton in Osborne County, and today, of course, his name is synonymous with nationally famous chocolates. Satisfy your sweet cravings at the Russell Stover candy factory and retail store, 1995 Marshmallow. Monday-Saturday 10 a.m.-6 p.m.; Sunday 12-5 p.m. 620.365.5590. **ee**

LAHARPE

Population 561

TLC Garden Center:
1007 W. U.S. 54. This lush garden center has your seed needs all wrapped up in brown paper in neatly labeled cubby-holes. You'll find very reasonable prices for all sorts of garden products—flowers, plants, shrubs, trees, home and patio decor, and gift items. Monday-Saturday 9 a.m.-5:30 p.m.; Sunday 10 a.m.-2 p.m. 620.496.1234. tlcgc.com.

MILDRED

Population 27

Mildred Store: 86 3rd.
Formerly known as Charlie Brown's, this grocery store's traditions are carried on by new owners Loren and Regena Lance. (The former owners were Charles Brown and his wife, Lucille, thus the *Peanuts* connection.) The deli still serves the popular Charlie Brown sandwich piled high with meat and cheese. This little store fills a big need in the community and has been a mainstay in Mildred for more than 100 years. Live music is a special treat every third Saturday of the month. Monday-Saturday 9 a.m.-6 p.m.; Sunday 9 a.m.-4 p.m. 620.439.5424. FB.

MORAN

Population 542

Moran Cemetery: From
1st, ½ mile south on Cedar (U.S. 59), then 1 mile west on

Nebraska. The GAR memorial, a native stone pyramid beside the flagpole, was dedicated in 1893 by Sanders Post No. 254. At its base a small white stone is inscribed, "In memory of our fallen comrades." Also of interest in the cemetery is the arch joining the gravestones for Robert McFarland and James Harclerode. According to newspaper accounts the men were brutally killed in 1884 while building a house on land whose ownership was disputed.

Anderson County

AROUND THE COUNTY

Prairie Spirit Trail:
A pioneer trail in its own right and following one of the first north-south rail lines in Kansas, the Prairie Spirit Trail opened to bikers and hikers in 1996. Now a Kansas state park, the trail runs 51 miles from the Old Depot Museum in Ottawa to Riverside Park in Iola where you can continue six more miles to Humboldt on the Southwind Trail (*see* p. 216). In Anderson County you'll find trailheads in Scipio, Garnett, Welda, and Colony. On your scenic trek you'll cross bridges and pass woodlands, prairie, and lakes, and catch glimpses of wildlife. Permits required for those over 16. 785.448.5496. bikeprairiespirit.com.

Samuel Tipton House
(NRHP): 27851 NW Barton. From W. 4th in Garnett, ½ mile north on Maple (U.S. 59), 11¾ miles west and north on K-31, 3 miles west on 4 (becomes 2000), then ½ mile

north on NW Barton. Built on what was known as Mineral Point, one of the highest points in the county, the house was sometimes called Mineral Point Mansion. This three-story sandstone structure was built circa 1857 for Samuel Tipton, credited with introducing Shorthorn cattle to Kansas. The home's lower floor was used as a post office, general store, and stagecoach stop. Monday-Saturday by appointment. Tour charge (minimum 6 people). Reservations required. 785.489.2444.

Lone Elm Cemetery:
Should you find yourself five miles west of Kincaid on U.S. 59, look for a giant stone "beehive" in the cemetery just north of Lone Elm. Not a beehive at all, but rather it's a stone structure protecting an old water well.

COLONY

Population 401

Prairie Spirit Trail: E. 1st
and Colony. If you started this hiking and biking rail trail (*see* p. 118) in Ottawa, you'll be on mile 40 when you reach Colony. It's 11 more miles on this linear

state park to its end in Iola. The scenic Prairie Spirit Trail is a hard-packed surface trail built on an old railroad grade. Permit required for those over 16. 785.448.6767. Bikeprairiespirit.com.

Hi Point Cafe and Convenience: 210 E. Broad. Three owners have pitched in to keep this friendly little combination convenience store and cafe going. It's known for its double cheeseburgers and applauded for its homemade pies. Most popular are the peanut butter, pecan, and apple. Cafe hours, daily 6:30 a.m.-2 p.m.; store hours, daily 6:30 a.m.-7 p.m. 620.852.3007. FB.

GARNETT

Population 3,307

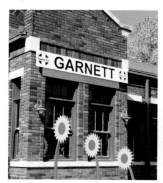

Prairie Spirit Trail Trailhead: 8th and Main. Renovated in 1996, this brick 1934 Santa Fe depot serves as Garnett's trailhead for the Prairie Spirit Trail (*see* p. 118). Sunflowers will greet you out front every day of the year, and old-fashioned street lights and landscaping line the trail through town. Restrooms and visitor information are available. Daily 7 a.m.-7 p.m. 785.448.6767.

Anderson County Courthouse (NRHP): 100 E. 4th. Revered architect George Washburn designed this majestic three-story

red-brick Classic Romanesque structure dedicated in 1902. The exterior and interior both have retained the historic ambience. Lady Justice stand above the front entrance on the west side, and a Statue of Liberty replica, donated by the local Boy Scout troop in 1950, stands on the northwest lawn. Monday-Friday 8 a.m.-5 p.m.

Arthur Capper Memorial: 416 S. Cedar. The state's first Kansas-born governor, Arthur Capper (1865-1951) entered the world in a house that once stood on this lot. Nationally known, he was also a U.S. senator, newspaper publisher, and philanthropist.

Lake Garnett and North Lake Park: 500 N. Lake. Drive around the lake to see the 1930s football stadium stonework, fence, and shelters constructed by the Civilian Conservation Corps and the National Youth Administration. National sports car races were held here from 1959 to 1964, and today the park is home to the Cornstock music event, go-kart races, and the Lake Garnett Grand Prix Revival. 785.448.5496. tinyurl.com/lakegarnett.

Walker Art Gallery: 125 W. 4th (Garnett Public Library). During the 1930s and 1940s Maynard Walker was a

primary promoter of Regionalist artists such as John Steuart Curry, Grant Wood, and Thomas Hart Benton. In 1951 Maynard donated his collection of paintings, which also included works by European artists George Grosz, Edouard Manet, and Jean Baptiste Corot, to the city to establish an art gallery in honor of his mother, Mary Bridget Walker. Monday-Saturday 10 a.m.-4 p.m. 785.448.3388. tinyurl.com/walkartgall.

Anderson County Museum: 410 W 6th. Having taken up residence inside the former Longfellow grade school, the museum interprets the county's history. May-September, Tuesday-Friday 1-4 p.m. 785.448.5740. historyandersoncoks.org.

Maloan's: 101 W. 4th. Since 1996 people have been investing in a good meal at this former corner bank. The pressed-tin ceiling and old wood floor provide a rich ambience for enjoying steaks, seafood, and pasta, and on Friday and Saturday nights, prime rib. A full bar is available. Thursday-Saturday 5-8 p.m. 785.448.2616. FB.

Prairie Belle's Kitchen: 130 E. 5th. The renovated historic downtown building, complete with exposed stone

walls and high ceilings, will add to your enjoyment of blended coffees, homemade baked goods, fresh salads, soups, and daily specials. Monday-Friday 6:30 a.m.-2 p.m.; Saturday 6:30-11 a.m. 785.448.2253. FB.

Yoder's Country Store:
22800 NW 1700. From Maple (U.S. 59), ½ mile west on 7th, ¼ mile south on Westgate, then ¾ mile west on 1700. It's just a short drive into the country for biscuits and gravy, deli sandwiches, and hard-packed ice cream. Yoder's also carries discount groceries, bulk foods, and fresh meats. Look on the south side of the road for a metal shed with a big parking lot. Monday-Saturday 7 a.m.-7 p.m. 785.204.1961. FB.

Bauman's Cedar Valley
Farms: 24161 NW Kentucky. From Maple (U.S. 59), ½ mile west on 7th, ¼ mile south on Westgate, 4½ miles south and west on 1700 (becomes Maryland, 1650, 1600), then 1 mile south on Kentucky. John and Yvonne Bauman and their six kids started farming in 2001 and even though they only farm 120 acres, they are an incredibly industrious family and have created a sustainable operation. Shop at the Farm Store for pastured turkeys, ducks, chickens, and eggs; grass and grain finished beef and pork; raw milk; and non-GMO animal feed. Reap the vegetables of the Bauman family's labor during the garden season. Monday-Wednesday, Friday 9 a.m.-5 p.m. 785.448.2239.

Schmucker's Country
Store: 19777 NW 1700. From U.S. 59 (Maple), 3¾ miles west on 4th (becomes 1750), ½ mile south on Louisiana, then 1½ miles west on 1700. Neighbors come to this Amish country store for straw hats, bonnets, and horseshoes. Additional items inside this metal building

include kitchenwares (such as the heavy-duty, long-handled spoons), bulk goods, simple toys, and home remedies. Monday-Friday 9 a.m.-5 p.m.; Saturday 8 a.m.-12 p.m. 785.448.6728.

Lodging: The Kirk House (785.448.6500, thekirkhouse.net); additional lodging (tinyurl.com/garnettlodge).

explorer extras...
In Garnett

Tuesdays are sale days at the Anderson County Sale Company, 430 N. Maple, which involves more than a regular livestock sale. The Amish arrive in their buggies, buyers and sellers come from miles around, and auctioneers ensure fast-paced action. An extraordinary auction of "stuff" starts outside at 9 a.m., and livestock bidding begins at noon. The sale barn opened in 1939, and Ron and Christy Ratliff keep the family business moving ahead. Cafe opens at 7 a.m. 785.448.3800. FB.

The Kirk House (NRHP) at 145 W. 4th, designed in 1913 by architect George Washburn, was built for Garnett banker Sennett Kirk and his wife, Bertha. The wood-frame home is an example of the Colonial Revival style.

Garnett House, 202 W. 4th, was built in 1858, and additions were later made to this hotel whose guest list included John Brown, Wild Bill Hickok, Buffalo Bill Cody, and Belle Starr.

The 1887 House of Eleven Gables, 230 W. 4th, was designed by a German architect in the tradition of the luxury houses of Germany.

Tulip-patterned bricks trim each of the 44 windows in the Harris House, an 1888 Victorian home, at 405 W. 4th. For tours, call 785.448.6767.

Shelley-Tipton House (NRHP) at 812 W. 4th is an elegant Italianate structure built in 1871 by S.S. Shelley. In 1887 it was purchased by Samuel Tipton, of Shorthorn cattle fame, as his retirement home.

At the corner of S. Oak and E. 4th the Donna Harris Memorial Park is accented with lovely landscaping, a fountain, and a mural painted by local high school students. The eye-catching mural depicts a large bright sunflower against a starry night sky.

Many buildings around the downtown square were built in the late 1800s. Among them you'll find good shopping for antiques, fabric, and gifts. **ee**

SE

GREELEY

Population 296

Gerth Cabin: From Brown, 1 block south on Main, 1½ blocks west on Bondi, then just south on Trego. Valentin Gerth, purportedly the first white settler in Anderson County, built this rough-hewn log house in 1856. Moved a few miles to this riverbank location, the cabin may have been used as a stop on the Underground Railroad. The cabin is not usually open, but just exploring around the outside environs make it worth a stop. Gerth and his wife, Mary, are buried in Greeley Cemetery just north of town. 785.448.6767.

Spencer's Crossing Bridge (NRHP): Also known as Greeley Bridge, this 1885 iron truss bridge spans 128 feet over Pottawatomie Creek. No longer used, it stands parallel to the new bridge. From U.S. 169, 1 mile north on Main, ¼ mile west on NE 2400, then ¼ mile north and west on 2370.

Popcorn Day: Friday is a good day to stop at the Bank of Greeley, 118 W. Brown. Popcorn is popped in a vintage popper in the lobby and is available free to customers and visitors alike. The Roecker family has owned and operated the bank since 1959, and the popcorn has been a tradition for almost 30 years.

Monday-Thursday 9 a.m.-4 p.m.; Friday 9 a.m.-6 p.m. 785.867.2010.

HARRIS

Unincorporated

St. Patrick's Catholic Church: 33721 NW Crawford. From Walnut, 5 miles west and north on K-31. A predominantly Irish parish completed this church, also known as Emerald Church, in 1899. After a fire in the 1930s it was reconstructed, and in the 1940s famous crooner Bing Crosby donated the *Sacred Heart of Jesus* statue that stands on a side altar. The church bell tower was removed in the 1990s due to water damage. But even without it, the red-brick Italian Renaissance structure looks majestic on its hilltop location. Because of the church's remote location, the doors are kept locked, but you can visit the nearby cemetery or enjoy a short walkabout and a beautiful view of the countryside. 620.364.2416.

SCIPIO

Unincorporated

St. Boniface Catholic Church: 32292 NE Norton. Head for the steeple! Carmelite priests have served this German Catholic parish since the 1860s, and the site of the original church is commemorated in the nearby cemetery. There you

will also find more than two dozen Carmelite graves. The "new" limestone church, whose steeple can be seen from miles away, was completed in 1891. Always open. 785.835.6273.

Old Scipio Schoolhouses: 32528 NE Norton. Look for the red metal roofs and you'll have found the schoolhouses, now the Rockers Photography studio. Standing close to each other, the stone school was built in 1875, and the brick school in 1912.

Scipio Supper Club: From the St. Boniface church, ¼ mile north on Norton, ¾ mile west on Scipio, just south on Nebraska. Story swapping about the best steak houses always includes Scipio. Although known to area folks since the 1960s, it's fun for the newbie to find this out-of-the-way, residence-turned-restaurant that's kind of cozy and kind of dark—like a supper club should be. KC strips, ribeyes, t-bones, and fresh-cut fillets are the main attraction in this perfect atmosphere for a great steak. Wednesday, Friday-Sunday 6 p.m.-9 p.m. 785.835.6246. FB.

Bourbon County

BRONSON

Population 313

Civil War Statue: Charles and Spruce (City Park). Posed in the middle of the park is one of only four white-bronze (cast zinc) Civil War statues in the state. Dedicated in 1907, this sentinel style soldier is more commonly seen in northern states.

First Horseshoe Tournament:
A small blue sign on the east side of town tells you that Bronson was home to the first horseshoe pitching tournament in the world! Although not the same horseshoe pits as those in the 1909 tournament, the pits in City Park at Charles and Spruce welcome you to bring your own horseshoes and play.

FORT SCOTT

Population 7,934

Frontier Military Historic Byway:
From Fort Gibson, Oklahoma, through Fort Scott, and north to Fort Leavenworth, this byway follows the old military road established between 1838 and 1845 to connect these forts. Supporters of both the free-state and proslavery causes also used this road during our state's territorial period. 913.758.2948. travelks.org/ksbyways.

Trolley Tour:
231 E. Wall (Visitor Information Center). The trolley driver doubles as guide offering an informative 50-minute tour around town in an old-fashioned trolley. You'll learn about the national cemetery, "painted ladies," the horse race track, Mark Twain's secretary's studio, Pill Hill, and all sorts of intriguing Fort Scott history. It's a marvelous starting point for your Fort Scott explorations. Tour charge. 620.223.3566. fortscott.com/trolley.php.

Fort Scott National Historic Site (NRHP; 8 Wonders of Kansas History):
1 Old Fort Blvd. Named for General Winfield Scott, the fort originally was established in 1842. Soldiers garrisoned here until 1853 to maintain peace

between indigenous and relocated Indian tribes. In 1855 the government auctioned the fort structures to newly arriving settlers, and the area became the nucleus of the town of Fort Scott. Soon proslavery and free-state citizens were caught up in the turmoil of Bleeding Kansas as they argued over the question of statehood. During the Civil War, soldiers returned to Fort Scott and it became the supply and logistical center for the Union Army of the West. Today this restored post, administered by the National Park Service, showcases 20 historic structures (11 original and 9 reconstructed) with excellent exhibits inside the buildings and on the grounds. May-October, daily 9 a.m.-5 p.m.; November-April, daily 8:30 a.m.-4:30 p.m. Admission charge. 620.223.0310. nps.gov/fosc.

Union Block:
Old Fort Blvd. and Oak. The two-story wooden structure just outside the fort's entrance was built around 1864 to help Fort Scott (town and post) defend against anticipated Confederate advances. Fortunately, no attacks occurred.

Fort Scott National Cemetery (NRHP):
900 E. National. The trolley-guided and self-guided tours point out gravestones for U.S. Colored troops, Native American soldiers, buffalo soldiers, Confederates from the 1864 Mine Creek battle (*see* p. 265), and memorials to those who never came home from various wars. A large glacial stone marks the grave of illustrious poet Eugene Ware (1841-1911) who also was an editor, Civil War soldier, author, and founder of the first Fort Scott public library. In 1862 President Lincoln designated these grounds a national cemetery. A historic rostrum and an 1870 brick home also are within the cemetery. 620.223.2840. tinyurl.com/natlcemetery.

Lowell Milken Center for Unsung Heroes:
1 S. Main. This state-of-the-art exhibition space recognizes unsung heroes who stood up for others, often at great risk to themselves. Their compelling stories are told through interactive kiosks and displays. Two of these brave heroes are Irena Sendler, a Polish social worker who rescued more than 2,500 Jewish children during WWII; and Ken Reinhardt, who befriended the first black students to attend his high school in Little Rock, Arkansas, in 1957. Additional heroes are recognized every year. The center is named for international philanthropist and education supporter Lowell Milken. Monday-Friday 10 a.m.- 5 p.m.; Saturday 10 a.m-4 p.m. 620.223.1312. lowellmilkencenter.org.

Gordon Parks Museum (8 Wonders of Kansas Art):
2108 S. Horton (Fort Scott Community College campus).

Gordon Parks, born in Fort Scott in 1912, was a pioneer for blacks in the fields of photography, filmmaking, and writing. His photos depicting poverty and racism, among other subjects, were potent pictures in *Life* magazine for 20 years. Impressive exhibits and artifacts are on display to help you know Parks and the topics he cared about. See his writing desk, a film camera and tripod, and some of his iconic photographs including those of the Tuskegee Airmen, Muhammad Ali, and American Gothic. Monday-Friday 10 a.m.-4 p.m. Call ahead, 800.874.3722, ext. 5850. gordonparkscenter.org.

Gordon Parks Gravestone: From 23rd, 1½ miles south on U.S. 69, then ½ mile west on Indian. Look for a black vertical stone in the cemetery's north end (section 7) by the road. On either side of the stone is a Parks' poem, "Homecoming" and "A Sign by the Road." His flat gray gravestone is behind this marker.

Historic Walking and Driving Tour: 231 E. Wall. The walking or driving tour brochure describes 46 sites and provides an excellent overview of the town, particularly of the architectral history of downtown buildings. Brochures are available at the Visitor Information Center, 231 E. Wall, or at fortscott.com/visit.php.

Fort Scott Downtown Historic District (NRHP):
Oak to Third and Scott to National. Despite fires, including the most recent in 2005, and the federal urban renewal project in the 1960s that demolished 85 historic buildings, the downtown still boasts 58 contributing buildings to the historic district designation.

Downtown: The red-brick main street creates a nostalgic ribbon down the center of a charming downtown. Gift and antique shops and cozy restaurants occupy the late 1800s buildings, even though a fire in 2005 destroyed nine buildings in the first block of south Main.

Brick History: In the early 1900s a large brick plant here produced 100,000 bricks every 10 days. The bricks cost two to four cents each, and a daily shipment filled approximately a dozen rail cars. Fort Scott bricks were used in the construction of the Panama Canal and for the Indianapolis Motor Speedway (nicknamed the Brickyard when its track was bricked in 1911). More than 10 miles of brick streets remain in Fort Scott.

First Presbyterian Church (NRHP): 308 S. Crawford. Three members made up the total congregation of this church when it was formed in 1859. When the 1888 church was razed, many of the bricks and materials were reused to build the present 1924 church. The auditorium, which seats 1,000, held the funeral for famed photographer and native son Gordon Parks in 2006. Monday-Friday 8 a.m.-3 p.m.

First Congregational Church (NRHP): 502 S. National. The local preservation alliance saved this 1873 church from demolition in 1973 and restored it in the years following. It now serves as an event center.

Post Office Art: 120 S. National. *Border Gateways*, a 1937 oil on canvas by Oscar E. Berninghaus, depicts pioneers in covered wagons coming into the newly established Kansas Territory in 1854. This WPA Section artwork, although inside the post office, is not publicly accessible. The PO staff would love to show it to you, though. Just ask at the window.

Vindeo del Alamo Winery: 102 S. National. Bobby and Denise Duncan moved here from south Texas to start their winery. Using pesticide-free and chemical-free methods and retaining as many natural minerals in the wine as possible is a priority. Sample the results or buy bottles at the restored 1922 Beaux Arts style tasting room, and pay a visit to the art gallery. Friday-Sunday 12-6 p.m. 620.215.6311. vinedodelalamowinery.com.

Twin Mansions: 742 and 750 S. National. A Boston banker built these two grand red-brick homes for his daughters and their husbands, who were to open banks in Fort Scott. The mansions were nearing completion when the Panic of 1876 struck. With no further support from the East, the banks never opened in Fort Scott. The sisters returned to Boston, never sleeping in their beautiful homes.

Nate's Place: 750 S. National. Guests at Lyons Twin Mansions can enjoy a complimentary breakfast at Nate's, inside one of the mansions. Also available to the public, breakfast offers many options including eggs Benedict and the signature sausage burrito. An array of healthy choices are served for lunch, and evening fine dining is a culinary treat. Tuesday-Friday 9 a.m.-2 p.m.; Thursday-Saturday 5-8 p.m.; Saturday-Sunday 8 a.m.-2 p.m. 620.223.3644. lyonstwinmansions.com.

Crooner's Lounge: 117 S. Main. Soft jazz, songs of Sinatra and Como, or other mood-setting music is the appetizer for a fine evening of delicious food and sophisticated drinks. Start with charcuterie and cheese or a beet salad and a martini while you study the menu of steak, seafood, pasta, and chicken dishes. Desserts are worth singing about too. Crooner's offers an intimate setting for you to enjoy live music or a show next door in a lounge or in the attached historic Liberty Theatre. Wednesday-Saturday 5-9 p.m. 620.224.9787. FB.

More Good Restaurants: Find pizza, burgers, and seafood at these popular local eateries. Papa Don's Pizza (22 N. Main, 620.223.4171); Nugrille (24 N. National, 620.223.9949); Sharky's Pub & Grub (16 N. National, 620.223.4777); and Marsha's Great Plains Deli (6 W. 18th, 620.223.6432).

Lodging: Lyons Twin Mansions (KBBA, 620.223.3644, lyonstwinmansions.com); Courtland Hotel (620.223.0098, courtlandhotel.com); additional lodging (tinyurl.com/fslodging).

explorer extras...
In Fort Scott

Built of red brick and limestone in the Modern Eclecticism style, the 1930 Bourbon County courthouse stands with solid authority on the square at 210 S. National. Visitors are welcome to go to the third-floor courtroom (if court is not in session) to view the 1929 D.H. Overmeyer mural *Justice Enthroned*. A Civil War cannon, war memorials, and a GAR monument guard the front lawn. Monday- Friday 8:30 a.m.-4 p.m. 620.223.0780.

Built in the Beaux Arts style, the 1904 two-story red-brick Carnegie library (NRHP), 201 S. National, still operates as the Fort Scott bibliotheque. Monday-Friday 9 a.m.-6 p.m.; Saturday 9 a.m.-2 p.m.

In 1910 W.C. Gunn donated the land for Gunn Park, 1010 Park, and some 20 years later the WPA added the main lake and stone shelter houses and walls. Newer additions include an 18-hole disc golf course, numerous biking and hiking trails, a dog park, and a second lake stocked with trout. Paddleboat and canoe rentals are available at West Lake. 620.223.0550. tinyurl.com/gunnpark.

For years Gunn Park had its own caretaker who lived on site with his family. In 1927 caretaker E.V. Kelley built two doll houses for his young daughters Nadine and Jenny. Quite unique, they are more like miniature houses, built outdoors and made of stone. In 2016 the local Kiwanis Club restored and rebuilt the wee buildings, and as you enter Gunn Park you'll see them to the south. The abandoned caretaker's home is nearby.

Named the National Avenue Bridge and painted bright rust orange, the 1933 Marsh rainbow single-arch bridge stands out as it spans the Marmaton River. From 1st, ½ mile north on National.

Pine Lawn Cemetery was established circa 1869 by the Jewish burial society as the interment grounds for the Jewish community that thrived in Fort Scott in the 1880s and 1890s. From E. Wall, 3 miles south on U.S. 69/K-7, ½ mile west on Ironwood, then ¼ mile south on 215.

Guinness World Records abound in Fort Scott—four records, to be exact. A team of Fort Scott residents laid a mile of pennies in the fastest time; a team also laid the longest continual line of coins; one

SE

resident ate the most McDonald's quarter pound cheeseburgers in three minutes; and the Mercy Health Center built the world's largest teacup! Read about these records at the Visitor Information Center, 231 E. Wall. Monday-Friday 8 a.m.-5 p.m.; Saturday 10 a.m.-4 p.m. tinyurl.com/fsguinness. **ee**

explorer extras...
In Fulton

Population 161

Since 1927 traffic has crossed the Little Osage River on the sturdy Marsh rainbow single-arch bridge. From E. Spruce, go ½ mile north on 215 (Old U.S. 69) and drive over the bridge.

Three distinct eras and architectural designs are apparent in the former Fulton School (NRHP) at 408 W. Osage. The red-brick two-story school building was built in 1917, the stone gymnasium was a 1936 WPA project, and the brick one-story cafeteria was added in 1964. Closed as a school in 1978, the building is now a community center. **ee**

explorer extras...
In Mapleton

Population 83

Some say it's like being in the Ozarks! Opened in 2003, Kansas Rocks Recreation Park provides trails for mountain bikers, hikers, utility vehicles, and four-wheel-drive vehicles (5 mph speed limit). As you might expect, you'll come across plenty of rocks! What you might not expect is the 200-foot elevation change in these 400 acres. Kanrocks, as the park is known, is a wonderful getaway to enjoy the outdoors in a beautiful rocky terrain. March-January, Saturday 8 a.m.-5 p.m. and Sunday 8 a.m.-4 p.m. Admission charge. 620.829.5328. kscrockspark.com. **ee**

Chase County

Once 400,000 square miles of tallgrass prairie covered North America. Now less than 4 percent remains—most of it in the Flint Hills of Kansas. It has never been plowed under because the steely flint close to the surface impedes even the best efforts of the plow shear. The gray and white rock exposed on the prairie, and which you can readily see dotting the hillsides, is interlayered limestone and flint, more scientifically known as chert. Flint, which is composed of the crystalline compound silica, was formed in this area more than 250 million years ago.

Each spring about 100,000 stocker cattle from all over the United States come to the Chase County prairie to graze for 90 to 150 days (between May and July) on some of the most nutritious grass in the world. On an average, most cattle gain two pounds per day during their visit to the lush Flint Hills.

AROUND THE COUNTY

Flint Hills Scenic Byway: The tallgrass prairie takes center stage for 47 miles between Council Grove and Cassoday on K-177. Expansive panoramic vistas of the glorious Flint Hills are punctuated with wildflowers during the warm months. 620.273.8469. travelks.com/ksbyways.com.

Tallgrass Prairie National Preserve (8 Wonders of Kansas): 2480B K-177. From Cottonwood in Strong City, ¾ mile west on U.S. 50, then 2¼ miles north on K-177. This National Park Service preserve protects and interprets the nationally significant—and vanishing—tallgrass prairie ecosystem. Choose from a variety of self-guided tours, or check the schedule at the visitor center for an informative bus tour through the prairie. The buildings of Stephen Jones' 1881 Spring Hill Ranch (NRHP) are open during the summer and include the massive three-story limestone barn and the majestic ranch headquarters. Also on the preserve is the one-room Lower Fox Creek School (NRHP), a lonesome stone schoolhouse that stands at the turnaround point of the Southwind Nature Trail, one of several hiking trails on the preserve. Trails open 24 hours; visitor center, daily 9 a.m.-4:30 p.m. For tours, call 620.273.8494. nps.gov/tapr.

Tallgrass Prairie Hiking Trails: Lace up your hiking boots and get ready to see a world like no other, which includes sharing this unique space with the great American bison. The Tallgrass Prairie National Preserve has more than 40 miles of backcountry hiking trails deemed moderately difficult and ranging from 4 to 13 miles in length. No pets are allowed on the backcountry trails, but four frontcountry trails are pet friendly. Trails open 24 hours. Maps are available at the preserve's visitor center and at tinyurl.com/tpnptrails.

BAZAAR

Unincorporated

Sharpes Creek Scenic Back Road: Back roads beckon you to follow them for an immersion into the Flint Hills scenery. Essentials to have with you are a spare tire, road map (often no cell service), and water. This 17-mile gravel drive through the rolling hills is especially good during the early summer or early fall when the wildflowers and grasses are at their glorious peak. From Palmer, ¼ mile east on Sharpes Creek across the railroad tracks, continue 11 miles stairstepping south and east on Sharpes Creek, then 6 miles west on 50 (becomes Little Cedar Creek) going toward Matfield Green. Grasses, creeks, pasture, cattle, and expanse accompany your route.

CEDAR POINT

Population 27

Historic Stone Mill: From U.S. 50, ½ mile south on 1st. The 1875 multistory Drinkwater & Schriver mill (NRHP) still stands on the banks of the Cottonwood River. And in the nick of time efforts are ongoing to save and restore this elegant piece of history, with a future addition of a museum. The best views of the old mill are from the street and the bridge, and visitors are welcome to walk by to see

the architecture. The original wooden water wheel is a clue to how special this site will be when finished. 816.808.1610. cedarpointmill.com.

Historic Bridge: The 1916 Cottonwood River Pratt truss bridge (NRHP) stands about ¾ mile west of Cedar Point on Main. It's a thrill to drive over these old bridges, and you can stop mid-bridge to take pictures of the river.

CLEMENTS

Unincorporated

Clements Stone Arch Bridge (NRHP): From U.S. 50, ½ mile southeast on G, then 1,000 feet south on a field driveway. Your destination is one of the most picturesque bridges in the state. With double arches, the Clements Bridge is one of the longest (127 feet), and between the arches an embossed stone records that the L.P. Santy Company was the architect for this 1886 bridge. The road was moved to save the bridge, and fundraising efforts hope to ensure its preservation.

Silver Creek Bridge: From G, ¼ mile northeast on U.S. 50, then 1 mile north on Fp. The declining but still charming stone single-arch bridge was built in 1900. It's a rarely visited structure, but make this short drive to see it before it succumbs to nature.

First Female Tattoo Artist: 6 miles south on G, 2 miles east on 100, the 1 mile south on J to Homestead Cemetery. A native of Lyon County, Kansas, Maud Stevens Wagner began a circus career in the early 1900s. After

leaving the circus she and her husband, Gus, traveled the vaudeville and county fair circuit as "tattooed attractions" while plying their trade. Both are buried in this rural cemetery. Maud was known as America's "First Lady Tattooer," as her gravestone clearly states. Inspired by Maud, entrepreneurs have opened Maud's Tattoo Company in Emporia, 720 Commercial.

Flying W Ranch: South of Clements. Josh and Gwen Hoy will customize your visit to their 7,000-acre cattle ranch whether you want to stay overnight or go horseback riding, fishing, hiking, help with a cattle drive, or watch a prairie burn. The many activities create a grand Flint Hills experience. 620.340.2801. flinthillsflyingw.com.

SE

COTTONWOOD FALLS

Population 874

Chase County Courthouse (NRHP; 8 Wonders of Kansas Architecture): 300 Pearl. The red roof on this 1873 limestone structure is no ordinary one, in fact every part of this majestic courthouse is quite extraordinary. John Haskell, the main architect for the state capitol, chose the Second Empire style for this structure. Standing in grand splendor at the south end of

Broadway, this oldest continuously operating courthouse in the state features a walnut staircase that leads to a bird's-eye view of the city from the third-story oval window. A lesser-known point of interest is the jail, which was used until 1971. Monday-Friday 8 a.m.-5 p.m. For tours, call 620.273.8469.

Historic Bridge and Dam:
From Main, ¼ mile north on Walnut (K-177), then southeast on an unnamed road. From the 1914 Cottonwood River Bridge (NRHP) you have a lovely view of the river and dam. In 1860, a drought year, cottonwood logs were used to form a dam that was needed to create water power for the grist mill. Later, a more solid dam was built with native limestone but eventually it was covered with concrete.

Community Connection Trail:
The Cottonwood River Bridge is the trailhead for this one-way, nearly two-mile sidewalk trail that parallels K-177 and leads you to Strong City. From there it connects with the Bottomand Nature Trail on the Tallgrass Prairie National Preserve.

Chase County Historical Museum (NRHP):
303 Broadway. The 1882 Chase County National Bank building is now home to colorful county history and includes two floors of exhibits about the nationally known Roberts rodeo family, area landmarks, and the nearby 1931 plane crash that killed eight including Notre Dame football coach Knute Rockne. A 1932 Rockne Studebaker, named in his memory, is also displayed. Tours to the crash site can be arranged. Tuesday-Saturday 10 a.m.-3 p.m. Donation welcome. 620.273.8500. FB.

Downtown:
With Broadway acting as the red (brick) carpet, it guides you through the Cottonwood Falls historic shopping district. A flag outside a shop means the door is open so please come inside. Hours are irregular as artists are sometimes at art shows or on location creating.

Emma Chase Friday Night Music (8 Wonders of Kansas Customs):
Music plays indoors at the Prairie PastTimes, 220½ Broadway, or on pleasant evenings out on the street at 331 Broadway (bring your lawn chairs). This tradition was started in 1999 by Sue and Monty Smith of the Emma Chase Cafe, and the event is named for this former cafe. Music night has grown in popularity to become part of the iconic fabric of Kansas. Each Friday night the strains of bluegrass, country folk, gospel, or old-time rock and roll envelop downtown. Friday 7:30-10 p.m. (except the first Friday in June during the Strong City Rodeo and on holidays). For Friday night schedules, call 620.273.8469. FB.

Prairie PastTimes:
220½ Broadway. An artist cooperative shares the distinctive art deco 1939 WPA building with

City Hall. The works of more than 30 Flint Hills artists and artisans come together in a joyous riot of color, textures, and creativity. April-December, Tuesday-Sunday 11 a.m.-5 p.m. and Friday 7-10 p.m.; January-March, Friday 11 a.m.-5 p.m. and 7-10 p.m., Saturday 11 a.m.-5 p.m., and Sunday 10 a.m.-3 p.m. 620.273.6003. FB.

Symphony in the Flint Hills Office and Gallery:
331-333 Broadway. The Symphony in the Flint Hills is an event that everyone should attend at least once in his or her lifetime. A symphony of music amidst wildflowers on the tallgrass prairie is an unforgettable experience, and thousands travel to the Flint Hills on a single summer day each year to hear a glorious concert by the Kansas City Symphony. In a lovely setting, you can bask in nature as the sun sets and cowboys herd cattle along the Flint Hills horizon. Symphony tickets are available here, and you can also shop and view special exhibits in the adjoining gallery. Daily 10 a.m.- 5 p.m. 620.273.8955. FB.

Flint Hills Gallery:
321 Broadway. Artist Judy Mackey finds inspiration for her paintings on location in the Flint Hills. The results are beautiful pastel scenes of nature and area landmarks, which adorn the walls of this tasteful gallery designed by her artist husband, Ken. The gallery also displays Ken's custom boot jacks, mirrors, and hat racks, which incorporate brass, copper, silver, leather, and wood. Browse and buy and take home a Flint Hills memory created by Judy or Ken. Tuesday-Saturday 10 a.m.-4 p.m. 620.273.6454. flinthillsgallery.com.

Salty Cow Mercantile:
322 Broadway. You'll find western wear, women's fashions, home

decor, and boots for the entire family inside this handsome two-story building that dates to 1927. Monday-Friday 10 a.m.- 6 p.m.; Saturday 10 a.m.-5 p.m. 620.273.6381. FB.

Tallgrass Antiques:
312 Broadway. Antique pieces, architectural salvage, and repurposed furniture provide wonderful decorator options for the creative homeowner. Friday-Saturday 10 a.m.-5 p.m.; Sunday 12:30-5 p.m. FB.

Cottonwood Falls Collectables: 311 Broadway. Enjoy your discovery of antiques and vintage, handmade, and upcycled items. Friday-Saturday 10 a.m.-5 p.m. 620.220.0212. FB.

Reyer's Country Store:
501 E. 7th. The sign above the door says "Feed & More" and that's what you'll find inside this family-owned feed (and more) store. Even if you don't need livestock supplies, stop in for utilitarian wares, handcrafted baskets, clothing, bird products, or more. Monday-Friday 8:30 a.m.- 5:30 p.m.; Saturday 8 a.m.- 12 p.m. 620.273.6229. FB.

Grand Central Hotel and Grill: 215 Broadway. Some of the best steaks in the state are served inside this 1884 hotel. A 1995 renovation exposed the building's original brick walls and stockyard brick floors that create a true Old West feel. Owner Suzan Barnes recommends the Grand Angelo steak as a filet or strip with shrimp or sauteed mushrooms. Ten oversized guest rooms, each branded in Chase County history, offer plush accommodations. Monday-Saturday 11 a.m.-8 p.m. 620.273.6763. grandcentralhotel.com.

Keller Feed & Wine Co.:
317 Broadway. Owners Bryan and Janice Keller Williams invite you to step up to the counter and order from a menu of old favorites such as a slab of smoked ham steak on a bed of garlic mashers with fried egg, smoked sausage, bacon, and covered in country gravy. Baked beans are served with a hint of sweet smoke and cloves in a Ball glass canning jar. Wine and beer also are available. The Williams' grow their own produce with help from the local high school ag class. Monday-Friday 7:30-11 a.m.; Friday 5-8:30 p.m.; Saturday 9 a.m.-8:30 p.m.; Sunday 9 a.m.-2 p.m. FB.

Lodging:
Clover Cliff Bed and Breakfast (KBBA, 620.343.0621, clovercliffranch.com); Grand Central Hotel (620.273.6763, grandcentralhotel.com); Mill Stream Motel (620.273.8114); Spring Street Retreat (316.393.3194, springstreetcwf.com); Stonehorse Bed and Breakfast (785.497.2904; stonehorsebedbreakfast.com); eight additional guest houses, retreats, and Camp Wood (chase countychamber.org/lodging).

**explorer extras...
In Cottonwood Falls**

Find an extensive display of Indian artifacts and arrowhead collections of longtime area residents Frank and George Roniger at the Roniger Museum, 315 Union. Tuesday-Wednesday, Friday-Sunday 1-5 p.m. 620.273.6412.

The Chase County All Veterans Memorial traces the history of U.S. military battles and includes such lesser-known conflicts as the 1916-1917 raid into Mexico, the 1900-1901 Boxer Rebellion, and the early-1800s Barbary Wars, even if Chase countians weren't involved. Plaques are within stone bases. From Walnut (K-177), just east on 210 into Swope Park.

The 1904 limestone Cottonwood Falls grade school with 1915 and 1962 additions patiently waits at 401 Maple for its next use.

Born in Cottonwood Falls, Dudley Doolittle (1881-1957) was a three-term U.S. congressman and, among other positions, held the unenviable post of federal Prohibition director for Kansas in 1920. He erected a tall rough-cut granite obelisk in honor of his parents, Joseph and May Doolittle, in Prairie Grove Cemetery. Plaques on either side of the monument share character descriptions of each parent. Also buried in the cemetery is Stephen Fuqua (Steve) Jones of Spring Hill Ranch, which is now part of the Tallgrass Prairie National Preserve. From Broadway, Prairie Grove Cemetery is 1¼ miles west on Main (becomes Lake).

Prairie vegetation grows naturally at this scenic byway overlook, which offers a

SE

360-degree view of the endless, rolling hills. Signs interpret the Flint Hills wildflowers and grasses, cattle, and wildlife. From 4th, 3 miles south on K-177. **ee**

ELMDALE

Population 54

Historic Buildings:
Although abandoned, some buildings still stand, lonely but defiant. A cornerstone of the native limestone City Hall states that it was built in 1936 by the WPA. The smooth stone face of the 1898 Peoples Exchange Bank appears at odds with the building's exterior side walls. On Campbell, the two-story limestone school, minus its bell tower, was constructed in 1895. Nearby is a 1915 red-brick auditorium.

Historical Markers:
Silver plaques on two limestone monoliths provide background about the 1951 flood (a line marks where the water crested) and the Jeffrey Brothers Mercantile Store (1872-1961).

Lake and Waterfall Scenic Drive:
From Spruce, 6 miles east on Lake. A narrow blacktop back road takes you on a scenic route from Elmdale to Cotton-wood Falls. At the Chase County State Lake scenic waterfalls might be flowing (depending on rainfall) in the early spring. To find them, from the dam on the lake's north end, walk ¼ mile to the east end of the dam and follow the primitive trail north to the falls. Keith Stokes, Kansas Explorer #5648, reports that these are some of the most beautiful waterfalls in the state. tinyurl.com/chasefalls.

MATFIELD GREEN

Population 46

Pioneer Bluffs: 695 K-177. Thanks to the Pioneer Bluffs Foundation you can tour this Flint Hills ranch (NRHP) home-steaded by Charles Rogler in 1859. Self-guided tours take visitors to the 1872 barn, the 1916 granary, the 1915 main barn, the windmill, and the garden. Guided tours of the 1908 Rogler family home also are available. The Pioneer Bluffs Foundation does a tremendous job preserving and restoring this historic ranch and sharing its connection to this tallgrass country. April-November, Friday-Saturday 10 a.m.-5 p.m. 620.753.3484. pioneerbluffs.org.

The Bank: 102 N. Reed (K-177). Small-town but big art talent is exhibited in this 1933 one-story former bank building. Variety in subjects and art styles are the riches inside this

Bank, plus, friendly folks are happy to answer your questions about Flint Hills art, people, and scenery. You may want to make a deposit here by making a purchase! April-November, Friday-Saturday 10 a.m.-5 p.m.; Sunday 1-5 p.m. 316.217.3319. matfieldgreen.org/thebank.

Bill McBride Studio:
640 K-177. Bill creates thought-provoking and imaginative sculptures using sticks, stones, bones, wire, and other bits of flotsam found on his 40 acres of Flint Hills prairie. How he combines natural and gathered items is creative genius! Call ahead, 620.481.6074. billmcbridestudio.com.

Buckeye Creek Art Studio:
2369 ZZ. Dale Hartley's exceptional artistry is in the form of subtly colorful glazed clay vessels made from local earthen materials, and in beautiful oil paintings that similarly reflect the colors of nature. Call ahead, 620.279.4543. dalehartley.weebly.com.

Larson and Rockne Memorials:
I-35 milepost 97 (Matfield Green rest area). A memorial honors Al Larson who gave his life saving fellow travelers in a flash flood near here on August 30, 2003. A monument to Knute Rockne, legendary Notre Dame football coach who died in a 1931 plane crash near this point, stands outside the service area. Inside, large photographic panels depict various aspects of Rockne's life. For tours to the crash site, call 620.273.8500.

STRONG CITY

Population 466

Santa Fe Depot and Railroad Park:
204 W. Topeka. The town was named for William Barstow Strong who was vice-president and general manager of the Santa Fe railway before becoming

president in 1881. It's fitting that City Hall is now located in this 1913 red-brick Mission style depot (NRHP). Historic photos and memorabilia line the walls. Monday-Friday 8 a.m.-4 p.m. 620.273.6345.

Stone Arch Bridge and Trail:

204 W. Topeka (Santa Fe depot). Fox Creek Bridge (NRHP) is a beautiful 1898 double-arch bridge in the wooded creek section of the Community Connection Trail, a biking and walking trail that connects Strong City with the Tallgrass Prairie National Preserve. The trail runs from the depot, ¼ mile north on Cottonwood, 3 blocks west on 6th, ¼ mile north on Pine under the U.S. 50 overpass, then ¼ mile west on 227 to the bridge. From here you can continue to the Tallgrass Prairie National Preserve Bottomland Trail. tinyurl.com/tpnptrails.

Strong City Opera House (RHKP):

501 Cottonwood. The 1901 former opera house, community center, and movie theater was constructed with native limestone from a nearby quarry, the same quarry that provided stone for the east wing of the state capitol. Renewed preservation efforts keep hopes alive that the building will be a viable resource for the community in the future.

Ad Astra Food & Drink:

318 Cottonwood. You've reached the culinary stars when you dine at Ad Astra in this historic Flint Hills town. Old favorites are prepared with a distinct new flair using locally sourced and fresh ingredients whenever possible. Even the fried brussel sprouts and homemade potato chips receive rave reviews as do the bison burger and the homemade desserts. Kansas craft beers are always available in the full bar. Thursday 5-8 p.m.; Friday-Sunday 11 a.m.-9 p.m. 620.273.8440. FB.

explorer extras... In Strong City

The city's railroad history theme continues at the community-built Strong City Park at 125 5th. Multiple play structures allow little engineers to climb, swing, and slide. **ee**

Chautauqua County

CEDAR VALE

Population 555

Hewins Park Pavilion (NRHP):

101 Salebarn. Since 1913 generations of Chautauqua County residents have attended events in this extraordinary structure. Inside, you can't help but exclaim over the impressive wood-frame gable and six radial arched wooden beams supporting the 40-foot-high roof. The pavilion is open on three sides allowing crosswinds to keep people cool during summer events. On the semicircular stage many bands have played over the years on hot summer nights while dancers waltzed, jitterbugged, discoed, two-stepped, and generally rocked across the concrete floor. Hewins Park, donated by local rancher Ed Hewins in 1882, is known for its large cedar trees, what one might expect in Cedar Vale.

Veterans War Memorial Park:

Monroe and Cedar. In the heart of downtown Cedar Vale is a thoughtfully designed veterans memorial with brick flooring and rough-cut limestone monuments bearing the names of veterans of wars from WWI to Operation Enduring Freedom.

Cedar Vale Museum:

618 Cedar. From 1904 when the L.C. Adam Mercantile opened in this building (NRHP) to when it closed its doors in 1953, this two-story brick structure served the community well. In 1970 the museum claimed it as its home and now it's stocked with community history including miniature replicas of old buildings, early homes, churches, stores, and other buildings that made up early Cedar Vale. Call ahead, 620.506.1260.

Hilltop Cafe:

1104 Walnut. A small-town cafe with local flavor puts out a fine, hand-breaded pork tenderloin sandwich, daily specials, hearty breakfasts, and a Sunday buffet. Monday-Saturday 6 a.m.-8 p.m.; Sunday 6 a.m.-2 p.m. 620.758.5075.

Otter Creek Bridge (NRHP):

From Caney, 3¼ miles north on 2. It's a pretty little bridge situated around a slight bend in the road. One of four camelback truss bridges remaining in Kansas, this bridge with a wooden-deck and 122-foot single span was built in 1936 by the WPA. Can you see the five angles on the truss that make it a camelback?

Big Caney River Bridge:

From Caney, ¾ mile east on Mill (becomes Heritage). Because Heritage was the original U.S. 166 many auto occupants have had the pleasure of crossing under the double rainbows of this 1930 Marsh arch bridge. It's still open to traffic, so you can cross it too!

SE

Caney River Pratt Truss Bridge: From Caney, ½ mile east on Mill, then ¼ mile north on a gravel road. Although it's closed to traffic, the bridge invites you to walk across it. Bridge fans will certainly notice that pins were used on this 1890s truss bridge instead of rivets!

CHAUTAUQUA

Population 108

Historic Chautauqua Springs:
From Main, ¼ mile east on Chautauqua. Osage Indians first enjoyed the medicinal benefits of these spring waters, and later the area became a popular healing resort hosting people from across the country, including Theodore Roosevelt and industrial tycoons of the era. In 1882 the springs were flowing at 180 gallons per hour. Two hotels, which long ago housed guests, are gone, but the old steps leading down to the drinking springs are yet evident. Today a rusted tea kettle, in a picturesque setting against the ruins, catches a small stream of ever-flowing spring water. Oaks and sycamores shade this tranquil healing place, and you may walk around the grassy, lush area where you'll find footbridges, picnic tables, and Initial Rock, a large boulder across the creek at the bottom of the cliff. Thanks go to the Green family for its efforts in preserving this historic area. 620.249.1981.

Black Dog Trail Campsite Marker:
K-99 and Olive. Beginning in 1803 Chief Black Dog and his Osage tribe traveled through this area twice a year on buffalo hunting trips. The sign here marks one of the Osage campsites on the hunting route, known as the Black Dog Trail (*see* p. 235).

ELGIN

Population 87

At some point around the turn of the century, Elgin was known as the biggest cattle shipping point in the world. By 1902 those days were over. An oil boom brought prosperity, but by 1924 the town had peaked. Today you can still see the second iteration of the sign that reads, "A Town Too Tough To Die," which stands in front of City Hall at Grand and Caney. Elgin had been a tough town but even by the late 1950s it was down to a liquor store, a filling station, and a cafe. When Margaret's Cafe closed in the early 1990s it was a sad end to a once prosperous, yet notorious, town. Today it feels a little "ghosty" as you drive down the wide bricked main street past the block of weathered downtown buildings.

Black Dog Trail Campsite Marker:
Grand and Main. The sign here marks one of the Osage campsites on the hunting route, known as the Black Dog Trail (*see* p. 235). Beginning in 1803 Chief Black Dog and his Osage tribe traveled through this area twice a year on buffalo hunting trips.

Cedar Creek Bridge (NRHP):
From Santa Fe, 1½ miles east on Wei Hockey (becomes Bronco). Built in 1927, this Marsh rainbow single-arch

bridge spans Cedar Creek. Remains of earlier bridge abutments are seen to the north.

Historic Railroad Bridge:
From Grand, ½ block north on Caney, 1¾ miles west on Dalton, then 1 mile north on 11. Drive the lush environs along the Caney River and look on the north side of the road to see the abandoned but still-solid stone railroad bridge built in 1886. Backtrack to Dalton and continue your scenic back road trip to Hewins (*see* next entry).

Elgin to Hewins Scenic Back Road:
From Grand, ½ block north on Caney, then 8½ miles west on Dalton. The drive west from Elgin is winding, tree-lined, and scenery-packed with rock outcroppings border-ing the narrow unpaved road. When you come to the little white Frontier Church you've made it to Hewins. In 1886 the Santa Fe railway made a station stop here for shipping cattle owned by Ed Hewins, one of the largest cattle ranchers in the world at the time.

Ozro Falls:
From Hewins, 1 block south on 8, 2 blocks west on Adams, 1¼ miles west on Dalton, 1 mile north and west on Eagle, then ½ mile north on 6th (no road sign). It's a bit of challenge to find this pictur-esque low-water bridge crossing the Caney River, and don't try to cross if the roads aren't dry. Stop at the big curve that leads down to the falls to survey the area before proceeding in

your vehicle. The falls are only about a three-foot drop but they extend from bank to bank across the river. The crossing is on the shallow limestone flat just above the falls, and is one of the prettiest scenes on Kansas back roads. Before pioneers settled here, this idyllic spot on Caney River was a campground for American Indians when they traveled the Black Dog Trail. Pioneers crossed here in covered wagons, and after settlement, the falls were a favorite picnic spot. The falls were named for a nearby town, now long gone.

Hewins to Cedar Vale Scenic Back Road:

From Dalton in Hewins, 3 miles north on 8, stairstep 5 miles west on Gallop, ¼ mile north on Heritage, ¼ mile west on Salebarn, then ½ mile northwest on Walnut. This route is on the cusp of the Chautauqua Hills and Osage Cuestas physio-graphic regions. Going west from Hewins you enter the Osage Cuestas and will see fewer trees and more level and open terrain.

explorer extras... In Niotaze

Population 80

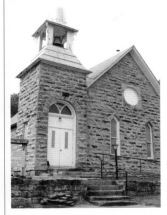

The church committee chose the lot at 301 N. F to build the Niotaze Methodist Episcopal Church (NRHP) so the congre-gation could view the valley

below. The pretty little church (complete with bell tower and steeple) was constructed in 1895 with rusticated sandstone quarried from the hill overlooking Niotaze. The church (now United Methodist) still operates and the view is still lovely. **ee**

explorer extras... In Peru

Population 133

About a half-mile east of Peru on the north side of U.S. 166 you can see the remains of a brick and tile plant that prospered around the turn of the 20th century. Drive by only. **ee**

SEDAN

Population 1,088

Hollow Park:
108 N. Sherman. Trash and junk once filled the creek, but the area has been transformed into a beautiful and tranquil site. A boardwalk

zigzags through flower beds then parallels the creek for a short distance to a small waterfall (if water is running). A gazebo and statue of Emmett Kelly accent a slope layered with vibrant flowers and shrubs. The 1874 St. Charles wooden one-room schoolhouse was moved to this location to add to the charm.

Red Buffalo Gift Shop:
107 E. Main. Art, upscale gifts, locally made products, gourmet foods, books, and small-batch Kansas roasted-coffee are a few of the delights at this classy

boutique. Thursday-Saturday 11 a.m.-5 p.m. 620.725.4022. FB.

Emmett Kelly Museum:
204 E. Main. Named for native son and famous circus clown Emmett Kelly (1898-1979), this museum features a small exhibit about Kelly's sad-faced character, Willie, and his circus career. Occupying a former opera house (RHKP) built in 1904, the museum also displays pieces of local history including a collection of about 75 radios and more than 1,500 decanters. June-August, Tuesday-Saturday 10 a.m.-5 p.m. 620.725.3193.

Buck's BBQ and Steakhouse:
1898 U.S. 166. A paleo dieters dream, Buck's fills up every hunter-gatherer with ribs, pulled pork, brisket, baked beans with brisket bits, steaks, shrimp, salads, daily specials, and more. A full bar is available. Monday-Saturday 11 a.m.-9 p.m. 620.725.5025. FB.

Green Door Cafe:
122 W. Main. On the other side of the green screen door you'll sit down to terrific burgers,

SE

breakfasts, and homemade desserts! Wednesday-Sunday 7 a.m.-7 p.m. 620.725.3280.

Main Street Cafe: 221 W. Main. If you're big into burgers, don't miss the Main Street. Referred to as the "Oh my!" burger, on the menu it's called the Hot Hamburger and is topped with a choice of fries, tots or curly fries, smothered with white gravy, and capped with grilled onions. Breakfast is served all day. Daily 6 a.m.-8 p.m. 620.725.3376. FB.

Safari Mark's Bar and Bistro: 102 W. Main. Take a seat on the first floor of the historic Bradford Hotel (NRHP) to enjoy burgers, steak, seafood, a full bar, a side of live music, and a dash of fun. Thursday-Saturday 11 a.m.-9 p.m. 620.725.4011. FB.

Scenic Butcher Falls: From Chautauqua, ¾ mile west on Main (becomes U.S. 166 Business), 1¼ miles northwest on K-99, then 3 miles west on Kansas. Park just off the road, go through the gate (clearly marked Butcher Falls; make sure you close the gate behind you), and follow the path about 250 feet to a natural stone-walled pool. If Pool Creek is running (depends on rainfall) you'll see water descending 14 feet from a ravine and gloriously splashing into the pool. The falls are named for Preston Butcher who acquired the property in 1889.

Lodging: Cabin on the River (620.725.4022, theredbuffalo.com).

**explorer extras...
In Sedan**

All of downtown is known as the Yellow Brick Road. Sidewalks are marked with two parallel yellow stripes, and in between the stripes 11,500 bricks have been laid to form paths through downtown. The heart of Sedan is filled with 1880s buildings that are home to numerous stores including Ackarman Hardware, 160 E. Main, that dates to 1879.

The 1918 Chautauqua County courthouse, 215 N. Chautauqua, was the last courthouse in the state designed by architect George Washburn. This Modern Eclecticism structure built of red brick occupies a full block square just north of downtown. 620.725.5800.

Gregg Theatre, 116 S. Chautauqua, was constructed in the late 1930s and now operates as a nonprofit run by volunteers. First-run movies shown on weekends and community theater performances share the space. 620.725.5403. FB.

The Chautauqua Gemstone is a 140-ton sandstone rock that in 1996 found itself in the

way of the U.S. 166 road crew. Sedan tourism champion Nita Jones said of the rock, "The Chautauqua Gemstone is hard as a diamond, warm as a ruby, desirable as an emerald and looks like a pearl. It's a jewel of Kansas." The huge 30-foot-tall boulder was moved to the side of the road and there it still sits about 12 miles west of Sedan on U.S. 166.

A two-mile hiking and biking trail connects the Old City Lake (from U.S. 166, 5 miles north on K-99) and the New City Lake (from U.S. 166, 2 miles north on K-99). The Civilian Conservation Corps built the 1935 lake and WPA funds yielded shelters and picnic tables. The 1965 city lake was constructed to supply the city's water. 620.288.1100. tinyurl.com/sedanoldlake. **ee**

Cherokee County

Kansas' Historic Route 66 Byway: Of the 2,448 miles of the famous Route 66, 13¼ miles pass through Kansas across the southeast corner of Cherokee County. It may be a short stretch but it has plenty of great explorer attractions—a charming narrow road, rainbow arch bridge, throwback market, a WPA park with a shallow wading creek, and three delightful towns. Long before this section of road became a Kansas Historic Byway, it was part of a new national highway network so designated on November 11, 1926. A bypass built in the early 1960s resulted in less traffic on the old route, leaving it for locals and for tourists to enjoy the nostalgic journey. 620.429.0190. travelks.com/ksbyways.

Frontier Military Historic Byway:

A designated Kansas Scenic Byway, the Kansas section of the military road starts at the Oklahoma border and passes through Cherokee County as it heads north, ending at the intersection of K-5 and K-7 in Leavenworth. Originally known as the Fort Leavenworth-Fort Gibson Military Road, this route was built in 1838-1840 to accommodate soldiers traveling between military posts. travelks.com/ksbyways.

BAXTER SPRINGS

Population 4,124

Route 66 Visitor Center (NRHP):

940 Military. You might guess from its iconic cottage style that this visitor center had a previous life as a Phillips 66 gas station. Built in 1930, it saw years of activity from Route 66 travelers. It now represents the past and is a sweet stop. Irregular hours. 620.856.2385. tinyurl.com/baxvisitor.

Baxter Springs Historical Museum:

740 East. Route 66, lead and zinc mining, Civil War battles, the Osage Indian tribe, and Mickey Mantle—you'll find excellent interpretations of these and more historic events and people inside this 20,000-square-foot museum. One of the most unique displays is the world's longest (1,100 feet) hand-carved wooden chain, carved from 1981 to 1994 by James Porter. Porter and his chain made an appearance on *The Tonight Show* in 1989. Continue your search for history

by picking up walking/driving tour brochures—for Civil War and historic sites and for downtown historic buildings. Tuesday-Saturday 10:30 a.m.-4:30 p.m.; Sunday 1-4 p.m. 620.856.2385. baxterspringsmuseum.org.

Black Dog Trail Marker:

740 East. Chief Black Dog was born around 1780 and for a time his migratory tribe's base camp was near present Coffeyville. In 1803 his Osages blazed what is now known as the Black Dog Trail, a 200-mile passage from present Baxter Springs to present Oxford. Thousands of Osages followed it on their semi-annual trek to hunt buffalo. Eventually, in the 20th century, the trail evolved into highways. Seventh Street was part of the trail and is designated by a historical marker north of the Historical Museum.

Battle of Baxter Springs:

198 E. 6th. Also known as the Baxter Springs Massacre, on October 6, 1863, William Quantrill's Confederate guerillas attacked Fort Blair in Baxter Springs. Soldiers at the fort fought off the attackers with the help of a Howitzer, but on leaving Fort Blair, the guerrillas came upon a Union wagon train led by General James Blunt. The Confederates, greatly outnumbering the Union forces, tragically massacred most of Blunt's command. A replica of the earth and log Fort

Blair is at this site, and a kiosk provides information.

Soldiers' Lot:

Baxter Springs Cemetery. From Military, 2 miles west on 12th/U.S. 166. Designated as an official Soldiers' Lot by the National Cemetery Administration, it is the final resting place for those killed in the 1863 Battle of Baxter Springs and other area engagements. The tall monument of a soldier with his hand over his rifle muzzle is the cemetery's centerpiece. The names of those who died are inscribed on it, and the men are buried in a common grave. A fence surrounding the plot is formed with cannon barrels protruding from the ground. Simple white gravestones for veterans from all wars flank the monument.

Rial A. Niles House (NRHP):

605 E. 12th. This 1870 red-brick home is impressive with a central cupola topping the Italianate structure. It also features walk-out windows and ornamental porch posts and arches. Built for business entrepreneur Rial Niles and his wife, Mary, the house has served as a social club, a church meeting place, and a residence. The stoutly built structure has survived two tornadoes, one in 1895 and more recently in 2014. Drive by only.

Outdoor Bas-Relief Mural:

1201 Military (south side of the American Bank). Images of mining, cowtown days, Osage Indians, Route 66, the famous wooden chain, and more town history compose this unusually

SE

designed mural. It was created in 1995 by Paula Collins of Denton, Texas. tinyurl.com/baxbasrelief.

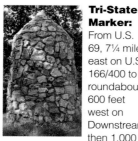

Tri-State Marker:
From U.S. 69, 7¼ miles east on U.S. 166/400 to a roundabout, 600 feet west on Downstream, then 1,000 feet south on an unnamed gravel road. At the dead end you'll come to an uncommon stone obelisk monument. Built in 1938 by the National Youth Administration, the marker designates the junction of Kansas, Missouri, and Oklahoma. The original stone marker endures, but unfortunately other tri-state signs have been stolen.

Angels on the Route:
1143 Military. The original owner of this lunch and gift shop liked angels, thus her business name. Inside a renovated 1865 dry goods store, Angels is a heavenly spot for lunch, a snack break for dessert and coffee, and souvenir shopping. Wednesday-Thursday 11 a.m.-3 p.m.; Friday-Saturday 11 a.m.-7 p.m. 620-856-2266. FB.

Good Restaurants:
Baxter Springs Smokehouse (2320 Military, 620.856.3287); Rice House Chinese (2932 Military, 620.856.2828); and Weston Cafe (1737 Military, 620.856.4414).

Kansas Route 66 Historic District (NRHP):
From Military, 5 blocks west on 3rd, then 3 miles north on Willow. Between the Willow Creek bridge and the Marsh rainbow single-arch Brush Creek bridge is a stretch of Route 66 that retains many remnants from its original construction—narrow road (only 25 feet wide), unpaved shoulders, box culverts, and the tree-lined roadsides. Drive this back route slowly and soak it in. It's subtly sublime.

explorer extras... In Baxter Springs

For a view of the lovely Spring River, from Route 66, travel 1 mile east on E. 12th to Riverside Park.

Johnston Library (NRHP), 210 W. 10th, has the appearance of a courthouse because in 1872 it was intended to be one. It was never used for that purpose, but it was a city hall and a college before Peter Johnston donated it to the city in 1905 for its library. It still serves as the town library.

A Baxter Springs veterans memorial at 13th and Park honors local veterans and the memory of all American veterans. Images of military action are superimposed on four large free-standing granite stones that represent each branch of the military. **ee**

COLUMBUS

Population 3,223

Cherokee County Courthouse:
110 W. Maple. Silver wheat shafts on the facade of this 1955 courthouse add an artistic glint, but the 1919 Seth Thomas clock in the 40-foot tower on the courthouse lawn is the real gem. Purchased as a memorial to WWI servicemen, the clock was placed in the 1889 courthouse tower.

Following the demise of the old courthouse, the original clock parts were discarded, and not until 1983 were they found and reassembled. One of the clock faces is on the current courthouse; the other three are on the free-standing tower containing the clock, which bongs on the hour and half-hour. Monday-Friday 9 a.m.-4:30 p.m. 620.429.2042.

Pop Bottle Collection:
110 W. Maple (county courthouse). How many courthouses display a collection of 1,300 pop bottles from all over the world? Courthouse maintenance man Ralph Houser has collected pop bottles for more than 34 years, and some (1,300) are displayed inside the courthouse. In addition to these he has another 2,000 bottles at his home! To see the collection, stop at the county clerk's office and ask for Ralph. Monday-Friday 9 a.m.-4:30 p.m. 620.429.9558.

Courthouse Square:
Iron cutouts of Columbus' ship the *Santa Maria* are docked on the square's street poles (remember, you're in Columbus). You can park in the middle of the street around the square,

which is bordered with late-1880s buildings.

Columbus Museum:

100 S. Tennessee. The ball of string you see here might be the second most famous one in the state, but it claims television fame! Ed Fouts, who wound this 826-pound ball (468 miles of string!), appeared on *I've Got a Secret* in 1953. Other exhibits feature Columbus native Merle Evans (bandleader for the Ringling Bros. and Barnum & Bailey Circus), local athletes, agriculture, history, industry, and downtown businesses. A driving tour brochure of historical homes and points of interest is available here and at the chamber office, 320 E. Maple. Tuesday-Saturday 1-5 p.m. 620.429.2160.

Post Office Art: 320 E. Maple.

Stop at the chamber office and ask to see the Section art sculpture on display here. Moved from the post office, the bas-relief is a sand sculpture entitled *R.F.D.* and produced by Waylande Gregory in 1940. You'll also see a large 1987 mural of historic Columbus by Duke Wellington, who died before the mural's completion. Monday-Friday 8:30 a.m.-2:30 p.m.

T.J. Losey Memorial:

1130 SE Wyandotte (City Cemetery). Take a seat on a bench as you admire the detail on the larger-than-life monument to Thomas J. Losey (1846-1936), a member of the 14th Kansas Cavalry during the Civil War. The memorial features a statue of Losey dressed in uniform with a sword on his belt and holding a rifle. A tree theme runs through the elaborate Losey monument extending to the benches and chairs that surround the family plot. T.J. lived to age 89, but his family died young—wife Flora Bell at age 47 and their two daughters as young children. The cut-off branches on the sculpted tree stump symbolize life cut short.

Lodging: Maple Common Hotel (620.429.3130, mapleuncommonhotel.com); Pitcher Pump (620.429.2776, pitcherpumpbedbreakfast.com); Smittle House (620.429.2420, smittlehouse.com); additional lodging (tinyurl.com/columbuslodging).

explorer extras... In Columbus

The Ottawa architectural firm of George P. Washburn and Son designed the one-story red-brick Carnegie library (NRHP), 205 N. Kansas, completed in 1913 and still serving the town.

The WPA built the 1930s stone structures, including the retaining wall and the interestingly designed (no longer used) swimming pool bathhouse, in City Park at Kansas and Grave. **ee**

GALENA

Population 2,994

Galena Mining and Historical Museum: 319 W.

7th (K-26). Amazing photos and artifacts capture the region's mining days from 1877 to the 1920s, when lead and zinc were the heart and soul of Galena. Once you visit this museum, inside a KATY railroad depot, you'll have a new appreciation of this town and its history. June-September, Monday-Friday 10 a.m.-4 p.m.; October-May, Monday, Wednesday, Friday 1-3:30 p.m. Donation welcome. 620.783.2192.

Schermerhorn Park:

3501 S. Main. From 7th, 2¼ miles south on Main/K-26. Just before Shoal Creek Bridge, turn east into the park. The arching entrance gate, stone terraces, and retaining walls, built by the WPA in the early 1930s, are fascinating features and transport you back to an earlier time. Wade or take a refreshing dip in the cool shallow waters of the spring-fed Shoal Creek, just as Route 66 travelers have done since the 1920s. Follow the drive to the parking lot behind the superintendent's house to find a wooded trail that leads you past limestone bluffs covered with lush Ozark vegetation and back to Schermerhorn Cave. Legend says the cave was a hideout for Jesse James. The spring that flows from the cave is home to the dark-sided salamander, the cave salamander, and the gray-bellied salamander, all of which are on the Kansas endangered species list. 620.783.5265.

Southeast Kansas Nature Center: 3511 S.

Main (Schermerhorn Park). On top of the elaborate WPA

SE

stone terraces, the handsome and modern nature center is in an excellent setting to help you discover the intricacies of Ozark Plateau flora and fauna. Watch small, living animals, use interactive displays to learn more about the threatened and endangered species that call this area home, and step out onto the wraparound deck to spot birds and other wildlife. A large collection of American Indian artifacts is also on display. Tuesday-Saturday 10 a.m-4 p.m.; Sunday 1-4 p.m. 620.783.5207. FB.

Schermerhorn House (NRHP): 803 E. 5th. The 1895 two-story Queen Anne home was originally the residence of prominent businessman Edgar Backus Schermerhorn, who donated the land for the park bearing his name. The house appears to have fallen on hard times, but it is still an impressive sight.

Pappy Litch Park: 500 block of S. Main. Named for a beloved local historian, the park features a gazebo and a granite monument honoring the mining history of Galena and the Will Rogers Highway (Route 66.) A federal weigh station that inspected commercial vehicles on Route 66 once stood on this spot.

Liberty Hall: 720 S. Main. Inside this 1887 restored IOOF building, now used for business offices, is a floor like nothing you've seen (or stepped on) before—you're walking on $4,000 worth of pennies! Do the math, kids. That's 400,000 pennies. It's thought to be the largest coin floor in the nation. The upper floor has been restored as an event center and features a copper ceiling and original wood beams and floor. The building occupants will gladly let you look around. 417.624.4444.

Main Street Deli: 5th and Main. Coming in for a bite to

eat, you'll find more than you expected. Gifts and art line your path back to the deli at the rear of this former Citizens State Bank. Try the house-smoked pulled pork sandwich on a Hawaiian bun, or any of the daily specials. Monday-Friday 10:30 a.m.-2:30 p.m. 620.783.5902. FB.

Streetcar Station Coffee Shop: 515 S. Main. You'll receive a warm Kansas greeting from owners Danny and Kathy Anderson and leave with a smile on your face. The Streetcar is a good station stop any-time, whether for biscuits and gravy, a homemade meatball grinder, a gourmet cup of cof-fee, or a smoothie. The shop's name pays homage to the streetcar that once ran on Main Street. A streetcar mural is an appropriate addition to the interior. Tuesday-Friday 6 a.m.-2 p.m.; Saturday 6 a.m.-12 p.m. 620.783.5554. FB.

Norma's Diner: 300 W. 7th. Home-style meals are the staple here, with a few surprises (like gyros) thrown into the menu mix. Norma's is a great choice for breakfast, especially for pancakes. Daily 7 a.m.-2 p.m. 620.383.1016. FB.

Mi Torito: 418 S. Main. A restored train depot is where you'll set your caboose down to dip chips in queso fundido while you wait for the sizzling fajitas. If you order the Kansas burrito you'll get a nod of approval from the waiter. Daily 11 a.m.-9 p.m. 620.783.2883. FB.

Cars on the Route: 119 N. Main. Visitors flock to see the fabled little 1951 International tow truck that inspired the Tow Mater character in the hit animated movie *Cars* (2006). The truck was once used to lift equipment from mine shafts. Have your picture taken next to the perky rusted truck and other vehicles that resemble

the movie's characters. Then step inside this renovated 1926 Kan-O-Tex gas station for hamburgers, fries and a pop. Be sure to shop for Route 66 souvenirs, and to see a few historic photos and memorabilia from bygone days. April-September, Wednesday-Sunday 10 a.m.-4 p.m. 620.783.1366. FB.

explorer extras... In Galena

A colorful outdoor Route 66 Postcard mural dresses up the side of the building at Main and 7th. A little pocket park in front of the mural is a spiffy place to take a selfie.

One of the last remaining native stone buildings in this area, Roosevelt School, 319 W. Empire, was constructed in 1937 by the WPA. It is a visible reminder of when Empire, 1 mile north on K-26 across Short Creek, was a separate community from Galena. The former school is now a private residence. Drive by only.

Find antiques imported from England inside a former and haunted bordello! Bordello Antiques, 206 N. Main, also provides refreshments in the tea room. Wednesday-Friday 10:30 a.m.-4 p.m.; Saturday 10:30 a.m.-5 p.m.; Sunday 1-5 p.m. **ee**

HALLOWELL

Unincorporated

Angelo's Deli: 9057 SW U.S. 160. Angelo's has supplied customers with groceries, gas, and bait since 1957. But it may be the unique sauce on white-bread sandwiches that keeps folks coming back to this charming hole-in-the-wall. Daily lunch specials are also served. Monday- Saturday 8 a.m.-5 p.m.; Sunday 10 a.m.-3 p.m. 620.597.2525. FB.

Lodging: Claythorne (620.597.2568; claythornelodge.com).

RIVERTON

Unincorporated

Nelson's Old Riverton Store (NRHP): 7109 SE Route 66 (U.S. 400) The ambience of this sweet reminder of the old Route 66 days probably hasn't changed much since it opened as Leo Williams Grocery in the 1920s. It's one of the most nostalgic stops in the state, where you can order a sandwich at the meat counter, buy Wonder Bread or Jello in the old-fashioned market, or pull an ice-cold pop out of an original Coca Cola cooler. Memorabilia of the "Mother Road" (Route 66) line the shelves and are stacked up to the pressed-tin ceiling, and an adjoining room is packed with every imaginable souvenir bearing the name Route 66. The Old Riverton Store is an explorer's haven! Monday-Saturday 7:30 a.m.-8 p.m.; Sunday 12-7 p.m. 620.848.3330. FB.

Riverton Kiosks: From U.S. 400 roundabout,150 yards west on Route 66/Beasley.

Get your kicks on Route 66 at the kiosks incorporating several well-designed, illustrated panels that portray area history and area attractions. Stopping here will help you uncover every bit of adventure along this historic route!

Brush Creek Bridge (NRHP): From Military, 2 miles west on Route 66. Drive or walk over this 1923 beauty, also known as the Rainbow Bridge, to appreciate the one-and-only surviving concrete Marsh arch single-span bridge on the entire Route 66.

SCAMMON

Population 467

St. Bridget Church: 406 N. Keith. While in Scammon, stop at the 1907 red-brick St. Bridget Church to see its original stained-glass windows. Each one is an artistic depiction of a different Bible story. Daily 9 a.m.-5 p.m.

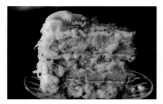

Josie's Ristorante: 400 N. Main. Grandmother Josie's recipes from Italy create a dining experience with a unique taste of the Old Country. Besides the authentic Italian, customers can also enjoy steaks and shrimp inside this old corner mining town company store. If you are a lover of Italian cream cake, don't leave without indulging in a slice with a cup of coffee,

or take it with you to savor later. Wednesday-Saturday 5-8 p.m. 620.479.8202. FB.

Carona Depot & Railroad Museum: 6769 NW 20. From K-7, 2 miles west on K-120, then ¼ mile south on 20. Railroad buffs will appreciate this historic depot where 1950s trains stand idly by on the sidetrack. Call ahead, 620.396.8594.

**explorer extras...
In Weir**

Population 661

Although taller, the brick cylindrical water tower at Weir is a near twin of the tower in Cherokee. Unlike Cherokee's 1896 structure, the 1889 Weir tower is no longer in use.

No longer operating, the little restored Texaco station on W. Main creates a nostalgic memory with its simple 1920s design, gas pumps, free-standing Texaco sign and pole, and large Coca Cola button sign.

Hosey Hill Cemetery is a fascinating cemetery filled with uncommon gravestones, Italian family names that reflect the heritage of the area, beautiful sculptures— and a grand stone elephant statue atop Inman E. Vandry's (1887- 1928) gravestone. A palpable quietness is felt in this rural setting. From Dreher, 1¾ miles west on Main. **ee**

SE

WEST MINERAL

Population 176

Big Brutus (8 Wonders of Kansas Commerce):
6509 NW 60. From K-7, 6 miles west on K-102 (becomes Scammon), then ½ mile west on NW 60. No name other than Big Brutus would befit this gigantic, massive, and enormous electric coal shovel. You can see this big guy long before you get there—like a multistory building plopped onto a rural landscape. And this thing actually moved! Big Brutus in action rumbled along at .22 mph (that's less than a quarter mile per hour) and removed the overburden (soil and rocks covering the coal seam) before smaller shovels came in and dug out the coal. One of the two largest electric coal shovels in the world still assembled, Big Brutus ran 24 hours a day from 1963 until 1974. For the full impact of this machine and the area's strip-mining history, start your tour in the visitor center museum to see displays, photos, and an informative video. You're welcome to walk up to Big Brutus and stand in its bucket.

And when you do, think about the fact that with one scoop this bucket picked up enough soil and rocks to fill three railroad cars! You may also climb up five stories to the "belly" of this big

boy and sit in the control seat. Memorial Day-Labor Day, daily 9 a.m.-8 p.m.; January-March, daily 10 a.m.-4 p.m.; remaining months, daily 9 a.m.-5 p.m. Admission charge. 620.827.6177. bigbrutus.org.

Mined Land Wildlife Area:
From the 1920s to 1974, only 2,000 acres of this 13,000-acre property were not surface mined. Now those scarred tracts of land, once stripped of overburden, have evolved into woodlands and grasslands that wind around a thousand deep pit lakes perfect for birding, canoeing or kayaking, or fishing. With more than 80 boat ramps, these lakes, both beautiful and eerie, are easy to access. Maps of the lakes are available at Big Brutus and from the Mined Land Wildlife Area office at 7545 NW Belleview (from Big Brutus, ½ mile south on NW 60, 1 mile west on Coalfield, 2 miles south on NW 70, then ¾ mile west on Belleview). Cabins available. Reservations required. 620.431.0380. tinyurl.com/minedlandinfo.

Coffey County

AROUND THE COUNTY

Wolf Creek Generating Station:
3 miles southeast of New Strawn. Wolf Creek, the only nuclear plant in the state, generates electricity by heating water to produce steam in this massive, domed structure. Steam turns turbines that spin a magnet inside an electrical generator, thus producing electricity. No gas, oil, or coal is burned as a heat source. With the property tax the plant pays to the county, it was possible

to fund a new library and fire department in each incorporated city in the county.

Observation Silo and Trails:
From Neosho in New Strawn, ¾ mile north on U.S. 75, 1¼ miles east on 17. The Wilson Cadman Wildlife Education Area provides three nature trails that guide you through a variety of habitats. Follow a short trail past a prairie barn to a concrete silo in the woods. For a great view, climb the 65 steps up a spiral staircase inside the silo to the observation deck.

Coffey County Lake:
From Neosho in New Strawn, 1¼ miles south on U.S. 75, 1 mile east on 15, then just north on Native. It's quite an experience, some say a bit eerie, to fish here and look across the lake at the Wolf Creek nuclear plant dome. One of the lake's purposes is to provide cooling water for the plant's generating station. Called the Crown Jewel of Kansas fisheries, this lake has one of the best predator-to-prey ratios in the country, allowing fish to thrive all year long. Because of the connection and proximity to the nuclear plant, photo identification and boat and vehicle registration are required at the lake gatehouse. For daily lake status, call 620.364.2475.

Beto Junction:
I-35 and U.S. 75. The name Beto was derived years ago from the initials of the larger towns (Burlington, Emporia, Topeka, and Ottawa) located on the highways that intersect at this point. Country Pride, a 24-hour convenience store, restaurant, gas station, and travel center makes this a popular stop.

Stone Fences:

Gene Merry, Kansas Explorer #54, says his granddad told him that wherever you see a stone (layered) fence, there's been a bad boy. Coffey County has a lot of stone fences! The reason may be the number of bad boys, but more likely it's due to an 1867 state law that provided a bounty of five cents a rod to those building stone or hedge fences.

Oil Pumps: You'll see many large oil pumps in the county, but have you noticed the small pumping units? In this area the oil-bearing formations are close to the surface (about 900 to 1,100 feet), thus making smaller pump units feasible.

BURLINGTON

Population 2,630

Outdoor Murals: Look in any block and you'll probably see a mural. Thirteen large outdoor murals decorate Burlington, and close to 100 adorn exterior and interior walls of public and school buildings throughout the county! A Jim Stukey mural at 6th and Neosho depicts early county officials, and a second Stukey mural, 2nd and Neosho, beautifully illustrates the Kansas Sampler Foundation's 8 Rural Culture Elements in Burlington. Maps of Coffey County murals are available at the visitor information dispenser located at the caboose at 4th and Neosho.

Post Office Art (NRHP):

107 S. 4th. *Boy and Colt*, an Arizona red sandstone sculpture, is a 1942 Section artwork by Robert Kittredge.

Old 75 Artists Gallery:

106 N. 3rd. Local, regional, and international artworks are exhibited here for your perusing and purchasing pleasure! Thursday 12-4 p.m.; Friday-Saturday 10 a.m.-5 p.m.

Restoration Capital of Kansas:

More than half of the 84 downtown business buildings have been restored or renovated in the past 20 years making Burlington the Restoration Capital of Kansas. Buildings date to the late 1800s, and downtown shops—selling collectibles, gifts, used furniture, women's clothing, and floral items—invite you to stop and see their buildings' interiors.

Carriage Works Factory:

3rd and Niagara. The 1875 factory along Rock Creek has been rehabilitated into a private residence. The mural at 519 Neosho depicts how it appeared as an operating carriage factory. Drive by only.

Excelsior Water Mill: From 4th, 4 blocks east on Kennebec. The mill stands erect and proud on the banks of the Neosho River after nearly succumbing to neglect. The sturdy three-story native stone flour mill was built in 1869 and later produced hydroelectric power for Burlington. After sitting empty for decades, the 5,000-square-foot building has been regally restored as a private residence. Drive by only.

Carnegie Library: 201 N. 3rd. The 1913 Carnegie library (NRHP) was designed by well-known Kansas architects George Washburn and Son. In 2006 Gene and Barb Merry completed a restoration of the beautiful red-brick library and converted it into the office of Merry Investments, the River City Art Gallery, and a meeting space. If the inside lights are on, you're welcome to stop to see the gallery or ask questions

about Burlington. Learn why it's called the Restoration and Pressed Metal Ceiling Capital of Kansas! 620.364.2615.

Catfish Capital of Kansas:

410 Juniatta. An unusual feature in the Coffey County Library is the mounted catfish and a fishing trophy! Years ago, catfish fishing contests were held between Burlington and nearby Chetopa, and a traveling trophy was awarded to the winner. According to this fish story, after a victorious Chetopa won the contest several decades ago, someone from Burlington stole the trophy and hid it. A few years ago the trophy mysteriously reappeared in the library and is now on permanent display. An accompanying video shows many trophy fish caught over the years. Monday-Thursday 9 a.m.-8 p.m.; Friday 9 a.m.-5 p.m.; Saturday 9 a.m.-3 p.m. 620.364.5333.

Catfish Mural: From 4th, 4 blocks east on Kennebec, then ½ mile north on Old Mill. On the east side of a cement block building a colorful mural is cleverly reminiscent of a 1950s postcard—a cheerful depiction of a little boy catching a big fish, and with a caption that reads, "Greetings from Burlington, Catfish Capital of the World!"

Burlington City Dam: From 4th, 4 blocks east on Kennebec, then ½ mile north on Old Mill. A serene place to cast a fishing line, have a picnic, or just watch the water flow over the city dam

SE

is Drake Park, a scenic spot on the Neosho River. Locals know the fishing is good for white bass, crappie, spoonbill, carp, and drum.

Coffey County Historical Museum:
1101 Neosho. A gun collection, doll collection, a stocked covered wagon, and a 1947 fire truck are only a few of the artifacts that tell of the county's early days. The museum complex comprises many outdoor entities including old-fashioned playground equipment, a windmill, and portions of an iron truss bridge. March-October, Monday-Friday 10 a.m.-4 p.m. and Saturday-Sunday 1-4 p.m.; November-February, Monday-Friday 10 a.m.-4 p.m. 620.364.2653. coffeymuseum.org.

Across the Borders:
320 Neosho. Owners Arthur and Venia Syring bring Tex-Mex to the Midwest by creating a diverse menu that includes favorite Mexican dishes as well as breakfasts, steaks, shrimp, chicken-fried steak, and chicken-fried chicken—all with a Tex-Mex flavor. You won't find fried taters and onions on the menu, but you can ask for them! The stained-lass windows by local artist Jim Stukey highlight Burlington's tie to each of the Kansas Sampler Foundation's 8 Rural Culture Elements. Monday-Friday 5:30 a.m.-8 p.m.; Saturday 5:30 a.m.-9 p.m. 620.364.1455.

The Bake-Ary Donut Shop:
401 N. 4th. The early birds come for wake-up smokies (smoked sausage wrapped and baked in flaky dough), biscuits and gravy, and of course warm-from-the-oven, melt-in-your-mouth donuts. Daily 5 a.m.-12 p.m. 620.364.2733.

Diners' Kafe: 1020 N. 2nd. It seems that many small towns have a home-cooking cafe that satisfies every comfort food craving, and Diners' does the job here. You can also custom-order a cake from a selection of 71 flavors! Other baked goods such as pies, cookies, and cheesecake are available too. Sunday-Monday 11 a.m.-2 p.m.; Tuesday-Friday 11 a.m.-8 p.m. 620.364.1340. dinerskafe.com.

Lodging: tinyurl.com/burllodging.

explorer extras...
In Burlington

Although he does give a close shave with his special old-fash-ioned straight razor, you're not encountering the demon barber of Fleet Street. Instead you'll enjoy meeting Jake Johnson, better known as "Jukebox Jake the Singing Barber of Neosho Street" at Jukebox's Barbershop, 406 W. Neosho. Jake cuts hair for men and boys, and, upon request, will strap on his guitar and harmonica and play a tune or two. A wall-sized mural pays tribute to Jake's longtime predecessor "Honest" John Deitrich, a beloved local barber who operated at this spot from 1960 to 2014. Tuesday-Friday 9 a.m.-6 p.m.; Saturday 9 a.m.-3 p.m. 620-490-1798. FB.

The County Poor Farm, a 180-acre farm once comprising a hospital, wash house, and large barn, was in operation until the 1951 flood wiped out the majority of the buildings. A two-story red-brick house still stands. From Kennebec, 1 mile north on U.S. 75. Drive by only.

The National Youth Administration (NYA) erected Kelley Hall in 1941, built with irregular sand-stone from local quarries. The football stadium, also a NYA project, was built of the same stone in 1947. Both are found in Kelley Park at 3rd and Alleghany at the south end of town. The park hosts one of the state's longest consecutively held annual fairs every July.

Finding round barns is a source of great pleasure for "barnies," and a lone, unused round barn awaits your viewing pleasure at 10 and Quail. The 1909 barn sports a jaunty wooden quilt block. From 4th, 4½ miles east on 11, then 1 mile south on Quail. Drive by only. **ee**

explorer extras...
In Gridley

Population 334

Nancy's Groceries, 507 Main, relies on steady regular cust-omers to keep it going. Any purchase you make provides a boost. If you're hungry, Nancy's provides lunch. Monday-Friday 8 a.m.-6 p.m.; Saturday 9 a.m.-5 p.m. 620.836.2563. FB.

You can learn about a town and its history in a variety of ways, but in Gridley you can do it visually with the informative and stylishly outdoor mural by Jim Stukey at 6th and Main.

No goosing in Gridley! Because of the many incidents of goosing in Gridley, city leaders in 1911 passed an ordinance against it. The Gridley ordinance is thought to be the only town in the nation to outlaw the practice. The city council's original minutes and the published ordinance can be seen at City Hall, 503 Main. Monday-Friday 7:30 a.m.-1 p.m. 620.836.3145.

Where do you go where everybody knows your name? Not the neighborhood bar, but rather the service station! Rodger's Oil Company, 603 Main, is affectionately known as Pete's, Dale's, the station, or the house of knowledge. If there's anything you want to know, just join the local men for a cup of coffee. They line up and wait for the door to open at 7:30 a.m. and have done so since 1963. Besides a great deal of very important information, you can also get gas at Rodger's. (Of course the best place to really learn anything is at the local library where the townswomen hold court.) Monday-Friday 7:30 a.m.- 6 p.m.; Saturday 7:30 a.m.-12 p.m. 620.836.2233. **ee**

LEBO

Population 915

Harold Spatz: Ogden and Broadway. A veterans memorial in this pocket park recognizes Harold "Skinny" Spatz, whose name is listed on a Flint Hills stone monument along with other local men killed during WWII. Sergeant Spatz's plane went down in General Doolittle's 1942 Tokyo Raid, and later Spatz was executed by the Japanese.

Outdoor Mural: Lebo's historic past and Welsh heritage are the subjects of Jim Stukey's large, colorful mural on the side wall at City Hall, 5 E. Broadway.

Historic Stone Jail: Under the water tower sits the little 1890 stone jail—empty, unused, and no customers of late. From Broadway, ½ block south on Pine.

LEROY

Population 548

Opothleyahola Memorial: A small native stone shelter honors Opothleyahola (Yahola), a Creek Indian leader who suffered great hardships when he and his followers were marched to Indian territory from Georgia and Alabama on the Trail of Tears in 1839. Siding with the Union during the Civil War, Yahola and about 1,000 of his followers formed the First Indian Home Guard in 1862 and were inducted into the army at LeRoy. A plaque in the shelter provides a detailed history of these events.

Gazebo: Main and Kansas (City Park). An old-fashioned gazebo with bandstand was constructed in 1981. An engraved granite marker has been placed beside its base in memory of Thomas Crabtree, John Scott, and Fredrick Troxel who founded LeRoy in 1855.

Outdoor Mural: 6th and Main. Depictions of many faces and places, all part of LeRoy's heritage, combine to form this colorful mural.

Luther's Store and Restaurant: 98 W. 6th. Stop here for your traveling supplies, Luther's old-fashioned beef jerky, or sandwiches made with hand-carved meat. Outside, take a seat in the enormous rocking chair at 6th and Reaper and have your picture taken! Monday-Friday 7 a.m.-8 p.m.; Sunday 7 a.m.-6:30 p.m. 620.964.2500. jerkyusa.com.

The Pizza Parlor: 608 N Main. Christine and Vernon Williams invite you into their parlor to settle into a comfy booth alongside a vintage limestone wall. There you can choose from hot bubbling cheesy pizzas, humongous crusty calzones, and quality sandwiches. Add to any of these a trip to the fresh salad bar. Vernon's mom, Wilda, worked long and hard to expose the limestone, but she left some of the plaster so you can sign your name on the "Great Wall." Monday-Saturday 10 a.m.- 8 p.m. 620.964.2100. FB.

Arnold's Greenhouse: 1430 K-58. From Main, 4½ miles west on K-58. It's a gardener's paradise—Kansas' largest selection of perennials and annuals (2,500 varieties of each) are found in this premiere greenhouse, which also features vegetables, herbs, aquatic plants, trees, shrubs, and some of the finest roses bushes in the state. George and Rita Arnold had no idea their garden would become such a large operation when they opened it in 1977. March-October, Monday-Saturday 9 a.m.-5 p.m. (longer hours during peak planting season). 620.964.2463. arnoldsgreenhouse.com.

SE

NEW STRAWN

Population 394

John Redmond Lake:

From Neosho, ¼ mile south on Main, ¼ mile west on 16th (Lake), then 1 mile southeast on Embankment. Situated on the Neosho River and in the Central Flyway, the reservoir is an important stopover for many species of migrating waterfowl. John Redmond was constructed in 1964 for flood control, recreation, water supply, and wildlife management. 620.364.8614. tinyurl.com/johnredmond.

WAVERLY

Population 571

Outdoor Mural: 3rd and

Pearson (K-31). Painted on a brick wall, the mural is a colorful memory of Ohio Days, a rural picnic that celebrated the town founders from Ohio.

Olive Ann Beech Marker:

Pearson and 1st (Waverly Park). A large sign pays tribute to Olive Ann Mellor Beech (1903-1993) who, with her husband, Walter, established Beech Aircraft in 1932. After Walter's death in 1940, she became the first woman to head a major aircraft company. Waverly is proud to be the birthplace of this outstanding woman, known as the First Lady of Aviation. She was awarded many honors, including induction into the Kansas, the National, and the International Aviation Halls of Fame.

Crawford County

The first commercial coal mining shaft dug in 1877 was just the beginning of the coal boom in Crawford County. The coal fields of southeast Kansas created jobs for thousands of Europeans who came to this country to escape poverty, oppression, and political injustice. An estimated 31,000 immigrants from 52 nations arrived in southeast Kansas between 1880 and 1940, bringing with them a diversity of languages, religions, cuisines, and lifestyles. Because of the origins of its ethnic population, the coal fields became known as the "Little Balkans" of Kansas. The miners hard work for little pay caught the attention of the Socialist Party in the early 1900s. Since most European miners tended to be pro-labor, they joined forces with the Socialists, thereby closely allying unions, strikes, and political activism with the area's coal mining industry.

AROUND THE COUNTY

Crawford County State

Park: From K-7, 1 mile east on K-277. The 500-acre park is located on the edge of the Ozarks. In the spring, redbud trees add even more beauty to this heavily wooded area. Hiking, biking, boating, swimming, and RV and tent camping are some of the amenities you can enjoy. State park entrance charge. Cabins available. Reservations required. 620.362.3671. ksoutdoors.com.

Civilian Conservation Corps (CCC) Memorial and Museum: From

K-7, 1 mile east on K-277. Just inside the state park entrance a memorial honors not only the CCC workers who built this lake in the 1930s but also the 3.5 million men who were part of the CCC, a New Deal federal program. Recognizing the park's history are a bronze statue of a CCC worker, a one-and-a quarter-mile memorial trail past artifacts used to build the lake, interpretive signage, and a small museum inside a unique stone structure formerly a water tower. Museum is always open.

Fried Chicken Capital of Kansas (8 Wonders of Kansas Cuisine):

Crawford County probably has more fantastic non-franchised restaurants than any other county in the state. And although the county is deservedly dubbed the Fried Chicken Capital of Kansas, you'll find much more than chicken here— everything from classic diners to Thai.

ARMA

Population 1,469

Arma Mural: 306 E. Washing-

ton. In 2009 local artist Gary Lofts and his wife, Susan, spearheaded a campaign to paint a large mural on the side of a 1907 downtown building honoring the town's centennial. It's a beauty and depicts the town's history including scenes of a miner, railroad and depot, a church, a Model T, and the former school bulldog mascot.

Veterans Memorial: 5th and

Washington. Built shortly after WWII, this memorial now honors local veterans who served in all wars. Flags representing four branches of the military fly in front of the memorial. Arma's V-J Day homecoming has been celebrated annually since 1946.

Ed Babcock Wood Sculptures:

All kinds of fun can be found in City Park, 251 N. 5th, from whimsical animals carved from logs by local chainsaw artist Ed Babcock, to playgrounds, horseshoe pits, and bocce courts. Wednesday-Friday 1-5 p.m.; Saturday 9 a.m.-1 p.m. 620.347.8355.

All American Grill:

102 E. South. It's old-fashioned home cooking—biscuits and gravy, burgers, hand-cranked curly Q's, and homemade onion rings—at this American grill. And every couple of days the owner whips up more than a dozen pies and desserts, including top favorites coconut meringue and Reese's peanut butter pie. Daily 8 a.m.-8 p.m. 620.347.4000. FB.

CHEROKEE

Population 712

Historic Water Tower:

The plaque on the tall cylindrical red-brick water tower reads, "Cherokee Water Works 1896." According to the city clerk, this water tower is the eighth oldest still in use in the United States. 620.457.8413.

Idle Awhile Bar: 201 S. Vine. Slow down, put your gears in neutral, and idle here awhile. According to owners Dan and Michelle Mortenson, that's what patrons have done since the 1890s when the building was constructed as a speak-easy. Today you can enjoy a cold beer or a wine cooler (all legal!). Speaking loud and clear is the delicious food—burgers, steaks, chicken, ribs, mountain oysters, and homemade desserts. Homemade bread comes with dinner. Tuesday-Saturday 11:30 a.m.-10 p.m. 620.457.8778. idle-a-while.com.

Mined Land Scenic Back Road:

From K-7, 5 miles west on U.S. 400, 2 miles north on 100, 2 miles east on 520, then 2 miles south on 120 and you're back to U.S. 400. You leave the blacktop at your first turn (north on 100) to drive through part of the Mined Land Wildlife Area—land once devastated in the aftermath of strip mining is now lush with woodlands, grasslands, and abundant water. One mile east on 520 you'll cross Lime Creek on the Hudgeon Bridge (NRHP), a picturesque 1923 bridge with lovely railings and turned balusters.

FRANKLIN

Unincorporated

Miners Hall Museum:

701 S. Broadway. On this site, prior to the 2003 tornado, stood a community hall where the Amazon Army (a women's protest group supporting striking miners) started its march in 1921. A new metal building now occupies the spot and serves as the Miners Hall Museum. From a pickax to a log sheet, mining and miner artifacts portray this cultural history. Displays feature life in the mines, social and home life, health and safety, and more. Monday-Saturday 10 a.m.-4 p.m. 620.347.4220. minershallmuseum.com.

Franklin Community Park and Memorial Garden:

Broadway and 5th. May 4, 2003, will not be forgotten in this area. On that date a vicious tornado destroyed much of this tiny village. In the Franklin Community Park a marker relates the tornado tragedy, and a plaque on a pecan tree explains the metal still wrapped and twisted around the trunk.

Longest Sidewalk (NRHP):

The sidewalk runs parallel to U.S. 69 Business from the south end of Franklin to E. Hector in Arma. When Franklin High School closed in the late 1920s, children had to walk to school in Arma. To provide safe passage, in 1937 the WPA finished a one-and-three-quarter-mile sidewalk between the two towns. *The Guinness Book of World Records* recorded this sidewalk as the longest walkway connecting two towns. Instead of leading you to school, today this long sidewalk invites you to take a leisurely stroll, skip, turn cartwheels, play hopscotch, push a baby stroller, pull a wagon, ride a bike, jog, walk your dog, and kick up your heels. Much more fun than school.

Jefferson Highway: Franklin is on the Kansas Frontier Military Historic Byway (travelks.com/ksbyways) but also is on the route of the Jefferson Highway, the first transcontinental road to traverse North America north to south. The Jefferson Highway Association was founded in 1915.

Strip Pit Alley Scenic Drive:

From U.S. 69 just south of Franklin, 4½ miles east on 620, 3 miles north on 270 to Mulberry, continue 6 miles north on 270 to Arcadia, then 4 miles west on Arcadia (becomes 710) to U.S. 69. Along the way you'll pass many strip pits, signs, and other vestiges of old coal

SE

mining camps. Many of these pits are from the 1930s, when massive coal shovels ripped into the earth (some to a depth of 100 feet) leaving barren land and piles of gob (discarded coal waste) in their wake. But now you'll see strip pits in their restored glory, brimming with water in a new wooded environment that attracts birds, wildlife, hunters, and fishermen.

FRONTENAC

Population 3,432

The town was laid out in 1887 on the site of Mine No.1 of the Cherokee-Pittsburg Coal Company. The following year an underground explosion killed 47 miners and became the greatest mine disaster in Kansas. The 1910 census recorded 21 nationalities (predominantly Italian) among Frontenac's 3,000 residents, establishing the town as "the melting pot of Kansas."

Wilderness Park: 907 W. McKay. From Parkview/U.S. 69, ½ mile west on McKay. You'll find more than four miles of walking trails in this wooded area, which is picturesque during the fall and shady during the hot summer. 620.231.4100.

Pallucca's Market: 207 E. McKay. Fresh spaghetti sauce, meatballs, chili without beans, homemade Italian sausage, fresh-cut meats, Frontenac bakery bread (8 Wonders of Kansas Commerce), and great selections of grated cheese, olive oil, and dry noodles—you'll find these and more at Pallucca's, which dates to 1909. Attilio Pallucca started his store as an Italian American

cooperative, trading on credit with the miners. Owned by the Pallucca family until 2013, new owners Ethan and Alyssa Edwards continue the market's century-old traditions. Monday-Saturday 9 a.m.-6 p.m. 620.231.7700. FB.

Barto's Idle Hour Steak House & Lounge: 201 S. Santa Fe. It doesn't have chicken in its name but it does on its plates—and it comes with a terrific reputation! Since 1951 Barto's has also provided hand-cut steaks (purchased from Pallucca's), shrimp—and dancing! Yes, all kinds of music, including polka, Friday and Saturday nights starting at 8 p.m. in the lounge. Tuesday-Saturday 4-10 p.m. 620.232.9834. FB.

GIRARD

Population 2,779

In 1868 Dr. Charles Strong killed a deer while hunting in this area. At the spot the deer fell, Strong drove a stake into the ground and announced that he would build a town on this site. A marker beside a deer statue on the town square at Prairie and Summit describes this unusual town beginning.

Crawford County Courthouse (NRHP): 111 E. Forest. Built in 1922, this Modern Eclecticism structure features marble walls and staircases. Stand at the center of the first floor and look up to

see the beautiful stained-glass ceiling above the third floor. A UH-1H Huey helicopter flown by a Kansas pilot is stationed on the courthouse square. Nearby are a granite wall inscribed with the names of all 777 Kansans who lost their lives in Vietnam, flags of the five military branches, a POW-MIA flag, Kansas flag, and American flag.

The Appeal to Reason:
When J.A. Wayland moved the socialist newspaper *The Appeal to Reason* to Girard in 1897 it became the largest circulated weekly paper in the world, and it set the stage for Girard to become an integral part of U.S. socialism. The post office at 115 N. Summit was built in 1918 to handle the huge volume of mail created by the popularity of Wayland's newspaper. About 75,000 copies of it were mailed out every week during 1919.

Little Blue Books:
Socialist Emanuel Haldeman-Julius became renowned world-wide as the publisher of the *Little Blue Books*. His goal was to print the world's great literature in an inexpensive (five-cent) format that working men and women everywhere could afford. Between 1919 and 1951 he and his wife, Marcet, printed more than 1,500 titles and sold more than 500 million copies. You'll find *Little Blue Books* in both the Girard Public Library and the Leonard H. Axe Library at Pittsburg State University.

Carnegie Library (NRHP): 128 W. Prairie. Two Ionic columns flank the front door of this 1906 building. Still serving as the Girard Public Library, it contains a collection of the Haldeman-Julius *Little Blue Books*. In 2002 an impressive addition was added to this historic limestone structure. While you're here, pick up a map for a driving tour of the town's historic sites (see next entry). Monday-Friday 9:30 a.m.-5 p.m.; Saturday 9:30 a.m.-3 p.m. 620.724.4317.

Historical Driving Tour:

Girard's history awaits you on this tour, which includes the 1887 home (NRHP) of publisher J.A. Wayland (721 Summit); the Haldeman-Julius House (RHKP; 310 N. Sinnett), home of the *Little Blue Books* publishers; the J.T. and Anna Leonard Home (NRHP; 211 N. Summit), the largest home ever built in Girard in a stunning Queen Anne style; the J.E. Raymond House (NRHP; 301 S. Osage), identifiable by its "onion dome"; and the home of Henry Laurens Call (608 N. Summit). Call was a Socialist lawyer, author, and lecturer, and in 1908 he built the first airplane west of the Mississippi. Call named it the *Mayfly* because "it may fly!" But it didn't. A 19-site driving tour brochure is available at the front desk of the public library, 128 W. Prairie.

Chicken Annie's of Girard:

498 E. K-47. 4 miles east of Girard on K-47. The Crawford County chicken legacy has spread to Girard thanks to the original Chicken Annie's descendants, who opened this restaurant in 1971. The chicken here is cooked to order so it may take a bit longer, but it comes straight from the fryer. Wednesday-Saturday 4-8:30 p.m.; Sunday 11 a.m.-8 p.m. 620.724.4090. FB.

Unincorporated

St. Aloysius Historic Site

(RHKP): From Summit in Girard, 8 miles west on K-47. The story of this historic site is an amazing one, beginning with a Catholic priest caught in a terrible storm. Hiding under his horse's saddle, he prayed for survival, promising to build a church on the site if his life was spared. He survived and in 1871 he built the church. When a second storm destroyed the wooden church, parishioners built a stone structure in 1881, which was used until a much larger church was completed in 1907. But the forces of nature continued to plague Greenbush, and in 1982 lightning struck St. Aloysius Church and destroyed it. Today its grand stone ruins remain as a haunting piece of Greenbush history. A steadfast group of parishioners has kept alive the story of St. Aloysius and has built a pavilion nearby and moved a one-room schoolhouse to the site. 620.724.8536.

Population 516

Gebhardt's Chicken:

124 N. 260. From U.S. 69 just south of Franklin, 4 miles east on 620, then ¼ mile north on 260. It started as a honky tonk, but in 1946 Ted and Maycle

Gebhardt turned their farm home into a restaurant, cooking fried chicken dinners as best they knew how. With almost 60 years of success under its belt, Gebhardt's must be doing something right! Sunday 11 a.m.-7:30 p.m.; Monday, Friday-Saturday 4-8 p.m. 620.764.3451.

Population 20,398

SE

Miners' Memorial: 2nd and Walnut. A beautifully landscaped area features a larger-than-life bronze statue of miner John Christian Ott and large polished granite monuments inscribed with names of miners who worked in the Weir-Pittsburg coal fields. Informational kiosks along a sidewalk tell more about the life of a coal miner.

Immigrant Park: 106 W. 2nd. In the block east of the Miners' Memorial the handsome brick Pritchett Pavilion graces the site where the old Europe Hotel and Frisco depot once stood. In the late 1800s and early 1900s these facilities received new immigrant families who came to

work in the coal fields. Plaques on the pavilion are inscribed with stories of these families and the difference they have made in the area. A nearby mural depicts the old hotel and depot.

Carnegie Library (NRHP):

308 N. Walnut. Because library funds provided by Andrew Carnegie (who was anti-union) angered area miners, Carnegie's money was accepted but his name was omitted from the library's exterior. This 1912 structure, now the Pittsburg Public Library, is one of the few Carnegie libraries in the country built with elements of Art Nouveau and the Prairie School style. Monday-Thursday 9 a.m.- 8 p.m.; Friday-Saturday 9 a.m.- 5 p.m.; Sunday 1-5 p.m. 620.231.8110.

Solidarity Mural: 308 N.

Walnut. Inside the Public Library, Wayne Wildcat's colorful mural illustrates the 1921 Pittsburg event involving 6,000 women marching in protest of mining conditions and in support of striking miners. The *New York Times* dubbed these courageous women the Army Amazons, and their march became a turning point in labor history.

Hotel Stilwell (NRHP):

707 Broadway. In 1889, in an attempt to make his little mining town appear more metropolitan

and thereby attract new capital, financier Arthur Stilwell constructed this grand downtown hotel. The grandeur is evident in the lobby, which features a stained-glass dome and medallions around the hanging lights. In its day, the hotel hosted such renowned figures as Susan B. Anthony, Theodore Roosevelt, and William Jennings Bryan. Above the outdoor balcony, a carved limestone griffin guards the property. Restored in 1997, the hotel today houses apartments. Lobby open Monday-Friday 9 a.m.-5 p.m. 620.235.1997.

Pittsburg State University Veterans Memorial Amphitheater: 1909 S. Rouse.

You'll feel a tug at your emotions as you walk the entryways lined with flags of the 50 states and the official seals of the five military branches. Dedicated in 2004, this memorial amphitheater features a half-sized replica of the Vietnam Veterans Memorial in Washington, D.C. The replica was part of the Moving Wall program that brought The Wall to those who couldn't travel to the nation's capital. Among other features, the amphitheater contains an eternal flame and a reflecting pool. Psuvetmemorial.org.

Timmons Chapel: 409 E.

Ford (Pittsburg State campus). This all-faiths chapel built in the Country English Gothic style is peaceful and picturesque, tucked among trees on a spot

that overlooks the university lake. The charming stone building is accented with a multi-color slate roof and a three-bell spire topped with a cross. Local philanthropist Bess Timmons funded the building of this church in 1966.

Professors' Row (NRHP):

E. Lindburg. It was a Sunday event in the late 1910s to drive past the fancy new Craftsman style homes of college professors Whitesitt (120 E. Lindburg) and Shirk (116 E. Lindburg). Although the structures were a basic rectangular form with linear ornamentation, these bungalows had welcoming porches, garages, and were quite a contrast to Pittsburg's usual Victorian and mining company homes.

Crawford County Historical Museum:

651 S. U.S. 69. Exhibits capture the area's history of coal mining, farming, printing, and ethnic diversity. Unique artifacts include a dress worn by 1967 Miss America Debbie Barnes and a 1938 aerial fire truck. Wednesday-Saturday 10 a.m.-4 p.m; Sunday 12-4 p.m. 620.231.1440. crawfordcountymuseum.com.

Signet Coffee Roasters:

206 S. Broadway. Choose from a selection of single-origin and blended beans, or enjoy a coffee from the coffee bar. Add homemade caramel, mocha mix, and whipping cream for extra deliciousness. Monday-Friday 7 a.m.- 4:30 p.m.; Saturday 7 a.m.- 12 p.m. 620.308.5326. FB.

Sweet Designs Cakery:
311 N. Broadway. Behind this brightly colored storefront are tasty homemade cakes, cookies, cupcakes, and ice cream. One bite and you'll smile with delight! Tuesday-Friday 10 a.m.-6 p.m.; Saturday 10 a.m.-2 p.m. 620.231.2253. FB.

Chicken Annie's Original:
1143 E. 600. From 20th, 4 miles north on U.S. 69, then 3½ miles east on 600. When Annie's husband, coal miner Charley Pichler, suffered a disabling accident in Yale Mine No.13 in 1933, she had to find work to support their family. In 1934 Annie started selling fried chicken out of her home, with side dishes of German potato salad, German coleslaw, a strip of green pepper, and a slice of tomato. That was the beginning of this now-famous restaurant. It is owned today by Annie's grand-children, who are still serving delicious fried chicken dinners. Tuesday-Saturday 4-8:30 p.m.; Sunday 11 a.m.-8 p.m. 620.231.9460. FB.

Chicken Mary's:
1133 E. 600. From 20th, 4 miles north on U.S. 69, then 3½ miles east on 600. When Joe Zerngast was no longer able to work in the coal mines in the early 1940s, his wife, Mary, started preparing meals to support the family. They began serving chicken dinners in their home, moved into an old mining camp pool hall in 1945, and have operated in their current location since 1966. The Zerngast family's third generation continues to compete with neighboring Chicken Annie's for the best and most mouth-watering chicken dinners. Tuesday-Saturday 4-8:30 p.m.; Sunday 11 a.m.-8 p.m. 620.231.9510. FB.

Pichler's Chicken Annie's:
1271 S. 220. From 4th, 4½ miles south on Broadway/U.S. 69 Business. Chicken Mary's granddaughter Donna married Chicken Annie's grandson Anthony, and together they created a new dimension to the area's chicken tradition by opening Pichler's Chicken Annie's! You know the food is something special coming from this chicken-cooking combo. Tuesday-Saturday 4-8:30 p.m.; Sunday 11 a.m.-8 p.m. 620.232.9260. FB.

Bob's Grill:
1014 N. Broadway. This is a working man and woman's throwback 1964 diner. You'll see white-collar folks, blue-collar folks, and everyone in between on the bar stools or at the counter visiting with neighbors, friends, and new faces in town. The food is as good as the friendly service! Breakfast and lunch are busy times, but Bob's is worth the wait. Monday-Saturday 5 a.m.- 1 p.m. 620.232.9738. FB.

Otto's Cafe:
711 N. Broadway (Hotel Stilwell). This retro diner looks just as it did when it opened in 1945 as an addition to Hotel Stilwell. It still has the 10-stool counter and the mauve and gray Formica countertop. Surrender to the temptation of the strawberry shortcake during berry season. And during any season, Otto's is a breakfast oasis. Daily 7 a.m.-2 p.m. (closed Wednesday). 620.231.6110. FB.

Typhoon Grill: 1014
S. Broadway. A richly decorated Asian interior is the perfect complement to the delicious and beautifully presented Thai dishes such as pineapple curry, rice soup, pad Thai, and tamarind chicken. Monday-Saturday 11 a.m.-8:30 p.m. 620.232.9900. FB.

Jim's Steak House & Lounge:
1912 N. Broadway. The vintage neon sign out front is a clue that Jim's has been around for awhile, and with good reason. This classic steak house is famous throughout the region for steaks, steak tips, and onion rings. One taste and you'll know why Jim's has been in business since 1938. Monday-Saturday 4:30-10 p.m. 620.231.5770. FB.

SE

Mall Deli:
202 E. Centennial (Meadowbrook Mall). Jim and Diane Martino have found the right recipe for creamy Italian dressing, French dips, subs, and more, as well as the best ingredients for serving their customers! The Mall Deli has been a pleasant dining stop since 1979, and folks line up for the experience every day at noon. You can buy bottles of the addictive creamy Italian dressing to tide you over until your next visit. Monday-Saturday 10:30 a.m.- 9 p.m.; Sunday 11 a.m.-5 p.m. 620.231.7590. FB.

Lodging:
Himmel House Bed and Breakfast (KBBA, 620.232.9497, himmelhouse. com); additional lodging (visitcrawfordcounty.com).

explorer extras...
In Pittsburg

From the local Harry's Cafe (412 N. Broadway, 620.232.2125) to the live music and comedy of T.J. Leland's (108 W. 6th, 620.404.8065), more restaurants and nightlife spots are listed at visitcrawfordcounty.com.

A folksy boy-meets-girl mural incorporates southeast Kansas themes (mining, chicken, and more) into the scene. The mural, created by Pittsburg State University students, is at the corner of 3rd and Broadway.

Pittsburg State University is the only college in the nation to have a gorilla as its mascot. A 1965 bronze *Gus Gorilla*, designed by Larry Wooster, stands on the south side of the Overman Student Center, 302 E. Cleveland. A new life-sized, one-ton bronze gorilla created by Tom Corbin was installed on the east side of Carnie Smith Stadium, 1705 S. Joplin.

A banana tree in Kansas? When your college mascot is a gorilla it stands to reason that a banana tree should be nearby. Enjoy a stroll through this beautiful campus to look for the trees, although they are set out only in warmer months. How will you know when you find a banana tree? It has bananas on it!

Restoration efforts are ongoing to return the 1920s Colonial Fox Theater (NRHP) at 409 N. Broadway to its full splendor. In the meantime, a mural of a movie screen has been painted on the north side of the building and movies are shown on it during the summer. June-September. 620.235.0622. colonialfox.org.

Built in 1923, Memorial Auditorium, 503 N. Pine, invites you to stop in to see its local art in the lobby gallery. Monday-Friday 8 a.m.-5 p.m.

Dozens of mausoleums adorned with columns, peaked roofs, and arches, dominate the landscape at Mount Olive Cemetery, 402 E. Quincy, and at Highland Park Cemetery, Broadway and Centennial, south of the university.

Kids love Lincoln Park, W. 9th. You'll understand why when you see its aquatic center, the miniature train, miniature golf course, fishing pond, and Kiddieland, an amusement park for small children. 620.231.8310. **ee**

Elk County

ELK FALLS

Population 99

Elk Falls Iron Truss Bridge (NRHP): 4th and
Montgomery. The flood of 1976 made it impossible to continue vehicular traffic across this 1893 bridge, but in 2001 the Friends of Elk Falls with help from AmeriCorp workers saved the bridge by replanking the floor. The 130x16-foot bridge on the northeast side of town has become a popular stop and offers a great view of the falls and the Elk River below.

Elk River Falls: 4th and
Montgomery. A grist and flour mill was built on this river in 1875 (the mill closed around 1900), but sometime prior to 1892 Jo Johansen constructed a sandstone milldam to create a water supply. A primitive path on the north side of the iron truss bridge takes you down to the water falling gently over a rock ledge.

Elk Falls Pottery: 1954 U.S. 160. Steve and Jane Fry are in their new studio on the north side of U.S. 160. If the gate is open, so are they! The Frys are masters of cleverness and efficiency so not only will you see the functional stoneware handcrafted from Kansas clays, but also their renovation talents. You might even observe potter Steve at his 19th-century treadle wheel, where he'll gladly explain this artistic process. Monday-Saturday 9 a.m.-5 p.m. Call ahead, 620.329.4425.

Rock Garden: When visiting Elk Falls Pottery, ask to walk around the rock garden. Steve and Jane Fry uncovered and renovated a "secret" garden, an overgrown and neglected spot once the pride of former owner Maude Frakes. The 1930s garden is filled with intriguing grassroots art including concrete and stone benches, gazebo, pergola, tipi, and other unusual shapes and designs created with stones Maude collected from across the country. During the Great Depression Maude hired out-of-work locals to help build her garden. Maude hosted a rally for Alf Landon in 1936, which gives you a clue as to the symbolism of the garden's eight concrete elephants.

Prudence Crandall:

U.S. 160 and Osage. In 1833 Prudence Crandall established the first black female academy in New England (Canterbury, Connecticut) and was arrested and imprisoned for doing so. She was later released, but the school was forced to close. Crandall moved to Elk Falls where she continued to advocate human rights. She is buried in Elk Falls Cemetery, on the north side of the middle section. On the west edge of Elk Falls at a small roadside pull over, a historical marker recounts the Crandall legacy.

explorer extras...
In Elk Falls

You may notice all the outhouses around Elk Falls, but you haven't seen anything until you see them all dressed up! The Elk Falls open house and Outhouse Festival happens the Friday and Saturday before Thanksgiving, and you must see it to believe it! The town's outhouses are decorated with quirky and creative themes. Not only is this wonderful fun, but it's a great opportunity to visit the world's largest living ghost town (Elk Falls) in the heart of the "Kansas Ozarks." If you miss the event, stop at Elk Falls Pottery, 1954 U.S. 160, and ask to see the three decorated privies in Outhouse Grove. 620.329.4425.

If you've had a secret desire to see a collection of outhouse memorabilia, you're in luck. Outhouse aficionado Homer Allison has placed his original collection in the one-room Pershing/Prairie Gem schoolhouse at Montgomery and 11th. Seventy miniature outhouses, photographs, decorative plates, and books on the subject are sure to impress you. If you just can't wait until the Outhouse Festival to see this, call 620.329.4425.

The striking art deco gymnasium is the last remaining building of the local school. The admirable WPA gymnasium is painted bright white, which accentuates the structure's clean lines. It's next door to the one-room Pershing/Prairie Gem schoolhouse, which was moved into Elk Falls from two miles out of town. **ee**

GRENOLA

Population 197

The town name may sound like a healthy cereal, but the name is the result of a compromise between neighboring towns that agreed to become one. Grenola combines of "Gre" from Greenfield and "Nola" from Canola.

Grain Elevator Museum (NRHP):

Main and Railroad. The Grenola Mill and Elevator served the community from 1909 to 1986, and now this elevator-turned-museum preserves the early days of Grenola through photographic exhibits and artifacts. Displays range

from wagons and buggies to period rooms and household items. Two one-room schoolhouses have been moved onto the site. May-October, Saturday 1-5 p.m. and Sunday 2-5 p.m. 620.358.3241.

Historical Marker: Main and Railroad. The native limestone marker next to the stone gazebo in a park recounts the longhorn cattle drives of 1881-1884, when Grenola was the largest single cattle shipping point in the United States.

HOWARD

Population 633

Elk County Courthouse (NRHP):

127 N. Pine. Described as a Romanesque Revival hybrid, this 1908 courthouse of yellow brick and limestone trim, and with a central clock tower, occupies a full block east of downtown.

Batson's Drug: 102 N. Wabash. When the town's grocery store closed, Batson's drugstore added groceries to its inventory—a courageous move in a small town, but a vital service for the community. When you find yourself in Howard, pay a visit to Batson's, buy a few gifts and groceries, and enjoy a treat at the old-fashioned soda fountain. Monday-Friday 8 a.m.-6 p.m.; Saturday 8 a.m.-2 p.m. 620.374.2265.

SE

Cookson's True Value Hardware:
114 N. Wabash. Inside this turn-of-the-century building with old wood floors and a pressed-tin ceiling, Cookson's has provided hardware for this area since 1953. Monday-Friday 8 a.m.-5 p.m.; Saturday 9 a.m.-12 p.m. 620.374.2340.

Hubbell's Rubble:
K-99 and Adams. In 1980 Jerry Hubbell started welding together some of the scrap metal he found around his farm. He became pretty creative and decided to share his designs with passers-by on K-99. You're welcome to stop and take pictures; lots of people do!

Howard National Bank:
147 N. Wabash. The former bank building, circa 1877, stands guard over downtown. The Gothic and Romanesque details are even more accentuated by the structure's aged, but still regal, appearance.

Benson Museum:
145 S. Wabash. Agricultural and local exhibits are displayed in several buildings that compose the Benson Museum. The complex includes a schoolhouse, cottage, and a 1920s service station with gas pumps and a red-tile roof. Call ahead, 620.874.4009.

Howard City Lake:
From Adams, ¼ mile south on K-99, then 1¼ miles east on Killdeer.

Also known as Polk Daniels Lake, its attractive stone arch entrance, shelter houses, and walkways are 1930s WPA projects. A popular fishing lake, it is surrounded by woods and prairie grass.

Poplar Pizza:
202 S. Wabash. Bryan and Mary Jo Miller established the original Poplar Pizza in 1982 on Poplar Avenue in Buffalo, New York. But after visiting this area, they opened a shop in Howard. Since 1995 business has been great! They serve real buffalo wings, New York-style pizza using a family secret sauce, sweet potato fries, and offer everything from char-grilled steak to pressure-fried chicken. The servings are plentiful and the price is a bargain. Tuesday-Saturday 11 a.m.-2 p.m. and 4-9 p.m.; Sunday 11 a.m.-2 p.m. 620.374.2525. FB.

Toot's Drive In:
1251 K-99. The burgers and fries are filling, the ice cream is cold, the pie is homemade, and since 1955 happy customers continue to count on Toot's. Daily 10 a.m.-9 p.m. 620.374.2345. FB.

Sweet and Spicy:
1229 K-99. Spicy Mexican burritos and tamales complement sweet donuts, cinnamon rolls, and cake. It's all here, plus burgers, sandwiches, and more. Monday-Saturday 5:30 a.m.-

2 p.m. and 5-8 p.m.; Sunday 7 a.m.-2 p.m. 620.374.3004. FB.

Benjamin Hobbs:
In 1933 local students created an endearing tribute to the county's first teacher, who had died more than 60 years earlier. The students donated funds to improve the gravesite of 23-year-old Benjamin Hobbs, who died in 1871. Although his grave was not in a field at the time, a wire-fenced field now covers the site, which is marked with a plaque, a decorative wrought iron fence, and a concrete foundation to protect the grave. From E. Washington, 2½ miles north on K-99, then east onto a small roadside pull over. If you walk east toward the wire fence you'll see a red sign noting Hobbs' birth and death dates and can view his burial site farther to the east.

Lodging:
Cattle Baron Inn Bed and Breakfast and RV Park (KBBA, 620.374.2503).

explorer extras...
In Longton

Population 318

Brenda Beaumont is doing a terrific job keeping her Longton Grocery store, 419 Kansas, operating in a small town. She and the community will appreciate you stopping by and picking up a few travel supplies for your exploring journeys. Monday-Friday 9 a.m.-5 p.m.; Saturday 9 a.m.-12 p.m. 620.642.3695. FB.

Between Nemaha and Montgomery on the north side of U.S.160 the crude cabin built of railroad ties in 1944 housed the 10-member

Fouch family. Water was carried in by buckets from a well and meals were cooked on a wood stove until the late 1960s.

The 1905 stone jail with a brick chimney still stands at 106 E. 5th. It's last-known inhabitant was in the early 1970s.

Chris Beougher grew up in the area and decided to try his hand at running a bar and grill. He's an energetic young fellow! Support him by stopping in for a greasy burger and homemade macaroni and cheese at Elk River Drive-In, 202 W. 2nd (U.S. 160). Monday-Saturday 8 a.m.-8 p.m. 620.642.3663. FB.

Old-timers say a cafe has always been in the old building at 417 Kansas as long as they can remember. It's changed hands and names a few times, but today the Cozy Inn Cafe is here serving made-from-scratch edibles that the locals love. Hardly a seat can be found on Sundays when owner Stephanie Henning and her crew fry up hand-battered, pan-fried chicken. Breakfast served all day and daily specials are other delicious reasons to stop here. Tuesday-Sunday 6:30 a.m.-2 p.m. 620.642.3911.

Lodging:
Silver Bell Motel (620.642.6145, tinyurl.com/longtonsilverbell). **ee**

explorer extras...
In Moline

Population 340

The oldest pedestrian suspension bridge in the state spans Wildcat Creek one block west of Main

at 515 N. Biddle. The cables and wood planks have been replaced on this 1904 bridge, but it still has a good swing and a fascinating rhythm.

A Masonic room, WWI photographic equipment, memorabilia from the oldest Chevrolet dealership in the nation, and more are found inside this three-story frame building, now the Shaffer House Museum, 2nd and Plum. The house, originally built in the late 1800s as a rooming house, took on the shape and style seen today in 1919 when Dr. C.E. Shaffer purchased it, added to it, and opened a private hospital. The structure later was used as an apartment building, and in 1973 it became the town's museum. June-August, Saturday and Wednesday 9 a.m.-12 p.m. 620.647.3406.

A U.S. Air Force T-33 trainer jet rests in City Park at 3rd and Maple. The plane had been on display in Independence for many years but had deteriorated over time and become the target of vandals. In the late 1990s Moline residents donated money to move the jet to their town, restore it, and place it in its new home. A fence now protects the aircraft. The first T-33 jet made its first flight in 1948; production ended in 1959.

Enjoy the friendly staff and the special—a hand-breaded chicken-fried steak with french fries on top and covered with gravy—at the Swinging Bridge Cafe, 304 Walnut. Monday-Saturday 7 a.m.-7:30 p.m. 620.647.4055. FB. **ee**

Greenwood County

AROUND THE COUNTY

From April to October Greenwood County pastures are filled with about 120,000 stocker cattle that come from all over the country to graze on the prairie's lush green grasses for about 90 days. Additionally, some 22,000 in cow herds are grazed year round and supplemented with hay and feed during the winter.

SE

EUREKA

Population 2,527

"Eureka, I Found It!":
1st between Main and Elm. Walk south on the path, cross a small rock-banked creek, and look on the west side. There a large native stone contains a tablet with an inscription that begins, "'Eureka, I found it', shouted a small band of hardy pioneers in August of 1857." It goes on to read that the cool clear water convinced these settlers that this was the "ideal place" for their town site.

Greenwood Hotel (NRHP):
301 N. Main. A major renovation of this 1883 three-story hotel was completed in 1926. The building's Spanish style architecture, popular in elite circles at that time, is

evident in the multicolored clay roof tiles, the thick geometric-patterned stucco, and the exposed window hoods. From serving as a small livestock exchange to becoming the site of many million-dollar oil-field deals in the 1920s, the hotel has hosted guests from all walks of life. The classic green-and-gold marquee is from 1926. In the 21st century, a second restoration has been completed on the hotel's first floor, which now contains an event center, offices, and retail stores. 620.583.2599. FB.

Greenwood County Historical Museum:

120 W. 4th. Ranching, farming, and oil-boom exhibits, plus historic photos of all the towns in the county (including the ghost town of Teterville) are featured in the museum's new building. You'll also learn about the area's orphan train children, black settlers, nationally recognized sculptor and Eureka native Jim Brothers, and dolls handmade by local women employed by the WPA. Excellent genealogical information is available. Monday-Friday 10 a.m.-4 p.m.; Saturday 10 a.m.-1 p.m.; November-February, closed Saturday. 620.583.6682. FB.

Historical Driving Tours:

Self-guided tour brochures for each quadrant of the county are available at the Historical Museum, 120 W. 4th. They direct you to a WPA constructed lake, stone bridges, ghost towns, cemeteries, oil-boom remnants, natural landmarks, and many more fascinating sites. 620.583.6682.

Post Office Art (NRHP):

301 N. Oak. *Cattle Roundup* is the title of this 1938 Section artwork by Vance Kirkland.

Utopia College: 708 E. 5th.

In response to fear of an impending third world war and the use of nuclear bombs, Roger Babson, a Massachusetts economist and philanthropist believed the Mid-west to be the safest place for people to sustain themselves—and he considered Eureka to be in the exact middle of the "magic circle" safe zone. He purchased several properties here in 1947 and founded a college where he could preach his message and prepare students to teach at his other colleges, thereby creating a larger network of believers. The college never met enrollment expectations and eventually folded in 1970. Two buildings remain—the main headquarters, a large white mansion of the Southern Colonial style at 708 E. 5th; and a three-story red-brick structure at 522 N. Nicholas. More information about Babson and his college is at the Historical Museum, 120 W. 4th.

Martyred John Rogers:

708 E. 5th. Roger Babson (*see previous entry*) erected a large granite marker in memory of his ancestor the Reverend John Rogers, who according to the inscription, was burned at the stake in 1555 for translating the Bible into English.

Robertson House (NRHP):

403 N. Plum. This eclectic Prairie School style structure is an exotic architectural specimen by Kansas standards, but its grandeur exemplified the rise of the area's oil industry in the early 1920s. Built in 1923 by oil contractor Russell Roy Robertson, the home was a symbol of his success in the new industry. But little did the next owner know when he bought the home just before the Great Depression that the price of oil would drop to 66 cents a barrel by 1933. Unfortunately, the house was sold at a sheriff's sale. A similarly designed house at 403 N. Maple is a Prairie-Italian Renaissance style hybrid. Drive by only.

Victorian Faces: 201

N. Main. Three identical female faces still watch over the former Eureka Bank built in 1879. The busts, a typical Victorian motif, are ornamenta-tion on the structure's arched window hoods. The Italianate building is now occupied by a local CPA business.

Greenwood Cemetery:

1407 E. 7th. Two mausoleums serve as great examples of the 1890s Classical Revival influence. The Leedy and the Thrall mausoleums both are massive stone structures elaborately adorned with Victorian detail (flower motifs, heavy columns, pilasters, and symmetrical facades). They stand off the fourth driveway to the east of the cemetery entrance.

Fall River Canoe Trips:

416 E. River. Rent your canoes from Lloyd Funk and launch at the Fall River Wildlife Area. It's a great family or group outing lasting two to three hours down

a four-and-a-half-mile scenic waterway that ends at Eureka. Shuttle service is provided. Reservations required. April-October. 316.841.0462.

Westside Service Station and Riverside Motel

(NRHP): 325 W. River. This former gas station and motel take you back to a time when Americans drove cross-country on smaller highways and through every small town along the way. Travelers needed roadside service stations, cafes, and lodging, which were sometimes combined into one property. This series of buildings was constructed in 1939 as a combination service station, cafe, and three cabins with carports. They were built in a regional architectural style known as Ozark Giraffe, a version of cobblestone-house construction. In the years that followed, larger cabins were added and smaller ones torn down. Today the buildings are a popular restaurant and bar known as Benny's Westside.

Benny's Westside: 325 W.

River. Good times are found inside this 1939 former service station and cafe, which are rich in history and architectural character. The service bay is now the bar, complete with a garage door that opens onto an outdoor patio. The sandwiches, soup, and service are superb. 620-583-8700. FB. Daily 11 a.m.-10 p.m.

Lo Mar Drive In:

916 E. River. Devout followers of this little red-and-white 1955 drive-in swoon when they hear the words Marshmallow Nut Cup. It's a

scrumptious heap of soft serve chocolate ice cream, velvety marshmallow topping, and crunchy chopped peanuts. You might find something similar elsewhere, but for some reason it tastes extra special here. The juicy burgers are made from Black Angus beef. Monday, Wednesday-Saturday 11 a.m.-7 p.m. 620.583.7810. FB.

Cindy's Copper Kettle:

815 E. River. The locals say, "When relatives come to town, we go to the Copper Kettle." That has to tell you something! We can tell you that the home cooking is fabulous and the chicken and noodles are a favorite. Tuesday-Saturday 6:30 a.m.-8 p.m.; Sunday 7:30 a.m.-2:30 p.m. 620.583.5716. FB.

Cake Batter Batter:

110 E. 3rd. Deanna Jensen hit a home run when she opened her bakery inside the historic Greenwood Hotel. Step up to the plate and order cookies, cupcakes, cinnamon rolls, sandwiches on homemade bread, soups, and fresh roasted coffee. If you haven't visited Deanna's bakery yet, well… batter late than never! During baseball season, hours may change. Monday-Friday 7 a.m.-6 p.m.; Saturday 7 a.m.-2 p.m. 620.583.2599. FB.

Lodging: Spring Creek Guest House (620.583.7271, double-arrowc.com); additional lodging (tinyurl.com/eurekalodging).

explorer extras… In Eureka

Revered architect George P. Washburn designed the 1914 Eureka Carnegie library (NRHP), 520 N. Main, a one-story brick and limestone structure of the Neoclassical style. A private business now occupies the building.

It's heartening to see restoration efforts, and the Santa Fe depot (NRHP) at 416 E. 5th has bene-

fited from just such an effort. The first depot was constructed in 1879, but as the oil and gas boom grew, the town required a larger depot. The current Prairie and Craftsman style brick and stucco depot was built in 1917 on the site of the original. Passenger service to Eureka ended in the 1950s, and freight service in 1971. A private business undertook the restoration and now occupies the very attractive depot.

You will enjoy a six-mile scenic drive around Eureka City Lake, completed in 1938 by the WPA, Civilian Conservation Corps, and the city. The 1930s craftsmanship is still evident in the native limestone inlaid dam, picnic shelters, and entrances. The lake was built for flood control, water supply, and recreation, and today the property incorporates a residential development. From 7th, 4½ miles north on State (becomes Lake), then east to the lake. 620.583.5858.

Take a seat on the Whittle and Argue Club Summer Annex bench on the south side of the Greenwood Hotel, 301 N. Main. The green bench dates at least to the 1950s when prominent Eurekans whittled and argued here. A message on the bench reads, "People with high tempers please use dull knives." **ee**

SE

FALL RIVER

Population 154

Fall River Grocery:

414 Merchants. The sidewalks are elevated in Fall River so step up and support this grocery store! Monday-Saturday 7:30 a.m.-6 p.m. 620.658.4615.

Fall River Lake and State Park: From U.S. 400, 1 mile north on Lake, then continue ¾ mile north on 534. The Fall River reservoir dam was completed in 1949 to diminish flood damage. Positioned between the cross timber area of the Chautauqua Hills to the east and the grasslands of the Flint Hills to the west, this area supports forested flood plains, blackjack oaks, and tallgrass prairie. Canoeing is popular here and mountain bikers will find two challenging trails. State park entrance charge. Cabins available. Reservations required. 620.637.2213. ksoutdoors.com.

Iron Truss Bridge: From U.S. 400, 2¼ miles north and east on Lake. Bear southeast at the fork just before the Fall River dam, and slowly proceed ½ mile down a narrow, winding blacktop toward the campground. You'll come to a pretty little one-lane truss bridge that takes you across the Fall River. For a distant view of the picturesque 1929 bridge, cross the dam on 20.

Fall River to Climax Scenic Drive: From the east end of the Fall River dam, 4¼ miles north and west on a twisting Badger Creek Rd., stairstep west and north on 55, then 10 miles west on 70 to Climax. This slow, leisurely drive to Climax takes you through hills and valleys, woodlands, and along Otter Creek. The early part of this drive borders Fall River Lake. Maps of the lake will help you and are available at the state park office.

HAMILTON

Population 255

Holmes Sundry: 101 E. Main. Every inch of space is put to good use in this old drug store, and an old-fashioned soda fountain dating to the 1920s holds a featured spot. Locals and visitors love this store and take advantage of the delicious meals and lunch specials that change daily. Buy and eat all you can—it's the heart and soul of Hamilton. Monday-Friday 6 a.m.-6 p.m.; Saturday 6 a.m.-3 p.m.; Sunday 7 a.m.-1 p.m. 620.678.3341.

explorer extras... In Madison

Population 671

The Madison Historical Society has worked hard to create a museum inside this 1879 Santa Fe Depot (NRHP). Nicely interpreted exhibits, interesting artifacts, and historic photos provide a window into the past of this sturdy town. 3rd and Boone. 620.437.2303.

Who says Kansas is flat? From Lincoln, drive south on 3rd up to the old water tower. You'll see why sleds are not allowed on this hill!

A renovated Gulf Station stands at Madison and 4th, complete with gas pumps that read 32 cents per gallon.

Although it closed in 1952, friends of the brown-brick District No. 8 School have restored it to become one of the grandest little one-room schoolhouses in the state. Next to it No. 8 Cemetery contains an unusual memorial on the southeast side near the road—a small sculpture of an elephant in ornamental saddle and headdress. It bears no identification other than a U.S. Vietnam Veterans medallion placed near the elephant's feet. From 3rd, 2¾ miles south and east on K-58. **ee**

explorer extras... In Neal

Population 49

This scenic route isn't for everyone, and it's for no one if the road is at all muddy. From Main, 1¾ miles east on U.S. 54, 1½ miles south on CC, then stop! Stop and walk down to Walnut River, to the Rocky Ford. Large flat rocks make it possible to drive across the river, but only in utility vehicles. This lovely area might just be something to view and admire, but not cross, and instead retrace your path back to the highway. **ee**

PIEDMONT

Unincorporated

Jim and Lila's Cafe: 100 Main. In 1963 Jim and Lila Wunderlick bought a cafe in downtown then in 1971 moved their business across the street to its present location. It's been there, open six days a week, ever since. Jim is gone now, and Lila is over 80, but she still does the cooking the same way she'd do it at home. Some say the fried chicken is the best they've ever had, and the chicken-fried steak is pan fried! It's a rustic, out-of-the-way spot where the local farmers and ranchers gather. It has all the charm you would expect, and then some, from a little place called Jim and Lila's. Monday-Friday 7 a.m.-3 p.m.; Saturday 7 a.m.-8 p.m. 620.864.2250.

North Branch Otter Creek Bridge (NRHP): From Walnut, 1 mile north on Main, ¾ mile west on U.S. 400, then 3¾ miles north on Fairview. J. Walter Sharp built this stone triple-arch bridge in 1908, and thankfully in 2004 the Greenwood County commissioners voted to save it. Instead of tearing it down, they built a new bridge beside it and left this old beauty for all to admire.

explorer extras...
Severy

Population 248

From K-99, 1 mile west on 400 to Q. When you see the silo at the corner you'll have found the Needle in a Haystack! The metal building beside the silo is a quilt shop stocking more than 3,000 bolts of quality cotton fabric along with the latest books, patterns, notions, and antique rolling pins. Look closely at the top of the silo. Do you see the giant needle and thread? Monday-Saturday 9 a.m.-5 p.m.; Sunday 1-5 p.m. 620.736.2942. FB.

The delightful former 1937 service station at Main and S, nattily spruced up, carries fresh produce, grass-fed beef, baked

goods, collectibles, antiques, and coffee. Severy Station is a pleasing stop for locals and visitors. May-December, Friday 7 a.m.-3 p.m. and first Saturday of the month 7 a.m.-3 p.m. 816.225.3855. FB. **ee**

TETERVILLE

Ghost Town

Teterville Scenic Back Road: It's a beautiful and unobstructed drive through the Flint Hills to find the remnants of Teterville. From Hamilton, stairstep 6¼ miles west and south on 4, stairstep 8½ miles west and north on 1 (becomes 7), north 3¼ miles on River, then 1 mile east on Teterhill. Look for the remains as you turn south into the pasture to go to Teter Rock (*see* next entry). Built during the 1920s oil boom, Teterville once boasted a population of more than 600, along with two general stores, a school, a post office, and shotgun houses for oil workers and their families. By the 1960s everyone and nearly everything was gone. Today only a few foundations and an old oil-heating tank remain.

Teter Rock: From the Teterville remnants, 1 mile south on a pasture driveway (look for signs to the Rock). Around the late 1870s James Teter piled rocks as a marker to guide pioneers searching for the Cottonwood River. Eventually the rocks were removed and used for construction materials. So in 1954 a 16-foot-tall rock slab was erected on this hilltop in honor of Teter. There's something about this jagged and giant rock slicing through the Flint Hills skyscape that makes this a powerful Kansas site.

Wild Mustangs: You might have glimpsed a wild mustang as you drove north on River to Teter Rock. But you're likely to see an entire herd from your high perch at the Rock. Look south into the valley where these horses often are contentedly grazing or running unfettered in the Flint Hills pasture. For the past 15 years mustangs have been brought to Kansas by the Bureau of Land Management from western states where the severe weather had made their living conditions in their natural habitat unstable. Today more than 4,700 wild horses roam more than 36,600 acres in the Flint Hills.

SE

Labette County

AROUND THE COUNTY

Pearson-Skubitz Big Hill Lake: Situated in the northwest part of the county, Big Hill Lake, run by the U.S. Army Corps of Engineers, is one of the clearest lakes in Kansas with more than 1,200 acres of surface water. It provides fishing and camping and features numerous parks, hiking trails, and 17 miles of equestrian trails. 620.336.2741. Camping reservations. 877.444.6777. tinyurl.com/bighilllake.

CHETOPA

Population 1,086

Memorial Marker: Maple/U.S. 166 and Locust. From 1st, ¼ mile east on U.S. 166, then south into City Park. As you enter the small park, look for the large, red granite marker with bas-reliefs of Chief Chetopah and George Lisle. The monument memorializes town founder Lisle, the settlers who helped build the town, and Lisle's friend Osage Chief Chetopah, for whom the town is named.

Catfish Capital of Kansas:

618 N. 11th. Record numbers of catfish are caught on the Neosho River throughout the year. Thanks to former Chetopa mayor Ron Wood, a large metal catfish from North Star Metal Works in Caney makes the perfect visual statement at the town entrance. A fishing pole hooks the giant fish next to the sign announcing Chetopa as the Catfish Capital of Kansas.

Paddlefish: From Maple/U.S. 166, 1 block south on 1st, then 1 block east on Locust. From mid-March to mid-May (when the river is high) fishermen try to catch the ancient-looking, scaleless paddlefish (locally known as the spoonbill) below the Neosho River dam.

Pecan Capital of Kansas:

The pecan tree is native to southeast Kansas, and groves of them are plentiful along U.S. 166 coming into Chetopa from the east. Pecan harvest, usually in late fall, utilizes a mechanical device that shakes the tree; a pecan harvester then picks up the fallen pecans.

Jeremiah Cook House:

706 Maple. Colonel Jeremiah Cook gained fame for his exploits

in the Union army and for his land and loan business. Cook, a state legislator, built this Italianate showpiece home with a prominent tower and wide eaves with paired brackets in 1886.

Stained-Glass Windows: 332 Maple. A stained-glass fan window of orange, yellow, blue, and pink brightens the imposing red-brick corner building. Built in 1900, it is a mix of Richardsonian Romanesque and Italianate styles. A smaller fan window of stained glass is set above the corner entrance. Originally a commercial structure, it currently is unoccupied

Hornets Nest: 937 Maple. The house-made hot sauce is a perfect compliment for any meal, especially the burgers, chicken-fried steak sandwiches, and homemade onion rings. With a nod to the school mascot, a hornets' nest hangs from the ceiling. It's a real one, but not active! Monday-Friday 10:30 a.m.-9 p.m. 620.236.7860. FB.

The Wulf's Den: 813 Maple. Open wide and use your fangs to bite into mile-high sandwiches such as Reubens, burgers, and Philly cheesesteaks. Tuesday-Sunday 11 a.m.-8 p.m. 620.236.2016. FB.

explorer extras... In Chetopa

Historic Chetopa is depicted in a colorful mural at the corner of 4th and Maple.

At the Chetopa Museum, 406 Locust, American Indian artifacts provide insight to the town's history and its namesake, Osage Chief Chetopah. April-September, Wednesday-Friday 1-4 p.m. 620.236.7121. FB. **ee**

Population 424

Edna Mattress Factory:

104 N. Delaware. Since 1962 owners Terry and Missy Hilderbrand have taken pride in producing high-quality traditional spring mattresses and latex foam beds. They also make custom mattresses to fit any size. Monday-Friday 8 a.m.-4:30 p.m.; Saturday 9 a.m.-1 p.m. 620.922.3440. FB.

First State Bank Building (NRHP): 100 Delaware.

Opening in 1887 as the International Bank, the two-story structure originally featured a Victorian facade, but in 1912 the ground floor was altered to reflect the Modern Classical Revival style. It served as a bank until 1978 when it became home to the Edna Historical Museum. 620.922.3841.

Art Deco Community Building: From Delaware,

½ block east on Main. Distinctively art deco with its pleasant lines and symmetrical design, the structure was built by the WPA in 1939 to serve as a community building, which it still does today.

Dalton's SteakOut:

1010 4000. Young Dalton Morgan's cooking and baking skills, learned from her mom, have gained her a loyal following for what she calls "classic cowgirl cuisine." The homemade light-and-crusty Vienna bread for the ribeye steak sandwich is especially popular. The Terry Special, named for the mattress factory owner, consists of two eggs over easy on a mattress of hash browns with scratch sausage gravy on top. Coffee lovers are giddy over the huge assortment of flavored iced and hot coffees. Tuesday-Friday 6:30 a.m.-2:30 p.m. 620.922.7280. FB.

explorer extras... In Mound Valley

Population 390

Why is a flagpole in the center of downtown's main intersection? No one knows why or how long it's been there. One theory is that town leaders placed it there for no particular reason. It does come in handy, though, for giving directions—"From the flagpole, go. . . ." In recognition of the mystery flagpole, every June the town hosts the Flagpole Festival.

You can almost see boys and girls of yesteryear skipping toward this charming 1904 red-brick rural schoolhouse, the former Globe School, with its tall bell tower. Not restored, but in decent condition, the school is unused today. 17036 Gove. From the flagpole, 3 blocks east to 5th, 2¾ miles north on Pecan (becomes Grove). **ee**

OSWEGO

Population 1,777

Historic Riverside Park

(NRHP): From 6th, 6 blocks north on Wisconsin. Thanks to the Oswego Lady's Entertainment Society, the town has Riverside Park. In 1887 the society

purchased an area overrun with scrub oak and brush for the purpose of developing a park. They deeded it to the city for one dollar in 1902. In the 1930s many structures—fountain, fishpond, shelters, pool and bathhouse—were built through a Kansas Emergency Relief Committee program and the WPA. An overlook atop a bluff offers a beautiful view of the expansive Neosho River Valley. A nearby historical marker describes the land's connection to the American Indians and the military. Narrow paved roads provide a lovely route through the park, which would make the Lady's Entertainment Society proud. 620.795.4433.

John Mathews Park:

4th and Union. In 1841 the U.S. government sent fur trader John Mathews to this area to serve the Osage Indians as a blacksmith. Mathews also owned a trading post, race track, stables, and tavern near this site. The well, which Mathews dug in 1841, is the only remnant of the Osage village, commonly known as Little Town. Mathews would later take the Confederate side during the Civil War and be killed by Union troops. A plaque and sign at the well recounts this area's early history.

Smith-Hollingsworth-Thomas Log House

(RHKP): 3rd and Merchant. This log cabin is the only visual reminder of the town's early settlement period. Pioneer James Smith built it in 1867, and later sold it to Elizabeth Hollingsworth, a pioneer mother of seven. The cabin, donated to the city by Nellie Thomas,

stands on its original site. At one time it served as a meeting place for the Baptist church, and later as a jail. A likeness of a pioneer mother and child is carved into a maple tree stump near the site.

Labette County Courthouse: 417 Merchant.

Some ideals are written in stone, such as the strong words "Justice" and "Equality" etched into the exterior of this 1948 structure. The front of the courthouse also lists the county's 16 original settlements.

Outdoor Mural: *Village of Little White Hair* at 4th and Commercial, illustrates the 1840s relationship between white trader John Mathews and the Osage Indian tribe.

Post Office Art (NRHP): 819 4th. *Farm Life* is the title of this 1940 Section artwork by Robert Larter.

Oswego Historical Museum: 410 Commercial.

Early history exhibits include display cases of WPA dolls and a collection of personal belongings of and photographs by Evelyn Briggs Baldwin, Arctic explorer (*see* next entry). This museum also is a resource for genealogical research. June-October, Monday-Friday 1-5 p.m. 620.795.4500. oswegohistory.org.

Evelyn Briggs Baldwin: This future Arctic explorer moved from Iowa to Oswego in 1869 with his parents and spent his youth here. He became a meteorologist and later went on two Arctic expeditions and

SE

led a third. He became a popular lecturer throughout the country, relating tales of his exploring adventures. The Historical Museum has an excellent collection of his personal belongings, photographs and items from his explorations, and copies of his book *The Search for the North Pole.* Baldwin is buried in Oswego Cemetery. From Commercial, 2¼ miles west and north on 6/U.S. 160. In the center of the east side, a tall red granite monument with an urn marks his grave.

Oswego Drug Store:
413 Commercial. Twenty flavors of fudge are made on site with real cream and butter. Try the samples to figure out which delicious piece (or pieces!) to buy. Monday-Friday 9 a.m.-6 p.m.; Saturday 9 a.m.-1 p.m. 620.795.2233.

explorer extras...
In Oswego

Built in a basic design, the one-story red-brick Carnegie library (NRHP), 704 4th, has been serving the town since 1912.

Originally built as a private residence in 1876, the brick Edwards House (RHKP), 910 Ohio, was one of the buildings of the Oswego College for Young Ladies from 1885 to 1920. By the time a devastating

1922 fire burned a dormitory and classroom, the college had already been sold to the Kansas Military Academy. The house, highlighted by its two-story porch supported by brick columns, is the last vestige of the college campus.

The spectacular Deming House at 918 6th combines several architectural styles, including Neoclassical, Dutch Colonial Revival, and Queen Anne. It was originally built in 1890 with additions in 1905 and 1906. The additions originally were part of the South American exhibits at the 1904 St. Louis World's Fair. After the fair ended they were disassembled and shipped to Oswego. **ee**

PARSONS

Population 10,164

Antietam Circle: From 16th, 1 mile east on Main, then ¼ mile south on Leawood to Oakwood Cemetery. Civil War veterans purchased the southwest corner of this impressive cemetery in 1886 and named it Antietam

Circle. A handsome cast-iron gateway donated by the DAR in 1911 leads to four bronze soldier statues each facing in different direction with many of the 300 Civil War graves encircling them. The two eight-inch cannons were gifts from the U.S. War Department in 1898, and a bald eagle sculpture stands atop the 1905 red-domed rotunda.

Carnegie Arts Center:
117 S. 17th. The 1909 Carnegie library (NRHP), now the Carnegie Arts Center, was built of Carthage stone cut in the Cyclopean style (a type of ancient masonry made with massive irregular blocks) and topped with a red clay tile roof.

First Presbyterian Church:
1700 Broadway. If the exterior of this 1907 Gothic Romanesque castle-like structure with turrets and imported Italian tiles doesn't impress you (and even if it does), step inside to see the 75 stained-glass windows! Monday-Friday 9 a.m.-12 p.m. 620.421.6300.

Parsons Historical Museum and Iron Horse Museum:
401 S. 18th. Rooms re-creating pioneer life, a large stone from the infamous Bender house, and a horse-drawn hearse are only a few of the exhibits at the Parsons Historical Museum. The Iron Horse Museum exhibits railroad memorabilia inside a replica 1885 KATY railroad depot. A locomotive and caboose are also on the grounds. May-October, Friday-Sunday 1-4 p.m. 620.717.1066. FB.

Parsons Arboretum:

2004 S. Briggs. The arboretum and wetlands were started in 1991 and are filling in nicely with trails, labeled trees, and shrubs. Two acres of wetlands, a large gazebo, a memorial tree area, nature trails throughout the 19-acre park, and an 18-hole disc golf course were developed on land deeded to the arboretum by the Union Pacific Railroad in 1991. The old municipal swimming pool bathhouse on site was converted into a visitor center. During the season, beautiful flower gardens enhance the visitor center area. 620.421.7088. tinyurl.com/parsonsarb.

Tale of the Turtle:

The 3,600 pound concrete turtle sculpture at the Parsons Arboretum was a beloved feature at the former skating rink. There he provided a place for generations of kids to sit while waiting for parents to pick them up—even after a drunk driver hit him and knocked off his head. The city moved the huge sculpture to the top of the wetlands dam and hired a sculptor to reattach his 350-pound head. Once again children can climb on the revived turtle, who is happily at home in the arboretum park. From Wilson and 21st, just north off Wilson.

Stan Herd Sculptures:

From U.S. 400, ¼ mile south on U.S. 59 (Tolen Creek Park, behind the travel plaza). Here you'll see two new giant stone sculptures by artist Stan Herd. *Ancient Head* is a 13-foot American Indian head and the second sculpture is a 32x24x6-foot turtle. A one-and-a-half-mile trail takes you past the sculptures and an 1895 stone cabin and around a pond.

Kitchen Pass Restaurant & Bar:

1711 11th. At this downtown spot expect great! Burgers, sandwiches, grilled salmon salad, blackened chicken, and a Kansas City strip dusted with a signature seasoning. Monday-Saturday 11 a.m.-10 p.m. 620.421.1907. FB.

Ernesto's Mexican Restaurante and Cantina:

200 N. Central. Chimichangas and beef fajitas with corn tortillas are only two of the many items cooked fresh daily and served to eager customers inside this colorful restaurante! Tuesday-Saturday 11 a.m.-1:30 p.m. and 4:30-8 p.m. 620.421.2930.

Circle's Pecans and Country Store:

2499 U.S. 400. From U.S. 59, 10 miles east on U.S. 400; or from McCune junction, 4 miles west on U.S. 400. Pecan growers since 1990, Circle's has expanded its business to include a restaurant and gift shop. You'll find fresh deli sandwiches, an array of baked goods (including sugar-free and gluten-free), and an assortment of pies—pecan is the top seller. Stock up on cracked pecans, flavored pecan candies, nut meats, jams, jellies, and much more. Monday-Saturday 9 a.m.-5 p.m. 620.632.4382. FB.

Lodging: Bricktoria Bed & Breakfast (620.423.3000, tinyurl.com/bricktoria); The Farmhouse (620.423.2216, experiencethefarmhouse.com); additional lodging (visitlabette.com).

explorer extras... In Parsons

Parsons is the Purple Martin Capital of Kansas, and houses for these tiny birds are found on Corning between 17th and 18th and on 18th between Corning and Belmont.

A replica of E.M. Viquesney's *Spirit of the American Doughboy* WWI memorial statue stands in front of the Municipal Building at 17th and Main.

In 1950 the Boy Scout troop donated the replica Statue of Liberty that stands in front of Parsons Middle School at N. 28th and E. Main.

It's the perfect place for your little ones to exercise their minds and enter a world of discovery. The vibrant and energetic environment inside Curious Minds Discovery Zone, 1810 Main, will stimulate brain cells and entertain young minds for hours. This hands-on museum is for children of all ages. Thursday-Saturday 10 a.m.-5 p.m.; Sunday 1-5 p.m. Admission charge (adults free). 620.778.2657. FB. **ee**

SE

Linn County

AROUND THE COUNTY

Frontier Military Historic Byway:
A designated Kansas Scenic Byway, the Kansas section of the military road starts at the Oklahoma border and passes through Linn County as it goes north to its terminus at the junction of K-5 and K-7 in Leavenworth. Originally known as the Fort Leavenworth-Fort Gibson Military Road, this route was built in 1838-1840 to accommodate soldiers traveling between military posts. 913.758.2948. travelks.com.ksbyways.

Original Military Road:
The county's only remaining section of the original Fort Leavenworth-Fort Gibson Military Road is found just east of Pleasanton. From Main in Pleasanton, go ¼ mile east on 10th, ½ mile south on Holly, then 1¾ miles east on 1000. A sign here states that the dirt road going ½ mile southwest to Mine Creek is the original military road.

Marais des Cygnes River:
With the river a dominant feature of the county, the origin of the name is of interest. Marais des Cygnes is a French translation of an Osage appellation meaning "marsh of the swans." According to American Indian legend, Coman and Osa, two young Indians from different tribes, fell in love. Coman's tribe was of the water; Osa's tribe was of the forest. Against the instructions of Osa's grandfather, a tribal elder who had forbidden the two to marry, the lovers set off down the river in Coman's canoe, only to be pulled under by a great and unforeseen force. Two swans appeared where the canoe had been moments before. The river has since been known as the marsh of the swans.

BLUE MOUND

Population 273

Ralph's Service:
107 N. 5th. Some might remember hearing the bell ring when you pulled into a gas station years ago. At Ralph's you still hear that yesteryear sound when you drive up to the gas pumps. An attendant comes right out to pump your gas, and if you need your windshield washed, just ask. What an old-fashioned treat! And it's a good stop too for a bottle of pop and a candy bar. Monday-Friday 7 a.m.-6 p.m.; Saturday 7 a.m-1 p.m.

Luna's Feedlot Cafe:
208 W. Main. Folks come here for the chicken-fried chicken, burgers, and for the rise-and-shine breakfasts, including made-from-scratch buttermilk pancakes. You'll find a lot of feed at the Feedlot. Monday-Saturday 7 a.m.-2 p.m. 913.756.2606.

CENTERVILLE

Unincorporated

Old Pump House:
4311 W. 1325. Laura Eastwood's husband attended an auction not long ago and came home with the news that she was the new owner of a 1918 oil pump house! It's a huge pump house, a two-story brick building with tall, stately windows on all sides. It didn't take long for Laura to turn it into an event center that hosts live music, dancing, weddings, and more. The building originally held equipment that pumped oil across the state to a refinery, and it closed in the 1940s. Admire it from the outside or for tours, call 785.448.7623. FB.

Farm & Feed:
212 E. Market. With the inventory that Howard and Bobbie Brown have, they need three buildings to hold it all! They stock everything from horse tack to hardware, gifts, kitchen tools, pet food, salt blocks, fencing, purses, jewelry, cowboy clothing, genuine leather goods, and feed. They also stock cold pop, bottled water, and cold candy bars in a cooler. And it's handy too that the post office sits between their buildings. Tuesday-Friday 10 a.m.-5 p.m.; Saturday 9 a.m.-2 p.m. 913.898.2266. centervillefarmfeed.com.

St. Philippine Duchesne Memorial Park:
8487 W. 1525. From Main, 2¾ miles north and east on 1077, then 2¾ miles south and east on W. 1525. Pass through a replica stockade entrance into the park, once the site of

Sugar Creek Mission. In 1838 900 Potawatomis were force marched 620 miles from their home in northern Indiana to the mission. The journey took 61 days, and during that time 39 Potawatomis, mostly children, died along what became known as the Trail of Death. In 1841 several nuns of the Sacred Heart order, including 72-year-old Sister Rose Philippine Duchesne, came to the mission to teach the children. Beyond the stockade entrance, the story of this tragic march and of Mother Duchesne is dramatically told through historical markers, memorials, pictures, and crosses. Mother Duchesne was canonized in 1988, the first female saint west of the Mississippi River.

LA CYGNE

Population 1,125

City of Swans:
Images of the graceful white bird adorn the town. Statues sit at the entrances to the park and cemetery and in front of houses. A swan is depicted on the town's welcome sign, and they are painted on the water tower and on windows of businesses and the museum. La Cygne's annual festival is the Swanfest, which takes place the second Saturday of every September. Founded in 1869, the town took its name from the nearby river,

the Marais des Cygnes, which is a French translation of an Osage appellation meaning "marsh of the swans."

La Cygne Historical Museum:
300 N. Broadway. A walk through the museum leads you to a drug store with old-fashioned remedies, a gun collection, the artwork of local artist Don Lutton, antique implements, and WPA dolls representing U.S. presidents and their wives. Volunteers work hard throughout the year documenting local history and creating rotating displays. May-October, Monday-Tuesday, Thursday-Friday 1-5 p.m. 913.757.2151.

Oak Lawn Cemetery:
Swan and W. 1st. Swans perched on top of brick pillars greet you at the entrance of this 1883 cemetery. Stately oaks stand over the cemetery's older section on the north end where several Civil War soldiers are buried. A memorial stone, next to a swan-shaped planter, has been placed in the cemetery to recognize those soldiers.

Isinglass Estate Winery:
16241 W. 381. Horses can be seen in their white-fenced pastures or in the equestrian arena practicing jumps. The estate is also home to cabins

and a meeting space, lakes, and a 20-acre vineyard. The winery and tasting room are inside a first-rate metal barn, and as you sample the wines you can view the stainless steel tanks and the Missouri oak wine barrels. The estate name, Isinglass, refers to a collagen used as a clarifying agent for wines. March-December, Saturday-Sunday 12-6 p.m. 913.226.2287. isinglassestate.com.

Lodging: Cabin Ridge (913.757.3999); additional lodging (tinyurl.com/linncolodging).

MOUND CITY

Population 682

SE

Woodland Cemetery:
N. 5th and Elm. Thirty Union soldiers killed in the 1864 Civil War Battles of Mine Creek and Marais des Cygnes are buried in the city cemetery. Ownership of the plots, known as the Soldiers' Lot, was later transferred to the federal government, which maintains them today. The remains of other Union and unknown soldiers were moved from different areas of the county to the Soldiers' Lot in 1888. A tall granite monument with a soldier statue was added in 1889. The cemetery is the final resting place of free-state activist James Montgomery; William Stillwell, a victim of the 1858 Marais des Cygnes Massacre; and local abolitionists Augustus and Susan Wattles.

Linn County Courthouse (NRHP):
315 Main. Inside this Queen Anne style courthouse are pressed-tin ceilings, gleaming wood doors, historic photos, and original furnishings.

The front door handle is the original hardware placed there in 1886, and upstairs in the courtroom take a step-back-in-time by walking across the creaky wood floors. The courthouse was a setting for the 1969 movie *The Learning Tree*, filmed by famed Kansan Gordon Parks. Monday-Friday 8 a.m.-5 p.m. 913.795.2660.

Mound City Historical Park: 7th and Main. During the Civil War, Union soldiers camped on the hillside that is now this historic and attractive park. Pioneer structures and artifacts help visitors imagine what life was like in the early days of the city. A 1915 bungalow, log cabin, 1888 depot, 1864 schoolhouse, barn, and windmill are part of the complex. You'll also see a gazebo, which marks a 1914 mineral well that spurred the construction of a short-lived sanitarium. A building at the park's west end houses an 1840s bandwagon left in town by a circus in 1865. May-October, Saturday-Sunday 1-5 p.m. 913.795.2074.

Sacred Heart Church:
727 Main. The church was built in 1941 as a shrine to Sister Rose Philippine Duchesne, who was canonized in 1988. The stone interior features stained-glass windows that tell her life story, and two murals portray her work at Sugar Creek Mission, where she taught Potawatomi children and nursed the sick in 1841. Call ahead, 913.795.2770.

Tranquility Village Cafe:
614 Main. Relax inside this dining area of soothing colors. Biscuits and gravy and Philly cheesesteak sandwiches are only a few of the popular menu items. Pets are welcome and have their own pet menu—at an outside dining area with Pork Chop, the owner's rescued terrier. The Tranquility complex includes well-tended flower gardens with a rustic touch, which you are welcome to stroll about, and a lovely shop with gifts, antiques, and plants. Monday-Thursday 7 a.m.-4:30 p.m.; Saturday 7 a.m.-6 p.m.; Sunday 8 a.m.-2 p.m. 913.795.0246. tranquilityvillage.com.

Lodging: Chestnut Guest House (913.471.4578, tinyurl.com/linncolodging).

explorer extras...
In Mound City

In 1904 the funeral for territorial abolitionist Susan Wattles was held at the 1868 Congregational Church at 5th and Spruce. The church is no longer in use.

The white front columns of the 1941 Mound City Library portend the richness and history of this structure. The forerunner of the library was the Mound City Literary Society founded by the town's young women in the 1870s. They originally named the society, and later the library, for Mary Somerville, a revered Scottish scientist and mathematician of the 19th century, but who had no personal

connection to this country. 913.795.2788.

The 1868 county jail (NRHP) at 318 Main, is the oldest original building still standing in Mound City. It now houses the antique store Three Chicks and a Pony. Wednesday, Friday-Saturday 9 a.m.-1 p.m. FB.

The redbuds in the spring and the sugar maples in the fall make

Mound City a beautiful place to visit. Sugar maples are indigenous and prolific in this area. You'll have a wonderful view of the area from Sugar Mound Lookout. From 4th, ½ mile east on Main to the hilltop. **ee**

PARKER

Population 268

Heritage Park: 125 W. Woodward. Nothing says "community" like a park. A sidewalk decorated with symbols and family names leads to a nicely constructed shelter with an outdoor kitchen. The sidewalk names reflect the community members who donated and helped make the park amenities possible.

Landers Creek Bridge (NRHP): From Main, 3 miles south on Center (becomes 1077), just west over the tracks into Goodrich (unincorporated town), then ¼ mile south on Main. This unique five-arch bridge is an example of the era (1920s) when both limestone and concrete were used in construction. As is usual, the bridge arches are under the road, but the concrete spandrel walls extend above the road to form guard rails. You'll know you're almost there

when the gravel road becomes a driveway. The bridge is no longer open to vehicular traffic.

Lodging: Walnut Hill Farm Bed and Breakfast (913.898.6595, walnuthillbnb.com).

PLEASANTON

Population 1,187

Mine Creek Battlefield State Historic Site

(NRHP): From U.S. 69, 1 mile west on K-52. In October 1864 approximately 2,500 Union soldiers routed approximately 7,000 Confederate troops, killing or capturing more than 1,000. It was the only Civil War battle fought on Kansas soil and was one of the largest cavalry engagements of the war. Inside the visitor center Civil War uniforms, weapons, and photographs interpret this historic event. More than two miles of trails with signage provide a close-up view of the battlefield. April-October, Wednesday-Saturday 10 a.m.-5 p.m. Admission charge. 913.352.8890. kshs.org.

General Pleasonton: Main and 9th. You'll find the bronze bust of the town's namesake, General Alfred Pleasonton, in the small, well-landscaped General Pleasonton Park. The plaque on the bust's base provides a brief timeline of his service in the military, including leading the charge of Union troops at the 1864 Battle of Mine Creek. Five years later, the town of Pleasanton (spelled differently from the general's name) was established.

Linn County Historical Museum:

307 E. Park. Bleeding Kansas, the Underground Railroad, and the Civil War are feature exhibits at this outstanding small-town museum. Other displays present the local story of lead and coal mining, military uniforms from the Civil War to the Gulf War, a buggy shop, period rooms, and much more. The genealogy library is one of the best in the region. Tuesday,

Thursday 9 a.m.-5 p.m.; Saturday-Sunday 1-5 p.m. 913.352.8739.

Cookee's Drive-In: 102 E. 12th. You can't miss this brightly trimmed drive-in with retro service— no buttons or intercoms here, just drive up and someone will come to your car and take your order. Housed in an original 1950s Valentine diner, Cookee's is a shot of nostalgia for baby boomers, and a glimpse into the past for their kids and grandkids. Diner classics—burgers, fries, and malts—are on the menu. Monday-Friday 11 a.m.-7 p.m.; Saturday 9 a.m.-7 p.m.; Sunday 11 a.m.-6 p.m. 913.352.8789. cookeesdrivein.com.

Lodging: Cedar Crest Lodge (913.352.6533, cedarcrestlodge.com).

explorer extras... In Prescott

Population 262

The 1883 two-story red-brick Prescott School building (NRHP)

at 174 W. 3rd, designed in the Italianate style, is now the city library. Congratulations to Prescott for its efforts to restore this historic structure. 913.471.4593.

The community restored a second school, the former Prescott Rural High School (NRHP), 202 W. 4th, which closed its doors in 2006. Constructed in 1924 in the Mission and Spanish Revival style, it was later used as an elementary and junior high school and is now the city hall.

The "Father of Rocky Mountain National Park," Enos Mills was the son of a Quaker family that farmed here when he was born in 1870. For health reasons, he left for Colorado at age 14 and began a lifelong love affair with the Rockies. Mills' interest led him to later be the driving force behind the creation of the national park in 1915. A sign noting this achievement stands at the site of his birth. From Main, 3 miles north on Ungeheuer, then ½ mile east on 600.

The Mine Creek Bridge (NRHP), a 110-foot steel and concrete Marsh rainbow single-arch bridge, was built in 1927. From Main, 5¼ miles north on Ungeheuer. **ee**

TRADING POST

Unincorporated

Trading Post Museum:

From U.S. 69, 600 feet east on K-52, then 1 mile southwest on Valley. Established in 1825 by French traders, Trading Post is one of the oldest existing settlements in Kansas. At the museum an 1827 map designates this site as "establishment de Chouteau," the name of a family

SE

operating this American Fur Company post and licensed to sell kettles, blankets, and other items to the Potawatomi and the Miami tribes during the 1830s and 1840s. April-October, Wednesday-Saturday 10 a.m.-2 p.m. 660.200.5566. FB.

Marais des Cygnes Massacre Memorial:
Trading Post Cemetery, just north of the Trading Post Museum. A tall granite monument pays tribute to victims of the 1858 Marais des Cygnes Massacre (see next entry). Inscribed on the memorial are the names of the free-state men who died or were wounded, a brief summary of the tragedy, and two stanzas of "Le Marais du Cygne," a poem by John Greenleaf Whittier written in response to the massacre. The poem appeared in the September issue of the *Atlantic Monthly* four months after the incident and drew national attention to the violence in Kansas Territory.

Marais Des Cygnes Massacre State Historic Site (NRHP): 26426 E. 1700.
From U.S. 69, ¾ mile east on K-52, 1 mile north on Wakefield, 2½ miles east on 1700, then ¾ mile north and west on a gravel road. Take the first left into the park and continue past the 1860s stone house to the massacre site and historical marker at the ravine. Twelve

historical markers guide you through this unattended site and recount the massacre. On May 19, 1858, proslavery border ruffians rounded up 11 local free-state men, marched them to this ravine, and opened fire. Six men were killed and five were wounded. Soon after the massacre, John Brown built a short-lived fort on the site, and in December that same year, in an act of retaliation, he went into Missouri to free 11 slaves. The massacre focused the nation's eye on Bleeding Kansas, the sobriquet applied to Kansas Territory during the Missouri border wars over the slavery issue. 913.352.8890. kshs.org.

Marais Des Cygnes National Wildlife Refuge:
24141 K-52. From U.S. 69, 1 mile east on K-52. Calling all bird watchers! This 15,000-acre wetlands wildlife habitat is dedicated to the management of waterfowl, wetlands, and bottomland hardwood forest. The refuge is named for the trumpeter swan (cygne), which historically was common in the Midwest and thought to have stopped at these wetlands during fall and spring migrations. 913.352.8956. fws.gov.

Lyon County

explorer extras... In Admire

Population 156

The Flint Hills Nature Trail passes through the northern tier of Lyon County. Access the trail in Admire at Main and 4th. Access points are also found in Allen and Bushong to the west. kanzatrails.org.

Just a short drive west of town is a graceful stone single-arch bridge crossing Hill Creek. Rock Bridge is hand-hewn and built in 1917 with limestone from a nearby quarry. Because it was

the oldest standing structure in Admire, the bridge was renamed Admire Memorial Bridge in 1986 in recognition of the town's centennial. From K-99, 1 mile west on South (becomes 330).

The former 1925 high school (elementary school after consolidation) has been converted for use as a community center at 100 E. 3rd. **ee**

Population 177

Historic Buildings: A number
of interesting historic structures reside in this tiny town—the two-story limestone 1907 Allen Hotel (324 Main); the old drug store (403 Main); the former State Bank, now City Hall (4 W. 5th); and a former school at 108 E. 7th. The school, now a child development center, was built in 1918 in the Neoclassical style but it's easy to recognize the "new" 1948 Streamlined design addition.

Keianna's Dive: 408 Main.
If you're looking for tasty vittles, this dive is a doozy. The menu includes homemade pies—pecan and chocolate cream are the favorites—and burgers, salads, lunch specials, and fried chicken every Thursday. Keianna's cooking keeps the locals happy! Monday-Saturday 10:30 a.m.-2 p.m. 620.528.3355. FB.

AMERICUS

Population 883

Rolling Hills Bar & Grill:

622 Main. This comfortable and casual spot receives high marks for fantastic food and friendly folks and offers such favorites as beef-n-bleu burger, aged hand-cut steaks, chicken-fried steak, homemade coconut cream pie, root beer floats, and more. Of special interest is the shrimp boil special on the first Friday and Saturday of the month! Monday-Saturday 11 a.m.-10 p.m. 620.443.7005. FB.

Harry & Lloyd's Bar and Grill:

608 Main. If you're a fan of comedies, you'll get the name of this bar and grill. If not, we'll give you a hint and say there's nothing "dumb" about the sports bar ambience of gleaming dark wood and exposed stone walls. And you might be "dumb and dumber" (now you get it?) not to try the fried tacos with pulled pork, barbecue sauce, and a side of homemade coleslaw. Monday-Saturday 5-9 p.m.; Sunday 3-7 p.m. 620.443.5066. FB.

EMPORIA

Population 24,799

Veterans Day Founder:

Alvin King, an Emporia shoe salesman whose nephew had died in combat in 1944, began a campaign in 1953 to change the name of Armistice Day to Veterans Day, thereby honoring veterans from all wars rather than only those from WWI. Kansas Congressman Ed Rees carried the message to Congress, and in 1954 President Eisenhower signed the bill proclaiming November 11 (formerly Armistice Day) as Veterans Day. In 2003 Congress officially declared Emporia the Founding City of Veterans Day. Commemorating Veterans Day (8 Wonders of Kansas Customs) is especially significant in Emporia.

All Veterans Memorial:

933 S. Commercial (Soden's Grove Park). In 1991 Emporia dedicated the first memorial in the nation to honor all veterans from the Civil War through the Gulf War. A Vietnam War-era Huey helicopter and a WWII Sherman army tank accompany the memorial, as does the Purple Heart Memorial. A first-rate and moving online tour is at allveteransday.org. 620.341.1803.

Veteran Monuments:

Veterans are respectfully honored with many memorials throughout Emporia. Civil War Veterans Monument (4th and Union, Fremont Park); Spanish-American War Memorial (S. Neosho and Kansas); Hispanic American World War II Veterans Memorial (205 S. Lawrence, St. Catherine's Church); Veterans Hall of Honor (1200 Commercial, Emporia State University, Memorial Student Union).

William Allen White

(8 Wonders of Kansas People): Born in Emporia in 1868 and raised in El Dorado, William Allen White attended the College of Emporia and the University of Kansas before returning to Emporia in 1895, when he purchased the *Emporia Gazette*. He rose to national fame with his 1896 editorial "What's the Matter with Kansas," which targeted the Populist Party. White's writings influenced local, state, and national politics for more than 60 years. White is buried at Maplewood Cemetery, 2000 Prairie.

Red Rocks State Historic Site:

927 Exchange. When you see the red Colorado sandstone house, you'll have found Red Rocks, the home of William Allen White and family. White lived here from 1899 until his death in 1944. The house was built in 1888 in the Queen Anne style and White bought it in 1899.

By 1921 the White family had converted it to its present Tudor Revival appearance. Red Rocks remained in the White family until 2001 when White's granddaughter Barbara White Walker and her husband, Paul, donated it to the State of Kansas. April-October, Thursday-Saturday 11 a.m.-5 p.m. Admission charge. 620.342.2800. kshs.org.

Emporia Gazette Museum:

517 Merchant (*Emporia Gazette* office). Early 20th-century newspaper equipment and artifacts dating to the William Allen White era are displayed including White's desk in the front office. Note the lion head, sunflowers, and keys that serve as doorknobs. White's great-grandson Christopher White Walker is the *Gazette's* current publisher. On slower news days the staff will be glad to give you a tour through the museum. Call ahead (ask for Regina), 620.342.4800.

William Lindsay White Memorial Park:

North of the *Emporia Gazette* office. Posted on bronze plaques in this memorial pocket park are a selection of editorials and musings by William Allen White and his son William Lindsay White, also a former *Gazette* editor.

SE

Peter Pan Park: W. Randolph and Neosho. William Allen White and his wife, Sallie, donated the land for this park in memory of their daughter, Mary, who died in 1921 at age 16 in a horseback riding accident. The Whites named it Peter Pan Park because Mary, like Peter Pan, never wanted to grow up. At the south edge of the lake is a bust of White, dedicated in 1950 by former President Herbert Hoover, along with White's moving editorial to his daughter. A statue of Peter Pan stands at S. State and Kansas near the wading pool.

Prairie Passage Stone Sculpture Garden: U.S. 50 Business and Industrial (Lyon County Fairgrounds). Eight limestone pylons represent prominent individuals throughout Emporia's history. Designed by Emporian Richard Stauffer, the monoliths were carved by the Kansas Sculptors Association team in 1992. The figures include William Allen White, internationally known editor of the *Emporia Gazette*; Alahe, an American Indian representing the "people of the east wind"; Nathaniel Lyon, a Civil War general for whom Lyon County was named; and Preston B. Plumb, an Emporia founder and U.S. Senator.

Lyon County History Center: 711 Commercial. Begin your exploration of the county and surrounding area in this former Montgomery Ward store built in 1928. Interactive exhibits showcase the Flint Hills, Veterans Day and the military, American Indians, natural history, immigration, farming, ranching, and transportation. A discovery area for kids encourages little

ones to learn about history through investigation and imagination. Tuesday-Saturday 10 a.m.-4 p.m. Admission charge. 620.340.6310. explorelyoncounty.org.

Emporia State University: 1 Kellogg Circle. Founded in 1863, the university has been known by many names, including Kansas State Teachers College from 1923 to 1974. In 1922 the Memorial Union became the first chartered student union west of the Mississippi River, and its original columned entrance remains today. Other points of

interest on campus include the 1938 football stadium wall built by the WPA, the Norman Eppink Art Gallery, and the 1890s one-room stone schoolhouse at 18th and Merchant. 620.341.1200. emporia.edu.

Memorial to Fallen Educators: 18th and Merchant (west of the stone schoolhouse). A remarkable memorial honors educators who have died while on the job, either by mass school shootings, classroom fires, knife fights, car crashes, or accidents. It was designed following the Sandy Hook Elementary School shooting and built by the National Teachers Hall of Fame in 2014.

National Teachers Hall of Fame: 1 Kellogg Circle (Emporia State campus). Exceptional teachers from around the nation are honored at this facility

that includes a gallery of teachers recognized for their exceptional teaching careers, a Wall of Fame where former students may honor their best teachers, a miniature display of classrooms through the centuries, and a gift shop. Monday-Friday 9 a.m.- 5 p.m. 620.341.5660. nthf.org.

Anderson Memorial Library (NRHP): 1220 C of E. Not only is this the second oldest Carnegie library in Kansas, it is also one of the most unique. Its symmetrical domed limestone design with temple-front motif renders it a "temple of knowledge." Dedicated in 1902 on the former College of Emporia campus, the library features a bronze plaque paying tribute to John Anderson. Anderson, president of the board of trustees of the College of Emporia, established the library in 1888. Andrew Carnegie built this building in 1899 as a memorial to Anderson, who'd had an early influence on Carnegie's life. The building has been restored and is privately owned. 620.343.7275.

Carnegie Library (NRHP): 118 E. 6th. Leaded-glass windows and exquisite woodwork served as a serene backdrop for readers inside this Carnegie library from 1906 to 1979. The red-brick building housed the Lyon County Museum until 2016. Currently it is not in use.

David Traylor Zoo of Emporia: 75 Soden. You'll enjoy the pleasant surroundings of this picturesque animal park, which is one of the country's smallest accredited zoos. The serenity of the ponds and

botanical areas contrast with the romping cotton-top tamarins, a new lemur exhibit, and the majestic bobcats and pumas commanding their lairs. The size of the zoo is perfect for small children. Daily 10 a.m.-4:30 p.m. Donation welcome. 620.341.4365. FB.

Soden's Grove Bridge (NRHP): 933 S. Commercial.
The 1923 Marsh rainbow single-arch bridge (pedestrian traffic only) is a great vantage point to view the waterfall over the old milldam where Soden's Mill once stood on the Cottonwood River. Built in 1860, the mill was destroyed by fire in 1944.

Cottonwood River Trail:
933 S. Commercial (Soden's Grove Park). This one-mile unpaved nature trail starts near the rainbow arch bridge, follows wooded areas along the river, and ends at Peter Pan Park at Randolph and Neosho.

Hallie B. Soden House (NRHP): 802 S. Commercial.
A wedding present from W.T. Soden to his daughter Hallie, this 1893 home was built by Charles S. Squires, one of Emporia's first trained architects, with lumber from Soden's sawmill. The original furniture came from Soden's furniture factory, also based in Emporia. Drive by only.

Colonel H.C. and Susan Cross House (NRHP):
526 Union. You almost can't tear your eyes away from this magnificent late-Victorian era Queen Anne style home constructed in 1894. The detailing and decorative elements on the doors and windows are mesmerizing.

Built for prominent banker and railroad executive H.C. Cross and his family, Cross died just a few months after the home was completed. Today it is a private residence. Drive by only.

Richard Howe House (NRHP): 315 E. Logan. This
two-story limestone home was constructed during the mid-1860s by stone mason and Welsh immigrant Richard Howe, whose fine masonry work can be seen on many of Emporia's finest structures. For tours, call 620.340.6310. explorelyoncounty.org.

More Historic Homes:
Drive down any residential street near downtown to find beautiful historic homes, many on the NRHP, including the Harris-Borman House (827 Mechanic); the Keebler-Stone House (831 Constitution); and the Mrs. Preston B. Plumb House (224 6th), built by Carrie Plumb as a memorial to her husband, U.S. Senator Preston B. Plumb.

Antiques: A number of fine
shops contribute to an excellent antique mall in the restored 1907 Poehler Mercantile at 301 Commercial. Tuesday-Saturday 10 a.m.-5 p.m.; Sunday 1-5 p.m. 620.341.9092.

Outdoor Murals: Colorful
murals are found around town and include *Spring in the Flint*

Hills by Stan Herd and Louis Copt (W. 6th and Merchant); *Our Flag Was Still There* by Marilyn Dailey (11th and Commercial); *Endurance* by Dave Loewenstein, Nicholas Ward, Itzel Lopez-Vargas, and team (behind Mulready's Pub, 717 Commercial); and *Day and Night Jazz* by Josh Finely (next to *Endurance*).

Emporia Arts Center:
815 Commercial. An airy, contemporary building provides open spaces that accentuate the rotating fine art and photography exhibits. Beautiful handmade art, jewelry, home goods, and more are available for purchase in the gift store. Tuesday-Friday 10 a.m.-6 p.m.; Saturday 10 a.m.-3 p.m. 620.343.6473. FB.

Granada Theatre (NRHP):
807 Commercial. An ornate example of the Spanish Colonial Revival style, this theater with a stucco facade was built in 1929 and has been beautifully restored. You won't find a bad seat in the house for the movies, concerts, and plays on the grand stage. Monday-Friday 10 a.m.-5 p.m. 620.342.3342. FB.

SE

Sweet Granada: 805 Commercial. Hundreds of handmade gourmet confections created with quality ingredients are waiting for you in this shop next to the Granada Theatre. Take your pick from dipped chocolates, truffles, caramels, fudge, molded candy sunflowers, chocolate-drizzled popcorn, and chocolate-dipped strawberries. You're sure to find plenty of gifts for the sweet folks in your life. Monday-Saturday 10 a.m.-7 p.m. 620.342.9600. FB.

Granada Coffee Company:
809 Commercial. Owner Rocky Slaymaker once built movie sets in Hollywood, and his classy but casual coffee shop looks like it came right from the silver screen! Adjoining the restored Granada Theatre, this charming spot serves specialty coffees, teas, and sandwiches. Monday-Friday 7 a.m.-7 p.m.; Saturday 8 a.m.-7 p.m.; Sunday 8 a.m.-2 p.m. 620.342.4001. FB.

Gravel City Roasters:
608 Merchant. Emporia's reputation is growing as the headquarters for "gravel grinders," those who bicycle on the many

gravel roads around the area. This bicycle-themed coffee shop is a great stop to enjoy locally roasted and specialty coffees that taste good anytime, and especially after a long ride. Monday-Friday 7 a.m.-8 p.m.; Saturday 8 a.m.-8 p.m.; Sunday 11 a.m.-7 p.m. 620.343.3919. FB.

Twin Rivers Winery and Gourmet Shoppe:
627 Commercial. Stop by for a flight (or a glass) of Twin Rivers handcrafted wine and pair it with cheese. You'll find cheeses, oils and vinegars, dips and sauces, bulk spices, and many other culinary delights in the gourmet shoppe. Monday-Saturday 10 a.m.-5 p.m. 620.208.9463. FB.

Radius Brewing Company:
610 Merchant. It's been a long time, since before the 1920s Prohibition days, that Emporia has had an operating brewery. But Radius Brewing is worth the wait! The huge silver brew vats are rightfully front and center in the

contemporary mosaic of wood, steel, and brick in this renovated downtown building. Local artwork graces the walls, and the aroma of artisan dishes of smoked gouda cheese soup and ribeye steaks floats through the hop-and-barley-infused air. Local author Cheryl Unruh, Kansas Explorer #2703, is a regular. She loves to watch the culinary team in the open kitchen prepare the pizza dough, tossing it high before slathering it with toppings and popping it into the wood-fired brick oven. A full bar features wonderful Bloody Marys,

Moscow Mules, and martinis made with house-infused vodka. Daily 11 a.m.-10 p.m. 620.208.4677. FB.

Pho BannLao:
409 Commercial. Laos is surrounded by Vietnam, Thailand, Cambodia and Myanmar, so you'll find familiar (pad Thai and pho) and not-so-familiar dishes (tom kha, a soup with a coconut milk base enriched with meat, fish, and vegetables) that reflect the influence of the countries neighboring Laos. For dessert, try the sliced mangos on a bed of sticky rice with warm coconut milk. Tuesday-Saturday 11 a.m.-9 p.m.; Sunday 12-8 p.m. 620.208.6666. phobannlao.com.

Amanda's Bakery and Cafe: 702 Commercial. Inside the historic Kress Building (NRHP) is a buzzing little cafe that makes divine sandwiches with thick slices of homemade bread. A stand-out is the creamy chicken salad with grapes. More fresh salads and home-baked goods are also on the menu. Tuesday-Friday 8 a.m.-3 p.m.; Saturday 8 a.m.-2 p.m. 620.340.0620. FB.

Commercial Street Diner:
614 Commercial. Rise and shine! This diner is the favorite breakfast spot in town. Look forward to big stacks of hot pancakes, flaky biscuits covered in thick sausage gravy, crispy hashbrowns, and eggs any way you want them. Tuesday-Sunday 6 a.m.-2 p.m. 620.343.9866.

Do-B's: 704 E. 12th. The burger so good it's named the OMG is made of ground choice chuck, topped with pastrami and grilled onions sauteed in a teriyaki glaze, and crowned with pepper-jack cheese and creole mustard. You have to try the OMG, and the next time you stop in try the Philly steak sandwich or a po' boy. Monday-Friday 11 a.m.-8 p.m.; Saturday 8 a.m.-4 p.m. 620.342.7294. FB.

Bobby D's BBQ: 607 Merchant. Known for its slow-smoked meat and its cheesy potatoes, Bobby D's has been featured on the popular TV series *Pit Masters.* Monday-Saturday 11 a.m.-9 p.m. 620.342.1990. FB.

Casa Ramos: 707 Commercial. The usual Mexican favorites are excellent, as are the unusual—the braised lamb shank dish and the molcajete, a big bowl of chicken and beef with mushrooms, onion, and tomato, all sizzling together in a flavorful sauce and topped with cheese. Daily 11 a.m.-9 p.m. 620.340.0640. FB.

Shangri-La Sushi and Teriyaki: 841 W 6th. Yes, Dorothy, you can get good sushi in Kansas! The bento lunch boxes are popular and are served with teriyaki, dumplings, and California sushi rolls. Monday-Saturday 11 a.m.-2:30 p.m. and 5-9 p.m. 620.412.5588. FB.

J's Carryout: 27 Commercial. Pick up lunch for a picnic at the zoo or in the park at this old-time burger stop. Monday-Friday 10:30 a.m.-7 p.m.; Saturday 10:30 a.m.-2:30 p.m.

Mulready's Pub: 717 Commercial. Friendly and full of fun-loving employees and customers, Mulready's knows no strangers! Pull up

a bar stool, meet your neighbor, tip the bartender, and enjoy a craft beer—23 on tap, including three nitro and 40 bottled selections. More than 100 brands of Scotch, bourbon, and whiskey are also served. Daily 2 p.m.-12 a.m. 620.208.2337. FB.

Brickyard 20 Ale House: 402 Merchant. You'll find 20,000 square feet of good times inside this former lumberyard. The beer (more than 20 on tap) seems even better with the live music, karaoke, trivia night, and, when the weather is nice, relaxing in The Yard, the biggest outdoor patio in town. Monday-Wednesday 5 p.m.-12 a.m.; Thursday-Saturday 5 p.m.-2 a.m.; Sunday 3 p.m.-2 a.m. 620.208.6084. FB.

The Bourbon Cowboy: 605 Commercial. It's all about the country music and dancing in this fine cowboy bar. A quality atmosphere and outdoor patio will make you want to kick up your heels. Tuesday-Saturday 4 p.m.-12 a.m. 620.481.9404. FB.

Lodging: Gufler Mansion (970.582.0207, FB); additional lodging (visitemporia.com).

explorer extras...
In Emporia

Dynamic Discs, 912 Commercial, a full-service disc golf supply company, started in 2005 in a basement while owner Jeremy Rusco was a student at Emporia State. The company has graduated to carry everything disc golfers need to play the game. Enjoy disc golf locally at the Emporia Golf Course, Jones Park, and Peter Pan Park. The Dynamic Discs showroom is

at 912 Commercial. Monday-Saturday 9 a.m.-5 p.m.; Sunday 1-5 p.m. 620.208.3472. FB.

It's party time! For Party Time Ham, that is, one of Fanestil Meats best-known, top-quality selections. A spacious new store at 4700 W. U.S. 50 offers fresh and frozen meats (ham, beef, chicken, and turkey), salsas, sauces, relishes, seasonings, nuts, cheese, milk, and more with many items produced in Kansas. Monday-Friday 8 a.m.-5 p.m.; Saturday 10 a.m.-4 p.m. 620.342.6354. FB.

Emporia Downtown Historic District (NRHP) covers 18 city blocks and includes 169 buildings that together interpret 150 years of community development. A downtown walking tour brochure is available at the Lyon County History Center, 711 Commercial, or at explorelyoncounty.org.

For almost 30 years E.J. Alexander drove his team of white horses from his 40-acre truck farm east of town to sell produce in Emporia. Children flocked to his wagon for rides and to eat the fruit and vegetables. E.J., a former slave, was born in North Carolina, never married, and lost track of his siblings. When he died in 1923, he bequeathed his 40 acres and all of his savings for the children of Emporia who needed protection and education. He set aside one acre for his own burial plot and for any children or families that could not afford a burial. A children's camp was later built on the site of his truck farm. You can see Alexander's

SE

gravestone, poignantly inscribed "The Children's Friend," at Camp Alexander, 1783 P5. From Commercial, 3¾ miles east on U.S. 50 (becomes 175), ½ mile north and east on P2, then 200 yards north on P5. 620.794.1830. campalexander.org. **ee**

HARTFORD

Population 366

Hartford Collegiate Institute (NRHP):
Plumb and College. In 1861 this two-story native stone building opened as a branch of Baker University, whose main campus is in Baldwin City (Douglas County). Classes were taught here until 1875, when the institute closed. This building is the only vestige of the college and is now a community meeting space.

Historic Jail: The circa 1880 strap-iron jail stands proudly as an open-air relic at Commercial and Plumb.

Neosho River Bridge (NRHP): From Commercial, ½ mile east on Plumb. Just west of the dike is a 1926 graffiti-marked, Marsh rainbow double-arch bridge. Cross the bridge to enter the Flint Hills National Wildlife Refuge, a large waterfowl management area noted for its diverse habitats that include wetlands, bottomland hardwood forests, grasslands, riparian areas, and agricultural lands.

explorer extras...
In Olpe

Population 542

Early German Catholic settlers established a parish here in 1885 and built the St. Joseph Church at 306 Iowa in 1910. If the door is open, step inside to see the beautiful altar, stained-glass windows, ceiling, and original woodwork. 620.475.3326.

Inside Olpe's Chicken House, the Coble family has served famous fried-chicken dinners since 1958. It's a delicious tradition! Steaks, seafood dishes, and especially the onion rings are also recommended. Monday-Saturday 11 a.m.-8 p.m. 620.475.3386. **ee**

READING

Population 231

Historic Jail: The original wooden jail built in 1870 sits under the water tower. Lawbreakers are happy to know it's no longer used. From 1st, ½ block north on Franklin.

The Miracle Cafe: 103 Franklin. Community members found all the wood scraps they could to build this new cafe after the 2011 tornado destroyed much of the town, including the historic home that the cafe first occupied. Salvaged tables and chairs from the original cafe are now the furniture of the new one, and other scraps have been incorporated as trim around the windows and doors. It's not only the place to find an excellent roast beef dinner or a breakfast omelet, but it's the heart of the community where locals and visitors come to reminisce, sign the guest book, have a piece of pie or a cinnamon roll with a cup of coffee. Hats off to the Reading folks! Monday-Thursday 9 a.m.-3:30 p.m.; Friday 9 a.m.-9 p.m.; Saturday 6-11 a.m. (breakfast only). 620.699.3009. FB.

Montgomery County

AROUND THE COUNTY

Little House on the Prairie: From 27th in Independence, 1¾ miles west on U.S. 160, 6¾ miles southwest on U.S. 75, 1½ miles south on 2700, then 1 mile west on 3000. Laura Ingalls Wilder, well known for her *Little House* books, lived here briefly with her family when she was a child in 1869-1871. Visitors will find an open rural setting comprising a reproduced cabin, an 1872 schoolhouse, post office, 1920s barn, 1880s farmhouse, and a gift shop. When the buildings are closed, signage is available to guide you through the delightful site. April-October, Monday-Sunday 10 a.m.-5 p.m. Donation welcome. 620.289.4238. littlehouseontheprairiemuseum.com.

Elk City Lake and State Park: 4825 Squaw Creek. From 27th in Independence, 1½ miles west on Main/U.S. 160, 1 mile north on 3325, ¼ mile west on 4600, 1½ miles north on 3300, then ¼ mile west on Squaw Creek. Six scenic hiking and nature trails, which meander through the colorful oak and hickory forest surrounding the lake, are the stand-out features of this park built in 1967. Birders will find neotropical fowl and pileated woodpeckers here, and everyone will enjoy great camping, fishing, swimming, and picnicking. State park entrance charge. Cabins available. Reservations required. 620.331.6295. ksoutdoors.com.

Hiking Trails at Elk City Lake:

The nationally recognized Elk River Hiking Trail stretches 15 miles one-way from the west edge of the lake dam to the U.S. 160 bridge on Elk River. This trail offers stunning views of the lake and the dramatic rock formations. The first step onto the nearly three-mile Table Mound Hiking Trail is a descent between two boulders, but then the trail becomes a moderate trek through scenic ravines and forests and across small creeks.

CANEY

Population 2,140

Both the town and Caney River were named for the numerous wild cane thickets that lined the river banks.

Safari Zoological Park:

1751 1425. From U.S. 75, 1½ miles east on 3rd. Tom and Allie Harvey's devotion to animals and providing them excellent habitats dates to 1989. An intriguing two-hour guided tour

will teach you about the habits and habitats of endangered animals (lions, tigers, bears, primates, and more), and you'll be amazed by the interactions of the animals and guides. This unique zoo is intimate, clean, and cheerful; it's small enough to be friendly yet large enough to be impressive. It's a comfortable place, no matter the weather, with covered paths and places to relax. Memorial Day-Labor Day, Monday-Saturday 10 a.m.-5 p.m.; changes in hours are posted on FB. Admission charge. Call ahead, 620.515.2885.

Wark Memorial Park:

300 E. 4th. The park is named in honor of Montgomery County native George Wark, a WWI general and a state senator. The park's environs contain a campsite marker along Black Dog Trail (*see* p. 235), established around 1803 by Osage Chief Black Dog as an annual hunting route. You will also see a sign designating 4th Street as part of the Blue Star Memorial Highway, a post-WWII tribute to U.S. armed forces. A four-pillared, red-brick shelter built in 1951 stands at the park's center and is dedicated to the memory of local window-glass workers. Delightful wood carvings created by Tom Zimmer are scattered throughout the park, and a life-sized metal sculpture of a saluting soldier stands near the flagpoles at the veterans memorial. The soldier's face is hauntingly realistic. It is not known who created the captivating sculpture.

Wedding Ring Design:

In Caney the wedding ring pattern isn't just for quilts. It was incorporated into the architectural design of a local house, which is no longer standing but lives on in a mural on 3rd between State and Spring. The wedding ring pattern also is integrated into the gazebo in Wark Memorial Park and into a home on W. 4th between Wood and Fawn.

Caney Valley Historical Museum and Complex:

310 W. 4th. A colorful Marion Bryant historical mural of Caney's early years preps you for your visit through area history. The museum complex includes a doctor's office and an 1871 one-room schoolhouse (above the entrance is printed "Knowledge is Power"). A historical marker notes that Caney's streets, laid in 1907, were constructed with bricks produced in the town's brick plants. Monday, Wednesday-Friday 9 a.m.-3 p.m. 620.879.2233. FB.

explorer extras... In Caney

Two-thirds of the way down the main driveway of Sunnyside Cemetery, look on the right for three historic plaques in the Mason family plot. The first plaque states that Jappa Mason was a teacher of oil magnate Harry Sinclair, Walt Disney, and future world explorer Martin Johnson. A second plaque notes that Captain Richard Mason of the 16th Arkansas Cavalry was severely wounded on this spot in 1862, and a third plaque reveals that Richard Colbert Mason was an inventor of oil industry devices. From 3rd, 3 blocks north on McGee, 1 block west on Taylor.

It's hard not to notice all the brick buildings, streets, and

SE

homes in Caney. By 1915 the town supported three brick plants, a smelter, three glass plants, a refinery, and the largest crude oil terminal in the world.

The native sandstone Caney High School football stadium at S. Main and W. 9th was built by the WPA in 1938.

The two-story native sandstone house at 133 N. State was built in 1889 as a hotel and stage coach stop. ee

CHERRYVALE

Population 2,288

Cherryvale Depot: 125 N. Depot. Now used for the offices of Watco, a short-line railroad company, this red-brick, turn-of-the-century structure was built in 1910 for the Santa Fe railway. Rare are the arched, covered drive-through entrance portico and waiting platform, a design seen on no other depot on the Santa Fe's southern Kansas lines. tinyurl.com/cvaledepot.

Logan Park: Liberty and Park. From 1895 to 1939 the Old Soldiers' Southern Kansas Reunion was held in this park, named in honor of General John A. Logan, the first commander of the local GAR post. The reunion drew orators that included Theodore Roosevelt and U.S. senator from Kansas Charles Curtis. Elsewhere in the park a plaque is dedicated to Spanish-American War veteran Frank Bellamy, possible author of "The

Pledge of Allegiance" (*see* next entry). Remnants of 1930s WPA improvements can be seen scattered throughout the park.

Pledge of Allegiance: From E. Main, ¼ mile north on 5700 to Fairview Cemetery. Controversy will always exist about whether Frank E. Bellamy, a Cherryvale high school student, actually wrote "The Pledge of Allegiance." In 1890 he entered the pledge in a contest sponsored by *The Youth's Companion*, but the magazine never acknowledged his entry. The words he wrote, supposedly, were printed in an 1892 issue, but a *Companion* staff member, Francis Bellamy, was given credit. Cherryvale's Bellamy, a Spanish-American War veteran, died in 1915 before he knew of the controversy and was never able to defend authorship. He is buried in Fairview Cemetery with a copy of his handwritten pledge beside his grave. Look for the flagpole and flag to find his grave.

Carnegie Library (NRHP): 329 E. Main. Much of the original woodwork remains inside this red-brick 1913 structure designed by the well-known Kansas architectural firm George Washburn and Son. Two tall white pillars and the embossed words, "Public Library," greet you at the entrance of this handsome building, which still functions as the town's library. Monday-Friday

11 a.m.-6:30 p.m.; Saturday 9 a.m.-2 p.m. 620.336.3460.

Cherryvale Historical Museum: 215 E. 4th. Inside this former Bell Telephone building well-displayed items include WPA dolls and beautiful glassware and china. In a not-so-delicate display, you will see hammers used by the murderous Bender family in the 1870s. The Bloody Benders, as the family is called in hindsight, ran an inn near Cherryvale and killed a dozen guests, robbed them, and buried them in the backyard. The family escaped the law and was never apprehended. Call ahead, 620.336.3350.

"Don't Spit on the Sidewalk": Cherryvale was once home to seven brick plants, including one that produced the "Don't Spit on the Sidewalk" brick. The slogan, stamped into the bricks, was made famous by Kansas State Board of Health officer Dr. Samuel Crumbine. The "Don't Spit" brick was only one of Crumbine's various campaigns to improve sanitation and combat disease. Many streets and buildings in town reflect the brick plants' presence. Cherryvale also was home to the largest zinc smelter in the world in 1898.

Just Us: 515 S. Liberty. This local restaurant is known for its plentiful buffet with something to please everyone—fried chicken, turkey, ribs, and plenty more. Thursday-Saturday 4-8 p.m.; Sunday 12-2 p.m. 620.336.3772.

ABJ's Cruiser Cafe: 215 N. Liberty. The most popular menu item? Chicken-fried steak with real mashed potatoes.

Too early for lunch or dinner? Breakfast offers biscuits and gravy among other morning favorites. Tuesday-Saturday 5 a.m.-8 p.m.; Sunday 5 a.m.-2 p.m. 620.702.6202.

MJ's Burger House:
107 W. Main. The burgers in this house are the real deal, and so big you can hardly get your mouth around them. But we know burger lovers will find a way! Monday-Saturday 7 a.m.-9 p.m.; Sunday 7 a.m.-2 p.m. 620.336.2952. FB.

explorer extras...
In Cherryvale

Vivian Vance is probably best known as Ethel Mertz, sidekick to Lucille Ball in the beloved television comedy *I Love Lucy*. Born Vivian Jones in 1909 in Cherryvale, she was the first (1954) Emmy Award winner for Best Supporting Actress. Vivian Vance Memorial Drive is on 6th, and the actress's childhood home is at 309 W. 6th. She also resided at 311 E. 5th.

Born in 1906 in Cherryvale, Louise Brooks ranks today as one of the silent screen's greatest stars. She—and her famous bobbed hair—also appeared in the *Ziegfeld Follies* theatrical shows on Broadway. Drive by her former homes at 320 W. Main and 531 E. 7th.

Leatherock Hotel, the 1912 railroad hotel at 420 N. Depot and Front, once hosted many a rail passenger as overnight guests. It is now the Leatherock Hotel Bed and Breakfast. leatherockhotel.com.

A beautiful stained-glass window at Cherryvale United Methodist Church, 305 W. 3rd, incorporates the figure of a Civil War soldier.

Pearson-Skubitz Big Hill Lake (*see* p. 257) provides many recreational opportunities, including a 17-mile horseback riding trail that winds along a scenic hardwood ridge and offers impressive views. From U.S. 169, 5 miles east on 5200. **ee**

COFFEYVILLE

Population 9,949

Dalton Gang Robberies:
October 5, 1892, was a tragic day in Coffeyville. That morning the notorious Dalton Gang (Grat, Bob, and Emmett Dalton; Bill Power; and Dick Broadwell) rode into town and boldly tried to rob two banks at the same time. The robberies failed, thanks to a quick-thinking bank teller who told the gang that the bank vault was on a timer, giving the town's citizens an opportunity to gather to defend their town. Four of the town's residents were killed in the resulting gunfight, as were Grat and Bob Dalton, Power, and Broadwell. Emmett Dalton was wounded, captured, and sentenced to life in prison. He served 15 years at the penitentiary in Lansing before he was pardoned.

Old Condon Bank (NRHP):
811 Walnut. One of the two banks involved in the 1892 robbery attempt by the Dalton Gang, Condon Bank (also known as the Perkins Building) has been restored to its vintage 1890s appearance. The chamber of commerce and visitors bureau are housed inside this two-story Victorian building, whose unique stamped-metal front facade is a gateway into a beautifully ornate and decorative interior. Monday-Friday 9 a.m.-5 p.m. 620.251.2550. tinyurl.com/condonbank.

Dalton Defenders
Museum: 113 E. 8th. The
feature display centers on the Dalton Gang robberies and honors the citizens who defended the town. Additional exhibits focus on major league pitching sensation Walter Johnson (*see* later entry), 1940 presidential candidate Wendell Willkie (who taught at Coffeyville High School in 1913), the town's six brick plants, and additional early history. An extra treat is a replica of one of the largest hailstones on record! It fell in Coffeyville in 1970. March-November, Monday-Friday 10 a.m.-4 p.m. Admission charge. Call ahead, 620.251.2550. daltondefendersmuseum.com.

Dalton Death Alley:
Just north of the newer Condon Bank, 814 S. Walnut. An audio recording relates the story of the Dalton Gang's fateful bank robbery attempt in October 1892, and the shootout that partly occurred in this alley.

Elmwood Cemetery:
16th and Elm. From 12th, ½ mile south on Elm. The isolated graves of three of the five Dalton Gang members— Bob and Grat Dalton and Bill Power—are in the cemetery's southeast section. Nearby, a trio of signs provides details of the robbery and aftermath. Charles Brown and George Cubine, two of the defenders killed during the 1892 Dalton raid, are also buried in this cemetery. A map is available at the visitor center, 807 Walnut.

Don Sprague Murals:
The most famous of Don's outdoor murals is on the sidewalk in front of the Old Condon Bank, 811 Walnut, and depicts the

SE

members of the Dalton Gang lying dead. If you wish, you may lie down next to them and have your picture taken. In each of his murals, Don has hidden his son's (Tim) name; the number of times "Tim" appears in each mural is noted by the number of dots behind Don's signature. Most of his murals can be seen between Elm and Walnut and between 7th and 10th. A driving map of all 15 Sprague murals is available at the chamber of commerce, 807 Walnut.

Chainsaw Sculptures:

8th and Beech. A tall orange carrot, a red rose petal on a giant stem, Campbell Soup cans, a keyboard, and the many more creative wood sculptures adorning this corner will make you smile. They are by Michael DeRosa's students of the Coffeyville Community College art department.

Brown Mansion (NRHP):

2019 S. Walnut. See how the wealthy lived in the early 1900s by touring this stunning mansion built in 1904 for W.P. Brown, the area's natural gas magnate. The Brown family lived here until 1973, when they sold the mansion to the local historical society leaving all of the original furniture, china, and furnishings inside. A 60-minute tour shares the magnificence of this mansion, from its third-story gymnasium to its signed Tiffany chandelier. The Browns are buried in Elmwood Cemetery. March-November, Thursday-Saturday, tours at 1 and 3 p.m. Call ahead, 620.251.2550. brownmansion.com.

Walter Johnson:

Baseball Hall of Famer Walter "The Big Train" Johnson pitched for the Washington Senators from 1907 to 1927, winning the World Series in 1924. Johnson was born in Humboldt but lived in Coffeyville during the baseball off-season. Avid baseball fans will enjoy seeing the town attractions that pay tribute to this great player—the monument and illustrated plaque behind the ball field backstop in Walter Johnson Park (from U.S. 169, east on 8th); the mural by Don Sprague (223 W. 9th); and the exhibit at the Dalton Defender's Museum (113 E. 8th).

Coffeyville Aviation Heritage Museum:

2002 Buckeye (Pfister Park). From 11th/U.S.166, 2 miles north on Buckeye, then bear left at the fork. The museum is at home in a 1933 hangar built by the WPA. Local residents Joe and Howard Funk built some 230 airplanes during the 1940s, and one is displayed here. Other exhibits focus on early aviation, area pilots, and Coffeyville's WWII army airfield. May-September, Saturday-Sunday 1-4 p.m. Call ahead, 620.515.0232.

Garden Thyme Tea Room:

805 McArthur. The charming cottage atmosphere is a delightful change of pace for lunch or a break where you can choose from 40 varieties of tea. Lunch offerings include the harvest salad with maple cider dressing, grilled sandwiches, soup, or the daily special. As an added treat, select any of the fine desserts—but someone in your group should definitely order and share the signature Aunt Cessie's pumpkin cake. Available with advanced notice is an elegant high tea with scones and finger sandwiches. Monday-Friday 10:30 a.m.-2:30 p.m. 620.251.4515. FB.

Lanning's Downtown Grill:

111 W. 9th. It's full of atmosphere, and the huge menu will please a variety of tastes. Unique choices abound for breakfast—cinnamon pecan pancakes, beef tips and eggs, and chicken-fried bacon—and delicious homemade desserts include cheesecake and cake balls. As Lanning's tagline says, it's the "best grill in the 'ville." A full bar is available. Monday-Wednesday 11 a.m.-9 p.m.; Thursday-Saturday 7 a.m.-9 p.m. 620.251.8255. FB.

El Pueblito's:

600 Northeast. No bad choices can be made here, it's all good, especially the chicken Jalisco burrito, carne asada, and the chips and cheese dip. Margarita lovers love it here. Monday-Saturday 11 a.m.-9 p.m.; Sunday 11 a.m.-3 p.m. 620.251.1618.

Dirty's Tavern: 128 W. 9th. Handmade pizza, burgers on homemade buns, buffalo wings, catfish, and more. We know you'll clean your plate at Dirty's! Monday-Saturday 5-9 p.m. 620.251.4811. FB.

Sunflower Soda Fountain: 125 W. 8th. It's a throwback to the old days, and comfort food reigns—meatloaf, cheesy party potatoes, and green beans. But that's not all. You'll also like the sandwiches, soups, and all the homemade sweets, such as cheesecakes, pies, cakes, and cookies. The ice cream treats are wonderful on a hot day! Monday-Friday 7 a.m.-5 p.m.; Saturday 11 a.m.-3 p.m. FB.

Utopia: 206 W. 10th. Hot, iced, and blended coffees; Italian sodas; lemonade; teas; and small batches of muffin tops, cookies, brownies, and more make for a perfect world at Utopia. Monday-Friday 6 a.m.-1 p.m. 620.688.6742. FB.

Lodging:
tinyurl.com/staycoffeyville.

explorer extras... In Coffeyville

Pfister Park, 1906 N. Buckeye, features a fabulous aquatic park and sprayground, historic WPA buildings and shelters, and many recreational opportunities. 620.252.6108. tinyurl.com/cvilleaquatic.

The 1928 Midland Theatre (NRHP), 212 W. 8th, is undergoing restoration. The Mission Revival style is evident on the brick, tile, and terra cotta facade.

A new bridge spans Onion Creek but just to the east the original Onion Creek Bridge (NRHP) still stands—a 1911 pin-connected Bedstead Parker truss with vertical end posts. From U.S. 166, ½ mile south on Overlook.

The brick and limestone Neo-classical Carnegie library (NRHP) at 415 W. 8th was completed in 1912. It now functions as a photography studio.

Montgomery County was one of several counties in the state with settlements formed by Exodusters, Southern blacks migrating North in search of a better life. The Bethel African Methodist Episcopal Church (NRHP) at 202 W. 12th, constructed in 1907, was the second church built by the congregation that settled here in the late 1870s.

Isham Hardware, 811 Union, the oldest hardware store in Kansas, opened in 1870. When the Dalton Gang came to town in 1892 to rob two banks, citizens fired shots from inside the hardware store during the ensuing shootout (*see* p. 275). A mural of Coffeyville, covering Isham's north exterior wall, depicts points of activity during the Dalton Gang raid. Monday-Friday 8 a.m.-5 p.m.; Saturday 8 a.m.-12 p.m. 620.251.0790. **ee**

INDEPENDENCE

Population 9,230

Riverside Park and Ralph Mitchell Zoo: 1736 N. 5th.
Golden lions at the entrance welcome you to this picturesque park founded in 1914. Take a five-cent carousel ride, a miniature train excursion for a quarter, and play a game of miniature golf for a dollar (on a course that features the history of Independence!). The *Corythosaurus* from the Sinclair Dinoland display at the 1964 World's Fair resides in Kiddy Land, along with Humpty Dumpty, Cinderella, and a really big shoe. The park's flower and sculpture gardens are exquisite in the summer. The 1925 Ralph Mitchell Zoo adjoins the park and features bears, cougars, and a 1932 WPA-built monkey island. The zoo's most famous inhabitant was Miss Able, the first (1959) American primate to ride a Jupiter rocket into space. Park ride hours, Memorial Day-Labor Day, daily 6:30-9:30 p.m. and Sunday 1-5:30 p.m.; zoo hours, April-October, daily 9 a.m.-7 p.m. and November-March, daily 9 a.m.-5 p.m. 620.332.2512. FB.

Riverside Park Shelter House and Band Shell:
Oak and Park. The entrance at the south end of the park will take you by the showcase building, the A.C. Stich Shelter. Built of stone in 1917, it incorporates an open porch on either side and a fireplace. It's been beautifully maintained over the years. The amphitheater around the band shell was built by the WPA in 1935.

William Inge Collection:
1057 W. College (Independence Community College). From Main, 1¾ miles south on S.10th, then ½ mile west on College. One of America's renowned playwrights, William Inge, a native of Independence, won a Pulitzer Prize for *Picnic*. His

SE

famous plays also include *Splendor in the Grass*; *Come Back, Little Sheba*; *Bus Stop*; and *The Dark at the Top of the Stairs*, all of which became successful motion pictures. The Inge Collection is in the Academic Building library and consists of motion picture lobby posters and cards, still pictures, press books, original manuscripts, and much more. Monday-Thursday 8 a.m.-4 p.m. Call ahead, 620.332.5468. indycc.edu/library.

Logan Fountain Sculptures:

Park and Oak (Riverside Park). The fountain was added to the park in 1948 as a memorial to Robert Logan, park supporter. A recent renovation has the fountain once again flowing in splendor around the well-landscaped area. On a brick oval sidewalk around the fountain, a life-sized sculpture of William Inge portrays him sitting on a bench with pen in hand. Nearby, three sculpture sets each depict a scene from his plays *Picnic*; *The Dark at the Top of the Stairs*; and *Come Back, Little Sheba*.

Independence Historical Museum and Art Center (NRHP):

123 N. 8th. Inside this former post office you are introduced to the area's most famous citizens—Alf Landon, Harry Sinclair, William Inge, Bill Kurtis, Vivian Vance, Laura Ingalls Wilder, and space-traveling chimpanzee Miss Able. The story of the nation's first night baseball game under lights, which was played in Independence in 1913, is told here, and sports fans will enjoy

the international fishing lure exhibit. The museum expanded its mission to include art, and now features a permanent collection and rotating exhibits. Tuesday-Saturday 10 a.m.-4 p.m. Donation welcome. 620.331.3515. ihmac.org.

Alf Landon Home (RHKP):

300 S. 8th. A dedicated group of Independence residents saved this historic home from demolition and moved it to its present location in 2005. Oil man Alf Landon served as governor of Kansas from 1933 to 1937, was the 1936 Republican presidential candidate, and is the father of Senator Nancy Landon Kassebaum Baker, although she never lived in this house. For tours, ask at Historical Museum. 620.331.3515.

Independence Downtown Historic District (NRHP):

Chestnut, Laurel, Myrtle, Main, and Maple between 5th and 9th. The advent of the industrial age and the oil and gas boom, which began here in the early 1900s, led to a glorious age in Independence architecture that can be admired within this historic district. As often happened in communities in the late 1800s, buildings were constructed of wood and succumbed to devastating fires, such as the 1875 fire in Independence. The city adopted an ordinance that required all future buildings to be constructed of steel, cement, and other incombustible materials.

Downtown: The many recessed entrances provide a nostalgic opening to friendly shopping experiences. Boutique clothing, home decor, hardware, jewelry, and gifts are but a few of the

shopping choices you will enjoy. Magnolia Scents by Design, 106 Pennsylvania, makes many of its products and offers candles, lotion, diffuser oils, body cream, and soaps. Outdoor sculptures add to the enjoyment of strolling in downtown.

Historic Church and Residence:

201 S. 5th. Gothic Revival fans will appreciate the First Presbyterian Church built in 1928 and modeled after Melrose Abbey in Scotland. Just to the south of the castle-like church, the yellow-brick mansion of Harry

Sinclair stands at 215 S. 5th. Sinclair, founder of Sinclair Oil, built this grand Neoclassical house in 1909. Among its many stand-out features is the double-enclosed porch with six large stone pillars over the main entrance.

Mount Hope Cemetery:

Elm and Penn. William Inge (1913-1973) and his family are

buried at the south end of the cemetery, just north of Oak and 5th. Look for a large gray granite Inge family stone. Not far from the cemetery entrance off Elm, a granite stone marks the grave of Dr. George Tann (1825-1909), a physician for Laura Ingalls' family. Added to the stone, a white sign reads, "A negro doctor that doctored the Ingalls for malaria in 1870." To locate Tann's gravestone, take the west drive to the center of the cemetery. A special feature in Mount Hope is the two-mile limestone retaining wall, built by the WPA in 1934, surrounding the entire cemetery. Look for the many sunburst designs incorporated into the rock on the outside of the wall.

Uncle Jack's Bar & Grill:

104 N. Penn. This restaurant was named for "Uncle Jack" Clark, who was raised in Independence and later moved to New York where he became a well-known fashion photographer and Renaissance man. The bar and grill is famous for its succulent aged steaks, hand-breaded fried mushrooms, and bleu cheese dressing. Monday-Saturday 11 a.m.-10 p.m. 620.330.7090. FB.

Brother's Railroad Inn:

113 S. Penn. Continuing his grandfather's tradition started in 1950, Mike Conway uses family recipes to create superb homemade Italian cuisine. Favorites include lasagna, fried ravioli, and baked ziti Al Forno con Salsiccia. Two of the specialty pizzas are the chicken bacon ranch and the

Maryland, a nod to grandpa who started the original Railroad Inn in Bowie, Maryland. Sandwiches, salads, steaks, shrimp, and more, plus gourmet desserts are also on the menu. Wednesday-Friday, Sunday 11 a.m.- 2 p.m.; Wednesday-Saturday 5-9 p.m. 620.331.3335. FB.

Vintage Steakhouse:

119 W. Main. Popular and elegantly prepared dishes include the honey Cajun pasta, tender steaks, and barbecued pork chops. Monday-Friday 11 a.m.-2 p.m. and 5-9 p.m.; Saturday 5-9 p.m. 620.577.2603. FB.

Ane Mae's Coffee & Sandwich House:

325 N. Penn. You'll be warmly welcomed by the staff, the locals, and the fresh flowers on the tables. This sweet spot is a bright, cheerful coffee shop offering fresh-baked pastries, mouth-watering paninis, homemade soups, quiche—and marvelous coffee! Monday-Friday 7 a.m.-5 p.m.; Saturday 7 a.m.-2 p.m. 620.331.4487. FB.

American Soda Fountain:

205 N. Penn. Hop on one of the shiny red stools at the counter of this 1947 soda fountain, or bring the whole family for an ice cream treat or lunch. Historic photos of Independence decorate the walls and accentuate that old-time feeling. Monday-Friday 7:30 a.m.-2:30 p.m. 620.331.0604.

Belmont Castle: 4471 4500.

From Penn, 2¾ miles east on Main/U.S. 160, then ¾ mile north

on 4500. This captivating stone home was a labor of love built for Dominica "Minnie" Calonder, an immigrant from Switzerland who grew up near the ruins of Belmont Castle in her homeland. Her family emigrated to America in the 1880s, but she never forgot her fanciful dream of living in a castle like Belmont. She eventually married Marell Tucker, who fulfilled her wish and built a home in the style of the original castle. Tucker, a carpenter, hauled the native stone from nearby Mouse Creek, and incorporated green-glass bottles to spell out the home's name on the front. Completed in 1932, the very unusual home is today a private residence. Drive by only.

Lodging:

tinyurl.com/indylodging.

SE

explorer extras...
In Independence

The red-brick Neoclassical Carnegie library (NRHP), 220 E. Maple, has served as the city's public library since it was built in 1907. This impressive library added a new section in 2007 and, because of energetic new programming and networking, it received the Best Small Library in America award in 2012. Local art, photography, and traveling exhibits change frequently. Monday-Friday 10 a.m.-6 p.m. 620.331.3030. FB.

The 1886 Montgomery County Courthouse, 300 E. Main (U.S. 160), was remodeled and expanded in the Modern Eclecticism style in 1931. The four two-story columns at the entrance add to the stately appearance of this government building.

A replica Statue of Liberty and a bronze statue of a little boy holding a folded flag stand in front of Memorial Hall (NRHP), 410 N. Penn. They were both presented the day this Classic Revival building opened in 1923.

The 1927 Booth Theater (NRHP), built in the Mission Revival style at 119 W. Myrtle, is waiting to be restored.

Two murals have been painted in recent years as part of the Astra Arts Festival in downtown. Look for the richly colored Dave Loewenstein mural at Laurel and Penn, and the Heidi M. Sallows American flag mural in the 100 block of Penn.

Get wet and wild at Riverside Beach Family Aquatic Center. Its swimming pool includes a Lazy River, 120-foot slide, shower tunnel, and much more fun. 5th and Oak. 620.331.4260. indyrec.com.

The magnificent Collegiate Gothic style 1923 high school (NRHP), 300 W. Locust, might remind you of a giant chocolate cake piped with elaborate decorative white icing. The red-brick building, now Independence Middle School, occupies a full city block. The 1939 gymnasium addition was a Public Works Administration (PWA) project. A second PWA structure, the 1940 Washington School (NRHP) at 300 E. Myrtle, is a sleek example of the Modern Movement style.

Miller Brothers Fast Gas at 928 E. Main and at 2706 W. Main still offers good old-fashioned service. Just give 'em a honk and someone will run out and pump your gas. 620.331.3616.

You'll find the four-arch Verdigris River rainbow bridge, designed

by J.B. Marsh, on Old U.S. 160, now a side road. Completed in 1928, it is formally known as the Dewlen-Spohnhauer Bridge (NRHP), named for two area servicemen who died overseas during WWI. From Penn, 1½ miles east on Main (becomes U.S. 160), then 500 feet northeast on Old U.S. 160. **ee**

Neosho County

CHANUTE

Population 9,255

Chanute-Wright Brothers' Memorial: 1 W. Main (Depot Plaza). A huge kinetic biplane sculpture stands as a memorial to Octave Chanute, a railroad and bridge engineer and an early aviation pioneer. The town's namesake never lived here, but he was responsible for building the railroad that came through the town. The biplane (representing the Wright brothers' aircraft) and life-sized silhouettes turn with the wind, and bronze plaques explain Chanute's contribution to aviation. This amazing sculpture was dedicated in 2003.

Santa Fe Depot (NRHP):
111 N. Lincoln. The restored Santa Fe depot houses the Safari Museum (*see* next entry) and the Chanute Public Library. Constructed in 1903, the depot was once home to

Santa Fe railway's Southern Division headquarters and a large Harvey House restaurant. The adjacent area has been developed into a plaza (*see* previous entry) featuring the Octave Chanute memorial, a gazebo, walking trail, and a small collection of rail stock.

Martin and Osa Johnson Safari Museum (8 Wonders of Kansas People):
111 N. Lincoln (Santa Fe depot). Between 1917 and 1936 explorers and naturalists Martin and Osa Johnson (Osa was a Chanute native) traveled to the exotic realms of Africa, Borneo, and the South Seas recording their adventures in documentary films, photographs, and writings. A video of their fascinating lives and diverse achievements

introduces you to your safari through this excellent museum with three impressive exhibit galleries. A featured exhibit is the replica of the Johnsons' zebra-striped plane *Osa's Ark!* On the grounds, the Frank Jensen metal sculptures *Sentinels of the Savannah* feature two life-sized giraffes, standing tall and overlooking their Kansas home. Tuesday-Saturday 10 a.m.-5 p.m.; Sunday 1-5 p.m. Admission charge. 620.431.2730. safarimuseum.com.

Johnson Graves: Elmwood Cemetery. At the corner of S. Malcolm and E. 14th a brown sign notes the nearby burial site of Martin and Osa Johnson (*see* previous entry). From the short gravel entry, follow the brick walkway to the brick horseshoe surrounding the Johnsons' graves.

Historic Austin Bridge (NRHP): S. Santa Fe and 27th (Santa Fe Park). King Bridge Company built this bowstring arch bridge over the Neosho River in 1872. This cast iron, 160-foot-long structure was moved to the park in 1999 and stands at the southern terminus of a three-mile hiking and biking path.

Chanute Art Gallery: 17 N. Lincoln. Special exhibits change every few months in this expansive and colorful art gallery that represents local and regional artists. Tuesday-Saturday 11 a.m.-3 p.m. 620.431.7807.

Cardinal Drug: 103 E. Main. Expect a thoroughly charming, old-fashioned soda fountain setting here! Enjoy soda fountain treats at the counter, which is in front of the 1914 solid oak back bar with mirror and cabinets, or take a seat at one of the

authentic ice cream chairs and tables. Your purchase is rung up on the solid brass 1908 cash register. Antiques and Coca Cola memorabilia are displayed throughout the store, making your experience here a delightful visit to an earlier era. Monday-Friday 9 a.m.-6 p.m.; Saturday 9 a.m.-2 p.m. 620.431.9150.

Good Eateries: Some fine choices for filling up in Chanute are the Grain Bin Restaurant (314 E. Main, 620.431.7373); El Pueblito (901 W. Cherry, 620.431.6006); and The Red Pepper (2110 S. Santa Fe, 620.431.4817).

Lodging: chanutechamber.com.

explorer extras...
In Chanute

Insects and other critters have a presence in Chanute these days! Don't worry, they don't sting or buzz, they don't even move. They only delight those who find them. Look on building walls, signs, and sidewalk. "Insects and Friends on Parade" began with local artist Bob Cross making insects in his welding class. More creatures are to be added to the "Parade"! Maps of this public art are outside the visitor information center at 21 N. Lincoln.

The six-story art deco building sporting gargoyles on each corner and beautiful terra cotta ornamentation was built as the Tioga Inn (NRHP) in 1929. Located at 12 E. Main, it now offers extended stay lodging.

District court is now held in the renovated Carnegie library (RHKP) at 102 S. Lincoln. The two-story yellow-brick Prairie School structure was built in 1906.

Brochures for driving tours of historic homes are available at the Safari Museum, 111 N. Lincoln, and outside the visitor information center, 21 N. Lincoln. The 1887 James and Ella Truitt House (NRHP), built in the Queen Anne style, stands in a serene setting at 305 N. Steuben.

If you stand at Main and Lincoln, you'll see a large Google logo in the middle of the intersection. It is the same logo you will see on your Mac computer when you first launch Google Earth. Because Google software engineer Dan Webb grew up near Chanute, he chose Chanute to be visible on the opening coordinates. tinyurl.com/googlechanute.

During the summer take a ride down the Lazy River or cool off in the spray features at the Maring Aquatic Center, 400 S. Highland. 620.431.4199. chanute.org.

Tour the lovely herb and flower gardens of Summit Hill Gardens at 2605 160. From K-39, 6 miles south on U.S. 169, then ¾ mile west on 160. Spend a relaxing time in this lovely setting shopping for all-natural, handcrafted soaps, creams, and other skin care products. The complex includes the restored 1874 Summit Hill School, the first school in Neosho County. Saturday 10 a.m.-4 p.m. For tours of the gardens and school, call ahead 620.212.3878. summithillgardens.com. **ee**

SE

ERIE

Population 1,121

Dinosaur Park: 4th and Walnut. Dinosaurs still roam in Erie, but in the form of fantastical sculptures created by Robert Dorris from scrap auto parts. This prehistoric menagerie of 12 creatures include a *Tyrannosaurus rex*, *Stegosaurus*, *Velociraptor*, *Triceratops*, *Brontosaurus*, and

Eryops. The city has created a landscaped park with specially constructed concrete pads for each dinosaur. Although you can see the sculptures from outside the fence that surrounds them, close-up tours are available the second Saturday and third Sunday of each month 12-4 p.m. 620.244.3461. eriedinosaurpark.com.

Bean Feed Capital of Kansas:
Erie is famous for its annual Old Soldiers and Sailors Reunion, a historic event that has taken place during the third week of July every year since 1873. It includes Erie's famous (free!) Bean Feed, where members of the American Legion Post cook more than 1,400 pounds of beans in 50 iron kettles that they fire up on the courthouse lawn. You're invited to step up with a bowl and spoon to see why Erie is called the Bean Feed Capital of Kansas!

Bean Feed Pipes:
1st and Butler. You'll see more than 50 black iron kettles, used each year for the famous Bean Feed, hanging on these white iron pipes when the big day comes each July.

Veterans Memorial:
1st and Main. An impressive black and gray granite veterans memorial stands on the courthouse grounds at 100 S. Main. The large monument lists the names of local veterans who have served in the armed forces, from the Civil War to the war in Iraq. Nearby under a pavilion, hangs a black kettle above a simple stone honoring all veterans.

explorer extras... In Erie

Discover the town history at the Mem-Erie Historical Museum, 403 S. Main. See an iron railing that came from the 1904 courthouse and look for a moon buggy too! April-September, Monday-Saturday 1-3 p.m. 620.244.5452.

The cream-colored trough in front of the museum was used to water horses and dogs in downtown Erie in 1914. Can you see the low trough for the dogs?

The cornerstone of the 1904 county courthouse has been embedded in a wall in front of the new courthouse built in 1962.

On State Street, just east of Butler, an artistic little concrete arch bridge (NRHP) is kept painted a sparkling white. The bridge, built in 1924 and all gussied up with turned concrete balusters, spans a tributary of the Neosho River. **ee**

ST. PAUL

Population 620

To advance Indian assimilation, religious denominations established more than 100 missions in Kansas, Missouri, Oklahoma, and Wyoming. Osage Mission was founded in 1847 in present St. Paul when Jesuit Fathers John Schoenmakers (known as the "Father of Civilization in Southeast Kansas") and John Bax, joined by the Sisters of Loretto, organized schools to educate the Osage boys and girls. When the Osages left Kansas in 1870, the schools became boarding institutions for white students until it closed in 1905. A historical marker on K-47 provides an overview of the mission.

Osage Mission Historical Museum:
203 Washington. The museum rests on the site of the original Osage Mission and schools (*see* previous entry). Museum exhibits interpret the important histories of the 1847 mission, the Osages in this area, and local pioneer history. Tuesday-Saturday 9 a.m.-1 p.m. 620.449.2320.

St. Francis Hieronymo Church:
208 Washington. St. Francis, the first church in the Diocese of Wichita, had its beginnings in 1847. The present church building was completed in 1884 in the Romanesque Revival style and has become an area landmark, noticed especially for its 79-foot-tall bell tower. Brochures inside the church foyer describe the interior and provide a timeline of area history.

St. Francis Cemetery:
From 5th, ¾ mile east on K-47. North of the north driveway are the graves of Jesuit Fathers Schoenmakers and Bax, who founded Osage Mission, and of several Sisters of Loretto, who operated the schools for Osage children.

Osage Mission Infirmary (NRHP):
325 Main. Built in 1872 and located at the Osage Mission, this building was the infirmary for the mission under the watchful eye of the Jesuits and the Sisters of Loretto. In 1912 it was moved to its present location to be used as a residence. A wood-frame house, it has a dormered, mansard roof and was constructed in the Second Empire style. The old infirmary most recently operated as a bed and breakfast. 316.882.7809.

St. Paul Supermarket:
514 Washington. In 2007 the locals voted to keep the grocery store operating in St. Paul, and the city stepped up to take ownership. A local couple manages it, and the city clerk spends one day a week helping out, doing payroll and other jobs. Make a visit to this clean, well-run store and pick up a few items to help support it. Monday-Saturday 8 a.m.-7 p.m.; Sunday 10 a.m.-6 p.m. 620.449.8950. stpaulmarketks.com.

St. Paul Cafe: 717 Washington. Clean, friendly, and with the kind of meals you've come to expect at a great small-town cafe. The burgers (made with locally raised beef) are top-quality and so are the homemade onion rings. 6:30 a.m.-1:30 p.m. 620.449.2222.

STARK

Population 71

Murphy's: 220030 K-39. From U.S. 59, 1 mile east on K-39. Rick Murphy built it and Portia Murphy stocked it. With those two involved, Murphy's will be high on the list for antique shoppers. When it opens in the summer of 2017, it will "have a little of everything," so you'll just have to come see. Monday-Saturday 9 a.m.-5 p.m. (or whenever Portia sees a car at the store). Call ahead, 620.754.3300. FB.

Colborn's Kitchen: 101 W. Main. Jeremy Colborn and his family have embraced Stark and the area and are thrilled to be serving "comfort family food," which includes chicken-fried steak, onion rings, ribeyes, homemade pies, and filling breakfasts. But it's the fried chicken that draws repeat customers back to this small-town cafe! Tuesday-Wednesday 7 a.m.-2 p.m.; Thursday-Saturday 7 a.m.-9 p.m.; Sunday 11 a.m.-2 p.m. 620.754.3222. FB.

Lodging: Murphy's Landing (620.754.3300, murphysatstark.com).

THAYER

Population 481

McLachlen Park: Neosho and Malcolm. From Galveston/U.S. 169, ½ mile west on Neosho. The historic band shell and little stone bridges add character to this picturesque park.

Thayer City Museum (RHKP): 201 W. Neosho. The community's history is kept safe in the former Thayer State Bank built in 1900. Call ahead, 620.443.0296. FB.

Thayer City Lake and Park: From Galveston/U.S. 169, 1 mile west on Montgomery, then ¼ mile south on Chase. It's a surprise and a delight to come across this beautiful city lake nestled among the trees. Take a picnic to the retro Roy Johnson Park and dine on concrete picnic tables under the trees.

Poor Boys Steakhouse: Enjoy a rich dining experience with any of Poor Boys perfectly grilled steaks, burgers, or shrimp, and especially with the prime rib on Fridays and Saturdays. Tuesday-Saturday 5-9 p.m. 620.839.5122. FB.

Big Ed's: 611 N. Galveston. Sterling Silver steaks and a delicious salad bar make Big Ed's a must stop for big eaters. It's now in its 25th year of business. Cash or check only. Wednesday-Saturday 11 a.m.-2 p.m. and 5-10 p.m. 620.839.5335.

Wilson County

ALTOONA

Population 396

Prairie Nut Hut: 1306 Quincy. U.S. 75 Business and K-47. Mountain oysters! Prairie Oysters! People must love 'em because this Nut Hut sells 100 pounds per week! Since 1940 customers have come here for the food and the tradition. The hut isn't fancy, and if you don't care for mountain oysters, the burgers are excellent, including the popular green chili burger. The barbecue sauce is homemade, shelled peanuts are complimentary, tossing the shells on the floor is mandatory, and the chicken-fried steak is made the Explorer Way. For a rare treat, order the Hopping Nut Plate—a combo of frog legs and mountain oysters. Tuesday-Friday 11 a.m-9 p.m.; Saturday 11 a.m.-8 p.m. 620.568.2900.

BUFFALO

Population 224

With our state animal in mind, it seems fitting for Kansans to visit Buffalo. Not famous for buffaloes, however, the town is known

SE

historically for its production of red bricks. The largest brick plant west of the Mississippi River in 1902, the Buffalo Brick Plant produced up to 125,000 bricks a day and employed 75 to 100 men. The building bricks were rated top quality and shipped nationwide. In 1939 the plant was reorganized as Buffalo Brick and Tile and as Acme Brick in 1954. It finally ceased operation in 1966 and was demolished in 1972. You can see the buffalo imprint on the sidewalk bricks at Main and Micro-Lite.

FREDONIA

Population 2,390

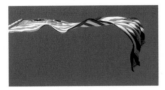

South Mound: From Washington, ¼ mile south on S. 7th, then 800 feet west on an unnamed road to the crest of the hill. It's a winding drive to the top of this mound, which rises just over 1,000 feet and offers a 360-degree view of Fredonia and the fertile Fall River Valley. An enormous 40x60-foot flag flies atop a 100-foot flagpole at the mound's summit. When you leave, take the road on the opposite side of the mound for a different winding descent.

First School: Washington between 5th and 7th. The stone retaining wall and steps mark the site of Mound School, Fredonia's first grade and high school, built in 1880. Students arriving by horse and buggy disembarked onto the elevated ground.

Courthouse Square: 615 Madison. A 1961 courthouse is the centerpiece of this historic town square. You'll also see restored metal park benches from 1915, a 1932 WPA bandstand, the clock tower from the original 1886 courthouse, and a veterans memorial. In the 1990s the town reproduced the old-fashioned electric street lamps, which now border the square.

Post Office Art (NRHP):

428 Madison. *Delivery of Mail to the Farm* is the title of this 1939 Section artwork by Lenore Thomas. The unique mural is a grouping of 10 glazed terra cotta sculptures fixed to the wall. The colorful figures tell a story of children receiving letters through the mail at their farm.

The Stone House (RHKP):

320 N. 7th. Step into the oldest house in Fredonia, which is home to the Fredonia Arts Council, one of the state's oldest art councils, dating to 1967. The 1872 stone home contains permanent and rotating local and regional art exhibits. Monday-Friday 10 a.m.-2 p.m. 620.378.2052. Fredoniaks.org.

Gold Dust Hotel (NRHP):

402 N. 7th. The three-story Italianate building commands the corner of the courthouse square, where it was constructed in 1885 as a hotel. It has been restored and converted into assisted living housing.

Wilson County Museum:

420 N. 7th. Early pioneer artifacts and area exhibits are displayed at this museum, housed in the 1915 former county jail and sheriff's residence. Monday-Friday 1-4:30 p.m. 620.378.3965.

Downtown Grill: 414 N. 7th. It comes highly recommended by the locals, who pack the bar stools at the old-time counter. The friendly aura inside this tiny diner means that probably someone will scoot down to make a place for you. An outdoor mural on the building's north wall represents what you'll find inside. 620.378.3287.

Stockyard Restaurant:

360 W. Madison. This isn't a livestock sales barn cafe. Your dining experience comes with white tablecloths and cloth napkins! More important are the Stockyard's juicy grilled steaks, jumbo shrimp, and prime rib, served with all the trimmings. There's one Cow Pie you'll welcome at your table—a warm brownie, topped with a scoop of ice cream and drizzled with chocolate and caramel sauce. Live music plays on some weekends. Monday 11 a.m.-2 p.m.; Tuesday 9 a.m.-5 p.m.; Thursday-Friday 11 a.m.-2 p.m. and 5-8 p.m.; Saturday 5-9 p.m. 620.378.2563. FB.

Tri-Mee Drive-In:

1017 Washington. "Tri" one of the popular loose-meat beef burgers at this little burger joint, in business for more than 50 years. The juicy regular burgers are good too, and big! Add a shake and some Spicy-Qs for a full meal. Monday-Saturday 11 a.m.-9 p.m. 620.378.2624. FB.

Old Mill Dam: From Washington, 1 mile south on Cement, 1¼ miles west on Golf Course (becomes Old Mill Dam Rd.), cross the railroad tracks, then immediately south and west 1,000 feet on Old Mill. Here,

at Fall River, the old linseed mill, the dam, and the falls create a postcard-perfect scene. You can walk down to the water and dam for a closer view of the old mill. The original structure was built in 1891, burned in 1898, and the current mill rebuilt in 1900. This lovely Fall River setting is depicted in a mural at Madison and 7th in Fredonia.

Historic Water Tower:
10980 Decatur. From 8th, 4½ miles west on Washington, then 450 feet south on Decatur. This old vine-covered, red-brick water tower rises high and features a crenellated parapet reminiscent of a medieval castle turret. It's quite a sight. Before electricity, gravity brought water from the tank in the wider north tower down to the nearby house and farm. The narrower south tower likely housed stairs leading to the top of the structure, which was built around 1900. It stands on what is locally known as the old Pratt place, formerly the farm of the Pratt family who once owned a local cement company.

Fort Row:
From Jackson, 9 miles north on 2nd (becomes Harper). No remnants of the old fort are visible, but a sign explains the area's role in a tragic story. Harassed by Confederate Indians in present Oklahoma, Creek leader Opothleyahola (*see* p. 243) and about 10,000 followers fled into Kansas in late 1861. In sub-zero weather, without food, appropriate clothing, or other protection, the refugees arrived here seeking aid. The small local militia stockade was not equipped to handle the thousands in need. Between the lack of assistance and the

extreme weather conditions, countless Creeks died. Opothleyahola and the Union army moved survivors to Fort Belmont in nearby Woodson County in early 1862. The story of this tragedy is on file at the Wilson County Museum, 420 N. 7th. tinyurl.com/fortrow.

explorer extras... In Fredonia

Sale days are Tuesdays at noon at the Fredonia Livestock Sale Barn, 360 W. Madison. Take in this slice of country culture. 620.378.2212.

See a textbook example of a Queen Anne cottage home (NRHP) built by A.C. Flack in 1895. The porch spindlework, the turret, and the high hipped roof are stand-out features of this graceful home at 303 N. 8th. Flack, a local doctor helped organize the Fredonia Telephone Company. The home is now a private residence. Drive by only.

To the north of the Flack home, at 321 N. 8th, is a wood-frame Folk Victorian house built in 1882 for Viola Gilmore. It was a wedding present from her husband, John, the local newspaper editor. Sadly, she died of an intestinal infection in Washington, D.C., while on her honeymoon and never saw her enchanted cottage. Viola is buried in Fredonia Cemetery, 1000 and Cement. Her tombstone is to the south-east of the sexton's office. ee

Population 2,421

Norman No. 1 Oil Well and Museum: 106 S. 1st. Striking black gold in 1892, the Norman No.1 was the first commercial oil well in Kansas. It was named for T.J. Norman, a blacksmith who owned the land on which the oil was found. A 67-foot-tall wooden replica of the historic oil derrick stands in front of the museum, and a marker at 1st and Mill designates the well's original site (NRHP). The museum features photos of the oil field and this prosperous time in Neodesha, but it also focuses on other area topics including Little Bear, chief of the Little Osage tribe; WPA dolls; and Fredonia natives Tom and Tammy Parish, clowns for the Ringling Bros. and Barnum & Bailey Circus. Tuesday-Saturday 10 a.m.-4 p.m. Donation welcome. 620.325.5316.

Post Office Art (NRHP):
123 N. 5th. *Neodesha's First Inhabitants* is the title of this 1938 Section artwork by Bernard Steffen.

Little Drummer Boy:
From Main, 1½ miles north on 8th, then 4 blocks west on Spruce to Neosho Cemetery. One of the cemetery's interesting gravestones, shaped like a drum, is that of Frank "Cutty" Cartwright, an orphan who was known locally as the "little drummer boy." In 1885 he was killed in a freak train accident and, improbably, was buried next to the engineer who drove the train that ran over him. To

SE

find Cutty's grave, enter through the cemetery's brick pillars at the northeast end of the old section and continue north. Cutty's gravestone is on your left, just past the drive to the GAR memorial marked by a cannon and a statue. Brochures for a cemetery walking tour are available at the chamber office, 1st and Main. 620.325.2055.

Brown Hotel (NRHP):

519-523 Main. After being widowed, Carrie Brown supported herself and her two young boys by managing a hotel in Coffeyville. She moved to Neodesha in 1892 and bought the Occidental Hotel, which burned down three years later. She quickly rebuilt and in 1896 her new red-brick structure, the Brown Hotel, opened. The hotel is rare example of a commercial building commissioned by a 19th-century businesswoman. It currently is empty.

Beef Burger Bob's:

621 Main. Wilson countians love their loose-meat beef burgers! The steamed and crumbled ground beef on a soft bun pair nicely with a side of Curly-Q fries. Homemade cinnamon rolls, pies, and other desserts are popular and go quickly! Monday-Friday 11 a.m.-7 p.m. 620.325.5500. FB.

Bumpy's: 1000 Main. This family-style sports bar and grill is a favorite local hangout. Customers rave about the hand-cut steaks, homemade soups, desserts, and the Thursday night chicken-fried steak. Tuesday-Saturday 11 a.m.-9 p.m. 620.325.2280. FB.

El Tapatio: 105 S. 4th. Family-owned, El Tapatio serves authentic Mexican cuisine, offering combination dinners and many specialities. Ask for a free sopapilla on your birthday! Monday-Saturday 11 a.m.-8:30 p.m.; Sunday 11 a.m.-3 p.m. 620.920.4040. FB.

Lodging:

tinyurl.com/neodesharv.

explorer extras... In Neodesha

Downtown offers a pleasant walk amid brick paths and old-fashioned street lamps and past historic business buildings. Take time also to see the grand historic homes on 8th between Iowa and Grant and the beautiful Victorian home at 703 Main. Walking tour brochures are available at the chamber office, 1st and Main. 620.325.2055. **ee**

Woodson County

AROUND THE COUNTY

Woodson State Fishing Lake:

738 Fegan. From U.S. 75 in Yates Center, 7 miles southwest on U.S. 54, stairstep 3½ miles south on Grouse (becomes Hereford), then ¾ mile southwest on Fegan. The Civilian Conservation Corps (CCC) constructed this enchanting lake in 1933 on land donated by Ben Fegan. The old-timers know it as Lake Fegan, and they definitely know about the big fish here. The handiwork of the CCC is most noticeable in the stone on the dam. Information is available

at the office on the west side of the lake. Note the decorative metal cutouts near the office. 620.637.2748.

NEOSHO FALLS

Population 136

Neosho Falls population has dwindled to 136 from a high of 1,200. It once was home to a power plant, grist mill, and many other businesses that supported a growing town. But relocation of the railroad coupled with the flood of 1951 had devastating effects on the town.

Neosho Falls Dam:

From Main, 1½ blocks east on 5th (becomes Water). The falls at the Neosho River are picturesque and a popular spot for photographers, artists, and fisherman. Look for the large carp whose fins are visible above the water as they search for food in the shallow stream. Iridescent mussel shells that you may see along the river banks were harvested at the turn of the 19th century by the Iola Button Factory to make into buttons.

Riverside Park:

From Main, ¼ mile east on 7th, then ¼ mile northwest on 200 to just across the bridge. It was here in 1879 that President Rutherford B. Hayes enjoyed a picnic at the county fair. A thick stand of towering trees of walnut, pecan, and hickory creates a comfortable shaded canopy still today. You can almost hear people cheering during the horse races that were once held in the pasture nearby.

Art Deco School: 106 Main. Only the skeleton remains of the unique 1939 Neosho Falls School and gymnasium. The art deco style school closed in 1969 and when demolition crews discovered that the building was made of solid concrete they discontinued work. Today the building stands stripped and empty but majestic in its stark beauty.

PIQUA

Unincorporated

Piqua might be small, but the Piqua Farmers Co-op bins aren't! The bins, along U.S. 54, store 1.5 million bushels of grain (corn, soybeans, wheat, and grain sorghum).

One Paved Street:

The reason that Piqua has even has one paved street (2nd) is because it is part of Old U.S. 54. One mile east on 2nd (becomes 140) you'll see a 1921 marker for the Kansas Federal Aid Project, which helped pay for the highway. The marker stands beside the cemetery fence and is on the Woodson and Allen county line.

Buster Keaton: 302 S. Hill (Rural Water District Office). Piqua is the birthplace of one of the greatest silent film stars

and filmmakers, Buster Keaton, especially famous for his comedic deadpan persona. His parents, vaudevillians traveling with magician Harry Houdini and their medicine show, were in Piqua when Buster was born in 1895. A small museum inside the water office is a haven of photos from Keaton's films and of his life. They were donated in 2002 by film historian Jeffrey Vance and Eleanor Keaton, Buster's second wife. Also exhibited is a life mask of Buster's face made by a movie studio to test lighting as a stand-in for the actor. A plaque telling of Buster's birth in Piqua stands outside the water office. Monday-Friday 8 a.m.-2:30 p.m. Call ahead, 620.468.2385. FB.

One Store Town:

201 2nd. Like a one-man band, this small-town general store has it all. At the Farmers Co-op Farm Store you can buy groceries, pick up a cold pop and a candy bar, have your tire fixed, and, on Tuesdays, get a haircut in the little barber shop in the back (7:30 a.m.-12 p.m.) Jay McNett charges $7 for the haircut and the conversation is free! Monday-Friday 7:30 a.m.-5 p.m.; Saturday 7:30 a.m.-12 p.m. 620.468.2535.

St. Martin of Tours Church:

From 2nd, ¼ mile south across U.S. 54 on Xylan. Regular mass is no longer held at the 1922 church, but you can see the steeple from miles away, and the doors are open. Visitors are welcome to stop in for a peaceful moment or to see the interior beauty. A statue of St. Isidore, the patron saint of farmers, stands outside. 620.365.2277.

St. Martin of Tours Cemetery:

Behind the church. Inside the cemetery you'll find an 18-foot-tall crucifix with gravestone for the priests who served the church positioned in a semicircle around it. A veterans memorial stands between the church and the cemetery and lists those from the Piqua area who served their country.

Silverado's: 112 2nd. This is a family-friendly bar, clean, and popular with the locals. Try the famous prime rib served every Saturday night, and on the first Saturday of the month, brave the crowd for the boiled shrimp. Shelia Lampe, Kansas Explorer #3460, also recommends the smothered chicken. Monday-Wednesday 11 a.m.-1:30 p.m.; Thursday-Saturday 11 a.m.-9 p.m. 620.468.2132. FB.

TORONTO

Population 273

Toronto is on the physiographic cusp of the northern end of the Chautauqua Hills and the southern end of the Osage Cuestas. Check the color code on your state map.

Toronto Lake and Cross Timbers State Park:

From Broad, ¼ mile east on K-105, then 1¼ miles south on Point. The cross timbers of the Chautauqua Hills is an old, even ancient, forest of post and blackjack oaks, with the oldest post oak dating to the 1720s. The best way to become familiar with the vegetation of this rare forest is by hiking its trails—a total of 15 miles of hiking and biking trails surround the lake. The Ancient Trees of the Cross

SE

Timbers Trail is an easy one-mile trek through the forest with accompanying interpretive signage. Its trailhead is adjacent to the gatehouse at Toronto Point off K-105. Other trails include the Chautauqua Hills Trail (1½ miles) and the Overlook Trail (1¼ miles), which provides the highest elevation overlooking the lake. Cross Timbers Park is especially beautiful to visit during the fall. State park entrance charge. Cabins available. Reservations required. 620.637.2213. ksoutdoors.com.

Lizard Lips Grill and Deli at Country Junction:

153 U.S. 54 (U.S. 54 and K-105). A combination deli, convenience store, and bait shop, this legendary explorer stop makes sandwiches with meat piled high, stirs up hot specials on cold days, and provides all the area information you need. Daily 7 a.m.-7 p.m. 620.637.2384. FB.

Hilltop Cafe and Grocery:

153 Westshore (Toronto Lake). It's convenient to have this little spot on the west shore for breakfast, lunch, and dinner. Pick up a few groceries and bait while you're here. Sunday-Wednesday 7 a.m.-3 p.m.; Thursday-Saturday 7 a.m.-7 p.m. 620.637.2700. hill-top-cafe.com.

Courtney's Places: 120 W.

Main. Courtney Neill started off with five "places" selling all sorts of items in one restored 1886 hardware store. But he discovered that customers really only needed one place—a pizza and pasta house, which has now expanded to seat even more diners. Cus-

tomers travel from as far away as Wichita and Kansas City on a regular basis for the sumptuous homemade Italian dishes, pizza, and decadent desserts, all highlighted with the genuine friendliness of chef Courtney. Pile your friends in the car and travel for a night out at this one delightful place! Cash and check only; no local ATM. Friday-Saturday 5-8 p.m.; Sunday 11:30 a.m.-1:30 p.m. (buffet) and 5-7 p.m. 620.637.0175. courtneysplaces.com.

YATES CENTER

Population 1,380

Woodson County Courthouse (NRHP):

105 W. Rutledge. Completed in 1900, this Romanesque Revival building was designed by George Washburn, who is credited with many of Kansas' beautiful courthouses. Inlaid into the red brick at the south entrance is a plaque reading, "Do unto others as you would have them do unto you." A large rock-faced veterans memorial wall stands on the southwest corner of the courthouse grounds. Monday-Friday 8 a.m.-5 p.m. 620.625.8605.

Courthouse Square Historic District (NRHP):

This historic district includes 43 structures built between 1883 and 1928, including the 1928 gazebo, a tribute to county soldiers and sailors who served in WWI. Many of the buildings are two-story sandstone and brick of Italianate design. Tour brochures are available at the chamber office, 110 N. Main. Monday-Friday 10 a.m.-3 p.m. 620.625.3235.

Woodson Hotel: 203 W.

Butler. For years this beautiful 1887 stone hotel (NRHP) sat in disrepair. With its many graceful details, it was one of the most sophisticated of the downtown Italianate buildings. Now renovated as apartments, this architectural icon once again graces the northwest corner of the courthouse square.

Woodson County Museum:

204 W. Mary. Inside the 1878 former First Christian Church (later a chicken hatchery) you'll find an extensive county museum filled with artifacts, including a 1926 fuel truck. Learn more about the ghost

town Kalida, the Woodson State Fishing Lake (built by the Civilian Conservation Corps in 1930), and the town founder Abner Yates. The museum complex includes a mounting stone with tie-up rings, an 1868 cabin, a country schoolhouse, and a small church. June-August, Monday-Friday 1-4 p.m. 620.625.6001.

Abner Yates: From Mary, 1 mile north on U.S. 75, then ¼ mile east on 120 to Yates Center Cemetery. In 1875 a debate ensued about the location of the county seat. A plot of land with water owned by Abner Yates was selected as the best site even though no one lived there. Yates donated ground for the courthouse, a city park, each church, and a plot of land for the first two children born. Yet he died a poor man in 1904. Citizens showed their appreciation for Abner and his wife, Mary, by pooling their money and erecting a respectable gravestone. The dark gray granite Yates stone stands at the east end of the main driveway.

The Feedbunk: 112 W. Rutledge. "Homestyle cookin' like Grandma's" is the motto, and grandma must have been one good cook! Enjoy the roast beef and mashed potatoes, fried chicken and pan gravy, pancakes that are astronomical in size and flavor, and delicious desserts. Decorated in Americana, this Feedbunk provides plenty of room for its hungry crowd. Monday-Tuesday 6:30 a.m.-8 p.m.; Thursday-Saturday 6:30 a.m.-10 p.m.; Sunday 6:30 a.m.-2 p.m. 620.625.8586. FB.

Hys Filling Station: 710 W. Mary. Customers drive out of their way for the Hys (pronounced Hies) burgers and homemade pies, including gooseberry and peanut butter. The pies are popular and between six and ten are made daily. Monday-Friday 11 a.m.-8 p.m.; Saturday 11 a.m.-2 p.m. 620.625.9001. FB.

Kalida: From U.S. 75, 2 miles east on W. Mary (U.S. 54), then 1½ miles south on Osage. Originally named Chellis, the name was changed to Kalida by Tom Davidson who bought the property in 1870. Kalida was the county seat in 1873, but when Yates Center was granted the honor in 1875, Kalida was moved. Today it is best known for the old stone gates that were left behind. Tom's son James attended the 1893 Columbian Exposition in Chicago and returned with architectural design ideas that he implemented in the gates at the south end of the property. They are rather astonishing to come upon out in the country. You may take pictures of the gates but do not enter the private property. Learn more about Kalida at the Woodson County Museum, 204 W. Mary.

Kalida Cemetery: From U.S. 75, 2 miles east on W. Mary (U.S. 54), 1 mile south on Osage, then ½ mile west on 100. The large stone burial plot is for the Tom Davidson family, who had come from Pittsburg and purchased the town site of Kalida in 1870. Tom's son James designed the cemetery entrance and family plot.

SE

explorer extras...
In Yates Center

The 1912 Carnegie library (NRHP) at 218 N. Main still serves as the public library. The red-brick and limestone building displays an eclectic mix of styles including Prairie School, Craftsman, and Classical.

In the 1920s the city paved its major streets with dark red bricks (NRHP), which have been well maintained ever since.

If you poke around the 100 block of E. Butler, you'll find a pretty nifty stone jail built in 1899. One of the desperadoes who broke out tried to steal a man's horse and wagon. He didn't get far before he was gunned down by the law.

On the south side of the building at Rutledge and State a mural by local art teacher Kathe Hamman depicts Creek leader Opothleyahola and local architecture, customs, and history.

Four murals by Kathe Hamman portray the area's local cultural heritage on the cinder-block archways at the entrance of DeLay Stadium, S. Lincoln and W. Chillis. Although the 1920 structure is no longer used as a stadium, it is kept busy with its soccer field and walking track.

The Woodson County Quilt Trail group has placed large, colorful quilt blocks throughout the town and county. Quilt trail and historical driving tour brochures are available at the chamber office, 110 N. Main, and at local businesses. FB. **ee**

South Central Kansas

Counties: Barber, Barton, Butler, Cowley, Harper, Harvey, Kingman, Marion, McPherson, Pratt, Reno, Rice, Sedgwick, Stafford, Sumner

EXPLORER ELEMENT EXAMPLES

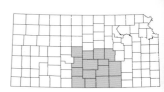

Architecture: Kingman County Courthouse, Kingman

Art: Coutts Museum of Art, El Dorado

Commerce: Family Food Store, Sawyer

Cuisine: Luciano's, Mulvane

Customs: Fairfield Polo Club, Haysville

Geography: Dyck Arboretum of the Plains, Hesston

History: Pawnee Rock State Historic Site, Pawnee Rock

People: Swiss Mennonite Memorial, Moundridge

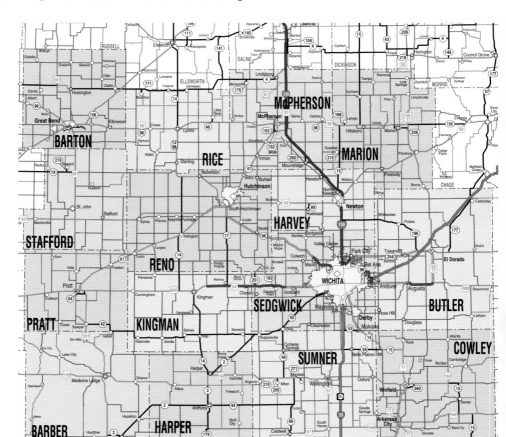

Barber County

AROUND THE COUNTY

Gypsum Hills Scenic Byway (8 Wonders of Kansas Geography):

The byway begins at the western city limits of Medicine Lodge and continues west to the intersection of U.S. 160 and U.S. 183 at Coldwater. The route is a straight 42 miles but on either side of the road you'll see red, beautiful red—buttes, mesas, canyons, and vistas. The land is rugged and rolling, expansive and enchanting. You may see cattle in the pasture land, abundant yucca, a few trees, and too many pesky eastern cedars, but it's the red that steals the show. Many of the rocks and much of the soil are stained red by iron oxide, giving the region its physiographic name, the Red Hills. Gypsum, a white rock, is found in layers within those red beds. One type of gypsum, selenite, forms large diamond-shaped crystals that litter road cuts appearing like broken glass. 620.886.9815. travelks.com/ksbyways.

HARDTNER

Population 173

Gypsum Hills Nature Museum:

301 E. Central. Bill and Janet Smith are collectors, museum organizers, and field guides. Inside a former school, their exhibits showcase insects from around the world, wildlife native to the area, fossils, butterflies, rocks, and minerals. Call ahead, 620.840.1037. FB.

Old Hospital: N. Main and Caddo. Town founder Jacob Achenbach bought the land for the Hardtner townsite, laid out the lots, brought in telephone lines and the railroad, donated a park to the city, and in his will left funds for a town hospital. Constructed in 1941, Achenbach Memorial Hospital has been renovated across the street from Achenbach Park. Drive by only.

Yur Place: 303 E. Central. Since 1988 the Sterlings have been keeping hungry customers happy. Tayla McNally, Kansas Explorer #4576, loves the lunch buffet and says it's "real home cooked food like Grandma used to make." Monday-Friday 6 a.m.-2 p.m. 620.296.4477. FB.

Sternberger Round Barn:

10866 Hackberry. From Main, 6¼ miles west on Hackberry. From the road you can glimpse this frame round barn with conical roof and central cupola. A gambrel dormer with hay hood is on the barn's south side. Drive by only.

Search for Buffalo Scenic Back Road:

Even if you can't find Ted Turner's 2,000 head of buffalo on the Z Bar Ranch, the beautiful Red Hills scenery is worth the drive. And sometimes you will see buffalo in herds of

20 to 150. Your drive begins at Hardtner. Go 19 miles west on Hackberry (look for buffalo after about 17 miles), then 4¾ miles north on Aetna. From here, you have two options in your buffalo search: (1) on paved roads, continue 15 miles north on Aetna to U.S. 160; or (2) on unpaved roads, go 10¾ miles east on Cottage Creek, then 11 miles north on Sandy Creek (becomes Lake City) to U.S. 160. You will cross cattle guards, so cattle and buffalo may be on the roads. If your search turns up empty, the drive through open prairie is nonetheless fantastic.

ISABEL

SC

Population 92

While surveying the townsite, Layton White heard that his daughter Isabel had just been born, so he named the town for her!

Golden Rule Oil Company Building:

Main and Ethel. This small tin-clad building with matching parapets on all four sides, was one of 23 stations in Kansas owned by the Golden Rule Refining Company. You can still see the faded name and logo on the front facade. The company was started in 1914 by Elbert Rule.

Thornton Adobe Barn (NRHP):
Although it is in Pratt County, the barn is close to Isabel. From Main, ¾ mile east on K-42, then 1¼ miles north on 110. Ed Thornton built the adobe structure as a dairy barn in 1942. The foundation is concrete, the haymow is wood framed, and the body of the barn is made from sun-dried adobe bricks and is covered with white stucco. Sections of adobe bricks are exposed on the exterior, but more can be seen inside. Signage explains the architecture and history of the barn, which is located in the Isabel Wetland Wildlife Area and is owned by the Kansas Department of Wildlife, Parks and Tourism. Always open.

explorer extras... In Isabel

Isabel was once known as the Windmill City because of the many windmills in town. One still stands across from the Community Store on Main Street.

The abundant gypsum in the area accounts for Isabel's large number of stucco houses. **ee**

KIOWA

Population 1,040

Land Rush Statue:
4th and Main. Kiowa was one of five official Kansas starting points for the Cherokee Strip Land Rush of 1893. To honor that heritage and his grandfather, James W. Polson, Cecil Tucker and his wife, Verna, have donated to the town this bronze sculpture of a horse and rider, and a woman handing claim stakes to the rider.

Kiowa Historical Museum:
107 N. 7th. Inside the former city hall and fire station, the museum captures the area's colorful history. Exhibits focus on the Land Rush and cattle shipping and note that temperance leader Carry Nation unleashed her hatchet-wielding campaign in Kiowa. Her hatchet is on display. Worth noticing is the whimsical figure at the bottom of the cast iron light fixtures that flank either side of the front doors. 620.825.4127. tinyurl.com/kiowamuse.

Carry Nation: 6th and Main. This temperance firebrand's saloon-smashing crusade (*see* p. 293) began in Kiowa on June 1, 1900—and so says the plaque on the historic native rock water fountain.

Hometown Market: 140 S. 6th. Even buying a few things will support this co-op grocery store, owned and operated by the people of Kiowa and surrounding area. Stop in for something you need! Sunday 12:30-5 p.m.; Monday-Saturday 8 a.m.-7 p.m. 620.825.4777. FB.

The Sideline: 629 Main. Out-of-towners and locals alike give thumbs up to the pizza—the dough and sauce are homemade. Tasty too are the sandwiches, spaghetti, salads, and ice cream. Monday, Tuesday, Thursday 11 a.m.-8 p.m.; Wednesday 11 a.m.-3 p.m.; Friday-Saturday 11 a.m.-9 p.m. 620.825.4233.

Plum Thickett Inn: 1215 Main. This full-service restaurant and bar is known for its weekend specials such as blackened prime rib. The steaks have a good reputation too, and the locals recommend the Italian nachos and the bust-your-buttons buffet. Tuesday-Saturday 11 a.m.-9 p.m.; Sunday 11 a.m.-2 p.m. 620.825.4218. FB.

Lodging: Schupbach Haus (KBBA, 620.825.4110, kbba.com); Bunkhouse Suites (620.886.1557, bunkhousesuites.com); Kiowa Motel (620.825.4040).

explorer extras... In Kiowa

The piece of petrified wood standing at 6th and Main was brought to Kiowa from Fort Supply, Oklahoma, by George Haskin around 1913.

Sadly deteriorating is this 1915 Mission style Santa Fe depot, 203 S. Railroad, built of locally mined gypsum. Note the terra cotta roof.

The former Elmore Hotel, known locally as the Kiowa Social Club, was built circa 1916. Because it was constructed next to the railroad, the architect added earthquake shocks to the foundation to absorb vibrations from the rail cars. Located on S. Railroad, the building currently is vacant.

At the 900 block of Main, South Barber School, a red-brick art deco former grade school, was

built in 1935. The tile detailing around the entrance is particularly striking. **ee**

MEDICINE LODGE

Population 2,041

Memorial Peace Park:
From Main, 1¾ miles east on U.S. 160 to Airport. Look for the overhead entrance sign welcoming you to the park. Here a marker relates the story of the 1867 Medicine Lodge peace treaty council, which involved U.S. soldiers and commissioners and as many as 15,000 Plains Indians including chiefs Satanta and Black Kettle. Contrary to general public impression, this treaty did not bring peace to the frontier. Nonetheless, every several years an iconic Peace Treaty Pageant is held in this park's natural amphitheater to celebrate the treaty signing. peacetreaty.org. 620.886.9815.

Peace Treaty Monument:
1st and Main. Stone statues of a soldier and a Plains Indian commemorate the signing of the 1867 peace treaty between the U.S. government and five tribes of Plains Indians.

Stockade Museum:
209 W. Fowler. The original 1874 stockade once stood in present downtown and purportedly covered about two blocks. In this replica stockade, the showcase exhibit features a copy of the 1867 Medicine Lodge peace treaty along with photos of the first reenactment (1927) of the treaty's signing. Other exhibits preserve the story of early Medicine Lodge and temperance crusader Carry Nation. A log cabin and old courthouse jail complete the museum complex. June-October, Tuesday-Sunday 10:30 a.m.-5 p.m.; November-May, Tuesday-Sunday 1-4 p.m. Admission charge. 620.886.3553. medicinelodgestockade.org.

Carry Nation Home
(NRHP): 211 W. Fowler. The home, on its original site, was declared a National Historic Landmark in 1976. Interpretive signs provide an excellent background of the temperance fighter Carry Nation (8 Wonders of Kansas People). Carry's hatchet, Bible, hat, valise, WCTU pin, and a few pieces of furniture are some of her personal items on display. Carry's passionate opposition to alcohol resulted from her first husband's alcoholism, from which he died. Her second husband, David Nation, a preacher, disapproved of her extreme views, and the couple divorced in 1901. A large portrait shows Carry with the divorce decree, which states that desertion—on her part—was the grounds for divorce.

Sagebrush Gallery of Western Art:
115 E. Kansas. Ranch country, cowboys, and livestock are artist Earl Kuhn's favorite watercolor subjects. Inside this gallery you'll find his stunning limited edition prints so lifelike you could step right into these western scenes. Monday-Friday 9 a.m.-5 p.m. (unless Earl is at an art show). 620.886.5163. earlkuhn.com.

Stucco Homes:
Barber County probably has more stucco homes than any other county in the state, and Medicine Lodge likely has the most. Gypsum, a natural and abundant material in this county, was readily used in making stucco. Many of the houses are constructed in the bungalow style.

Lustron Home:
203 S. Spring. This enamel-coated, all-steel, prefabricated home was built here in 1949. These unique homes, never needing paint, were a popular answer to the post-WWII housing shortage.

Gyp Hills Scenic Back
Road (8 Wonders of Kansas Geography): From U.S. 281, 3¼ miles west on U.S. 160, 6 miles south on Gyp Hill, 7 miles west on Scenic, then 7 miles north on Lake City. Small green signs whose white letters read "Scenic Drive" help guide the way. Approximately a 20-mile round trip, this beautiful drive takes unpaved roads through rolling hills and red mesas past Flower Pot Mound and other landmarks. You will cross cattle guards, so watch for cattle on the road.

Lodging:
Bunkhouse Bed & Breakfast at Wildfire Ranch (620.739.4788, bunkhouse-atwildfireranch.com); Gyp Hills Guest Ranch (620.886.3303, gyphillsguestranch.com).

explorer extras...
In Medicine Lodge

Medicine Lodge was named by the Kiowa Indians when they discovered the healing qualities of the river and built medicine lodges nearby.

Several downtown businesses display plaques telling the history of the buildings. Examples include the Grand Hotel, 124 S. Main, built in 1885 as a first-class hotel, and the 1884 First National Bank (now SCTelcom), 101 S. Main.

David Nation, Carry Nation's second husband, is buried in Highland Cemetery on U.S. 281. A small white stone near the northeast side of the stucco cemetery building marks his grave.

The four corners of the 1874 stockade, long since gone, are marked by historical signs at the Barber County Courthouse (118 E. Washington), People's Bank (121 S. Main; behind the bank on Washington), the Police Department (114 W. 1st), and the school district office (100 E. 1st; between the office and the Presbyterian Church). The stockade, complete with watchtowers and built entirely of native logs, was constructed to protect the area from Indian raids.

At 2nd and Walnut, the original school bell rests prominently on a tall architectural remnant of the 1889 former school.

A replica Statue of Liberty stands at 320 N. Walnut in front of Medicine Lodge Grade School.

A black iron water fountain and trough unit is part of the 1912 Wisner Memorial Foundation at 1st and Main. Dr. Henry Wisner, a Barber County rancher, made the donation for the water unit.

An equatorial sundial stands southwest of Barber County

North High School, 400 W. Eldorado. From U.S. 281, east on W. Eldorado, then north on the first drive to the school.

Enjoy a half-mile hike on the Red Cedar Nature Trail or the longer hiking loop at Barber State Fishing Lake. From U.S. 160, 1½ miles north on U.S. 281. **ee**

SHARON

Population 162

Martina McBride:

Sharon is the hometown of singer Martina McBride, as signs on K-160 tell you. This famous country-western star grew up as Martina Schiff and attended grade and high school in the blond-brick school at the end of N. Broadway.

Martina McBride Park:

N. Broadway. Walk under the entrance arch into an area of playground equipment, picnic shelters, and the most dominant feature, the water tower! Two plaques explain that the Federal Emergency Administration of Public Works, one of the

"alphabet" agencies of the New Deal, built this tower in 1938.

Wisner Library: 102 S. Broadway. Inside this beautiful 1910 pillared and brick building you'll find most books kept in

old glass-front wood bookcases. The small library is named for Dr. Henry Wisner, a Barber County rancher. Hours irregular.

Bull Pen: 103 E. Benton. It's known for steaks, barbecue buffet, and chicken-fried. Take a look at the display case featuring memorabilia of hometown girl Martina McBride. Wednesday-Saturday 5-9:30 p.m. 620.294.5240. FB.

SUN CITY

Population 54

Buster's Saloon: 104 W. Main. This legendary Red Hills watering hole was named for Buster (C.A.) Hathaway, who started it in 1946 as Hathaway's Tavern. But soon it became known simply as Buster's. As you enter through the double screen door under a tin awning, imagine all the cowboy boots that have crossed this wood floor and rested on the bar's brass foot rail. It's a pasture-to-plate menu and as owner Harry Dawson says, "It's a meat eater's heaven." The Angus beef is grass fed here in the Gyp Hills, and you'll taste the goodness in each bite of the steaks and burgers. Sure to quench your thirst is the famous ice cold fishbowl beer. Grill hours, Thursday-Sunday 11 a.m.-9 p.m. 620.248.3215. FB.

River Road Scenic Back Road:

From Main, ¼ mile north on Sun City, 9½ miles northwest on River (becomes Sun City), then 1½ miles west on Wilmore into unincorporated Belvidere (Kiowa County). This sandy winding road parallels the Medicine Lodge River. As you near Belvidere, physiographic changes from the Red Hills to the High Plains are revealed in the topography and vegetation. In season, wildflowers line your route in stunning fashion.

Barton County

Early Explorers (1600–1865)

Kansas Wetlands Education Center:

592 NE K-156. From U.S. 56, 6½ miles northeast on K-156. This is best point to embark on your journey into the Cheyenne Bottoms Wildlife Area. No matter what your level of knowledge about wetlands, bird migration, and the development of Cheyenne Bottoms, the exhibits and conversation here will fascinate and educate you further. Monday-Saturday 9 a.m.-5 p.m.; Sunday 1-5 p.m.; November-March, closed Monday. 620.566.1456. wetlandscenter.fhsu.edu.

Observation Tower:

From the Kansas Wetlands Education Center, ¼ mile southeast on K-156, then ¾ mile northwest on Cheyenne Bottoms Rd. You're not as high as the birds, but the elevated view will help you see the expanse of the wetlands. Follow the public access roads from here around Cheyenne Bottoms.

Cheyenne Bottoms Wildlife Area (8 Wonders of Kansas):

5 miles south of Hoisington or 6 miles north of Great Bend on U.S. 281, then 2 miles east on NE 60 to NE 20, and follow the public access roads within the wetlands. Cheyenne Bottoms, a 41,000-acre wetland basin, is one of the world's most important migratory stops for North American shorebirds. More than 350 species have been recorded here—more than 130 species nest in the area, and nearly 70 species are permanent residents. Considered the largest marsh in the nation's interior, Cheyenne Bottoms has been designated a Wetland of International Importance. Tens of thousands of geese, ducks, and shorebirds migrate through here during spring and fall. Interpretive signs are along the route through this very impressive area. 620.793.7730. tinyurl.com/cheybott.

Wetlands & Wildlife National Scenic Byway:

Begin at K-4 and U.S. 281 in Hoisington. Anchored by Cheyenne Bottoms Wildlife Area on the north and Quivira National Wildlife Refuge (Stafford County) on the south, this 77-mile route through the Arkansas River Lowlands connects human and bird migratory paths and provides excellent bird-watching opportunities. The area is characterized by irregular hills and sand dunes created by the river as it winds its way through the Central Plains. Although the route doesn't go through any town, eight towns are easily accessible. Your route ends near St. John (Stafford County). 620.792.2750. travelks.com/ksbyways.

Small-Town Scenic Drive:

If you enjoy driving and finding little places off the beaten path, head to northern Barton County in the Smoky Hills region. Look skyward and follow the church steeples and grain elevators, which lead you from one small town to the next. Start in Olmitz (population 115) at NW 90 and NW 105 and follow the county blacktops to Galatia (population 39), Susank (population 34), Beaver (unincorporated) to end in Odin (unincorporated). Post rock fences, abandoned homesteads, limestone buildings, and lush crops accompany you through this hilly landscape, and a little bar and grill await you in most of the towns. The clock towers on the churches in Olmitz and Odin are landmark pieces.

SC

Heartland Farm:

From K-96 in Great Bend, 13¾ miles west on 10th (becomes Barton, becomes X), then ½ mile south on 390. This peaceful farm is owned by the Dominican Sisters, who offer group tours of their organic gardens, straw-bale house, silo chapel, labyrinth in the virgin prairie, and small alpaca herd. Donation welcome. Reservations required. 620.923.4585. heartlandfarm-ks.org.

BEAVER

Unincorporated

Beaver Brewery at Mo's

Place: 1908 Elm. It's all about the craft beer and the drive to this little farming burg with the dominating grain elevators. Inside a nondescript metal building, Dale Kaiser and Austin Bell are keeping alive the brewing tradition started by Len Moeder. The seven popular craft beers are on tap, and a small menu offers specialty burgers, hand-cut fries, homemade cole slaw, and on weekends, steaks. Wednesday-Saturday 11 a.m.-9 p.m. 620.587.2350. FB.

Beaver Creek Stone

Bridge (NRHP): NE 50 and NE 230. From Elm, ¾ mile west on NE 190, then 4 miles north on NE 50. A small single-arch bridge sits under the road, and a big cottonwood stands nearby. Look for the decorative keystones on either side of the bridge with WPA and 1941 inscribed on each.

Bridge #218 (NRHP):

From Elm, ¼ mile east on 190, 3 miles north on Vine (becomes

NE 60), then 600 feet west on NE 220. Although not having a spectacular name, this sturdy little country bridge over a Beaver Creek tributary has stood the test of time. It's different in that some parts of the bridge (guardrails and curbing) are made from concrete; the walls for the double span are made of limestone. The concrete curb bears the inscription, "WPA 1940."

CLAFLIN

Population 641

Miller's of Claflin: 200 Main. A furniture tradition since 1903, Miller's is notable for its impact on the town, both economically and visually. Drive downtown and you'll think you've entered a living history museum. Miller's has duplicated the look and color of actual buildings that stood in Claflin prior to a series of fires. The interiors showcase new furniture or are used as warehouses. Monday, Thursday 9 a.m.-8 p.m.; Tuesday-Saturday 9 a.m.-5 p.m. 800.748.8314. millersofclaflin.com.

Squeegy's Bar & Grill: 217 Main. Come casual, come hungry. The daily special offers a comfort food such as meatloaf or smothered steak, which comes with mashed potatoes, veggie, and a trip through the salad bar. Tuesday-Saturday 11 a.m.-2 p.m. and 4-9 p.m. 620.588.3625. FB.

explorer extras...
In Claflin

Bailey's Food Bin, 101 Main, is one of the finest small-town groceries you'll find anywhere.

You're welcome to use the "comfort station" while you're here. Monday-Saturday 8 a.m.- 8 p.m.; Sunday 11 a.m.-5 p.m. 620.587.3496. baileysfoodbin.com.

The white-and-red 1930s White Eagle filling station in the 200 block of Main is a steadfast icon. Although no longer a service station, "Bloomer Garage" appears in faded print across the front.

You'll hear the Immaculate Conception church bells, 310 Main, peal out a hymn every day at noon except on Tuesday—the day the tornado siren is tested.

The locals are proud of their nifty nine-hole, grass-green Claflin Golf Course. It's waiting at 1178 NE 150 for you to tee up and make par. Try to ricochet a drive off the windmill at hole 6! Greens fee. **ee**

ELLINWOOD

Population 2,114

Underground Tunnel

Tours: 1 N. Main. In the 1880s the town was populated by German immigrants who, in their home country, had used tunnels as a practical access to businesses in basements. Several tours now take you under Ellinwood. On the west side of Main you're led down back stairs, past coal chutes, and into former underground business areas. A tour on the east side of Main takes you under the historic Wolf Hotel. Admission charge. Reservations required. Thursday-Monday. 620.639.6915. historicwolfhotel.com.

Dick Building (RHKP):

2 N. Main. This looming Italian-ate building is a historic anchor and icon on this busy corner of Main and U.S. 56. Constructed in 1887, it stood over underground businesses. In 1900 Mathias Dick bought the building and opened a hardware and farm implement store. Not until 1982 did restoration of the tunnels and underground shops begin, initiated by Dick's granddaughter and her husband, Adrianna and Dan Dierolf. Today the Dick Build-ing houses two antique stores.

Ellinwood Emporium:

2 N. Main. On the ground level inside the Dick Building you will enjoy your hunt for antique treasures. Emporium owner Rick Casagrande gives exceptional tours of the underground tunnels. Monday, Thursday-Saturday 10 a.m.-
5 p.m.; Sunday 12-5 p.m. 620.564.2498.

Draney's Antiques: 4 N.

Main. Also in the Dick Building are Ron and Becky's eclectic inventory of items related to oil, gas, fishing, hunting, sports, and cars. Thursday-Saturday 10 a.m.-5 p.m. 620.639.5329.

Ellinwood Packing Plant:

701 W. Santa Fe. Cases and freezers in the plant's retail store contain some of the best Kansas raised beef, pork, and poultry. The steaks, burgers, and sausages served in regional restaurants probably came from this plant. Be sure to try the famous Hillbilly bacon. Bring a cooler and fill it with quality meat from the heartland. Monday-Friday 8 a.m.-5:30 p.m.; Saturday 8 a.m.-1 p.m. 620.564.3156.

Gather: 19 N. Main. Running

this combination coffee shop, lunch spot, and soda fountain is how Rod and Danielle Weber spend their retirement. Danielle makes homemade breads and Rod concocts the specialty coffees and soda fountain treats. The syrups comes in dozens of flavors including special ones for diabetics. A daily special, sandwiches, and a salad bar are available for lunch. Rod and Danielle love being here and so will you. Tuesday-Friday 7 a.m.-4:30 p.m. 620.617.3225. FB.

Lone Wolf Restaurant:

111 E. 1st. A former Knights of Columbus building is now a popular stop for made-from-scratch meals. Aged steaks from Ellinwood Packing are hand cut and burgers are hand pattied and charbroiled. The hot food bar at lunch and the Explorer Way chicken-fried steak are among the popular options. Monday-Saturday 11 a.m.-2 p.m. and 5-8 p.m. 620.564.2829. FB.

Annie Mae's: 518 E. Santa Fe.

Fill up on daily lunch specials, burgers, and sandwiches during the week, and steaks and pizza on weekends. Monday-Friday 11 a.m.-2 p.m. and 5-9 p.m.; Saturday 8 a.m.-9 p.m. 620.564.3676. FB.

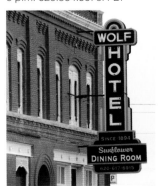

Lodging: Historic Wolf

Hotel (KBBA, 620.617.6915, historicwolfhotel.com).

explorer extras...
In Ellinwood

The look of downtown is enhanced with bright golden wheat shocks on each light pole. The art was inspired by the interior decor of the historic Wolf Hotel.

You'll see one of the state's 91 remaining Lustron homes at 523 W. 6th. These easily constructed homes made from prefabricated enameled steel are popular finds with enthusiasts of this housing style developed post-WWII.

The Schulte-Lyon Kimpler Building is the oldest wooden building in town, built in 1874. See it on the east side in the 100 block of N. Main.

The attractive 1931 art deco band shell (NRHP) on N. Main is the prominent feature in Wolf Park. The land for the park was donated by Fred Wolf in 1930.

Beneath the tall spire, working clocks enhance all four sides of the tower on the 1900 native stone St. Joseph Church, 214 N. Main.

The 1892 Saints Peter and Paul Church (RHKP), 498 NE 110, is steadily being restored following damage from a 2007 tornado. A striking archi-tectural specimen, the gable-front, two-story brick building features a dominant bell tower that has now been reconstructed. The church, known as "Land-mark of the Plains," is 5 miles north of town on NE 110. To see the interior, call ahead, 620.556.7310. ee

SC

GREAT BEND

Population 15,901

The town was founded at a great bend in the Arkansas River. Thus, its name!

Visitor Center: 3111 10th. Look for the awning and a big sign welcoming you to Great Bend. At the visitor center you can pick up brochures, learn about the Wetlands & Wildlife National Scenic Byway, and the many things to see in Great Bend and the area. Monday-Friday, 8 a.m.-12 p.m. and 1-5 p.m. For your convenience, a 24-hour accessible visitor resource center is in the entrance of the building. 620.792.2750. visitgreatbend.com.

Barton County Courthouse: The white exterior, numerous columns, and large arched windows create a stunning 1918 Classical Eclecticism stone structure. Inside, marble interior walls and stairs complete the grandeur. Monday-Friday 8 a.m.-5 p.m. 620.793.1800.

Jack Kilby Plaza: In front of the courthouse. The magnificent larger-than-life statue of Jack Kilby was sculpted by local artist Chet Cale. Kilby, a Great Bend native, invented the monolithic integrated circuit, known as the microchip, which paved the

way for the modern information age. The sculpture includes Kilby and two children, which symbolizes the transmission of knowledge from one generation to the next. Kilby won a Nobel Prize in Physics for the invention.

Courthouse Grounds: The double-block courthouse square includes a memorial band shell, the Kansas Quilt Walk, a synthetic ice rink (winter), and a Civil War statue honoring war veterans. The 1915 statue, an original by sculptor Frederick C. Hibbard, stands atop a base containing several inscribed plaques.

Outdoor Murals: A dozen colorful murals of various depictions adorn the streets of Great Bend. You'll see *El Baile/The Dance* at 10th and Main, and the *Clara Barton* mural at 16th and Williams. Four can be found on Main or just to the west, and three more are in Brit Spaugh Park, 2123 Main.

Great Bend Zoo: 2123 Main (Brit Spaugh Park). A pleasant stroll beneath the huge cottonwoods takes you by animals from all seven continents. Look for the birds, monkeys, servals,

lions, white tigers, and bears, oh my! A visit to the Raptor Center contains quality interactive displays where you learn more about birds of prey, such as eagles, owls, and hawks. Walk or drive along the network of ponds to view larger animals. Daily 9 a.m.-4:30 p.m. 620.793.4226.

Oscar Micheaux (1884-1951): Raised in Great Bend, Micheaux became the first black to produce a full-length motion picture (1919) with an all-black cast. The grave of this famous filmmaker and author can be seen at Great Bend Cemetery, Broadway and Coolidge. From the Broadway entrance, go north (cemetery office is on your right) into the cemetery to the dead end,

west to the second blacktop driveway, then south at the Y. Micheaux's gravestone is the fourth one along the road to the east. Learn more about Micheaux at the Barton County Historical Museum.

Barton County Historical Museum: 85 S. U.S. 281. The museum complex includes a schoolhouse, depot, post office, Waupun windmill, 1873 stone house, blacksmith shop, 1898 church, and an implement building. The main museum interprets county history through theme displays, and additional exhibits recognize Great Bend's famous citizens including filmmaker Oscar Micheaux, basketball star Jackie Stiles, and Nobel Prize winner Jack Kilby. A highlight is a 1950s Lustron home complete with period furnishings. April-October, Tuesday-Friday 10 a.m.-5 p.m. and Saturday-Sunday 1-5 p.m.; November-March, Tuesday-Friday 10 a.m.-5 p.m. Admission charge. 620.793.5125. tinyurl.com/barton-museum.

Lustron Homes: You gotta love the Lustron! And Great Bend has been designated the Lustron Home Capital of Kansas. Eighteen Lustrons, prefabricated, all-steel homes popularized after WWII, were built by local company Brack Implements. You can see these compact, efficient houses on Broadway at W. 3410, E.1444, and E.1416; on Coolidge at 1307, 1310, and 1406; and on Harding at 1317, 1410, 1411, and 1417. The Abel home (NRHP), 2601 Paseo, and the Nagel house (NRHP), 1411 Wilson, are both deluxe two-bedroom models. Visit the Barton County Historical Museum to view a fully furnished Lustron.

Kansas Oil & Gas Museum and Hall of Fame: 5944 W. 10th. Whether you have a great or mild curiosity about the oil industry, this museum helps you understand the effects this resource has had on our daily lives. Learn about oil

extraction and efforts to protect our environment. Individuals significant to the Kansas oil industry are honored in the Hall of Fame. April-September, Monday-Friday 1-5 p.m. 620.793.8301.

Shafer Art Gallery: 245 NE 30 Rd. (Barton Community College campus). From 24th, 2 miles north on U.S. 281, then 1¾ miles east on NE 30 Rd. Each of the 28 Gus Shafer bronze sculptures tells a vivid story. Additional permanent exhibits feature works of Sandzen, Audubon, Picasso, Matisse, and other artists. In the lobby, four large murals by artist Pat Potucek beautifully depict the formative years of the area. Monday-Saturday 10 a.m.-5 p.m. 620.792.9342.

Rosewood Wine Cellar: 1901 Lakin. The historic brick building adds to the "rustic, ranch-elegance" environment where shelves are filled with specialty meats, jellies, honey, bath products, candles, pottery, and handcrafted wines. All products are made by client-employees with developmental disabilities. The wines are produced at Rosewood Winery (see p.303). Monday-Saturday 10 a.m.-6 p.m. 620.603.6410. rosewoodcreations.com.

Heart of Kansas Mercantile and Miss Pretty Pickles: 1212 and 1214 Main. Shoppers looking for all things Kansas will find them in this warm and inviting

store filled with gifts, books, foods, useful kitchen items, home decor, Redbarn pet products, and local and statewide art. Through a connected door is a bright and fun boutique stocked with women's and children's clothing and accessories, and gifts for babies. Monday-Friday 10:30 a.m.-5:30 p.m.; Saturday 10 a.m.-3 p.m. 620.786.2333. FB.

Fuller Brush Factory Outlet: 15 SW 40. From K-96, 2¾ miles west on 10th (W. Barton County), 1/4 mile south on Airport (SW 40), and take the first drive west to the parking lot. You don't have to wait for the Fuller Brush man to knock on your door, you can go directly to the factory outlet. The company was started in Boston by Alfred Fuller in 1907, and in 1972 a manufacturing facility opened in Great Bend. Household cleaning, cooking, and personal care items can be purchased right where they're made. Monday-Friday 9 a.m.-5:30 p.m. fuller.com. 800.522.0499.

B-29 Memorial: 9047 6th. From K-96, 2¾ miles west on 10th (W. Barton County), 1 mile south on Airport, then just west on 6th. Great Bend Army Air Field opened in 1943 as a B-29 bomber training facility. A symbolic memorial with intersecting arches represents the emblem of the Global 20th Air Force (the 20th was established in 1944 to perform bombardment missions against Japan).

SC

A miniature B-29 cast in stainless steel is the memorial's centerpiece. Learn more about the WWII training facility at the Barton County Historical Museum. b29memorial.com.

Great Bend Army Air Field Hangar (NRHP):

South of the B-29 Memorial. The hangar was used for maintenance and modification of aircraft for air fields engaged in combat training in south-central and southwest Kansas during WWII. Damage to the hangar from a 2008 tornado is still evident.

Norden Bombsight Storage Vaults (NRHP):

South of the B-29 Memorial. The two concrete bunkers, with eight-inch-thick walls, served as storage for bombsights that aircraft used when conducting high-altitude strategic bombing exercises. The bunkers sit vacant across the road to the south from the Piper hangar.

National Hot Rod Association (Sunflower Rod and Custom Association) Drag Strip

(RHKP): 455 W. Barton County. From U.S. 281, 5¾ miles west on 10th, then ¼ mile south on G. On the site of the WWII bomber training field, this drag strip held the first (1955) NHRA drag racing competition. Races are still held here today. srcadragstrip.com.

Perks Coffee: 1216 Main. Fresh roasted coffee and mouth-watering baked goods are sure to perk you up at this

coffee shop and quick lunch stop. Homemade bierocks and a daily lunch special await you here too. Monday-Friday 6:30 a.m.-7 p.m.; Saturday 8 a.m.-7 p.m. 620.786.2334. FB.

Great Bend Coffee:

2015 Lakin. Another great coffee and lunch stop, this one is inside a glorious 1928 Modern Gothic building originally built as a Masonic lodge. A large menu includes brick-oven baked hot sandwiches and pizza. Monday-Friday 7 a.m.-3 p.m.; Saturday 8 a.m.-3 p.m.; Friday-Saturday 5:30-8:30 p.m. 620.603.6465. greatbendcoffee.com.

Granny's Kitchen:

925 E.10th. Look for the little cream-colored house on the south side of E. U.S. 56. When a place offers 18 different omelets, makes biscuits and gravy from scratch, and serves breakfast burritos and pancakes, you know you want to be here for breakfast, served anytime. Wednesday-Sunday 7 a.m.-2 p.m. 620.793.7441.

Classic Inn: 1 S. Patton. From 10th, 1 mile south on Patton (U.S. 56). Two golden lion statues greet you as you enter this combination American Asian (Chinese and Vietnamese) restaurant. Linh Reiter offers a welcome smile and a scrumptious lunch buffet

for a quick meal, or a broad menu with everything from steaks and liver and onions to Pho and a local favorite, fried rice noodle salad. Monday-Saturday 11 a.m.-2 p.m. and 5-9 p.m. 620.792.3100.

Mary's Kitchen:

2424 10th. If you want the real deal in Mexican food, come to Mary's for the barbacoa tacos, tortas, and burritos, and on Saturdays delicious pozole and menudo. Monday-Saturday 5 a.m.-3 p.m. 620.792.2912.

HandleBar and Grill:

807 10th. The decor is motorcycles and handle bars and you'll find locals, visitors, families, and bikers enjoying the atmosphere and the food. Tuesday-Sunday 11 a.m.-8 p.m. 620.603.6676. FB.

More Good Restaurants:

Leann's Restaurant (2520 10th, 620.793.6491); and The Page: An American Bistro (2920 10th, 620.792.8700).

Lodging: visitgreatbend.com.

explorer extras...
In Great Bend

Chet Cale is a professional sculptor working with stone, bronze, clay, and wood. His Stone Street Arts studio and gallery is in an old red-brick hatchery at 510 Stone. Call ahead, 620.282.0160. chetcale.com.

The red and earth tones add zest to the Crest Theater (NRHP) facade and marque—both fabulous 50s! Well-known

theater architect Robert Boller incorporated geometric and Art Moderne design in this 1950 building at 1905 Lakin. It is now home to the Great Bend Community Theatre. gbct.net.

The B&B Metal Arts design at the entrance of the Great Bend Sports Complex, 41 McKinley, is quite a hit, in more ways than one. Local athletes posed for the depiction of seven ballplayers in action. From 10th, ¾ mile south on McKinley.

Enjoy a seven-mile, one-way hike or bike ride along the Arkansas River levee and the flood control ditch. A trailhead (with parking available) is from K-96, 2 miles west on W. 10th (becomes W. Barton County). tinyurl.com/gbbikehike.

Enjoy the drive along Broadway, from Morton (three blocks west of Main) to Harrison. You'll see diverse styles of grand historic homes, from Mediterranean at 2818 Broadway to Mission at 2816 Broadway.

Few poor farm buildings have survived, but the former Barton County Poor Farm home is intact and one of the best in the state. The three-story red-brick structure is now part of a church complex. From K-96, 1¾ miles west on W. 10th (becomes W. Barton County). Drive by only.

Santa Fe Trail Park, 10th and Frey, is a beautiful spot with landscaped gardens and a

pond. A DAR Santa Fe Trail marker stands at the edge of the park near 10th.

The Fort Zarah historical marker stands in a roadside park about 1 mile east of Great Bend on U.S. 56. The fort was established in 1864 to protect wagon trains and provide annuities to Plains Indians who had signed peace treaties.

Get wet and wild at Wetlands Waterpark, a new aquatic park providing terrific fun in the water! In Brit Spaugh Park, 2303 Main. 620.792.1516. greatbendwaterpark.com. **ee**

HOISINGTON

Population 2,685

Cemetery Folk Art: E. 9th and Cedar. From Cedar, enter the eastbound drive in Hoisington Cemetery, take the first drive north to the end, then east to Post 21. Here you'll find the first of several folk art gravestones created by local man Phil Webb. Something tugged at his heartstrings several years ago when he noticed graves without headstones. The first marker he created was for Creola Paxton who he learned loved to sew— and those are the exact words he inscribed on her marker

along with a cross, a needle, and a spool of thread. You'll find many more of these irregular concrete blocks with small figures and bright splashes of paint that tell you something about the deceased.

Post Office Murals (NRHP): 121 E. 2nd. *Wheat Center* is the title of the large farm scene, a 1938 Section artwork by Dorothea Tomlinson. The lobby also displays three scenes by a local artist Bob Booth depicting the modernization of harvest.

B&B Metal Arts: 1143 N. Susank. You'll see B&B Metal works throughout Barton County and other cities around the state. Should you need a customized sign, ornamental iron, streetscape, copper wall banners, or life-sized sculptures, visit brothers Bruce and Brent Bitter in their shop. Monday-Friday 9:30-11:30 a.m. and 1:30-4:30 p.m. 620.653.4000. bbmetalarts.com.

Municipal Building Sundials: 109 E. 1st. Sundials on each side of the tall column are unique accessories on the art deco Municipal Building. Unusual and distinctive, they've been known to keep perfect time! The building was built by the WPA in 1939.

High School and Stadium (NRHP): 218 E 7th. The native limestone stadium was a 1937 WPA project, which was followed by the construction of Hoisington High School, completed in 1940. This handsome blonde-brick three-story school with art deco ornamentation and carved detailing was a PWA project.

SC

Tap Room: 170 S. Main. The sign says cold beer and hot food, and locals give both high marks. Started in 1952, this dive bar posts a host of signs that add character and humor and go down well with the frosty beer and Becky's homemade bierocks. Monday-Saturday 9 a.m.-12 p.m. 620.653.2611.

Lodging:
hoisingtonks.org/lodging.htm.

**explorer extras...
In Hoisington**

Barton County is the only Kansas county named for a woman, Civil War nurse Clara Barton. Learn more about this courageous woman in a lobby display at the Clara Barton Hospital, 250 W. 9th. FB.

In the William Lebert Park, 149 N. Main, colorful signs describe the Wetlands & Wildlife National Scenic Byway and the 2001 tornado that hit Hoisington. A brass plaque pays tribute to Bill Lebert, a banker and community supporter.

Make a retro stop at the Man-weiler Chevrolet dealership, 271 S. Main. The Streamline Art Moderne building (NRHP) constructed in 1944 displays the classic curved showroom, rounded corners, glass blocks, and colorful neon Chevrolet sign. FB.

Diners were the main structures built by the Valentine Manufact-uring Company. But the Wichita-based company also designed small prefabricated buildings for use as ice cream stores and liquor stores. When Prohibition ended in Kansas in 1948, several of these were sold throughout the state. The Liquor Box at 168 W. 2nd is one of the few

remaining in the state. 620.653.2991.

Hoisington history is worth exploring at the Hoisington Historical Society Museum. You'll find it inside the restored 1905 home at 120 E. 2nd. Call ahead, 620.653.4320. **ee**

ODIN

Unincorporated

Holy Family Church: 1387 NE 90. Step inside to see the simple but beautiful interior of this 1896 native limestone church with a classic spire. The cemetery behind it contains many ornate gravestones inscribed with names of German immigrants who settled here. 620.587.3628.

 Odin Store: 890 NE 140. Edgar and Sue Jacobs have created a community atmosphere in "The store," as it is known, since 1972. The friendly owners provide the area with a place to buy gas, pick up a few groceries or sandwiches, and to meet friends and family for a meal or a cold brew. If you're in a hurry, just grab a cold drink or candy bar out of the cooler. Monday-Saturday 7:30 a.m.-12 a.m.; Sunday 9 a.m.-6:30 p.m. 620.587.3370.

PAWNEE ROCK

Population 247

Pawnee Rock State Historic Site: From U.S. 56, ½ mile north on Centre. Years ago this natural landmark stood much taller, but in the 1870s settlers and the railroad

quarried much of its rock for building purposes. With the help of interpretive signs and a monument, you will appreciate the importance and striking qualities of this former observation point on the Plains. A Dakota sandstone lookout tower stands atop the rock. The 360-degree view is much different today, but imagine spotting a covered wagon train traveling the Santa Fe Trail (now U.S. 56) some 175 years ago. Can you find

the memorial plaque to William Becknell, "Father of the Santa Fe Trail," on the face of the rock? kshs.org.

Santa Fe Mercantile: 300 U.S. 56. Owner Linda McCowan Waite has a talent for blending unique items and making customers smile. Find a wide variety of antiques, Pinterest-type craft supplies, Kansas prairie items, and farm objects. Wednesday-Sunday 1-5 p.m. 620.617.7121. FB.

Rosewood Winery: 1171 SW 20. From Centre, 3 blocks east on Santa Fe, 4¾ miles north on SW 110, then ¾ mile west on SW 20. Rosewood Creations has developed innumerable first-class job opportunities for those with developmental disabilities. One of those is this winery, located on a ranch north of Pawnee Rock where many types of jobs, and a horse therapy program, take place. Come for a wine tasting in a one-of-a-kind setting. Rosewood Wines—The Fox, Shining Spark, Copper Profits, and Coosa Pat—are named for the therapy horses. Thursday-Friday 1-5 p.m. 620.982.4487. rosewoodcreations.com.

Butler County

AROUND THE COUNTY

100 Cow Hill Scenic Back Road: 267 Pioneer. You need to try this rugged route just for the name alone! From 116th in Beaumont, stairstep 7¾ miles south and west on Squier (becomes Beaumont-Latham), 1½ miles west on 190, 1 mile south on Rattlesnake, 2½ miles east on 200, ½ mile south on Wiedeman, then 2 miles east on 216 (becomes Oxen as you cross into Elk County). Along the way you'll likely see buffalo, definitely a wind farm, and lovely Flint Hills scenery. Just past the Green Ranch sign, you'll come to a descent so steep you could stack 100 cows on top of each other, thus the nickname (unofficial) of this road. Dry weather roads.

Stone Bridges Scenic Back Road: From Main in Elbing, 5¾ miles east on 160. At this point you'll see the Whitewater River Masonry Bridge, a single-arch bridge built in 1910. Continue to the single-arch Henry Creek Bridge by backtracking west on 160

to Diamond, 2 miles south on Diamond, then 2½ miles east on 140. Nine more stone bridges can be found throughout the county. A guide is available in El Dorado at the city hall, 220 E. 1st, and at District 142, 142 N. Main; or on p. 4-5 of tinyurl.com/tourbridges.

Bois d'Arc and the Little Walnut River Pratt Truss Bridge (NRHP): From U.S. 400 in Augusta, 7 miles south on U.S. 77, 2½ miles east on 170, 1¼ miles north on Hopkins Switch, then ¾ mile east on 157 Terr. Here you'll come face to face with the only remaining building (an abandoned 1890s limestone structure) of Bois d'Arc, a little village settled in 1867. Turn south to cross the bridge over the Little Walnut River. This 102-foot-long 1885 truss bridge with wooden plank surface is for one-way traffic. Go slow, hold your breath, and drive across—then do it again!

ANDOVER

Population 12,265

Andover Tornado Monument: 100 block of N. Andover. Three flag poles within a v-shaped native limestone wall stand as a tribute to the survivors and victims of the devastating April 26, 1991, tornado. This monument is across from the Catholic church, which was demolished in the tornado and later rebuilt.

Andover Historical Museum: 937 N. Andover. Inside the former library, this museum tells the local story. Call ahead, 316.775.3656.

AUGUSTA

Population 9,203

Augusta Historic Theatre (NRHP): 523 State. This 1935 art deco theatre was one of the first in the nation whose interior was completely lit with neon. The wall murals; ornamental plaster designs in black, silver, salmon, and green; and stenciled ceiling give the theatre an intriguing Egyptian appearance. augustahistorictheatre.com.

Downtown: A dominant red-brick street serves as a wonderful accent to the nicely landscaped business district. Stop at the Downtown Augusta office inside the 1909 Frisco depot (RHKP) at 618 State for brochures or public restrooms. Shopping opportunities include the Cross Eyed Cow antique shop (601 State, 316.831.7733); Boutique 1631, a women's clothing store (513 State, 316.775.1631); and the Brick Street Flower Company (502 State, 316.775.1648). downtownaugustainc.com.

Post Office Mural (NRHP): 119. E. 5th. *A Kansas Gusher* is the title of this 1940 Section artwork by Donald Silks, which depicts a farm scene with an oil well geyser in the background.

Augusta Historical Museum: 303 State. The oil industry has been vital to Augusta's history, and its saga is told here in addition to exhibits about the town, pre-1800s through the 1950s. The C.N. James Log

SC

Cabin (NRHP), built as a trading post in 1868, served many purposes and is one of the few log cabins remaining in Kansas on its original site. C.N.'s wife, Augusta, was the inspiration for the town's name. Visit the blacksmith's shop complete with tools and coal-fired forge from the late 1800s. Monday-Friday 11 a.m.- 3 p.m.; Saturday 1-4 p.m. 316.775.5655. augustahistoricalsociety.com.

Kansas Museum of Military History:
135 S. U.S. 77. From 5th, ¼ mile south on Walnut. Look for a round-top structure. A group of veterans created this aviation and military museum to tell the events of WWII to the present conflicts. More than 10,000 artifacts— including a Huey helicopter, Kiowa helicopter, and Vietnam-era gun truck—are in the collection. May-October, Monday 11 a.m.-4 p.m.; Wednesday-Friday 11 a.m.-5 p.m.; Saturday 9 a.m.-4 p.m. 316.775.1425. FB.

Brick Street Cafe:
507 State. Word on the street is that Brick Street is your stop for creative soups, sandwiches, and yummy breads. Tuesday-Saturday 8 a.m.-2:30 p.m. 316.260.1515. FB.

Sugar Shane's Cafe:
430 State. The pan-seared white fish is the big seller here, but the burgers and chicken-fried steak get high marks at this beach-themed cafe. As they say at Sugar Shane's, "no matter the latitude, it's a tropical attitude." Monday-Saturday 11 a.m.-9 p.m.; Sunday 11 a.m.-2 p.m. 316.201.1099. sugarshanescafe.com.

explorer extras... In Augusta

Make an old-fashioned stop at Miller's Five Drive-In, 330 State, where you step up to the outside window to order your food, drink, or an ice cream. Tuesday-Saturday 11:30 a.m.-7 p.m. 316.775.9989. FB.

In Garvin Park near Augusta City Lake, a new nine-hole disc golf course features glow-in-the-dark (black light) DreamCatcher baskets, natural tee boxes, and colorful signage. From 7th (U.S. 54), 1¼ miles north on State, 2 blocks west on Sunflower, then jog north.

Made entirely of native rock, two unusual and artistic features each comprise a low semicircle wall enclosing picnic benches with a tall stone wood-burning grill completing the circle. Built in 1940 as a National Youth Administration project, they can be seen in the southwest part of Garvin Park. From 7th (U.S. 54), 1¼ miles north on State, 2 blocks west on Sunflower, jog north, then continue west into the park.

Former English teacher Frank Jensen based many of his fascinating metal and steel sculptures on classical literature. You can see them from U.S. 400 as you drive by his home called Henry's Sculpture Hill, an homage to Henry David Thoreau. From Osage, 4½ miles east on U.S. 400. sculpturehill.com. **ee**

BEAUMONT

Unincorporated

Through the first half of the 1900s Beaumont was one of the most important shipping points in the Flint Hills. Each spring thousands of cattle were shipped here by rail from Texas and Oklahoma to pasture on the area's bluestem grass. The stockyards could handle 9,000 at a time. When the cattle arrived they were counted, weighed, and then driven by horseback to pasture. By the 1950s trucks had taken over the cattle transport business. Multiple large markers to the north and east of the Beaumont Hotel (see later entry) convey the area's history.

1885 Frisco Wooden Water Tower (NRHP):
SE Main. The last remaining Frisco wooden water tower of its kind in the United States,

it provided water for steam locomotives and for the cattle stockyards. Beaumont was a railroad cattle shipping point dating to 1880. 620.843.2591.

Frisco Ponds (NRHP):
South of the wooden water tower. These retention ponds, developed in 1885, held the water supply for the steam engines on the Frisco railroad. From the ponds the water was piped into the wooden water tank. In 2007 the ponds were restored and provide excellent fishing for guests of the Beaumont Hotel. Signage west of the water tower tells more of the history.

Beaumont Hotel (NRHP):
11651 SE Main. This historic hotel opened in 1879 as a stagecoach way station and hotel for cattlemen and railroaders. In 1953 a native grass airstrip was created to accommodate cattle barons flying in to check their herds. Today visitors fly here to eat at the Beaumont Cafe or to spend the night. 620.843.2422. hotelbeaumontks.com.

Beaumont Hotel Cafe:
11651 SE Main. Choose from the formal dining room or the 1950s-style diner with stainless steel accents, Formica counter, and 13 chrome stools. Cowboys, motorcyclists (second Sunday

of each month), and hungry travelers frequent this historic stop. And everyone is sure to be pleased with the ribeye, prime rib, burgers, sandwiches, salads, and more. January-February, Friday-Saturday 7 a.m.-7 p.m. and Sunday 7 a.m.-3 p.m.; March-December, Wednesday-Friday 11 a.m.-8 p.m.; Saturday 7 a.m.-9 p.m.; Sunday 7 a.m.-3 p.m. 620.843.2422. beaumonthotelks.com.

Old Frisco Railroad
Bridge: From Main, 4½ miles west on U.S. 400, then ¼ mile north and east on Stony Creek. Built for the Frisco railroad in 1936, this structure displays a unique art deco style. "Frisco Line" is engraved on the bridge on either side of the roadway that passes under it.

Lodging: Beaumont Hotel (KBBA, 620.843.2422, beaumonthotelks.com).

BENTON

Population 872

Infinity Art Glass:
120 N. Main. Artist Scott Hartley creates luminous hand-blown glass objects of all shapes and sizes. He's glad for the public to watch his demonstrations and tour the studio. A small gift gallery sells his work. Tuesday, Thursday 12:30-5:30 p.m.; Saturday 10 a.m.-2 p.m. 316.778.2115. infinityartglass.com.

Stearman Sky Tours:
You can sit in the front open cockpit of those 1943 Stearman PT-17 biplanes you see taking off and landing at the Stearman Field. These are the planes that served as primary trainers for cadets during WWII. Enjoy a 20- or 40-minute "sky tour" any day, year round (depending on weather) with Greg Largen or Randy Hardy. One person per ride. Ride charge. Reservations required. 316.644.3257. stearmanskytours.com.

Stearman Bar and Grill:
14789 SW 30th. Situated beside the Lloyd Stearman Field, named for aviation pioneer Lloyd Stearman, this trendy bar and grill is highlighted with vintage airplane decor. Customers can watch classic planes come and go from the airfield as they dine on the Biplane cheeseburger, Flyover Philly, or Red Baron ribeye, to name a few. A full bar is available. The spacious patio is open when the garage door is up. Watch out, you might get spritzed (by water) when it's really hot! Daily 7 a.m.-9 p.m. 316.778.1612. stearmanbarandgrill.com.

SC

CASSODAY

Population 128

Large shipments of cattle are brought into Cassoday from all over the country to "go to grass" in the Flint Hills. The railroad, which came to Cassoday in 1923, once shipped the herds, but today cattle trucks have surpassed railroad delivery.

Cassoday Country Store:
15133 NE K-177. Fill up here with gas, convenience store items, or breakfast, lunch,

or dinner. A buffet lunch is available during the week, and burgers on weekends. Monday-Saturday 7 a.m.-7 p.m.; Sunday 8 a.m.-6 p.m. 620.735.4423. FB.

Cassoday Historical Museum: Washington and Beaman. Inside an original Santa Fe depot, the museum preserves Cassoday's heyday as a railroad cattle shipping point. 620.735.4431.

Teter Rock: From Washington (K-177), 11¾ miles east on 1st (becomes 150). This odd, man-made rock formation is in Greenwood County (see p. 253), but easier to locate from Cassoday.

**explorer extras...
In Douglass**

Population 1,690

Downtown has a pleasant nostalgic look, and one sweet spot is the old stone post office, 315 S. Forrest. It still operates and welcomes you to support it with a purchase of stamps. Monday-Friday 9 a.m.-12:30 p.m. and 2-4:30 p.m. 316.746.2691.

The limestone community building (NRHP), 206 S. Forrest, was a 1937 WPA project. It is still used as the community building today.

A wonderful collection of pioneer artifacts at the Douglass Pioneer Museum, 314 S. Forrest, captures the past of this small town. Monday, Wednesday, Friday 9-11 a.m. and 1-3 p.m. 316.746.2319.

Triangle M Restaurant, 326 S. Forrest, has a different dinner special each night, such as

meatloaf, ham and scalloped potatoes, and chicken and noodles. They're also known for Mexican food (after 4 p.m.), cinnamon rolls, and mouth-watering home-baked pies of all kinds. Tuesday-Saturday 6 a.m.-9 p.m. 316.746.2071. ee

EL DORADO

Population 12,852

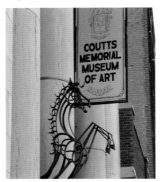

Coutts Museum of Art: 110 N. Main. The classic columns and handmade doors from Mexico are your entry to a quality showcase of art on three floors. Antique furnishings and Persian rugs create pleasant surroundings for the works of well-known artists such as Renoir, Thomas Hart Benton, and Frederic Remington. You will also find the largest Makk collection in the United States plus a sizable Prairie Printmakers collection. The works in this museum were purchased from all over the world primarily by local attorney Warren Hall Coutts Jr. The museum was named in memory of his son who was killed in 1965. Tuesday-Friday 9 a.m.-5 p.m.; Saturday 12-4 p.m. 316.321.1212. couttsmuseum.org.

Sculpture Alley: Just north of Coutts Museum. This plaza showcases two bronze sculptures and a 10x25-foot Flint Hills mural. Artists Phil Epp and Terry Corbett incorporated 570 colorful ceramic tiles to create the mural.

Butler County Courthouse (NRHP): 205 W. Central. George Washburn was the architect for this very impressive 1908 Romanesque Revival courthouse constructed in red brick with limestone accents. Standing on the front lawn, the Freedom Memorial honors armed forces and home-front supporters. A replica Statue of Liberty is nearby, and Lady Justice holds a place atop the courthouse.

Butler County Historical Society Museum and Kansas Oil Museum: 383 E. Central. The story of oil is an important one in this area, from its geology and boomtowns to the people and their social history. Kids can play and learn through a special hands-on exhibit, and all ages marvel at the working scale model oil refineries and rotary rigs. At the Kansas Oil Hall of Fame you're introduced to such entrepreneurs as Al Derby and W.G. Skelly. On the museum grounds are replica stores of a typical 1920s oil town, a "shotgun" house, and oil-field equipment. Aside from the oil history, the county museum presents an excellent portrayal of the Flint Hills and life in Butler County, from Native American habitation through the development of farming and ranching. Tuesday-Friday 10 a.m.-4 p.m. and Saturday 12-5 p.m. Admission charge. 316.321.9333. kansasoilmuseum.org.

Stapleton No.1: From N. Haverhill, ¾ mile west on 6th, ¼ mile northwest on Parallel, 1 mile north on Boyer, ½ mile north on W. Refinery, then sharp left after the cattle guard. Stapleton No.1 was the 1915 discovery well in the El Dorado oil field. Soon Oil Hill, a boomtown to support the industry, sprang up nearby. Use your imagination to picture 2,500 oil-field workers living here in "shotgun" houses. A stone monument and an oil rig mark the well site. Enhance your visit to this historic spot by first stopping at the Kansas Oil Museum. 316.321.9333.

Riverside Park: Central and River, just east of the Walnut River. No doubt you'll climb on one of the giant (and inviting) low sycamore limbs before you even see the iron truss fishing bridge over the river. Walk across the bridge and, if you like, continue on a sidewalk trail through the woods. This hiking and biking trail runs five miles to El Dorado Lake.

El Dorado Lake and El Dorado State Park:

618 NE Bluestem. Early in the year you might see bald eagles around the lake. The lake (completed in 1981) and park offer all the usual recreational opportunities and a variety of nature trails. A rare equestrian camping facility is located here along with a 12-mile horse trail. State park entrance charge. Cabins available, reservations required. 316.321.7180. ksoutdoors.com.

Downtown: It's very pleasant to stroll the red-brick sidewalks and enjoy the sculptures, old-fashioned street lamps, planters of flowers, trees, benches, and enticing storefronts. Find classy home decor gifts at Walter's Flowers (124 N. Main, 316.321.1740) or women's clothing at Robin's (113 W. Central, 316.321.3280). More than 100 properties make up the El Dorado Downtown Historic District (NRHP).

Sweet 120: 142 N. Main. Joyce Parker sees opening this chocolate shop as her community service to the town! Maybe you can give back to her by buying delicious gourmet chocolates (made by Sweet Granada in Olpe) or the chocolate-laced popcorn.

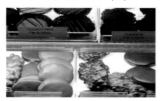

What a sweet sacrifice! Monday-Friday 7 a.m.-6 p.m.; Saturday-Sunday 10 a.m.-2 p.m. 316.452.5200. sweet120.com.

BrewCo. Coffeehouse and Dilly Deli: 142 N. Main. Inside the Historic District 142 building in the heart of downtown El Dorado, BrewCo. Coffeehouse and Dilly Deli offers freshly built breakfast and lunch sandwiches using homemade spreads and

locally sourced award-winning meats. Or just stop in for a specialty coffee or smoothie. Monday-Friday 7 a.m.-6 p.m.; Saturday 8 a.m.-5 p.m.; Sunday 9 a.m.-3 p.m. 316.322.0211. district142.com.

Walnut River Brewery:

111 W. Locust. You can't help but love it here, especially when owners/brewmeisters B.J. Hunt and Rick Goehring brazenly admit that "everything unapologetically screams Kansas when you step into the brewery." The real stars of the show, however, are the exceptionally tasty brews that they concoct— Falconer's Wheat, Warbeard Irish Red, and Teter Rock Kölsch. You'll enjoy this immersion in handcrafted beer and Kansas inside an old brick building just off the main street. Tuesday-Friday 3-10 p.m.; Saturday 11 a.m.-10 p.m.; Sunday 12-5 p.m. 316.351.8086. walnutriverbrewing.com.

Willie's: 151 N. Main. Inside a historic building with pressed-tin ceiling, wood floor, and brick walls, this popular downtown sports bar and grill serves good food and good times. On the walls, photos and memorabilia preserve the yesteryears of El Dorado sports. 316.452.5546. Daily 11 a.m.-9 p.m.

Charlie G's: 212 E. Central. Charlie is carrying on two great local culinary traditions. He serves his mom's chili, of Susie's

SC

Chili Parlor fame, and the veal burger of Job Lunch (once located in this building). Real buttermilk pancakes and cinnamon rolls make this a good breakfast stop too. Monday-Friday 6 a.m.-5 p.m.; Saturday 6 a.m.-2 p.m. 316.452.5844.

Beijing Bistro: 1905 W. Central. Two generations of the Chen family, who immigrated from Taiwan in the 1970s, operate this modern Asian food bistro. Award-winning chef Ping-Chen uses freshness, quality, and presentation to make traditional favorites such as kung pao and moo shu chicken, and be sure to try the sushi and sashimi. Daily 11 a.m.-10 p.m. 316.321.9999. beijingbistro.com.

El Dorado Livestock Auction/Real Deal Cafe: 2593 SE U.S. 54. At this fairly new livestock auction facility the cafe is just as the name implies—the real deal when it comes to home cooking. The cafe opens at 10 a.m. on Thursdays; the sale starts at 11 a.m. 316.320.3212. eldoradolivestock.com.

Lodging:
tinyurl.com/eldolodging.

explorer extras... In El Dorado

Enjoy spray features at North Main Park, 1000 N. Main, and at Graham Park, 1600 Edgemoor. Take your dog for a romp in Dog Park, 400 E. Locust.

Placed in the same path as the tornado that took 13 lives in 1958, the Tornado Victims' Memorial in Graham Park features 13 pillars and a large abstract Aeolian harp that captures the wind. 1600 Edgemoor.

A 1940 WPA project and still used today, McDonald Stadium was named for longtime high school baseball coach (1944-1969) James McDonald. The rare design of the grandstand at 210 N. Griffith incorporates concrete supports that extend through the roof. A granite monument in front of the post office at Vine and Central pays tribute to Pulitzer Prize-winning editor William Allen White, who was raised in El Dorado.

Built in 1912, the Eclectic Neoclassical Carnegie library (NRHP) stands at 101 S. Star. Constructed of native limestone, it features a red-tile roof. Today the former library houses a private business. Drive by only.

Town undertaker James Oldham built the striking native limestone Queen Anne home (NRHP) at 321 S. Denver. The

1885 house features a two-story tower. Drive by only.

The circa 1918 Mission and Spanish Revival red-brick Missouri Pacific depot (NRHP) has been restored and converted for use as an event center at 430 N. Main. **ee**

explorer extras... Near Leon

Population 691

See the picturesque 1905 stone single-arch Hickory Creek Bridge at 140 and Ellis. From U.S. 400 just south of Leon, 2 miles south on Chelsea, ½ mile east on 120, 2 miles south on Cole Creek, then 2 miles east on 140.

Pioneer Memorial: U.S. 400 and Mill (Leon Cemetery). "In memory of all the fearless pioneers," is how the memorial's long message begins. The monument is dedicated to all the early settlers buried here in unmarked graves. **ee**

explorer extras... In Potwin

Population 439

Look into the pasture north of Munson and NW 80 to see the indention swale that is a remnant of the Cherokee Trail. Brown signs mark the trail, which was an old Indian route that gold seekers and emigrants followed on their way to California. cherokeetrail.org.

Potwin's first bank, 126 N. Randall, now houses the public library. You'll find the restroom inside the vault of this 1904 limestone building. 620.752.3421. **ee**

explorer extras...
In Rose Hill

Population 3,942

Phil Brinkley's Jurassic Art along the road is a head turner. Fantastical creations using automotive parts, farm equipment, or whatever is around, are molded and welded into all sorts of metal creatures that soar, ride, and leap on motorcycles, segways, and vehicles. They'll bring a smile and sense of wonderment to your world, at least for a little while. From N. Rose Hill, ¼ mile west on Rosewood (becomes SW 170) to 256 W. Rosewood.

Polecat Bridge (NRHP), a little 1901 stone single-arch bridge, is a beauty, even though you can see the scars on the railing from a car hitting it. From Rosewood, 6 miles south on N. Rose Hill (becomes Butler), then 1½ miles east on SW 230. **ee**

Population 1,420

Towanda Area Historical Museum (NRHP):
401 Main. Formerly a Masonic lodge, this two-story limestone building now preserves area heritage. Look especially for the display of the legendary Whitewater Falls Stock Farm (*see* next entry). Wednesday, Friday 1-4 p.m.; Thursday 12-4 p.m. 316.536.2500.

Whitewater Falls Stock Farm Barn:
From River Valley, 1½ miles west on K-254, just north on Adams, ½ mile west on Old Hwy 254, 2 miles north on Santa Fe Lake, short jog east on Parallel, ½ mile north on Santa Fe, just east on 4,

then just north on Falls. You've arrived at this amazing barn, well worth the drive to find! J.W. Robison, a Percheron horse breeder, built this 64x120-foot wooden barn in 1908. It had 50 stalls, steam heat, gas lights, its own water plant, and a balcony. It almost looks too fancy, even in its deteriorated state, to be a barn! The good news is that owners Duane and Amanda Busenitz are restoring it. You may take pictures but do not enter the barn. In dry weather, carefully continue just north on Falls through the tree line to a low-water bridge (*see* next entry). Don't attempt to cross unless the road is dry. FB.

Low-Water Bridge Scenic Back Road:
From K-254, 1¾ miles north on River Valley, 1 mile west on Parallel, 1 mile north on Diamond, ¾ mile west on 10, then ½ mile south on Falls. If the roads are dry and you're up for adventure, try this back-road route across the low-water bridge to the Whitewater Falls Stock Farm Barn. Just before the bridge you'll come to a curve where you should stop and walk ahead to be sure the road is dry. What you'll see ahead may surprise you—a long low-water bridge. Cross the bridge, go through the tree line, and there is the Whitewater farm barn!

Skewed Iron Truss Bridge:
From 3rd, ½ mile west on Main (becomes River Valley), ¾ mile west on K-254, ½ mile north on Arapaho, 1¼ miles west on 15, then 1 mile north on Santa Fe Lake. If this 1928 West Branch Whitewater River

Bridge looks a little out of kilter it's because it is. It's called a skewed bridge and is designed that way because the road and the river intersect diagonally, and the skew allows the bridge supports to be parallel to the river banks.

Population 710

Oldest Bank in Butler County:
126 S. Main. Organized in 1891, the Bank of Whitewater is at home in the 1897 bank building and is still locally owned and operated. The antique clock in front of the building is a reproduction.

Mom's Cafe:
213 S. Main. This classic small-town cafe, known for its homemade jams, jellies, and pies, is popular with the locals because of the comfort of Mom's food. Tuesday, Saturday 6 a.m.-2 p.m.; Wednesday-Friday 6 a.m.-8 p.m. 316.799.1904.

SC

Grace Hill Winery:
6310 S. Grace Hill. The label names alone make you curious— Peckerhead Red (sweet red), Leaning Shed Red (dry red), and Dodging Tornadoes (semi-sweet red)—and those are just the reds! Tasting is free for small groups (fewer than eight people). Bring a picnic and enjoy a glass of wine on the

patio and observation deck. Monday, Thursday 10 a.m.-4 p.m.; Friday-Sunday 12-6 p.m. For vineyard tours, call 316.799.2511. gracehillwinery.com.

Cowley County

AROUND THE COUNTY

Stone Arch Bridges:
Cowley County is the Stone Bridge Capital of Kansas. Built between 1890 and 1920 from local limestone, 16 stone arch bridges are still standing (below the road) and are awaiting your discovery! If you are bridge hunting, do not go onto private property to photograph the bridges. Bridge brochures are available in the Chamber of Commerce offices in Arkansas City, 106 S. Summit; and Winfield, 123 E. 9th. A stone bridge map is at cowleycounty.org/visit. 620.442.0236.

Waterfall: From U.S. 77,
13½ miles east on U.S. 166. From the Cowley State Fishing Lake entrance, turn west onto the driveway and follow it to the end. If rain has been plentiful, you'll see a beautiful 25-foot waterfall cascading over the rocks into the creek below.

Cowley County Barn Quilt
Trail: Cowley is one of 22 counties involved in Kansas Flint Hills Quilt Trail project. More than 100 brightly colored wooden quilt blocks are placed on buildings throughout the county. Watch for them as you explore. A map is at cowleycounty.org/visit. 620.221.9951.

Cotton Fields: Every year more cotton is grown in Kansas (in 2016 16 counties produced cotton). In September and October look roadside in the Winfield, Oxford, and Wellington (Sumner County) vicinities, as well as in Harper, Sumner, Pratt, and Reno Counties. The white fluffy stuff is visible in the wide open bolls just before it's harvested. The oldest active cotton gin in Kansas is in Winfield. Outside of Cowley County you'll also find gins in the towns of Anthony, Cullison, and Moscow. For group tours, call 620.222.4818. kansascotton.com.

explorer extras...
In Atlanta

Population 194

Atlanta displays a red Santa Fe caboose at 5th and Walnut. The antiques and crafts inside are available for perusal and purchase when you see the American flag flying. 316.945.5464.

At Iron Horse Antiques, 319 Main, you'll uncover a wealth of reasonably priced treasures and collectibles.Open most weekend afternoons. 620.394.1378.

Hungry explorers, don't overlook the made-from-scratch breakfasts, homemade desserts and pies, dinner specials, gluten-free items, and healthy choices at the Lil Red Rooster

Cafe, 323 Main, run by the capable and friendly Connie Gillespie. Tuesday-Thursday 8:30 a.m.-2 p.m.; Friday-Saturday 7 a.m.-7 p.m., Sunday 7 a.m.-3 p.m. 620.394.2022. FB. **ee**

ARKANSAS CITY

Population 12,305

Cherokee Strip Museum:
31639 U.S. 77. When the gun fired at noon on September 16, 1893, the great Cherokee Strip Land Rush was under way! It was a race for land, and when all was said and done 42,000 claims had been staked in a 50x200-mile area, primarily in Oklahoma Territory. Those who had come for land had spent days or months primarily in seven Kansas towns to secure permits and make preparations for the race. Museum exhibits and historic photos present a fascinating overview of this largest land race in world history. More area history is presented in displays of the 1942 Strother Army Air Field,

early Arkansas City businesses, and American Indians. Featuring live farm animals, a garden, and pond, the Bill Baird Memorial Pioneer Farm and Garden gives visitors a sense of farm life and animal husbandry at the turn of the 19th century. Tuesday-Saturday 10 a.m-5 p.m.; Sunday 1-4 p.m. Admission charge. 620.442.6750. cherokeestripmuseum.org.

Cherokee Strip Marker:
From the Cherokee Strip Museum, ½ mile south on U.S. 77, then just west on 312th. A large granite marker atop a stair-step limestone base memorializes the thousands of pioneers who participated in the 1893 land rush.

Historical Markers:
From the Cherokee Strip Museum, ¼ mile north on U.S. 77 to the roadside park. The first of three historical markers recounts the Cherokee Strip Land Rush, a second notes U.S. 77 as a Blue Star Memorial Highway (dedicated to those who served in WWII), and a third recognizes the famous Chisholm Trail (the early cattle drive route from Texas to Kansas).

Ireland Hall (NRHP): 300 W. Central. Identified by its arches, gargoyles, lion heads, dragons, rock-faced masonry, and a colorful facade, this former high school is now home to several departments of Cowley College.

The 1890 Silverdale Limestone building was constructed with a vermilion mortar that was not waterproof, which eventually resulted in the exterior's rosy hue.

Downtown: As a result of a 1914 oil boom, many early 20th-century commercial structures are now part of a 70-property Arkansas City Commercial Center Historic District (NRHP). Whether you can identify the architectural style or not, the ornamentation and grandeur of many of these buildings will impress you. The district is downtown on Summit and on either side of Summit on 5th. The 1924 Burford Theatre at 118 S. Summit has been restored and is now open as a multipurpose venue.

Antiques and More:
Enjoy shopping downtown for antiques and repurposed items at Land Rush Antique Mall (208 S. Summit, 620.307.5858); Bee'tween Friends (206 S. Summit, 620.307.6580); Mylissa's Garden Antiques (309 S. Summit, 620.442.6433); and Calvert's Antique Station (501 S. Summit, 620.442.1211).

Pamalou's at Graves Drug: 212 S. Summit. The powder blue-and-white counter and floor will draw you to the 1947 soda fountain. Take a seat on one of the stools and order a treat or homemade lunch special. Tuesday-Friday 8:30 a.m.-5 p.m. (lunch 11 a.m.-3 p.m.); Saturday 10:30 a.m.-1:30 p.m. 620.442.8317. FB.

Public Art: 215 S. 2nd (Cowley College campus). A group of four delightful bronze statues in front of the Brown Center depict a violin player, a singer, a dancer, and a child reading a book. Three Gary Kahle stainless steel sculptures can also be seen on campus.

Scripture Hill: From Summit, ¾ mile east on Kansas to the roundabout, then 1 mile north on U.S. 77, and look to the west. In 1897 a railroad dispatcher created this 475-foot-long message for everyone on the northbound train to see. Spelled out in stone, it reads, "Christ died for the ungodly." Each letter is 18 feet high, 12 feet wide, and 3 feet deep.

Steamy Joe Coffee House & Bakery: 216 W. Central. You are greeted with home-baked goodies and the wonderful aroma of fresh roasted coffee. The many rooms in this house-turned-coffee shop, provide the perfect spot for relaxing with your favorite beverage and pastry. Monday-Friday 7 a.m.-8 p.m.; Saturday 7 a.m.-4 p.m. 620.307.5798. FB.

Brick's: 301 S. Summit. Looking for a classic throwback dining experience? Head to the brick building with the clock on top. Don't miss the breakfasts at this oldie and goodie. Daily 6 a.m.-3 p.m. (closed Tuesday). 620.442.5390.

SC

Greendoor La Familia:

714 W. Madison. They know how to do things right at this family-owned Mexican restaurant that has been an Arkansas City tradition since 1976. Tuesday-Saturday 11 a.m.-2 p.m. and 4:30-8 p.m. 620.442.1685. greendoor-lafamilia.com.

Daisy Mae's Cafe:

511 W. Madison. The ham and beans with cornbread on Wednesdays and Saturdays, the daily specials, and the chicken-fried steak keep the locals happy at this popular cafe. Monday-Saturday 6 a.m.-8:30 p.m.; Sunday 6 a.m.-3 p.m. 620.442.9877.

Ark City Kayak Rentals and Tours:

27801 27. The slow-moving waters of the Arkansas River make it easy for kayak novices to learn or practice their kayaking skills. Explore the area in a whole new way—from the water. Rental and tours are offered year round, depending on conditions. 620.660.3250. arkcitykayakrentals.com.

Inspiration Point:

30811 Horizon (Camp Horizon). From Summit, 4 miles east on Madison (becomes 292), ½ mile south on 101, 2 miles east on 296, then 1 mile south on Hillcrest. Park at the camp office and walk about 100 yards south between the cabins to the tall wooden cross at the overlook. Standing on the large flat stones at the summit, you'll have a fabulous view of the valley and the Arkansas River. From there you can, if you'd like, hike the one-mile trail down to the river. The campground also offers 10 challenging miles of trails for hikers and mountain bikers. 620.442.5533. horizoncenter.org.

Chaplin Nature Center:

27814 27. From Summit, 3 miles west on U.S.166, 2 miles north on 31, just west on 272, then just north on 27. If the visitor center is open, start there to see the displays about area wildlife. The six hiking trails are very enjoyable and include routes along the river, into wooded areas, and through a reconstructed prairie. Trails are open daily. The nature center is owned by the Wichita Audubon Society. 620.442.4133. wichitaaudubon.org/cnc.html.

Lodging:

tinyurl.com/arkcitylodging

explorer extras... In Arkansas City

The 1992 Stan Herd outdoor mural, 100 block of N. Summit, pays tribute to the Cherokee Strip Land Rush.

The rotunda at Wilson Park, Summit and Maple, was built in 1918 for the traveling Chautauqua circuit. This popular form of community entertainment and culture featured speakers, musicians, entertainers, ministers, and specialists on various topics.

A 1910 Santa Fe locomotive has made its last stop and now rests on the east side of Wilson Park at Summit and Maple. A sign next to Engine No. 2542 includes part of a speech by John Landreth, general manager of the Santa Fe railway, on dedication day in 1955. The sign also shares the interesting story of moving the engine six blocks from the tracks to the park.

The superb limestone trim on the 1907 Neoclassical Carnegie library makes a drive past the stately red-brick building worthwhile. This former library, 217 W. 5th, is in private ownership. **ee**

BURDEN

Population 536

Around Town: Explore the town until you've found the historic jail, several wooden quilt blocks, the limestone Emerald Bank, a wishing well, and a map mural.

Sassy Lady Cafe:

503 Elm. Inside an 1876 home (painted with a Sassy touch!) you'll find made-from-scratch biscuits and gravy, sandwiches on homemade bread, and desserts that change daily. Steaks made from locally sourced meat are served Friday nights. Cast iron skillet-fried chicken is the Sunday feature. Stop by for antique shopping too. Monday-Friday 7 a.m.-8 p.m.; Saturday-Sunday 7 a.m.-2 p.m. 620.438.2040. FB.

CAMBRIDGE

Population 84

Thee Chapel:
From Main, ¼ mile east on U.S. 160, then north into a pasture. Local residents reconstructed this old fishing cabin as a small chapel, a place for peace and contemplation. The pews date to the early 1900s. Always open. 620.221.9951. cowleycounty.org/cambridge.

Cambridge Log Cabin:
From U.S. 160, 3½ miles north on Main (becomes 281). Catchy signs along the highway let you know when you're close to this newly constructed cabin, which resembles the one built here in 1872. Inside are artifacts and information about the cabin's history. According to local lore, the stone dugout behind the cabin was used as living quarters while the original 1872 cabin was being constructed. The cabin is always open. cowleycounty.org/cambridge.

Stone Arch Bridge:
From U.S. 160, 4½ miles north on Main (becomes 281), then ¼ mile east on 275. The Walter Sharp Bridge Company built this stone double-arch bridge in 1917. One of the arches is filled in but the other remains picturesque.

DEXTER

Population 279

Henry's Candies:
21172 K-15. Chocolates, rock candy, taffy, and peanut clusters are just a few of the homemade sweets you'll find at Henry's candy factory. A window offers a view into the kitchen, and usually on Sundays at 1:30 p.m. you can watch the candy cooks at work. Henry's is currently operated by the third and fourth generations of a candy-making family that continues the tradition begun by ancestor Tom Henry. Tom, by the way, stirred up the original chocolate and caramel bar in 1919 that eventually sold worldwide as Oh Henry! Daily 9 a.m.-5 p.m. 620.876.5423.

Historical Outdoor Mural:
105 S. Main. A local stone arch bridge, a champion harness horse for whom the town was named, the discovery of helium, and the Black Dog Trail— all pieces of Dexter's past— are featured in this weathered outdoor mural.

Black Dog Trail Campsite Marker:
From Main, 200 yards west on Hawkins. Beginning in 1803 Chief Black Dog and his Osage tribe traveled through this area twice a year on buffalo hunting trips. The sign here marks one of the Osage campsites on the hunting route, known as the Black Dog Trail (*see* p. 235).

Helium Well:
109 Main (west side of Main in Helium Memorial Park). Helium was first discovered in Dexter in 1903. The site of the first well is surrounded by a circle of stones, and signage tells the history of the discovery.

Historic Hitching Rail:
The old hitching rail still stands alongside the corner bank at Main and Central. The Dalton Gang robbed this bank in 1892— the gang's last successful robbery, occurring the day before the Daltons' fateful bank holdup in Coffeyville.

Grouse Valley Grill & Grocery:
501 K-15. Wanda and Randy Waldeck are the friendly owners who serve one of the best burgers in the state. Juicy, hand-pattied, and locally sourced meat is topped with fresh veggies and served on a butter toasted bun. Biscuits and gravy are prepared for breakfast. Pick up a few grocery items, have a cup of coffee, and get to know the townsfolk while you're here. Monday-Saturday 6 a.m.-7 p.m. 620.876.5617. FB.

Grouse Creek Scenic Back Road:
The lush Grouse Creek Valley is your companion along this winding drive, and it's a delightful route on which to enjoy this part of the county. From Central, 1 mile southwest on Main (becomes 231), 11 miles south and west on Grouse Creek, then 8 miles west on U.S. 166 to Arkansas City.

Stone Barn:
20438 K-15. From 206th, ¾ mile north on K-15. In 2011 artist Kelly Unrein painted the faces of four Kansas legends (Robert Docking, Amelia Earhart,

SC

Dwight Eisenhower, and Bob Dole) on the tin roof of the 1878 stone barn owned by Grady and Shannon Martin. Drive by only.

Lodging: Stone Barn Log Cabins (620.886.1703, stone-barnfarmks.com/logcabins).

ROCK

Unincorporated

Stone Arch Bridge:
From U.S. 77, 1 mile east on 26, ½ mile north on 91, then ¾ mile east on 22. Built circa 1910, this double-arch bridge over Rock Creek is a beauty.

Solid Rock Cafe:
301 S. Winfield. You'll find solid food here—solid good, that is, and made from scratch. Try the Bomb burger, filled with your choice of cheese and served with homemade mashed potatoes and gravy. On second Saturdays, hand-breaded catfish is the special. Homemade pies and cakes are available anytime. Monday 7 a.m.-1 p.m. and Tuesday-Saturday 6 a.m.-3 p.m.; June-September, also Friday-Saturday 5-8 p.m. 620.986.550. FB. 620.986.5500

SILVERDALE

Unincorporated

Silverdale to Oklahoma Scenic Back Road:
From B, 3¼ mile south on 141 (County Rd. 1). Silverdale is a charming little burg and this route takes you past its most illustrious business, the Born Stone Company, founded in

1949. It's then just several miles to Oklahoma, but along the way you'll cross over three sizable rivers, one with an iron truss bridge, and see a farm with horses and a grand old limestone barn. Make sure to come back to Kansas!

Made Straight: From B, ¼ mile north on 141 (County Rd. 1), then just under 2½ miles west on 296 (if you get to 111 you've gone too far west). On the north side of 296 an aged rectangular limestone wall is inscribed, "Made Straight 1934." The county commissioner's name is also on the stone. The sign refers to the completion of the straightening of the road, which originally had many switchbacks to help horses and wagons climb Horseshoe Hill. To make it easier for cars to ascend the hill, the road was "made straight" despite the difficult task of cutting through the bedrock.

explorer extras...
In Udall

Population 748

On May 25, 1955, Udall was wiped out by a vicious tornado, one of the deadliest to ever touch down in Kansas. It killed 83 residents, injured 270, and destroyed 192 buildings. In City Park a large native stone memorial beside the water tower is inscribed with the names of those who perished. On Main, just west of K-55.

One room in the Udall Community Historical Society Museum, 109 E. 1st, features photos, articles, and interviews relating to the devastating tornado of 1955. Also on exhibit are the histories and records of early Udall families and

the community. Wednesday 3-5 p.m.; Sunday 1-3 p.m. 620.782.3004. **ee**

WINFIELD

Population 12,333

Architectural Tours:
A 21-stop driving tour features historic homes built by architect William Caton, and a second driving tour showcases 28 historic homes ranging in style from Italianate Vernacular to Greek Revival. A walking tour takes you to Baden Square, formerly St. John's College founded in 1893. Pick up tour brochures from the Chamber of Commerce, 123 E. 9th, or at tinyurl.com/catontour. 620.221.2420.

County Map: 311 E. 9th. A large map detailing the towns, townships, and rivers in the county is etched into the stone face of the 1962 Cowley County Courthouse.

War Memorials: 401 E. 9th. The 777 Kansas servicemen and women killed or missing during the Vietnam War are listed on this replica of the Washington, D.C., Vietnam Veterans Memorial. Another nearby memorial recognizes veterans in all wars up through WWI. Inscriptions in the walkway provide information about each war.

Island Park: N. Main. Just southeast of the park entrance, along the street, four limestone carvings by David Chapman honor the Walnut Valley Festival. Plaques on the stone entrance recount this park's Chautauqua history from 1887 to 1913. Note the man-made waterfall on the west side of the park and the playground on the east. Do watch out for geese and ducks as you drive around.

Outdoor Murals: The 1999 Maggie Bicker mural on the Island Park restroom resembles an English cottage. On the side of the 1941 Webber Land Company building, 810 Loomis, are Maggie's old-time depictions of Webber employees.

The Beginning Mural: 900 Main (inside RCB Bank). More than 80 years of Winfield history is spread over the bank's entire back wall. Artist Sue Jean Covacevich did a masterful job including historic events, people, and places in the colorful mural. She finished the mural in 1952 and revised it in 1975 when the bank expanded. Monday-Friday 9 a.m.-5 p.m. 620.221.1650.

Antiques: Looking for collectibles, antiques, or repurposed items? You'll find them at Junk Generation (420 Main, 620.229.1959); Winfield Restorations (601 Main, 620.402.6460); Virginia Jarvis Antiques (701 Main, 620.221.1732); Trunk N Treasures (1016 Main, 620.218.3335); and

Finneus & Arbuckle (115 E. 6th, 620.218.4654).

Liermann's Saddle and Boot Shop: 1008 Main. Manager Maria Kerr's great-grandfather brought his leatherworking craft from Bavaria to America, and in 1881 opened this shop—the oldest boot shop in the state. This historic business also stocks hats, tack, bits, saddles, belts, wallets, and anything leather. The backroom is a treasure trove of old leather tools and equipment. If you ask, Maria is happy to show it to you. Monday-Wednesday, Friday 9:30 a.m.-5 p.m.; Saturday 9:30 a.m.-3 p.m. 620.221.1498.

Cowley County Historical Museum: 1011 Mansfield. The county's varied history is preserved at this two-story limestone former school. Displays recognize Winfield State Hospital and two nationally known manufacturers—Binney & Smith Company, which opened its Crayola product factory in Winfield in 1952; and Gott Manufacturing, producer of water coolers, and founded in Winfield in 1916. Tuesday-Sunday 1-4 p.m. 620.221.4811. cchsm.com.

Wheat State Wine Company: 23622 Springhill Farm. From 19th, 1¼ miles south on U.S. 77, just east on Quail Ridge, 2¾ miles south on Pike, 4¼ miles east on 212, then just south on Springhill Farm. A group of community-minded entrepreneurs doing things the right way are growing vines,

making wine, and hosting a variety of entertaining events. Come enjoy the country setting and sample or buy wines, which include Flat Pick, a light fruity wine; Dandy Horse, a dry white; and Plowboy, a sweet wine. Friday-Sunday 12-6 p.m. 620.229.9463. wheatstatewineco.com.

College Hill Coffee: 403 Soward. Inside this 1926 bungalow you'll find all the specialty coffees and sodas you desire plus made-from-scratch baked goods, soups, sandwiches, quiches, cheese-cakes, and more. Monday-Thursday 6:30 a.m.-6:30 p.m.; Friday 6:30 a.m.-10:30 p.m.; Saturday 7:30 a.m.-3 p.m. 620.229.8155. collegehillcoffee.com.

Burger Station: 113 E. 7th. Your ticket to a great burger awaits you at this carry-out Station, an institution in Winfield since 1952. Monday-Saturday 10:30 a.m.-8 p.m. 620.221.9773.

Neives' Mexican Restaurant: 119 E. 9th. You'll like the feel of Neives' the minute you step inside the door. By the way, the food is great too. Try the fried Chickenancho! Daily 11 a.m.-9 p.m. 620.229.7600. FB.

SC

Biederman's Bistro:
801 Main. A wide array of tasty meals and daily specials are on tap at this full-service bistro. Tuesday-Saturday 7 a.m.-8 p.m.; Sunday 11 a.m.-2 p.m. 620.221.0888. FB.

Kathryn's at Millington Place: 124 E. 9th. Casual and fine dining provides many options in this multiple-room restaurant. Dry-aged steaks, shrimp po' boys, homemade soups, and cocktails are just a few of the delicious choices. Tuesday-Saturday 7 a.m.-9 p.m. 620.402.6607. FB.

El Maguey: 1515 E. 9th. Start with the fresh salsa served with warm chips. Follow that with the enchiladas rancheras stuffed with shredded beef, peppers, and onions. That's only one of the many muy bueno entrees, which, by the way, is even better with an ice cold margarita! Monday-Saturday 11 a.m.-9 p.m.; Sunday 11 a.m.-3 p.m. 620-221.4940. FB.

Lodging: Barns at Timber Creek (KBBA, 620.221.2797, timbercreekbarns.com); additional lodging (visitwinfield.com).

explorer extras... In Winfield

In 1927 Dean Leroy Allen put the Southwestern College nickname (Moundbuilders) into action. Since that time students and faculty have been decorating rocks and placing them on a

mound during an annual ceremony. It's a one-of-a-kind tradition among colleges worldwide! You can see the growing mound at the northeast side of the parking lot at 1st and College. At this point take note too of the long flight of 77 steps leading to Christy Hall, a feature since 1910.

The many rows of white gravestones at the Kansas Veterans' Cemetery, 1208 N. College, is a site for reflection and respect. The inscription on the prominent pavilion reminds us, "No one is ever buried alone. All are buried with honor."

Now privately owned, the 1912 Carnegie library (NRHP) is at 10th and Millington. The two-story red-brick building features an arched doorway with limestone pilasters extending above the roof line.

If you like great music of all kinds plus a lively time, don't miss the Walnut Valley Festival, famous for its picking and fiddling contests. About 15,000 attend this event at the Winfield Fairgrounds the third week of each September. wvfest.com. **ee**

Harper County

AROUND THE COUNTY

Runnymede Historical Marker: From 14th in Harper, 7 miles northeast on K-2. In the late 1880s a typical English village was developed near here to attract Englishmen and

teach them American farming methods. For a time 100 young men lived on this virtual dude ranch, but the colony failed within five years. Nothing of Runnymede remains today.

ANTHONY

Population 2,254

Harper County Courthouse: 201 N. Jennings. This 1908 red-brick and limestone George Washburn structure is one of the most well-maintained and preserved courthouses in the state. Stop in the district court clerk's office and ask to see the historic courtroom. The staff will be very glad to show it to you. Monday-Friday 8 a.m.-5 p.m. 620.842.3721.

Jetts: 102 W. Main. Jetts has operated since 1912 and is the last in a chain of Jetts stores that once operated in Kansas and Oklahoma. Inside this modern facility you'll find men's, women's, and children's clothing, shoes, and accessories. It's one of a handful of stores in the state still carrying Merle Norman cosmetics. Monday-Friday 9:30 a.m.-5:30 p.m.; Saturday 9:30 a.m.-5 p.m. 620.842.5159. jettsstore.com.

K.Lane's Boutique: 118 W. Main. Anthony is never at a loss for fine apparel. K.Lane's offers women's clothing and accessories. Tuesday-Friday 9 a.m-5 p.m.; Saturday 9 a.m.-4 p.m. 620.842.3867. k-lanes.com.

Farmhouse 5: 610 W. Main. Owner Cheris Coggins, her husband, and three children make up the 5 in the name of this home decor business. It has become so popular that

they opened Urban Interiors in Wichita in 2017. Cheris excels in finding one-of-a-kind furniture and home decor rich in texture, style, and quality. She also carries boutique clothing and accessories and designs fabrics and furniture sold at both stores. Monday-Friday 10 a.m.-5:30 p.m. 620.842.2944. FB.

Irwin-Potter Drug:
202 W. Main. Eleven stools wrap around the horseshoe counter at the cozy little 1950s soda fountain. Order the specialty cherry limeade and watch it being made with an old-fashioned lime squeezer. It's a delightful return to the fab 50s! Monday-Friday 8 a.m.-6 p.m.; Saturday 8 a.m.-1 p.m. 620.842.5119. FB.

Anthony 9-11 Memorial:
W. Main (Memorial Park). In response to the 9-11 tragedy, the community of Anthony raised and sent money to the family of a fallen firefighter. A relationship developed between town and family, and the bond has impacted Anthony. A memorial built with steel from the World Trade Center, limestone from the Pentagon, and soil from the field in Pennsylvania stands in this park. Two beams of light glow at night in memory of the Twin Towers. In 2006 Governor Kathleen Sebelius signed a bill designating this monument the official 9-11 Memorial of Kansas. It is a fitting and touching tribute to the heroes of 9-11 and to the human spirit that binds us all. 620.842.5434. 9-11memorialanthonyks.org.

Post Office Mural (NRHP):
121 W. Steadman. Turning a Corner is the title of this 1939 Section artwork by Joe Jones. It depicts a 1930s wheat harvest.

Historic Airmail Arrow:
From LL&G, 2 miles west on K-2. A 1929 airmail remnant can be seen at the Municipal Airport north of K-2. In the early days of night-flying mail service, giant concrete arrows were constructed, flat on the ground, to guide pilots. Each arrow, painted bright yellow, was at the base of a tall tower supporting a beacon light that illuminated the arrow. Placed every 10 miles, each illuminated arrow directed the pilot on his route. At Anthony the tower and beacon still stand, and much of the arrow is visible, although it has been shortened due to highway expansion.

Historic Anthony Theater (NRHP):
220 W. Main. The beautiful 1936 art deco theater is undergoing restoration but it still shows movies every two weeks. The theater has the distinction of being the first building in town to have "refrigerated air." 620.896.7378. FB.

Historical Museum:
502 W. Main. The late 1880s and early 1900s in Anthony are the focus of this museum, housed in a brick 1928 Santa Fe depot. Thursday-Saturday 10 a.m.-5 p.m. 620.842.3852.

Carry Nation Was Here?:
125 E. Main (Idle Hour Bar). The bar's interior still preserves the damage by Carry Nation or one of her temperance supporters in 1900—well, we think it does. The hatchet marks are easily seen and there are plenty of them. Although no documented proof exists, the boys at the bar insist the marks were made by the crusading Carry! Monday-Saturday 11 a.m.-12 a.m. 620.842.3015. FB.

Dinner Bell:
611 LL&G. You won't find a deep fat fryer in Chad and Penny Gerdes' restaurant. Everything is prepared in an iron skillet or is baked. The noodles, gravy, and mashed potatoes are made from scratch, the way Chad's mom, Debbie, taught him. Monday-Friday 11 a.m.-2 p.m. 620.842.3433. FB.

Kristy's Kafe:
110 W. Main. Family recipes dominate the menu that includes sandwiches, pasta, Tex-Mex, and homemade pizza (try the popular baked potato pizza). Kristy's is a great stop for families and large groups. If you see a message on the restroom door from George, he's just the harmless spirit who hangs around here. Tuesday-Saturday 11 a.m.-8 p.m. 620.842.3722. kristyskafe.com.

SC

Roadrunner Diner: 416 W. Main. Take a seat on one of the eight stools inside this 1930s Valentine Diner. It's wonderfully old-time; you'll see original equipment and even the old payment slot (find out what that was for!). Regulars love the old-fashioned burgers, the Explorer Way chicken-fried steak, and much more, including the soft serve ice cream. Monday-Friday 6 a.m.-2 p.m. and 5-8:30 p.m.; Sunday 6 a.m.-2 p.m. 620.842.3055.

Lodging:
tinyurl.com/anthonylodging.

explorer extras...
In Anthony

The 1911 Carnegie library (NRHP), still serving the town, stands at 104 N. Springfield. The one-story red-brick structure is built in a rare Jacobethan style. By the way, Jacobethan is a coined term meaning the combination of the Jacobean and Elizabethan architecture styles.

Note the bright yellow terra cotta design on the front of the 1934 Municipal Building at 104 N. Springfield. Now used for everything from pancake feeds to recreation basketball, the building continues to be a community asset.

Four outdoor murals enhance the town and include a railroad scene by Mike Fallier and Joe Burnett at Main and LL&G, and a mosaic tile design featuring an agricultural theme at Jennings and Main. 620.842.5456.

In 1908, to select a style for their church, the First Congregational Church (NRHP) committee traveled to several communities to see their churches. The search resulted in a Gothic Revival brick building featuring three towers and stained-glass windows honoring Anthony's founders. See it at 202 N. Bluff.

Washington Elementary School at 215 S. Springfield was designed in the lovely Spanish Eclectic style in 1928.

Anthony City Lake and Park is a busy place thanks to all it has to offer—water recreation; tent camping and RV sites; a go-cart track; nine-hole, grass green golf course; and more. From Main, 2 miles north on LL&G, then ½ mile west on 20. 620.842.5434. anthonykansas.org. **ee**

ATTICA

Population 600

Dying Protest: From Main, ¾ mile west on C (U.S. 160), 200 feet south on a connector road, then ½ mile east on NW 60 to Attica Cemetery. When Nathaniel Grigsby, childhood friend of Abraham Lincoln and a Union veteran, died in 1890 he left a unique epitaph on his headstone for all to read: "Through this inscription," he began, "I wish to enter my dying protest against what is called the Democratic party." To read what else Nathaniel had to say, enter at the main gate and take the paved road that curves left to section 3E (east side). Grigsby's is the northwestern-most gravestone in that section.

Krazy Horse: 618 C. This is a meat-and-potatoes kind of place with Krazy menu names like Grilled Yard Bird (chicken breast) and Oink Fritter (breaded tenderloin). Grilled steaks, fresh salads, and daily specials satisfy most any craving. Wednesday-Saturday 11 a.m.-2 p.m. and 5-9 p.m.; Sunday 11 a.m.-2 p.m. 620.915.7299. FB.

Dari Cone: 134 C. Not just ice cream treats, this Dari serves burgers, sandwiches, chicken, and more. And customers say the staff is great. Monday-Tuesday 11 a.m.-7 p.m.; Wednesday-Friday 11 a.m.-4 p.m. 620.254.7779. FB.

explorer extras...
In Danville

Population 36

Danville has the only post office in the state set in an old (1961) gas station. You can't pump gas there but you can buy some stamps and help this little post office survive. Monday-Friday 11 a.m.-1 p.m.; Saturday 10:30 a.m.-11:45 p.m.

Even miles from Danville you can see the high-rising steeple of the historic Immaculate Conception Catholic Church dedicated in 1907. For a close-up look at this red-brick beauty, keep your eye on the steeple and you'll find it.

If you see a guy sitting at his picnic table beside the Copper Club garage, you've found Joe. He'd love it if you asked to see his collection of oil cans, cigar boxes, license plates, bottle openers, key chains, and more stored in his garage. Ask him about the Harley-Davidson distribution business in Danville. It's a pleasure to spend time with him. From Ryan, ½ block east on Main, then south into the alley. 620.962.5428.

Calvary Cemetery is home to many interesting gravestones and an impressive veterans memorial. Around Memorial Day the many flags flying at this prairie setting create a moving scene. From U.S. 160, ¼ mile south on 80. **ee**

explorer extras... In Duqoin

Unincorporated

Rainbow Arch Bridge:
From Main, ¾ mile south on 20. Marsh arch bridge lovers will love seeing this lovely one archer. Look for the 1929 Kansas Highway Commissioner plaque on this bridge, which carries traffic safely over Sand Creek. **ee**

explorer extras... In Freeport

Population 5

Freeport is the smallest incorporated town in the state. Of its five residents, one is the mayor and the rest make up the city council. 620.962.5211.

You're invited to the Freeport coffee, which takes place the first and third Thursdays of each month from 9-11 a.m. in the old red-brick bank building at Grand and Main. The mayor and his city councilwoman wife host the coffees, and usually

more than a dozen come. Bring some baked goods (or not). They (all five residents) love it when company comes to Freeport! 620.962.5211.

The door bolt of the historic Presbyterian Church is only there to keep the door from flying open on windy days, so go on in and look around (and remember to bolt the door when you leave). This wood frame building with semicircular pews is on the American Presbyterian/ Reformed Historical Sites Registry. It is on the northeast side of town on Church Lane. 620.962.5221. **ee**

HARPER

Population 1,412

Red Fish: It's not hard to spot the red fish on top of this unique 1886 standpipe water tower. When the 120-foot tower was erected, a nine-and-a-half-foot red fish was placed at the top as a weather vane. In

1892 when a tornado hit Harper, the fish was bent double, and the pole that held it was damaged. The fish was repaired and has remained a town symbol ever since.

Historic Fountain (RHKP):
Main and Central. The Harper Study and Social Club donated the fountain to the city in 1909. Complete with troughs, it was used as a watering station for 60 years. In 1983 the handsome

and detailed fountain was restored and, minus the watering troughs, placed at the center of the downtown intersection. A large brass plaque on the fountain relates its history. One of the original water troughs is now at home in City Park.

City Park: Main and Maple. The Harper Social and Study Club built this very pretty park around 1932 with assistance from the WPA. Note the stone arch entrances, complete with star, sunflower, horseshoes, and bears!

SC

Early Courthouse:

300 block of Main. Originally built in the 1870s as the county courthouse, its use as such was discontinued when the town of Anthony became the county seat by defeating Harper in the county seat wars. The former courthouse then was used as the Harper Normal School and Business College, later as a church, and now is vacant—but nonetheless, dignified.

Runnymede Church (NRHP):

11th and Pine. This 1890 Episcopalian church was moved into Harper from the English settlement town of Runnymede (see p. 316). The town, a failed social experiment, was north of Harper.

Beal Orchard & Country Store:

131 NE 100. From Main, ¾ mile north on Central, then ½ mile east on 100. Trek out to the family-owned orchard and "pick your own" peaches, apples, and nectarines from the thousands of trees planted by Steve Beal and Daylene Hinds. These hard-working folks also grow a variety of your favorite vegetables and sell grass-fed beef by the package. The country store stocks a treasure of jellies, sauces, old-fashioned candies, Kansas honey products, soaps, and sand plum jam. May-November, Wednesday-Friday 10 a.m.-5 p.m.; Saturday 10 a.m.-2 p.m. Call ahead, 620.896.7044. FB.

Red Rooster:

524 W. 14th. This Red Rooster has a lot to crow about. You'll find out why when you sit down at this cute cafe and order some super home cooking. The daily specials—Mondays fried chicken and Tuesdays meatloaf—are highlights as are the real mashed potatoes and gravy. Customers also praise the sweet tea and the pecan crumb apple pie. It's not on the menu but if you want chicken and waffles, just ask! Breakfast is served until 10:45 a.m. and again at 5-8 p.m. Monday-Friday 6 a.m.-2 p.m. and 5-8 p.m; Saturday 6 a.m.-2 p.m. 620.896.2409.

Fence Post Supper Club:

700 E. 14th. Breakfast, lunch, and dinner offer stick-to-your-ribs food such as steaks, pork chops, and fried chicken. Daily specials, sandwiches, salads, and not-often-seen-on-a-menu items such as frog legs and mountain oysters are popular too. Daily 6 a.m.-10 p.m. 620.896.2204. fencepostharper.com.

Petros Drive-In (formerly D & J):

609 E. 14th. It's known far and wide for its thirst-quenching cherry limeades, scrumptious nu-burgers (crumbled hamburger), and foot-long chili cheese dogs. Customers like to invent flavored concoctions such as vanilla-marshmallow cokes and anything else they can dream up for owner Petros Gridzlas to make. He's always happy to oblige. April-September, daily 11 a.m.-7 p.m. 620.896.2057.

explorer extras... In Harper

Aviation pioneer Lloyd Stearman built the house at 221 E. 14th as a high school project. His father built the 1907 Martha Kiefer House (RHKP) at 1310 Central.

James Knox Clark operated a transfer/hauling business in Hutchinson when he was hired by the new Harper Town Company to haul belongings from the train to the new settlement. He did such a good job that he was asked to move his business to Harper. He was reluctant to do so, but when he was promised his choice of farmland he made the move. When you see "Clark 1877" boldly painted on the red barn 1 mile east of Harper on U.S. 160, you'll see the place he chose. The land is still in his family.

Mike Fallier painted the mural at 914 Main, which depicts a train coming into Harper. Around town you'll see several murals that were painted by local schoolchildren. ee

WALDRON

Population 10

Tammy Faye Bakker Messner: From Main, 1 mile east on 100. Many are surprised to learn that once-famous evangelist and TV talk show host Tammy Faye Bakker is buried in this secluded prairie cemetery. She and her former husband, evangelist Jim Bakker, rose to fame through their Christian-based PTL (Praise The Lord) network. After a widely publicized scandal, they divorced and she later married Roe Messner, a Waldron native and church builder. Tammy Faye, known for her teary testimonials and heavy eye and face make-up, died of cancer

in 2007. Her fans often leave tubes of lipstick and mascara at her gravesite. To find her grave walk north two-thirds of the way into the cemetery and look for the large Todd stone on the west side. From there, three rows to the west are three flat gray granite markers. One is Tammy Faye's.

Harvey County

AROUND THE COUNTY

Harvey County West Park: 2733 West Park. From Burrton, 5 miles east on U.S. 50, 3 miles north on Golden Prairie, ¼ mile west on 24, north into the park, and follow the signs to the bait shop. Nearby, a trail begins with a most unusual starting point—a very long, wire-mesh suspension footbridge that extends 168 feet across the fishing lake! After you cross, take a one-mile trail through

the woods or just keep going back and forth over the bridge! Equestrian trails and picnic areas are also available in the park. 316.283.5420. tinyurl.com/harvcowest.

Historical Marker: From 30th in North Newton, 6 miles north on K-15. An upside-down pilaster capital from the 1906 Harvey County courthouse contains four brass plaques describing early area trails— the Chisholm, the Cherokee, the Pike's Peak, the Black Beaver, and Meridian Road.

BURRTON

Population 888

The Barn: 307 W. Dean (U.S. 50). People are flocking to this restaurant with Mason jar chandeliers and a 100-year-old grain bin opened up to serve as the bar. In the first 10 months since opening in October 2015, the Barn has sold 10,000 of the large and hand-breaded chicken-fried steaks. What a testimony! The Farmer Burger, grilled salmon, and peanut butter cream pie are just a few of the other favorites. Daily 11 a.m.-9 p.m. 620.463.8056. FB.

HALSTEAD

Population 2,083

Riverside Park: From 2nd, ¼ mile north on Main. A plaque on a granite stone records that the Harvey County Old Settlers Picnic was first held here in 1896. In more recent years the park gained recognition as one of the primary filming locations for the motion picture *Picnic*. (Although the plaque states the filming was in 1956, it actually occurred in May 1955). Movie buffs might recall the springy pedestrian bridge appearing in film. Spanning the Little Arkansas River, it was built in 1938 and remains on its original site in the south part of the park.

Flood Gates: You can almost imagine entering a medieval walled city as you approach Halstead from the north on K-89. Massive gates hang between concrete pillars, and high earthen walls border either side. Are they here to guard the town and the tall grain elevators that appear like castles? It's not quite so dramatic. What you're actually seeing are huge flood prevention structures built in 1994. The gates stand at the bridge entrances over the Little Arkansas

SC

River, and will close if the river begins to rise toward flood stage. No medieval mystique, but nonetheless important.

The Old Hardware Store:

208 Main. Take a delightful step back in time inside this beautifully restored historic building. The Old Hardware Store has been selling hardware since 1885, and it seems that very little has changed (although the original, authentic hardware now ranges to the 1970s). The century-old interior retains its wood floors, pressed-tin ceiling, and original counters, and an old ladder rolls along on a trolley to reach the upper shelves. Closer to ground level, you'll find hardware tucked away in turn-of-the-century bins and in more than 200 drawers. Besides offering antique hardware and some other antique pieces, the Old Hardware Store offers a marvelous experience! Monday-Saturday 9 a.m.-5 p.m. 316.835.2446. theoldhardwarestore.com.

Post Office Art (NRHP):

319 Main. *Where Kit Carson Camped* is the title of this 1941

Section artwork by famed Kansas landscape artist Birger Sandzen. See the mural inside the 1939 post office.

Kansas Learning Center for Health: 505 Main. This

facility is considered the oldest rural health museum in the nation. Designed for guided group learning, a browsing tour is also open to the public. The

interactive, hands-on activities create exciting opportunities to learn about health, especially with Valeda, the health education transparent woman, on hand! Monday-Friday 9 a.m.-4 p.m. Admission charge. 316.835.2662. learningcenter.org.

Halstead Historical Museum: 116 E. 1st. A 1917

brick depot (NRHP) houses excellent displays about historic Halstead. Learn about Dr. Arthur Hertzler, the "Horse and Buggy Doctor"; the filming of *Picnic* in Halstead (and see the film's actual swan boat); the story of the Halstead hospital, clinic, and school of nursing; and Halstead natives—Adolph Rupp Kentucky Wildcat basketball coach (1930-1972); and Jim Roper, first to win a national drag car race (1949). March-December, Saturday-Sunday 2-5 p.m. Donation welcome. 316.835.2267.

Halstead Cemetery:

From 3rd, 1¾ miles north on Main (becomes Hertzler). To find the grave (and a handsome memorial bench) of Dr. Hertzler (1870-1946), go east into the cemetery's northernmost driveway, then just south at the first crossroads. Also of interest in the cemetery's northwest corner is a plaque on a large natural stone affirming that "A daughter of a soldier of the American Revolution," Elizabeth Burch Brown, is buried in this cemetery.

Fairview Cemetery:

12th and Halstead. From U.S. 50, 2 miles north on Halstead. Outside the white fence, a plaque on a large natural stone states that "The widow of a soldier of the American Revolution," Rebecca Keys Burch, is buried in this cemetery. Burch is the mother of Elizabeth Burch Brown, buried in Halstead Cemetery (*see* previous entry).

Lodging: Spring Lake

RV Resort (316.835.3443, springlakervresort.com).

explorer extras...
In Halstead

In the early 1900s the electric-powered Arkansas Valley Interurban Railroad provided passenger and light freight service through Halstead from Hutchinson to Newton and into Wichita. The old Interurban station still stands at Spruce and 2nd, and six Interurban bridges (abandoned) can be seen east of town. Two close together are, from Spruce, 3¼ miles east on 6th (becomes SW 37 gravel road). On the north side you can spot the multiple-span bridge nestled among dense trees. Continue ¼ mile farther east to see the second bridge. tinyurl.com/avlbridges.

Christian Bergtholdt, a German Mennonite immigrant from

Bavaria, built the exquisite Queen Anne home (NRHP) at 205 E. 5th. The house was constructed in 1885 after Bergtholdt had achieved financial success from his grain elevator and mill. **ee**

HESSTON

Population 3,736

Dyck Arboretum of the Plains:
177 W. Hickory. The Kansas flora is showcased at this lovely prairie garden. Take a stroll on the half-mile path around the lake surrounded by 13 acres of landscaped native wildflowers, grasses, shrubs, and trees. Scientific and common names of plants are noted on the easy-to-read labels. In addition to native plants you'll see ceramic sculptures, created by Kansas artist Conrad Snider, with inspirational quotations that enhance and give deeper

meaning to this natural setting. Visitor center and gift shop hours, Monday-Friday 9 a.m.-4 p.m.; arboretum, always open. Donation welcome. 620.327.8127. dyckarboretum.org.

Hesston Public Library:
300 N. Main. A warm and inviting library with a modern touch awaits you. Not only filled with good books but it offers good coffee, snacks, and art. Created by local art instructor Hanna Eastin, a clever bookends sculpture feature ceramic books with library donors' names as

the book titles. A small room near the front of the library displays a collection about the 1990 tornado that devastated Hesston. In the back, many clocks let you know the exact times in different parts of the world. Monday-Friday 9 a.m.-6 p.m.; Saturday 9 a.m.-2 p.m. 620.327.4666. FB.

King Memorial Park:
Lincoln and Ridge. The plaque on the shelter house tells you that the park is a memorial to Raymond and Yvonne King who died October 2, 1970, in the airplane crash that killed members of the Wichita State University football team. This beautiful park is a fitting tribute to the Kings, longtime supporters of the Hesston community. 620.327.4311.

Emma Creeks Antiques:
100 N. Main. The hardware store building dates to 1887, and its "old bones" form a great backdrop for the vintage oak furniture, glassware, metal toys, and much more. You'll enjoy this buy, sell, and trade store! Thursday-Saturday 10 a.m.-5 p.m. 316.772.7324. FB.

Lincoln Perk:
709 E. Lincoln. Drive through or stop in for a fresh roasted perk-me-up. Homemade scones, muffins, and the like pair nicely with your drink of choice. Lunch offers soups, salads, and sandwiches. Monday-Saturday 7:30 a.m.-5 p.m.; Sunday 7:30 a.m.-2 p.m. 620.327.2349. FB.

Water's Edge:
701 S. Main. Eat well at this restaurant inside the Hesston Wellness Center. In addition to the regular menu,

the buffet on Thursday nights (except the fifth Thursday in the month) is a crowd pleaser with its fried chicken, waffles, burgers, and Mexican. Wednesday-Friday 7 a.m.-2 p.m.; Thursday-Saturday 5-8 p.m.; Saturday 7-11 a.m.; Sunday 11 a.m.-2 p.m. 620.327.4099. watersedgehesston.com.

Lodging: Cottonwood Grove RV Campground (620.327.4173, cottonwoodgrove.com); additional lodging (tinyurl.com/hesslodging).

explorer extras... In Hesston

Underground irrigation keeps the 18-hole municipal golf course, 520 Yost, in great condition. Greens fee. 620.327.2331. hesstongolf.com.

Let your kids out of the car to play in the spray park (Aquatic Park), just south of King Park parking lot at Ridge and Lincoln.

Let your dogs out of the car to play in Hesston Dog Park, just west of Old U.S. 81 at 505 W. Lincoln. **ee**

NEWTON

Population 19,117

During its cowtown days (1871-1872) Newton was the western terminal of the Santa Fe railroad and a railhead for the famed Chisholm Trail, and was known as "the wickedest city in the West." But these days were short-lived as the rails soon extended to Dodge City. Cowboys were replaced with sodbusters, including a large group of Mennonites who brought Turkey Red wheat to Kansas.

Harvey County Historical Museum:
203 N. Main. The 1904 Carnegie library (NRHP) is the home of this museum, whose fascinating permanent and rotating exhibits give life to

the history of Newton and the surrounding towns. Tuesday-Friday 10 a.m.-4 p.m.; 3rd Thursday 6-8 p.m.; 1st and 3rd Saturdays 10 a.m.-4 p.m. 316.283.2221. hchm.org.

Blue Sky Sculpture

(8 Wonders of Kansas Art): From Main, ½ mile east on 12th, then ¼ mile north on Kansas to Centennial Park. An impressive and large free-standing tile sculpture by artist Phil Epp celebrates the blue prairie skies by positioning the viewer in a juxtaposition between the sculptural imagery and the natural sky. Collaborative artists are Terry Corbett and Conrad Snider.

Community Mural: 304 N.

Main. In 2010 Kansas artists David Lowenstein, Erika Nelson, and Matthew Farley painted this colorful mural with help from local volunteers. Entitled *The Imagineers*, it depicts a group of people around a table "engaged in the process of building, playing, restoring and imagining."

Carriage Factory Gallery

(NRHP): 128 E. 6th. Works of Kansas artists are displayed on three floors against the historic backdrop of this carriage factory. The original factory and a blacksmith shop were built on this site in 1883, and the present factory, housing

the gallery, was constructed in 1903. In addition to the art exhibitions are an excellent gift shop and a courtyard of outdoor art. Tuesday-Friday 12-5 p.m.; Saturday 10 a.m.-5 p.m. 316.284.2749. carriagefactoryartgallery.com.

Warkentin House

(NRHP): 211 E. 1st. This opulent 1887 house was built for Mennonite entrepreneur Bernhard Warkentin. He was largely responsible for the major Mennonite migrations to America in the 1870s, the introduction of Turkey red wheat, and in establishing the Kansas wheat milling industry. This

home's leatherette wainscoting, ball-and-spindle fretwork, and dentil block design dispel the myth that all Mennonites were austere people. April-May and September-December, Saturday-Sunday 1-4:30 p.m.; June-August, Tuesday-Sunday 1-4:30 p.m. Admission charge. 316.283.3113. FB.

Downtown: Specialty shops in Newton's well-kept business district ensure that you won't go home empty handed. Visit the Kitchen Corner (607 N.

Main, 316.283.4253); Main Street Company (611 N. Main, 316.283.5745); Charlotte's Sew Natural (710 N. Main, 316.284.2547); and Faith & Life Bookstore (606 N. Main, 316.283.2210).

Prairie Harvest: 601 N. Main. Make this your stop for fresh organic produce, bulk foods, spices, and Kansas products, and choose from healthy deli options. Baked on

site, the whole grain breads, zweiback, and the famous peppernuts create an aroma that make these products hard to resist. Other breads are baked a block away by Crust & Crumb Co. (a locally owned artisan bread company) and delivered warm to the Prairie. Monday-Friday 10 a.m.-7 p.m.; Saturday 9 a.m.-5 p.m. 316.283.6623. prairieharvestks.com.

Anderson Book & Office

Supply: 627 N. Main. The Andersons have run this family operation since 1892, which will intrigue you if you have a zest for old-fashioned buildings and their accessories. The entryway floor is imprinted, "The Golden Rule Store," the name of the early JC Penney store that occupied this building prior to the Andersons. Kansas books, gifts, office supplies, and more offer an engaging variety to peruse and purchase. Monday-Saturday 9 a.m.-5:30 p.m. 316.283.3570. FB.

Newton Bike Shop:

131 W. 6th. The shop's passion is to create and foster a love for cycling. Buy a bike, trade a bike, repair a bike, talk bikes, get bike gear, and find the best

bike adventures. Guaranteed you'll feel the pedal power. Newton Bike even provides a hostel for those cycling through the area. Monday-Friday 10 a.m.-6 p.m.; Saturday 10 a.m.-3 p.m. 316.243.2070. newtonbikeshop.com.

CaNewton Canoe and Kayak Rental:
5 blocks west of Main on 4th. Canoe Newton. Get it? Even if you don't, you will enjoy canoeing or kayaking on the Sand Creek River, an experience made easy by Marc and Lisa Fitzroy. Ring the doorbell on the fence north of the boat ramp, and soon you'll be outfitted for fun on the river. Paddleboats are available weekends. April-September, Monday-Friday 5:30-dusk and Saturday-Sunday 10 a.m.-dusk. 316.288.5756. canewton.com.

Sand Creek Trail:
600 block of W. 5th. At Athletic Park, hop on the bike and hike path that parallels Sand Creek. The two-mile (one way) northeasterly route takes you to Centennial Park at 12th and Kansas. 620.284.6083. tinyurl.com/sandcreekbike.

Athletic Park:
600 block of W. 5th. Near the north entrance of the 1909 park, a 17-foot statue sculpted in 1942 by Max Nixon honors Mennonite farmer pioneers (NRHP). South of the statue is the historic Newton Stadium (NRHP), a 1936 WPA project. The stadium and the accompanying Fischer Field host various athletic and community events.

Genova Italian Restaurant:
1021 Washington.

It didn't take long for people to find out about the outstanding Italian cuisine served in this strip mall. Step in to the rich aromas of homemade pasta, tomato sauce, and freshly baked bread. First-timers may want to start with the Sampler Platter. The tiramisu or lemoncello dessert is the perfect ending to whatever you choose. Warning: the warm garlic rolls served with a delicious chunky Mediterranean dipping oil before dinner are addicting! Tuesday- Saturday 11 a.m.-9 p.m.; Sunday 11 a.m.-3 p.m. Reservations recommended. 316.587.8099. genovaitalianrestaurant.com.

Back Alley Pizza and Norm's Coffee Bar:
125 W 6th. It's a hot spot in town due to the rapid fire way they make the pizza and the jolt you get from fresh and hot java beverages. Order at the counter then watch the staff hand toss

the pizza dough, slather it with toppings, and pop it in the fast-baking Italian pizza oven. Monday-Saturday 8 a.m.-8 p.m. 316.804.4924. FB.

The Breadbasket:
219 N. Main. The soup and salad bar is fresh and mouth watering and comes with homemade breads. Soup specialties include green bean and ham, a thick chicken and noodle, and chicken borscht. Save room for the terrific homemade pies. A Low German buffet on Friday and Saturday nights features verenike. Order at the counter. Monday-Thursday 6:30 a.m.-5:30 p.m.; Friday-Saturday 6:30 a.m.-8 p.m.; Sunday 10:30 a.m.-2 p.m. 316.283.3811. newtonbreadbasket.com.

Druber's Donuts:
116 W. 6th. A Newton landmark, this donut shop has a very unique time schedule to accommodate Amtrak travelers and college students. Its business week starts Sunday evening at 11:30 p.m. and closes 1 p.m. the following day. This schedule continues through the week until Saturday when the shop closes at 1 p.m. Sunday 6 a.m.-12 p.m. Druber's also serves light lunches, but the hot donuts are the best! 316.283.1206.

SC

Gillispie Meats:
420 E. Broadway. Inside this unassuming stucco, cream-colored building with blue trim is one fine butcher shop run by a dedicated owner Roger Gillispie. He sells fresh and frozen meats of all kinds, and customers drive many miles for the ham loaf and bierocks. If you like, Roger is happy to make sandwiches for you from the deli meats and cheese. Tuesday-Friday 9 a.m.-6 p.m.; Saturday 9 a.m.-4 p.m. 316.283.1661.

701 Cafe: 701 N. Main. The slogan for this down-to-earth, friendly stop is "Gourmet All Day!" And that's what you'll get with the sandwiches, wraps, fresh salads, and homemade sides. Gluten-free, vegetarian, and vegan options also are available. Monday-Friday 10:30 a.m.-2:30 p.m.; Thursday 5-8:30 p.m.; Saturday 11 a.m.-8:30 p.m. 316.804.4573. FB.

Beck's Farm: 7620 S. Anderson. Sarah and Scott Beck started their orchard more than 17 years ago with the help of their children and friends, and they are still going strong. Besides "pick your own" sweet, juicy peaches, you might find fresh fruit and vegetables from Hawaii, Alabama, Georgia, Kansas, and wherever else Sarah can make a trade. June-September, Monday-Saturday 10 a.m.-6 p.m. and Sunday 12-5 p.m. 316.282.2325. becksfarm.com.

Lodging: tonewton.com.

**explorer extras...
In Newton**

The grand old mill, 301 N. Main, a Second Empire style building, was constructed in 1879 as the Monarch Steam Mill. In 1886 Bernhard Warkentin purchased it and converted it to a roller mill (NRHP) to handle the Turkey Red hard winter wheat. The historic structure has had several lives, and survives today as Old Mill Plaza housing several businesses.

In Okerberg Park, 4th and Plum, four brass plaques fixed to a limestone pilaster capital from the 1906 Harvey County courthouse provide a history of the Chisholm Trail and the area.

Beside the sidewalk trail just east of the Ash Street Bridge, a plaque states that more than two million longhorn cattle crossed Sand Creek from 1867 to 1871 near this point at Ash and 8th. The crossing was on the Chisholm Trail, the cattle drive route from Texas to Kansas.

A plaque on the sidewalk at 5th and Main tells the story of the first water well in Newton, dug in 1871. Should you want to see the actual well site, carefully dodge the traffic to find the little concrete marker in the middle of the intersection!

Formerly a Santa Fe depot (NRHP), the 1929 Tudor Revival train station, 414 Main, was modeled after Shakespeare's house at Stratford-upon-Avon. The station continues to provide train service.

Excellent Mexican food awaits you at Casa Fiesta (1607 N. Main, 316.283.7960); El Toro (121 W. 5th, 316.283.4044); and Acapulco (217 W. Broadway, 316.283.6026).

The 1906-1907 Santa Fe steam engine commands attention in its permanent home under a shelter in Military Park, 7th and Oak.

The Main Street Historic District (NRHP) comprises 52 buildings in the 200 to 800 blocks of N. Main. Walking tour brochures are available at the visitors bureau,

201 E. 6th; at Anderson's, 627 N. Main; or at tonewton.com/history.html.

A nine-hole disc golf course awaits you and your expertise at Centennial Park. A dog park is here too, awaiting you and your dog! From Main, ½ mile east on 12th, then ¼ mile north on Kansas. 316.284.6083. **ee**

NORTH NEWTON

Population 1,793

Kauffman Museum: 2801 N. Main. Pioneer life and Mennonite migration from Russia and Prussia are interpreted in an award-winning exhibit comprising quotations, photos, and historic artifacts. An official Save America's Treasures project, an exhibit of Mennonite immigrant furniture from the Vistula Delta of present Poland is an outstanding display. A late 1800s farmstead presents seasonal heritage vegetable and flower gardens, and a tallgrass prairie reconstruction accents the entrance of this exemplary museum. Tuesday-Friday 9:30 a.m.-4:30 p.m.; Saturday-Sunday 1:30-4:30 p.m. 316.283.1612. kauffman.bethelks.edu

Bethel College: 300 27th. Bethel is the oldest Mennonite college in North America, founded in 1887. Beautiful limestone buildings highlight this campus.

Thresher National: 300 27th. Eric Preheim grew up near Augusta, Georgia, home of the Augusta National and the Masters Golf Tournament. When he established the disc golf course on the Bethel College campus, he named this

2,474-foot, nine-hole course the Thresher National. tinyurl.com/threshernatl.

Sand Creek Trail: 29th and Goerz. A North Newton starting point for this trail is Memorial Grove, east of the tennis courts on the Bethel College campus. The North Newton part of the trail is approximately two miles long and is composed of either sidewalk or wood chips. Eight interpretive signs along the route explain local history and culture. 316.283.7990. tinyurl.com/sandcreektrail.

Lodging: Serenity Silo, Barnview Cottage, and Woodland Hideaway (316.283.5231).

SEDGWICK

Population 1,696

Downtown Historic District (NRHP): The district encompasses the majority of the west side of the 500 block of N. Commercial. Buildings here date from the 1880s to 1930, the oldest one standing at 523 Commercial. A nearby historical plaque relates its story.

City Park: Madison and 4th. At this corner you'll see a charming bear that Doug Bough carved from a walnut tree trunk in 1993. Embedded in a rock monument nearby, a plaque recounts the history of the town.

Cy's Hoof and Horn: 425 N. Commercial. Wipe your boots and walk up the cattle chute-like ramp into a warmly lit interior where you'll soon dig into Cy's renowned chicken-fried steak and the aged steaks hand cut in-house. Cy Lampe, inspired by his grandmother's home cooking and hard work, built this eatery in 2001. Monday-Saturday 11 a.m.-10 p.m. 316.772.5329. hoofandhornsupperclub.com.

WALTON

Population 233

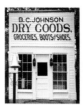

First Business: Look for the old storefront for BC Johnson Dry Goods. It was the first (1872) business building in Walton, and it's still standing! Later the building operated as a post office, but currently is vacant.

Fountain of Brotherhood: 400 block of Main (City Park). A large rustic stone monument with a nonoperating fountain boasts five beautifully carved limestone insets. It was presented to the community by the Walton Mennonite Church in honor of the Turkey Red Wheat Centennial in 1974.

Turkey Red Wheat: From Main, ½ mile northeast on U.S. 50. At the roadside pullover, a historical marker summarizes the history of Turkey red wheat and its journey to Kansas via the Mennonite colonists. The hard winter wheat helped Kansas earn its nickname the "Wheat State." The nation's leading wheat producer, Kansas continues to be known as the breadbasket of the world.

Black Flame: On the night Ted Pankratz died, his son Tim dreamt of a black flame. In the center of Walton Cemetery, that flame is on Ted Pankratz' gravestone in the form of a black granite abstract sculpture. Creating the flame was a family project, and son-in-law Bryan Saner was the sculptor. From U.S. 50, 1 mile north on Walton to the cemetery.

Whistlestop Cafe: 106 N. Main. On Tuesday mornings you might notice the husbands at one table while the wives get together at another, each group catching up over coffee. Customers know this

is the place for breakfast (it's served all day). If you like oatmeal, order a bowl with honey and milk, and add a handful of raisins in honor of Jonah Reimer. A longtime and devoted Whistlestop customer, Jonah is no longer with us, but his tradition lives on. Tuesday-Sunday 8 a.m.-2 p.m.; Thursday 5-8 p.m. 620.837.3136.

Kingman County

AROUND THE COUNTY

Greenwood Cemetery: From U.S. 54/400 in Kingman, 7½ miles south on K-14, 5 miles east on SE 70, then 1 mile north on SE 70 Ave. It's not often you cross a cattle guard to enter a cemetery, but in some rural areas it is needed to keep the free-range livestock out. Clyde Cessna's family is buried in this cemetery, and on the back of the Cessna family stone an inscription reads, "Aviation Pioneer." In front of this stone, Clyde's small and simple marker causes one to reflect on this famous aviator's career and his contribution to early flight and aircraft construction.

CUNNINGHAM

Population 475

Cunningham Museum: 100 W. 1st. Volunteers keep this museum, located in a former grocery store, going strong. To see it, call Donna Glenn and in five minutes she'll meet you and open the doors. Among the exhibits inside are historic military equipment, a toy collection, and a 1930s paper prom dress. A former calaboose stands nearby, sans prisoners! 620.298.2744.

SC

KINGMAN

Population 3,158

Kingman County Courthouse (NRHP):

130 N. Spruce. This outstanding red-brick with limestone trim courthouse is a 1908 Roman-esque Revival hybrid, the work of well-known architect George Washburn. The interior detail has much to appreciate. For example, the 1x1-inch lobby floor tiles have each been indi-vidually laid! Another point of amazement is the courtroom—with a fireplace! Monday-Friday 8 a.m.-5 p.m. 620.532.2521.

Kingman County Museum (NRHP):

400 N. Main. The museum is at home in the 1888 former city hall and fire station, a red-brick and limestone building with a quirky feature—the splendid 80-foot tall tower you see was built back in the day as a cotton-hose drying tower for the fire station. It is the only remaining one in the state. Museum exhibits feature Kingman County natives aviator Clyde Cessna and Major League baseball player Don Lock, plus the exciting adventures

of Cannonball Green and the Cannonball Stage Line. March-December, Friday 9 a.m.-3 p.m.; Saturday 9 a.m.-12 p.m. 620.532.5274.

Stan Herd Outdoor Murals:

Two 1998 Stan Herd murals on the museum's north wall depict the flight of the first Cessna airplane and Cannonball Green driving his stagecoach.

Post Office Mural (NRHP):

425 N. Main. *In the Days of the Cattlemen's Picnic* is the title of this 1942 Section artwork by Jessie Wilbur. The scene is of men and women preparing for a rodeo, a historic annual event sponsored by the Cattlemen's Association of Kingman.

Buffalo Sculptures:

From Marquette, 1 mile east on U.S. 54/400. Artist Glenn Stark's buffalo (two adults and a calf) creations stand on a hilltop on the north side of the highway to welcome you to Kingman. Sometimes a live llama joins them at the hilltop.

Glenn Stark Sculptures:

Main and Sherman. Giraffes, bears, a moose, a dinosaur, and howling wolves keep company with a settler plowing,

a cowboy on his horse, totems, and more in Santa Fe Park. When grassroots artist Glenn Stark died in his 90s, about 20 of his colorful and imaginative concrete sculptures found a new home here.

National Guard Armory

(NRHP): 111 S. Main. The first constructed in the state by a municipality, this armory is one of only three built in Kansas prior to WWII. Erected in 1937 during the Great Depression, this PWA structure displays an art deco facade and glass-block windows. It is now home to the Kingman Area Chamber of Commerce. 620.532.1853.

Kingman Historic Theatre:

237 N. Main. The 1950s orange-powder blue-and-white marquee on this 1920 brown-brick building extends a colorful invitation to come inside for a movie and all the trimmings. The roomy balcony is for adults only. FB.

Riverside Park: 100 E. 1st. What a lovely park. The drive around it follows the quarter-mile oval horse race track used in the early 1900s. Enjoy the South Fork Ninnescah River and the tall cottonwoods along a mile sidewalk trail in the park. Old-fashioned street lamps guide you during the late evening, and several walking bridges cross the river; one leads to an Outdoor Wildlife Learning Sites (OWLS) site with a butterfly and hummingbird garden, native grass and flower garden, and a nature trail. Bring your fishing pole and try your luck at Hoover Pond, a 1934 WPA project.

Walnut Hill Cemetery:
From East D (U.S. 54/400), 1 block north on Marquette. Here you'll find a zinc Civil War statue of a soldier at parade rest. Unusual additions on the upper tier of the base are the relief busts of Abraham Lincoln, and Civil War Generals Ulysses Grant, William Tecumseh Sherman, and Philip Sheridan.

Cleo's Floral and Cafe
Cleo's: 229 N. Main. Espresso, smoothies, snow cones, and light lunches are enjoyed amidst the flowers and gifts. For the cafe only, enter at the former barber shop between Kingman Theatre and Cleo's Floral. Monday-Friday 9 a.m.-5 p.m.; Saturday 9 a.m.-12 p.m. 620.532.3883.

Jeri's Kitchen: 312 N. Main. Exposed brick walls add to the open atmosphere in Jeri's, known for comfort food favorites including fried chicken, roast beef, pulled pork, daily specials, and a Sunday brunch buffet. Monday-Saturday 4:30 a.m.-8 p.m.; Sunday 6 a.m.-2:30 p.m. FB.

Smitty's Carry-Out:
233 East D (U.S. 54/400). If you're hankering for a burger, look no further than Smitty's. Smitty's is known far and wide for their fresh meat burgers, hand-cut fries and out of this world hand-battered onion rings. Monday-Saturday 11 a.m.-8 p.m. 620.532.1883. FB.

Grumpy's Steakhouse:
130 West Avenue A. Grumpy's slogan is, "Where happiness is a steak away." The char-grilled burgers and hand-cut steaks accompany friendly service, making everyone happy at Grumpy's! Tuesday-Saturday 11 a.m.-9:30 p.m. 620.532.2442. FB.

Lodging: Savannah House Bed & Breakfast (620.955.6179, FB); additional lodging (cityofkingman.com/lodging).

explorer extras...
In Kingman

Red-brick streets accentuate the many turn-of-the-century downtown buildings.

The 1914 one-story red-brick Carnegie library (NRHP) at 455 N. Main still serves the town. The building's Neoclassical style is evident in the moulded wood pediment with egg-and-dart motif and dentil eaves.

The 1910 red-brick Santa Fe depot (NRHP) holds its place at 201 E. Sherman. The brown-brick Missouri Pacific depot, built in the 1910s, is just off the walking path west of the swimming pool (212 W. Main).

A replica Lady Liberty statue at Main and K-14 shares a small red-brick plaza with a memorial honoring local veterans. **ee**

MOUNT VERNON

Unincorporated

Creations Restaurant:
4996 NE 150. From U.S. 54/400, 3½ miles north on NE 150. The Creations burger, French dip sandwich, and chicken-fried steak are all made-from-scratch delicious. Visitors to Cheney Lake, 1 mile east, appreciate the breakfast buffet on Saturdays

and Sundays.Wednesday-Saturday 8 a.m.-7 p.m.; Sunday 8 a.m.-3 p.m. 316.542.9888.

NORWICH

Population 487

Ye Olde General Store:
307 S. Main. Diversified stock—house paint and auto, farm, and garden supplies—gives customers what they need. In turn, customers give life to this thriving store, which also serves as the local post office! Monday-Friday 8 a.m.-6 p.m.; Saturday 8 a.m.-4 p.m. 620.478.2229. FB.

SC

RedZ: 246 N. Main. Looking to cool off with an ice cream treat? You've found it at this red-brick corner building sporting an original pressed-tin ceiling and wood floors. The soda fountain has a new counter and back bar, and besides cool treats it offers good eats—pizza, burgers, sandwiches, and smoked meats. Monday-Friday

9:30 a.m.-2 p.m.; Saturday 6 a.m.-7 p.m. 620.478.2401. FB.

Rowan's Honey Shop:
218 S. Main. Whether you want honey-related items or to learn more about beekeeping, Rowan's is happy to help. This unique shop makes and sells "honeymade" sauces, liquid honey, jellies, jams, lip balm, moisturizers, and beekeeping equipment. You can even buy a package of bees with a mated queen! Friday 8 a.m.-4 p.m.; Saturday 9 a.m.-12 p.m. 620.478.2275. rowanshoneyshop.com.

Eagle Grocery: 242 S. Main. There's a new grocery store in town and the locals are so pleased! You too can support this little two-aisle store. Buy spices; they don't always move so quickly! Monday-Saturday 7 a.m.-7 p.m.; Sunday 11 a.m.-3 p.m. 620.478.2282. FB.

WATERLOO

Unincorporated

Historic Riggs Arboretum:
From NE 20, 2 blocks north on Grove, then 1 block west on Elder. For a walk through the oldest arboretum west of the Mississippi, ask John Riggs, grandson of John Walter Riggs who established this 10-acre site in 1887, for permission. It's worth it just to see the amazing bark pattern on the Kansas champion Loblolly Pine! Trails take you past two more Kansas champions—American Yellowwood and Laurel Oak—and 70 other varieties of trees from around the world. 785.227.3787.

ZENDA

Population 90

The Lumber Yard Steakhouse: 311 N. Main. Inside, old lumberyard shelves display antiques, and original racks now hold bottles of wine. The outside is just an ordinary metal building, but the steaks and atmosphere inside are anything but! Tuesday-Friday 11 a.m.-2 p.m.; Thursday-Friday 5-9 p.m.; Saturday 11 a.m.-10 p.m. 620.243.6000. FB.

Zenda Community Museum:
101 N Main. Zenda history and school trophies are displayed inside a former bank. Behind the museum a building has been constructed just for "Bonnie's Little Zenda." Bonnie Bailey spent two years creating 36 intricate scale model buildings of Zenda's turn-of-the-century Main Street. It's impressive! Call ahead, and don't be surprised if you reach the Country Cottage Beauty Salon. That's where you'll find museum volunteer Betty Green. 620.243.7365.

**explorer extras...
In Zenda**

The Zenda jail, ½ block east of the Lumber Yard Steakhouse, still has the iron rings that shackled prisoners.

The Zenda post office, 210 N. Main, is in a white stucco building with a recessed arched entrance. Buy some stamps to help support this little PO, and enjoy a conversation with the clerk. Monday-Saturday 9:30-11:30 a.m. 620.243.5041.
ee

Marion County

AROUND THE COUNTY

Marion Reservoir:
Constructed by the federal government, the reservoir lies between the towns of Marion and Hillsboro off U.S. 56. Many recreational opportunities are available, from fishing and skiing to bird watching, hiking, and camping. Completed in 1968, the lake was built for flood control and as a water supply. 620.382.2101. tinyurl.com/marionres.

BURNS

Population 217

Pizza Rehea's: 110 E. Broadway. Customers say it's the best pizza they've ever had—it must be the secret sauce or the homemade dough made by owner Rehea Huls. Monday, Wednesday-Friday 10:30 a.m.-7 p.m.; Tuesday 10:30 a.m.-4:30 p.m.; Saturday 10:30 a.m.-1 p.m. 620.726.5524.

DURHAM

Population 108

Santa Fe Trail Ruts:
From 6th, 1½ miles south on K-15, 2 miles west on 270, ½ mile north on Falcon. Durham is near the Cottonwood Crossing of the Santa Fe Trail, and several traces of the trail are still visible in the area, especially at this location. Look for a small sign on the road.

Cottonwood River Crossing of the Santa Fe Trail: 290 and Falcon. From Douglas, 1¼ miles west and north on 5th (becomes 285),

then ¼ mile east on 290. A little kiosk displays three interpretive panels about the Cottonwood Crossing on the famous trail. Nearby is a Santa Fe Trail marker placed by the DAR.

Mystery Building:
507 S. Douglas. It's an attractive building, this narrow structure with tile exterior (looks like bricks), multicolored awning tiles, a small ceramic inset, and decorative features that appear to be eagles. But everyone, even the locals, are stymied about the building's origin.

Main Street Cafe: 517 S.
Douglas. Some come for breakfast just for the homemade syrup and pancakes! It's also a favorite destination for the Friday night German buffet that features verenike, sausage, and cherry moos. The reasons for its popularity go on and on— the catfish, honey glazed ham, chicken-fried chicken, and the homemade pies are just a few of them. Monday-Saturday 6:30 a.m.-2 p.m.; Friday 5-8 p.m. 620.732.2096. wedelcafe.com.

FLORENCE

Population 447

Harvey House Museum
(NRHP): 221 Marion. Nearly 140 years ago Fred Harvey established a line of restaurants

to accommodate Santa Fe railway passengers. In 1877 the Harvey House in Florence became the first to offer lodging along with its dining facilities. Only a third of the original building remains, but displays capture the essence of this unique business that operated until 1900. Groups may make reservations for a Harvey House meal served by Harvey Girls. Call ahead, 620.878.4296.

City Tree Farm: From Main,
¼ mile east on 4th, then north just before the Cottonwood River Bridge, and park on the dirt path. A large stone sign marks the tree farm, and from it you can see the 1,700 black walnut trees that were planted along the Cottonwood River in 2006. With help from the Kansas Forest Service, local volunteers planted this hardwood forest that will mature in 2060. At that time the city can sell the trees for their valued hardwood.

Stringtown: From the Tree
Farm, cross the bridge and continue ½ mile east on a brick road. It is thought that this area earned the name Stringtown because main street was strung out along the river. Businesses operated here until the 1951 flood wiped them out. The only remaining evidence of this unofficial town is the red-brick road.

Hillcrest Cemetery:
From 8th, ½ mile north on Marion. An inscribed gray granite monument in the northwest corner is the only recognition of the 300 Russian

Mennonites buried here who died during the winter of 1874-75 from a smallpox epidemic. A space was carved in that stone to hold the one gravestone found for one of those 300—young Lelah Kirgan. Another "of interest" story here is that of Bertha "Teeny" Williams, who, after the cemetery records were lost in a fire, researched and re-recorded every burial plot. Read her fascinating research findings posted in the cemetery gazebo.

Crystal Spring: From 8th,
¾ mile north on Marion, 1 mile west and north on 130, ¼ mile north on Whitetail, then ¼ mile east on a narrow driveway. The water for the city of Florence comes from Crystal Spring, one of the largest single springs in the Flint Hills. The fun is exploring the babbling spring and the rock path above the little 1949 springhouse. A historical marker tells you more about the spring.

Florence Water Tower
(NRHP): U.S. 50 and U.S. 77. The 1888 water tower represents the first waterworks system in the community. Its water supply comes from Crystal Spring, one of the largest artesian wells in Kansas. The water in this unique tower is 99.967 percent pure, a fact proudly proclaimed on the tall cylindrical structure.

Flint Hills Market and
Bakery (NRHP): 423 Main. Four giant windmill heads act as ceiling fans, and that's quite a sight! This former opera house has been converted into a destination market, bakery, and deli. Here you'll find organic

SC

and gluten-free items, plus regular groceries, gifts, baked pizza, sandwiches served on bread made in-house, bierocks, salads, and more. Oh yes, and the very yummy pies and cakes. Monday-Saturday 9 a.m.-5:30 p.m. 620.878.2258. FB.

explorer extras... In Florence

Town and Country, 410 U.S. 77, is a classic old roadside diner serving daily specials. It's a hopping place and beloved by the locals. 620.878.4487.

The picturesque Bichet School (NRHP), a native limestone country school with classic bell tower, served a French-speaking settlement here from 1896 to 1946. Local stonemason Oscar Johnson created the decorative work on the quoins, lintels, cornices, and round window. The original stone outhouses and cave storm shelter are still intact. From U.S. 77, 4½ miles east on U.S. 50, then ¼ mile north on Bluestem. **ee**

GOESSEL

Population 517

Mennonite Heritage Museum Complex: 200 N. Poplar. A tribute to Russian Mennonite pioneers who settled the area in 1874, the complex displays countless artifacts in a replicated immigrant house and barn (combined as one unit), and two authentic farmhouses,

a bank, and two schools. In season the heritage flower and vegetable gardens are beautiful sights. A full-sized wheat straw replica of the Liberty Bell is in the Turkey Red Wheat Palace along with P.H. Friesen's murals and a large array of farm equipment. An excellent gift shop sells Mennonite heritage gifts such as the Dutch Blitz game. May-September, Tuesday-Saturday 10 a.m.-5 p.m.; March-April and October-November, Tuesday-Saturday 12-4 p.m. Admission charge. 620.367.8200. goesselmuseum.com.

Alexanderwohl Mennonite Church: 1304 K-15. From Main, 1 mile north on K-15. Built in the Dutch Mennonite style in 1886, the structure features a wraparound balcony and proscenium arch in the sanctuary, both rare architectural designs in a Mennonite church. On the grounds is a threshing stone used by the immigrants. 620.367.8192. alexanderwohl.org.

Bethesda Hospital:

305 E. Main. The original structure was the first Mennonite hospital in North America. In 1928 the Bethesda Hospital and Home Society constructed this building, which is now occupied by a private business. The hospital history is on file at the Mennonite Heritage Museum.

Immigrant Graves:

From Main, 1 block south on Cedar. The tiny cemetery of the Mennonite Brethren Church of the Schellenberg community is still evident even though the church no longer exists. Most gravestones are those for infants and young mothers born in South Russia.

Pine Edge Golf Course: 468 130. From Main, 1 mile north on K-15, then 1½ miles east on 130. Former dairyman Myron Schmidt built this nine-hole, grass-green short course. Hole three is 126 yards—if you don't hit your ball far enough it will land in the pond; if you hit it too far, it will hit the twin silos. Sharpen your wedge at Pine Edge! Greens fee. 620.367.2664. FB.

Keith's Foods: 216 E. Main. Order sandwiches at the meat counter in this agreeable little grocery store. They'll make 'em exactly as you want 'em. And the coldest pop in the state is in these coolers! You might find a few items you need for your home pantry too. Shelving holds vintage product containers that make for an old-fashioned look. Monday-Saturday 8 a.m.-7 p.m. 620.367.2203.

Branding Iron: 106 N. Cedar. Lunch and dinner entrees are made with locally sourced ingredients whenever possible. The Bison Burger is the bomb! Monday-Thursday 11 a.m.-1 p.m.; Monday-Friday 5-7 p.m.; Saturday 11 a.m.-1:30 p.m. and 4:30-7 p.m. 620.367.2363. FB.

HILLSBORO

Population 2,903

Mennonite Settlement Museum: 501 S. Ash. The Peter Paul Loewen House (NRHP)

is the last remaining Mennonite style Russian clay-brick house-barn in North America. It is now a museum focusing on the early lifestyle of Russian and Polish Mennonites and their 1870s settlement in Kansas. The complex includes a replica 1876 Jacob Friesen windmill, the

original of which stood at the Gnadenau settlement. Admission charge. Call ahead, 620.947.3162.

Schaeffler House
(NRHP): 312 E. Grand. This Queen Anne home was built in 1909 by German Lutheran immigrants who founded the Schaeffler Mercantile Company. Tour charge. Call ahead, 620.947.3162.

Heritage Alcove at the Center for Mennonite Brethren Studies (Tabor College library): 400 S.
Jefferson. This little-known gem displays personal belongings brought with the Mennonite immigrants who settled Gnadenau. Of special interest (especially to Kansas wheat growers) might well be the original Turkey Red wheat seed that was stowed away in young Anna Barkman's trunk when she and her Mennonite family sailed from Crimea in 1874. You'll also see a trunk belonging to Abraham Schellenberg, Mennonite immigrant from Molotschna (South Russia) along with his various tools, several pieces of china, clothing, and other personal items. A prized

artifact is the prototype of a plow invented by Heinrich Sommerfeld. To fully appreciate this museum, ask for Peggy Goertzen when you arrive. Monday-Friday 9 a.m.-12 p.m. and 1:30-4 p.m. 620.947.3121, ext. 1211.

Gnadenau (Grace Meadow) Cemetery:
From D, 2 miles south on Ash (becomes Indigo). This is the burial ground for the Krimmer Mennonite Brethren, a group of Mennonites who came from Crimea in South Russia in 1874. The gravestones provide evidence of these families' origin, and a plaque provides background about them and their trip from South Russia.

Historic Mennonite Brethren Church:
Nighthawk and D (across from Tabor College). Built in 1893, the church is a typical example of a one-room meetinghouse, characterized by simplicity and a white exterior. It is believed to be the oldest existing Mennonite Brethren church building in the United States still used for worship.

Ebenfeld Mennonite Brethren Church:
1498 Kanza. From Lincoln, 1¾ miles east on D, then 4 miles south on Kanza. This three-story wooden structure is home to what is thought to be the first organized Mennonite Brethren congregation in North America. A nearby plaque summarizes its history. The 1926 Ebenfeld School stands across the road. 620.947.3704.

Norel Farms Bakery:
207 N. Main. Man cannot live by bread alone, but you may want to when you try Rachel's homemade wonders. Sprouted wheat, home-ground

flour, gluten-free, pumpernickel, and cinnamon raisin are just a few of the choices. But wait, there is more than bread! Muffins, cookies, pies, donuts, pizza crust, cinnamon rolls, bierocks, and homemade soup in season. All homemade for you to enjoy. Monday-Saturday 5:30 a.m.-4 p.m. 620.947.2343. norelfarms.com.

Lodging:
cityofhillsboro.net/lodging.html.

explorer extras...
In Hillsboro

Many folks drive many miles to buy the home-style German sausage at Dale's Supermarket, 108 W. Grand. 620.947.3501. FB.

Get this. For 30 years the building that now houses Odds 'N Ends Boutique, 209 S. Main, was the office of Drs. Eitzen and Ens. The Low German pronunciation of Eitzen is "Ahdz," so patients would joke about going to Drs. Ahdz and Ens, and that's how Odds 'N Ends got its name! Great story, and a great store with kitchenware, glassware, house decor, and gifts in every nook and cranny. Monday-Saturday 10 a.m.-5:30 p.m. 620.947.2361.

A replica Statue of Liberty, a 1950 Boy Scout project, stands in Memorial Park as does a veterans memorial. From Ash, 1 block west on D, then 1 block south on Memorial.

Since 1970 the famous Hillsboro Arts and Crafts Fair has been held the third Saturday of each September. Set in a six-block area of downtown, it draws more than 40,000 shoppers. **ee**

SC

explorer extras... In Lehigh

Population 169

At Prospect and Main, the concrete block building with a red-brick front and tin roof supposedly was a machine repair shop in the early 1900s. Note the 10 windows with arched window heads. Two mill

rocks used to grind wheat from 1898 to 1914 are displayed in City Park on Main. **ee**

LINCOLNVILLE

Population 195

Miniature Castles:

310 Kansas and from Main, ¼ mile south on U.S. 77. Small but tantalizing are two miniature rock castles made by Dr. John Wesley DeMand, a local physician. Constructed with limestone in the 1930s, they were built on top of old cellars, and at one time included glass in the windows and a light bulb inside. Drive by only.

Amelia Park Bridge

(NRHP): From Main, 3¼ miles south on U.S. 77/56, then ½ mile west on 260. The cast concrete balustrade with spindles adds an interesting touch to this 1914 reinforced concrete bridge over Clear Creek.

explorer extras... In Lost Springs

Population 68

At a roadside pullover an illustrated sign notes the location of Lost Spring (NRHP), a watering hole where travelers on the Santa Fe Trail stopped from 1821 to 1866. In 1859 Lost Spring Station, a hotel and tavern, was established. Nearby is a stone marker placed by the Old Settlers of Marion County in 1908. From Berry, 2½ miles west on Broadway (becomes 340).

At Smith and Broadway is a superb Santa Fe Trail marker erected in 1908 by the DAR. The inscription on the ornate bas relief brass plaque reads, "This marks the route of the Santa Fe Trail. Kansas City to Santa Fe 1822-1880."

The post office in Lost Springs is inside an old one-room schoolhouse at 125 Berry. Your purchase of stamps will help keep this inviting little PO open. Monday-Friday 1-5 p.m.; Saturday 12-1 p.m. 785.983.4813.

Al's Cafe, 101 Berry, has been serving great Mexican food since 1973 and draws customers from miles around. Ask for Al's special—a tostado on a soft flour shell. The

homemade refried beans are especially popular too. Wednesday-Saturday 11 a.m-8 p.m. 785.983.4827. FB. **ee**

MARION

Population 1,862

Central Park: Main and Elm. The centerpiece of this charming and historic park is the 1884 fountain and a wooded walking path along Luta Creek that offers a nice respite. In the park's southeast corner you'll find an 1860 historic spring, still running. Now beautifully landscaped, the spring once was a watering site for passing pioneers. Today the park's old-fashioned playground equipment provides good fun for children.

Marion County Courthouse (NRHP):

200 S. 3rd. The 1907 limestone Richardsonian Romanesque courthouse, enhanced by a prominent clock tower and entrance stone carvings, impressively occupies a full block square. Monday-Friday 8 a.m.-5 p.m. 620.382.2185.

Marion City Library:

101 Library. This red-brick, tile-roofed 1912 Santa Fe depot has been converted into a handsome library. One section is in the old freight room, and the ticket office is now the Kansas room, well stocked with Kansas books. 620.382.2442. FB.

Marion City Museum:
501 E. Main. The ornate wood ceiling and elaborate stained-glass windows inside this former 1887 church provide a fitting backdrop for the city's museum. Fine exhibits guide you through Marion's colorful past May-October, Thursday-Saturday 10 a.m.-4 p.m. 620.382.9134.

Bearly Makin' It Antiques:
308 Main and 1953 Sunflower. If two local couples have been buying, selling, and trading antiques and collectibles since 1994 it makes sense that their inventory has grown—a lot! In fact, they had to buy an old alfalfa mill on the edge of town to hold everything. Featured on the popular TV program *American Pickers*, the Ogdens and Maggards have quite a following. Call ahead to make sure the mill is open as the owners are often out picking. Saturday 10 a.m.-5 p.m. 620.382.6393 or 6311. bearlymakinitantiques.com.

Gallery 101 of the Flint Hills:
106 E. Main. In this very fine gallery you are surrounded by eclectic art representing a wide variety of mediums and subject matter by Kansas artists. Jan Davis is the owner and artist who keeps art alive through exhibits and classes. Tuesday-Friday 10 a.m.-5 p.m. and Saturday 10 a.m.-1 p.m. 620.382.7501. gallery101flinthills.com.

Trace Of Copper:
1216 Commercial (U.S. 56). The very fine brass and metal sculptures, primarily of rural Kansas subjects, are the work of Ern Hett's grandson Tracy. With these the family's metal sculpting tradition enters its third generation. Monday-Friday 8 a.m.-4 p.m.; Saturday 10 a.m.-12 p.m. 620.382.2099.

Historic Elgin Hotel: 115 N. 3rd. Now a boutique hotel, the Elgin was known as one of the most elegant hotels in Kansas. Constructed of limestone in 1886, it was built in the commercial palace style.

Marion Cemetery:
From E. Main, ½ mile north on Eisenhower. In the back of the cemetery is a nine-foot-tall limestone tree branch containing a scroll, hand, vine, and other artistic expressions. This unusual gravestone is for Judge Reuben Riggs (1810-1873) who died in a blizzard on the way to a buffalo hunt. The inscription tells us he was an honest judge and a poor man's friend.

CB Baked Goods:
420 E. Main. You can find the usual yummy baked goods—cinnamon rolls, sticky buns, cookies, and bierocks—and the unusual Bolsos, a bread pocket stuffed with various fillings such as pizza, ham and cheese, or a breakfast mix. The locals love 'em! Tuesday-Friday 8 a.m.-1:30 p.m. 620.381.0288.

The FamLee Bakery:
330 E. Main. Home-baked goodness inside this 1890 native limestone building include scones, muffins, cinnamon rolls, biscuits and gravy, soups, and deli sandwiches, all of which come highly recommended by Teresa Huffman, Kansas Explorer #3737. Tuesday-Friday 5:30 a.m.-2 p.m.; Saturday 5:30 a.m.-12 p.m. 620.381.2253.

Copper Shed: 1832 140. From Main, 5 miles south on 3rd (becomes Sunflower), then ¾ mile west on 140. The Copper Shed was founded by craftsman Ern Hett, and his family is continuing the tradition. Pieces created from copper, brass, other metals, old machinery parts, and antiques are on display and for sale. Kansas symbols, such as sunflowers, wheat, and the state

SC

seal, are favorites. Many one-of-a-kind antiques, primitives, and rustics help create an antique wonderland. Call ahead, 620.382.2041. FB.

Marion County Poor Farm:
1649 Old Mill. From 3rd, 4 miles west on Main (becomes 190), then 2¾ miles south on Old Mill. Cedars obscure the view of what was once an impressive limestone structure built by the

county in 1890. Residents worked the 160-acre farm to make it self-sufficient. It closed in the early 1960s. Drive by only.

Poor Farm Cemetery:

1649 Old Mill. A short distance north of the poor farm home, a gate leads to a small cemetery. Most of the short or flat gravestones, hidden among the grasses, have a first initial and last name. One flat stone simply says, "Negro Boy," but neither he nor some of the others buried here lived at the poor farm.

Marion County Park and Lake (NRHP): 1 Office.

From 3rd, 2 miles east on U.S. 256, then 1¾ miles south on Upland. From 1936 to 1939 Civilian Conservation Corps (CCC) camp workers built this lake, the stone bridge railings, stone arched bridge, picnic tables, and stone outbuildings. A bronze statue commemorates the 300 black WWI veterans who composed the CCC camp. Drive or bike around to the south side of the lake where a large sign announces that a Guinness world record was set here in March 2012 when 1,272 marshmallows were roasted simultaneously! 620.382.3240. marioncountyparkandlake.com.

Lodging: Historic Elgin

Hotel (NRHP, 620.382.3200, historicelginhotel.com); Country Dreams Bed & Breakfast (KBBA, 620.382.2250, country-dreamsbedandbreakfast.com).

explorer extras...
In Marion

Pick up visitor information including a brochure and map of the Marion County Auto Tour of Santa Fe Trail at the Marion County Economic Development Office, 230 E. Main.

Lovely historic homes are found in Marion at 202, 301, and 404 E. Santa Fe. A guide to more historic homes is at tinyurl.com/marionhomes.

Maybe it's the location or the simple rainbow arch design that makes it seem this bridge is floating above Clear Creek. It's definitely a head turner for those traveling east of town on U.S. 56.

The city hall, 203 N. 3rd, with striking art deco details was a 1938 WPA project. **ee**

PEABODY

Population 1,155

Peabody Downtown Historic District (NRHP):

Stroll down Walnut between 1st and Division and take a close look at these 1880s buildings,

most of them limestone. One particularly stunning structure is the 1919 former Berns-Sunflower Theatre (NRHP) at 114 N. Walnut. Note the sunflowers and the beautiful terra cotta and clay tile, typical features of the Beaux Arts style.

Peabody Museum (NRHP):

106 E. Division. A gift from F.H. Peabody, Santa Fe railroad vice president, this former 1874 library was the first free public library in Kansas. Now a museum, its treasures include a doll collection and Victorian-style dollhouse, the early-1900s popcorn popper from the Sunflower Theatre, and photos of the famous trotting horse races and Chautauquas that

took place in City Park at the turn of the century. Call ahead, 620.983.2512.

Morgan House (NRHP):

212 N. Walnut. This 1881 Queen Anne home was the residence of W.H. Morgan, longtime editor of the Peabody Gazette. An 1886 fountain stands outside. Call ahead, 620.983.2512.

Peabody Printing

Museum: Next to the Morgan House. A tour of the 1870s-1920s printing equipment helps visitors appreciate the full spectrum of the industry's evolution. Call ahead, 620.983.2512.

Carnegie Library (NRHP):

214 N. Walnut. Still operating as a biblioteque, the 1914 Neoclassical building retains its original woodwork and the marble-tile entry. Tuesday 9 a.m.-12 p.m. and 2-8 p.m.; Wednesday-Friday 2-5 p.m.; Saturday 9 a.m.-12 p.m. 620.983.2052. peabody.lib.nckls.org.

Flint Hills Gypsies:

111 N. Walnut. Vintage wallpaper borders, doorknobs, a bejeweled guitar (minus the strings), brooches, vintage clothing, hats, Pinterest-type items, and regular antiques tease your imagination in this long, narrow historic building (NRHP). Owner Morgan Marler loves to treasure hunt so his customers, and gypsies, can find their treasures right here. Friday 12-5 p.m.; Saturday 10 a.m.-5 p.m.; Sunday 1-5 p.m. 620.947.1606. FB.

Mennonite Centennial Memorial: 1st and Walnut.

Plaques on a limestone obelisk pay tribute to the Mennonite immigration to the Peabody area starting in 1874. From this point, many immigrants formed settlements around Hillsboro.

State Bank Park: 200 block of N. Walnut. The Peabody Opera House, which once stood on this site, is where early-1900s orphan train children gathered and waited for their new families to claim them. Now a pocket park, it contains reminders of the past such as steps from the First Presbyterian Church and the stately clock that once stood in front of the Stroud jewelry store.

WWII POW Camp: 122 W. 2nd. Known as the Eyestone Building (NRHP), it housed the Nusbaum Eyestone Ford Agency in the 1920s on the first floor with the Motor Inn Hotel on the second. But during WWII, POWs were housed here. If you stand at just the right spot west of Vine on 2nd you can still see one of the guard towers.

Peabody City Park (NRHP): W. 2nd and Locust. The drive around the park is on a former trotting horse race track. The Kansas State Fair was held here in 1885 as were Chautauquas from 1907 to 1920. The octagonal floral exhibition hall dates prior to the state fair. WPA-era projects include the athletic stadium, picnic tables, grills, benches, and plantings. The swimming pool, playground equipment, and disc golf are from modern times.

Prairie Lawn Cemetery: From Walnut, ½ mile east on 9th, then ½ mile north on Cemetery. This beautiful rural setting is the final resting place for more than 140 Civil War Union veterans. It's unusual to see a red-brick street out in the country, but you'll find it on your way to the cemetery. It was part of Old Old U.S. 50.

Stone Barn: From Maple, 3½ miles east on U.S. 50. The large three-story limestone barn was built in 1887 by T.B. Townsend, a wealthy contractor from Ohio. He never lived here, but an overseer ran his diverse farming operation.

Coneburg Inn: 904 N. Peabody. "EAT" spelled out in large letters on the metal building lets you know you've arrived at the Coneburg Inn, the home of good food and good times. A scratch kitchen, full bar, monthly live music, karaoke, and the famous fried pickles make a trip to Lindsey Marshall's "burg" a great idea. Tuesday-Saturday 12-9 p.m.; Sunday 8 a.m.-8 p.m. 620.983.2010. FB.

Pop's Diner: 128 N. Walnut. The Garbage—and it's finger-lickin' good—is a popular breakfast of hash browns, onions, green peppers, tomatoes, ham, and an egg on top if you want it. Burgers are the mainstay for lunch at this comfort food diner. Monday-Saturday 6 a.m.-2 p.m. 620.983.2307.

Lodging: Prescott House Bed and Breakfast (KBBA, 316.215.1864, kbba.com).

explorer extras... In Peabody

Since the 1960s the Peabody Sausage House, 109 W. 9th, has been a favorite stop for the secret-recipe pork sausage. Monday-Friday 8 a.m.-12 p.m. and 1-5 p.m.; Saturday 9 a.m.-12 p.m. 620.983.2160. **ee**

Unincorporated

Tiny Pilsen was settled as a Czech community around 1874. If you read A Shepherd in Combat Boots before coming to this town it will add meaning to your visit.

St. John Nepomucene Church: 275 and Remington. Father Emil J. Kapaun, who has been nominated for sainthood, held his first Mass in this 1915 red-brick and limestone Gothic structure. The exterior is accented with a red-tile roof and copper shingles. The interior was renovated in 2002, and the bas-relief Stations of the Cross and stained-glass windows are breathtaking. Daily 9 a.m.-5 p.m. 620.382.3369.

SC

Chaplain Kapaun Statue: Southwest of the church. Father Kapaun (8 Wonders of Kansas People) served as a chaplain in the Korean War, and this inspirational bronze statue depicts him aiding a wounded soldier. Kapaun was captured by the communists in 1950, and while in captivity his unselfish courage and his ministry endeared him to his fellow prisoners of war. tinyurl.com/father-kapaun.

Father Kapaun Museum:

Rectory south of the church. The museum preserves the memory of Father Kapaun with a collection that includes his vestments, military foot locker and some of its contents, and other artifacts. Safely stored in the museum vault is the Medal of Honor that Kapaun received posthumously from President Obama in 2013. Tuesday, Friday 1-4 p.m. 620.382.3369. tinyurl.com/hfpmc-kapaun.

Father Kapaun Memorial:

Cemetery behind the church. At the base of the large cross stands a small memorial stone to Father Kapaun, who died in 1951 while in captivity. He was buried in a Korean POW camp.

explorer extras...
In Tampa

Population 108

Concerned citizens raised money to open this much needed grocery store—the community-owned Tampa Trail Stop at 319 Main. It's run by volunteers, who appreciate business from the locals as well as from Kansas explorers! Monday-Friday 10 a.m.-1 p.m. and 4-7 p.m.; Saturday 10 a.m.-1 p.m. 785.965.7254. FB.

Hungry from your day on the trail? Or need a hearty start to your exploring adventures? The Santa Fe Trail Cafe, 303 Main, provides a filling breakfast or chicken-fried steak, chicken-fried chicken, and burgers. Monday 11 a.m.-2 p.m.; Tuesday-Friday 7-9:30 a.m. and 11 a.m.-2 p.m.; Saturday 5-8 p.m.; Sunday 11 a.m.-2 p.m. 785.965.2054. FB.

Noting the route of the Santa Fe Trail through this area, a stone marker was placed at 330 and Limestone in 1914. Across the road a trail "Crosses Here" sign is posted near where wagon ruts are still visible on the south side of Tampa Cemetery. **ee**

McPherson County

AROUND THE COUNTY

Olive Springs Schoolhouse Gallery:

From I-135 exit 72, 7½ miles east on Smoky Valley, then just north on 24. The 1885 one-room Olive Springs school, on its original location, is the home gallery of artist Maleta Forsberg, well known for her watercolor, oil, and acrylic paintings of landscapes and animal, bird, and floral scenes. Call ahead, 785.254.7833.

CANTON

Population 764

Prairie Trail Scenic Byway:

U.S. 56 and 27th. Canton is the southeast end of this 80-mile byway that ends at Mushroom Rock State Park (*see* p. 60) in Ellsworth County. From the buffalo tram ride at Maxwell Wildlife Refuge in Canton to the "castle" at Coronado Heights, the Swedish village of Lindsborg, and the western history in Ellsworth, this is a charming route through the mixed-grass prairie. travelks.com/ksbyways. 785.227.2549.

Oil Boom: Canton became a city in 1880 thanks to the coming of the Santa Fe railway. In the 1920s the area experienced an economic boom when "black gold" was discovered and oil derricks sprang up across the prairie. Today working and abandoned pump jacks dot the landscape, and oil-field equipment lies along U.S. 56 just west of town and at the north end of Main—all reminders of Canton's connection to the industry. One of the last steel derricks marks the entrance to the McPherson County Fairgrounds (from Railroad, ½ mile north on Main).

Hot and Cold Water

Towers: 4th and Railroad. In 1956 Claudia Fisher thought it would make for a good tourist attraction if the two side-by-side water towers were labeled Hot and Cold. Her prognostication proved correct!

Last of the Carnegies:

203 N. Main. Designed by Kansas architect George P. Washburn, the 1921 Canton Township Carnegie Library (NRHP) is the last Carnegie library built in Kansas. A unique element on the building is the book return slot—a miniature door (complete with a doorknob) under the windows at the entrance. Open the door and return your book! It's not clear whether the book return was part of the original design, but we're sure you've never seen one like it before. Tuesday-Thursday, Saturday afternoon. 620.628.4349.

Three Sisters Victorian Tea and Treasures:

105 N. Main. Vintage, antique, and repurposed treasures abound. Reservations required for tea time and evening meals. Tuesday-Saturday 10 a.m.-4 p.m. 620.628.4484. FB.

Stars and Stripes Military

Museum: 104 W. Allen. Guide Cheryl Everhart tells compelling stories about items on display here, such as the letter of condolence from President Kennedy to the parents of the first Kansan killed in Vietnam, William Joe Everhart. Learn about women's roles in the military, see a Fort Riley camouflaged Bible, and hear more about local war heroes. Call ahead, 620.628.4484.

Historic Jail: 106 W. Allen. Once called Canton Prison, the strap-iron jail was built in 1883. To see it, inquire at Three Sisters. 620.628.4484.

Soda N' Suds: 116 N. Main. A 1930s soda fountain is now inside a former laundromat, thus the Suds! On random days either Explorer Way chicken-fried steak or homemade bierocks is the daily special, but Thursdays are pan-fried chicken with pan gravy day! Tuesday-Friday 11 a.m.-6 p.m; Saturday 11 a.m.-2 p.m. 620.350.8006.

Maxwell Wildlife Refuge (8 Wonders of Kansas Geography): 2565 Pueblo. From Railroad, 6½ miles north on Main (becomes 27), then 1¼ miles west on Pueblo. Maxwell Wildlife Refuge is a beautiful mixed-grass prairie home to herds of 160 buffalo and 70 elk. Pueblo is an open range public road through the refuge, and for a two-mile stretch (from the first cattle guard on Pueblo to Battle Hill) you may find buffalo in your path. For an unobstructed panoramic view of the Smoky Hills prairie, climb to the top of the observation tower just west of the visitor center gate. Tram rides take you into the pastures where you'll almost always see buffalo (elk appear more often in the winter), and in season the wildflowers and grasses are abundant in their glory. Tuesday,

Thursday, Saturday. Tour charge. Reservations required. 620.628.4455. maxwellwildliferefuge.com.

Edgar Miller Grave: From Main, 2 miles east on U.S. 56, ½ mile north on 29, then ¼ mile east on a field driveway to Jones (Fairview) Cemetery. The story is that in 1864, during a summer of unrest on the Plains, 18-year-old Ed Miller rode horseback to find medical help for a woman in Marion. On his way home he was killed by Indians close to this location where he is buried. A small granite stone near a DAR marker indicates his grave. Others were later buried here as well, thus creating a cemetery. 620.628.4993.

explorer extras... In Canton

At the McPherson and Marion county line 3 miles east of Canton on U.S. 56, a map engraved on a large natural stone marks where the Chisholm Trail intersected with the Santa Fe Trail. **ee**

CONWAY

Unincorporated

White Over Bends: From Conway, 1 mile east or west on U.S. 56. This area has been developed through the years as an underground refined petroleum storage facility. These facilities can be identified by the organized array of short white pipes (pipeline over bends) on the surface. Petroleum products are transported through miles of underground pipelines throughout the state, then directed to the over bends, which create space for products to be stored below the surface in salt caverns. These salt caverns house many refined products such as gasoline, diesel, propane, and butane.

Fractionation and Storage: From Conway, 2½ miles west on U.S. 56. The tall towers in this area are a fractionation (a separation process in which a mixture, in this case natural gas liquids, is divided into smaller quantities) and storage facility owned by Williams Mid-Continent. The process here is to further refine fractionate products and offer a purer product to end users.

ELYRIA

Unincorporated

Kaw Indian Peace Treaty Site: From Comanche, ¼ mile southeast on Old U.S. 81. A historical marker summarizes the 1825 treaty between the U.S. government and American Indian tribes to ensure peaceful relations for travelers on the Santa Fe Trail.

Brookscape Gardens: 799 Old U.S. 81. Once you find your way here you'll love the charming country environment created by Michael and Arlene Daniel. Plants hang in buckets from the silo, the old garage is now the retail store, the former dairy barn is the office, and a beautiful wooden pergola with a stone patio is your entrance to it all. What a delightful setting to buy plants, garden supplies, equipment, and decor. March-December, Monday-Friday 10 a.m.-6 p.m. and Saturday 9 a.m.-4 p.m. 620.241.7433. FB.

GALVA

Population 905

Galva Historical Museum: 204 S. Main. Volunteers have created clever exhibits such as the local farm truck timeline from the 1920s to the present. Learn more about the Santa Fe Trail history in this area, and in the school display section don't miss seeing the football

SC

helmet that "crowned" the 1948 homecoming queen. First Sunday 2-4 p.m.; second Saturday 10 a.m.-12 p.m.; third Thursday 7-9 p.m. Call ahead, 620.245.7677.

Rendezvous Coffee Company: 305 E. U.S. 56. The small-batch roasted coffee ensures a cup full of flavor every time. Smoothies and locally baked goods will also help start your morning right. Monday-Saturday 6 a.m.-4 p.m. 620.654.3697. FB.

Tin Roof Pantry: 1315 21. About a mile south of town you'll find Nancy Becker hard at work preparing delicious pastries, baked goods, frozen meals, and bulk foods for you to take home to your pantry. Monday-Friday 8 a.m.-5 p.m.; Saturday 9 a.m.-12 p.m. 620.654.3721.

Hungry Mann's Cafe: 220 E. U.S. 56. You know it's special when the cars are parked two deep. If you've never had corn-bread and sausage gravy for breakfast, you can have it here! Mann's makes its own sausage in-house, and the pancakes are served with a homemade secret-recipe syrup. Burgers, sandwiches, and salads are available daily, but watch out on Wednesdays when the locals line up for the fried chicken buffet and on Fridays when it's all about the Explorer Way chicken-fried steak. Monday-Friday 6 a.m.-2 p.m.; Friday 4:30-8 p.m.; Saturday 6-11 a.m. 620.654.3500. FB.

Empire and Trails: From Main, 1 mile east on U.S. 56, then 2 miles south on 22.

Now a quiet area in the country, it was once a bustling spot with covered wagons traveling on the Santa Fe Trail and stopping at nearby Fuller's Ranch (1855) for rest, water, and food. In 1871 Joseph Colby built the first permanent residence that started the town of Empire. In 1879 the railroad missed the town, and the buildings and people moved north to a railroad campsite that became Galva. A marker at this site mentions Fuller's Ranch, the town of Empire, and the Santa Fe Trail. An illustrated sign describes the Crossing of the Running Turkey Creek and the Cherokee Trail (gold seeker trail) meeting up with the Santa Fe Trail here. Brown signs mark where the Cherokee Trail crossed Iron Horse just east of 22.

Empire Cemetery: From Main, 1 mile east on U.S. 56, then 2½ miles south on 22. One of the most beautiful and well-kept cemeteries in the state, it had its beginnings serving the short-lived nearby town of Empire.

explorer extras... In Galva

If it's hot outdoors, cool off at KD's Tropical Sno Shack, a nifty little spot at 115 S. Main where sno kones come in fun flavors, for example KC Chief, Wild Cat, Jayhawk, and Wicked Witch. 620.241.1379. FB.

From 1st, go 1 block north on McPherson to walk the still-in-progress Sunflower Santa Fe Trail. From McPherson it's open

1 mile to the east or west and parallels an active Union Pacific rail line. **ee**

Population 1,391

Stan Herd Mural: 113 S. Main. On a building wall south of the Prairie State Bank, a 1986 Stan Herd mural depicts Inman around 1910. Some of the structures he included are still standing—the depot, the faded-red mill, and the corner limestone building, formerly an Oddfellows lodge. For fun, pull up to the bank's drive-through window and tell them you're just there to look at the mural.

Inman Museum: 101 Main. A continued work in progress, this museum has a lot of life! Inman in the late-1800s is presented in exhibits filled with artifacts from businesses, from the wheelwright to the mercantile. Also inside is a small replica of the last-standing adobe German Russian church in America. Outside, an 1880s-1920s farmstead includes a house, summer kitchen, barn, and brooder house. The museum complex is also comprised of an 1887 Rock Island depot and a 1909 telephone office. Sunday 1:30-4 p.m. Donation requested. 620.585.6659. inmanmuseum.com.

Historic Flour Mill: Gordon and Spruce. Although faded and abandoned, the 1908 Enns Mill was once one of finest and produced Best Flour and Dixie Lilly. Few small-town mills still operate and this one ceased operation in 2001.

Cornerstone Market:
217 S. Main. Like so many small grocery stores, this store operates for the community good. You'll find such specialties here as the homemade German smoked sausage and the locally produced Knackies Bear-B-Cue sauce. Owners Saundra, Beth, and Mark Goertz believe in their motto: "Love where you live, shop local." Monday-Friday 7:30 a.m.-7 p.m.; 8 a.m.-5 p.m. 620.585.6950. cornerstoneinman.com.

The Country Store:
104 Ranch Land. From Main, continue just north across the tracks and Old K-61. A iron cutout of the store name and a small sewing machine image lets you know you've arrived. Inside the metal building you'll find 72-inch tablecloth fabric, buttons that match fabrics, zippers, baby burp towels, head coverings, and other hard-to-find items. Monday-Friday 9:30 a.m.-5 p.m.; Saturday 9:30 a.m.-12 p.m. 620.585.6601.

Neufeldt Variety:
114 S. Main. When you open the door of this historic building, you'll enter a charming store where you can feel good about shopping locally. Variety is the

right name to describe what you'll find—jewelry, plush toys, greeting cards, Russell Stover candy, home decor, a large selection of jigsaw puzzles, gift items, books, and more. Monday-Friday 9 a.m.-5 p.m.; Saturday 9 a.m.-2 p.m. 620.585.2293.

Inman Harvest Cafe:
112 S. Main. Goulash for breakfast? It's made with hash browns, onions, scrambled eggs, sausage, and cheddar cheese, and it's a big seller! But so is the hot roast beef sandwich with beef slow-cooked for 12 hours. Verenika Day (Thursdays) features traditional Russian Mennonite verenika, German sausage, gravy, zwieback, cherry moos, and more. As owner Katy says, "This is who we are... on a plate!" Fried Chicken Fridays and an accompanying buffet produce yet another bountiful harvest for any customer—and we haven't even talked about the pies yet! Tuesday-Wednesday, Saturday 6 a.m.-2 p.m.; Thursday-Friday 6 a.m.-8 p.m. 620.585.6925. FB.

Jim's Appliance:
103 S. Main. If you're looking for friendly hometown service for every kind of appliance—and any color of stand mixer under the sun—this is the shop to visit. Monday-Friday 8 a.m.-5:30 p.m.; Saturday 8 a.m.-4 p.m. 620.585.6422. jimsappliancesofinman.com.

Main Street Pizza:
100 S. Main. Try the chicken ranch or German pie (Canadian bacon and sauerkraut) pizza at this popular local eatery. Pasta, burgers, sandwiches,

and dessert pizza with cream cheese, chocolate chips, streusel, and frosting will make your sweet tooth's pizza dream come true. Daily 11a.m.-1:30 p.m. and 5-8 p.m. 620.585.2188. FB.

Lake Inman:
11 and Cheyenne. From Main, 3 miles east on Center (becomes Cherokee), then ¾ miles north on 11. It's the largest natural lake in the state—a half-mile-wide circular sinkhole. In the late 1860s when Major Henry Inman made the trek on the Fort Harker Trail from present Kanopolis to Wichita he camped at this body of water. Because in his reports he often referred to the lake, it became known as Lake Inman.

Blaze Fork Drainage System:
Buckskin and 10. This unique network of drainage channels was excavated to drain the original lakes and marshes west of McPherson and east of Inman. In 1916 Mennonite farmer John Schrag converted a 2,000-acre lake between McPherson and Conway into farmland by making a 15-foot-wide cut through a ridge to lead the water into the Blaze Fork Valley. Resulting floods in the Blaze Fork watershed instigated a domino response of channelization and additional drainage projects in the lower areas of the valley. This network of ditches and laterals is still in operation today, although some of the more flood-prone land has been developed into the McPherson Wetlands. A half mile east of 10 and Buckskin a bridge crosses the channelized Blaze Fork with laterals on either side of it leading into the main Big Ditch. 620.241.7669.

SC

Sinkholes: Oil exploration in the 1930s initiated these sinkholes scattered throughout the area. Seven sinkholes ranging in size from 1 to 10 acres and up to 15 feet deep can be seen at road intersections. The largest is four miles north of Inman on 8, and the first and still growing sinkhole is at 10 and Arrowhead. Local legend has it that Sinkhole Sam, a mysterious creature also known as Foopengerkle, lives in the sinkhole at 10 and Arrowhead.

Lodging: Serendipity Guest Cottage Bed & Breakfast (620.242.3026, FB); The Barn at Harlin and Laurie's (620.960.3860).

**explorer extras...
In Inman**

The handsome limestone building (NRHP) at 100 N. Main was built in 1893 as the Oddfellows lodge. One of the first buildings in Inman, it was used as a meeting hall for social groups and nearly a dozen organizations. It was remodeled in 1991 to become the area library.

At 113 S. Main, the small engraved stone west of the Stan Herd mural marks the final resting place of Inman Sam (1976-1990), the town cat who worked at the grain elevator and slept in nearly every downtown business. **ee**

LINDSBORG

Population 3,481

Wild Dala Horses

(8 Wonders of Kansas Customs): In Sweden, 18th-century lumberjacks carved small Dala horses in their off hours at their logging camps. When they returned home, they passed them out to village children. During the 19th century it became customary to paint these wooden horses. Fast forward to the Wild Dala

Horses of the Swedish town of Lindsborg. They're amazingly colorful, they're fun, and they're all over town—more than thirty of these four-foot-tall painted, wooden horses adorn the street corners of downtown. Cleverly designed and created by local artists, the horses have names like Hello, Dala!; Fala the Dala Brick Road; and Dalallama Telecomma. Pick up a brochure at the Travel Information Center, 118 N. Main, so you can fala the Dala tour around town.

Downtown: In a delightful two-block stretch, the brick streets and an eclectic mix of galleries, independently owned eateries, a wine tasting room, and specialty shops make it a special treat to spend the day in Little Sweden, the nickname given to this Swedish-settled town. Below are some highlights, but so much more awaits your discovery. visitlindsborg.com.

Hemslöjd (8 Wonders of Kansas Commerce): 201 N. Main. Traditional Swedish Dala horse signs are made here, and on many days you can watch a wood craftsman and artist Shirley Malm create them. Shirley painted many of the Wild Dala horses placed around town, and she's happy to answer any questions you may have about

these dazzling creatures or Swedish Folk Art. Dala horses and Scandinavian gifts are also for sale at Hemslöjd, which, by the way, is Swedish for "handicrafts." Monday-Saturday 8 a.m.-5:30 p.m.; Sunday 12-5 p.m. 785.227.2053. hemslojd.com.

Connected–A Fair Trade Store: 131 N. Main. It's the most lavishly stocked fair-trade store in Kansas. But what is fair trade? The Connected website tells us, "We, as fair traders, are committed to giving economically and socially marginalized people a market for their goods that pays them up front and fairly." You'll feel good about shopping here! Monday-Saturday 10 a.m.-6 p.m.; Sunday 12:30-5 p.m. 785.212.1801. connectedfairtrade.com.

Tröllslända Toy Store: 112 N. Main. This dragonfly (as tröllslända means) carries you to Scandinavian and European stores renowned for classic toys. And on the shelves, tin robots, stuffed animals, and so much more wait for you to carry them home! Science and creative games are in abundance here too. Monday, Wednesday-Saturday 10 a.m.-5:30 p.m.; Sunday 12-4 p.m. 785.212.1492. trollslandatoystore.com.

Rendezvous Adventure Outfitters: 113 N. Main. Whether you want to gear up for Kansas exploring or need more serious outfitting for international outdoor adventures, make your first rendezvous at this new store. Besides gear, it provides guided hikes in central Kansas.

Monday-Saturday 10 a.m.-5 p.m. 785.227.9810. rendezvous-adventureoutfitters.com.

Old Mill Museum Complex:

120 Mill. The standout feature is the Smoky Valley Roller Mill (NRHP), a grand three-story brick structure with polished wood chutes, belts, levers, wheels, augers, sifters, and bins—the only things missing are the noise and grain dust flying. Built in 1898, it is the best-restored mill in the state and rests on its original site along the Smoky Hill River. Within the museum complex the Swedish Pavilion (NRHP), prefabricated in Sweden as a Swedish exhibit building for the 1904 St. Louis World's Fair, serves as the anchor

for a collection of early settlement buildings. Museum exhibits relate the county history including the impact of the Swedish and Mennonite immigrants on local culture. Monday-Saturday 9 a.m.-5 p.m. Admission charge. 785.227.3595. oldmillmuseum.org.

Small World Gallery: 127 N. Main. Between the pressed-tin ceiling and the polished wood floors, the walls are filled with the beautiful photography of Jim Richardson, a *National Geographic* photographer. Works of local artists also are displayed as is the handcrafted jewelry of Kathy Richardson and Briana Zimmerling. Monday-Thursday 10 a.m.-5 p.m.; Friday-

Saturday 10 a.m.-7 p.m.; Sunday 11 a.m.- 4 p.m. 785.227.4442. smallworldgallery.net.

Chestnut Studios: 118 S. Main. An exquisite historically restored interior and delightful merchandising make this artist cooperative a place to appreciate independent artists and makers. Monday-Saturday 10 a.m.-5 p.m. 620.755.5338. FB.

Birger Sandzen Memorial Gallery (8 Wonders of Kansas Art): 401 N. 1st.

Birger Sandzen (1871-1954) was a Swedish immigrant who studied with great European artists to become a prolific American oil painter. His legacy is recognized in contemporary art museums and collections worldwide. Sandzen's beautiful landscapes are readily recognizable by their thick pastel brushstrokes on wall-sized canvasses. Tuesday-Saturday 10 a.m.-5 p.m.; Sunday 1-5 p.m. 785.227.2220. sandzen.org.

Lester Raymer's Red Barn Studio Museum: 212 S.

Main. Even the walk on the red-brick path to this fairy-tale looking barn is enchanting. The Red Barn Craft Studio (NRHP) is a Raymer work of art in itself. The working studio of the late Lester Raymer, an internationally known artist, the

Red Barn now holds exhibits of his paintings, printmaking, ceramics, carvings, and metalworks but also displays some of the handcrafted toys he made each year for his wife. The most famous of his art is the sun quilt. Stitch by colorful stitch, it became a Raymer masterpiece incorporating 16 different sun faces and four corner sunbursts. The quilt can occasionally be glimpsed on the CBS program *Sunday Morning.* Tuesday-Friday 10 a.m.-5 p.m.; Saturday-Sunday 1-5 p.m. Donation welcome. 785.227.2217. lesterraymer.org.

Post Office Mural (NRHP):

125 E. Lincoln. *Smoky River* is the title of this 1938 Section artwork by famous Lindsborg artist Birger Sandzen. The landscape scene depicts the tree-lined Smoky Hill River and, in the background, two farms tucked into green fields under a sky of billowy clouds.

Courtyard Gallery:

125 N. Main. Immerse yourself in a two-level smorgasbord of Midwest art with an emphasis on Kansas artists. Monday-Saturday 10 a.m.-5 p.m. 785.227.3007. courtyardgallery.com.

Courtyard Bakery: 125 N. Main. Stroll a brick passageway back to the airy courtyard bakery. Natural light streams from the atrium across a vast mural of an outdoor gazebo scene by oil painter Maleta Forsberg. In these pleasant surroundings, make your

SC

selection from house-baked cookies, cinnamon rolls, almond flavored kringlor bars, and more at this self-serve bakery where you pay on the honor system. Monday-Saturday 9 a.m.-5 p.m. 785.227.3007.

Blacksmith Coffee Shop and Roastery: 122 N. Main. Sweden is one of the top coffee-drinking countries in the world so it seems natural that an artisan micro-roaster would be here in Little Sweden. The coffee making that happens here is steeped in tradition as deep as the history of the Holmberg and Johnson Blacksmith & Wagon Shop (NRHP) in which this coffee shop is located. At this 1900 building, countless homesteaders and cowboys had their horses shod and wagon wheels fixed. Now, quite a different (and more pleasing!) aroma emerges from the brick chimney, one that lures in customers to try exotic, single-origin Arabica bean coffees. A light breakfast and lunch menu includes house-made pastries, espressos, pour-over coffee, and teas. Monday-Saturday 6 a.m.-6 p.m. 785.212.6077. blacksmithcoffee.com.

The White Peacock Tea and Coffee Company: 124 S. Main. Gourmet fair-trade coffees, teas, healthy foods, tasty pastries, gluten-free treats, and chocolates entice you to relax awhile in a warm, bohemian environment, or take in the fresh air on the secluded pergola courtyard behind the building. Monday-Friday 7:30 a.m.-6 p.m.; Saturday-Sunday 9 a.m.-6 p.m. 785.212.6108. whitepeacockcoffee.com.

The Swedish Crown: 121 N. Main. Swedish flavors come to life under the care of Chef Shana Everhart in this iconic restaurant that has been a favorite of many for more than 40 years. Start your

meal with the Smoked Salmon Plate (capers, dill cream, and rye crisp bread), and for your entree try the Swedish Dinner, a sampling of potato sausage, Swedish meatballs, and dill potatoes. Complete your meal with a lingonberry sundae or ostkaka (a type of cheese cake) with lingonberries. Tastefully prepared American dishes are served too, some with a Swedish twist. Tuesday-Saturday 9 a.m.-9 p.m.; Sunday 9 a.m.-3 p.m. 785.227.8422. theswedishcrown.com.

Öl Stuga: 119 S. Main. In this iconic ale house you'll find the locals hanging out, having a brew, or enjoying one of their favorite deli sandwiches such as the German sausage or the Brent Nelson, made with smoky cheesy sausage. Monday 4-11 p.m.; Tuesday-Saturday 11 a.m.-11 p.m. 785.227.8762. FB.

Farley's Bar and Grill: 101 N. Main. Here you'll find classic and upscale pub food and (in this Swedish town) a few dishes with an Irish twist. Inside a historic bank building, Farley's has updated with contemporary renovations including sports programming on large screens. Sidewalk dining is enjoyed by families, cyclists, and motorcyclists. Daily 11 a.m.-9 p.m. 785.212.6030. FB.

Swedish Country Inn: 112 W. Lincoln. Guests or drop-in visitors are welcome to partake in a typical and well-presented Swedish breakfast. Come hungry! Breakfast offers Swedish meatballs, lingonberries, eggs, porridge, cheese, pickled

herring, fruit, waffles with lingonberry syrup, rye bread, and more! The cuisine is as delightful as the lovely Country Inn itself. Daily 7-10 a.m. 785.227.2181. swedishcountryinn.com.

Coronado Heights (NRHP; 8 Wonders of Kansas Geography): From Main, ½ mile west on Lincoln, 2½ miles north on 13, 1 mile west on Winchester, then north up a winding road. Standing high on a hill, Coronado Heights was created by the WPA in 1936 as a picnic and campground area and has been a favorite cross-country stop ever since. It was named for the Spanish explorer Francisco Vásquez de Coronado who supposedly came through this area in 1541 in search of gold. The remaining Dakota sandstone structures here are oddly unique and range from picnic tables and a fireplace to the famous "castle." Equally impressive is the 360-degree view of the Smoky Valley—square mile after square mile of cropland. Go to the castle roof for this top-of-the-world experience! The Heights is marvelous for kite flying, picnicking, or practicing yoga at sunrise. lindsborghistory.org.

Lodging: Seasons of the Fox, A Bed and Breakfast (KBBA, 785.227.2549, seasonsofthefox.com); Swedish Country Inn (785.227.2985, swedishcountryinn.com);

Trädhuset and Vetehuset (855.872.3487, lindsborgvacationrentals.com); additional lodging (tinyurl.com/lindlodging).

explorer extras... In Lindsborg

A full-service independent grocery, Scott's Hometown Foods, 215 N. Harrison, makes its own Scandinavian foods from old recipes—potato sausage, cheeses, rye bread, and more. Come to the deli case to assemble a Coronado Heights picnic. Monday-Saturday 7 a.m.-9 p.m.; Sunday 11 a.m.-6 p.m. 785.227.2296. scottshometownfoods.com.

The striking 1874 Bethany Lutheran Church, 320 N. Main, is characteristic of Swedish churches. The gleaming white exterior and tall steeple are picture perfect against a blue Kansas sky.

Rent a quadricycle, made for two to six riders, at the Hemslöjd, 201 N. Main, and pedal yourself around this splendid town. Or bring your own bicycle or walk the two-and-a-half-mile sidewalk Valkommen Trail that follows an old rail bed. The trail incorporates a historic railroad bridge over the Smoky Hill River at the south end of the route (tinyurl.com/valkommenbike). More fun includes a game of chess on an outdoor board (bring your own chess pieces) at Viking Valley

Playground in Swensson Park, and a trip down Thor's Revenge water slide at the swimming pool, 520 S. 1st. 785.227.8687.

Swensson Park at Swensson and Main is home to the new Viking Valley playground, the 1936 WPA memorial band shell, and many vestiges of the past.

We doubt you'd like to live and raise your family in a 6x12-foot dugout for six years like early Swedish pioneer Gustaf Hoglund did from 1868 to 1875. Legend has it that the family used its wagon for the roof. Later Gustaf and his wife, Maria, built a frame house over their underground nest and used the dugout for the cellar. The dugout is still visible. From Main, 1½ miles west on Swensson, then ¼ mile south on 12. tinyurl.com/hoglunddugout.

A statue of Carl Aaron Swensson, founder of Bethany College in 1881, stands on a large limestone base on 1st, just north of Olsson. Carl's wife, Alma, was a founder of Bethany's Messiah Festival in which a large chorus and orchestra have performed Handel's masterwork for more than 130 years.

Captive Rock is caged outside the Old Mill Museum Complex, 120 Mill. Found during road construction in the 1960s, the rock exhibits markings that are probably the work of pioneer children instead of being Indian petroglyphs as was once speculated.

If you'd like a break from self-serve at the gas pump, stop at Petersen Oil at 300 S. Cole. Leroy Petersen or his crew will come to you, fill 'er up,

check the oil, and wash your windshield. He's been serving customers since 1964. **ee**

MARQUETTE

Population 643

Kansas Motorcycle Museum: 120 N. Washington. First you'll marvel at the more than 100 motorcycles from

eras past and present. But it's the historical photos and posters that capture the vigor and living-on-the-edge tension of motorcycle racing. Whether you're a biker, racer, pleasure rider, or none of the above, you'll enjoy learning about this culture. Even the motorcycle workshop will rev your engines! The museum is centered around the six-decade career of Marquette's racing legend Stan Engdahl. Dedicated volunteers help keep this intriguing museum operating. Monday-Saturday 10 a.m.-5 p.m.; Sunday 1-5 p.m. 785.546.2449. ksmotorcyclemuseum.org.

Museum Complex: 202 N. Washington. The pillared facade of the Marquette Museum was built in 1910 to house the Luther League, a young people's organization. Today this facility is preserving the story of this Swedish town, founded by immigrants in 1869. The complex also includes Range School, a 1906 one-room country school, and the 1916 Missouri Pacific depot from Falun. Call ahead, 785.546.2292.

SC

Opera House Block:

100 block of Washington. A colorful mural announces the Opera House Block, and a metal plaque on the long corner building informs us that it was the first brick building in Marquette (1887). The old opera house occupied the back half of the second story.

ArtSpace Gallery and Studios:

115 N. Washington. Looking for fanciful, contemporary American art? Artist and owner Rich Thibodeau will help you find that perfect piece for your collection. Friday-Sunday 1-4 p.m. 785.546.2455. FB.

City Sundries:

104 N. Washington. A step through the recessed entrance is a step back in time. The original cabinets in this old drug store still remain, now displaying modern gifts. After you look around, take a seat for an ice cream treat at the old ice cream tables beside the 1901 marble soda fountain, complete with original back bar and mirror. Freshly made sandwiches and wraps are also available. Monday-Saturday 10 a.m.-5:30 p.m.; Sunday 12-5:30 p.m. 785.546.2234.

explorer extras... In Marquette

Set your eyes on the most colorful light pole in Kansas at 115 N. Washington. Artist Mri

Pillar turned an ordinary solar light pole into a vertical work of art by covering it with a mosaic of colored glass, stone, and other materials.

Washington Street Historic District (RHKP) comprises the entire block between 2nd and 3rd. The buildings here were constructed between 1886 and 1919. Metal posters of Chief Sitting Bull, George Washington, Lucille Ball, and 27 other nationally known figures peer down from second-story windows.

Besides its comfortable shade trees, the 1924 City Park at N. Washington features Dakota sandstone gates, bandstand, and fountain. A veterans memorial also stands in the park.

The fine gifts and crafts at Washington Street Emporium, 100 N. Washington, will entice you to invest your dollars inside this 1886 bank building (RHKP), complete with pressed-tin ceiling and original teller cage. If it's not open when you are in town, stop next door at Piper's Fine Foods, 102 S. Washington, and ask Mary Piper to open up for you. Saturday 10 a.m.-4 p.m. 785.546.2271.

The Marquette Community Library, 3rd and Washington, operates inside an 1887 former bank building. The teller cages are a functioning part of the library. 785.546.2561.

The 1888 Hanson-Lindfors House (NRHP), 211 E. 5th, is a 19-room showcase home. Adjoining it is the historic cabin where the Marquette Town Charter was signed in 1874. Call ahead, 785.546.2292.

A mural on the north side of the Kansas Motorcycle Museum, 120 N. Washington, depicts a

biker on the Prairie Trail Scenic Byway. The mural was the work of Naomi Ullum and Central Christian College students. The scene of Marquette life on the south side of Marquette Lumber and Hardware was painted by numerous citizens.

Marquette Pioneer Trail is a three-mile, asphalt-surface trail for bicycles, walkers, and wheelchair users. Near the trailhead, E. 5th and Harold, you'll find a new nine-hole disc golf course.

Historically in Sweden, last names was patronymic, meaning one referred to Carl, for example, as Olof's son. Over time this practice led to names being shortened and Carl Olof's son became Carl Olofsson. Names such as Olson, Larsson, Swenson, and Gustafson are common in Marquette Cemetery and other cemeteries with Swedish burials. From Washington, 1 block east on 6th, ½ mile north on Swedonia (becomes 5th), then ¼ mile west on K-4. **ee**

MCPHERSON

Population 13,322

McPherson Museum & Arts Foundation:

1111 E. Kansas. A new building gave museum staff room to showcase both McPherson history and the museum's art collection. Exhibits feature the McPherson Globe Refiners basketball team that won the first-ever gold medal in that sport at the 1936 Olympic Games; McPherson as the Light Capital of Kansas; H.H. Nininger, the "Father of Modern

Meteoritics"; and an original Nipper dog (RCA Victor's mascot). The art collection ranges from American Indian pottery to works by Anna Larkin, court sculptor for the king of Sweden. June-August, Monday-Friday 8-5 p.m. and Saturday-Sunday 1-5 p.m.; September-May, Monday-Friday 8-5 p.m. and Saturday 1-5 p.m. Admission charge. 620.241.8464. mcphersonmuseum.com.

Outdoor Murals: Colorful murals around town portray area highlights including the McPherson Globe Refiners basketball team (Kansas and Ash); All Schools Day (123 S. Main); McPherson College Auto Restoration (Main and Euclid); Central Christian College (Main and Marlin); Maxwell Wildlife Refuge (Main and Sutherland); and the veterans memorial (401 N. Main). Matthew Richter painted the Maxwell mural and Naomi Ullum was the main artist for the others. tinyurl.com/macmurals.

Santa Fe Trail Signage: 1111 E. Kansas. Illustrated signs describe and provide locations of Santa Fe Trail sites, including road ranches, that are near McPherson.

McPherson Opera House (NRHP): 221 S. Main. A three-story architectural showpiece, this restored red-brick structure is accented

with limestone cornices, arches, and decorative bricks. It was lit by electricity on opening day in 1889! The restoration, including all ceiling stenciling and scrollwork detail, resulted in a masterful rebirth of this charismatic building. Dancers, musicians, and other performers appreciate the intimacy of this 500-seat facility. 620.241.1952. mcphersonoperahouse.org.

Visual Arts Alliance of McPherson Gallery (VAAM): 223 S. Main (first floor of the Opera House). The tall windows are perfect for admitting natural light and for showcasing local and regional art (on display and for sale). Select from fine photography, blown glass, sculpture, pottery, jewelry, painting, and weaving. Tuesday-Saturday 10 a.m.-5 p.m. 620.241.5774. FB.

McPherson County Courthouse (NRHP): 117 N. Maple. The 105-foot tower with working clocks on four sides augments this beautiful limestone Romanesque Revival courthouse built in 1894. An impressive bronze statue of General James McPherson astride his horse stands on the west side of the square. McPherson, for whom the town was named, was the highest ranking Union officer to die on the battlefield during the Civil War. Veterans memorials also adorn these lovely grounds. Monday-Friday 8 a.m.-5 p.m. 620.241.8149.

Downtown: Retail stores in this Kansas Main Street community have made McPherson a shopping destination. A sampling of stores include The Cook's Nook (219 N. Main, 620.241.7180); One Door North, The Gallery at The Clayworks (107 N. Main, 620.241.8411); The Well Coffee Shop (101 N. Main, 620.241.1840); and Stitches Quilt Shop (102 S. Main, 620.241.2986).

Craft Coffee Parlor: 120 N. Main. It's not only about the coffee in this cool, laid-back downtown coffeehouse. Tasty treats include scones, house-made granola, breakfast wraps, waffles, cookies, and vegan salted pecan balls. Monday-Wednesday 7 a.m.-6 p.m.; Thursday-Saturday 7 a.m.-10 p.m.; Sunday 12-6 p.m. 620.755.5212. craftcoffeeparlor.com.

Neighbors Cafe: 204 S. Main. Being here is like crawling out of bed and stumbling into Mom's kitchen. The radio is on, breakfast aromas are swirling, and folks are chatting. Unlike Mom, however, owner Shelly sometimes gets on the bullhorn to make an announcement! In addition to the giant hubcap-sized cinnamon rolls, breakfast features Fancy Browns—golden hash browns with diced ham, green peppers, and onions topped with cheddar cheese. Breakfast is served until closing. Lunch is also available and are to-die-for desserts. Tuesday-Saturday 6 a.m.-1 p.m. 620.241.7900. neighborscafe.com.

Main Street Deli: 108 S. Main. This renovated 1883 bank building now houses a delicious bakery and deli— a great find for you and your

SC

friends. Hearty soups come in a crusty French bread bowl, and the General McPherson sandwich combines wheat bread, raspberry mustard, roast beef, Swiss cheese, spinach leaves, and tomato! Desserts are made from scratch, and the fruit pies are renowned in this region. Gluten-free options are available. Monday-Saturday 11 a.m.-8 p.m. 620.241.1888. FB.

Knackies Meat & Sweets:

111 S. Maple. After years in the catering business and making the famous Knackies Bear-B-Cue sauce, it was a natural step for Steve and Kay Knackstedt to open a restaurant so everyone can enjoy the succulent, sweet sauce on platters of smoked ribs, brisket, sausage, turkey, and more. Order a side of cheesy Bear Claw potatoes to really do it right. Tuesday-Friday 11 a.m.-2 p.m.; Thursday-Friday 5-8 p.m. 620-504-6030. bear-b-cue.com.

Woodies Smokehouse:

206 S. Centennial. Formerly known as Woodies BBQ Shack, the name change hasn't affected the menu. Those who eat at Woodies are fanatical fans. The crowd pleasers are the smoked ribs, brisket, and spicy baked beans. If they run out of food, they close early. Daily 11 a.m.-8 p.m. 620.245.5820. FB.

Lodging: visitmcpherson.com

explorer extras... In McPherson

Walking and driving tours lead you past the historic homes on Walnut and Maple between Marlin and Seitz. Tour brochures are available at the Kansas

Travel Information Center inside the McPherson Museum, 1111 E. Kansas.

Beautiful Lakeside Park, at Kansas and Lakeside, is home to a 1939 WPA band shell, the ducks and swans on the lake, and the Swan Court garden area. McPherson Water Park is nearby at 511 Lakeside. mcphersonwaterpark.com.

Krehbiels Specialty Meats, 1636 Mohawk, is a fresh and certified meat market that carries beef, pork, ostrich, turkey, jerky, a variety of sausage—and large bones for dogs! Monday-Friday 9 a.m.-6 p.m.; Saturday 9 a.m.-3 p.m. 620.241.0103. healthymeats.net.

Especially in the evening, it appears that the south side of McPherson is home to a city of lights, many stories high and many acres wide. What you're seeing is one of two oil refineries owned by CHS, the nation's largest farmer-owned cooperative refinery. It processes about 95,000 barrels of crude oil each day, and the majority of it comes from Kansas producers. The crude oil is refined into gasoline and diesel fuel products for distribution in the central and northern United States.

Travelers on K-135 have long noticed the red-brick church with the simple cross on the steeple just north of McPherson. New Gottland Lutheran Church was built in 1910, and each October a bazaar is held to fund the maintenance on this country church. From I-135 exit 65, 1 mile east on Pawnee. **ee**

Population 1,753

Moundridge Museums:

406 W. Cole. For many years the Cole House Museum was the only attraction showcased by the Moundridge Historical Association. The 1875 home of Thornton and Drusilla Cole is one-of-a-kind in that it is outfitted with original furnishings, quilts, and textiles. To this site, dedicated and ambitious volunteers have now added the Heritage Museum, an agricultural building, blacksmith shop, and depot. Along with displays portraying town history, the Heritage Museum features the fascinating story of Civilian Public Service, an alternative to military service for conscientious objectors. Tuesday 9 a.m.-12 p.m. 620.345.8979. Admission charge. moundridgekansas museums.com.

Christian Marker:

From Cole, 1 mile south on Christian. Founded in 1875, Christian was the first town in the area. Although nothing of the town remains, a limestone marker tells us that in its heyday Christian supported a store, post office, and blacksmith shop.

Happy Hollow Gift Shop:

420 N. Wedel. Quality service and excellent inventory will make shopping a joyful experience here. Find kitchenware, home

decor, puzzles, baby clothing, handbags, cards, table linens, and more. Monday-Friday 9 a.m.-5 p.m.; Saturday 9 a.m.-12 p.m. 620.345.3135. FB.

Modd's Sweets and Eats:
1321 S. Christian. Want something sweet to start your day? Modd's waffle with brown sugar syrup and peanut butter will satisfy your craving. And for some healthy eats, try Modd's colorful and healthy wraps for a light lunch. Specialty coffees, espressos, and baked goodies are only a request away. Monday-Friday 6:30 a.m.-3 p.m.; Saturday 7 a.m.-12 p.m. 620.345.2944. FB.

Quincy's Bar and Grill:
128 S. Christian. A varied menu includes charbroiled burgers, chicken, salads, sandwiches, and more. The house specialty is slow-roasted prime rib on Thursdays to Saturdays for dinner. Monday-Saturday 11 a.m.-10 p.m. 620.345.3232. FB.

Swiss Mennonite Memorial:
From Christian, 4 miles west on Cole (becomes Arrowhead), ½ mile north on 18, then ¼ mile east on Aztec. Although the 1882 Hopefield Church is the oldest Mennonite church building in continuous use in Kansas, it's the memorial that is the most impressive. The globe atop the white stone monument is intriguing, and the many plaques describe the Swiss Mennonite migration from Russia, the Anabaptist history, and list the names of original

immigrant families. A second memorial marker stands at 18 and Arrowhead in front of the pines.

Lodging:
Underhill Farms Country Inn (KBBA, 620.345.8415, underhillfarms.com).

Pratt County

explorer extras...
In Coats

Population 86

Is it a rock garden or a petrified wood garden? You decide. Frank Lockert brought the rock here from Barber County in the early 1930s. A cottage in the back of the garden at 404 Main is faced with some of the petrified wood as is a little wishing well. Other native stone is also mixed into the landscape. Although the garden is past its prime, it's interesting to see, but please stay on the sidewalk. **ee**

explorer extras...
Near Cullison

Population 104

The J.R. Rice Barn and Granary (NRHP) are separate buildings, the frame horse barn completed in 1909 and the granary in 1907. The grand 80x40-foot barn is accented with a cupola atop its gambrel roof. From Main, 2 miles west, then ½ mile north on 110. Drive by only or call ahead for a tour, 620.388.6239. **ee**

Two extraordinary sculptures carved from cedar immediately capture your attention as you drive into the Cullison (Sunset) Cemetery. The angel with long wings widespread and the Virgin Mary nearby bring a solemn and unexpected beauty in this peaceful prairie setting. Both were carved by Cullison native Dayle Lewis. From U.S. 54, 800 feet south on Cullison/Main, ½ mile west on Central, then ¼ mile south on a gravel road to cemetery.

PRATT

Population 6,986

Pratt is the gateway to the High Plains, located on the cusp of the Arkansas River Lowlands and the High Plains. The rolling grasslands are interrupted by the Ninnescah River, and to the northwest you'll find sand hills and dunes.

Hot and Cold Water Towers:
N. Main and Green. It started as a joke in 1956. No one remembers who, but someone labeled two abandoned water towers Hot and Cold. They have fooled many a passerby, and the water towers have now become a tourist attraction. The addition of a lovely flower garden beneath the towers invites you take a few minutes to meander through the short paths and sit in the shade of the famous towers.

Pratt County Historical Museum:
208 S. Ninnescah. Many galleries exhibiting an abundance of artifacts capture the history of the county. Walk along an impressive boardwalk down an old-time Main Street and peer into typical turn-of-the-century shops. The Miss Kansas event, held in Pratt since

SC

1955, warrants a large display, and miniature train enthusiasts will be amazed at Gene Rose's miniature trains and pioneer village setting—everything is hand carved, from the trains to the horses. The WWII Pratt Army Air Field exhibit provides background before you visit the All Veterans Memorial. Monday-Friday 1-4 p.m; Saturday-Sunday 1-3 p.m. 620.672.7874. prattcountymuseum.org.

B-29 All Veterans Memorial: 40131 Barker (Pratt Airport). From U.S. 400, 4 miles north on Main/U.S. 281, then just west on Flint. The Pratt Army Air Field, 1943-1945, was one of the first B-29 bases in Kansas and a pioneer of the B-29 program. Two military planes and a helicopter bring high-flying attention to this impressive memorial. Tribute is paid to the B-29 bomb groups that trained here and to area veterans. A circular walking path with informational signs connects the memorial with the B-29 Museum. 620.672.1944 or 8321. prattveteransmemorial.org.

Parachute Building (NRHP): From the B-29 All Veterans Memorial, ¼ mile south on Barker, ½ block west on Kennedy, then just south on Morris. You can identify this building by its 40-foot-tall loft (in front of the shorter one-story parachute packing building). The facility was used to dry, inspect, clean, and reassemble

the parachutes of the B-29 crews that trained here during WWII. The platoon that served in this building consisted of seven women, two who were members of the Women's Army Corps, and a male sergeant. This parachute tower is one of two remaining in Kansas. A large interpretive sign nearby presents the fascinating history of these architectural reminders of Kansas' involvement in WWII. For tours, call 620.672.8321. prairiebombers.org.

B-29 Museum: Inside the Parachute Building. This new museum features exhibits and archives from the B-29 bomb group. Memorabilia includes letters from a flight surgeon, photos, a flight jacket containing a Japanese language hand-book, and a survival map. For tours, call 620.672.8321. FB.

Norden Bombsight Vaults (NRHP): From the B-29 Memorial, 1 block west on Flint. The two well-preserved concrete bombsight vaults served as storage for the bombsights that aircraft used when conducting high-altitude strategic bombing exercises. The Norden Bombsights were classified as secret during most of WWII.

Earl H. Ellis VFW Post #1362 (NRHP): 701 E 1st. Members of the post funded and helped build this 1939 native stone building. During WWII it served as a social center for troops from the Pratt Army Air Field. Named for a native son, Earl Ellis was known as the "Father of Amphibious Warfare" for his genius in military planning during WWI.

Vernon Filley Art Museum: 421 S. Jackson. Since 2014 Pratt has been home to a first-class art gallery, utilized both for exhibits and to enhance cultural life in Kansas. Fulfilling Mimi Filley's

dream that her art collection remain in Pratt, Mimi and her husband, Vernon, donated their lifelong collection to the museum, which Mimi helped fund. The aesthetically pleasing and historically significant art showcases diverse pieces in a variety of mediums. Tuesday-Friday 10 a.m.-4 p.m.; Saturday 1-4 p.m. Admission charge. 620.933.2787. vernonfilleyartmuseum.org.

Lemon Park: S. Pine and Santa Fe. The one-mile nature trail leads you through the woods and over a creek, or you can walk the lighted sidewalk trail around the park. Either way you're among 40 varieties of trees on this land donated to the city by Mr. and Mrs. George W. Lemon. Take time to see the tree sculp-tures and stroll the boardwalk to the middle of the pond.

Blue Moon Coffee House: 210 S. Main. Once in a blue moon you'll find the perfect blend of comfy, casual, and coffee. Sink into an oversize chair to sip away your cares with assorted coffees and specialty drinks. If you drop in for lunch, try the wraps or ham sliders. Monday-Friday 7 a.m.-5 p.m.; Saturday 7 a.m-1 p.m. 620.508.6232. FB.

The Uptown Cafe and Club D'Est: 202 S. Main. Try many selections made from award-winning Kansas beef or choose from seafood, chicken, and a host of sandwiches and

salads. Monday-Saturday 11 a.m.-8 p.m.; Sunday 11 a.m.-2 pm. 620.672.6116. uptowncafe-clubdest.com.

Woody's Sports Bar and Grill: 418 S. Main. Burgers are the mainstay here, and the Woody burger is almost big enough for two! Monday-Saturday 11 a.m.-10 p.m. 620.672.7744. FB.

The Chapeau Food & Drink: 701 N. Main. The main event is the pizza-taco, which originated in Pratt in the 1960s. Wash it down with the ice cold beer while you look for your favorite "chapeau" among the dozens on display in this kitschy bar and grill. Monday-Friday 11 a.m.-2 p.m. and 6-10 p.m.; Saturday 6-10 p.m. 620.672.2012. FB.

Nature Center and Aquariums: 512 SE 25. From Main, 2½ miles east, then 1 mile south on 25. Tall cottonwoods surround the Pratt Education Center that Professor Lewis L. Dyche started as a fish culture school for KU students in 1913. The two-story brick building operated by the Kansas Department of Wildlife, Parks and Tourism provides a great opportunity to learn about Kansas wildlife through displays of live and preserved animals. A grassland exhibit explores wildlife common to different grass regions, and the 12 aquariums include fish

species native to our state. Monday-Friday 8 a.m.-4:30 p.m. 620.672.0776. tinyurl.com/prattedcen.

explorer extras... In Pratt

With 13 parks in this nature-loving community, the inspiring Avenue of Flags Park is south of U.S. 54 on Haskell. tinyurl.com/prattparks.

Tots love splashing around in the town's two old-fashioned wading pools—in Zerger Park at Main and Thompson, and in Gebhart Park at 2nd and Hamilton. While in the latter park, look closely for remnants of a 1936 National Youth Administration park project. Summer 1-4 p.m. tinyurl.com/prattparks.

Built in 1930, the art deco Barron Theater at 313 S. Main features an elaborate facade and neon marquee. It is no longer used as a theater.

The regal 1910 Gebhart House (NRHP), 105 N. Iuka, was built in Colonial Revival style by S.P. Gebhart, publisher of the *Pratt Union* from 1896 until his death in 1935.

Also known as Hotel Parrish, the eight-story, art deco former Hotel Roberts (NRHP), 120 W. 4th, was constructed in 1930 and served as a hotel until the 1970s. Renovations in 2015 resulted in the building coming into use again as loft apartments named Parrish Lofts.

Many Victorian homes grace the town of Pratt, especially along S. Oak and Pine and in the 100 to 400 blocks of N. Main.

The Gene Wineland outdoor mural at 4th and Main captures a distance view of the Pratt grain elevators and water towers.

The community loves its disc golf, and the popular Hot and Cold Water Tower Classic,

named for the iconic local water towers, is held each spring at the 27-hole course in May Dennis Park at Mound and Logan. **ee**

Population 128

Family Food Store: 201 Main. The outside does not portend the treasures within. Started as a learning laboratory for Greg and Ruby Wolf's six home-schooled children, the Wolfs now operate a popular bakery, deli, and bulk-food store. Sandwiches are made with freshly baked bread, and homemade casseroles and pizzas are in the freezer waiting for a ride home with you. Baked goods come as singles or in a pack, but you really should buy the pack as you can't eat just one! Thursday 11 a.m.-8 p.m.; Friday 7 a.m.-8 p.m.; Saturday 7 a.m.- 4 p.m. 620.594.2483.

Reno County

ARLINGTON

Population 466

Arlington Trading Co.: 103 W. Main. You'll enjoy antique shopping in this former Westinghouse Appliances building. The original sign above the door is your clue that good stuff is inside! April-November, Thursday-Saturday 10 a.m.-2 p.m. 620.538.2416.

 Carolyn's Essenhaus: 104 E. Main. In the morning, people head straight for the pastry bar, pick out some goodies,

and drop money in the jar. This essenhaus (German for "eating house") is famous for its homemade breads, donuts, pies, and bienenstich (German for "bee sting"), a type of coffeecake with streusel topping. Other than these sweet treats, Carolyn's also offers pan-fried chicken on Wednesdays and Russian Mennonite verenike and fixings on Friday nights. Monday-Friday 6 a.m-8:30 p.m.; Saturday 6 a.m.-2:30 p.m. 620.538.4711. FB.

BUHLER

Population 1,332

Adrian's Boutique: 118 N. Main. Buhler has become a shopping destination, and one of the main reasons is this boutique. Customers have been coming here for more than 30 years and have become addicted to the selection and quality—and to the fun of shopping in this unique gift store. Monday-Saturday 10 a.m.-5 p.m. 620.543.6488. adriansboutique.com.

Pam's Sugar Shack: 110 N. Main. It's a little shop packed to the brim with all sorts of candies, nuts, and gummies! A sweet stop to satisfy your sweet tooth. February-December, Wednesday-Saturday 12-6 p.m. 620.543.2250. FB.

Town Hall Antiques:
101 S. Main. The inventory is ever changing and ever exciting inside this original town hall building. Wednesday-Friday 12-5 p.m.; Saturday 9 a.m.-4 p.m. 620.960.1203.

Downtown: From flooring to cabinets, groceries, and clothing, a shopping variety is found in two short blocks: Bartel Kitchen & Bath (207 N. Main, 620.543.6767); Neufeldt's Flooring (110 W. 2nd, 620.543.2274); Mane Street Style Salon and Boutique (216 N. Main, 620.543.2433); Play It Again Thrift Boutique (215 N. Main, 620.543.5298); and Hometown Food Store (116 N. Main, 620.543.2230).

Mustard Seed:
214 N. Main. Step through the recessed entrance of the timber facade into the warmth and the aromas of roasting coffee and home-baked goodness. Cindy Kaufman's cinnamon rolls and quiche are made daily and don't last long. Uniquely crafted sandwiches, salads, and soups offer a mix of hearty and light with something for everyone. Verna Lee Penner, Kansas Explorer #9, purrs when she bites into the Cranky Turkey, made with smoked turkey, handcrafted cranberry cream cheese, and sprouts on grilled wheatberry bread. Excellent coffees, teas, artisan sodas, and homemade desserts are here too waiting to please you. Tuesday-Saturday 8:30 a.m.-4 p.m. 620.543.2200. FB.

LaVon's Bakery & BBQ:
216 N. Maple. An old meat cooler showcasing specials of the day is the first thing you'll see you as step down into this cozy tucked-away eatery. Bierocks, enchiladas, pigs-in-the-blanket, beef brisket, smoked pork sandwiches on homemade buns, and homemade pies are daily fare. Pan-fried chicken brings a crowd on Wednesdays,

and verenika with ham gravy is served on Fridays until it's gone. Find a nook and cranny inside or eat on the veranda. Wednesday-Friday 11 a.m. to 6 p.m. 620.543.2411. lavonsbakeryandbbq.com.

Mamma Lou's: 111 N. Main. If you're lucky enough to find an open table, Mamma Lou (Mary Lou Lowe) will fill you up with a delicious breakfast or lunch. She's right when she says, "The food will make you smile!" Monday-Friday 7 a.m.-4 p.m.; Saturday 7 a.m.-2 p.m. 620.543.5139. FB.

Sunflower Metal Designs:
13209 E. 82. From Main, 2½ miles east on 82. Julie Gaeddert Ball and her father, Leon Gaeddert, began by making metal sunflowers to dress up the entrance to their farm's corn maze. And they haven't stopped since! Julie's original designs include scripture and inspirational wall art, religious scenes, and life-sized sunflowers. The only thing that slows her down is the farm's sweet corn business and helping run the maze. Call ahead, 620.727.6420. sunflowermetaldesigns.com.

Lodging:
Grand Staff Bed and Breakfast (KBBA, 620.543.6518, grandstaffministries.com).

explorer extras...
In Buhler

Paying tribute to the area's settlers is a granite plaque on a large brick monument at 82nd and Wall. Its inscription begins, "On this knoll stood our Mennonite Forefathers who left Russia in search of religious freedom, viewed the land and settled in these parts in 1874 to 1880."

John J. Wall, co-owner of the 1892 Buhler Mill and Elevator Company, built the house at 103 N. Maple in 1900. Twelve years later the Heinrich P. Ratzlaff family purchased the home and it is now known as the Wall-Ratzlaff House (NRHP). **ee**

HAVEN

Population 1,233

Haven Outdoor Mural:
116 S. Kansas. In 2001 Marty Hoskinson of Haven Sign Company created the colorful and artistic mural depicting Haven history.

Hardware Haven:
104 N. Kansas. A haven for hardware store junkies, this longtime store business operates inside a 100-year-old building complete with original wood floors, pressed-tin ceiling, and flour sacks lining the walls. Monday 12-5:30 p.m.; Tuesday-Saturday 8:30 a.m.-5:30 p.m. 620.465.3451. FB.

Willie Burger: 109 S.
Kansas. Brothers Jesse and Jacob Oehlert named the cafe and the signature burger for their grandpa, Wilbur Oehlert, and we're sure he'd approve of the open-faced crumbly beef

burger on toasted homemade bread. They also serve their Uncle Craig Sailsbury's prize-winning chili, and Mom, Sandra Williams, is in the kitchen making everything from scratch. Tuesday-Friday 11 a.m.-9 p.m.; Saturday 10 a.m.-9 p.m.; Sunday 11 a.m.-2 p.m. 620.466.5122. FB.

Indian Creek Bison Ranch:
13010 E. Lake Cable. Jerry Schmidt begins the ranch tour with a history of bison on the Great Plains and their connection with American Indians. Jerry will tell you everything you could want to know about bison while you enjoy an amazing close-up view of more than 20 of these magnificent animals. Admission charge. Reservations required. 620.921.5184. indiancreekbison.com.

Lodging: Whitetail Acres Bed
and Breakfast (620.465.3670, whitetailacres-kansas.com).

HUTCHINSON

Population 41,889

Cosmosphere (8 Wonders
of Kansas): 1100 N. Plum. Your journey into space history begins in the shadow of an actual SR-71 spy plane, a T-38 astronaut training jet, and a full-scale space shuttle replica. The Hall of Space Museum features one of the most significant collections in the world of U.S. and Russian space artifacts including the actual *Apollo 13* command module and a flown *Vostok* spacecraft. The chronological interpretation of the space race acquaints you with the personalities involved, and educational shows in the IMAX Dome Theater, planetarium, and Dr. Goddard's Lab are indeed out of this world. An affiliate of the Smithsonian Institution, the Cosmosphere is like no other place on Earth! Monday-Thursday 9 a.m.-5 p.m.; Friday-Saturday 9 a.m-7 p.m.; Sunday 12-5 p.m. 620.662.2305. cosmo.org.

Strataca - Kansas
Underground Salt Museum
(8 Wonders of Kansas):
3650 E. Ave. G. Adventure awaits as you go deep inside the only salt mine in the Western Hemisphere with an underground museum. Equipped with hard hat, you will descend 650 feet in a dark elevator to caverns that are 275 million years old. Once there you will find an amazingly large, lighted, salt-lined hallway with hands-on displays, videos, and artifacts. Your ticket includes

access to gallery exhibits, a train ride on the Salt Mine Express, and a tram ride (called the Dark Ride) where you will learn about original salt mine workers, their environment, equipment, and their treacherous trip down the shaft. Want more? Sign up for the Safari Shuttle, a tram tour beyond the original museum boundaries into the raw mine area virtually untouched for more than 50 years. Tuesday-Saturday 9 a.m.-5 p.m.; Sunday 1-5 p.m. Last tour at 3 p.m. Admission charge. 620.662.1425. underkansas.org.

Reno County Museum:
100 S. Walnut. Excellent permanent and rotating exhibits highlight county events, from weather disasters and presidential visits to health, war, politics, and more. The museum grounds feature a claim house, outhouse, windmill, and jail. Tuesday-Friday 9 a.m.-5 p.m.; Saturday 11 a.m.-5 p.m. Donation welcome. 620.662.1184. renocomuseum.org.

Reno County Courthouse
(NRHP): 206 W. 1st. The stunning and grand exterior of this art deco limestone courthouse complements its

SC

beautiful interior of marble columns, bronze newel posts, a chandelier, exquisite murals, and Japanese inlay. Take the elevator to explore all six floors—it's an old-fashioned ride with a friendly elevator operator. Monday-Friday 8 a.m.-5 p.m. 620.694.2934.

Historic Fox Theatre
(NRHP): 18 E. 1st. Known as the State Movie Palace of Kansas, this art deco theatre has been completely restored to its 1931 grandeur. The marquee is original and was the first flashing display of neon in Kansas! Today the stage is home to live performances and movies. 620.663.5861. hutchinsonfox.com.

Hutchinson Art Center:
405 N. Washington. Inside the newly remodeled center, a splendid permanent exhibit includes works by Birger Sandzen, John Steuart Curry, Lester Raymer, Thomas Hart Benton, and Hutchinson's own Alex Potter. Fine items also are for sale in the commercial gallery. Tuesday-Friday 9 a.m.-5 p.m.; Saturday-Sunday 1-5 p.m. 620.663.1081. hutchinsonartcenter.net.

Post Office Mural (NRHP):
1st and Poplar. *Threshing in Kansas* is the title of this 1942 Section artwork by Lumen Martin Winter.

Avenue A Park: Main and A. *Ad Astra*, a Dave Loewenstein mural depicting a Ferris wheel, a beautiful blue sky with constellations, and a grand wheat shock, is a poetic expression

of Hutchinson. Also within the park near Cow Creek, a Beth Van Atta sculpted grasshopper sits ready to jump. Follow the creek to the park's west end to a cooling spray ground. A large Jose Ray mural depicts a large whimsical figure scrunched under the eaves of the former Midwest Feed building.

Outdoor Murals: The mural (400 S. Main) by Julie Black, Brady Scott, and Jocelyn Woodson depicts the artists' interpretation of Kansas. *Imagine* (11 W. Ave. B), by Brendan Martinez, presents vibrant color and action. The Julie Black and Jocelyn Woodson mural (14 W. Ave. B) portrays a theme of empowerment.

Downtown: Sculptures (tinyurl.com/sculptwalk), numerous antique stores, and quality specialty shops create an inviting vibe in downtown. Start your shopping at Bluebird Books (2 S. Main, 620.259.6868); Apron Strings (1 S. Main, 620.259.7339); and Jackson Meat (13 W. 6th, 620.662.4465). If you're in town for the evening, check into a performance at Stage 9, an intimate theatrical venue (9 S. Main, 316.350.7529). Additional information (downtownhutchinson.com).

Smith's Market: 211 S. Main. Since 1933 this small market has provided satisfied customers with a variety of fresh fruits and vegetables, bulk candy and seeds, dried fruits, pastas, salad dressings, coffee, and friendly service. The Pat Potucek murals on the back wall add to the old-time market atmosphere. Monday-Saturday 7 a.m.-6 p.m.; 620.662.6761. smithsmarketks.com.

The Room: 2 E. 2nd. The Room is a new type of entertainment being played across the country. It's a team bonding adventure that will test your communication skills, ability to work with a team, and talent to decipher clues. And it's an exciting time to spend with friends and family. Friday 4-10 p.m.; Saturday 10 a.m.-10:30 p.m.; Sunday 12:30-8 p.m. Reservations required 1 hour in advance. 620.314.5306. theroom-hutchinson.com.

Carey Park: 1100 Carey Park. The historic fountain at the park's entrance (south end of Main) is a fitting tribute to Emerson Carey, founder of Carey Salt Company and a state legislator. The park is further enhanced with the Salt City Splash Aquatic Center, 1601 S. Plum, which includes a skateboard park, walking trail, and footbridges.

Hutchinson Zoo and Train: 6 Emerson Loop East (Carey Park). Featuring animals native to Kansas, this child-friendly intimate zoo provides a petting area of domestic animals and a telescope to view the buffalo across the pond. Kids love the Dinosaur Dig where they look for fossils, and a ride on the 16-gauge railway is fun during the summer months (ride charge). Start your visit in the log-cabin visitor center. Daily 10 a.m.-4:45 p.m. Donation welcome. 620.694.2693. hutchgov.com/zoo.

Dillon Nature Center:
3002 E. 30th. Just east of K-61 on 30th. Pleasant trails take you through trees, native grasses, wildflowers, gardens, and more. You can fish at the pond (bring your own pole), but the bonus might be the Playscape where you can splash in little stone creeks, pump water into your mud-pie kitchen, and play the chimes and drums. Above all, get dirty (sandy)! If you need a cleaner experience, excellent nature exhibits inside the center will garner your interest. Trail hours, daily 9 a.m.-dusk; visitor center hours, Monday-Friday 8 a.m.-5 p.m., Saturday 10 a.m.-5 p.m., and Sunday 1-5 p.m. 620.663.7411. tinyurl.com/DillonNC.

Sand Hills State Park:
From K-61, 1 mile east on 56. You're in sand dune country, and trails in the sand are what you'll find here. Up and around the dunes and through the grassland prairie, 14 miles of hiking and horseback riding trails are yours to enjoy. Interpretive signage adds to your experience. Reservations required for campground. 316.542.3664. ksoutdoors.com.

Jillian's Italian Grill: 216 N. Main. The upscale atmosphere here provides a pleasant cosmo-politan feel augmented with strains of cool jazz in the back-ground. A gleaming wood bar is an inviting place for a cocktail before dinner, and an excellent wine cellar features many Euro-pean reds to accompany a delicious Italian meal. A wood-fired pizza oven anchors a more casual area in the restaurant. Tuesday-Thursday 11 a.m.-9 p.m.; Friday-Saturday 11 a.m.-10 p.m. 620.663.8466. FB.

Roy's Hickory Pit BBQ:
1018 W. 5th. Come early because it closes when the food is gone! Roy's gets packed fast (you'll see cars and trucks parked in ditches every which way). For years this unassuming place has served some of the very best barbecue anywhere! Tuesday-Saturday 11 a.m.-2 p.m. 620.663.7421. roysbbq.com.

Skaets Steak Shop:
2300 N. Main. Skaets is steaks spelled backwards! This popular, longtime breakfast veteran is equally known for its steaks and burgers. It's cute and cozy, and the locals fill it up fast. The service is fast, though, so there'll be a place for you! Tuesday-Thursday 6 a.m.-9 p.m.; Friday-Sunday 6 a.m.-10 p.m. 620.662.9845.

Antojitos Mexicanos El Barbas: 601 E. 4th. Order authentic Mexican food at the counter to carry out or eat in. Don't be shy about asking questions, but there's no question that the tacos de carne asada, gorditas, and burritos are top-notch. Corn and flour tortillas are made in-house. Monday-Saturday 9 a.m.-9 p.m., Sunday 9 a.m.-3 p.m. 620.669.8845. FB.

Firehouse Cafe: 1824 E. 4th. Firehouse is the decor here, and when you pay your bill you'll be staring at an old hose-drying tower behind the counter. This former two-story red-brick Fire Department Station #4 is the place to fire up for good eating and to put out your hunger. Monday, Wednesday-Sunday 8 a.m.-1 p.m. 620.669.8836.

Anchor Inn: 128 S. Main. It's the longtime anchor in this town for Mexican eating, and serious devotees continue to crave the tostadas, cheese enchiladas, fajitas, flour tacos, and the red beer. Monday-Friday 11 a.m.-2 p.m. and 5-8 p.m.; Saturday 11 a.m.-9 p.m. 620.669.0311. FB.

Carl's Bar: 103 N. Main. This popular watering hole is inside a nifty historic downtown building. The Cody Special, named for Cody Heitschmidt, Kansas Explorer #5089, combines smoked sausage, ham, pepper jack cheese,

SC

jalapenos, and a secret sauce. Carl's also serves an excellent Reuben and offers many more selections in this kick-back-with-friends environment. Tuesday-Saturday 11 a.m.-9 p.m. 620.662.9875.

R-B Drive In: 201 E. Ave. A. It's been a local institution since 1948 and it remains the choice of many who love a perfectly greasy hamburger, hand-cut fries, hand-breaded pork tenderloins, limeades, and ice cream. Go inside or pull into the stall and honk for service! Monday-Saturday 10:45 a.m.-4 p.m. 620.662.9713. rbdrivein.com.

More Good Restaurants: Airport Steakhouse (1100 Airport, 620.662.4281); Allie's Deli and Coffee Shoppe (101 N. Main, 620.665.5400); Bogey's (1718 N. Plum, 620.665.8189); and Metropolitan Coffee (1329 E. 17th, 620.662.8401).

Lodging: visithutch.com.

explorer extras... In Hutchinson

A little pocket park with two cannons surrounds the Soldiers and Sailors Memorial (NRHP) at 1st and Walnut. A statue of Abraham Lincoln stands atop this 1918 monument, and additional statues flank each corner.

A 10-foot-tall granite memorial to President Warren G. Harding,

who, during a brief stop here in 1923, helped harvest wheat on this site. A plaque commemorates the man and the event. From Main, 5 miles west on 4th, than just west of the cemetery.

In George Pyle Park, Walnut and E. Ave. B, environmental enthusiasts will appreciate the large colorful sign entitled "Stormwater Treatment Protects Water Quality." And this beautiful park provides examples of how to do just that. Of additional interest in these environs are the free-standing concrete bollards representative of 1910s architecture. When President Harding spoke here in 1923, the park was named Sylvan Park.

The cornerstone on the northeast corner of Memorial Hall, 101 S. Walnut, states that it was laid by President William Howard Taft on September 26, 1911.

The handsome red-brick and limestone Carnegie library (NRHP), 427 N. Main, most recently served as the Union Labor Temple. The 1904 building currently is empty.

Brochures for a self-guided architectural tour of downtown Hutchinson are available at the Reno County Museum, 100 S. Walnut, or at tinyurl.com/hutchtour.

A little-known trolley railroad system, the Arkansas Valley Interurban (AVI), provided passenger and freight service to Wichita, Hutchinson, and Newton. Beginning in 1911, it ceased operation in 1938 due to the growing popularity of automobiles. The AVI terminal (NRHP) at 111 E. 2nd has changed little in its appearance from the time it was built in 1915.

Frank D. Wolcott House (NRHP), 100 W. 20th, one of the earliest

homes (circa 1919) to be built in the stately Hyde Park subdivision, is a wonderful example of the Craftsman bungalow style that was becoming popular during this period.

The longest grain elevator in the nation (under one head house) is in Hutchinson at 11th and Halstead. It's only 67 feet short of a half mile long.

Hutchinson has been the proud home of the official Kansas State Fair since 1913 (kansasstatefair.com). The fair is held each September, but any time of the year you may step onto the fairgrounds, and east of the Administration Building, 2000 N. Poplar, you will see a large mint green and yellow ear of corn standing on a bed of sunflowers. The local Ladies Columbian Club raised money to build this sculpture and its base and display it at the 1893 World's Fair in Chicago.

Something special happens every third Thursday evening of each month. Interactive art, music, history, and shopping draw diverse crowds to downtown, all of which have helped revitalized the area. FB.

A plaque at Washington and 1st recounts the events of a huge gas explosion that happened there on January 2001. The explosion was due to pressurized gas escaping from an underground storage facility.

On the east side of Memorial Park Cemetery, 5905 W. 4th, you will find Petland, an area set aside for pet owners to bury their beloved companions. Some of the gravestones and tree sculptures that honor the pets are beautifully detailed and unique. From Main, 5 miles west on 4th. **ee**

LANGDON

Population 42

City Hall: 18 S. Front. This sweet city hall that doubles as a library is usually open Saturday mornings. Formerly a house, it became the city hall in the late 1980s and is marked with a flagpole and a post rock sign reading, "Fairfield Falcons."

MEDORA

Unincorporated

This sand hills route from Medora to Nickerson offers a fine sampling of the Arkansas River Lowlands ecosystem—tall cottonwoods, sand hills, pastureland, tree-lined creeks, and cedars dominate the countryside. From Old K-61, ¾ mile north on Medora, 4 miles west on 95, 1 mile south on Plum, then 8½ miles west on 82 to Nickerson.

Polk's Farm Market:
8315 N. Old K-61. Take the Medora exit off K-61 to find the fruit stand that has been providing fresh fruits and vegetables since 1978. August-December, daily 1-7 p.m.

Becker's Bunkhouse (NRHP): 4918 E. Main. Ranson Hotel, built in 1905 to accommo-date train passengers, was one of the first buildings constructed in tiny Medora. As times changed, it became a service station, and in the 1950s-1990s it was a grocery store and residence. Today the former hotel is Becker's Bunkhouse and sells Old West antiques and collectibles. It's operated by Representative Steve Becker unless he's in Topeka during legislative sessions. Usually Thursday-Saturday 10 a.m.-4 p.m. Call ahead, 620.543.6444. FB.

NICKERSON

Population 1,049

Historic Gleaner: Railroad and Nickerson. Why is an old but shined up Gleaner resting on the corner? It's a permanent fixture here to acknowledge Nickerson's Baldwin brothers, who invented the Gleaner in 1923, the first self-propelled combine harvester. A large plaque tells its history.

Hedrick's Exotic Animal Farm: 7910 N. Roy L. Smith. You can stay overnight in one of the animal-themed rooms; take a tour of the kangaroos, zebras, camels, giraffes, Indu-Brazilian Zebu, ostriches, pot-bellied pigs, and more; or just drive slowly past the farm on the east side of Nickerson on K-96. You'll see animals not usually seen in a Kansas pasture. Tour charge. Call ahead, 620.422.3245. hedricks.com.

Berridge IGA Store:
115 N. Nickerson. The meat department, low milk prices, and friendly service are the draw at this independently owned grocery. 620.422.3298. berridgeiga.com.

City Hall: 15 N. Nickerson. A colorful 1970 mural of early Nickerson depicts the round-house that was moved to Newton and the 1881 city hall that was destroyed in a fire. Monday-Friday 8 a.m.-5 p.m. 620.422.5981.

Sunshine Cafe:
3 N. Nickerson. Start your day with the special crumbly peanut butter topping on your pancakes. Sunshine's does chicken-fried steak the Explorer Way, serves hand-breaded pork tenderloin, and makes chicken and noodles from scratch. Try the homemade pies too! Tuesday-Friday 6:30 a.m.-8 p.m.; Saturday-Sunday 6:30 a.m.-2 p.m. 620.422.5153.

Flick's Bar & Grill: 10 S. Nickerson. Try the Foreman burger with bacon, pepper jack and cheddar cheese, and served with the famous Flick's sauce. The burgers are so juicy you'll need extra napkins! But wait, there's more. In fact, more than 75 menu items, from beer-battered cod to gizzards. Monday-Friday 11 a.m.-8 p.m.; Saturday 11 a.m.-3 p.m. 620.422.6060. FB.

Lodging: Hedrick's Bed & Breakfast Inn (KBBA, 620.422.3245, hedricks.com).

SC

PARTRIDGE

Population 241

The Potluck:

12205 W. Illinois. From U.S. 50, 2 miles north on Partridge, then 1¼ miles west on Illinois. A weathered dairy barn and the array of farm products inside is the Potluck. Choose from chemical-free vegetables, raw milk, fresh eggs, and more. Buying large amounts of vegetables qualifies for a bulk rate. You might even take home a homemade bird-house or two. Come anytime, if no one is home, pay on the honor system. Monday-Saturday daylight. 620.567.2093.

Glass Springs Dairy:

5702 W. Longview (Hutchinson). From K-61, 4½ miles east on Longview. Inside the small sales building on Jacob Beachey's dairy farm you may select from raw milk, yogurt, kefir, cream, butter, cheese, pastured eggs, pastured chicken, and beef along with assorted jams, jellies, relishes, and pickles. Monday-Saturday daylight. 620.669.8127.

Lodging: Homespun Hideway Guest House (620.567.2093, airbnb.com/rooms/7734371); The Roost (620.567.2093, airbnb.com).

PLEASANTVIEW

Unincorporated

Glenn's Bulk Food Shoppe:

6405 W. Morgan. For more than 30 years Glenn's has sold natural and gluten-free foods, kitchen-ware, bulk grains, spices, flour, canning supplies, dry mixes, frozen fruits and vegetables, meats, cheese, and gifts. New owners have expanded by adding a deli. Monday-Friday 9 a.m.-6 p.m.; Saturday 9 a.m.-5 p.m. 620.662.2875. glennsbulkfood.com.

Country Fabrics: 6411 W.

Morgan. Since 1977 owner Janet Headings had carried a large selection of fabric for quilts, tablecloths, and garments, as well as stocking notions, hankies, ironing board pads, and hot-pad gloves. Monday-Saturday 9:30 a.m-5 p.m. 620.662.3681. FB.

More Shopping:

pleasantviewkansas.com.

Dutch Kitchen: 6803 W. K-61.

This Amish-inspired restaurant is known for its home-style meals and homemade cinnamon rolls, sticky buns, breads, and pies. Order your favorite pie from 72 choices and pick it up the next day. Coffee is half price until 11 a.m. Monday-Saturday 6 a.m.-8 p.m. 620.662.2554. FB.

explorer extras... In Plevna

Population 98

Formerly the Plevna State Bank, the well-kept 1900 red-brick building at 301 S. Main is now home to City Hall. 620.286.5617.

Across from City Hall, the 1937 red-brick art deco gymnasium was constructed with New Deal funding. The building is now a community center.

If the area has had a wet spring, you'll be greeted in the serene Plevna Cemetery by carpets of beautiful flowers—Indian blanket and purple poppy mallow (cowboy roses). The flowers are at their blooming best during the early summer months. From Main, ½ mile west on W. 3rd.

Some of the best cottonwood trees are grown in the sand hills of the Arkansas River Lowlands. To find the Kansas champion Plains cottonwood, from 3rd in Plevna, go 6½ miles north on Avery (a sand road). On the east side of the road, this magnificent tree is 30 feet 8 inches in circumference and stands 90 feet tall. To experience a mile's worth of cottonwoods looming above and alongside you, backtrack ½ mile south on Avery, and go west on 4th. **ee**

PRETTY PRAIRIE

Population 688

When pioneer Mary Jane Collingwood reached this level land with no rocks or trees, she commented, "My, what a pretty prairie!" Thus, the town was named. Her descendants became giants in the area grain business.

Skating Rink: 122 E. Main. The Youth Center Roller Rink is a long-standing icon—the rink's wood floor dates to about 1949. And today's kids continue the long-held tradition—skating here and loving every minute! September-May, most Saturdays 7-10 p.m. Admission charge. 620.459.6908.

The Links at Pretty Prairie: 1 Power Drive. At the west end of town a nine-hole golf course features bluegrass fairways and bentgrass greens. Nearby is an 18-hole disc golf course. Greens fee. 620.459.4653. prettyprairiegolf.com.

Pretty Prairie Steakhouse: 112 W. Main. Looking for a juicy, succulent, hand-cut steak? You'll find it here, and the homemade bread pudding with amaretto sauce is the perfect ending to your perfect meal. The Lil' Rascals Lounge displays memorabilia of the original Our Gang. Carl Switzer, who played *Little Rascals* Alfalfa, lived in Pretty Prairie as an adult in the late 1950s. Tuesday-Saturday 11 a.m.-2 p.m. and 5-9 p.m.; Sunday (buffet) 11 a.m.-2 p.m. 620.459.6700. FB.

Collingwood Barn: 22002 S. Partridge. Brenda Pace is offering a grand opportunity for you to tour the restored 1913 Collingwood barn, built by John "Mart" Collingwood, grandson of Mary Jane Collingwood, founder of Pretty Prairie. One of the largest barns in the state, it was built in the shape of a Maltese Cross and has four wings. Call ahead, 720.331.6788. Collingwoodbarn.com.

explorer extras...
In Pretty Prairie

Since 1937 the town has been home to Kansas' largest night rodeo. The 14-foot bronco iron cutout on the city building, 119 W. Main, acts as an invitation to come to Pretty Prairie the third weekend of every July to see real rodeo action. **ee**

SOUTH HUTCHINSON

Population 2,552

Salt Marker: From Main, ¼ mile west on Des Moines. A historical marker tells the area's important story of salt, discovered in 1887. By 1910 26 salt companies had been founded in the vicinity. A second marker explains salt processing, and a half-ton block of mined salt is displayed nearby.

Reno County Veterans Memorial: From Main, ¼ mile west on Des Moines. Names of more than 14,000 Reno County veterans are etched in seven granite panels at this stately memorial north of the K-96/U.S. 50.

Religious Shrine: 612 S. Maple. With ceramic and concrete, artist Fred Henze created this detailed and modern shrine of Our Lady of Guadalupe in 1979.

Voss Water Park: Walnut and B. You can't keep the kids away from this fun little water park where they can splash and laugh to their hearts content. Summer months, daily 10 a.m.-9 p.m.

Central Livestock: 811 N. Main. If you've never experienced a livestock sale, try it. Amish will be here with tractor-pulled trailers. Walk up the ramp and find a place in the bleachers. You'll feel and see the action around you, from the cattle moving about the ring to the subtle motion of the bidders. A cafe is open for breakfast and lunch. 620.662.3371. centrallivestockks.com.

SYLVIA

Population 216

Cruising Sylvia: Drive slowly through this small town and you'll find interesting structures including a little white building resembling a European cottage (Main and C); a metal jail protected by canopy (130 S. Main); two churches with unusual architecture (E and Main, F and Main); and the red-brick Sylvia Rural High School (203 W. Old K-50). The 1926 school (NRHP) closed in 2014.

Brownlee House: Southwest of Sylvia. A fairy-tale house, that's one Kansas explorer's impression of this most unusual frame farmhouse built in 1917 but tinkered with from 1957 to 1995 by Don Brownlee. An organ and 500 pipes somehow fit inside the house, as do secret doors, clever inventions, carvings in unexpected places, and surprises that shouldn't be revealed ahead of your tour. Tour charge. Call ahead, 620.486.2962.

Lodging: Prairie Oaks Inn (KBBA, 620.486.2962, prairieoaksinn.net).

SC

YODER

Unincorporated

Drive the rural roads around Yoder to capture the essence of farm life. At first Amish farms may be hard to distinguish, but look for those without electric lines but often with two or three houses, white curtains in the windows, pumping windmills, and buggies. Tractors are allowed but not with cabs. In season, the Amish flower gardens are lovely. Please refrain from taking photos of these private and quiet people.

Yoder Hardware
& Lumber: 9816 S. Main. Ceramic mixing bowls, large crocks, canning jars, kerosene lamps, and a full-line of Radio Flyers wagons. Yoder Hardware carries modern items too, but the Amish influence is very apparent. Monday-Friday 8 a.m.-5 p.m.; Saturday 8 a.m.-2 p.m. 620.465.2277.

Birthday Marker: Red Rock and Main. Under the tree and surrounded by a white fence, a granite sign proudly marks Yoder's 100th birthday in 1989.

More Businesses:
Blue Shed Antiques and Flea Market (3301 E. Switzer); The Farm at Yoder, offering a petting zoo and wagon rides (620.465.2604); additional businesses (yoderkansas.com).

Kansas Station: Next to Yoder Meats. This gift and confection shop also carries handcrafted items and Kansas and wheat-strawboard products. It's also your station for local information. Monday-Saturday 9 a.m.-6 p.m. 620.465.3807. yoderkansas.com.

Yoder Meats:
3509 E. Switzer. It's mainly a meat market, but you'll also find Amish cheese, baked goods, Kansas products, pet products, and more. Bring a cooler to pack with award-winning meats. Fresh cold deli sandwiches and hot food during the week are available for lunch. Monday-Saturday 9 a.m.-6 p.m. 620.465.3807. yodermeatsks.com.

Carriage Crossing Restaurant & Bakery:
10002 S. Yoder. You might see Amish buggies in the parking lot but most assuredly you'll find good food inside. Specialties include grilled pork chops, country-fried steak, smoked sausage links (made with Yoder Meats) and, of course, home-made breads and pies. Monday-Saturday 6 a.m.-9 p.m. 620.465.3612. yoderkansas.com.

Bull's Eye Grill: 3408 E. Red Rock. You're on target here for burgers, fries, and shakes, plus a few sandwich and salad choices. Customize your burger from a long list of toppings including sauerkraut, grilled mushrooms, pepperoni, and bleu cheese. Follow that up with building your own sundae for dessert. Monday-Saturday 11 a.m.-8 p.m. 620.465.2855. yoderkansas.com.

Amish Cemetery: From Yoder Rd., 1½ miles east on Red Rock. Note the plain gravestones and the horse hitching rail, which is a cable running through a hedge post.

Country Variety Store: 5805 E. Red Rock. From Yoder Rd., 1¾ miles east on Red Rock. Plain fabrics, quilt batts, straw and wool hats, roasting

pans, and small toys are among the items inside this country store on an Amish farm. Notice the hitching post and absence of electric power lines. Daily 8 a.m.-5 p.m. (closed Wednesday and Sunday).

Rose's Pastries: 3610 E. Longview. From Red Rock, 1 mile north on Yoder Rd., then just east. For more than 14 years, Rose has been baking delicious rolls, breads, pies, cakes, turnovers, cookies, and gluten-free products. Be sure to try the Amish-style cinnamon rolls with caramel frosting. Her little shop is only open Friday 6 a.m.-6 p.m. 620.474.6869. rosespastries.com.

Borntrager Dairy:
10610 S. Halstead. From Yoder Rd., 1 mile west on Red Rock, then ¾ mile south on Halstead. Choose from fresh dairy products, meats, home-canned goods, and bread-and-butter pickles—all raised or produced on the farm. Monday-Saturday daylight. 620.615.2211.

Yoder Wood Products:
10409 Yoder. Leroy Keim is a talented Amish craftsman creating cabinets, chairs, tables, gazebos, and other custom wood products. He'd enjoy a visit from you. Monday-Friday 8 a.m.-5 p.m.; Saturday 8 a.m.-12 p.m. 620.465.1180.

Miller Cabinets:
1204 E. Longview. From Yoder Rd., 2½ miles west on U.S. 96, just south on Sandcreek, then ¼ mile west on Longview. Beautifully handcrafted cabinets made here are available at Miller's showroom and workshop. Monday-Friday 8 a.m.-5 p.m.; Saturday 8 a.m.-12 p.m. 620.669.1420.

Lodging: Sunflower Inn (KBBA, 620.465.2200, sunflowerinnofyoder.com); The Little House in Yoder (tinyurl.com/LittleHouseYoder); Hitchin' Post RV Park (620.727.2356, tinyurl.com/hitchinpostRV).

Rice County

AROUND THE COUNTY

Dozens of Santa Fe Trail historic sites are found in Rice and surrounding counties. Trail guides available at the Stone Corral kiosk (see next entry) will help you find these remarkable remnants and learn the stories behind them. tinyurl.com/sftrailquivirachap.

Camp Grierson and the Stone Corral Site:

From Lyons, 15½ miles east on U.S. 56, 5 miles south on 31 (Plum), then ¾ mile west on P. On the east side of the Little Arkansas and south of P are faint remains of Camp Grierson, established in 1865 to protect the river crossings and trading post during a period of Indian unrest. The camp was manned again in 1867 by a company from the 10th Cavalry black regiment and named for Captain Benjamin Grierson. Rifle pits and some burial indentations (the interred have been moved to Fort Leavenworth National Cemetery) are still visible. Across the road and on the west side of the river is where the Stone Corral once stood. Today nothing remains of the 300x200-foot stone corral although it once contained a trading post and living quarters. The primitive signage at Camp Grierson is not accurate.

Santa Fe Trail Swanson's Swales (NRHP):

From Lyons, 15½ miles east on U.S. 56, 4¼ miles south on 31 (Plum), then about 600 feet west into the farm driveway to the covered wagon. You're welcome to then follow the trail south into Swanson's pasture to see the wagon swales (ruts) that are among the best on the entire Santa Fe Trail. Look for indentations, some of which are eight feet wide. The large width is due to the double and triple teams of oxen and mules hitched to the wagons to make it easier to ford the nearby Little Arkansas River.

Santa Fe Trail Fry's Ruts (NRHP):

From Lyons, 15½ miles east on U.S. 56, five miles south on 31, then 1¾ mile west on P. A small sign directs you into the pasture where you'll continue about 300 yards south to an iron cutout of a wagon and oxen. From this vantage point you can see the historic ruts to the east and west and can imagine the pioneer journey in covered wagons. The wagon trail through this pasture, now owned by the Fisher family (descendants of the Fry family), is the route that led to or from the lower crossing of the Little Arkansas River less than 1 mile to the northeast.

Santa Fe Trail Ralph's Ruts:

From 8th in Chase, 4 miles west on U.S. 56, then ¾ mile north on 4. The gate reads "Ralph's Ruts," recognizing that Ralph Hathaway owned the land containing the Santa Fe Trail wagon ruts. It's always difficult to know if you're actually seeing the grassy trail ruts, but aerial photos at the Coronado Quivira Museum (*see* p. 362) in Lyons will help you know what to look for.

ALDEN

Population 147

Prairie Flower Crafts:

205 Pioneer. In 1970 Sara Fair Sleeper responded to the need for a quilting shop and turned several abandoned downtown buildings into a fabric, quilting supply, and knickknack store. Sara retired in 2013 at the age of 96 and Paula Royer stepped in to take over. With more than 5,000 bolts of fabric on hand, Alden remains a go-to town for your fabric and quilting needs. Monday-Saturday 10 a.m.-4:30 p.m. 620.534.3551. prairieflowercrafts.com.

explorer extras... In Bushton

Population 272

On the flat plains rises a tall complex of towers, furnaces, storage tanks, pipes, and lights. What goes on here? You're seeing Oneok Hydrocarbon, a plant that gathers, processes, stores, and transports natural gas. The plant is at 777 Y.

Bushton, Geographic Center of Kansas 67427

The Kansas Geological Survey determined that the state's center is about 1½ miles southeast of Bushton. The center point is on private property and not publicly accessible.

At the Farmer Township Community Library, 313 S. Main, ask friendly librarian Nikole Smith any questions you may have about Bushton being the geographic center, the artistic and colorful library bench, the old (but still used)

SC

book check-out system, the library's name, the longtime librarian Grandma Barbara Orth, or anything else about the area. Monday, Wednesday 1-5:30 p.m. 620.562.3568. FB.

Like many, you may have grown up using the Atom Pop Corn Popper (introduced in 1948) to make your evening treat. Did you know this UFO-looking aluminum vessel is made in Bushton? QuinCraft Products, 319 S. Main, produces and rolls these out to retailers nationwide. Stop by QuinCraft and buy one—they make great gifts, and they make great popcorn too! Monday-Friday 8:30 a.m.-12 p.m. and 1-5:30 p.m. 620.562.3249. atompoppopper.com.

It's not known how many Lustron homes were built across the country, but these post-WWII prefabricated houses (a response to the housing shortage) were popular for their enamel-coated, all-steel (never needs painted) construction. The Lustron at 385 6th was constructed by Brack Implement of Great Bend.

Local history is preserved at the Bushton Museum, inside the old bank building at 218 S. Main. The 1940s soda fountain is the centerpiece. Call ahead, 620.562.3213.

Stop at the Thunderbird Center convenience store, 221 S. Main, from 11 a.m.-1:30 p.m. for the day's hot lunch special or a grilled hamburger. Homemade biscuits and sausage gravy are the big draw on Saturday mornings from 8-10 a.m. Store hours, Monday-Friday 6 a.m.-8 p.m.; Saturday 8 a.m.-8 p.m. 620.562.3392. ee

CHASE

Population 468

Longshot Bar and Grill:
517 Main. It's not a long shot to expect good eating at this bar and grill. Steaks on Fridays and Saturdays, and Explorer Way chicken-fried steak every day are always winners. Monday-Friday 11 a.m.-2 p.m. and 5-9 p.m.; Saturday 11:30 a.m.-11 p.m. 620.938.9900.

Lodging: Ralph's Ruts Retreat (620.257.8155, tinyurl.com/ralphsrutsretreat).

LITTLE RIVER

Population 549

Little River was named for the Little Arkansas River.

Garden of Eden Grocery:
275 Main. As soon as you step into this store with its original wood floors the nostalgic feeling will urge you to buy a few things. Owner David Nelson (usually behind the meat counter) and Little River citizens will appreciate your support! Monday-Saturday 6 a.m.-8 p.m.; Sunday 12-5 p.m. 620.897.6224. FB.

Burke Hotel: Main and Kansas. William H. "Bill" Burke, a prominent stockman, grain man, and banker in Little River, ran on the Democratic ticket for governor in 1940 but was narrowly defeated. The 1921 red-brick former hotel bears his name, and "Burke Grain and Live Stock Co." is largely embossed on the old red-brick scale house beside the grain elevator.

Oliver's Beef & Brew:
245 Main. Beef and brew are definitely the staples here. The popular steaks and burgers are even more appreciated because the meat comes from the local grocery store. The salads and homemade carrot cake receive high marks too. Tuesday-Saturday 11 a.m.-8 p.m. 620.897.5216. FB.

LYONS

Population 3,737

Rice County Courthouse (NRHP):
101 W. Commercial. Accented with red brick and limestone, this 1911 Romanesque Revival edifice features a small mural on each of its floors. On the main level, look for a likeness of Coronado embedded in floor tiles. On the north lawn a bronze sculpture depicts kids hanging out and listening to the radio. Also on the grounds, a stately 1918 Civil War Union Memorial stands beside an eternal flame.

Davis Walking Trails:
1145 E. U.S. 56. This half-mile sidewalk trail starts east of Celebration Centre where you will see two bronze sculptures. It's a pleasant stroll among native trees and grasses with benches and a gazebo along the route. 620.257.5390.

Coronado Quivira Museum:
105 W. Lyon. Showcased inside are the histories of the Quiviran Indians, Coronado's trek through the area, the Santa Fe Trail,

and the settling of Rice County. Spanish explorer Francisco Vásquez de Coronado met up with the Quivirans during his 1541 exploration into this region, but these American Indians likely had been in this area for hundreds of years prior. Marvelous exhibits include replicated Quiviran grass huts, interpretations of the natives' daily rituals, and descriptions of the entourage that accompanied Coronado during his search for gold. Heritage galleries include a display about the origin of the famous Lyons water tower Christmas bell (*see* p. 364). Tuesday-Friday 9 a.m.-5 p.m.; Saturday 9:30 a.m.-2 p.m. Admission charge. 620.257.3941. cqmuseum.org.

Yummy Yummy Asian Cuisine and Grill: 105 W. 1st.

The reviews are off the charts for the fresh Asian dishes. Broccoli with garlic sauce, honey walnut chicken, vegetable egg fu young, and salt and pepper shrimp are some of the yummy offerings served inside the former and historic Ly-Kan Hotel. Try out Yummy Yummy's modern interpretations of classic dishes. Tuesday-Sunday 11 a.m.-9 p.m. 620.257.2888. yummyyummyasianlyons.com.

Scrambled Sam's: 802 W

Main. You'll love this breakfast and lunch joint especially when the cook flips those sweet cream

pancakes onto your plate. Hearty appetites will find the breakfast Belly Buster (eggs, breakfast taters, cob-smoked bacon, and buttermilk biscuits) very satisfying. Tuesday-Sunday 6 a.m.-1 p.m. 620.680.2634. FB.

El Rinconcito Mexican Store: 201 E. Main.

Look for the small orange building at the "rinconcito" (corner) of K-14 and U.S. 56. Inside are some of the best authentic Mexican dishes in the area. Try the tortas, tacos, tamales, or the special of the day. With a bottle of Jarritos and a few condiments from the salsa bar, you're set. Monday-Saturday 9 a.m.-9 p.m.; Sunday 9 a.m-4 p.m. 620.257.5600.

El Potrillo: 821 W. Main.

You won't have a problem finding something delicious among the diverse selections of authentic Mexican cuisine. Vegetarians will appreciate the many options available to them. Monday-Saturday 11 a.m.-9 p.m.; Sunday 11 a.m.-3 p.m. 620.257.3000.

Father Padilla Cross:

From Grand, 4 miles west on U.S. 56. This large concrete cross was erected in 1950 in memory of Father Juan de Padilla, the first Christian martyr in the United States, and in remembrance of the first cross that Coronado erected on the Great Plains. Padilla met the Quiviran Indians in 1541 when he came through the area with Coronado. He returned as a missionary in 1542 only to be slain by hostile Indians that same year. South of the cross once stood a large Quiviran

village; its lodges were similar to those replicated in the Coronado Quivira Museum.

Buffalo Bill Mathewson Well and Cow Creek Crossing:

From U.S. 56, 1 mile south on 12. A simple, modern pavilion protects the site of Bill Mathewson's 1860s hand-dug well on the east side of Cow Creek. He also operated a trading post nearby for Santa Fe Trail travelers who crossed Cow Creek at this point. A 1906 DAR trail marker is nearby. Mathewson earned his nickname because of the number of buffalo he killed to feed drought-stricken settlers in 1860-1861.

Lodging:

tinyurl.com/lyonslodge.

SC

explorer extras... In Lyons

In Workman Park, Main and Commercial, an old-fashioned drinking fountain stands beside a 1945 plaque that expresses gratitude to J.W. and Mahala Workman for donating the land for this park in 1882.

Constructed in 1929-1930, the art deco Lyons High School (NRHP), 401 S. Douglas, opened for fall classes in 1930. The school operated until 2014.

Stop in and say hello to Bubba, the friendly green and yellow parrot, at Woydziak Hardware, 109 West. He might wave to you first! Bubba is a good reason to visit this local hardware store, which also has a great selection of housewares, tools, and things you can't find elsewhere.

During the month of December it's worth the drive to Lyons to see the crown of red lights in the shape of a holiday bell with a white star on top that shroud the city water tower. This shining symbol had its beginnings in 1938 when courthouse custodian Oscar Laudick made the 40-foot-diameter frame to drape

over the water tower. Learn more about this iconic ornament and see early photos at the Coronado Quivira Museum. **ee**

STERLING

Population 2,299

Sterling Lake: 5th and Van Buren. A location for the 1955 filming of the movie *Picnic*, this 1937 lake with bridge and bathhouse, all built by the WPA, is today a lovely park and a pleasant place to fish and stroll. 620.278.3411.

Downtown: In this quintessential small town, old-fashioned street lights accentuate historic buildings and tree-lined avenues, each bearing a handsome street sign. Brochures for a historic downtown walking tour are available at the Main Street office inside the First Group Insurance building, 136 S. Broadway. Plaques on some of the restored structures provide the building's history.

Dillons Grocery Store: 212 S. Broadway. Future grocery store magnate John S. Dillon started his business

in Sterling in the early 1900s with a small general store. In 1912 the grocery-buying public had become accustomed to delivery and charge accounts, but Dillon changed all that the following year when he opened his first cash food market in Hutchinson. One of the older Dillons stores still stands in Sterling at 212 S. Broadway. John Dillon is buried in Sterling Community Cemetery.

The Emporium: 108 S. Broadway. Jerry Bourgain loves collecting Sterling memorabilia and he shares it here in the former Truehart Clinic building. The story of Dr. P.P. Truehart, who had the first radiation equipment west of the Mississippi, is also told here. Call ahead, 620.278.3473.

Cooper Hall (NRHP): 125 W. Cooper. This 1887 building was the original structure on the campus of the former Cooper College. On the building's west side, look for the larger-than-life bronze statue, *Divine Servant*, sculpted by Max Greiner. It symbolizes the college's focus on servant leadership.

Sword in the Stone: This mysterious gift of a stone and sword appeared in front of Cooper Hall on the morning of December 24, 2012. The school's mascot name, "SC Warriors," is etched on the side of the stone, and a gleaming sword protrudes from the top, in imitation of the legendary King Arthur fable. The "gift" remains where it was first left, and to this day no one knows by whom.

Veterans Memorial: 5th and Van Buren. A new and impressive tribute to Sterling veterans stands at the entrance to Sterling Lake. Plaques set into the curved limestone wall honor military troops.

Broadway Market: 105 S. Broadway. For years inside this historic building, the *Sterling Bulletin* churned out the news. The headlines today are the scrumptious sandwiches (such as the ham, apple, and havarti panini), delicious soups,

and excellent desserts. Owner Linda Stubbs has created a welcoming atmosphere amid the hum of coffee grinders and espresso machines. Tuesday-Friday 7:30 a.m.-5 p.m.; Saturday 7:30 a.m.-1 p.m. 620.278.6494. FB.

Sterling Cafe: 131 S. Broadway. This longtime local cafe is still supplying Sterling with wonderful edible comforts—especially the daily fried chicken! Wednesday-Saturday 6 a.m.-8 p.m.; Sunday 6 a.m.-2 p.m. 620.278.3099. FB.

TNT Dairyland: 452 S. Broadway. Dynamite ice cream treats—banana splits, floats, parfaits, and candy bar shakes—are served here as are broasted chicken dinners, burger, and tacos. April-October, daily 11 a.m.-9 p.m. 620.278.2297. FB.

Lodging: tinyurl.com/sterlodging.

explorer extras... In Sterling

The 1917 red-brick Carnegie library (NRHP) at 138 N. Broadway still houses the local bibliotheque. Nearby are remnants of a saber and rifle embedded in a 1918 rough concrete marker that serves as a war memorial.

The grand 1898 D.J. Fair home at 204 E. Monroe and the 1877 Patent stone house at 130 W. Monroe are just two of the many beautiful historic homes found around town.

A little vintage water fountain stands in front of the early 1900s Municipal Power and Water Plant building at 333 N. Broadway. Although the plant no longer supplies all of the city's power needs, it has been updated to operate during periods of high power demand.

The 1903 Santa Fe depot, 229 S. Broadway, was renovated in 1984 as a law office. A plaque on the east side of the brick building tells more about the depot, which originally featured separate male and female waiting rooms!

In Sterling Cemetery, 500 E. Cleveland, the black-faced granite Haran gravestone pays a touching tribute to the lives of Lonita and John Haran by providing a record of, among other things, their hobbies, favorite sports teams, work, children, and their pets Pretzel and Lucy. The marker stands along the driveway in the cemetery's southwest section. **ee**

Sedgwick County

ANDALE

Population 966

Andale Library Outdoor Mural and Bike Rack:
328 Main. The Andale Middle School raised the funds to create this lovely mural depicting children reading. Painted by Phyllis Hooker, it's on the north wall of the library. Take a close look at the nearby bike rack built by Robert Bell. It spells out "BOOKS." 316.444.2363. andalelibrary.info.

Landmark Church:
318 Rush. The dominating spire of the St. Joseph Catholic Church is an important social and cultural landmark for the town. The church, built in 1913, has an active community today.

Brunin Family Cafe:
320 Main. Dedicated to "real food," Brunin's makes chicken-fried steak the Explorer Way! Among the many old-fashioned staples, the homemade cinnamon rolls with melted butter are well worth the indulgence. Ron Brunin's daughters, Amiee and Andrea, keep the cafe open now that their dad is gone, and he's probably smiling down on them with pride. Monday,

Thursday-Saturday 6:30 a.m.-1 p.m.; Sunday (breakfast) 7 a.m.-12 p.m. 316.445.2699. FB.

BENTLEY

Population 526

Pribbenow Variety Store:
111 S. Wichita. Seeing the need for a grocery store in her hometown, Tracy Pribbenow moved back to Bentley and re-opened the general store that her grandparents had once owned. There's a little bit of everything on the shelves including milk, eggs, fresh fruit, canned and boxed food, ice cream, and pop. Stop by and pick up a few items or a snack for the road. Daily 9 a.m.-9 p.m. 316.796.1001. FB.

Bentley Corner Bar & Grill:
102 N. Wichita. Bentley's can whip up a thick, juicy burger cooked just the way you want it. Enjoy a cold one as you dig in to steaks on Wednesday nights and Mexican food on Thursday evenings. Tuesday-Saturday 6 a.m.-8 p.m. 316.796.0233. FB.

SC

CHENEY

Population 2,133

Cheney Lake and State Park:
16000 NE 50. Because of the wind, Cheney Lake has garnered a national reputation as one of the best lakes for sailing. Completed in 1965, this reservoir was built as a water source for Wichita and to provide flood control, recreation, and fish and wildlife management. State park entrance charge. Cabins available, reservations required. 316.542.3664. ksoutdoors.com.

Souder's Historical Museum:

39925 W. 39 S. In the 1960s Floyd and Norma Souder began preserving the area's history by creating a pioneer village. They re-created historic buildings and added a one-room schoolhouse from nearby Kingman County and 1880s Santa Fe depots from Cheney and Garden Plain. Artifacts and historical information from the area are displayed inside the buildings. Although Floyd and Norma are gone, the pioneer village continues to serve its purpose in this country setting. April-October, Saturday-Sunday 10 a.m.-6 p.m. Donation welcome. 316.303.5067. FB.

Benny's Burgers & Shakes:

610 N. Main. Expect good burgers, fresh-cut fries, and a variety of ice cream goodies, notably the colorful Flavor Burst ice cream. Benny's is one of the few places in the state with a Flavor Burst machine, which automatically injects the flavor into the soft ice cream. Customers love it! Sunday-Thursday 11 a.m.-9 p.m.; Friday-Saturday 6 a.m.-9 p.m. 316.542.9934. FB.

Hank is Wiser Brewery:

213 N. Main. Of course you'll be all the wiser too if you try Hank's home-brewed suds. Hank Sanford had been brewing beer at home for 15 years when he opened here in 2005. This small family-owned brewery has nine taps both for house beers and rotating seasonal beers from other breweries. Also available are 50 different kinds of bottled beers and a full liquor bar. The brews go great with the Beer-B-Que sandwich, and the beer memorabilia decor adds just the right touch. Thursday (beer only) 5:30-10 p.m.; Friday-Saturday 5:30 -11 p.m. 316.542.0113. FB.

China's Bar & Grill:

127 N. Main. Chinese and American cuisine come together in a fun and friendly atmosphere where there's something for everyone. Try the egg rolls or the catfish, and stay for the karaoke on Friday and Saturday nights. A full bar is available. Tuesday-Sunday 11 a.m.-9:30 p.m. 316.540.6013. FB.

CLEARWATER

Population 2,530

Historic Windmill:

600 E. Ross (City Park). An 1890 windmill once used as a watering station for settlers' horses now proudly stands in the park. Signage tells you that after operating on a nearby farm for more than 90 years, the windmill was refurbished and erected here as a symbol of the area's clear water.

Veterans Memorial:

534 N. Tracy (Clearwater Cemetery). In the north end of the cemetery a granite veterans memorial lists the names of those who died in wars from WWI to the present. The inscription reads, "In memory of those who died in the search of peace."

Golf Course and Tee Time Cafe:

14100 W. 95. Play the nine-hole, public grass-green course, then take the edge off your appetite at the adjoining Tee Time Cafe. French toast made with homemade bread is a good start for your day. The locals recommend teeing off on the salads, wraps, sandwiches, and daily specials. Tuesday-Friday 7 a.m.-2 p.m. and 5-8 p.m.; Saturday 7 a.m.-2 p.m. 620.584.3006. teetimegolfandcafe.com.

Walt's Old Fashioned Hamburgers:

800 E. Ross. Walt's has been grilling old-fashioned burgers and stirring up shakes and malts since 1948. The fries are hand-cut and sprinkled with Walt's zippy special seasoning. Monday-Friday 11 a.m.-8:30 p.m.; Saturday 11 a.m.-5 p.m. 620.584.2727.

Armando's Mexican Grill:

117 E. Ross. The brightly decorated restaurant with the scent of warm tortillas, chilis, and onions is an inviting welcome. Armando's is known as much for its good service as for its tasty Mexican dishes. Daily 11 a.m.-2 p.m.; Tuesday-Saturday 5-9 p.m. armandosmexicangrill.com. 620.584.3020.

explorer extras... In Clearwater

The Clearwater Historical Museum, 149 N. 4th, portrays town history, as does the museum's outdoor mural by local artist Yancy Lough. Sunday 1-4 p.m. 620.584.2444. clearwaterhistoricalsociety.com.

Thought to be the oldest existing school in Sedgwick County, the Richmond Hill School (RHKP), a one-story, wood-frame building, was constructed in 1875 near the Chisholm Trail. In 2008 when the school was slated for demolition, the community moved it from its rural location to its new home on the west side of the museum.

Clearwater was formed when the Chisholm Trail came through the area in 1867. The famous route is marked on the south side of the Historical Museum and at the Chisholm Trail Sports Complex, 908 E. Ross. From 4th, ¼ mile east on Ross to the sports complex, south into the parking lot, then walk a short distance south. ee

COLWICH

COLWICH

Population 1,345

Sacred Heart Catholic Church: 311 S. 4th. The 1906 brown-brick church with a tall double spire is clearly the center of this community.

St. Mark's Catholic Church (NRHP): 19230 W. 29 N. From Chicago, 3 miles south on 167 W., then 1½ miles west on W. 29 N. It's worth the short drive to see this stately 1906 limestone structure with a four-sided clock tower. If the doors are open, step inside to see the strikingly beautiful barrel-vaulted ceiling, which includes a painting of the Trinity in the apse above the altar.

Syl's Restaurant: 205 W. Wichita. Serving made-from-scratch comfort food since 1976, that's Syl's! Monday-Friday 8 a.m.-1:30 p.m. 316.796.1044.

Gambino's Pizza Original: 339 S. 1st. Dan and Maria Seiler started the first Gambino's here in 1984 and the franchise in 1986. In 1991 they sold the franchise but retained their original store and recipes, which the franchise changed after the sale. You can taste the difference, which is evident by

the number of customers who drive miles to eat inside this pleasant stone building. Wine served by the glass or by the bottle makes your meal even more enjoyable. Daily 11 a.m.-8 p.m. 316.796.1121. gambinosoriginal.com.

DERBY

Population 23,047

Foley Round Barn: 9449 S. Woodlawn. In 1910 W.C. Foley built a round barn around an existing silo. In the 1940s the subsequent owner added wings for his expanded dairy operation. Today it functions as an event center. Drive by. 316.788.2276. roundbarn.webs.com.

Water Park: 1900 E. James (Rock River Rapids and Family Water Park). You'll find many ways to enjoy the tree-house-themed water playground with six wild water slides and a Lazy River. 316.788.3363. rockriverrapids.com.

Derby Historical Museum (NRHP): 716 E. Market. The local museum is at home in an old 1923 schoolhouse. Among its exhibits is one of the largest displayed collection of arrowheads in Kansas, an 1870s log cabin, and a collection of 40,000 buttons. Call ahead, 316.788.9003. derbykshistorymuseum.org.

Derby Donut: 1710 E. Madison. Eclectic and never boring are the colorful donuts and cupcakes with dozens of toppings. The maple long johns groan under the weight of two full slices of bacon on top, the cinnamon rolls are delicious, and the decorated cookies are as much fun to look at as they

are to eat. And if you need more sugar, Derby Donut stocks more than 100 varieties of glass bottled, cane sugar sodas. Monday-Friday 4 a.m.-4:30 p.m.; Saturday 4:30 a.m.-3 p.m.; Sunday 4:30 a.m.-12 p.m. 316.789.0330. FB.

Sig's Gourmet Butcher Shop: 300 S. Baltimore. Family-owned and operated for four generations, Sig's specializes in aged Angus beef and fresh pork and chickens as well as sausages, hickory-smoked bacon, and spiral cut hams. Stop at the deli for a sandwich. Tuesday-Saturday 9 a.m.-6 p.m.

Pizza John's: 208 S. Baltimore. These "purveyors of round meals and flat snacks" has been cranking out locally loved thin crust pizza since 1969. The seasoning sprinkled on the pie after it's baked ratchets up the flavor! Monday-Saturday 11 a.m.-10 p.m. 316-788-2011. pizzajohnsderby.com.

EASTBOROUGH

Population 771

Started in 1937 when it was one mile east of the Wichita city limits, this town is now surrounded by Wichita—the only city in Kansas completely surrounded by another city. Its main entrance is on the west side, entering on Douglas from Woodlawn. As you drive the half mile east before entering Wichita again, don't exceed the 20 mph speed limit. Urban legend has it that it's a famous speed trap. Although only four-tenths of a square mile in size, this is one of the wealthiest cities in the state and features beautiful homes and landscaping.

SC

GARDEN PLAIN

Population 866

Frosty Treat: 203 W. Harry. It's in an original old Valentine diner, so look for the brass plate with the heart and arrow. Valentines are prefabricated, square-sided diners providing stools and a small counter. These small box-like buildings were first made in Wichita in the 1930s by founder Arthur Valentine and were sold nationwide. Monday-Friday 11 a.m.-2 p.m. and 4:30-7:30 p.m.; Saturday 11 a.m.-7:30 p.m. 316.535.8303. FB.

GODDARD

Population 4,582

Tanganyika Wildlife Park: 1000 S. Hawkins. Visitors enjoy a close-up supervised experience interacting with exotic and endangered animal species. Walk among the kangaroos and hand feed the giraffes. From a safer distance, watch the lemurs, white tigers, and monkeys. Near or far, you'll enjoy connecting with the animals! May-September, daily 9 a.m.-5 p.m.; October-April, hours irregular. 316.794.8954. twpark.com.

Lake Afton Public Observatory: 25000 W. 39 S. (near Lake Afton County Park). Take this opportunity to view the dazzling night sky! Programs are offered for the public Fridays and Saturdays at 7:30 p.m. The observatory's museum features interactive astronomy exhibits. Admission charge. 316.448.6909. lakeafton.com.

Ginger Asian Cuisine: 19894 W. Kellogg. The lunch specials are the star. Monday-Thursday, Saturday 11 a.m.-9:30 p.m., Friday 11 a.m.-10 p.m. 316.550.6338.

HAYSVILLE

Population 11,004

Historic Vickers Station: 140 N. Main. Fill up with Haysville information at this 1956 former Vickers service station. Now housing the local chamber of commerce, the little red-and-white structure survived an F4 tornado in 1999 that ripped out the interior but left the exterior intact. The iconic batwing roof survives! 316.529.2461. haysvillechamber.com.

Fairfield Polo Club: 9420 S. Broadway. This polo club is the seventh oldest in the country, having been a sanctioned club since 1931. The public is welcome to watch a 90-minute game, so bring a blanket, lawn chairs, and a picnic. It's a thrill to see the horses' strength, hear the thundering hooves, and watch skilled players in a sport we rarely see in Kansas. This aristocratic game is played about three times a week from mid-May through September. 316.686.7314. wichitapolo.org.

KECHI

Population 1,961

Karg Art Glass: 111 N. Oliver. This striking log building is home to one of the finest

art galleries in the state. Owners Rollin and Patti Karg, well-known artists in fluid glass design, feature various art mediums, but the showcase room is a glass color trove of swirls, swoops, and solids of every size and beautiful shape. Watch glass blowers most mornings. Monday-Saturday 8:30 a.m.-5 p.m.; Sunday 11 a.m.-4 p.m. 316.744.2442. rollinkarg.com.

Shopping: Once famous for its antique stores, Kechi today hosts a delightful variety of shops. Find vintage, repurposed, handmade, and new items; honey and bee products; and more at the following: Vintage Rhinestone (137 N. Oliver, 316.258.4748); The Cottage Market (137 N. Oliver); and Junk in the Trunk (237 E. Kechi, 316.299.9988).

Quilt Shops: Quilts, supplies, fabric, related items, and crafts are at Kechi Quilt (118 E. Kechi, 316.616.8036); and Cindy's Quilts-n-More (147 N. Oliver, 316.708.2706).

Geno's Bar B-Q: 140 S. Oliver. Look for the little house to find the ribs, brisket, links, and sides that customers rave about. It's small but the food and service are grand. Carry out is popular at this tiny, often packed place. Friday 5-8 p.m.; Saturday 12-7 p.m.; Sunday 12-3 p.m. 316.744.1497. FB.

MAIZE

Population 3,823

Nancy's Amaizen Sandwiches:
5125 N. Maize. The grilled homemade chicken salad with chopped cherries

on marble bread served with baked beans and a delicious cherry limeade make for a scrumptious meal. All 25 sandwich choices are equally scrumptious! Daily 7 a.m.- 3 p.m. 316.722.9904. FB.

Chamber Music At The Barn:
4055 N. Tyler (Prairie Pines Tree Farm). From 37th N., ¼ mile north on Tyler. First-rate musicians and a gorgeous country setting combine to create one of the top cultural experiences in Kansas. Dining and sipping wine in the gardens and strolling through the ground's floral beauty is a pleasant prelude to the main event in the beautiful log barn. The summer concert series ranges from jazz to opera. 316.264.4662. cmatb.org.

MOUNT HOPE

Population 816

Bardshar Barn:
From Ohio, 1¾ mile east on Main (becomes 101). With good reason people have been gawking at the grand Bardshar Barn since 1915. A concrete wainscot wall forms the base, and the remainder of this splendid barn was built with cast-concrete blocks made by the barn's owners. Cupolas and a gambrel roof add to the grandeur. Please don't drive in the yard, but you may take pictures from the road.

Woodland Park:
From Main, ¼ mile north on Ohio, then just west on Oak. Bring your fishing pole, worms, and walking shoes to enjoy this stocked fishing lake. If the fish aren't biting, take a walk around the lake on a one-mile hiking trail, or relax in the gazebo that overlooks the water.

Wetland Marsh:
From Ohio, 2 miles east on Main (becomes 101), 1 mile south on N. 247, then ½ mile east on W. 93. The next half mile comprises the largest remaining wetland in Sedgwick County. It's a small remnant of an ancient and expansive wetlands complex that once extended to the McPherson Wetlands. Over time the area has been drained and to create farmland, but a few fragments, like this one, remain. The marsh is a nice stop for bird spotting.

PARK CITY

Population 7,499

1865 Peace Treaty:
From I-35 exit 14, ½ mile west on 61 N., then ¼ mile north on Broadway. A bright state historical marker on the west side of Broadway summarizes the 1865 Little Arkansas council that involved hundreds of members of the five Plains tribes that camped near here to negotiate a peace settlement with the U.S. government. One mile farther west at 61 and Seneca, a large 1925 DAR plaque memorializes this historic encampment along the Little Arkansas River where the treaty was signed. The agreement allowed for safe passage of settlers and traders on the Santa Fe Trail. But peace

was fleeting and within two years another treaty was negotiated near Medicine Lodge.

Lodging:
tinyurl.com/parkcitylodge.

explorer extras...
In Peck

Population 1,650

Boudreux's Burger Barn burgers are seared on a very hot griddle creating that perfect crusty edge, and the fries are thin and hand-cut. You'll find this country burger stop in a log-cabin style building at 1499 N. Meridian. Monday-Saturday 11 a.m.-7 p.m. 316.524.2763. FB. **ee**

VALLEY CENTER

Population 7,011

Splash Park:
716 McLaughlin. Hot days? Splash around and cool down in Splash Park— great fun for you and the kids. June-September, daily 10 a.m.-6 p.m. 316.755.7320. tinyurl.com/vcsplash.

Valley Center Historical Museum:
112 N. Meridian. The local museum made its home in an 1880s house and filled it with artifacts and archives that keep the history of Valley Center alive. Call ahead, 316.744.2275. tinyurl.com/vcmuseum.

Big Larry's Burgers:
328 S. Meridian. Don't worry, Larry's has normal sized burgers too. But if you're up for a challenge try the gigantic, six-tiered cheese-burger. How you bite into it, we're not sure, but we're sure you'll figure out a way! The fresh-cut fries can be ordered with a variety of

SC

decadent toppings. As if that weren't enough, Flavor Burst ice cream, shakes, and malts will tempt your sweet tooth. Monday-Saturday 11 a.m.-10 p.m. 316.755.9858. FB.

Spirit's Pub: 231 E. Main. Jami Tracy, Kansas Explorer #5185, and husband, Mike, hardly ever miss the bimonthly wine tastings at Spirit's. On a more frequent basis, owner Keith Moss also prepares a wicked brisket, pulled pork, chicken-fried steak, and chicken and noodles. Monday-Saturday 11 a.m.-9 p.m. 316.351.5711. FB.

WICHITA

Population 386,552

Wichita is a city with a vision to become a cultural mecca in the Midwest. It continues to increase its visibility of art, entertainment, landscaping, and historic preservation to make this largest city in the state one of the most pleasing to visit.

Keeper of the Plains
8 Wonders of Kansas Art: 650 N. Seneca. A giant bridge, suspended in a majestic bow-and-arrow-inspired design, is your pathway to the plaza. Here artist Blackbear Bosin's 44-foot, five-ton colossal steel statue, *Keeper of the Plains*, rises skyward on a 30-foot promontory above the confluence of the Little Arkansas and Arkansas Rivers. Each evening the Ring

of Fire lights at the base of the statue and burns for 15 minutes. Nearby, a concrete wall shares the Plains Indian story through replica artifacts and informational plaques. tinyurl.com/keeperoftheplains.

Mid-America All-Indian Center Museum: 650 N.
Seneca. The excellent exhibit galleries host outstanding American Indian art and artifacts to help you better understand Plains Indians culture and to provide insight into local American Indian personalities. Of special interest is the career of artist Blackbear Bosin, creator of *Keeper of the Plains*. Tuesday-Saturday 10 a.m.-4 p.m. Admission charge. 316.350.3340. theindiancenter.org.

Botanica, the Wichita Gardens: 701 Amidon.
Themed gardens, water features, and beautiful statuary make this a wonderful oasis in a busy city. A treehouse, bridges, outdoor musical instruments, color, and things to touch make the children's garden an enchanting place. But the 87-foot-long porcelain clay celadon Fu Cang Long treasure dragon by artist Jennie Becker just might be the crème de la crème of this very lovely outdoor environment. The dragon, with a

pearl in its mouth, awaits you in the Chinese Friendship Garden. April-October, Monday-Saturday 9 a.m.-5 p.m. and Sunday 1-5 p.m.; November-March, Monday-Saturday 9 a.m.-5 p.m. Admission charge. 316.264.0448. botanica.org.

Old Cowtown Museum:
1865 W. Museum Blvd. After the visitor center's introduction to Wichita's cowtown history, step out onto the boardwalk and dirt streets of this late 1860s-1870s living history museum. With more than 50 buildings (27 original) and costumed reenactors (during the summer) you'll feel part of early Wichita and thoroughly enjoy the experience. Chickens, Percheron horses, a cow, and sheep are on hand to greet you in the 1880s farmstead. April-October, Tuesday-Saturday 10 a.m.-5 p.m. and Sunday 12-5 p.m.; November-March, Tuesday-Saturday 10 a.m.-5 p.m. Admission charge. 316.350.3323. oldcowtown.org.

Exploration Place: 300 N.
McLean. Look inside a seven-foot-tall mouth, sit inside an airplane, take the controls of a flight simulator, watch a film in the dome theater, see a display of 1950s Kansas—and that's just getting started. Exploration Place is endless fun, endless discovery, and endless high-tech exploring! Tuesday-Saturday 10 a.m.-5 p.m.; Sunday 12-5 p.m. Admission charge. 316.660.0600. exploration.org.

Wichita-Sedgwick County Historical Museum:

204 S. Main. Start your journey of Wichita and Sedgwick County in the majestic 1892 limestone original city hall. Top-notch exhibits reflect early Wichita (when it attracted buffalo hunters and traders and became a wicked cowtown) and focus on Wichita's automotive industry, oil's enormous effect on city development, and the aviation industry that made Wichita the Air Capital of the World. The history of the Dockum Drug Store sit-ins and Wichita's connection to the first electric guitar are among the lesser-known but equally interesting stories examined. Tuesday-Friday 1 a.m.-4 p.m.; Saturday-Sunday 1-5 p.m. Admission charge. 316.265.9314. wichitahistory.org.

Museum of World Treasures:

835 E. 1st (Old Town). A haven for American and world history buffs, this world-class museum features an extraordinary and well-displayed collection of artifacts ranging from a Nazi Germany surrender document to Ulysses S. Grant's Civil War flag, items of European royalty, Egyptian mummies, and a Mayan burial urn. The Hall of Presidents is an additional highlight. Monday-Saturday 10 a.m.-5 p.m.; Sunday 12-5 p.m. Admission charge. 316.263.1311. worldtreasures.org.

Kansas African American Museum:

601 N. Water. The Calvary Baptist Church (NRHP) is a fitting venue to better understand the 20th-century black experience in Wichita.

The museum also showcases the significance blacks have had in Wichita culture, historically to the present. Documents, photos, and artifacts combine to create compelling exhibits. Tuesday-Friday 10 a.m.-5 p.m.; Saturday 12-4 p.m. Admission charge. 316.262.7651. tkaamuseum.org.

Kansas Aviation Museum:

3350 S. George Washington Blvd. At one of the most fascinating museums in the state, airplanes and airplane-related items help you grasp the vital role Wichita played in the aviation industry. Amelia Earhart, Howard Hughes, and other celebrities walked the halls of this stunning 1935 art deco WPA structure (NRHP) that once housed Wichita's original Municipal Airport. Take the stairs up to the control tower to see actual airplanes built in Wichita and a vast view of the city. Tuesday-Friday 9 a.m.-3 p.m.; Saturday-Sunday 9 a.m.-5 p.m. Admission charge. 316.683.9242. kansasaviationmuseum.org.

Kansas Firefighters Museum:

1300 S. Broadway. Engine House No. 6 (NRHP) was the last Wichita station operating with horse-drawn equipment. Inside the nicely renovated 1909 station, the museum exhibits early fire trucks and engines (some horse-drawn) as well as historic photos and many fire-related artifacts. South of the museum a Kansas Fallen Firefighters Memorial includes a wall with the names of fallen firefighters. Saturday 11 a.m.-3 p.m. Admission charge. 316.264.5990. kansasfirefightersmuseum.com.

Great Plains Transportation Museum:

700 E. Douglas. Displays of railroad lanterns, tools, and other artifacts are inside; and locomotives, cabooses, a baggage car, and more await you on the tracks. Year-round, Saturday 9 a.m.-4 p.m.; April-October, Sunday 1-4 p.m. Admission charge. 316.263.0944. gptm.us.

WATER Center:

101 E. Pawnee. The water treatment system in Herman Hill Park was designed due to decades of groundwater contamination under downtown. The plant not only treats more than a million gallons of water daily but also teaches the public about water treatment and the importance

of water. The modern architecture of the Water Center is a beautiful backdrop to outdoor fountains, a large and impressive free-standing fish observatory, and pleasant trails that lead across a creek and into the park. Inside, a museum features aquariums and interactive exhibits that provide exciting learning experiences.

SC

Outdoor features, open dusk to dawn; museum hours, Monday, Wednesday, Friday 1-4:30 p.m. For tours, call 316.350.3386. FB.

Great Plains Nature Center: 6232 E. 29th N. This center is a great primer for all ages to learn about the woodlands, prairies, lakes, and wetlands. You can view the root system of the famous big bluestem grass, and kids will love the hands-on exhibits and the giant aquarium. More than two miles of paved nature trails are at your disposal in the adjacent Chisholm Creek Park. Monday-Saturday 9 a.m.-5 p.m. 316.683.5499. gpnc.org.

Sedgwick County Zoo: 5555 Zoo Blvd. Naturalistic habitats showcase more than 3,000 animals and 400 species in visitor-friendly exhibits from Africa, Australia, South America, Asia, and North America. Among other interesting scenes are the elephants frolicking in the world's largest elephant pool. The free tram tour is an efficient way to move around the zoo. Daily 10 a.m.-5 p.m. Admission charge. 316.660.9453. scz.org.

Sedgwick County Courthouse and Memorial: 504 Main. The 1888 Sedgwick County courthouse (NRHP) is a stunning limestone Romanesque Revival building. On the south grounds the magnificent Soldiers and Sailors Civil War monument (NRHP) recognizes each of the four branches of the Union military (artillery, cavalry, infantry, and navy) with full-sized bronze statues.

Law Enforcement Memorial: Main and Central. Since 1871 29 City of Wichita and Sedgwick County law enforcement officers have lost their lives in the line of duty. To honor them, replicas of these fallen officers' boots, sculpted by Connie Ernatt, are lined across a stone ledge. Identifying plaques are placed above each pair. Look for this memorial behind the large statues of a lion and lioness.

Section Art (NRHP): 401 N. Market. Exhibited inside the former post office (now a federal courthouse) are two 1936 Section art murals: *Kansas Farming* by Richard Haines and *Pioneer in Kansas* by Ward Lockwood. Enter from the west side. Monday-Friday 9 a.m.-5 p.m.

Wichita Art Museum: 1400 W. Museum Blvd. Cross an enthralling walkway of brightly colored, intermingled glasswork by Dale Chihuly to reach one of the finest art exhibits in the country. The collection comprises more than 8,000 pieces with an emphasis on exceptional American art. A quality hands-on interactive area is a fascinating learning experience for kids. A cafe offers a light lunch menu, and a new Art Garden melds art and nature for a peaceful outdoor retreat. The Tom Otterness sculpture on the south side of the building disturbs the tranquility a bit as it depicts the fragmented body parts of two giant figures as they are overcome by chubby little characters. Tuesday-Saturday 10 a.m.-5 p.m.; Sunday 11 a.m.-5 p.m. Admission charge (Saturday is free). 316.268.4921. wichitaartmuseum.org.

Ulrich Museum of Art: 1845 N. Fairmount (Wichita State campus). The museum is Wichita's premier venue for contemporary works by artists of national and international significance. It's also well known for its Martin H. Bush outdoor sculpture collection of more than 70 works that are placed around campus. One of the beloved works is Tom Otterness's whimsical *Millipede*, which sits just south of the museum at Perimeter and Fairmount. Tuesday-Friday 11 a.m.-5 p.m.; Saturday-Sunday 1-5 p.m. 316.978.3664. ulrich.wichita.edu.

Douglas Avenue Sculptures: Douglas between Main and Topeka. Be amused and delighted at 13 life-sized bronze sculptures adorning this area. For example, you may come

upon a barefoot businessman taking a cool break on a summer day or a small boy pushing an old-fashioned pedal car over fountains of water. The bronze replica of the Woolworth soda fountain, which once stood on this spot at 206 E. Douglas, captures a defining moment in the history of Wichita's desegregation struggle.

Orpheum Theatre (NRHP):
200 N. Broadway. Opened in 1922 as a vaudeville house, this grand historic theatre has lived many lives, and today it offers an outstanding performing arts venue. The original and stunningly beautiful atmospheric design of a Spanish garden or court is being restored. 316.263.0884. wichitaorpheum.com.

The Troll:
777 W. Central (behind the Westar Energy plant). If you've never seen the troll you may jump out of your shoes the first time you do. In 2007 local artist Connie Ernatt was commissioned to create the five-foot, 200-pound troll to add intrigue and fun to the walk along the river. To find the creature day or night in his hidey-hole (a green light illuminates him at night), follow the river path from the *Keeper of the Plains*, 650 N. Seneca, east across the river, then south toward the Vietnamese Monument (*see* next entry). About halfway along, the sidewalk splits; take the east sidewalk and look underground through the grate.

Vietnamese Monument:
777 W. Central. Along the river behind the Westar Energy plant, life-sized bronze statues portray the camaraderie of an American

and a Vietnamese soldier. The monument and large plaque are from the Vietnamese American community of Wichita in "memory and honor of American, Vietnamese and Allied soldiers who fought to resist the North Vietnamese Communist aggression." The plaque provides a moving history of the South Vietnamese struggles.

Veterans Memorial Park:
339 Veterans Parkway. One of the most comprehensive and moving veterans memorials in the state, it features numerous bronze sculptures and separate recognition for WWII, the Korean War, Vietnam War, Pearl Harbor, U.S. Marine Corps, U.S. Merchant Marines, U.S. Submarine, *USS Wichita*, Operation Freedom, and Gold Star Mothers. The John Stevens Pavilion displays 13 flags with the history of each.

Maple Grove Cemetery:
1000 N. Hillside. Interred in this cemetery of historical mystique are dozens of notable individuals including James R. Mead, a Wichita founder; Donald "Cannonball" Green, stagecoach operator; and Joseph McCoy, promoter of early railroad cattle trade. 316.682.4821. maplegrovecemetery.org/roster.html.

Highland Cemetery:
1000 N. Hillside. This "Resting Place of Pioneers" includes the grave of Buffalo Bill Mathewson, marked by a tall ornate stone monument and sculpture.

Piatt Memorial:
Piatt and 20th. A granite monument memorializes the tragic events of January 16, 1965, when a KC-135 refueler took off from McConnell Air Force Base and crashed into the neighborhood near Piatt and 21st. Twenty-three residents and seven air crewmen were killed, and 10 homes were destroyed. piattparkmonument.com.

Obama's Great-Grandfather:
11800 W. Kellogg (Resthaven Gardens of Memory). In the Garden of the Good Shepherd section, plot space 3-C-2, rests Ralph Waldo Emerson Dunham, the great-grandfather of President Barack Obama. Emerson is buried next to his second wife, Martha Mae Stonehouse.

Lawrence-Dumont Stadium:
300 S. Sycamore. It's seen many renovations since it was built in 1934 as a WPA project, but today this concrete stadium is home to the Wichita Wingnuts of the American Association of Independent Baseball and to the National Baseball Congress World Series. The Walk of Fame is beyond the outfield inside the ballpark. A monument to stadium promoter Raymond "Hap" Dumont stands at McLean and Maple, outside the stadium. 316.264.6887. FB.

Kansas Sports Hall of Fame:
515 S. Wichita. Memorabilia and photos tell the inspiring story of the state's magnificent sports history. Among the many

SC

legendary Kansas sports heroes honored here are Wilt Chamberlain, Barry Sanders, Jess Willard, Jackie Stiles, and Walter Johnson. Monday- Friday 10 a.m.-4 p.m. 316.262.2038. kshof.org.

Old Town District:

Wichita's premier entertainment district is in the heart of the converted brick warehouses and brick-lined streets. It offers night clubs, arts, entertainment, distinctive restaurants, casual bars, live concerts and theatre, upscale hotel suites, contemporary retail shops, a Saturday farmer's market, and special events. oldtownwichita.com.

Historic Delano District:

W. Douglas and Sycamore. Delano sprang up as a cowtown on the Chisholm Trail and now forms Wichita's Historic Delano District, a rejuvenated area of unique independently owned shops such as Hatman Jack's (601 W. Douglas, 316.264.4881); eateries including La Galette French Bakery & Deli (1017 W. Douglas, 316.267.8541); and bars, for example The Monarch (579 W. Douglas, 316.201.6626). Historicdelano.com.

Chisholm Trail Marker:

W. Douglas and McLean. A large rough-cut limestone marker, erected in 1941, preserves the passing of the famous trail through this area and states that "Over 300,000 head of stock arrived over this route" between 1865 and 1874.

The Workroom: 150 N. Cleveland. If you're thinking about customizing your home decor design, the Workroom is the place to start. Chic and upbeat, it's filled with ideas, from custom-made furniture to fine art by area artists, accessories, and vintage pieces. Visit with the staff about custom window treatments, pillows, and bedding. If you can imagine it, they can make it. And, fans of Wichita, this is where you can buy "be proud of Wichita" flag swag! Monday-Friday 11 a.m.-4 p.m.; Saturday 10 a.m.-5 p.m. 316.295.4520. theworkroomict.com.

Coleman Factory Outlet Store and Museum: 239 N. St. Francis. In the early 1900s William Coleman invented lanterns, heaters, and all types of camping equipment. Vintage Coleman products are displayed at the front of the store. Monday-Friday 9 a.m.-6 p.m.; Saturday 9 a.m.-1 p.m. 316.264.0836.

Spice Merchant: 1308 E. Douglas. Inside the original 1908 Mentholatum Company Building (NRHP), the Spice Merchant carries innumerable cooking accessories and kitchen decor, 150 bulk teas, 40 freshly roasted coffees, and about 160 bulk herbs and spices. On a historic note, the Mentholatum Company was founded in Wichita in 1889. Monday-Saturday 9 a.m-5 p.m. 316.263.4121. thespicemerchant.com.

Nifty Nut House:
537 N. St. Francis. You might go nuts trying to choose from among the thousands of candies here. This business

began in 1937 and has evolved into a destination attraction with legions of devoted customers. Monday-Friday 8 a.m.-5:30 p.m.; Saturday 9 a.m.-4 p.m. 316.265.0571. niftynuthouse.com.

Cocoa Dolce:

2132 N. Rock (Bradley Fair). Savor the sweetness of life through the artisan chocolates created by founder Beth Tully and her team. Extend your stay by visiting the Cocoa Dolce Chocolate Lounge and indulge in a glass of wine or a scoop of gelato to accompany a sampling of confectionary splendor. Monday-Saturday 10 a.m.-9:30 p.m.; Sunday 12-7 p.m. 316.866.2906. FB.

Cero's Candies:

3429 E. Douglas. The history of this sweet spot dates to 1885 and although the owners have changed, the commitment to creating quality candies continues. Monday-Tuesday, Friday 9 a.m.-6 p.m.; Wednesday 11 a.m.-6 p.m.; Saturday 9 a.m.-4 p.m. 316.264.5002. ceroscandies.com.

Micro-breweries: Wichitans love their beer! The city's vibrant and close-knit craft beer

community is a destination for enjoying top-notch brews: Aero Plains Brewing (117 N. Handley, 316.448.2811); Central Standard Brewing (156 S. Greenwood, 316.620.8515); Hopping Gnome Brewing Company (1710 E. Douglas); River City Brewing Company (150 N. Mosley, 316.283.2739);

Third Place Brewing (630 E. Douglas, 316.833.2873); and Wichita Brewing Company & Pizzeria (8815 W. 13th and 535 N. Woodlawn, 316.440.2885).

Restaurants: Wichita offers a diverse and voracious line-up of wonderful eating opportunities and foods, from donuts and pizza to ethnic and fine dining. The following is a sampling:

Old Mill Tasty Shop: 604 E. Douglas (Old Town). Take a seat on a stool at one of the most complete and classic old-fash-ioned soda fountains in the state. It's a dandy with its marble counter, brass rail, stools, and wooden back bar with mirror. Booths and tables are also available in this friendly, upbeat, and tasty shop. Excellent biscuits and gravy, sandwiches, and soups are just a few of the favorites! Monday-Thursday 11 a.m.-3 p.m.; Friday-Saturday 8 a.m-8 p.m. 316.264.6500.

Doo-Dah Diner: 206 E. Kellogg. This hugely popular scratch diner is named for Wichita's famed moniker (origin unknown). On the sweeter side, try the banana bread French toast topped with a mixture of candied apples, pecans, and apple butter. On the serious side is the Beefy Doo-dad (German style beef, cabbage and onion mix, mashed potatoes, and mushroom gravy drizzled with horseradish sauce). Guaranteed to make your

taste buds sit up and take notice. Wednesday-Friday 7 a.m.-2 p.m.; Saturday and Sunday (buffet) 8 a.m.-2 p.m. 316.265.7011. Reservations recommended. doodahdiner.com.

Public at the Brickyard: 129 N. Rock Island. Sarah Green, Kansas Explorer #4645, is a fan of the bison Prairie Sliders with a side of haricot vert (skinny green beans tossed with tamari and pine nuts), along with a Kansas brew on tap. The chicken and waffles, Uncle Jessy pizza, Cuban sandwich, and about anything else on the menu is bound to tempt (and please) you. Tuesday-Saturday 11 a.m.-10 p.m.; Sunday 10 a.m.-9 p.m. 316.263.4044. publicoldtown.com.

Georges French Bistro: 4618 E. Central. The results are amazing when chef Georges Youssef adds his culinary talents to crepes, seafood, steak frites, and the fresh seafood bar. A large wine and cocktail list allows you to select the perfect pairing with your choice of modern French cuisine. Monday-Saturday 11 a.m.-9 p.m. Reservations recommended. 316.831.1325. georgesfrenchbistro.com.

My Tho: 500 E. Central. Everyone who eats here enthusiastically says, "Best pho in town." Although the menu includes much more, you can't go wrong with pho—noodle soup of broth, rice noodles, herbs, and beef or chicken. Thursday-Monday 10 a.m.-9 p.m. 316.262.5452. FB.

Molino's: 1064 N. Waco. Mucho gracias to Molino's for bringing contemporary and authentic Mexican cuisine to Wichita. One of the original recipes is for pirata, a fusion of a taco and panini with choice of filling and topped with melted cheese, lettuce, pico de gallo,

guacamole, and sour cream. Delicioso! Daily 11 a.m.-9 p.m. 316.977.9336. FB.

Tanya's Soup Kitchen: 1725 E. Douglas. In this "food hot spot," as it is called, you can choose from many creative made-from-scratch soups and sandwiches. Can't decide? Tanya's offers a "flight of samples" so you can try all the soups. Vegans, vegetarians, carnivores, there's something for everyone here. Monday-Saturday 11 a.m.-3 p.m.; Friday-Saturday 5-8 p.m. 316.267.7687. tskwichita.com.

B&C Barbecue: 355 N. Washington. A barbecue buffet! What better way to fill up on smoked, hand-seasoned pulled pork, ham, turkey, hot links, ribs, and chicken. It's not a fancy place, just the place to come for a midday barbecue fix. Monday-Saturday 11 a.m.-2 p.m. 316.263.8815. wichitabcbbq.com.

SC

NuWay Cafe: 1416 W. Douglas. This white-brick, red-trimmed eatery is probably the oldest restaurant in town, dating to 1930. A seat at the U-shaped counter is a little hard to find as customers continue to clamor for the famous sandwiches (made of steamed and crumbled hamburger) and the root beer floats. Although crowded, the NuWay is worth the wait. Daily 10:30 a.m.-9 p.m. 316.267.1131.

Donut Whole: 1720 E. Douglas. The big white rooster on top of the building tells you there's a lot to cock-a-doo-dle-doo about here! Every cake donut is made from scratch

daily using locally sourced ingredients. Great coffees and teas are at your fingertips. Drive through, open 24 hours; store hours, daily 6 a.m.-12 a.m. 316.262.3700. FB.

Mediterranean Restaurants: Wichita is well known for its Mediterranean food. Make it your Explorer quest to try baba ganoush, fattoush salad, kebabs, falafel, or hummus at each of these. Mediterranean Grill (335 S. Towne East Mall Dr., 316.651.5599); MIF Deli (5618 E. Central, 316.651.5599); N&J Cafe (5600 E. Lincoln, 316.681.3975); Bella Luna Cafe (2132 N. Rock, 316.634.0008); and Byblos Deli (3088 W. 13th N., 316.943.3999).

More Good Restaurants: In addition to all the above, outstanding eateries are found at visitwichita.com. Also, look for food trucks around town.

Lodging: Delano Bed and Breakfast (316.201.3120, delanobedandbreakfast.com); Inn at Glenstrae (316.631.2883, theinnatglenstrae.com); additional lodging (visitwichita.com/hotels).

explorer extras... In Wichita

The 1915 limestone Carnegie library (NRHP) built in a lavish Beaux Arts style is one of the most beautiful libraries in the state. Currently used for offices, it is at 220 S. Main.

The 10,450-square-foot Campbell Castle (NRHP) at 1155 N. River Blvd. was built in 1888 for Kansas cattleman Col. Burton Harvey Campbell. The carriage house was a tiny 3,000-square-foot structure. Currently the castle is empty.

Frank Lloyd Wright considered his 1915 design of the Allen-Lambe House, 255 N. Roosevelt, one of his best. Tours, Tuesday and Friday 10 a.m. Admission charge. Reservations required. 316.687.1027. flwrightwichita.org.

The John Mack Bridge (NRHP) at 2700 S. Broadway is the nation's longest Marsh rainbow arch bridge still used for regular vehicular traffic. Built in 1931, this beautiful bridge comprises eight rainbow arches.

The simple red-brick building with an early Pizza Hut sign is where it all started—the original Pizza Hut. Located at 3786 S. Perimeter on the Wichita State campus, it was moved there from its original site at Kellogg and Bluff. Drive by only.

Beautiful and richly colorful bas-relief sculptures and decorative panels by Bruce Moore adorn the exterior of the 1929 art deco Wichita North High School, 1437 N.

Rochester. Note particularly the intricate American Indian motif on the six-story tower.

Detailed statues of a trapper and American Indian stand atop the natural rock fountain at East High School, 2301 E. Douglas. The sculpture is a memorial to J. Hudson McKnight (1861-1925), an alfalfa farmer who once owned the land where the school now stands. East High School, completed in 1923, was the city's first high school. A massive red-brick building, its striking Collegiate Gothic style and vast campus in the center of Wichita make it an urban landmark.

It's always fun to see grassroots art. You'll enjoy Gary Pendergrass' steampunk art in the 3800 block of W. 17th and Dan Beck's carved limestone creatures at 225 N. Poplar.

Watermark Books & Cafe, 4701 E. Douglas, is a wonderful independently owned cafe and bookstore that has brought quality books to the area since 1977. The Kansas section features memoirs, cookbooks, guidebooks, and classic and contemporary fiction by Kansas authors or set in Kansas. A cafe offers a light lunch, coffees, and teas. Monday-Friday 8 a.m-8 p.m.; Saturday 8 a.m.-5 p.m. 316.682.1181. watermarkbooks.com.

Bike, wheelchair, inline skate, or walk along the scenic 10-mile asphalt Arkansas River Bike Path. Follow it from W. 21st N. at Big Arkansas River Park to Garvey Park at Washington and Galena. tinyurl.com/arkriverpath.

The North Riverside Park comfort station (NRHP) was a 1934 Civil Works Administration project and one of the art deco buildings in Wichita that utilized Carthalite, a local trade name for a concrete mortar mixed with crushed glass and pigmentation. The comfort station was built to provide restroom facilities for those who visited the Park Villa shelter. Both red-brick structures are restored and utilized today.

History and architecture buffs, or anyone with an interest, can find many Wichita historic landmarks at tinyurl.com/wichitalandmarks.

In Naftzger Park, 601 E. Douglas, take a sip from the 1918 fountain named for fiery temperance leader Carry Nation. A block west at 517 E. Douglas, the Eaton Place building was known as the Carey Hotel when Carry Nation threw rocks through its saloon mirror in 1900.

Enjoy the upbeat flavor of Wichita's local bars. Local music is playing at Barleycorn's (608 E. Douglas, 316.866.6792) along with a mean trivia contest on Wednesday nights. Good-time dive bars are Lucky's Everyday (1217 E. Douglas, 316.201.6910) and Kirby's Beer Store (3227 E. 17th N., 620.239.7990, FB). For something a little fancier try the Wine Dive (4714 E. Douglas, 316.613.2772).

Wichita nightlife, from comedy to theatre, and more attractions are at visitwichita.com (select Things to Do). **ee**

Stafford County

AROUND THE COUNTY

Quivira National Wildlife Refuge (8 Wonders of Kansas): 1434 NE 80. From Main in Stafford, 6 miles east on U.S. 50, then 8½ miles north on NE 140. It's the sheer number of migrating birds that make this wildlife haven, started in 1955, so appealing to birders. From September to December a half million Canada geese and 27 variety of ducks pass through more than 20,000 acres of Quivira's prairie grasses, salt

marshes, sand dunes, canals, dikes, and woodlands. Bald eagles are also visible during the winter months. The visitor center provides a history of the refuge plus information about endangered birds, how birds follow highways in the sky, and why the marshes here are salty. Ask staff about which birds you might see on a particular day. Pick up a bird list, a 14-mile driving tour brochure, and ask about the nature trails. Visitor center hours, Monday-Friday 7:30 a.m.-4 p.m. 620.486.2393. tinyurl.com/visitquivira.

Wetlands and Wildlife National Scenic Byway: Birds in flight by the thousands are best seen in the spring and fall months along this 77-mile

byway connecting two of the world's most significant natural wetlands—Quivira National Wildlife Refuge and Cheyenne Bottoms (see p. 295). Depending on the time of day and season you might witness thousands of shorebirds, waterfowl, and even spy a few endangered whooping cranes. This area is a natural wonderland for photographers, hikers, and bikers. Small towns along the route offer their own versions of rural culture to help make this an adventurous experience. 620.793.1800. kansaswetlandsandwildlifescenicbyway.com.

SC

Martin Cemetery (NRHP): From St. John, 2½ miles south on U.S. 50. The only reminders of the Joseph Martin family, black settlers from Illinois, is found in this little half-acre burial ground south of St. John. Approximately 20 people are buried here, with only a few marked graves dating from 1906 to 1954. Drawn by the promise of good land and unlimited opportunities, the Martin group arrived here circa 1878, just prior to the vast Exoduster migration to areas in eastern Kansas.

Stafford County Country Club Golf Course: 143 SE 20. From U.S. 50, 1 mile south on U.S. 281, 2 miles east on SE 10, then ½ mile south on SE 20. Since 1957 golfers have been teeing up to play nine holes on this well-maintained bluegrass course. The public is welcome! Greens fee. 620.204.0931. FB.

Tree Groupings: From western Reno County through Stafford County you'll notice unusual clumps of trees on the south side of U.S. 50. These plantings resulted from the Beautification Act of 1965, influenced by Lady Bird Johnson. The act provided for beautifying roadways by removing billboards, screening junkyards, and landscaping roadsides. The tree clumps in this area include Russian olive, golden raintree, conifer, Osage orange, and other varieties.

Shelterbelts: Planted to slow the wind and decrease soil erosion, shelterbelts can be seen in many areas of the state, but good examples are along the north side of U.S. 50 in Stafford County. The Civilian Conservation Corps planted many in the 1930s as part of a Soil Conservation Service program. Look for long, wide rows of trees. A variety of species were planted because the survivability factors for each were not entirely known.

HUDSON

Population 128

Stafford County Flour Mill

(8 Wonders of Kansas Commerce): 108 S. Church. Head for the tall grain elevators to find one of the few remaining independently owned flour mills in the nation. The mill has been making flour specifically for the home baker for more than 100 years, and it's famous as the home of Hudson Cream Flour. In 2013 the mill began using a wind turbine to produce the majority of the power needed to make the flour. You're welcome to stop at the brick scale house

to see the scrapbook about the mill's history or to buy products. Monday-Friday 8 a.m.-5 p.m. 620.458.4121. hudsoncream.com.

Wheatland Cafe: 112 N. Main. On Sundays you'll find parked cars lining downtown Hudson and their occupants (eager customers) walking to this 1914 red-brick cafe. The Bauers know how to cook the old-fashioned way, and the Sunday buffet is filled with the fruits of their labors. Pan-fried chicken, bone-in ham, homemade breads, real mashed potatoes, and more, plus a variety of desserts and homemade ice cream. You'll agree that the walk is worth it! Sunday 11 a.m.-2 p.m. 620.458.4761.

MACKSVILLE

Population 545

WPA Band Shell: From Main, 2 blocks east on Halveson. What is unusual about this beautiful 1939 WPA stone band shell? Rocks from 48 states are incorporated into its structure.

Farmington Cemetery: Broadway and Pauline. "Lest We Forget" is inscribed on a gray granite marker that remembers veterans of the Civil War, Spanish American War, and WWI. Nearby, the back of Patricia Wood's red granite gravestone offers these wise words, "Life is like a piano. What you get out of it depends on how you play it." The stone's front is engraved Patricia L. Wood, 1948-2012, "Mother of Timber & Drift." Several years ago Today did a segment on unique names, and Timber

Wood and Drift Wood enjoyed their few minutes of fame.

Ironman Studios & Gallery: 133 E. Broadway.
Brian Williamson is an auto body technician by trade and a metalwork artist by passion, and the two join forces at this aesthetically pleasing concrete building. Brian created the "Welcome to Macksville" signs, and his many creations are displayed and for sale in his retail shop. Monday-Friday 8 a.m.-5 p.m. Call ahead, 620.348.5802.

Edna's Bar & Grill: 115 W. Broadway. Since 1952 Edna's has been standing in this spot. Those that haven't been here for a few years will notice a big change—the place has been spruced up inside and out. But unchanged (and as good as ever) are the big, hand-pattied burgers and the cold beer. Edna's is the home of the Big Dad half-pound burger with ham, bacon, cheese, and egg, and if you enjoy finding the best burgers in the state, you have to stop at Edna's. Tuesday-Friday 11 a.m.-2 p.m. and 5-8:30 p.m.; Saturday 11 a.m.-2 p.m. 620.348.4685. FB.

JT Cafe: 119 E. Broadway. Expect good, filling breakfasts and a daily crock pot buffet—homemade of course! Monday-Friday 6 a.m.-2 p.m.; Saturday 6-9:30 a.m. 620.320.5462.

SEWARD

Population 63

Mom's Bar and Grill: 420 Lincoln. The chicken-fried steak is made the Explorer Way, and other favorites include ribeye steak, mountain oysters, and homemade pies (especially the coconut meringue). The locals just love going to Mom's. Grill hours, Monday 11 a.m.-2 p.m.; Tuesday-Saturday 11 a.m.-8 p.m. 620.458.3554. FB.

explorer extras... In Seward

From Mom's Cafe, take a drive or walk two blocks north on tree-lined Lincoln to see the former combination historic school and fire station. Notice the bell tower complete with the old bell. The old school currently stands empty.

"Viva Cristo Rey! Viva la Virgen Guadalupe!" Those were the last words spoken by 14-year-old Jose Luis Sanchez del Rio before he was killed by captors in the Mexican Cristero War in 1928. A bugler for his Cristeros unit, he was told his life would be saved if he shouted "Death to Christ the King." He refused and was killed. He was beatified in 2005. A sign across from the 1915 red-brick St. Francis Xavier Church at Lincoln and 8th further relates this tragedy. **ee**

ST. JOHN

Population 1,262

Church of Jesus Christ:
5th and Exchange. In 1875 William Hickerton brought a wagon train of 35 families to this area, which he named Zion Valley. The first structure built was the Church of Jesus Christ, also called the Mormon Temple. An elder declared the town would never be destroyed by a tornado as long as someone from the faith lived in town. Services are no longer held in the little white church, but a brass plaque on a limestone base preserves its history.

Park on the Square:
Main and 3rd. The triple-deck Victorian fountain surrounded by flowers is the focal point of this beautiful park square. From 1909 to 1913 members of the local Hesperian Club raised the $5,000 needed to purchase the "fountain popular for the times." Large trees, benches, old-fashioned street lamps, and a Statue of Liberty replica complete the park's picturesque setting.

Stafford County Courthouse: 209 N. Broadway. An unusual triangular shape is the trademark of this 1929 Modern Eclecticism blond-brick structure with limestone trim. The interior retains much of the original fixtures, woodwork, and other decorative details of that time period. The landscaping in front adds a warm touch.

Gray Photo Studio (NRHP):
116 N. Main. Work is ongoing to restore the early 1900s studio and residence of William R. Gray, who produced more than 30,000 photos from 1905 to 1947 using the glass plate negative process. The collection has been fully restored and is archived at the Stafford County Museum. FB.

Carol Long Pottery:
991 NE 10. Carol has worked as a ceramic artist for more than 30 years creating functional and decorative pieces. Her works are exceptional and highly sought after for their meticulous detail, beauty, and masterful color and design. Monday-Friday 9 a.m.-5 p.m. 620.549.3859. carollongpottery.com.

WPA School: 505 N. Broadway. The 1939 high and grade school is painted a stark white to accentuate the crisp art deco lines common in buildings constructed during the New Deal era. Later additions to the school were made in 1963.

Delp Christmas Tree Farm:
2 NE 30. The tree farm began in 1959 and is believed to be the first of its kind in the state. Started by Cecil Delp as a 4-H project for his sons, Phil and Tony, the farm at its largest had nearly 300,000 trees. Tony now runs the operation and sells to individuals during the holiday season and wholesales year round throughout the Midwest. Opens the Friday after Thanksgiving. delptreefarm.com. 620.549.3273.

Lodging: Pine Haven Retreat RV Park (620.549.3444, pinehavenrvpark.com).

STAFFORD

Population 1,019

Stafford County Historical Museum:
100 N. Main. Ask at the office for a tour of the museum complex, whose feature is the stately former Farmer's National Bank building (NRHP) built by J.D. Larabee in 1886. In a

SC

separate structure, the museum houses the famous glass plate negative collection from the W.R. Gray Studio of photography in St. John. The plates number more than 30,000 and cover a time period from 1905 to 1947. The Gray collection is considered the largest of its kind in the United States that is specific to one location. A fascinating record of everyday life, the images depict work, school, vehicles, homes, pets, farms and farm animals, and more. Four exhibits feature 100 photos from the collection. Additional highlights are an intricately carved horse-drawn hearse and several antique cars. Monday-Friday 9 a.m.-3:30 p.m. 620.234.5664.

First Methodist Episcopal Church (NRHP): 219 W.

Stafford. Very uncommon for churches of this period, the exterior of this 1926 structure is of the English Collegiate Gothic style, identified by the streamlined form of this nearly square brown-brick building. The interior's Prairie School style is evident by the beautiful stained-glass ceiling windows and stained-glass pyramid lamps hanging from it. Fans of architect Frank Lloyd Wright will see his imprint here, which is not surprising since this church was designed by Wichita architect Don Buel Schuler who previously had worked for Wright. Monday-Friday 9 a.m.-12 p.m. 620.234.5055.

Nora E. Larabee Memorial Library (NRHP): 108 N.

Union. This 1907 Corinthian style red-brick library is a memorial to the only daughter of J.D. and Angeline Larabee,

leading citizens of early Stafford. An exquisitely beautiful stained-glass window contains a tasteful portrait of Nora (1875-1904). Note the gargoyle

rain spouts! Monday-Saturday 2-6 p.m. 620.234.5762.

Stafford Cemetery:

From S. Main, ¾ mile west on U.S. 50. The resting place of one of Stafford's early influential families, the Larabee Mausoleum is the cemetery's largest memorial. East from the mausoleum, a unique 1908 GAR monument replicates a tree trunk and incorporates sculptures of a Bible, peace lily, rifle, and canteen. The large marker was carved from limestone by a local stonemason.

Joan's Cafe: 454 Martin (U.S. 50). Owner Joan Clark treats folks like family and welcomes you to stop by for home cooking. Whether you choose breakfast, daily specials, or the Sunday buffet, save room for pie. The two most popular home-baked pies are rhubarb, and you guessed it, coconut meringue. Monday-Tuesday 6 a.m.-7 p.m.; Wednesday-Sunday 6 a.m.-2 p.m. 620.234.6958. FB.

The Gathering Place:

105 N. Main. In this casual but upscale atmosphere, those who gather here appreciate

the fresh, quality ingredients in everything from cinnamon rolls and wraps to salads and the "Chef Inspired Burgers"—for example, the California Dreamin' with avocado, red onions, and provolone cheese. A secret recipe makes the cinnamon cream pie extra special. Order it before it's gone! Wednesday-Thursday 7 a.m.-8 p.m.; Friday-Saturday 7 a.m.-9 p.m. (closed daily 2:30-4:30 p.m.). 620.234.5400. FB.

Elroy's Pizza: 115 S. Main. Leroy and Ollie Meyers started this popular pizza business in 1985. The name came from the moniker (Elroy) that the local school kids gave Leroy, their beloved bus driver. Speaking of names, the Alan pizza derived from a customer who ordered his pizza with alfredo sauce, canadian bacon, steak, jalapenos, mozzarella, and sprinkled with real bacon pieces. The next day people phoned in asking for "that pizza Alan had!" It's been on the menu ever since. Tuesday-Sunday 4-9 p.m. 620.234.5408. FB.

Lodging: Henderson House Inn and Retreat Center (KBBA, 800.888.1417, henderson-bandb.com); Stafford Motor Inn (620.234.2000, staffordmotorinnks.com).

Sumner County

Belle Plaine Travel Information Center:
770 N. I-35. I-35 milepost 26, 2 miles south of K-55. Artistic panels on the building's exterior pay homage to our state's history. Inside, the center is an excellent resource providing maps, directions, brochures, weather and highway information, and a gift shop. Daily 9 a.m.-5 p.m. 620.326.5123.

A red granite Chisholm Trail Marker can be seen in a former roadside park near Wellington Lake. The land where the marker stands was donated to the City of Wellington by Fred Rose, who traveled the famous trail as a child. From Plum in Wellington, 7¾ miles west on U.S. 160, 1 mile south on Mayfield, then 1 mile east on W. 20 S.

Population 497

Salter House Museum (NRHP):
220 W. Garfield. In 1887 Susanna Madora Salter, a 27-year-old mother and a member of the Woman's Christian Temperance Union, became the first woman in America to be elected town mayor. Argonia men may have nominated her as a joke, but she received two-thirds of the vote! She proved to be a good mayor and furthered the cause for women's rights. Her father, Oliver Kinsey, who had been the first mayor of Argonia, built a seven-gabled house for his daughter in 1884, which is now open as a museum. In a separate building, the Argonia Community Museum is adjacent to the Salter House Museum. 620.435.6171.

Salter Gravestone:
Argonia Cemetery. From N. Main, ½ mile east on U.S. 160. From the cemetery's center entrance, follow the left fork to the north end. At the curve are the graves of Susanna Madora Salter and her husband, Lewis. Susanna died in 1961 at the ripe old age of 101. North of the Salter graves a flat stone marks the resting place of a son who died at age 11 days in 1888, during Susanna's term as mayor.

Argonia Outdoor Mural:
100 block of N. Main. Artists Christi and John Jackson featured Argonia's famous native Susanna Madora Salter among their depictions of Argonia history.

Argonia Memorial River Walkway and Argonia River Park:
A sidewalk stretching from S. Main to the Chikaskia River creates this half-mile walk, bordered by cropland and a county road. The walkway meanders through trees and past benches and flower gardens and leads into the park along the river. 620.435.6553.

Lodging:
Argonia River Park (620.435.6553, tinyurl.com/argoniarv).

Population 1,630

Bartlett Arboretum:
Dr. Walter Bartlett started the arboretum (NRHP) in 1910, and it was open to the public until 1942; then again from 1961 until the mid-1990s. The 20 acres is now home to massive cypress, oaks, and champion Japanese maples, and current steward Robin Macy and the Soil Sisters (volunteers) are restoring the bridges, pathways, and grounds. A beautiful and spiritual oasis, the grounds are open during arboretum events, by reservation, or by chance. Donation suggested. Call ahead, 620.488.3451. bartlettarboretum.com.

Population 1,035

Historical Markers:
From Central, 2 miles south on Main (U.S. 81). Large iron cutouts of a horse-drawn chuck wagon and drovers on horseback stand as a tribute to the cattle drives that came through this area on the Chisholm Trail in 1866-1887. Signage relate the history of Caldwell, the Chisholm Trail, and the Cherokee Strip Land Rush.

Heritage Park:
102 S. Main. Old-fashioned street lamps and gazebo set the tone in this lovely park that captures

SC

pieces of Caldwell's history. Among them is a large sign summarizing Caldwell's history as the Border Queen. You'll also see a Brenda Almond mural depicting the progression of life on the Plains, a bronze etching by Harold Holden illustrating a Chisholm Trail roundup, and a limestone Chisholm Trail marker. In a kiosk across the street, pick up a brochure for a walking tour that takes you to 19 historical markers in the downtown district.

Border Queen Museum:

5 S. Main. Caldwell was one of the nine Kansas starting points for the 1893 Cherokee Strip Land Rush. An estimated 15,000 white settlers gathered here on September 16, 1893, to race into the former Cherokee territory to stake their claims. Photographs and artifacts tell the saga of the Chisholm Trail and preserve the culture and history of this area on the Kansas and Oklahoma border. Call ahead, 620.845.2145.

Gunfighters: 103 S. Main.

Cowboys with red bandanas around their necks and guns in hand stand on top of the Stock Exchange Bank positioned for a gunfight. But alas, they are only metal sculptures re-creating the image of Wild West days in this old cowtown.

Post Office Mural (NRHP):

14 N. Main. *Cowboys Driving Cattle* is the title of this 1941 Section artwork by Kenneth Evett, a student of famed Regionalist artist Thomas Hart Benton.

Boot Hill Cemetery: From

N. Main, ¼ mile west on G, then ¾ mile north on Sunflower. Near

the entrance of Caldwell City Cemetery, a wrought-iron fence surrounds a small plot of old gravestones. A historical marker tells us the stones (but not the graves) were moved here from Caldwell's Boot Hill cemetery. The original Boot Hill contained 60 burials dating from 1871 to 1884, but the gravesites have long since been lost under farmland. The small replica cemetery adjoins the larger city cemetery, which encompasses many interesting gravestones.

Last Chance Bar & Grill:

30 S. Main. The owners didn't let a fire that swept through this restaurant in 2015 close them down. The Last Chance has a second chance in this beautifully renovated building where the made-from-scratch burgers, steaks, and pork chops are as good as ever. Tuesday-Sunday, 5-9 p.m. 620.845.2434.

Red Barn Cafe: 624 S. Main.

Burgers, biscuits and gravy, bierocks, reasonable prices, and friendly service—those are the basics in this Barn, which is always buzzing with the locals. Come early for the daily blue plate special. 620.845.2171.

explorer extras... In Caldwell

Spanning Central at Main a large iron arch reads "Caldwell" and "1871" (the year the town was founded) and includes detailed cutouts of Caldwell's two main historic beginnings—cattle drives and the railroad.

Look for the Mesker facade—galvanized sheet metal stamped with intricate design—on the upper floor of the 1910 Cunningham Building, 11 S. Main. The Mesker material was named for the Midwestern family that manufactured the product.

On the one-story red-brick 1912 Carnegie library (NRHP) note how the entrance on the west side is the same as on the east, a rare design for a Carnegie. The building, 8 N. Osage, no longer functions as the town library.

Father M.K. Berry, the first resident priest of St. Martin of Tours Church, 428 N. Main, liked Spanish Mission architecture so much that he offered to personally raise half the funds for the church building if he could choose its style. Completed in 1924, the church exterior is cement-based stucco and is very obviously of the Spanish Mission style. 620.845.6763.

Most buildings in historic downtown Caldwell were built between 1883 and 1888. The restored 1879 opera house at Central and Main functions today as a community and event center and showcases historical artifacts. The large chandeliers were removed from the state capitol during a renovation and purchased by an individual who donated them to the opera house. 620.845.2145. **ee**

CONWAY SPRINGS

Population 1,243

Conway Springs Springhouse (RHKP):
Spring and Cranmer. Named for its mineral spring, the town became a focal point for visitors from across the country to bathe in and drink from the spring waters. The original 1909 springhouse (refurbished in 1999) stands on its original site beside the spring, surrounded today by the nicely landscaped City Park. From the springhouse, walk down eight steps to better see the water flowing from the spring.

Hired Man's Grocery & Grill:
424 N. 5th. When the town's old grocery store closed, Conway Springs lifers Clint and Jenny Osner opened a new one. The name Hired Man came from Clint's early designation when he helped his uncles at the farm. Shop or grab a bite here and the community will benefit. Store hours, Monday-Friday 7:30 a.m.-8 p.m.; Saturday 8 a.m.-5 p.m.; Sunday 8:30 a.m.-1 p.m; grill hours, Monday-Friday 11 a.m.-2 p.m. 620.456.3663. hiredmans.com.

explorer extras...
In Hunnewell
Population 66

At the east end of town at Main and S. Hoover, a grand red granite marker relates a thorough history of the Cherokee Strip Land Rush and a brief history of Hunnewell. **ee**

MULVANE

Population 6,287

Outdoor Murals:
As part of a town revitalization project, two large murals were designed by

talented twins Grant and Gavin Snider and were painted by a group of dedicated volunteers. Grant's brightly colored design at 1st and Main features popular local icons including the little red caboose, the grain elevator, and the Santa Fe depot. Equally striking is Gavin's *Welcome to Mulvane* mural at 2nd and Main, which reflects the town's railroad heritage. Grant and Gavin are 2004 graduates of Mulvane High School.

Mulvane Historical Museum:
300 W. Main. A 1910 red-brick Santa Fe depot is home to this museum, which exhibits local history and the compelling story of Laura Cobb. Cobb, a 1910 graduate of Mulvane High School, became a navy nurse and was stationed in Manila in 1942 when the Japanese captured the island of Luzon. While in captivity, she was chief nurse at the Los Baños prison camp. After 37 months the more than 2,000 prisoners were rescued by a U.S. Army Airborne task force. Tuesday-Saturday 10 a.m.-4 p.m. 316.777.0506. FB.

Laurie's Kitchen:
113 W. Main. Breakfast is queen in this bright and cheery kitchen and is served all day. A special treat is the breakfast buffet on Saturdays. But this Kitchen provides more than breakfast. The "lumpy" mashed potatoes, meatloaf, and other comfort foods are evidence of scratch cooking. Menu options are available for vegetarians. Tuesday-Sunday 6 a.m.-3 p.m. 316.777.9198. FB.

Luciano's: 216 W. Main. Luciano Mottola, originally from northern Tuscany, met tourist Nancy Farber and followed her back to America. They married, settled in Nancy's hometown, Mulvane, and opened this destination restaurant in 2005.

The genial and elegant chef is passionate about his cuisine. Favorites include Pasta Con Salsiccia (Italian sausage, fresh carrots, spring onions, tomatoes, real cream, and parmesan blended with fettuccine pasta) and an old family recipe, Mottola Sugo di Carne, prepared with a meat sauce that cooks for four hours. Also popular are the salads served in crunchy parmesan cheese bowls. Monday, Wednesday-Saturday 11 a.m.-9 p.m.; Sunday 11 a.m.-8 p.m. 316-777-0045. restaurantlucianos.com.

Wyldewood Cellars:
951 E. 119 (I-35 exit 33). The largest U.S. producer of elderberry products, Wyldewood is well known for its internationally award-winning wines, including Sand Plum Wine and Spiced Wine. You'll also find jellies, syrups, and even fudge and honey made with elderberries (the elderberry concentrate is said to have many health benefits). Other Kansas products and wine accessories are sold here too, and you're welcome to sample the wine! Monday-Saturday 9 a.m-6 p.m.; Sunday 12-5 p.m. 800.711.9748. wyldewoodcellars.com.

SC

explorer extras... In Mulvane

The double parallel parking in the middle of the street is not a sight you see everyday! But trail towns often formed with an extra wide street to allow wagon trains to pass or to circle. Stores formed along both sides of the wide street. Thus, the street remained wide when it was paved or bricked in later years, often in the 1920s.

You'll find Cobb Park, a pleasant park named for a local physician, at the west end of Main next to the Mulvane Historical Museum. It hosts an 1897 jail, a 1940s caboose, and a replica of a historic fountain that once stood downtown and was used to water horses. **ee**

OXFORD

Population 1,021

Red Feather Boutique:

101 N. Sumner. Behind the crisp white walls of this historic bank building this chic boutique offers classic and trendy styles for women of all ages. Jewelry and hats with a Kansas theme are on hand here too. Wednesday-Friday 10 a.m.-5 p.m.; Saturday 10 a.m.-2 p.m. 620.455.3814. FB.

Oxford Old Mill: 170 N. Old Mill. From Main, ½ mile north on Sumner, ¼ mile east on Cottonwood, then ½ mile north on Old Mill. Upon arriving, you have a marvelous view of this pictur-esque 1876 stone mill (NRHP) on the riverbank below. Walk down to the south side to see the mill race. Inside this iconic structure, wooden beams and stone walls provide a rustic setting for a unique dining experience. Oxford High School students run the restaurant and serve a home-cooked meal that

changes each week. Sunday 11 a.m.-2 p.m. Reservations required. 620.455.3456. FB.

Stage Line Marker: From Sumner, 2 miles east on Main (becomes 10). At the junction of 10 and 11 a limestone marker holds a 1938 DAR plaque honoring "The Pioneers' Stage Line Mail Coach 1871." Nothing remains of the way station that once stood here.

SOUTH HAVEN

Population 357

Muffin Top Bakery & Confections: 113 N.

Main. Deb Ray rises early in the morning to make cream puffs, muffins, cupcakes, lemon bars, scones, and more to tickle your fancy and tempt your sweet tooth. She also makes home-made quiche, soups, salads, and sandwiches for lunch. But Deb is best known for her beautifully crafted and delicious custom cakes. South Haven is so lucky! Tuesday-Friday 9 a.m.-5 p.m.; Saturday 9 a.m.-12 p.m. 620.892.2048. FB.

Kay's Corner Cafe: 230 S. Main. This country cafe's home cooking is just waiting for you to enjoy it. Great breakfasts, hand-breaded chicken-fried steak, and cheesy fries are three good reasons to come to Kay's Corner. Tuesday-Sunday 7 a.m.-3 p.m. 620.892.5166.

WELLINGTON

Population 7,967

National Glass Museum:

117 S. Washington. Collectors and novices will be thrilled by the brilliance of thousands of

pieces of colored glass inside this National Depression Glass Association Museum. Learn the fascinating history of this mass produced and affordable glass that brought a little joy

into people's lives during the Great Depression, one of the world's worst economic upheavals. May-December, Thursday-Friday 11 a.m.-4 p.m. and Saturday 11 a.m.-2 p.m. 620.326.6400. ndga.net.

Panhandle Railroad

Museum: 425 E. Harvey (Sellers Park). As is this one, many remarkable museums are established thanks to collectors who are willing to share. Highlights of P.H. Wiley's extensive railroad collection include trainman uniforms, Santa Fe furniture, watches (critical for precise timekeeping), and the prized piece—a bell from a Prairie steam locomotive. The museum is housed in the 1886 Park House Gallery (RHKP), a structure originally built for the short-lived Wellington Power and Light Company. Tuesday-Saturday 10 a.m.-4 p.m. Donation welcome. 620.399.8611.

Carnegie Library (NRHP):

121 W. 7th. This beautifully renovated 1916 Neoclassical

structure still houses the Wellington Public Library. Its buff-brick exterior is handsomely accented with carvings, cornices, and moldings. Inside, the lower level features traveling art exhibits, and on the front and west lawns, the bronze statues of a girl and a boy reading will make you smile. 620.326.2011.

Sumner County Courthouse: 501 N.

Washington. Inside this 1952 Modern Movement style courthouse, a lobby display case contains the skull of a Columbian mammoth. The bones of this mammal, thought to be 125,000 years old, were discovered in the early 1990s in the county landfill. A sign with the bones provides background. Also in the lobby a large county map is superimposed over a colorful mural depicting a rural pioneer scene. Monday-Friday 8 a.m.-5 p.m. 620.326.7941.

Chisholm Trail Museum:

502 N. Washington. A 1916 former hospital now has 40 rooms filled with artifacts and historic photos illustrating daily life in the Wellington area. June-October, daily 1-5 p.m.; May and November, Saturday-Sunday 1-5 p.m. 620.326.3820. chisholmtrailmuseum.us.

Downtown Wellington Historic District (NRHP):

When an 1881 fire and an 1892 tornado destroyed downtown buildings, community leaders took the opportunity to coordinate their rebuilding efforts. The result was a series of structures in matching design. These made Wellington home to the second longest Italianate historic district in the state. You can see this beautiful row of buildings in the 100 block of Washington, one part of the historic district, whose boundaries roughly are 10th, 4th, Jefferson, and Washington. All historic district structures are included in the historical walking/driving tour. Brochures are available at the visitor information kiosk, 123 N. Washington. 620.326.7466. wellingtonkschamber.com.

Edwin Smith House

(NRHP): 114 S. Jefferson. This pink stucco home makes you wonder if an architect from Miami's South Beach invaded the Kansas plains. Built in 1935, the Pink House, as it is known, was designed in the attractive Spanish Eclectic style, rarely seen in the Midwest. Edwin Smith, son of a town founder, expanded his father's business into a mercantile empire. Drive by only.

No. 7 Coffeehouse:

115 S. Washington. Direct-trade coffees, teas, and this breakfast showstopper—smoked ham and cheese on a grilled cinnamon roll—are among morning favorites. Nosh on sandwiches, soups, and salads for lunch. Monday-Saturday 6:30 a.m.-2 p.m. 620.326.6777. FB.

Andy's Grill & Bar: 1604 N.

A. This cement-block building with white trim and forest green letters has been a familiar sight for restaurant goers since 1972. Regulars know that the seafood, steaks, burgers, and sandwiches are top-notch. Tuesday-Friday 11 a.m.-1 p.m.; Monday-Saturday 5-8:30 p.m. 620.326.2776.

Bravo's Italian Bistro:

107 W. Harvey. It's the simple, homemade goodness that brings out the best in the Italian dishes. Customers agree that the lasagne is outstanding and they also recommend the spaghetti (homemade pasta with a deep rich marinara sauce). Portions are large but try to save room for the luscious Italian lemon cake. Daily 11 a.m.-9 p.m. 620.326.3748. FB.

Mexican Cuisine:

Two excellent stops for homemade Mexican are El Chile Verde (119 W. Harvey, 620.326.5337); and Fabiola's (302 N. Washington, 620.326.6554).

SC

explorer extras... In Wellington

The mural by Maggie Bicker at 7th and Washington captures a progressive story of Wellington history, from pioneer settlement to the coming of the railroad, wheat, and the aerospace industry.

Kids can crawl all over the Santa Fe steam locomotive at Sellers Park, 501 E. Harvey. Engine No. 1067 has been at home here since 1957. ee

Southwest Kansas

Counties: Clark, Comanche, Edwards, Finney, Ford, Grant, Gray, Greeley, Hamilton, Haskell, Hodgeman, Kearny, Kiowa, Lane, Meade, Morton, Ness, Pawnee, Rush, Scott, Seward, Stanton, Stevens, Wichita

EXPLORER ELEMENT EXAMPLES

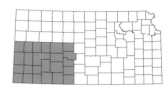

Architecture: Kiowa County Commons Building, Greensburg

Art: Jerry Thomas Gallery and Collection, Scott City

Commerce: Sharp Bros. Seed, Healy

Cuisine: Black Bison Pub, Syracuse

Customs: Large Sundials, Dodge City

Geography: Rugged Red Canyons Scenic Back Road, Comanche County

History: Santa Fe Trail Center, Larned

People: C.J. "Buffalo" Jones, Garden City

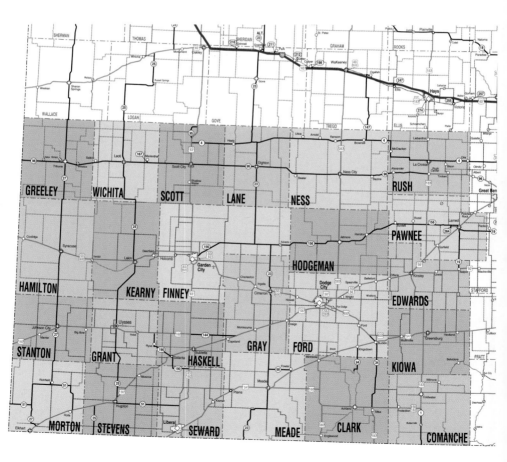

Clark County

Big Basin Prairie Preserve:

From Main in Ashland, 14½ miles west and north on U.S. 160 (becomes U.S. 283). This sweeping and rugged mixed-grass prairie of the High Plains is where the buffalo roam—and roam and roam. You may see a herd somewhere on the 1,800 glorious acres that form the Big Basin Preserve, a National Natural Landmark. Look for Big Basin signs and enter the preserve on the east side of U.S. 283 by crossing a cattle guard. Follow a driveway 1 mile east and north to a scenic overlook of the basin, a massive sinkhole that is one mile in diameter and 100 feet deep. This geological feature was created thousands of years ago by underground salt and gypsum formations that naturally dissolved over time. Return to the main driveway and continue ¼ mile east to a fork.

The fork's east road leads ¼ mile to the parking area above St. Jacob's Well. The south road leads ½ mile to a stone marker. Watch for ruts; they can be deep on these dirt roads. tinyurl.com/8wondersbigbas.

St. Jacob's Well:

From U.S. 283 Big Basin entrance, 1½ miles east on a service road to the parking area. The Little Basin is about 280 yards in diameter and 35 feet from rim to floor. Within the Little Basin is a small funnel-shaped pond (84 feet in diameter) that has attracted visitors dating to prehistoric times. The pond, named in more recent years for a biblical reference to Jacob's well, has never been known to go dry. A primitive path leads down to the serene spring-fed pool, which is surrounded by trees and rocks. Legend has it that the well has no bottom, but others say it is 58 feet deep. tinyurl.com/8wondersbigbas.

Living Waters Monument:

From St. Jacob's Well, 800 feet west to the fork, then ½ mile south. The hilltop marker is visible almost as soon as you enter the Big Basin preserve. Originally a loose mound of stones, the marker was placed here in the 1870s for early travelers, settlers, and cattle drovers to indicate water at St. Jacob's Well. Later the stones were cemented together to create a more permanent structure, which was named Living Waters Monument. In 1958 a plaque, which included scripture from John 4:10 and a description of the Plains Indians and St. Jacob's Well, was placed on the monument by the county historical society. You can see that this plaque is missing, stolen by vandals.

Clark State Fishing Lake:

From Minneola, 4¼ miles south on U.S. 283, 8½ miles east on G, 1 mile north on 15, then 2½ miles east to a fork. One mile on the fork's north road takes you to the lake; 3½ miles on the south road leads you on an unpaved perimeter route around the canyon and provides a grand view of the picturesque lake below. Porous sandstones, known as mortar beds from the Ogallala Aquifer, create the rimrock. Their light tan color contrasts with the red Permian rock beds. Cottonwood trees, sumac, yucca, and wildflowers vary in color through the seasons and augment this pleasing picture. A federal project, the lake was built by the Civilian Conservation Corps in 1934. From the northeast side of the lake, you will connect with the blacktop K-94. tinyurl.com/clarkcolake.

SW

State Fishing Lake to Ashland Scenic Back Road:

From Lake, 1¾ miles north and east on K-94, then 16 miles south on Clark County Lake Rd. This southern unpaved road from the lake to U.S. 160 at Ashland is one of the most breathtaking "dare-to-do-dirt" adventures you can take in southwest Kansas. It's 16 miles of unending vistas, no oil pumps, no telephones poles, nor anything else to impede your view of rolling hills, craggy creek-bed valleys, and a panorama of pure blue sky above the undulating prairie earth.

ASHLAND

Population 853

Pioneer-Krier Museum:

430 W. 4th (U.S. 160). The feature exhibit focuses on Harold Krier, an Ashland native and an internationally known precision aerobatic pilot who wowed crowds with his daring feats during the 1950s and 1960s. A colorful museum display includes one of his stunt planes, many photographs, memorabilia, and show bills. Krier died in a parachute accident in 1971 and is buried in Highland Cemetery. Other exhibits feature local pioneers and area notables such as opera singer Rodney Hardesty, world-record miler Wes Santee, and Notre Dame football coach and athletic director Jesse Clair Harper. Tuesday-Friday 10 a.m.-12 p.m. and 1-4 p.m. 620.635.2227. pioneer-krier.com.

Highland and St. Joseph Cemetery:

From Main, 1 mile east on U.S. 160, then ½ mile north on 21. An easily seen natural sandstone marker was erected in honor of Gerard Berryman. He was a Confederate soldier during the Civil War, and while his family built the monument to him, they also recognized all soldiers, both Union and Confederate, buried in this cemetery. Highland is also the resting place of acrobatic pilot Harold Krier. His grave is north of the small rock church and west off the cemetery's main driveway.

Clark County Courthouse:

913 Highland. A map of the county and natural landmarks is etched in stone on the front of this brick 1951 Modern Movement courthouse.

First National Bank (NRHP):

622 Main. This 1887 Romanesque structure is one of Ashland's most striking downtown buildings. Its ornamental design combines orange and red bricks and incorporates two styles of arches. Now operating as the Stockgrowers State Bank, it is truly a unique architectural accomplishment on the western Kansas landscape.

Sam's Pizza Barn:

509 W. 4th (U.S. 160). The dough is made from scratch at this local favorite garage-turned-pizza parlor. It also offers a large selection of wings. Daily 5-9 p.m. and Monday, Friday 11 a.m.-2 p.m. 620.635.4041. FB.

Ranch House Restaurant:

411 W. 4th. Stop here for a cup of coffee, a hearty breakfast, and a visit with the local guys who are here each morning solving the world's problems. Daily 6:30 a.m.-1:30 p.m.; Monday 5-8 p.m. 620.635.2535.

Red Hills Tavern:

320 W. 4th. The burgers, steaks, and sandwiches are the talk of the town in Ashland. Eat hearty, and rehydrate with a cold one. Monday-Friday 11 a.m.-1 p.m. and 5-9 p.m.; Saturday 5-10 p.m. 620.635.4137. FB.

Monte Casino Marker:

From Main, ¼ mile east on 4th (U.S. 160), then 3 miles north on Clark County Lake Rd. A large 1940s hilltop sandstone marker designates the site of Monte Casino Monastery. The short-lived monastery was built in 1876 by three Benedictine brothers. Note the three white crosses embedded into the monument. Nothing remains of the monastery.

Keiger Creek Bridge:

From Main, 8½ miles west on U.S. 160. This bridge across

the creek takes you through one of the most beautiful cuts of the Red Hills.

Lodging:
tinyurl.com/ashlandstay.

explorer extras...
In Ashland

Ashland Grade School (NRHP) at 210 W. 7th was constructed in 1937 through the Public Works Administration program. Erected by the WPA, a separate federal program, are the county highway department building (Highland and 10th) and the Girl Scout Little House (NRHP; 448 W. 6th). Both were built with locally quarried stone in 1937. The Girl Scouts still meet in their Little House.

Lustron homes are small prefabricated houses that became popular following WWII. Fewer than 100 of these still stand in Kansas. The surf blue Stein House (NRHP), a private residence at 420 Cedar, is the only Lustron in Clark County. Drive by only.

A row of historical area photos are set in round wood frames along the south side of the Bank of Ashland on 8th. The geodetic benchmark embedded into the bank's front wall was placed there in 1934 by land surveyors to determine elevation. **ee**

explorer extras...
In Englewood

Population 76

More than 60 percent (350,000 acres) of Clark County burned during the wildfires of March 2017. Englewood suffered the most damage per capita of any town in Kansas losing 10 percent of its 70 houses.

You know you're in ranch country when the cemetery entrance has iron cutouts of cowboys, cattle, and covered wagons. In Englewood Cemetery, playing cards etched into the gravestones for R.H. Roberts (1916-2002) and Merle Dreitz (1941-2004) hold special meaning for these men. From Claremont, 2½ miles north. **ee**

explorer extras...
In Minneola

Population 742

Town company president M.A. Low named Minneola in 1887 by combining the names of his daughters—Minne and Ola.

The town is proud of its sunflowers! Big, cheery metal *helianthuses* pop up from the Minneola welcome sign and are a lovely greeting.

The Boy Scout cabin at Oak and Locust, built by the WPA in 1935, incorporates a bas-relief sculpture of a woman on its south exterior wall. It was carved in 1933 by local artist Max Granke, but who the woman is or why she is on the cabin is not known.

Home Town Market, 135 S. Main, is a successful community-owned grocery. Stop in and support the store by buying a few explorer supplies, and if you're hungry take advantage of the lunch specials, 11:30 a.m.-12:30 p.m., and the pizza on Friday and Saturday nights. Monday-Friday 8 a.m.-7 p.m.; Saturday 8 a.m.-5 p.m. 620.885.4326.

Comanche County

AROUND THE COUNTY

Gypsum Hills Scenic Byway (8 Wonders of Kansas Geography):

Your route begins at U.S. 183 just north of Coldwater and extends east on U.S. 160 to the city limits of Medicine Lodge. The route is a straight 42 miles but on either side of the road you'll see evidence that you're in the Red Hills region—flat mesas, deep canyons, high buttes, and expansive vistas. The rocks and soil are stained red by iron oxide, giving the Gypsum Hills its physiographic name, the Red Hills. Closer to Coldwater you're also in High Plains country where grass pastures punctuate the landscape and come alive with wildflowers in the springtime. 800.684.6966. travelks.com/ksbyways.

Rugged Red Canyons Scenic Back Road:

From 2nd in Coldwater, 3 miles south on Central (becomes U.S. 183), 11 miles east on L, 6 miles southeasterly on 24/South Loop, 1 mile south on X, 3½ miles east on Q, 2½ miles north on N/North Loop, 4½ miles east on North Loop (becomes Estill in Barber County), then 6¼ miles north on Aetna to U.S. 160. This back-road beauty of a drive starts out through typical rolling red hills, but farther east the larger and more jagged the red canyons become. You're in open pasture with few obstructions. Charred cedar trees are evidence of the 2016 Anderson Creek fires. As you drive into Barber County, the red hills become littered with gypsum, a natural white mineral deposit. On this trip, unpaved roads are your route through this incredibly breathtaking part of the state.

SW

COLDWATER

Population 854

Heritage Memorial Park:
Main and New York. A walkway bordered by flowers and shrubs in this beautiful little park is one of the most elegant tributes in the state to county veterans of any war. Black stand-alone monuments list the names of those who served from the area.

Outdoor Mural:
104 W. Main. Stan Herd's elegant design of pioneer agriculture adorns an exterior wall of the Comanche County Museum. The scene connects a head of wheat, a Hereford steer, and a grain elevator. It is now Comanche County's logo.

Comanche County Museum:
104 W. Main. One of the most interesting exhibits showcases the Comanche Cattle Pool. A group of cattlemen combined their herds to form the largest cattle ranch ever established in Kansas. By 1884 the Comanche Cattle Pool contained 84,000 cattle and covered about 4,000 square miles of open range. It dissolved in 1885 after a devastating blizzard—and the advent of fence laws. Call ahead, 620.582.2859.

Coldwater Country Club Golf Course:
From Main, ¾ mile south on Central, ½ mile west on J, then 1 mile south on

Washington. It's not every golf course that has 10 holes, but this one does. Club members realized they had an ideal spot to add just one more feature—a swimming pool, a practice green, or another hole. They decided on a 10th hole, and although it's the shortest on the course at 110 yards, it's one of the most challenging. Greens fee. 620.582.2940.

Coldwater Lake:
From Main, ¾ mile south on Central, ½ mile west on J, ¼ mile south on Washington, then west into the entrance. Dedicated in 1980, Lake Coldwater is the only lake in southwest Kansas that allows water-related sports. It is also a wonderful site for camping and RVs. 620.582.2702. coldwaterks.com.

Dave's Pizza Oven:
100 N. Central. Since 1984 Dave has been rolling out made-from-scratch pizza dough. Ham-and-cheese pizza, breadsticks, and a pizza buffet have put him on the pizza map. Dozens of large maps of the county, United States, and the world cover the walls, but what's happening in Dave's pizza world is what really matters! Monday, Wednesday-Saturday 11 a.m.-9:30 p.m. 620.582.2775. davespizzaoven.com.

Auntie M's Pie Shoppe:
202 S. Central. You'll want to click your heels three times and go home to Auntie Em's just to sample her baked goodies—donuts, muffins, cinnamon rolls, cookies, and pies, pies, and more pies! She's also busy making daily specials—meatballs and cheesy potatoes, for example—all from scratch. Monday-Friday 7 a.m.-2 p.m. and 5-8 p.m.; Saturday 7 a.m.-2 p.m. 620.582.5886. FB.

The Kremee:
400 N. Central. Burgers, fries, and ice cream are the order of the day. Dine in or carry out from the window. Monday-Thursday 10 a.m.-8 p.m.; Friday-Saturday 10 a.m.-2 p.m. 620.582.2831.

explorer extras... In Coldwater

A restored neon marquee in red and blue enhances the tan-brick facade of the 1938 Chief Theater (NRHP), 122 E. Main. First-run movies are shown on weekends in this historic picture house in downtown Coldwater. 620.582.2705. FB.

The 1927 buff-brick Comanche County courthouse (NRHP), 201 S. New York, was built in the Classical Revival style. A projecting pavilion at the main entrance and the dressed lime-stone window sills and lintels showcase the classical styling.

In 2014 Tiffany Sowa commissioned 17-year-old Carlos Casas-Sanchez to paint an outdoor mural on her building at 136 E. Main, telling him he could create whatever he wanted. You'll enjoy seeing his youthful exuberant celestial masterpiece, best viewed from New York Street.

Tiffany Sowa and her daughter Camille have painted several murals, one of which features a lighthouse. With glow-in-the-dark paint, the lighthouse is a beacon in the night. You'll see it in the alley behind the Prairie Plaza Apartments at 205 S. Central. **ee**

PROTECTION

Population 530

Stan Herd Art Gallery:
404 N. Broadway. A Protection native, Stan is internationally known for his earthworks—using soil, crops, and other earth elements to create such large images that they can only be seen in their entirety from the sky. Stan's art gallery, adjacent to the Protection Township Library, is filled with his paintings, photos of his earthworks and murals, and other colorful tidbits. Monday-Friday 12-6 p.m. 620.622.4886.

Polio Protection Plaque:
Broadway and Walnut. Protection from polio was the mission of the Salk vaccine. And in 1957 Protection was selected to be the first town to inoculate all its citizens under the age of 50 with the vaccine. As we know, the vaccine was a success. A plaque next to the old-fashioned water fountain tells the polio/Protection story.

School Buildings:
210 S. Jefferson. What a difference 20 years makes in the world of architecture.

The Modern Movement style of the 1950 Protection Grade School (NRHP), now South Central Grade School, can easily be identified by its clean and simple lines. It provides an interesting contrast to the detailed 1930 Collegiate Gothic design of the 1930 Protection High School (NRHP), now South Central Middle School. The two schools, side by side and connected by a walkway, reflect obvious changes in architecture in just two decades.

Protection Community Venture:
221 N. Broadway. A community-owned grocery store means citizens have stepped up to invest and ensure that the townspeople have access to groceries. Support from the outside (travelers and explorers!) is a bonus. Monday-Saturday 7 a.m.-8 p.m.; Sunday 11 a.m.-5 p.m. 620.622.4406. FB.

Don's Place:
230 N. Broadway. Don opened his establishment in 1973 when he was 23 years young. Remarkable! He makes chicken-fried steak the Explorer Way and is famous for his homemade cream pies and donuts. Breakfast is served all day. Tuesday-Saturday 6 a.m.-8 p.m.; Sunday 7 a.m.-1:30 p.m. 620.622.4365.

WILMORE

Population 55

The Carousel:
210 N. Main. Just honk! When Ernie and Christy Griffin are home (usually April-June and October-December), they will come out at the sound of your horn and start those horses running! Ernie always wanted a carousel, and found

this beauty online. It was made in 2002 in Venice, Italy, and was in shopping malls in Minnesota and Texas before making its way to Kansas. Locals helped build a bright yellow-and-red gazebo to protect the ride, then helped put together the spinning tea cup, sleigh, and 13 horses on the carousel itself. Rides are free! 620.738.4420.

Catalog House:
210 N. Main. Before they purchased the carousel, Ernie and Christy Griffin bought and restored the 1913 Sears, Roebuck & Co. house just north of the carousel. Back in the day, families could order a complete house from the Sears catalog. All parts of the house—everything from the wood, to the nails and the final varnish—were shipped by rail to the buyer.

Stan Herd Outdoor Mural:
Railroad and Taft. Stan's depiction of the coin toss that decided the town's name dresses up the south base of the grain elevator. Local cattlemen and ranchers Thomas Jackson Wilmore and C.C. Pepperd participated in a coin toss to determine whose name would be given to the town. You know who won, since you aren't standing in Pepperd, Kansas, to view the mural.

SW

explorer extras... In Wilmore

This little town rests in a beautiful valley on Mule Creek, four miles north of U.S. 160 and six miles east of Coldwater.

The red-brick Federated Church at the south end of Main is the only remaining active church

in Wilmore. Dedicated in 1928, it retains the original semicircular pews in its small and intimate interior.

The 1910 alarm bell that was rung in case of emergencies is now restored and proudly displayed in front of the community building at Taft and Railroad. **ee**

Edwards County

explorer extras...
In Belpre

Population 82

Local cattleman Henry Laird funded the 1912 library, just west of Wheeler and Dudley. The small tan-brick building with arched portico bears his name. A veterans memorial stands just east of the library.

If you're looking for primitive, have a look at the old steel-cage jail at Dudley and Burdick. It'll make you appreciate your freedom! **ee**

KINSLEY

Population 1,408

National Foundation for Carnival Heritage Center:
113 E. 6th. Between 1904 and the 1980s Kinsley was home

to six carnival companies. Housed on the first floor of an old mercantile building, this museum pays tribute to the area's carnival heritage with its wonderful collection of old broadsides, artifacts from early carnival games, and historic photographs. Of primary focus is the stunning collection of carved carousel animals by nationally known animal sculptor Bruce White, a former resident of Coldwater. This museum isn't fancy, but you won't find content of this sort anywhere else in the state! It's a great one-of-a-kinder. For tours, call 620.659.2201.

Palace Theater (NRHP):
223 E. 6th. One of the finest examples of shoebox style (a functionalist style of modern architecture), this renovated theater has run movies continuously since it opened in 1917. A volunteer group operates the theater. 620.659.2225. FB.

Midway USA: U.S. 56 and U.S. 50. A sign on the west edge of town states that Kinsley is exactly midway between San Francisco and New York—1,561 miles each way! An exhibit about "Midway USA" is in the county museum (*see* next entry).

Edwards County Museum and Sod House:
U.S. 56 and U.S. 50. Featured is an enlarged 1939 *Saturday Evening Post* cover depicting two cars passing each other, each going to a world's fair on different coasts. The illustration is set in the middle in Kinsley, thus inspiring the town's nickname "Midway USA." Other displays portray early Edwards County history, the Santa Fe Trail, and a replica sod house. A steam engine, wooden windmill, and 1884 church on the museum grounds complete the complex. A veterans memorial stands east of the museum. May-September, Monday-Saturday 10 a.m.-5 p.m.; Sunday 2-5 p.m. 620.659.2420 or 877.464.3929. edwardscountymuseum.info.

Public Library and Bookworm:
208 E. 8th. Worthy of a photo is the charismatic wooden bookworm greeting visitors at the Kinsley Public Library. Four Kinsley High School students designed and built the sculpture (2001) to inspire young readers. Famed carousel sculptor Bruce White worked with the students and shared his tools and guidance. Monday, Wednesday 9 a.m.-7 p.m.; Tuesday, Thursday, Friday 9-11 a.m. and 1-5 p.m.; Saturday 1-5 p.m.

Historic Baseball Stadium:
Niles (U.S. 183) and Park (South Park). Baseball has been a part of this town's history since the Kinsley Stars and the Red Stockings baseball teams took the field beginning in 1877. Baseball teams still play at the 1934 wood and stone stadium at South Park. The stadium, a federal Civil Works Administration project, replaced the town's first baseball stands, built in 1904, after they burned down. The roof has been replaced with metal, but the benches are still red-and-white-painted wood, representing the high school colors and the colors of the original two baseball teams.

Civil War Statue (NRHP):
From E. 6th, ¼ mile north on Niles, 2¼ miles west 1st, then ½ mile north on Hillside Cemetery Rd to Hillside Cemetery. Local artist David Lester created this work, designed to honor Civil War soldiers, in 1917. Unlike other war statues of this era, this elaborate but primitive monument is made of hand-molded concrete. Lester served as a private in the 27th New York volunteers during the war, and in 1878 he and his wife moved to Kansas. Due to the effects of the environment, the statue has been encased in a protective metal building, but windows allow a view inside. A sign on the building relates the history of the statue.

A.L. Moffat: Hillside Cemetery (see previous entry). With a touch of humor, the small red granite gravestone for A.L. Moffat is inscribed, "A.L. Moffat 1885-1972 Lawyer Office Upstairs." The stone is in section C1, block

1, plot 5. In Kinsley, the door at 113 E. 6th still reads, "A.L. Moffat, Lawyer." In the second-story windows of the 100 block of E. 6th, colorful paintings portray local citizens from the past. Among them is "upstairs lawyer" A.L. Moffat.

First Cemetery: From 6th, ¼ mile north on Niles, then 1¼ miles west on 1st. This lonely cemetery was only active for about eight years, from 1878 to 1886, when it was abandoned for lacking a clear title for the land. A granite monument in the cemetery provides additional background. Research by the public library determined the causes of death for those buried here were typhoid, diphtheria, meningitis, prairie fires, murder, and being run over by a wagon.

Battle of Coon Creek: From Niles (U.S. 183), 2½ miles east on U.S. 50. On the south side of the highway, a historic marker captures the story of an 1848 battle between a large group of Plains Indians and an army train of 60 wagons along the Santa Fe Trail. The Indians sustained heavy casualties and when a young Apache returned to re-cover one of their own, the soldiers held fire. Legend has it that this young man was Geronimo, a future Apache leader.

Good Company:
512 Niles. Jennifer Gleason's gift store includes a selection of home furnishings and specialty foods. But the real draw is the artfully embellished serving utensils and other tableware she creates, drawing inspiration from her prairie upbringing. Monday 1-5 p.m.; Tuesday-Friday 10 a.m.-5 p.m. 620.659.2222. FB.

Bossy Sister Quilting:
209 E. 6th. All the quilting fabric, notions, and gift items that quilters adore are inside this beautifully restored downtown building with a gleaming original

wood floor and pressed-tin ceiling. Wednesday-Friday 10 a.m.-6:30 p.m.; Saturday 10 a.m.-4 p.m. 620.338.5168. FB.

Navanod Treasures:
213 E. 6th. Spend some time looking for that special treasure or hunting down a hard-to-find item. Three storefronts are filled with antiques, and, if they don't have it, they'll help you find it. Formerly known as Highway 56 Antiques, new owner Mike Donavan gave the store a new name—his name, spelled backwards! Monday-Saturday 9 a.m.-5 p.m.; Sunday 12-5 p.m. 620.659.2334.

Stacy's Town Square:
612 Niles. This is an all-purpose store. Inside you can have your hair done; rent a tuxedo; order party balloons; buy skin care products, gifts, and home decor; order a breakfast donut; grab a pizza or a sandwich for lunch, or an ice cream treat anytime. Monday-Friday 8 a.m.-7 p.m.; Saturday 10 a.m.-2 p.m. 620.659.2605. FB.

Good Restaurants:
Red Rooster (524 Massachu-setts, 620.233.6049); Strate's Kountry Kitchen (E. U.S. 50, 620.659.3299).

SW

explorer extras...
In Kinsley

A carnival mural by Jessica Charity White-Saddler brightens the corner at Marsh and 6th. In the 100 block of E. 6th colorful images by Larry Caldwell and high school students decorate the second-floor windows by portraying some of the early tenants of the building.

Architecturally significant homes are the prefabricated Lustron home (703 E. 4th); a turn-of-the-century mansion (417 5th); and a hexagonal house, although an addition has altered its appear-ance (5th between Emerson and Niles). **ee**

The Classical Revival style Edwards County courthouse built in 1928 has a substantial presence on the large block it occupies at 312 S. Massachusetts.

The terrain around Kinsley fluctuates from sand dunes and High Plains vegetation (sage, yucca, and pasture) west and south of town, to the Arkansas River Lowlands (flatter landscape, cottonwood trees, cropland) east of town. **ee**

**explorer extras...
In Offerle**

Population 194

A 1991 Dennis Burghart mural at Main and U.S. 50/56 captures the area's history, from cattle drives to railroads. In an early farm scene, a mother and daughter bring lunch to the field.

A DAR marker in City Park at Walnut and U.S. 50/56 denotes that the "dry route" cutoff of the Santa Fe Trail started one mile north and later one mile south of this point during the trail's active years. In both cases, the route eventually connected with the longer "wet route," which followed the Arkansas River, near Dodge City.

Two circa 1915 wood-frame grain elevators stand high against the sky east of town along U.S. 50. The one to the east is a cribbed structure built of two-by-four lumber and covered with steel siding patterned to look like brick. The second, the Gano elevator (NRHP), is a wood-studded structure covered with galvanized steel sheets. It is one of the few grain elevators in Kansas listed on the national register. The two structures are reminders of a time of intense competition in the grain storage industry in southwest Kansas, when even the smallest town had two, three, or more elevators to store grain before it was shipped across country by rail. From Walnut, 3½ miles east on U.S. 50. **ee**

Finney County

AROUND THE COUNTY

Ravanna Ruins Scenic Back Road: From Campus in Garden City, 23 miles east on K-156 to the granite marker,

7 miles north on K-23, then 4½ miles east on Lake. From a distance, the vertical stone ruins of the Ravanna school look like a mini Monument Rocks rising on the plains. In the 1880s Ravanna and Eminence, two thriving towns, each vied to become the county seat of Garfield County. Alas, the official survey showed that the county boundaries did not meet the required square miles for organization. The area was annexed to Sequoyah County (which was renamed Finney County) in 1893, and the towns died. On this route you will see expansive horizons and vistas and pass by mixed-grass prairie, huge cropland areas, and undulating terrain.

Ravanna to Eminence Scenic Back Road: From K-156, 7 miles north on K-23, 3½ miles west and south on Lake, then ½ mile west on Eminence. Should you want to see the site of the other player (the town of Eminence) in the Garfield County saga, take a High Plains drive to Eminence Cemetery, near where the town once stood.

Beersheba: This first Jewish agricultural colony in Kansas was established in present Finney County in 1882 by about 60 Jewish immigrants from Russia, sponsored by the Hebrew Union Agricultural Society. Farming efforts were not successful so many established businesses in Ravanna and Eminence. A historical marker at a rest area just west of K-23 and K-156 recalls the colony's short-lived existence. From Campus in Garden City, 23 miles west on E. Kansas (becomes K-156).

Jewish Cemetery:

From Kansas in Garden City, 4 miles north on U.S. 83, then 4 miles west on Lowe to Chmelka. Four gravesites are the only visible remains of a small community of Jewish settlers in this area. Also known as Toper Cemetery, the burial ground recorded its first burial in 1884 and its last in 1933.

GARDEN CITY

Population 26,966

Town Name: The story goes that a traveler at the train station asked Luticia Fulton the name of the emerging town. Luticia's husband, William, and his brother James were the first to file on land in Finney County and suggested the name Fulton Town. When Luticia said that she didn't like the proposed name, the traveler, inspired by Luticia's garden, said, "You ought to call it Garden City." The name stuck. You can see a modern version of Luticia's flower garden on the Historical Museum grounds, 403 S. 4th. At the former Santa Fe railway station in the 100 block of N. Main a handsome brick and sculpted stone memorial by Kansas artist Kivel Yankey relates the tale of Luticia Fulton and the naming of the town.

Finnup Park: 403 S. 4th. This spot on the Arkansas River once hosted thousands of wagons traveling on the Santa Fe Trail. Today the 110-acre park is home to the city's zoo, education center, museum, and

pool. A granite Santa Fe Trail marker placed by the DAR is on the park's north side along Maple.

Finney County Historical Museum: 403 S. 4th (Finnup Park). The museum features relevant exhibits and interpretive signage about the area's varied history, which includes cattle, cowboys, feed yards, the packing industry, irrigation, sugar beet factories, the big swimming pool, and C.J. "Buffalo" Jones, who is credited with saving the American bison. Follow a timeline from the Paleo-Indian period (9000 BCE) through the Santa Fe Trail and homesteading eras. The most unusual object here is the world's largest hairball, found by employees at a local meat packing plant in

GIANT HAIRBALL

1993. The 1883 home of William and Luticia Fulton, one of the county's founding families, stands on the museum grounds, as does an 1890 one-room schoolhouse. June to mid-August, Monday-Saturday 10 a.m.-5 p.m. and Sunday 1-5 p.m.; mid-August to May daily 1-5 p.m. 620.272.3664. FB.

Lee Richardson Zoo:

403 S. 4th (Finnup Park). This 1927 zoo, one of the oldest still operating in the state, has numerous options for you to meet a variety of animals. You may drive the zoo's perimeter to view many exhibits, or walk to the pedestrian exhibits. Nearly

300 animals are at home in modern, spacious enclosures with many animal enrichment activities. Watch playful North American river otters in the new Kansas Waters exhibit, and enjoy close-up views of mountain lions, jaguars, and bobcats at Cat Canyon. The Wild Asia exhibit features lovely Asian plants and architecture. From visiting the sun bears and snow leopards to the African lions and Bactrian camels, your time at the zoo is both educational and entertaining. April-August, daily 8 a.m.-7 p.m.; September-March, daily 8 a.m.-5 p.m. Admission charge for perimeter drive, which closes one hour earlier than pedestrian viewing (free). 620.276.1250. FB.

Safari Shoppe: 403 S. 4th. At the Safari Shoppe you'll learn about giraffe feedings, the zoo train, and renting safari cycles, strollers, wagons, and wheelchairs. Sack lunches, refreshments, and souvenirs are also available. April-August, daily 10 a.m.-7 p.m.; September-March, daily 12-5 p.m. 620.276.2661. folrz.com.

Finnup Center for Conservation Education:

312 E. Finnup. Visitors will appreciate the interactive

SW

displays here to learn about the area's natural and animal world. Public restrooms are available. Monday-Friday 8 a.m.-5 p.m. 620.276.6243.

The Big Pool: 504 Maple (Finnup Park). This block-and-a-half-sized swimming pool is so big that a boat once pulled a water skier through its waters! Hand dug with local labor in 1922, it holds 2.5 million gallons of water. The restored WPA bathhouse bears the sleek art deco design of the 1930s. New splash park features were added in 2006. A sign near the parking lot and an exhibit at the Historical Museum tell more of the pool's amazing history. June-July, daily 1-6 p.m. Admission charge. 620.276.1255. FB.

Historical Tours:
The visitor guide to Garden City and Holcomb includes a historical walking tour to more than a dozen sites, such as Silk Stocking Row (NRHP), the prominent Finnup family homes (NRHP), and the Bungalow Historic District (NRHP). A driving tour showcases additional historic locations. Brochures are available at the chamber office, 1511 E. Fulton Terr., or at tinyurl.com/gck-guide.

Finney County Courthouse: 311 N. 9th. A
statue of C.J. "Buffalo" Jones welcomes you to this 1929 Modern Eclecticism limestone courthouse with art deco detail. A plaque explains the fascinating life story of adventurer and plainsman Buffalo Jones,

who, among other accomplishments, rebuilt local buffalo herds, thereby helping save this noble beast from extinction. A replica Statue of Liberty stands on the grounds.

Historic Windsor Hotel (NRHP): 419 N. Main. Once
called the "Waldorf of the Prairies," this massive 1887 four-story hotel is undergoing renovation. The square tower over the main entrance has been restored with the gabled dormer window on each side

and ornamental railing. John Stevens, a town founder, built this grand Italian Renaissance structure, accented with a full-length skylight in its vaulted ceiling. It closed as a hotel in 1977. 620.290.6331. FB.

Downtown: Designated a Kansas Main Street community, downtown continues to thrive with events, art, architectural restoration, interpretive historical signage, and thriving businesses. Enjoy the many stores of antiques, clothing, bicycles, gifts, and jewelry as well as restaurants, coffee shops, and more. 620.276.0891. gcdowntown.com.

Garden City Arts:
318 N. Main. Absorb the art of southwest Kansas at this gallery featuring regularly changing local and regional exhibits. A gift shop offers a wide variety of art, pottery, sculpture, paintings, and jewelry. Tuesday-Friday 12-6 p.m.; Saturday 10 a.m.-5 p.m. 620.260.9700. gardencityarts.org.

Outdoor Sculpture:
3rd and Kansas. Garden City artist Javier Rivas sculpted *Friends and Frogs*, a life-sized bronze depicting five children of different ethnicities playing together and trying to catch frogs around a pond. A total of 18 public art pieces can be seen throughout the community including in downtown and the public library. Brochures listing locations of all the pieces are available at Garden City Arts, 318 N. Main.

Valley View Cemetery:
2901 N. 3rd. One of the most unique tombstones in the state may be the deteriorating upright stone topped with a rusted auto engine and goggles hanging off to one side. Michael Runnels died in 1927 when his car crashed into a train. One theory holds that Michael loved his car so much that he wanted

to die with it. Another theory purports that the grave marker was created to remind young people to drive carefully. This peculiar monument stands in the northeast quadrant of the cemetery under a cedar tree. Bronze plaques in the cemetery office relate the interesting history of Valley View and provide gravesite locations of town founders C.J. "Buffalo" Jones, William Fulton, James Fulton, and John Stevens. Locations are also given to the graves of the Herb Clutter family from Holcomb and to the infamous bank-robbing Fleagle Gang of the 1920s, and to a monument remembering 13 young American Indian men who worked in the sugar beet fields, died during the influenza epidemic of 1918, and were buried here in unmarked graves.

Sandsage Bison Range and Wildlife Area Tour:
From Fulton, 1¼ miles south on Main (U.S. 83). Here you'll board a Suburban or an open-air tram to travel through the sandsage prairie to the oldest publicly owned bison herd in Kansas. On your way to find these big, shaggy beasts

you'll view such wildflowers as western spotted bee balm, gaillardia, daisy fleabane, prickly pear cactus, larkspur, and shortgrass prairie vegetation. You might also meet up with a variety of wildlife including magpies, burrowing owls, black tailed jack rabbits, and prairie dogs. Donation welcome. Reservations required. 620.276.9400. fofgr.com.

Patrick Dugan's:
301 N. Main. Relax and enjoy a speciality coffee, a cup of tea, or an iced drink along with a pastry or breakfast sandwich in the comfortable and laid-back atmosphere of this corner coffee shop. Monday-Saturday 7 a.m.-5:30 p.m. 620.271.9131. FB

Traditions Soda & Sandwiches:
121 Grant. The sign above the old-fashioned soda fountain lists prices from the 1950s: ice cream soda 19 cents and sundaes, three dips, 24 cents. Things cost a little more today, but the strawberry ice cream soda is every bit as good and goes great with the popular Chubby Checker sandwich made with corned beef, turkey, tomato, lettuce, red onion, mustard, and mayo on buttered grilled sourdough! Monday-Saturday 9 a.m.-5 p.m. 620.275.1998.

Samy's Spirits:
1301 E. Fulton. Samy's pays homage to the rich tradition of the cattle industry in this area. You'll also find a pleasingly diverse menu that includes Italian, Mexican, Mediterranean, and Cajun dishes such as marinated chicken shawarma, blackened catfish, penne alla vodka, and fish tacos. Monday-Saturday 6 a.m.-10 p.m. 620.275.7471. FB.

Pho Hoa One:
713 E. Fulton. Pho Hoa opened in 1987 and has garnered legions of fans. One of the menu favorites is #38 (Bun Thit Nuong), a big bowl of steaming rice noodles topped with succulent grilled pork and sprinkled with peanuts. Pho, Vietnamese rice noodle soup, is extra delicious because owner and chef Ha Nguyen makes her broth using beef bones. Everything is made to order so preparation may take more time, but it's worth the wait! Monday-Tuesday, Thursday-Saturday 10 a.m.-2:30 p.m. and 4:30- 8:30 p.m.; Sunday 10 a.m.-3 p.m. 620.276.3393.

Ninja Sushi & Steak House:
416 N. Main. Nick Xu, Michael Zhang, and Daniel Ma are the owners of this dynamic new restaurant in downtown Garden City. Everything is superb—the soba and udon noodle dishes, the hibachi and bento dinners, and the sushi and sashimi. Daily 11 a.m.-9 p.m. 620.287.8089. FB.

Tequila's Mexican Grill:
1715 E. Kansas. Meda Munoz came from Mexico chasing the American dream. His genial personality and hard work have paid off with this popular restaurant. Everything on the huge menu is excellent—queso, fajitas, shredded beef entrees, plentiful orders of chips and salsa, lip-smacking margaritas, and Mexican beers. The service is fast and friendly, just one more reason why Tequila's is a favorite spot. Daily 11 a.m.-10 p.m. 620.275.4362.

Hanna's Corner:
2603 N. Taylor. The breakfast hot spot in town, Hanna's is known for large

SW

pancakes and fluffy biscuits and sausage gravy. But Hanna's is a lunch and dinner spot too, offering hot roast beef sandwiches, smothered pork chops, meatloaf, and more. Tuesday-Saturday 5:30 a.m.-8 p.m.; 6a.m.-1:30 p.m. 620.276.8044. FB.

Mexican Cuisine: Thanks to the diversity of its residents, Garden City has many variations on the Mexican theme. Casa Mariachi (1408 E. Fulton, 620.287.8188); El Zarape (2501 E. Fulton, 620.275.8181); Las Margaritas (301 N. Main, 620.271.9328); and Tacos El Tapatio (1203 E. Fulton, 620.275.6462, cash only).

More Good Restaurants: Napoli's, homemade pizza and Italian (2225 S. Air Service at the airport, 620.271.1490); Thai Arawan, serving Chinese and Thai (902 E. Fulton, 620.805.6280).

Lodging: Sunnyland Bed and Breakfast (RHKP, 620.276.0500, sunnylandbandb.com); additional lodging (visitgck.com).

**explorer extras...
In Garden City**

Step into various cultures at the town's ethnic markets. The Mexican market, El Remedio (1005 E. Fulton) carries nopalitos (sliced cactus palms) for salads, and a variety of chilis, pinatas, and canned Mexican products. The Vietnamese market, Savan Market (713 E. Fulton) stocks live crabs, rice paper, mudfish, and other Asian specialties. The African Store (911 W. Mary), provides immigrants from Somalia with a familiar grocery and a household store.

Buffalo Dunes, an 18-hole course at 5685 S. U.S. 83, is one of the top municipal golf courses in the state and consistently receives high rankings from national golf publications. 620.276.1210. buffalodunes.org.

Take a walk, a jog, or a bike ride on the three-and-a-half-mile paved Talley Trail that crosses the city from west (N. Lee) to east (E. Spruce). Seven gazebos placed along the landscaped trail serve as resting places, and a spot at Willowbrook Lane (east of N. 8th) has been enhanced with benches and a water tower to cool off people and pets. tinyurl.com/talleytrail.

Parrot Cove Waterpark, an indoor tropical-themed water park at 990 Stone Creek is one of the newest attractions in town. Float on the Lazy River or take one of four water slides—two are suspended four stories off the ground! Admission charge. 620.805.5303. parrotcovewaterpark.com.

Lustron homes, an efficient post-WWII invention, were made from prefabricated steel, inside and out! Garden City comprises eight such homes. See them at 407 Laurel; 405 and 1016 N. 4th; 310 and 312 Hudson; 211 and 901 N. 11th (with a detached Lustron garage); and 1203 N. 9th.

Stevens Park at Main and Pine is a distinctive downtown park boasting a 1931 band shell. The park's large trees providing plenty of shade have been the backdrop for countless events.

A tetra what? Look for the tetrahedron at the Garden

City Regional Airport, 2225 S. Air Service. The large, bright orange, triangular-shaped object on the tarmac is a special piece of equipment that indicates wind direction. It was first used by U.S. Army pilots who trained at the airfield during WWII, and it was restored in 2008. From Campus, 8 miles east on U.S. 50.

"Eat Beef, Keep Slim" is still proudly displayed on the grain elevators at Brookover Feed Yards north of town along U.S. 83. Earl Brookover established the first commercial feed yard, called "the yard that started it all," in the High Plains in 1951. Learn more about the cattle industry and commercial feed yards at the Historical Museum. From Kansas, 1½ miles north on Taylor (U.S. 83). ee

HOLCOMB

Population 2,118

Clutter Memorial: Park and Jones (Holcomb Community Park). In 2009 the town dedicated its park to the memory of the Herb and Bonnie Clutter family. The monument with a plaque about the family and the 1959 tragedy stands on the park's north end. The murder of this family was later memorialized in Truman Capote's *In Cold Blood*.

El Rancho: 305 N. Main. Since 1971 this family-run restaurant has pleased customers with their favorite dishes—enchiladas, chimichangas, tacos, and burritos—plus American fare and breakfast. Monday-Tuesday, Thursday-Saturday 10 a.m.-1:30 p.m. and 5-8:30 p.m. 620.277.2238. elranchoholcomb.com.

Ford County

AROUND THE COUNTY

Wagon Ruts: From 2nd in Dodge City, 10 miles west on U.S. 50/400. Most visible in the spring are the Santa Fe Trail wagon ruts (NRHP) near Howell. A sidewalk leads into the prairie grasses where you'll see historical markers and have the best view of the ruts. Looking out across the plains, it's easy to envision traders and their wagons rumbling along this trail, well-traveled from 1821 to 1880. 620.227.8188.

Amish Cemetery: From U.S. 400 in Dodge City, 5 miles south on U.S. 283, 4 miles west on Saddle, 1 mile north on 107, then ¼ mile west on Ridge. In 2014 descendants of an Old Order Amish Community came from Iowa to repair gravestones in this small cemetery. The last families left the community in 1929 and even the cemetery became abandoned over time. Now 28 of the 35 gravestones have been replaced and with due respect.

explorer extras... In Bloom

Unincorporated

Skeletal remains of the town still provide provocative textures, colors, and angles. The 1936

WPA Bloom High School gymnasium at 200 East is the stand-out remnant with its native red sandstone walls. The school closed in the early 1960s and only its entrance remains. An unidentified building, similar in construction to the gymnasium, still stands in good condition to the west along Main. A Spanish style service station with three service bays faces U.S. 54 as does the original Rock Island depot. Both stopped expecting traffic long ago. Bloom was once one of the largest wheat shipping stations on the Rock Island line west of Hutchinson, and it still serves as a grain storage facility today.

The Fort Dodge-Camp Supply Military Road passed several hundred feet west of the large state historical marker that stands ¾ mile east of Bloom on U.S. 54. The marker summarizes the history of this 90-mile ungraded prairie trail established in 1868 to transport supplies from Fort Dodge to Camp Supply in present Oklahoma. **ee**

BUCKLIN

Population 798

Main Street Market: 102 N. Main. Step inside this clean-as-a-whistle market and follow the old wood floors to the back. You might find Loretta Vice making the syrup for the most scrumdiddlyumptious limeades you've ever tasted. Besides groceries and limeades, you can find sandwiches, salads, and daily specials for lunch Monday through Friday. This cozy little market is good for Bucklin—and good for you if you shop here! Monday-Saturday 7 a.m.-8 p.m. 620.826.9860.

City Park: From Main, 1 block east on Grace. What a lovely park it is! Its stage, with a striking arrangement of arches, was erected in 1933 by the local En Avant Club. The low stone wall that surrounds the entire park, the star-shaped planters, the wishing well, and a picnic shelter were constructed in 1936 as a WPA project.

explorer extras... In Bucklin

Take a close look at the beautiful native rocks on the exterior of this WPA auditorium at 101 S. Nebraska. The 1936 building has been nicely preserved and now serves as the American Legion meeting hall.

An ace playing card is painted on the water tower, on the school sign, and is etched into the sidewalk. Why? Because the Bucklin High School mascot is the Aces. The junior high mascot is the Deuces! **ee**

DODGE CITY

Population 28,159

Francisco Vásquez de Coronado came through the area in 1541, Zebulon Pike in 1806, and in 1821 William Becknell passed this way when he opened the Santa Fe Trail. When the Santa Fe railroad reached this vicinity in 1872, the town of Dodge City was born. Buffalo hunters and soldiers from nearby Fort Dodge populated the town in its earliest years. But Dodge City is most famous for its cattle drive days of 1875-1886, when Texas longhorns came up the trail to the railhead to be shipped to stockyards in Chicago. Dodge City soon was branded "Queen of the Cowtowns."

Visitor Center: 400 W. Wyatt Earp. Built to look like a historic depot, the visitor center is the place to pick up tour brochures and other area information, and

SW

buy your tickets for the trolley tour of historic Dodge City. Memorial Day-Labor Day, daily 8:30 a.m.-6:30 p.m.; remaining months, Monday-Friday 8:30 a.m.-5 p.m. 800.653.9378. visitdodgecity.org.

Boot Hill Museum (RHKP; 8 Wonders of Kansas History): 500 W. Wyatt Earp. Feel the spirit of the Wild West!—the lawmen, gunfighters, cattle trails, and cowboys that made Dodge City famous. The main museum is a reconstructed 1870s western town, including a re-created

Boot Hill cemetery. A boardwalk runs along Front Street, where you'll find a general store, the famous Long Branch Saloon, a collection of more than 200 guns, and exhibits and audio-visual programs that depict life in the 19th century. The Boot Hill building houses exhibits about American Indians, the American bison and buffalo hunters, cattle drives and cowboys, ranching, homesteading, and Hollywood's impact on the area, including a pleasing and nostalgic display about the beloved *Gunsmoke* television series. In the summer you might come across a gun-fight reenactment, a variety show at the saloon (additional

charge), or the opportunity for a chuck wagon dinner. Memorial Day-Labor Day, daily 8 a.m.-8 p.m.; remaining months, Monday-Saturday 9 a.m.-5 p.m. and Sunday 1-5 p.m. Admission charge. 620.227.8188. boothill.org.

Trail of Fame: Follow this walking tour through the Old Dodge City historic district. The trail is marked with statuary and sidewalk medallions recognizing the famous and infamous who had major influence in the area's western heritage. Have your picture taken with an eight-foot bronze of famous Old West lawman Wyatt Earp (Central and E. Wyatt Earp). Or sit down at a card table with the likeness of Doc Holliday (beside the visitor center). More than 20 bronze medallions have been installed in the sidewalks between the Santa Fe depot (201 E. Wyatt Earp) and Boot Hill Museum (500 W. Wyatt Earp). Tour maps are available at the visitor center, 400 W. Wyatt Earp. dodgecitytrailoffame.org.

Kansas Teachers' Hall of Fame and Gunfighters Wax Museum: 603 5th. The purpose of the first (1977) teachers' hall of fame in the country is to honor outstanding Kansans in the field of education for grades K-12 and vocational schools. In addition, the facility exhibits school artifacts including early books, globes, water dipper,

and desks. Your admission also admits you to the kitschy throwback Gunfighters Wax Museum attraction. June-August, Monday-Saturday 10 a.m.-5 p.m. and Sunday 1-5 p.m.; September to mid-December, Thursday-Saturday 10 a.m.-2 p.m. Admission charge. 620.225.7311. teachers-hallfamedodgecityks.org.

Santa Fe Depot and Harvey House (NRHP): 201 E. Wyatt Earp. This beautifully renovated 1898 depot, Harvey House hotel, restaurant, and Harvey Girl dormitory has been converted to a 170-seat dinner theatre. The depot features its original pressed-tin ceiling, mosaic tile floor, and light fixtures. The Harvey House hotel lobby and dining room, vacant since 1948, is the new home of the Convention and Visitors Bureau. 620.225.1001.

Depot Theater Company: 201 E. Wyatt Earp. Inside the historic Santa Fe depot, this long-running attraction offers state-of-the-art dinner theatre, experimental productions, cabarets, and much more. 620.225.1001. depottheaterco.com.

Carnegie Center for the Arts (NRHP): 701 2nd. One of the most unique Carnegie libraries in the state, this 1907

CARNEGIE ART CENTER

structure has rounded architectural features and stained-glass windows. The building now hosts regularly changing exhibits of local and regional art. February-December, Tuesday-Friday 1-5 p.m.; Saturday 11 a.m-3 p.m. 620.225.6388. FB.

2nd Avenue Art Guild:

608 N. 2nd. The works of determined and passionate local artists are exhibited and for sale in the town's newest art gallery. Friday-Sunday 12-5 p.m. 620.255.1447. 2ndaveartguild.com.

Outdoor Murals:

On the 1930s First National Bank building (2nd and Spruce), Stan Herd has painted a five-story mural replicating Frederic Remington's *The Old Stage-Coach of the Plains*. Stan also has created a pictorial chronology of local history on the National Beef Packing plant exterior (2000 E. Trail).

El Capitan: 2nd and W. Wyatt Earp. A life-sized bronze sculpture of an imposing Texas longhorn commemorates the Dodge City cattle drive days of 1875-1886.

Cowboy and Oxen Sculptures: 501 W. Spruce.

In front of the former Municipal Building (NRHP) stand two commemorative features by Dr. O.H. Simpson. The cowboy statue was sculpted from cement with modeling skills Simpson learned as a dentist. The statue was unveiled at the 1929 dedication of the Municipal Building. The oxen memorial, consisting of two

concrete oxen heads, is thought to be crafted in 1932.

Wright Park: 71 N. 2nd. This park was platted in 1883 by Robert Wright, an 1860s plainsman who rose to prominence as an eminent Dodge City cattleman and entrepreneur. The park's signature structure is the grand 1919 Hoover Pavilion, a Spanish style stucco building named for George Hoover who is credited with platting the Dodge City town site and who became its mayor and a prominent businessman. Within this beautiful and historic park is a zoo, band shell, and the Liberty Garden (*see* following entries). A DAR marker and a plaque note the presence of the Santa Fe Trail, 1822-1872.

Historic Band Shell:

71 N. 2nd (Wright Park). The Cowboy Band plays every Tuesday evening during June and July at 8 p.m. in the 1934 stone and stucco band shell. Formed around 1881, the Cowboy Band performed at President Benjamin Harrison's 1889 inaugural celebration.

Liberty Garden: 71 N. 2nd (Wright Park). Just east of the Hoover Pavilion is a memorial commemorating 9-11. A four-foot section of steel from the Twin Towers is placed under a U.S. flag and between replicas of the towers. Two additions that now complete the memorial are a piece of Indiana Limestone, once part of the Pentagon facade, and a piece of Pennsylvania sandstone from the hemlock grove next to the crash site of United Flight 93.

Wild West Heritage Buffalo and Longhorn Exhibit:

Comanche and U.S. 50. At the south end of the Boot Hill Casino & Resort you can see buffalo and longhorn cattle year round. The exhibit describes the impact that livestock played in the development of Dodge City and southwest Kansas. A Walk of Fame features "western" inductees ranging from Hollywood stars to local icons.

SW

Mueller-Schmidt House
(NRHP): Vine and A. Built in 1881, this three-story house is the only stone home in Dodge City and is the oldest building in town still on its original site. June-August, Monday-Saturday 9 a.m.-5 p.m. and Sunday 2-4 p.m. Tours only. Donation welcome. 800.653.9378.

Dodge City Downtown Historic District (NRHP):
Generally bounded by Wyatt Earp, W. Third, N. Vine and E. Central. Contributing to the historic district are 76 structures built from 1886 to the 1970s, the majority of which are from the 20th century. Several factors combined to reduce the number of extant late-1800s buildings, including 1880s fires that took the original Front Street. Modern commercial construction occurred during the first three decades of the 1900s and continued during the post-WWII years, but

with a nod to the past, a replica of old Front Street was constructed in 1958. What remained of Dodge City's historic core, however, was doomed by the Urban Renewal plan of the 1970s, which demolished many structures. Today's historic district recognizes the growth and development of the town and its collection of commercial buildings from various periods.

Historic Architecture
(NRHP): Among the more interesting buildings included in the Downtown Historic District (*see* previous entry) are the following. The 1913 Ford County courthouse (Central and Gunsmoke) is a grand stone structure in Modern Eclecticism style. The 1928 Lora Locke Hotel (100 Gunsmoke) now serves as the county government offices, but the ornate lobby is still intact. Although not in the Downtown Historic District but nonetheless on the national register is the 1916 Sacred Heart Cathedral (903 Central), a beautiful example of Spanish Colonial Revival architecture.

National Weather Service:
104 Airport. From Central, 2½ miles east on Wyatt Earp (U.S. 56), ¾ mile north on Airport (airport entrance). Weather is important everywhere, but it's really important in western Kansas! Take a behind-the-scenes tour to see how the Weather Service researches and forecasts our rain or shine. Reservations required. 620.225.6514.

Winter Livestock:
1414 E. Trail. Established in 1936, Winter Livestock is one of the oldest and largest independently owned cattle auction barns in the nation. A sale starts every

Wednesday at 8:30 a.m., and visitors are welcome to experience today's cowboy culture. The sale barn cafe is a dandy, especially for breakfast. Cafe hours, Monday-Friday 7 a.m.-2 p.m. 620.225.4159.

Feed Yard Overlook:
From Central, 3 miles east on Wyatt Earp (U.S. 56). Here you can view the vast cattle feed yards, which have a capacity of 60,000 head. Cattle arrive weighing 600 pounds and leave in 140 days weighing 1,000 pounds or more. Signage explains more about the feed yard industry.

Boot Hill Casino
& Resort: 4000 W. Comanche. The first state-run gaming facility isn't as wild and wooly as gaming houses of the 1880s. But excitement floats in the air at this Old West themed casino. 620.682.7777. boothillcasino.com.

Boot Hill Distillery:
501 W. Spruce. Spirits are running high at Boot Hill Distillery. This unique distillery is housed in the former Municipal Building (NRHP) that was built in 1929 on the original Boot Hill Cemetery site (the interred had been moved in 1878). Grain for the distillery comes from local farmers Roger and Hayes Kelman and Chris

Holovach. It is processed at a local mill before being distilled and bottled. In the lounge at a historic bar, originally in a tavern on Front Street, you can order cocktails made with Boot Hill spirits. Friday-Saturday 1-7 p.m. Tours at 1, 3, and 5 p.m. Tour charge. 620.371.6309. boothilldistillery.com.

Dodge City Brewing:

701 E. 3rd. This brewery is the first in modern times in southwest Kansas. In the taproom you can enjoy a variety of hand-crafted beers and brick-oven pizza. Owner Larry Cook is a certified beer judge and has brewed award-winning beer since 2005. Wednesday-Thursday 4-10 p.m.; Friday-Saturday 11 a.m.-11 p.m.; Sunday 11 a.m.-8 p.m. 620.371.3999. dodgecitybrewing.com.

Cup of Jo-nes:
909 W. Wyatt Earp. Stop in or drive through for a cup of your favorite speciality coffee, tea, or other beverage. Delicious cinnamon rolls, fresh sandwiches, quiches, wraps,

salads, and soups are available, too. Monday-Saturday 6:30 a.m.-2 p.m. 620.789.5282. FB.

Kate's:
305 E. Trail. At this longtime favorite, the locals probably would recommend the chili-cheeseburger and homemade fries. But it's all good here, including the friendly service and giant ice-cold goblets of beer. Monday-Saturday 11 a.m.-10 p.m. 620.225.9466.

Guymon Petro Bar & Grill:
301 4th. The distinctive brick structure began its life as the Guymon Petro Mercantile Company, a wholesale grocery distribution operation that opened in 1902. A restaurant now operates inside this building, renovated in a rustic industrial style. The eclectic menu offers such dishes as voodoo shrimp and chipotle glazed quail. Two recipes are from the 1870s Harvey House days—fried chicken castaneda and Harvey House beef stroganoff. Dancing on the weekends. Grill hours, daily 11 a.m.-9 p.m. 620.371.7500. FB.

Osaki Hibachi Sushi:
2100 W. Wyatt Earp. Pick hot hibachi-grilled beef tips or chicken, or choose the cool taste of sushi rolls made fresh at the sushi bar. Try the special salmon family roll with spicy salmon inside, fresh salmon on top, and salmon eggs sprinkled over everything. Tuesday-Sunday 11 a.m.-9:30 p.m. 620.227.5235. FB.

Saigon Cafe Bistro:
202 E. Frontview. This small but busy Vietnamese restaurant has loyal customers who adore the flavorful pho—rice noodle soup—and the spring rolls and noodle bowls. Monday-Saturday 11 a.m.-2:30 p.m. 620.225.0682.

Central Station Bar & Grill:
207 E. Wyatt Earp. It's a one-stop spot for cocktails, dining, watching sports at the bar, and dancing in the club. A huge menu features mesquite grilled steaks, seafood, Mexican, pasta, salads, soups, and a variety of desserts. Grill hours, Monday-Saturday 11 a.m.-2 p.m. and 5-10 p.m. 620.225.1176. FB.

Casey's Cowtown Steak House:
503 E. Trail. Bask in the glow of the many stained-glass windows while enjoying a reasonably priced steak. Secret

seasonings make the Angus beef a steak house special. Monday-Saturday 11 a.m.-10 p.m.; Sunday 9 a.m.-2 p.m. 620.227.5225.

El Charro:
1209 W. Wyatt Earp. El Charro has been a local favorite since it opened in 1978. You'll see why when you taste the chicken enchiladas. They are extra good but only one of many popular entrees at this well-loved Mexican restaurant. Monday-Friday 11 a.m.-2 p.m. and 4:30-9 p.m.; Saturday 11 a.m.-10 p.m. 620.225.0371. FB.

Tacos El Torito:
105 N. 2nd. It's the place for Mexican take-out at nearly all hours of the day and night. Customers crave the tortas, carne asada tacos, and menudo. Monday-Thursday, Friday-Saturday 11 a.m.-4 a.m.; Sunday 11 a.m.-2 a.m. 620.227.9990.

Bella Italia:
312 W. Wyatt Earp. Tuck a napkin under your chin and dig into hearty pastas—ravioli aglio, spaghetti bolognese, and cioppino bella. You'll find much more to love on Bella's large menu. Daily 11 a.m.-10 p.m. 620.225.1800. FB.

Lodging:
Boot Hill Bed & Breakfast (620.225.0111, boothilldodgecity.com); additional lodging (visitdodgecity.org).

SW

explorer extras...
In Dodge City

Two unusual—and huge—sundials are at the east end of the Santa Fe depot, 201 E. Wyatt Earp. One tells Central Time and one Mountain Time. These decorative stone sundials, each more than 40 feet across, were designed in 1897 when the depot was built. Some years earlier, in 1883, railroads had set the four standard time zones nationwide. The Santa Fe railway in Dodge City drew a figurative line through its depot—trains heading east from that line recognized Central Time; trains heading west recognized Mountain Time. A sundial was placed on either side of the line to recognize the distinction and provide a visual aid to passengers. The sundials were restored in 1927 and again in 2004.

Next to the red caboose near the Santa Fe depot at 201 E. Wyatt Earp, a large sign details the unique history of a little Mexican village that developed in the nearby rail yard. It was home to workers from Mexico recruited by the railroad in the early 1900s. The sign tells of the workers' contribution to the development of Dodge City.

At Dodge City Downs, a Hispanic-operated track, quarter horses race for the finish line. Races are held year round, usually every other Sunday. September-April, 1 p.m.; May-August, 3 p.m. Bilingual organizers can answer your questions. 620.430.1768. dodgecitydowns.com (select FB).

During the summer watch a movie under the stars at the 1947 South Drive-In Theatre, 1019 McAtor. 620.225.4301. FB.

A white obelisk and a plaque commemorate the site of Fort Atkinson, which originally stood south of this marker. Created to protect travelers on the Santa Fe Trail, the small

post was built entirely of sod buildings. Field mice became such a problem that the commanding officer requisitioned cats from Fort Leavenworth! The fort only lasted four years, from 1850 to 1854. The plaque also notes that Caches, a famous campsite and a location of an early army headquarters, was just northwest of the marker. From Central, 4 miles west on U.S. 56, then just north on 107.

Sixteen miles of brick streets were laid in Dodge City between 1912 and 1925, and nearly 15 miles of them still survive, including two-and-a-half miles that are part of the Downtown Historic District (NRHP). Notice the diagonal weave pattern, especially at intersections, designed to prevent heavy vehicles from tearing up streets when making turns. ee

FORD

Population 221

R&V Blue Hereford Restaurant: 809 N. Main. Everything here speaks to tradition. Just ask the members of "the zoo," a group who has gathered here for coffee and meals since 1980. They have their own table, a sign with their names, and their photos on a nearby wall. Look for their preferred dishes, labeled Zoo Favorites, on the breakfast menu. Besides the camaraderie, the restaurant is known for the Sunday lunch buffet, all-day breakfast, and homemade pies. Tuesday-Saturday 7 a.m.-8 p.m.; Sunday 7 a.m.-2 p.m. 620.369.2841. FB.

FORT DODGE

Unincorporated

The Fort Dodge military post was founded in 1865 to protect the Santa Fe Trail from Indian attack. It is the oldest permanent settlement in the area. The complex became a soldiers' home in 1890 after the fort closed. The Kansas Soldiers' Home is still open to military veterans and their spouses, and it's not unusual to see citizens putting around in their golf carts in this friendly town. Visitors are welcome to take a self-guided tour by following the historic markers and stone signs. These tell about this unique community and identify its historic buildings, including stone homes built before 1875. Fort Dodge has all that its residents need, including assisted living quarters, a nursing facility, medical care, and more.

Fort Hays-Fort Dodge Road: Sheridan and U.S. 400. Just west of the Kansas Soldiers' Home a wood-framed sign notes that Fort Dodge was the western terminus on the 1867 Fort Hays-Fort Dodge Road. For about a year this supply route connected Hays to the Santa Fe Trail that ran through Fort Dodge. Usage of the road ended as railroads continued pushing westward.

Memorial Fountain: Patton and U.S. 400. A refreshing spot on the Fort Dodge campus is a circular fountain presented to the Kansas Soldiers' Home by Elizabeth Jackson in memory of her son James Wagnor, who lost his life in 1942 while a Japanese prisoner of war.

Fort Dodge Cemetery and Kansas Veterans Cemetery (RHKP): 11560 U.S. 400. From Sheridan, ¼ mile east on U.S. 400. A final resting place of military service men

and women, the cemeteries are a poignant stop on the High Plains. At the visitor center a memorable epitaph reads, "No one is ever buried alone, all are buried with honor."

Coronado Cross Park:
From Sheridan, 1½ miles east on U.S. 400. A 38-foot concrete cross was erected in 1975 to commemorate the site where Spanish explorer Francisco Vásquez de Coronado crossed the Arkansas River and on June 29, 1541, celebrated the first Mass west of the Mississippi. From the parking lot, take a short walk north over a little bridge and past yucca and other High Plains vegetation to a slight hilltop where the cross stands.

Population 806

Band Shell:
Main and A. This small but picture-perfect stone band shell was a 1938 WPA project. It's used for the town's homecoming parade and showcases the nativity scene at Christmas. It's easy to imagine sitting in a lawn chair on the red-brick Main Street listening to a town concert, which are still held here today.

Kelly's Corner Grocery:
301 N. Main. The pressed-tin ceiling and red-and-cream tile floor are reminiscent of the 1950s in this store decorated with vintage grocery products. In the back a deli serves ice cream treats from the soda fountain, sandwiches, and homemade cinnamon rolls. Monday-Saturday 7 a.m.-7 p.m.; Sunday 10 a.m.-4 p.m. 620.385.2311.

Windmill Restaurant:
410 S. Main. Jose Venancio was employed here 12 years before he bought the restaurant in 2009. He's a generous, hard-working family man who prides himself on serving delicious fajitas, enchiladas, tamales, and other Mexican American fare. Monday-Saturday 11 a.m.-3 p.m. and 5-8 p.m. 620.385.2523.

Wind Turbines:
The first of the enormous windmills in Kansas sprang up around the tiny burg of Spearville in 2006. The turbines, powered by blades more than 100 feet long, can be seen on the horizon miles before you reach them. An estimated 300 to 400 turbines now dot the prairie landscape near this town. A kiosk with graphics and information sheds more light on the subject. From Main, ½ mile east on U.S. 50, just north on 126, then west into a parking lot in a field.

Unincorporated

Immaculate Heart of Mary Catholic Church
(NRHP): 131 Spur. From Main in Spearville, 6½ miles east on U.S. 50, 6½ miles south and east on 132, ½ mile west on Iron, ½ mile south on 131 Spur. Built in 1913, this Gothic Romanesque Revival church is accented with stained-glass windows handcrafted in Munich, Germany—and recently restored. A beautiful structure of brick and limestone trim, its tall spire pierces the open skies of western Kansas. Although church services discontinued in 1997, the Windhorst Heritage group takes excellent care of the building and opens it for for daily viewing. Daily 8 a.m.-5 p.m. 620.659.3470. windthorstheritage.org.

Grant County

Wagon Bed Spring:
From U.S. 160, 8 miles south on K-25, at the curve continue 3¼ miles south on Wagonbed Springs, then 1 mile southwest across a cattle guard into a pasture. Wagon Bed Spring, also called Lower Cimarron Spring (NRHP), was an oasis on the route followed by most travelers on the Santa Fe Trail. But it also was the most dangerous stretch of the trail

SW

due to Indian hostilities. Today the spring contains no water, but years ago buffalo and other wildlife, American Indians, and travelers relied on this vital watering spot. Explorer and trader Jedediah Smith was killed by

Indians in this area in 1831, and the Mormon Battalion camped here in 1846 on its way to fight in the Mexican War. A historical marker and the remains of a wagon bed detail the spring's fascinating history. Wagon Bed Spring was designated a National Historic Landmark in 1960. 620.356.3009.

HICKOK

Unincorporated

Ulysses Watch and Clock Shop: 8549 E. U.S. 160. From Colorado in Ulysses, 8¾ miles east on Oklahoma (U.S. 160). Leonard Goossen has kept time in this location since 1983. Watch for a sign on the shop door; Goossen does double duty as a farmer and his sign lets you know if he's out planting wheat or harvesting a crop. Monday-Friday 8 a.m.-5 p.m. 620.356.4913.

Wagon Wheel Cafe and Bakery: 8551 E. U.S. 160. From Colorado in Ulysses, 8¾ miles east on Oklahoma (U.S. 160). Made-from-scratch breads, buns, cinnamon rolls, and pies; delicious biscuits and gravy and daily specials— that and more is baking at this country kitchen. Monday-Thursday 11 a.m.-2 p.m.; Friday 8 a.m.-8 p.m. 620.424.1368.

ULYSSES

Population 6,274

The city (Ulysses) and the county (Grant) were named for General and President Ulysses S. Grant, and the area is renowned for its annual Grant County Home Products Dinner in September. As you

drive this region you'll notice huge acreages of irrigated cropland and some of the largest cattle feedlots in Kansas.

Historic Adobe Museum (RHKP): 300 E. Oklahoma. Formerly a county shop completed in 1938 by the WPA, this adobe building is now home to an innovative museum that invites you to experience this area's history. Of primary interest are the photos, personal accounts, and artifacts examining the 1930s—the challenges and devastation of the Dust Bowl juxtaposed with

the boom of the developing gas industry (8 Wonders of Kansas History). A sod house and an Indian encampment relate stories of the region's pioneers and American Indians, and the 1950s display is pure fun. The Historic Adobe Museum is a certified interpretive visitor center for the Santa Fe National Historic Trail. Monday-Friday 9 a.m.-5 p.m.; Saturday-Sunday 1-5 p.m. 620.356.3009.

Old Town Site: From the Adobe Museum, 2 miles east on U.S. 160. Nothing remains of the original Ulysses town site. But along the highway is a clever metal cutout of horses

towing an old bank on a wagon heading west. The sculpture was designed and fabricated by local Earl Seger and his family, and represents the town of Ulysses being moved from one site to another. Look west and imagine a booming town with a population of around 1,500. That was the original Ulysses in the early 1900s. To raise money the town sold bonds, mostly to investors in the East. But when the bonds came due in 1908, Ulysses had no money to pay them. To escape the debt, the residents moved the town three miles west to its present site. The old hotel at the Adobe Museum complex is the center third of the Edwards Hotel, built in 1887 on the original town site. When the hotel was moved to the new Ulysses, it was cut into thirds.

Grant County Courthouse (NRHP): 108 S. Glenn. Art deco, earth tone tiles accent the brick exterior of this 1930 Modern Eclecticism courthouse. Note the gargoyle street lamps at the center entrance.

Mary Queen of Peace Catholic Church: 804 N. Colorado. One of the most unique and beautiful structures in western Kansas, this church is a classic example of hyperbolic paraboloid architecture and probably the only triple-roof, lattice-type, hyperbolic paraboloid church in the world. Built in 1963 by George Pitcher and Company, this unique

building includes a surrounding canted concrete base and continuous interior stained-glass windows. Daily 8 a.m.-8 p.m. 620.356.1532.

Main ARTery: 103 S. Main. The arts are alive and well in southwest Kansas, and this gallery is an engaging setting to connect with all mediums. It also offers art supplies, custom framing, paint parties, classes for all ages, and much more. The gallery displays the work of 24 artists and provides space to 20 vendors selling antiques and crafts. Tuesday-Friday 10 a.m.-5:30 p.m.; Saturday 10 a.m.-4 p.m. 620.424.3828. mainarterykansas.com.

Russ Binney Park: 200 W. Santa Fe. Longtime community advocate and businessman Russ Binney would appreciate this lovely little retreat that bears his name. Resting above the site of the old swimming pool, the park features grasses, shrubs, and flowers that can easily adapt to temperatures in this region. Common sage, blue spirea, and rudbeckia are only a few of the plants that augment the sidewalks and gazebo. A water fountain and a tiered limestone pond with lily pads and a waterfall add a nice touch to the surroundings.

Bear Creek Coffee Company: 107 N. Baughman. A renovated grocery store has made a successful transition into a little gem of a coffee shop. But besides specialty lattes and espressos, Bear Creek serves mouth-watering homemade scones and is a favorite lunch stop for chicken orchard salad, lobster bisque soup, and daily

specials. Tom Hauser, Kansas Explorer #6140, tells us he gets hungry just thinking about the BLT! Monday-Saturday 7 a.m.-2 p.m. 620.424.3414. FB.

Alejandro's: 816 W. Oklahoma. The stuffed sopapillas smothered with green chili sauce and the chili rellenos are excellent. And American offerings are equally good—steaks, seafood, and hand-breaded chicken-fried steak. Monday-Saturday 11 a.m-2 p.m. and 5-9 p.m. 620.356.3163. FB.

El Ranchito Cafe: 111 E. Oklahoma. Yes, more is better when it comes to fantastic Mexican cuisine in southwest Kansas. Folks have enjoyed it at the El Ranchito since 1968. Try the local favorite, the El Ranchito special—meat, beans, lettuce, tomato, sour cream, and avocado slices on a fried tortilla shell. Monday-Saturday 11 a.m.-9 p.m.; Sunday 11 a.m.-2 p.m. 620.356.9255. tinyurl.com/elranchito-ulysses.

Paleteria y Neveria Cuauhtemoc: 211 N. Main. Paleteria means popsicle, Neveria means ice cream parlor, and Cuauhtemoc was the last Aztec emperor. Owner Armando De La Pena is a Kansas State University graduate with a degree in criminal justice. But he followed his other calling to create ice cream concoctions in a traditional Mexican style. Armando's favorite flavors are pecan and cheesecake, but stop inside this nevería and discover your own favorites! Daily 1-8 p.m. 620.356.2290.

Corporate East Tavern: 1104 E. Oklahoma. Enjoy your "It's 5 o'clock somewhere"

cocktail and follow it with a great steak dinner, burger, wings, or the flavorful fish tacos. Monday-Saturday 5 a.m.-9 p.m. 620.356.4010. FB.

La Estrella Restaurant: 117 S. Main. The newest Mexican restaurant in town serves breakfast all day on Saturdays and Sundays. Customers love the tacos nortena—similar to tacos de carne asada—with choice of asada (steak), pollo (chicken), or ground beef (for the gringo!) and served with a grilled jalapeno and sliced avocado. Wednesday-Monday 10 a.m.-10 p.m. 620.339.1183. FB.

explorer extras...
In Ulysses

Illustrating Grant County industries, a mural by Ulysses native Armando Minjarez can be seen at the soccer field just east of the Grant County Civic Center, 1000 W. Patterson. armandominjarez.com.

The lustrous dove gray Lustron home at 123 N. Missouri is one of 91 Lustrons—popular housing following WWII—still standing in the state. The telltale signs of these structures are their box shape, low roof line, window awnings, and zig-zag design in the porch support pillars. Drive by only.

Memorial Park at 400 S. Main is a haven of shade under towering elms, blue spruce, and oaks, and a circle of benches in the park's center is surrounded by planters of cheery flowers. A marble stone pillar memorializes Dan C. Sullivan, a well-known rancher, grain man, oilman, legislator, and philanthropist. **ee**

SW

Gray County

CIMARRON

Population 2,236

Cimarron Crossing Park:

From A (U.S. 50), ½ mile south on Main. In 1822 William Becknell, known as the "Father of the Santa Fe Trail," first traveled what would become the trail's "dry route"—the cutoff route heading straight south to the Cimarron River. Although it was the most direct passage to Santa Fe, it was a dangerous section of the trail—hostile Indians and no water. In 1878 Cimarron was settled and named for the nearby river. Historical markers for the trail and a map are in the park along a half-mile paved walking path.

Gray County Courthouse:

300 S. Main. Built of brown brick with limestone trim, the 1927 courthouse occupies a full block square. Its Modern Eclecticism style features four grand pilasters. Remnants of a fish pond can still be seen piled under the evergreens on the north side of the grounds. On the pond site, a very striking veterans memorial now stands in respect to those who served from the county.

Old Gray County Courthouse (NRHP):

117 S. Main. Constructed 1886, this courthouse was the center of a heated county seat battle in 1889. A dozen men from nearby Ingalls, which had vied to become the county seat, raided the courthouse, stole the county records, and left three men dead in a bloody gunfight. On the front of the building, bullet holes from the gunfight are a visual reminder of the historic and deadly battle.

Clark Pharmacy and Soda Fountain:

101 S. Main. Jim and Sandy Coast passed the ownership baton to Matt and Kimberly Monical, both Cimarron natives who went away to college and returned home to raise their family. They expanded the business to include women's and children's clothing, home furniture, and a decor and gift shop (Blush Boutique, 103 S.

Main), and to sell cupcakes and other goodies from the in-house bakery. The interior of this full-service pharmacy retains the old pressed-tin ceiling and the beautifully tiled 1920s soda fountain (with its shiny spigots), which continues to serves old-fashioned treats. Monday-Friday 8:30 a.m.-6 p.m.; Saturday 9 a.m.-3 p.m. 620.855.2242. clarkpharmacy.com.

Canal Street:

From A (U.S. 50), 1 block north on Cedar. In the 1880s Asa Soule's mammoth Eureka Canal (*see* p. 409) ran through here to irrigate land in Gray and Ford Counties. In the 1930s when the ditch was filled in, the area was named Canal Street. You can still see earthen mounds between Ingalls and Cimarron on either side of U.S. 50 indicating where the canal once ran.

explorer extras...
In Cimarron

The venerable Cimarron Hotel (NRHP), 203 N. Main, opened in 1887 under the name of the New West Hotel. For a century it operated almost continuously as a hotel, its three-story brick facade of Second Empire style and its shady front porch welcoming guests to its once-plush interior. Today it is a private residence and stands as one of Cimarron's only reminders of its boomtown days in the 1880s.

Schedule a free, half-hour tour of Forget-Me-Not-Farms and you'll see everything from cows being milked on the carousel to milk being loaded onto the trailers. Reservations required (online preferred). 620.855.2844. 22502 R. forget-me-not-farms.com.

The native stone county shop building, 104 W. D, was erected in 1936 by the WPA to house maintenance equipment. The old shop is now used for storage. **ee**

explorer extras....
In Cimarron

At the corner of D and S. Main the small white concrete building with a blue wooden door is an innocent looking little thing. Would you guess it was constructed in 1920 as a jail? Locals report that it was the lockup as late as the 1930s, and anyone thrown into this unconditioned and unheated clink suffered through the heat and cold. **ee**

COPELAND

Population 298

Copeland Cafe: 201 Santa Fe. Homemade everything makes everything taste better. Savory, moist pot roast is served with potatoes, carrots, and a buttery homemade dinner roll. Follow that with a slice of peach pie with sugar crystals atop the crust. The coffee is excellent as are the homemade pancakes with warm homemade syrup. Cinnamon rolls and pies are made fresh daily. Monday-Saturday 7 a.m.- 8 p.m. 620.668.5563.

Outdoor Mural: Allen and Travis Bailey painted *Prairie Learning* in an apt location— on the side of the public library, 109 Santa Fe.

INGALLS

Population 297

Founded in 1884, the town was named for John J. Ingalls, a U.S. senator from Kansas who submitted Ad Astra per Aspera *for the state motto. A popular Latin phrase meaning "To the*

stars through difficulty," it was adopted as the official state motto in 1861.

Santa Fe Trail Museum:
204 S. Main. At home in two adjacent Santa Fe depots— the 1892 Ingalls depot and the 1918 depot relocated here from Montezuma—the museum features panels about each county town, the early history of the 1931 Spanish style St. Stanislaus Church, and fascinating photos of the Dust Bowl's "Black Sunday." A mural and exhibits preserve the saga of Asa Soule's legendary canal (*see* next entry). May-October, Monday-Saturday 9-11 a.m. and 1-4 p.m. 620.335.5220.

Eureka Canal (NRHP):
Also known as the Soule Ditch, this irrigation canal was the 1883 brainchild of Asa Soule. His plan was to build an irrigation ditch that would direct water from the Arkansas River west of Ingalls almost 100 miles east to Coon Creek in Edwards County. His canal did not work as he hoped, but traces of it can still be seen east of town starting at 13105 M and continuing east on the north side of U.S. 50. Mounds of dirt excavated during construction mark the route. One of the giant pumps for drawing water from the Arkansas into the Eureka Canal is exhibited outside the Santa Fe Trail Museum.

St. Stanislaus Catholic Church: 200 Rush. This
beautifully tended Spanish

style church was dedicated in 1931. Additions and interior modernization came in the 1970s, but great care was taken to preserve the exterior of the elegant entrance when a new entrance was added. 620.335.5202. ststanislausingalls.com.

Santa Fe Trail Markers:
A DAR trail marker in front of the museum, 204 S. Main, was originally placed along the trail's "mountain route" (a northwesterly route following the Arkansas River to Bent's Fort, Colorado), but it was moved to this site when U.S. 50 was under construction. A second DAR marker, at Main and Kansas, indicates where the trail left the "mountain route" south of present Ingalls to connect to the "dry route," a shorter but more dangerous journey.

Welborn "Doc" Barton House (NRHP): 202 S.
Edwards. Architecturally this rural Folk Victorian structure with eight exterior doorways is a unique design with each room having at least one door to the outside. Barton built the home in 1880 in Cimarron, and in 1896 it was sawn into three pieces and moved to Ingalls where it was reassembled. Barton and his brother Al drove 3,000 head of cattle from Texas to near Pierceville (west of Ingalls) in 1872 where they established the first working ranch in western Kansas. Today his house is unoccupied.

Ingalls Cafe: 120 S. Main. Ruthie Edmonson does most all her cooking from scratch, including the caramel pecan rolls and the real mashed

SW

potatoes, in this clean and friendly little cafe. Mark a Saturday night on your calendar and treat yourself to prime rib, the only night of the week it's on the menu. Vanilla soft serve ice cream is available anytime. Monday-Saturday 6 a.m.-8 p.m.; Sunday 7 a.m.-2 p.m. 620.335.5501.

MONTEZUMA

Population 955

Stauth Memorial Museum:
111 N. Aztec. Look for the copper roof! This facility features the worldwide travel adventures of Montezuma residents Claude and Donalda Stauth. Claude played in the Dodge City Cowboy Band, thus an entire museum section is devoted to the musical instruments that he collected as he traveled. In addition to its quality travel exhibits, the museum also features the Wall Western Collection (a permanent exhibit of Frederic Remington miniature bronzes) and the Fry Wildlife Collection. When the Stauths bequeathed their estate for the museum they stipulated that it remain free to the public and that the ladies bridge club, of which Donalda was a member, would always be welcome to meet here. The ladies still play here twice a month. Tuesday-Saturday 9 a.m.-4:30 p.m.; Sunday 1:30-4:30 p.m. 620.846.2527. stauthmemorialmuseum.org.

Street Names:
As one local said, we have street names you can't pronounce and can't spell!

The town founder named the town for Aztec emperor Montezuma, and he named the streets for historical figures associated with the conquest—Cortez, Mesita, Maldonodo, Mexitli, and Escalanta are a sampling.

Adobe House:
102 N. Tovar. A touch of the Southwest is evident in this attractive flat-top home made completely from adobe blocks in the 1930s. Drive by only.

WPA Projects:
The 1933 and 1935 work of the WPA is found in the Boy Scout stone cabin and the stone walls around it and the park at Tovar and Cortez.

Coffee Connection:
105 W Mexitli. You'll feel very good about spending money in this nonprofit cafe—all profits go back into the community. Coffee and baked goods start out your mornings, and soups, sandwiches, wraps, and salads are just right for lunch. Monday-Friday 7 a.m.-5 p.m.; Saturday 7-11 a.m. and 7-10 p.m. 620.846.7761. FB.

Montezuma Drug:
300 N. Aztec. You can't beat this locally owned pharmacy, in business since 1914, for cherry limeades, root beer floats, shakes, twist cones, and other frosty treats. Monday-Wednesday, Friday 9 a.m.-5 p.m.; Thursday, Saturday 9 a.m.-1 p.m. 620.846.2202. FB.

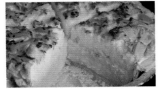

Brianna's Cafe:
203 N. Aztec. It's known for its fabulous pies, especially the coconut

cream and peanut butter. But customers also come from miles away for the fried chicken and the French toast with caramel syrup. Monday-Saturday 7 a.m.-8 p.m.; Sunday 10 a.m.-3 p.m. 620.846.7231. FB.

Gray County Wind Farm:
From Aztec in Montezuma, 2½ miles east on U.S. 56. Built in 2001, it was the first wind farm in the state. Its 170 wind turbines covering nearly 20 square miles are designed to gather energy from wind and convert it into electricity. Each tower is 207 feet high and weighs 147,000 pounds; each blade is 77 feet in length and weighs 3,300 pounds. All in all, the wind farm is an amazing sight. More information is available at the kiosk on U.S. 56 and at Stauth Memorial Museum, 111 N. Aztec. 620.846.2527.

Greeley County

Greeley County is in Mountain Time Zone (MT).

Greeley County was established in 1887—the last of the 105 Kansas counties to be created.

Horace Greeley Influence:
Several place-names in the county derive from *New York Tribune* founder and editor Horace Greeley (1811-1872), who supported Kansas entering the Union as a free state. He is also credited with coining the maxim, "Go West, young man." The county itself bears his last name, a small town has his first name, the county seat of Tribune is named for his newspaper, and a short-lived town was named for his dog Hector. Another short-lived town was named for Greeley's successor editor, Whitelaw.

Jack Rabbits:
The black-tailed jack rabbit is found throughout the state, but it's

more common on the western Kansas prairies. Stay alert. If you see a creature with large hind feet and ears about 5 inches long bounding along about 40 miles per hour, you've seen a jack rabbit! This speedy creature is the mascot of Greeley County high school in Tribune.

GAR Cemetery:

From Broadway (K-27) in Tribune, 11 miles west on Kansas (K-96), 2 miles north on 6, then ½ mile west on O. This cemetery contains seven Civil War veterans' graves and an interesting monument to the Rogers brothers, who died in the blizzard of 1886.

TRIBUNE

Population 766

Horace Greeley Museum

(NRHP): 214 E. Harper. Historic county photos line the walls inside this limestone structure, built in 1890 as the Greeley County courthouse but no longer used as such. The hallway with its original wood floors is flanked by exhibit rooms inviting visitors to examine Dust Bowl photos and artifacts. Admire the woodwork in the historic courtroom and visit the original jail cells in the basement. Thursday 9 a.m.-3 p.m. MT. 620.376.4996. horacegreeleymuseum.org.

Metal Ring Sculpture: 616 2nd. In front of the current courthouse stands an 11-foot metal sculpture made entirely from 544 wagon wheel hub bands metal rings. This 1941 stellar monument is in commemoration of the early Greeley County pioneers. Local welder Clyde

Smith created the sculpture by welding the bands together into its pyramid shape. Placed inside the pyramid are a sod-breaking plow, picket pins, and a hitching post.

Gooch's Foods:

503 Broadway. Since 1948 the Gooch family has operated this clean, full-service grocery store, an indispensable institution in these remote surroundings. Stop in and pick up a few supplies. Monday-Saturday 7 a.m.-6 p.m.; Sunday 8 a.m.-1 p.m. MT. 620.376.4621. FB.

Dixon Drug TrueValue:

422 Broadway. More than a drug store, Dixon's is a contemporary twist on an old-fashioned general store. Kellee and Chris Dixon bought the business in 1989 and have worked hard growing this hometown pharmacy. They've also added a wide range of merchandise— from clothing to shovels. Monday-Friday 8:30 a.m.-5:30 p.m.; Saturday 9 a.m.-2 p.m. MT. 620.376.4224. FB.

Colleen's Place: 311 4th.

Enjoy the hunt for antiques, vintage items, collectibles, and furniture. Thursday-Saturday 1-4 p.m. MT. 620.376.4633.

Greeley County

Republican: 507 Broadway. If you have questions about Tribune or the county, visit with Dan and Jan Epp at the newspaper office. The paper has been owned and operated by the Epp family for more than 80 years. 620.376.4264. gcrnews.com.

Peggy's Place:

Broadway and Harper. When local resident Bill Hamann returned home to spend his retirement years, he spruced up this empty corner lot into a beautiful green space with lush flowers, trees, and landscaping. He named it for his mother, Peggy.

Star Theater: 415 Broadway. It's a lucky small town that has a movie theater, and thanks to volunteers who run the ticket window, the concession stand, and are the clean-up crew, Tribune is one of those towns. Friday-Sunday. For movie hotline, call 620.376.4612. FB.

Veterans Memorial:

Broadway (K-27) and Zenaide. The beautiful and distinct monument is dedicated to the local men and women who have honorably served their country.

Prairie Ridge Golf Club:

From Lawrence, ½ mile north on Broadway (K-27), then ¼ mile southwest on the driveway to the clubhouse. Enjoy nine holes on large grass greens and buffalo grass fairways. Greens fee. 620.376.2548. tinyurl.com/tribgolf.

Alley Bar & Grill:

108 Ingalls. This vintage bowling alley is ready for you to bowl that perfect game! The grill feeds hungry competitors and

SW

cheering supporters. Monday, Wednesday-Saturday 5:30-10 p.m.; Sunday 11 a.m.-7:30 p.m. MT. 620.376.4808. FB.

Karen's Kitchen:
416 Broadway. The burgers, Mexican food, and the popular pork tenderloin sandwich are served in quick fashion, but slow down and take a moment to look around. At Karen's there is more to life than eating! Monday-Friday 9 a.m.-1:30 p.m. and 4:30-7 p.m. MT. 620.376.2223. FB.

The Trench Bar & Grill:
208 W. Kansas. Wayne and Emily Moritz have created a relaxed and fun-filled environment. Emily's excellent specials—pizza, Mexican, Rocky Mountain oysters, and more—are served four nights a week, and Saturday night is steak and shrimp night. Grill hours, Monday, Wednesday, Friday-Saturday 6-8 p.m. MT. 620.376.2900. FB.

Lodging:
greeleycounty.org/lodging.

explorer extras...
In Tribune

At the county fairgrounds you'll see the skeleton of a home-owned carnival. Come fair time (first week of August), the seats

come out of the shed and the gears are oiled as volunteers bring these carnival rides to life. From Broadway, 4 blocks west on Fairgrounds.

It's worth the drive past the 1931 Greeley County Community High School at 400 W. Lawrence to see its art deco styling, beautiful terra cotta detailing, and the relief panels of lavender, blue, orange, and green at the central entry. The school's interior underwent a major renovation in 1988 and still serves as the high school.

Unlike most poor farms, the Greeley County farm comprised smaller units, made of adobe bricks and stucco. The farm closed in 1946 and today only crumbling walls remain. If you walk around the remnants, watch out for snakes. From Broadway, 1 mile east on K-96, then 1 mile south on 17, west side of the road.

It has been noted by avid bird watchers that the group of trees south of the railroad tracks on the east side of Broadway is a resting spot for migrating birds. Bring your binoculars during the early spring and fall months—the times for your best chance to see a wide variety of birds. From Kansas (K-96), 1 block north on Broadway. **ee**

Hamilton County

Hamilton County is in Mountain Time Zone (MT).

Although feed yards are the main industry here, Hamilton County is home to five dairies.

IN COOLIDGE

Population 93

Trail City: A quarantine law against Texas trail cattle, passed by the Kansas legislature in 1885, stopped all trail herds from entering Kansas. As a result Texas cattlemen, including Martin Culver, proposed a National Cattle Trail (bypassing Kansas) for herds trailing from Texas to Montana. Culver went so far as to found the town of Trail City, Colorado, on the state line a few miles west of Coolidge. Due to its immediate cowboy activity, Trail City became known as the wickedest town on the Arkansas River. Culver moved his family from Texas to Coolidge, but nearby Trail City only lasted a few years. The Trail City name, however, was not lost and shows up still today in Coolidge.

Martin Culver: From Manchester, 1 mile north on Main (becomes C) to Coolidge Cemetery. Buried in this cemetery, Martin Culver (*see* previous entry) died in 1887 at the age of 48 from a ruptured appendix. His gravestone is in the shape of a cross and his grave is bordered with concrete and small round stones.

Santa Fe Trail Marker: Oak and U.S. 50. Set on the actual trail, this DAR marker is the westernmost indicator of the "mountain route" in Kansas. The "mountain route" was a slightly northwestward course of the Santa Fe Trail and followed the Arkansas River through Kansas

to Bent's Fort in Colorado. A thousand residents once populated this thriving border town that was incorporated in 1886. It's quieter now.

Potter's Opera House (RHKP): 110 Walnut. Town blacksmith Garner T. Potter built this native limestone opera house during 1886. It served many purposes including a church and a Masonic lodge and even hosted masquerade balls. Although the old opera house is now abandoned, the determined community has plans to renovate it.

Historic Buildings:
Two limestone structures, the 1886 limestone City Hall (210 Wheeler) and the 1888 Coolidge State Bank (Coolidge and Maple), are monuments to the town's prosperous (and rowdy) cowboy days. The bank is long abandoned, but the city council still meets in the City Hall building. The old saloon from Trail City (see earlier entry) was moved to Coolidge and is now the Trail City Bed & Breakfast (111 Elm).

Historic Water Tower: From Manchester, ¼ mile north on Elm. The 1887 brick and limestone water tower features nearly

four-foot-thick walls and an unusual arched entrance. A wooden tank originally sat on top of the brick base and captured artesian water, which was discovered in the region in 1887. Today the tower is on private property. Drive by only.

Historic Jail: From Spruce, 400 feet west on U.S. 50. On the south side of the road the lone limestone building, built around 1888, once served as the city jail. Many a cowboy or rowdy character must have spent time here after a night on the town!

Cousin Eddie's Visitor Center & Antique Store:
210 Coolidge. Ever since Clark W. Griswold and his family stopped in Coolidge to visit his cousin Eddie in the hit movie National Lampoon's Vacation, fans have made the journey here looking for the fictional farm where Eddie lived—and maybe sighting Aunt Edna. Visitors from all over the world have come to this former 1888 general store just to say they've been to Coolidge, Kansas. Store owner Lori Lennen has stocked the building with a wide array of antique and vintage furniture and collectibles. Tuesday-Saturday 11:30 a.m.-5:30 p.m. MT. 620.372.2414.

Western Trail Cafe:
204 W. U.S. 50. A cafe has occupied this building since the 1940s, and in 2013 the new owners renovated and spruced it up, inside and out. The menu is small but has all the dishes that cowboys like—the burgers are juicy, the sandwiches huge (the hand-breaded chicken-fried steak sandwich is a hand-

ful), and the ribeye steaks are seasoned and cooked to perfection. Wednesday-Saturday 11 a.m.-2 p.m. and 5-8 p.m. MT. 620.372.2401.

River Road Scenic Back Road (section 1): From Manchester, 1 mile south on Main (becomes B), then 16 miles east on River. For a truly dare-to-do-dirt adventure through the Arkansas River Lowlands take this sandy drive that parallels the river. Your 16-mile, back-road journey to Syracuse is flanked with cottonwoods and pasture, a beautiful combination of southwest Kansas scenery. It's also a great birding trail where you might spot western kingbirds, western meadowlarks, pheasants, and magpies.

Lodging: Trail City Bed & Breakfast and Log Cabins (KBBA, 620.372.2414, trailcitybb.com).

KENDALL

Unincorporated

Santa Fe Trail Marker:
Main and A. The DAR placed a marker near the location of the Aubry cutoff. The point was named for French Canadian Francis X. Aubry, who was always on the lookout for a shorter route

SW

on the Santa Fe Trail, an effort that earned him the nickname "Skimmer of the Plains."

Kendall Cemetery:
U.S. 50/400 and A. Not far from the native limestone entrance pillars you'll see a large round reservoir with a rusted water pump no longer in use. These are vestiges of the cemetery's 1936 WPA improvements.

River Road Scenic Back Road (section 3):
To continue the route that started in Coolidge (see p. 413) and then continued from Syracuse (see p. 415), go 18 miles east on River (becomes 358, J, K and again River) to Lakin (see p. 418, Kearny County). When you leave Kendall to begin this section of the back-road route, you should be north of the Arkansas River and north of the railroad tracks. Highlights along this route include the Amazon Ditch, Hartland, and Indian Mound, all in Kearny County (see p.418).

(see p. 413)
(see p. 415)
(see p. 418, Kearny County)
(see p.418)

SYRACUSE

Population 1,754

Hamilton County Museum:
102 N. Gates. This museum, in a former hardware store, preserves Syracuse newspapers dating to 1938, early vehicles, tools, guns, and other county artifacts. A highlight is the collection of Harvey House pieces including a glass cake stand, dishes, serving tray, and an original Harvey Girl uniform. Tuesday-Saturday 9 a.m.-4 p.m. MT. 620.384.7496. hamiltoncountymuseum.org.

DAR Marker:
102 N. Gates. After the 1908 Santa Fe depot was torn down, the red granite DAR marker noting the location of the Santa Fe Trail was moved to its current position in front of the Hamilton County Museum.

Depot Baggage Room:
From A, 400 feet south on Main, 250 feet east on a service road, then just north of the railroad tracks. This tan stucco building is the only remnant of the town's Harvey House, built here in 1908. Harvey Houses were a series of restaurants and hotels built along the Santa Fe railway to serve passengers. Notice the original wooden doors, capped by detailed arches. The former baggage room now provides storage for the BNSF Railway.

Hamilton County Courthouse:
219 N. Main. Built in 1937 of blond brick with limestone trim, this Modern Eclecticism courthouse stands at the north end of the business district. It was built with funds from the Federal Emergency Administration of Public Works, which is so stated on the building's southwest cornerstone.

Northrup Theatre (NRHP):
116 N. Main. Local businessman Frank Northrup built this classic art deco theatre in 1930, and his daughter, Muriel Ellis, painted the stenciled ceilings and walls in 1949. The original

pastel marquee, mosaic tiles, multicolor fluorescent wall lights, original seats, and Naugahyde wall add authenticity. For tours, call 620.384.5459. First-run movies are shown Friday-Sunday. 620.384.7688. FB.

Syracuse Sand Dunes Park:
From A (U.S. 50), 1½ miles south on Main (K-27). With an abundance of sand dunes it's easy to make your own style of fun. ATVs, dune buggies, 4-wheel drives, and roll cage-protected vehicles will encounter rolling dunes, bowls, and flat areas that appeal to sand dune dragsters who feel the need for speed. The 1,300-acre park is the state's largest sand dune park, and one of the largest in the Midwest. Permits required for unregistered vehicles. Admission charge. 620.384.2480. syracuseks.gov/sand-dunes.

Tamarisk Golf Course:
811 E. Golf Course. From A (U.S. 50), ¾ mile south on Main (K-27), then ½ mile east on Golf Course. Tee off on what local golfers say is one of the most challenging nine-hole courses in western Kansas. The fairways are lined with tamarisk bushes, a type of evergreen that thrives in saline soil. Daily 7 a.m.-7 p.m. MT. 620.384.7832. tamariskgc.com.

Syracuse Commission Company:
109 S. Main. A variety of cattle auctions begin here around 10 a.m. every Friday. Enhance your experience at VP's sale barn cafe. Among homemade offerings are apple, cherry, and coconut cream made-from-scratch pies and chocolate caramel sundaes. Cafe hours, Friday 7 a.m.-4 p.m. MT. 620.384.5259.

Black Bison Pub:
122 N. Main. Native son Matt Gould moved home after serving in the military, and decided the town needed a pub. He

renovated a two-story building and created a perfect setting for serving Kansas foods in a trendy, polished-wood interior. The pub is now in the hands of Tommy and Janet Thomaczek, and the food and drink still celebrate Kansas! The bar serves an impressive array of craft cocktails and 30 different beers. For dining, bison burgers

and steaks are the stand-out specials, and other favorites include homemade hummus and fish and chips. Monday-Saturday 11 a.m.-2 p.m. and 4-10 p.m. MT. 620.384.6348. FB.

Ramble-N-Restaurant:
606 W. U.S. 50. Fresh-cut steaks and home cooking entice the locals to amble in to the Ramble-N. Tuesday-Sunday 6 a.m.-9 p.m. MT. 620.384.7425.

KC's Mexican American Restaurant:
401 W. U.S. 50. It's Mexican with a seafood flair! Everyone seems to love the shrimp fajitas at KC's. Monday-Saturday 6:30 a.m.-8 p.m. MT. 620.384.5519.

Porky's Parlor:
12 N. Main. Hungry for a quick meal on the road? Pick up burgers, fries, fresh salads, and Mexican food at Porky's drive-through window. Or take a seat in the dining room. Either way, don't forget the ice cream! Daily 11 a.m.-8 p.m. MT. 620.384.6655. FB.

River Road Scenic Back Road (section 2):
The first River Road route we recommended was from Coolidge (*see* p. 413) to Syracuse. Now, from Santa Fe (U.S. 50), go 1¼ miles south on K-27, then 13 miles east on River to Kendall. The geographical combination of Arkansas River Lowlands landscape and High Plains vegetation such as yucca, sagebrush, and cottonwood trees makes this sandy route along the river an interesting one. Irrigated crops border the road in places.

Lodging:
tinyurl.com/syracusestay.

explorer extras... In Syracuse

Standing in Syracuse Cemetery, the solemn and moving Western Kansas Memorial Wall is a tribute to veterans, not limited to Hamilton County, from all branches of the military. From U.S. 50, ¾ mile north on K-27, then ¼ mile west on an unnamed paved road.

When the Arkansas River bed is dry, it's a great route for hiking and off-roading. When the river is running, it's a great route for canoeing. Wet or dry, you can't lose! For many years the Stock Tank Parade was held on the river, and during wet years you still might see some folks in stock tanks floating downstream as you drive by on U.S. 50. **ee**

Haskell County

Cattle feeding is a major industry in Haskell County. In fact, the county annually ranks first or near the top for the number of cattle on feed. The area also contains rich and fertile irrigated land that produces wheat, corn, soybeans, milo, sunflowers, alfalfa, and cotton. Oil and natural gas production are also a primary part of the economy.

SATANTA

Population 1,127

Janet's of Satanta:
217 Sequoyah. Janet Lawson never intended to go into the clothing business, but a funny thing happened. One day her husband told her that he'd bought a clothing store. Janet turned out to be a natural sales and business person, and has operated this successful women's clothing store since 1966. Well-dressed women throughout southwest Kansas have traveled to this fashionable shop for years. Tuesday-Friday 10 a.m.-5 p.m. 620.649.2319.

Cimarron River Company:
108 S. Sequoyah. If you appreciate exquisite and authentic American Indian jewelry and art, you'll be enthralled with this store. You'll find vintage and new jewelry for men and women, home decor, artwork, and accessories, all hand picked by owner Connie Miller, a respected and certified retailer. Tuesday-Saturday 10 a.m.-4 p.m. 620.649.3373. FB.

SW

Triple J's:
111 Sequoyah. It's the pizza with homemade crust and generous toppings that the locals rave about. Creative combinations include the chicken enchilada with chicken and green chile sauce; and Jared's special, a sauceless pie

with both bacon and Canadian bacon. Tuesday-Saturday 11 a.m.-9 p.m.; Sunday 5-9 p.m. 620.649.2277. FB.

Nieto's Cafe #2: 124 Sequoyah. Authentic Mexican and traditional American dishes are rolled into one delicious cafe. What more could you want? Seconds! If you're traveling a little farther south and west, Nieto's #1 is in nearby Hugoton. Monday-Saturday 10 a.m.-2 p.m. and 5-8 p.m.; Sunday 10 a.m.-2 p.m. 620.649.3004. FB.

Population 1,407

Haskell County Historical Museum: 605 E. Watkins. From Wooten, 3 blocks east on Courthouse, ½ block south on Winters, then 2 blocks east on Watkins. Along with its early county history displays, the museum houses important photograph collections including 1939 aerial photographs of the Santa Fe Trail that show the wagon ruts in Haskell County, and a collection of F.M. Steele, a noted traveling photographer who recorded—with beautiful clarity—everyday life in Kansas at the turn of the 19th century. The museum complex includes a historic ranch home, a Santa Fe depot and 1967 Santa Fe caboose, agricultural equipment, and a rural schoolhouse. Tuesday-Saturday 1-5 p.m. 620.675.8344. haskellcountymuseum.com.

Haskell County Courthouse: 300 S. Inman. In 1978 a new and larger courthouse was constructed to meet the needs of the county. The architects and planners were sensitive to the past and saved remnants from the old, beloved courthouse as a reminder of the county's growth and heritage. These artifacts and an explanatory plaque are at the 1978 courthouse sign at Inman and Choteau.

Macias Restaurant: 600 W. La Lande. No need to choose between Mexican and American fare, both are on the menu. Add some spice to your life and mix it up! Try a breakfast burrito, the hand-breaded chicken-fried steak, or the highly recommended buffet. Breakfast is served any time! Daily 7 a.m.-2 p.m.; Monday-Friday 5-8:30 p.m. 620.675.2867. FB.

Hodgeman County

Duncan's Crossing: From Main in Hanston, 7½ miles north on Highway (becomes 228), 3 miles east on West. Markers near the Hodgeman and Ness county line note Duncan's Crossing, a significant point on the Fort Hays-Fort Dodge Road, a military supply route in 1867-1868. John O'Loughlin established a toll bridge here in 1867, and in 1872 George Duncan bought the land and built a trading post on the site. Eventually the bridge washed out, and Duncan let people ford the Pawnee River here at no charge; thus the name Duncan's Crossing. Near the crossing, an illustrated bronze bas-relief plaque is "Dedicated to the pioneers who faced the dangers of prairie trails and frontier life to establish homes in

this community." It was placed by the Hodgeman Community Ladies Aid Society in 1929.

St. Mary's Catholic Church (NRHP): 14920 SE 232. From Main in Hanston, 7½ miles south on Highway (becomes 228), 4 miles east on H, then 2 miles south on 232. Irish born settlers erected this native limestone Gothic Revival church in 1904, but a devastating fire in 1928 left only the stone walls. The church was rebuilt with the original walls intact and rededicated that same year (1928). It ceased serving as a church in 1997, and today it is almost startling to come across this lonely Gothic structure in the rural High Plains.

Optical Illusion: From Wash in Jetmore, 7 miles south on Main (U.S. 283) to F. Just past the Jetmore Municipal Airport, and at the top of the hill, you'll see the Wright grain elevators. They are easy to spot and are only a couple of miles away—or so it appears. Actually they are more than 14 miles in the distance!

Fort Hays-Fort Dodge Road Markers: From Wash in Jetmore, 12 miles south on Main (U.S. 283), then 1½ miles east on Antelope. In a fence line stands a small post rock marker for the Fort Hays-Fort Dodge Road. Behind it an unusual formation—a barbed wire ball atop three large rock posts—marks the crossing point of this military supply route.

HorseThief Reservoir:
19005 SW K-156. From Main, 9½ miles west on K-156. Water is important, and scarce, in western Kansas and conserving it is an everyday fact of life. Enjoying this vital element for recreation is a much appreciated bonus. Part of the largest watershed district in the United States, this reservoir was constructed between 2009 and 2015. It offers 42 campsites with electricity and water, primitive sites, and a bathhouse. Yurts, canoes, and stand-up paddleboards are available to rent, and recreational amenities include hiking, biking, and equestrian trails; 3D archery; disc golf; mud volleyball; basketball; and a small climbing wall. You may also bring your jet skis, sailboats, and ski boats. Entrance charge. Cabins available, reservations required. 620.253.8464. horsethiefres.com.

HANSTON

Population 206

Bruce's Country Kitchen:
206 Washington. If you're looking for a red schooner and a bacon cheeseburger to go with your game of pool you've come to the right place. And, breakfast fans, breakfast is served all day. For a little nostalgia, slide a few coins in the old-time juke box and enjoy the tunes, both old and new. Monday-Saturday 10:30 a.m.-11 p.m. 620.623.2511.

Lodging: The Guest House
(KBBA, 620.357.5561, theguesthouseonline.com).

JETMORE

Population 879

Haun Museum (NRHP):
421 Main. The main part of this limestone museum building once stood as the first house on the 1879 Jetmore town site.

Exhibits here feature prehistoric remains and artifacts unearthed prior to the construction of HorseThief Reservoir, local Santa Fe railway history, and a one-room schoolhouse. Memorial Day-Labor Day, Friday-Saturday 11 a.m.-5 p.m. and Sunday 1-5 p.m. 620.357.8831.

Hodgeman County Courthouse (NRHP):
500 Main. The Haun family donated the land for the courthouse square, and in 1929 the Italian Renaissance structure made from Carthage granite and fine gray brick and trimmed with white limestone was completed. The green terra cotta roof tiles provide a striking accent. Visit the second floor to see historic photos, and the third floor to view the courtroom's original woodwork, fixtures, and furniture. Monday-Friday 9 a.m.-5 p.m. 620.357.642.

Kenyon Nature Park:
W. Bramley and Kenyon. Established in 2007, this park is a quarter-mile nature trail whose concrete path winds through lovely patches of wildflowers and tall shade trees. Benches are conveniently located along the way, and a picturesque bridge crosses a small stream.

Judy's:
303 Main. Judy's made-from-scratch pancakes spill over the plate, her French fries are homemade, and she hand patties the burgers. You can't find more down-home goodness than that. Monday-Friday 7 a.m.-8 p.m.; Saturday 7 a.m.-2 p.m. 620.357.8537.

Lock Restaurant:
509 Main. It's your lucky day when you eat at this popular

restaurant serving some of the tastiest Thai, Lao, Vietnamese, and American cuisine in the state. Lock (pronounced Luck) Pharathikoune, a native Laotian, started the eatery in 2013. It's proven so popular that she has opened another in WaKeeney. Customers love the egg drop soup and the

sweet and sour sauce. Her pho is fresh and flavorful, and she whips up a mean pad Thai. Tuesday-Sunday 10 a.m.-8 p.m. 620.357.6310.

Hideout Bar and Grill:
615 S. Main. With the restaurant on one side and the bar on the other, the Hideout welcomes you to enjoy a hearty meal or to relax with friends and a beer. Taco Tuesday is popular and so is the steak or chicken fajita salads served anytime. Grill hours, Monday-Saturday 11 a.m.-10 p.m. 620.357.8888. FB.

Message on the Hillside:
From Park, ½ mile south on U.S. 283. As you leave Jetmore you'll see stones on a hillside forming the words "Christ Died for Me." In 1912 a crew building the county high school started to lay the stones, but only "Christ Died" was in place when the workers were called to another job. A Sunday school class finished the project two years later. In 1932, when a new highway was slated to run exactly where the message lay,

SW

a group moved the stones to their present location.

Lodging:
tinyurl.com/stayhodgeco.

explorer extras...
In Jetmore

In 1888 the First National Bank was constructed on the corner at 423 Main. Built with native limestone, it is an eclectic mix of Italianate, Romanesque Revival, and Queen Anne architeture. Today the building's only occupant is a hair salon in the back.

A large mural on the side of the old lumberyard depicts the rural home setting of the lumberyard's original owner. The mural, at Main and Highway, was painted by the 1982 Jetmore High School art class.

Campers and explorers, load up on snacks and supplies at the Jetmore Food Center, 100 W. Washington. Monday-Saturday 8 a.m.-8 p.m.; Sunday 9 a.m.-6 p.m. 620.357.6554.

The native limestone rock wall that surrounds Fairmount Cemetery was built by the WPA in 1935. Inside the walls the tall beehive-shaped memorial, also made from native limestone, stands "In honor of all veterans who answered their country's call." From Park, 1 mile south on Main (U.S. 283). ee

Kearny County

AROUND THE COUNTY

Amazon Ditch: From Main in Lakin, 12½ miles west on U.S. 50, 2¼ miles south on D, then 2¼ miles east on 358 (becomes River) to the headgate. Or from

Main in Kendall, 6 miles east on River. Entrepreneurs such as Asa Soule of Eureka Canal fame and C.J. "Buffalo" Jones knew that to make this part of the country prosper they needed to tap into the Arkansas River for irrigation. In 1887 Soule and Jones started the 42-mile Amazon Ditch that runs from five miles west of Hartland east to the Finney County line. It was the largest irrigation feature ever constructed in Kansas. The ditch is still in use (and owned) by irrigation farmers today. In wet years it can be quite a sight to see the volume of water rushing through the gates. As you travel east on River you'll

see signs indicating when you are on the old Santa Fe Trail. 620.355.6422.

Hartland: From the Amazon Ditch headgate, 4½ miles east on 358 (River). Or from Main in Lakin, 8 miles west on Railroad (becomes 358 and River). Once the county seat of Kearny County, Hartland had its beginnings in 1885 with a prime position near the railroad and the river. It grew to be a bustling town of more than 2,000. When Lakin won the county seat in 1894, Hartland began its slow decline and by 1957 the book was closed for good on the former thriving town. At the town site a large sign recounts Hartland's history, and a Santa Fe Trail marker stands nearby.

Indian Mound (NRHP): From the Amazon Ditch headgate, 4 miles east on River, then 2½ miles south and east on J (River). Or from Main in Lakin, 5½ miles west on Railroad (becomes 358 and River). From the parking lot look north to see a sharp rise (not far from an irrigation canal bridge). This natural occurring formation was used as a waymark, first by American Indians and later by travelers on the Santa Fe Trail. It was significant because this location was the last opportunity for travelers to choose between following the trail's "mountain route" (longer but with more water) or the "dry route" (shorter but with less water). By 1870, when the Kansas Pacific Railway reached Kit Carson, Colorado, this section of the trail was abandoned. A sign between the bridge and the rise provides details about Indian Mound, and a DAR marker commemorating the trail stands on the hilltop. The mound is on private property but the public is welcome.

Charlie's Ruts (NRHP): From Main in Lakin, 4½ miles east on U.S. 50 to a roadside pull over. In the parking lot a historical marker tells the story of nearby ruts formed by freight wagons on the Santa Fe Trail. This section of the trail includes 12 intact swales (ruts). They are

widely known as Charlie's Ruts or Bentrup's Ruts for Charles Bentrup, the landowner who preserved them. Visitors are welcome to walk through the gate to stand in the actual ruts and visualize what it must have been like for travelers on this trail from 1821 to 1872. The site is now owned by the Kearny County Historical Society.

Kropp Land Monument:

From Main in Lakin, 7½ miles west on U.S. 50, then just north on J. In 1936 Vernon Kropp, a funeral director from Texas, erected this large gray granite monument to help him locate land he had purchased. To make it uniquely his, the monument was regally adorned with his initials VK, a fancy family crest, and the Latin phrase "Vitam Impendere Vero," which means "To Devote One's Life to Truth."

DEERFIELD

Population 687

Great Eastern Ditch:

Main and Moreland. The canal that you see running west to east through town is part of the Great Eastern Ditch, conceived and chartered by Buffalo Jones in 1881. It provided water, diverted from the Arkansas River, to irrigate crops during the dry years. It is still used for that purpose.

Historic Texaco Station

(NRHP): 105 W. 6th. Back when traveling long distances by automobile was a new thing,

service stations, like this 1923 Tudor Revival station, popped up across the country. This little structure was a "Texaco Registered Restroom" station, a designation signaling that the bathrooms were clean, and which also attracted a wider clientele enabling petroleum companies to sell products other than petroleum. The station, beautifully restored and awaiting your admiration, is owned by the Kearny County Historical Society and is open during special events. 620.355.7448.

LAKIN

Population 2,185

Kearny County

Courthouse: 304 N. Main. The Federal Emergency Administration of Public Works completed this brick and limestone Modern Eclecticism courthouse in 1939. Near the entrance a group of six limestone benches contain etched designs of cattle, wheat, corn, sunflowers, an oil well, and a covered wagon, each symbolizing the history and economy of this county. Beside the benches a large upright limestone slab depicts a map of the county and townships.

Kearny County Museum:

111 S. Buffalo. Santa Fe Trail buffs will be delighted with

the biographies of significant personalities connected with the trail, a 1939 aerial map of the Santa Fe Trail in Kansas, and an 1831 Conestoga freight wagon. In addition you'll see fossils, turn-of-the-century exhibits, and a small display about Fred Harvey's XY Ranch. The ranch was six miles east of Lakin and supplied all the beef for the Harvey House restaurants. On the museum grounds you're welcome to explore an 1876 Santa Fe depot, an 1893 schoolhouse, the 1875 O'Loughlin home, farm machinery, restored windmills, and a 1909 12-sided barn. Tuesday-Friday 9 a.m.-4 p.m. 620.355.7448. kearnycountymuseum.org.

Wooden Windmill:

U.S. 50/400 and K-25. It's a rare one, and an original, and it once stood at the 1890s farmstead of early settler John O'Loughlin.

Lakin High School:

407 N. Campbell. This large dark-red-brick 1931 school boasts Spanish Colonial Revival styling with twin terra cotta arched entrances that showcase ornate colorful relief panels in vivid blue, green, and orange.

DAR Marker: A red granite stone, placed by the DAR in 1906, marks the Santa Fe Trail,

SW

which ran in front of the present high school at 407 N. Campbell.

Flashbacks Diner: 210 W. Santa Fe Trail. Inside a former Dairy Queen you'll definitely encounter flashbacks to the 1950s—cherry-red booths and chairs and gray formica tables. Not many places serve fried okra but you'll find it on the menu along with your favorite burgers, hot dogs, cherry limeades, and shakes. Daily 10 a.m.-10 p.m. 620.355.7060. FB.

Jacked UP BBQ: 108 N. Main. Ivan Nolde has jacked up his cooking skills in his scratch kitchen making fall-off-the-bone ribs and beef brisket like nobody's business. You'll see the difference in his daily specials, such as smoked turkey and dressing and chicken fettuccini alfredo, and in the homemade cobblers, pies, brownies, cinnamon rolls, and bread bowls for the soup, even in the homemade ice cream. Tuesday-Friday 11 a.m.-2 p.m.; Thursday-Saturday 5-9 p.m. 620-355-8090. FB.

Lodging: tinyurl.com/lakinlodging.

**explorer extras...
In Lakin**

At Lakin Cemetery a stately veterans memorial comprises five large gray granite monuments and flags representing each of the service branches. The memorial remembers the service men and women from Kearny County who served in each of the wars from the Civil War to Vietnam. From N. Main, ¾ mile east on U.S. 50.

Nothing remains of Chouteau's Island, a Santa Fe Trail site. A historical marker at a roadside pull over recounts its early significance on the trail. From Main, 1½ miles west on U.S. 50. **ee**

Kiowa County

AROUND THE COUNTY

Haviland to Belvidere Scenic Back Road: From U.S. 50, 3¾ miles south on 51, 1 mile east on M, 2 miles south on 53, 750 feet east on O, 5½ miles south on 73, then ½ mile east and south on 76 to Belvidere. The back roads from Haviland to Belvidere offer some of the best jaw-dropping grassland vistas in the state. In this area that borders the High Plains and the Red Hills physiographic regions the scenery changes from slow-moving cattle on the road in front of you to a prairie spectacle of gently rolling hills offset by craggy stone outcroppings that seem to go on forever.

IN BELVIDERE

Unincorporated

Beautiful View: From Dodge, ½ mile north on 76, bear left at the fork and

cross a cattle guard, then ¼ mile west on 76 to a roadside pull over. A short way from town, this panoramic view of the breathtaking landscape gave Belvidere its name, which means "beautiful view" in Italian.

Old Schoolhouse: Northeast corner of town. On this old schoolhouse, now the community center, notice the two doors—one was the entrance to the grade school, the other to the high school. An interior plaque memorializes Doc Carpenter, the lumberyard manager who cared for horses and trained his last horse at the age of 92.

Halley's Junction: 101 N. High. It's been around forever so you know to overlook the dusty layers and the clutter, all of which add to the experience. The old red-brick store with its creaky wood floors and pressed-tin ceiling feels like a step back in time—even the second hand seems to move a little slowly in its sweep across the clock face. Old tools hang from pegboards, antiques and collectibles cover every surface, and owner Hank Halley and his wife, Diana, hold court at a table in the middle of the large open room. If you need directions they are happy to point you down the right path, and they might share a story or two. Buy a cold pop, some snacks, or sandwiches from the freezer. April-October, Monday-Friday 9 a.m.-4:30 p.m. 620.862.5234.

Belvidere to Wilmore Scenic Back Road: Going west out of Belvidere, you're on the road to Wilmore, and it's a goodie for explorers. From 76, 6¼ miles south and west on Dodge (becomes 70), just east on County Line, 1½ miles south on 23, then 5 miles west and south on C. The red-sand route bordering mostly pasture is rugged in this area. You'll see more cattle than houses or humans, and although the road is relatively flat, the buttes and canyons are all around you. Look for Wilmore's grain elevator in the distance.

Soldier's Creek Cemetery: From 76, 1½ miles east on Dodge (becomes Wilmore), just south on Sun City, then ¼ mile east on unnamed road. You'll see many cowboy gravestones decorated with horses, ranch names, and sentimental phrases. Look for the large chunks of petrified wood that have been used as markers, and handmade gravestones with hand-painted names.

Population 785

Greensburg was changed from a quiet little prairie town to one forced to make tough decisions. An EF5 tornado destroyed 95 percent of the town in May 2007, but in its wake a disheartened but determined citizenry knew they would rebuild. But how? Back to status quo or go in a "green" direction? The town's name implied which way to go but would they have the courage to do it? Despite growing pains, this county seat has remade itself like no other prairie town has had the chance to do.

Green Tours: It's a fascinating exploration for fans of green infrastructure, or for anyone curious about the amazing survival and remaking of a modern city. To tour the town, bicycles are available to borrow for no charge at the Big Well Museum, 315 S. Sycamore. Self-guided tour brochures are available at the museum's visitor center or at tinyurl.com/greensburgtour. For guided tours, call 620.723.4102.

The Big Well (NRHP; 8 Wonders of Kansas) Museum & Visitors Center: 315 S. Sycamore. Completed in 1888, this 109-foot-deep by 32-foot-wide water well was excavated without machines, but with simple tools operated by hand—shovels, picks, half barrels, pulleys, ropes, and mules. It served as the city's water supply until 1932. Recognized as the world's

largest hand-dug well, it was covered and opened as a tourist attraction in 1939 and operated until the 2007 tornado. The bigger and grander museum opened in 2012. Photos and graphics of the tornado's devastation, along with items gathered after the storm, are displayed on the well's perimeter walls. You'll also find information about the history of Greensburg and, of course, the big well. A grand white circular metal staircase leads visitors into the well where you can toss a coin and make a wish. Another set of stairs leads to the top level of the museum, high above the well, for a bird's-eye panoramic view of the community. The famous 1,000-pound pallasite meteorite discovered in Kiowa County, the largest pallasite found to date, is on display inside the museum. Monday-Saturday 9 a.m.-5 p.m. and Sunday 1-6 p.m. Admission charge. 620.723.4102. bigwell.org.

SW

Memorial Plaza: Northwest of the Big Well Museum. From 1915 to 2007 the Weaver and Emily (Beck) Fleener family home stood on the northeast corner of the block shared by the Big Well Museum. After the 2007 tornado the Fleener-Beck family donated its property to the city for a plaza to memorialize this dramatic time in

Greensburg's history that took their home and those of their neighbors. A gray granite marker lists the names of the 10 residents whose lives were lost the night the devastating tornado hit Greensburg. Stop for a moment of quiet reflection on the cost of that storm.

Water Tower Sculpture: Southwest of the Big Well Museum. The old city water tower was a crumpled heap after the tornado and was purchased for scrap iron by the former Wichita-based Caster Iron Company. The company created a red and blue sculpture from parts of the water tower and donated it as a memory piece to Greensburg. The red ball is from the top of the old tower.

Kiowa County Commons Building: 320 S. Main. The city library, county museum and soda fountain, the K-State Research and Extension office, and a media center with an internet-based TV and radio station all share space inside this 20,000-square-foot building. On the roof top a closed-loop geothermal system and thin-film solar panels provide the power.

Whenever the building is open, you're welcome to come inside, take the stairs to the top, and exit outside for a closer look at this example of green infrastructure.

Soda Fountain: 320 S. Main. Although the 1917 Hunter Drugs is no longer in business, its beloved 1950 soda fountain survived the tornado. The beautifully restored fountain, now a living history exhibit at the Kiowa County Historical Museum serves banana splits, sundaes, shakes, and sodas. Take a seat at the counter to watch the soda jerk make your treat. A life-sized cutout of Hunter Drugs' long-time beloved soda jerk Richard Huckriede, better known as Dickie, stands next to the counter with his story. Monday-Friday 10 a.m.-5:30 p.m.; Saturday 10 a.m.-5 p.m. 620.723.2331. FB.

Kiowa County Historical Society Museum: 320 S. Main. The museum's exhibits burst forth in beautiful detail with large photo cutouts of historic figures including Donald "Cannonball" Green, the flamboyant stagecoach driver who operated the Cannonball Stage Line and for whom Greensburg

is named; and Sheriff Mable Chase, who in 1924 became the first woman in the United States to be elected sheriff. Learn about other county towns, including Belvidere's bustling cattle ranching history, and stroll down the hall with a miniature version of historic Greensburg. Monday-Friday 10 a.m.-5:30 p.m.; Saturday 10 a.m.-5 p.m. Admission charge. 620.723.1125. FB.

Kiowa County Memorial Hospital: 721 W. Kansas. The hospital is the first LEED Platinum Certified Critical Access Hospital in the United States. Designers created this first-of-its-kind energy efficient hospital, and visitors are welcome to visit the main lobby and lower level areas. A lobby sign details the green enhancements, and if you are interested in a tour, ask at the desk. Landscaping includes native plants such as sandhill plum, and signage informs readers of the reasons and ideas for environmental conservation. 620.723.3341. FB.

5.4.7 Arts Center: 204 W. Wisconsin. This ultramodern community arts center is committed to presenting regularly changing fine art and photography exhibits, performances, and activities for community members and visitors. The building is the first LEED (Leadership in Energy and Environmental Design) Platinum Certified building in Kansas. It was designed and built by Studio 804, a nonprofit organization of University of Kansas students. 5.4.7 is the month, day, and year that the EF5 tornado struck the town. Monday-Wednesday 1-5 p.m.; Thursday-Friday 10 a.m.-5 p.m. 620.723.2600. 547artscenter.org.

Where'dya Find That

Antiques: 148 S. Main. Owner Erica Goodman will help guide you on a treasure hunt through this trove of quality antiques wonderfully displayed inside the two-story historic Robinette Building (NRHP). It is the only historic commercial building to have survived the 2007 tornado. People will ask, "Where'd ya find that?" when they see your new find. Monday-Saturday 10 a.m.-4 p.m. 620.723.1112. FB.

Twilight Theatre & Community Auditorium:

200 S. Main. The curtains have risen on this plush new theatre that shows first-run movies and includes a stage for live performances. The theatre was built from the ground up after the original, constructed in 1916 as an opera house, was destroyed in the 2007 tornado. Tuesday-Thursday 10 a.m.-7 p.m.; Friday 10 a.m.-9 p.m.; Saturday 7-9 p.m; Sunday 2-8 p.m. 620.723.1092. FB.

Crazy Mule Food & Brew:

106 S. Main. Find contemporary twists on old and new favorites—lamb sliders with red-onion relish and green chili fries—on this crazy and fun menu. Or pick a lighter option like the sweet field salad with toasted pecans, strawberries, and grilled chicken. A full bar serves Crazy Mule-inspired cocktails such as Mascara on a Mule and Sister Sara. Tuesday-Saturday 11 a.m.-2 p.m. and 5-9 p.m.; Sunday 10 a.m.-1 p.m. 620.723.9025. FB.

Reggie's Pizza: 321 W.

Kansas. The two most popular pizzas? The Overland (Reggie's version of the supreme) and the Heart Attack (a five-meat pizza). Owner Mike Wilson loves pizza and the pizza business so you can count on fresh vegetables, homemade dough, and personal service. Thursday-Tuesday 11 a.m.-8 p.m. 620.723.2200. FB.

Pueblo Nuevo: 801 E.

Kansas. Steaming platters of pineapple fajitas, chili rellenos, chicken enchiladas, and homemade chimichangas smothered in queso make this a delicious stop. Tuesday-Sunday 11 a.m.-8 p.m. 620.723.3057.

Kook's Meat and Deli: 101

S. Sycamore. Come early for lunch or else the daily special will be gone, as will some of the best homemade pies, including the reigning favorite: peanut butter pie. Steak night every Thursday is especially popular too. Monday-Friday 7 a.m.-8 p.m.; Saturday 9 a.m.-2 p.m. 620.723.2121. FB.

Cannonball Bar and Grill:

403 E. Kansas. It's not as flamboyant as town namesake Cannonball Green reportedly was, but he would have approved of this bar and grill. It's a friendly local hangout with much visiting between tables while customers wait for their daily special or burger. Wednesday-Monday 4-10 p.m. 620.723.2866. FB.

Lodging: greensburgks.org.

explorer extras... In Greensburg

Several fragments and noticeable damage are still visible from the 2007 tornado. The steps that once led into Fran's Antique Store (once housed inside the former First Christian Church) stand on their own at Sycamore and Wisconsin.

A bit of humor is needed when devastation cuts into a community. Art was unleashed on a damaged tree stump by an unknown creator who sculpted it into a cowboy riding a tornado with the old water tower crumpled beneath it. See it at the Cannonball Golf Course, 200 block of S. Poplar.

Greensburg's namesake was a colorful Cannonball Green, who ran a stage line connecting the railroad to towns across southwest Kansas and who helped found the town of Greensburg in 1886. Find out more about this exuberant

SW

character on the historical marker in the rest area on the north side of the highway. From Main, 1 mile east on U.S. 50/400. **ee**

HAVILAND

Population 686

Haviland Hardware: 114 N. Main. This 1911 hardware store is a blend of the old and the new. Under original pressed-tin ceilings, you'll still find hardware and groceries—and a place to hook up your wireless laptop at no charge. The coffee is always on! Monday-Friday 7 a.m.-4:30 p.m.; Saturday 7-10:30 a.m. 620.862.5202. FB.

Barclay College: Haviland is probably the smallest town in the state with an institution of higher learning. Still operating today, Barclay College, on N. Kingman, dates to 1917 and promotes a Bible-centered environment for learning.

Beautification Project: Two murals seem to stretch all the way across the intersection of Main and Walnut. One, depicting a rising sun, green prairie, clouds, and elevators on the horizon, invites you to "Come, and rest awhile" on the nearby patio with tables and chairs. The second mural continues with the same green prairie and includes images of a covered wagon and historic buildings.

Origins, A Divine Coffeehouse: 121 N. Main. Customers appreciate the fair-trade coffee, delicious frappes, and refreshing Italian sodas. The pineapple paradise

smoothie is a perfect start to the day, and the ham and cheese toastie with ham, provolone, and homemade spinach dip is a top choice for lunch. Monday-Friday 7 a.m.-9 p.m.; Saturday 8 a.m.-6 p.m. FB. 620.862.7250.

MULLINVILLE

Population 251

Fromme-Birney Round Barn (NRHP; 8 Wonders of Kansas Architecture): From U.S. 54, 3¾ miles south on 10, then 1¾ miles west on O. On its original site, this grand 1912 barn stands as a lonely vestige out in the country. You can imagine it filled with draft horses as you walk round and round on its dirt floor, looking at the stalls and tack, climbing the stairs to the loft, and hearing the wind whistle through the cracks. Storyboards and photos

explain the efficiency of round barns and relate the history of this beautiful structure and the family who owned it. The Fromme-Birney barn, 70 feet wide and 50 feet high, is a rare breed of barns still standing in Kansas. Our hats are off to those who restored it in 1995.

Shop for gifts and leave what you owe in the jar. Always open. Donation welcome. 620.548.2266.

Country Cafe: 401 S. Main. This small but bustling diner puts everyone in a good mood. The terrific breakfasts include a serving of real butter with the pancakes, and the sausage, egg, and cheese biscuit receives high marks. One bite into the chicken-fried steak will tell you it's made the Explorer Way, and it comes with real mashed potatoes. The homemade pies are not to be missed. Monday-Saturday 6 a.m.-8 p.m.; Sunday 7 a.m.-1:30 p.m. 620.548.2568. FB.

M.T. Liggett Metal Sculptures: U.S. 400 west of town and U.S. 54 east of town. M.T. Liggett delivers extreme political statements on whirligigs and signs welded together from discarded machinery or anything else lying around his farm. His messages and motion displays draw plenty of attention, and his zingy signs in the shape of whimsical birds, demons, dragons, and bugs go on for more than a quarter mile both west and east of Mullinville.

Mullinville Compression Station: From Main, 3½ miles east on U.S. 54/400. What happens at a compression station? Natural gas is highly pressurized as it travels through an interstate pipeline. To ensure that it continually remains under pressure, compression is required periodically along the pipe. Thus the need for compressor stations, which are usually placed at 40- to 100-mile intervals.

Veterans Memorial:

U.S. 400 and Main. This striking memorial to the veterans of Kiowa County is a countywide project, with residents from Greensburg and Haviland contributing to it. Nearly 1,800 names of county veterans, past and present, are inscribed on large gray granite tablets, above which is written, "We shall not forget."

Lane County

AROUND THE COUNTY

Grain Bin Scale House:

From Main in Dighton, 7 miles west on Long (K-96), 2 miles south on Eagle, then ½ mile west on 130. Vance and Louise Ehmke's grain bin also serves as a scale house and living quarters. It measures 42 feet in diameter, 31 feet to its peak, and can hold 25 semi-truck-loads of any commodity. In keeping with the exterior, the interior sports a rustic flare. Enjoy as you drive by. 620.397.2350. ehmkeseed.com.

Playa Lakes: From Main in Dighton, 8 miles west on Long (K-96), then 3 miles south on Dodge. A playa is a naturally occurring low spot caused by subsurface salt deposits that dissolved thousands of years ago. With more than 23,000

playas in western Kansas, you see them often as mudholes, buffalo wallows, or just low spots. Usually they are round and shallow, and ducks and other waterfowl love them; but tractors see them quite differently. At this location is the largest playa in Lane County, a 136-acre low spot. Monitoring wells are collecting long-term data in a University of Kansas and Kansas Geological Survey study of how playa lakes add to aquifer recharge. More than 10,000 years ago Clovis People hunted mammoths, camels, prehistoric horses, and other game at this important site. It was also an important stopover for many other nomadic Indian tribes.

DIGHTON

Old Bank Gallery (RHKP):

146 E. Long. Showcased here are the watercolors, pastels, colored-pencil works, and bronzes by award-winning artist Patrycia Herndon. But her greatest work might be the restoration of this 1888 First National Bank building. The 1890 bank teller cage from

Alamota (a town east of Dighton) is the centerpiece of Patrycia's studio and gallery. Her water-colors of flowers are breath-taking—and for sale! Monday-Friday 10 a.m.-3 p.m. (unless at an art show). 620.397.2273.

Dighton Opera House (RHKP):

146 E. Long and 140 S. Lane. It takes a bit of viewing this building from the front, sides, and back to realize that it's actually L-shaped and wraps around the Old Bank Gallery (see previous entry). Built in 1908, it is now used as a woodworking shop and for storage, and is not open to the public. While you're looking up at this unique structure, note the second story, which housed the opera house and a lodge hall.

Lane County Courthouse:

144 S. Lane. The courthouse was built in 1931 of yellow brick with limestone trim in the Modern Eclecticism style. On either side of the main entrance two lime-stone bas-relief panels depict the town's cultural heritage. They were sculpted by well-known Hays artist Pete Felten for the Dighton centennial. The courtroom is rich in historic orn-amentation, boasting a large painting of a sod house created in 1961 by local artist Mary A. Bosley for the state centennial. A display case at the courtroom entrance contains items con-fiscated at an earlier time including alcohol (moonshine), drug paraphernalia, and weapons. Monday-Friday 8 a.m.-5 p.m. 620.397.2805.

SW

Lane County Community High School and Stadium

(NRHP): 200 S. Wichita. The high school and stadium, both still in use today, were New Deal projects. The blond-brick high school, built through the Federal Emergency Administration of Public Works in 1936, was designed by Glen Thomas, an architect best known for his stunning work on Wichita North High School. Look for his signature bas-relief panels of carved bison on either side of the entrance, and the striking geometric ornamentation in vivid reds and blues. The native limestone stadium was a 1937 WPA project, built with stone from the former courthouse in Ravanna in nearby Finney County (*see* p. 394).

Lane County Museum:

333 N. Main. Exhibits present the county's heritage, including the story of the "Lane County Bachelor," a ballad written by Ness County resident Frank Baker in 1886. You'll also find out about jack rabbit drives, droughts, and prairie fires, and what Lane County produces for the world—oil, cattle, and grain. A sod house stands on the museum grounds. Tuesday-Saturday 1-5 p.m. 620.397.5652. FB.

Historic Gas Station:

239 E. Long. Fans of early gas stations will admire this 1937 Farmers Oil station and garage. Elements of the Mission style design, typical for that period, are evident in the white stucco walls and a red-tile roof of this well-preserved structure. The service bays were added in the 1940s. It is now privately owned.

Dighton Bowl & Diner:

530 E. Long. Memorabilia of all sorts deck the walls inside this diner, where bowling and hot daily specials combine for a perfect game. Grill hours, Monday-Thursday 7 a.m.-8 p.m.; Friday-Saturday 7 a.m.-2 p.m. 620.397.5518.

Lodging: Wild Horse Canyon Bed & Breakfast and Shady Porch Guest House (KBBA, 620.397.5914, wildhorsecanyonbnb.com).

HEALY

Unincorporated

Sharp Bros. Seed Company:

1005 Sycamore. Located in the most thriving unincorporated city in Kansas, Sharp Bros. has a reputation far and wide for top-quality seed for home, farm, and commercial landscapes. This company sets the standard for native grasses but also carries custom seed mixes and specialties such as Monarch butterfly and honey bee wildflower blend! For all your seed needs, shop Sharp! Monday-Friday 8 a.m.-12 p.m. and 1-5 p.m. 620.398.2231. sharpseed.com.

Healy Oil Co.: 1002 N. Dodge. You'll find certified mechanics at this Sinclair gas station, so if you're having car trouble or need new tires, Healy is the place to be. Fill up on gasoline or enjoy a home-cooked meal from the convenience store kitchen. Monday-Saturday 7:30 a.m.-5 p.m. 620.398.2300. healyoil.com.

Hometown Pride:

1002 Elm. A privately owned grocery store in an unincorporated town, that's impressive. The town may be small but its residents support what they have. Monday-Saturday 10 a.m.-6 p.m. 620.398.2299.

Meade County

On the cusp of the Red Hills and High Plains physiographic regions, Meade County offers exhilarating views, especially on its back roads. From dry sagebrush desert conditions to rugged red hills and, in season, wildflower accents, this landscape defies monotony.

AROUND THE COUNTY

Ancient Deposits Scenic Back Road:

From Carthage (U.S. 54/160) in Meade, 8 miles south on 23, 4 miles east on V, stairstep 12¾ miles east and south on 22 (becomes W, 23, X, 25, Aa, 26), 5 miles east on Ee, then 21 miles north and west on 31 (becomes Aa, 30, Y, 29, S, 27) to U.S. 160. At 17½ miles into the journey, just east of 25 on Y, you'll find Mennonite names in the tiny Kleine Gemeinde Cemetery.

Throughout your drive through southern Meade County, a handful of homes and a few cattle herds are set against this red, rugged, and remote route, whose geography has resulted from erosion of ancient sea deposits. For a paved-road version of this back-road drive, visit Meade State Park.

Meade State Park and Fishing Lake: From Carthage (U.S. 54/160) in Meade, 8 miles south and 5 miles west on K-23. This was the first designated state lake in Kansas, carved out of the Turkey Track Ranch in 1927. Today the beautiful setting offers 80 acres of water for fishing, and more than 400

acres for camping, wildlife habitat, hiking, biking, and viewing a variety of eastern and western migratory birds. State park entrance charge. Cabins available, reservations required. 620.873.2572. ksoutdoors.com.

Jones and Plummer Trail Marker and Scenic Overlook: From U.S. 54/160 in Meade, 9½ miles south and west on K-23. Here a wood-framed sign relates the saga of the Jones and Plummer Trail, which ran from present Oklahoma to Dodge City. It was started in 1874 by buffalo hunters Charles Jones and Joe Plummer to deliver hides to Dodge City and beyond. At this marker, the scenic overlook provides a vast view and wondrous spectacle of craggy canyons.

FOWLER

Population 558

Fowler Swimming Pool and Bathhouse (NRHP):
308 E. 6th. It's a long swim around this big oval pool measuring 90x120 feet. The deep "end" is actually in the middle, where the diving platform stands. The pool and bathhouse were constructed as WPA projects and have kept folks cool every summer since 1937. June-August, daily 1-7 p.m. 620.646.5309.

Neon 57: 102 E. 5th. This soup, salad, sandwich, ice cream, and homemade (delicious!) dessert cafe creates a 1950s spark inside a former movie theatre. A seven-stool ice cream counter adds chrome and color, but it's the booth

made out of the back end of a 1957 Chevy that takes the cake! Owner Lynne Zortman is known for her coconut cream pie and raspberry sour cream pie and other favorites include apple crumb, blueberry banana cream, and pecan. Lynne helps her accountant husband during tax season so the 57 is closed during March. Tuesday-Friday 9 a.m.-4:30 p.m. 620.646.5775.

Duck Inn Bar and Grill:
410 Main. Known for its kid-friendly, family atmosphere, it's a popular spot to duck in for sandwiches and daily specials. If you're a burger fan, you'll find them big and filling! As their motto says, "Duck Inn and Waddle Out." Tuesday-Friday 5:30-9 p.m. 620.646.5431. FB.

**explorer extras...
In Fowler**

Drive by 608 N. Pine to see a well-kept, maize-yellow Lustron home. One of the advantages of these prefabricated homes, popular after WWII, is the enamel steel panels on the exterior that never need to be painted!

SW

Fowler residents claim that the town's old cement jail is the smallest in the state—and they put a plaque on the front to let you know it. The 1912 jail house stands under the water tower on the north end of Main. **ee**

MEADE

Population 1,634

Dalton Gang Hideout and Museum (NRHP): 502 S.

Pearlette. The Dalton Gang brothers used the home of their sister, Eva Whipple, as a hideout during the late 1880s and built an escape tunnel from the house to the barn where they kept horses for a quick getaway. The National Youth Administration (NYA) rebuilt the barn, which had burned, and the tunnel in 1941, and much of the landscaping, the wishing well, outdoor fireplace/grill, and retaining wall enclosing the property were rebuilt by the NYA and the WPA during the same period. The 96-foot-long, 32-inch-wide, 6½-foot-high dirt tunnel was converted by the WPA into a walkway with stone walls and cement floor, and visitors are welcome to try their hand at slipping through this escape route. Inside the museum you'll learn about all 15 Dalton siblings (only a few were outlaws) and the exploits of the notorious gang, and you'll see saddles, guns, and other western artifacts. Monday-Saturday 9 a.m.-5 p.m.; Sunday 1-5 p.m. Admission charge. 620.873.2731. oldmeadecounty.com.

Old Town: Dalton Gang

Museum grounds. South of the museum a Wild West town facade has been built for historical reenactments and gunfight competitions. Kids get a kick out of standing in the old casket propped up on the undertaker's wall and having their picture taken from behind the bars of the jail cell.

Heritage House:

Dalton Gang Museum grounds. The 19th-century home of John Wherle was the first in Meade to have indoor plumbing. The home also features doors leading outside from every room in the house. For hours, see Dalton Gang Museum.

Meade County Historical Museum: 200 E. Carthage.

The six flags in front of the museum represent the six countries that once claimed the territory from which Meade County was carved. Inside, neat little vignettes interpret the

county's yesteryears including the historic Jones and Plummer Trail. Amazing photographs capture the dark and dirty days of the infamous 1930s Dust Bowl. Two block southeast, an outdoor display features early farm equipment. Tuesday-Saturday 10 a.m.-5 p.m.; Sunday 1-5 p.m. 620.873.2359. oldmeadecounty.com.

Meade County Courthouse: 200 N. Fowler.

The building contains no name or sign to indicate it is the courthouse, but there's no mistaking that this grand structure is the seat of county government. Tall white columns are the focal point of this 1923 building. A closer look at the exterior reveals that the lighter colored bricks form a repeating diamond pattern within the darker red ricks. Remnants of the original courthouse, including a bas-relief limestone sculpture reading "1888" and a limestone slab step are on the southwest corner of the courthouse square.

Historic Telephone Building: From Carthage

(U.S. 54/160), ½ block north on Spring Lake. This 1932 stunner of a small blonde-brick building is the work of architect Glen Thomas, who designed the outstanding Wichita North High School and the high school in Dighton. Terra cotta buffalo heads created by Bruce Moore, who later earned worldwide fame, look out from the top of two columns flanking the front door. Bas-relief sculptures, including those of a tipi and a buffalo against blue sky backgrounds, adorn the building's front corners to the left and right of the entrance. This structure was created for the Southwestern Bell Telephone Company and is used today by AT&T.

Rusty Nail: 512 W. Carthage.

Breathe in the rich scent of leather as you enter this repair shop, where owner Mike Nail fixes most any shoe, boot, saddle, or leather good you bring him. You'll also find new leather goods (many that Mike has crafted) and Southwest style jewelry for sale. Mike has been in business more than 40 years and knows his stuff! Monday-Friday 8 a.m.-6 p.m.; Saturday 8 a.m.-3 p.m. 620.873.2144.

Hoodoo Brown:
From Fowler, 1 mile east on Carthage. Situated on the Jones and Plummer Trail, the area south of the cemetery was once the farmstead and trading post of Hoodoo Brown. After the death of his daughter Grace in 1887, Hoodoo sold the land to a cemetery association, which named the cemetery Graceland as a tribute to his daughter. A red marble memorial to Grace stands in the cemetery's south-central section.

Meade City Park:
N (U.S. 54/160) and 19. Enjoy a rest among the shade trees and the WPA shelter houses, or take a dip in the pool at this pleasant city park. A limestone marker and wooden sign on the north edge of the park tell the story of Hoodoo Brown's Road Ranch, a place for provisions for travelers on the Jones and Plummer Trail

from 1879 until the new town of Meade was established in 1885.

Bob's Drive-In:
801 E. Carthage. Bob's has served hand-pattied burgers since 1968. The shakes, sundaes, cherry lime-ades, and soft serve ice cream cones are popular too at this drive-in. Sunday-Friday 11 a.m.-9 p.m. 620.873.2862. FB

Chuckwagon Restaurant:
807 W. Carthage. Explorers will be happy to know that the chicken-fried steak is made the Explorer Way—fresh meat, hand breaded, and grill fried. Even better, it's served with real mashed potatoes and gravy. The Chuckwagon takes its name seriously, with a salad bar in a miniature version of a chuck wagon, complete with canvas cover. Monday-Saturday 6 a.m.-9 p.m.; Sunday 6 a.m.-2 p.m. 620.873.2414.

Cancun Mexican Grill:
144 W. Carthage. This casual and friendly restaurant is known for its wide variety of Mexican cuisine including sizzling fajitas, seafood, steaks, vegetarian dishes, burritos, enchiladas, and more. Tuesday-Friday 11 a.m.-2 p.m. and 4-9 p.m.; Saturday 11 a.m.-3 p.m. 620.873.2100.

Lone Tree Incident:
From Fowler, 1½ miles west on U.S. 54/160. At a roadside pull over a historical marker relates the tragic encounter in 1874 between 25 Cheyennes, led by Chief Medicine Water, and a group of surveyors. The bodies of the six men from the surveying party were found and tempo-rarily buried in a common grave near a solitary cottonwood tree.

explorer extras...
In Meade

First Presbyterian Church of Meade Center: 402 W. Carthage. A lovely 1888 white church with a tall, slender center tower has always been admired by passers-by. It is privately owned and remains empty.

Golfers can enjoy an 18-hole experience at the nine-hole Meade Golf Course by playing twice through, but starting from a different spot in each tee box.

The course sports native grass roughs and Bermuda grass fairways with paved cart paths throughout. You won't find a flat green or fairway on it. Locals say it's a challenging course. Greens fee. From Carthage, 1 mile south on K-23, 250 feet west on O. FB **ee**

SW

PLAINS

Population 1,085

Widest Main Street:
Grand. Known as the widest main street in the United States and once featured in *Ripley's Believe It or Not*, Grand spans 155 feet five inches from storefront to store-front. A row of trees is planted down the middle of the street,

and you can park on either side of the median or against the curbs—four parking areas in one! Another fact you might want to know is that it takes 69 kids stretching arm-to-arm to reach from storefront to storefront! tinyurl.com/widemain.

Angell Plow Outdoor Mural: 411 Grand. This long 1980 Stan Herd mural depicts the use of the Angell one-way disc plow. Considered an important contribution to agriculture, this implement was invented by local wheat farmer Charlie Angell during the 1920s. His invention, which was especially suited to farming on the semi-arid plains, was patented and widely used from the 1930s to the 1960s.

C.J. Angell: From Grand, 800 feet east on U.S. 54/160, just south on B, then ¼ mile west on Iowa to the Plains Cemetery. A large red granite marker, the gravestone for Charlie Angell, notes C.J. Angell as "Inventor of Angell one-way disc plow."

Plains Tavern: 301 Grand. This isn't just a tavern, it's where all the locals meet for lunch and dinner. For generations the Cox family has kept this tavern clean and family oriented. It's the home of the famous Saturday night ribeye, whose secret seasonings are charcoal-grilled into locally purchased meat. Specials are served everyday at noon, and the burgers are terrific! Monday-Saturday 10 a.m.-10 p.m. 620.563.7131.

Applehutch Farm: 6083 S. From Grand, ½ mile east on Iowa, 3 miles south on 5, then 1½ miles east on S. Two tall, dark blue silos mark the Applehutch, where you pick your own fruit in season (usually late July through October). Choose from peaches, pears, grapes, apples, pumpkins, and gourds, or buy a few fruit-related items (fruit dryers and peelers) in the retail store. The website tells you what's ripe for picking! 620.629.1447. applehutch.biz.

Morton County

AROUND THE COUNTY

Cimarron National Grassland Range Office: 242 E. U.S. 56. From Morton in Elkhart, ¼ mile east on U.S. 56. Self-guided auto tour brochures; bird and wildlife charts; and camping, hiking, and horseback riding information are available here and at tinyurl.com/cimgrass. Monday-Friday 8 a.m.-12 p.m. and 1-5 p.m. 620.697.4621.

Cimarron National Grassland: From Morton in Elkhart, 2 miles east on U.S. 56, 7½ miles north on K-27, then east into the park and follow the signs. Established after the

Dust Bowl to prevent further soil erosion, the Cimarron National Grassland is dominated by three ecosystems—shortgrass prairie, sandsage prairie, and wooded riparian. The Sea of Grass, a self-guided auto tour, takes you 30 miles through the three ecosystems and along the National Historic Santa Fe Trail, marked by limestone posts. The 23 miles of the Santa Fe Trail form the longest portion

of this famous route on public land. You can bike, hike, or ride horses on a companion trail. If you don't want to follow the entire auto tour, take time to stop at the Santa Fe Trail historic sites of Middle Spring (NRHP) and Point of Rocks (NRHP). To find these, follow the above directions 7½ miles north on K-27, cross the Cimarron River bridge, and turn west. More than 345 bird species (including roadrunners), as well as pronghorn, elk, and mule and whitetail deer, live in the grassland.

Eight Mile Corner: From Morton, ½ mile south on U.S. 56, 7¾ miles west on A. You'll see a 1903 windmill whose weather vane bears the names Kansas, Oklahoma, and Colorado. It's around here that the three states meet, but the exact location has changed

over the years. In 1990 a brass plate, whose inscription implies it is at the point where the states meet, was imbedded in the middle of Road A, 50 feet southwest of the old windmill. In the late spring yucca bordering the roadway are in bloom.

ELKHART

Population 2,138

Morton County Historical Museum: 370 E. U.S. 56.
Start your county explorations at this excellent museum. Acquaint yourself with the Point of Rocks Ranch, the adobe city hall, the POW camp that stood on the site of the present El Rancho Motel, the Dust Bowl, the old Tucker Hospital, and Olympic track stars who grew up in Morton County. A Charles Goslin mural visually transports you to the Santa Fe Trail or out on the prairie among the buffalo. This museum has been designated an official interpretive facility for the Santa Fe National Historic Trail. Tuesday-Friday 1-5 p.m. Donation welcome. 620.697.2833. mtcoks.com.

City Hall: 433 Morton. The
WPA built this adobe building in 1937. To see evidence of its 18-inch-thick adobe walls, ask the city clerk to open the closet door! She also is glad to give you a quick tour. The original adobe bricks are visible throughout the building. Monday-Friday 8 a.m.-5 p.m. 620.697.2171.

WWII Memorial: At the
entrance to City Hall you'll see an unusual 1941 WWII veterans memorial—a small monument with an attached drinking fountain. Stop and take a sip and say a silent thank you for their sacrifice.

Olympic Champions:
Two track celebrities hail from this small western Kansas town. An illustrated red granite monument to Glenn Cunningham and Thane Baker stands near City Hall, 433 Morton.

Doric Theatre: 508 Morton.
New life has been breathed into this historic building. It first opened as a vaudeville theatre in 1918, then silent moving pictures were added. The "talkies" came next, and the theatre continued operating until the 1980s. In 2015 the multistate Mitchell Theatre chain, owned by a local farm family and headquartered in Elkhart, restored and reopened the theatre. First-run movies are shown on weekends, and independent films are screened on week nights. The balcony is open for cocktails, and of course the popcorn is buttery and delicious. 620.697.4111. dorictheatre.com.

The Flying Monkey:
350 Morton. It will take flying monkeys to carry you away from the coffee bar and gigantic cinnamon rolls! Other homemade treats such as donuts and breakfast biscuit sandwiches are morning favorites, and for lunch try the signature sandwich, the T-Bird—smoked turkey, hickory bacon, and American cheese snuggle under smears of homemade tomato jam on slices of whole wheat bread. Tuesday-Friday 10 a.m.-4 p.m.; Saturday 7-11 a.m. 620.697.6659. FB.

Big C's Cafe: 969 U.S. 56.
Brenda and Chad Herron love making homestyle meals including the Explorer Way chicken-fried steak and the coconut shrimp. Breakfast is all about the fluffy pancakes and breakfast burritos, and lunch might be meatloaf one day and barbacoa tacos the next. No matter what you order on which day, it's all good. Tuesday-Friday 6:30 a.m.-8 p.m.; Saturday-Sunday 6:30 a.m.-2 p.m. 620.697.4268. FB.

Lodging: Cottage Inn Bed
& Breakfast (620.697.1010, cottageinnelkhart.com); Cimarron Bed and Breakfast (580.696.4672); additional lodging (tinyurl.com/stayelkhart).

SW

explorer extras... In Elkhart

Whistle Stop Park walking path (two and a half miles) parallels U.S. 56 and starts at Morton and U.S. 56. Enjoy this pleasant stroll through a lovely green space with trees, benches, and old-fashioned street lights.

Named for Glenn Cunningham, world record-setting miler and Olympian who grew up in Elkhart, Cunningham Park on Main Street is bordered by a 1930s WPA stone fence.

The county-owned Point Rock Golf Club, 619 Airport, is an enjoyable nine-hole, grass-green course. The signature seventh hole includes a pond and a retaining wall in front of the green, the fourth and fifth holes are built over an airport runway, and the fourth is only 30 yards from Oklahoma, so you have the opportunity to hit your ball clear out of the state! 620.697.9801. **ee**

RICHFIELD

Population 42

Stained-Glass Windows:

451 Walnut. The paneled, multi-colored stained-glass windows in the United Methodist Church are especially vibrant from inside the church where the sunlight makes the wooden rafters glow. This original church, named the Plumer Presbyterian Church,

---

was established in 1888. The current church, a red-brick structure built in 1910, is thought to be the oldest structure in Morton County.

Morton County WPA Bridge (NRHP):

From Main, 6¼ miles west on K-27 to the curve, then 4 miles north on 9. A 1939 WPA project, this stone five-arch bridge spanning Bear Creek is constructed of area limestone. Unfortunately, the bridge lost some of its beauty when culverts were placed inside its under-road arches.

In Rolla explorer extras...

Population 428

Roll down to the Rolla Roller Rink at 311 Washington! Inside the old American Legion hall, this 1950s wooden rink is open during the school year. Skate for free! Friday-Saturday 6-10 p.m. 620.593.4433.

The beautiful outdoor mural, at 215 Washington south of the Rolla Senior Center, is by local artist Janis Hollis. In this serene rural depiction, a cowboy gazes down a long stretch of highway into the sun setting on a pink, range, and lavender horizon. White grain elevators rise in the far distance, and a green cornfield stands in the foreground. **ee**

Ness County

AROUND THE COUNTY

Stone Bridge Tour:

The abundance of native limestone provided a natural resource for building bridges throughout the county. The following historic bridges are found south of K-96. The tour starts from Bazine.

1. 1935 Bazine Vicinity Triple Arch Bridge: From Main, 4 blocks west on Burgess, 1¼ mile south Dd, then 1½ miles west on 110.

2. 1935 Walnut Creek Tributary Triple Arch Bridge: From bridge #1, ¾ mile west on 110.

3. 1934 Ness County Triple Arch Bridge (WPA; NRHP): From bridge #2, ¾ mile west on 110, 9 miles south on Cc, then ¾ mile east on 20.

4. 1928 Pawnee River Tributary Double Arch Bridge (NRHP): From Bridge #3, ¼ mile east on 20, 2 miles north on Bb, 2 miles east on 40, then ¼ mile north on Dd.

BAZINE

Population 327

WPA Building: 212 N. Main. A city building constructed by the WPA in 1936 using locally quarried limestone still stands solidly next to the fire station and in front of the water tower. The city uses it for storage.

Model Stock Farm:

From Farnesworth, 3 blocks south on Main. Three native limestone buildings remain from a circa 1900 Model Stock Farm.

This type of farm was similar to today's experiment stations—researching and demonstrating improvements in agricultural techniques, efficiency, and building layout. The large barn, smaller stone building, and home tucked into a grove of trees reflect the concept that farm buildings should be beautifully designed as well as utilitarian.

Scary Bridge: From Farnesworth, 2 blocks south on Main, then 2 blocks east on Burgess. "Scary bridge" was the name that Marci Penner, Kansas Explorer #2, gave to this 1905 bridge when she drove over it. "Scary" primarily was due to the clatter from its corrugated tin deck. But the tin has been in place since 1982, so the bridge is perfectly safe!

Bazine Limestone:
204 S. King. You'll notice the abundance of limestone structures in this county, and if you'd like to know how the stone is quarried and used as building resource, Glenn Schniepp is the man to ask. Glenn offers free tours of his quarry where you'll see shells, shark teeth, and many other fascinating fossils. Individuals and groups are welcome. Call ahead, 785.398.2545. bazinelimestone.com.

Historic Cenotaph:
From Burgess, 6¾ miles south on Austin (becomes Dd) to St. John the Baptist Cemetery. A cenotaph (an empty tomb or a monument erected in honor of an individual or a group whose remains are elsewhere) has been placed here for local man John O'Brien who died at the 1876 Battle of the Little Bighorn

in Montana along with General George Custer and members of the Seventh U.S. Cavalry. O'Brien and the other cavalrymen are buried in Montana.

Hilltop Crosses:
From Main, 2¾ miles east on K-96. Three rock crosses mark the hillside where the words "Christ Pilot Me" are laid in stone. Most visible from the west, the crosses date to 1940 and were a project of the Bazine churches. At the corner just west of the crosses, turn south to see a limestone memorial and informational plaque.

BEELER

Unincorporated

George Washington Carver (8 Wonders of Kansas People):
From Hamilton, 900 feet west on K-96. At this point a historical marker summarizes the life of scientist George Washington Carver, who once lived near Beeler. While in Beeler, he purportedly told a neighbor that he felt something was under the ground in this area, but he wasn't sure what it was. He left the area in circa 1888, and in 1929 the first oil well was drilled a few miles south of Beeler.

George Washington Carver Homestead (NRHP): From Hamilton, ¼ mile east on K-96, then 1½ miles south on 523. Here a memorial rock honors George Washington Carver and marks the site of his homestead. Carver filed a homestead claim on 160 acres in 1886 and built a sod house, but no buildings stand on the land today. When Carver sold this property he used the money to attend college and, as we know, he later became a world-renowned scientist. More than 1,500 attended the 1953 dedication of this memorial that honors this famous man.

Welcome to Beeler:
E. Broadway. A handcrafted "Beeler Welcomes You" sign made from windmill blades and two limestone posts makes for a charming entrance into town.

WPA School: Broadway and Hamilton. The red-brick Beeler High School closed in 1972 and now serves the community as a meeting hall. The handsome little Tudor Revival style building was constructed by the WPA in 1936.

Indian Hill: From Hamilton, ¼ mile west on K-96, then 3¾ miles north on C. To mark a hilltop, landowner Warren Sherwin commissioned local artist Brad Dinges to sculpt a steel figure of the horse and Indian rider. The drive to see the sculpture takes you through beautiful Ness County scenery.

**explorer extras...
In Brownell**

Population 29

An old deteriorating two-story wooden building stands at 5th and Davis. It's listing just a bit and although time is after it, the fires of March 2017 couldn't put it down! A former hotel, it has also housed a sporting goods store and a bar. The old dear is empty now. **ee**

SW

NESS CITY

Population 1,437

Ness City is in the Smoky Hills physiographic region, but as you go west you heading toward the High Plains region. The countryside starts to spread out and you can see forever.

Skyscraper of the Plains (NRHP; 8 Wonders of Kansas Architecture):
102 W. Main. When this four-story stone building with 13-foot ceilings was completed in 1890 it was the tallest building

between Topeka and Denver and deemed the "Skyscraper of the Plains." For decades it was home to the Ness County Bank as well as a host of other organizations. Brass doorknobs and fixtures with a sunflower design attest to this building's quality of detail, as does the oil painting, finished in 22-karat gold, that adorns the vault door. More than 60 photos of historic Ness County grace the walls. Call ahead, 785.798.2812.

Prairie Mercantile:
102 W. Main (basement floor). Shop for Kansas-made and Kansas-proud food, books, pictures, wheat weavings, limestone carvings, quilts, and more at the Mercantile before and after you explore the stunning bank building in which it is housed. Wednesday-Friday 1-4 p.m. 785.798.3337.

Ness County Courthouse:
202 W. Sycamore. J.C. Holland and Sons designed this 1918 Modern Eclecticism limestone structure that features decorative roundels.The front roundels in the top center on each side of the building originally contained working clocks. The dust storms

of the 1930s clogged the mechanisms so badly that they ceased working. In the mid-1970s local art teacher Jack Simpson painted Kansas images—the state seal, sunflowers, a bison, and a windmill—in each of the roundels.

Noah Ness Statue: 202 W.
Sycamore. A Civil War soldier with the Seventh Kansas Cavalry, Corporal Noah V.B. Ness, is the namesake of Ness County, the only Kansas county named for a corporal. The bronze statue of Corporal Ness, sculpted by H.T. Holden, stands in front of the courthouse as a tribute to those who served their country.

Veterans Memorial and Park: From Pennsylvania,
1 block west on Main. The attractive memorial in a nicely landscaped corner park was dedicated to those who served to ensure "that their efforts will never be forgotten."

Ness County Historical Museum: 123 S. Pennsylvania.
Inside an old mercantile building with the original floor and ceiling, the museum portrays the county story and showcases famous area residents including scientist George Washington Carver, Kansas governor and U.S. senator Andrew Schoeppel, and major league baseball players Chief Hogsett and Smokey Joe Wood. Tuesday-Friday 1-5 p.m. 785.798.3298.

Oil and Ag Museum:
212 Sycamore. The museum preserves the area's oil boom days and displays a collection of agricultural equipment. Call ahead, 785.798.3298.

Stan Herd Mural: U.S. 283
and K-96. A Stan Herd mural in a community is always an honor. One of his newer (2010) murals appears on the parapet of a former 1920s corner service station. It depicts historic Ness City from the 1870s through the 1890s.

Lion Block (NRHP):
216 W. Main. A look at the top of the building tells you why it's called the Lion Block. Local stonemason Henry Tilley carved the stone lion atop the parapet, along with the highly decorative circular and triangular motifs. The convention of the time was to call such buildings "blocks," and the name does not refer to city blocks as it does today. This Italianate style structure, constructed in 1887, was used for commercial retail space. It currently is empty.

Cactus Club: 124 S.
Pennsylvania. Decorated in a Southwest theme, this restaurant attracts locals and visitors with its noon buffet and daily specials. The grilled chicken salad with fresh greens, tomatoes, green peppers, hard-boiled eggs, cheddar cheese, and tender hot-off-the-grill chicken is a delicious meal in itself. Monday-Saturday 5:30 a.m.-2 p.m. and 5-8:30 p.m.; Sunday 8 a.m.-2 p.m. 785.798.3639.

Cuppa Joe: 108 E. Sycamore.
Run in for a cup of coffee, but if you have time stay for a piece of delicious homemade pie or a cinnamon roll. You might be lucky and find them coming

right out of the oven! A small lunch menu features sandwiches on homemade bread, salads, and daily specials. Monday-Friday 6 a.m.-2 p.m. 785.798.2600. FB.

Frigid Creme: 501 W. Sycamore. It's a favorite stop in the summer for locals and travelers along K-96 who crave a creamy cold treat or a good ol' burger, corn dog, and fries. May-September. 785.798.2424.

**explorer extras...
In Ness City**

Post rock fence posts surround Ness City's first schoolhouse, constructed in 1879. The local historical society maintains this one-room school at K-96 and Sycamore. 785.798.3298.

You might call the old shed the county event calendar. For more than 60 years it's been a tradition to paint announcements of activities, the birth of a child, high school graduation, remembrances of a loved one, community events, or a soldier's homecoming on this graffiti-covered Quonset. Some think that the layers of paint applied over the years are the only thing keeping the metal shed upright! It's a surprising piece of art on the prairie, but it's one that will warm your heart. From U.S. 283, 3¾ miles east on K-96.

Since 2007 volunteers have operated an impressive group of carnival rides and games during the Ness County Fair. Members of the Ness County Amusement Company say that the smiles they receive are all the payment they need. See the carnival in operation every July at the fairgrounds at 500 N. Court, which is also where you can visit the rides resting during the off-season. FB. **ee**

UTICA

Population 157

Vic's Shortbranch Saloon: 271 S. Ohio. The 1920s bar and polished old wood floor are evidence that the Shortbranch is a longtime fixture in the community. You'll see why when you bite into the half-pound Angus burger or the daily special. Delicious steaks are a special menu item in the evenings. Join the fun—lots of pool has been played here and lots of lies have been told! Monday-Saturday 11 a.m.-12 a.m. 785.391.2267.

Wertz Street Social Emporium: 222 E. Wertz. This 1909 lumberyard is now known for its pan-fried chicken buffet for lunch on Thursdays and for top-notch steaks and drinks on weekends. Thursday 11 a.m.-2 p.m.; Friday-Saturday 6:30-10 p.m. 785.391.2342. FB.

Utica Community Cafe: 142 S. Ohio. At this community-owned cafe you can meet the community folks who fill it up everyday. Come in for a home-cooked meal and become part of the family. Daily 7 a.m.-2 p.m. (closed Thursday). 785.391.2278.

Pawnee County

BURDETT

Population 248

Agriculture is king in Burdett. The Golden Valley farmers co-operative grain elevators at the south edge of town can hold 1.9 million bushels of wheat, corn, milo, and soybeans.

Clyde Tombaugh: Clyde Tombaugh is the town's most famous native son. He graduated from Burdett High School in 1925, and in 1930 he was credited with discovering what was thought to be our ninth planet, Pluto. The International Astronomical Union now considers Pluto a dwarf planet, but Tombaugh's efforts were still remarkable. Read more about him and his famous discovery on a historical marker on the west side of town at Maple and Broadway.

SW

Miniature Golf Course:

From U.S. 156, ¼ mile north on Elm, then 1 block east on Michigan. Brainstormers had a great idea when they renovated their 1977 community miniature golf course using a Pluto theme to honor their famed native son Clyde Tombaugh. In 2014 the cobalt-blue miniature golf greens and facts about Pluto and space were put in place, and the free course opened once again. Golf clubs and balls are found near the park restrooms.

City Park: Michigan and 345th. Beside the miniature golf course is a stone shelter house built with rocks from the old Browne and Mather house. Displayed inside the shelter is a lintel from the 1879 Mayer and Johnson Flouring and Grist Mill. The little historic water fountain, still working, provides a cool drink.

Moosette's Cafe:

204 Broadway. Leonard Mostrom is better known as Moose, and his wife, Kathy, is Moosette! Thus the name for this swell little eatery, which even features a moose burger (actually it's beef). The fresh-ground meat comes from the Ellinwood Packing Plant, so you know it's good, and the burgers are dressed up with an onion ring, bacon, tomato, and swiss cheese. The daily specials and homemade desserts are delicious too! Tuesday-Saturday 7 a.m.-2 p.m. 620.525.6660. FB.

GARFIELD

Population 191

Town Name: U.S. 56 and Pawnee (Downey Memorial Park). The bell in the tiny Garfield Memorial Wayside Chapel

(a replica of the original church) was given to the town in 1875 by Ohio congressman James A. Garfield, who became the 20th president of the United States in 1881. The bell was a thank you to former citizens from his Ohio district who had emigrated to Kansas and renamed their town in his honor.

West Roadside Park:

U.S. 56 and 3rd. Here you'll find a Santa Fe Trail marker placed by the DAR in 1906, and a large sign noting that Camp Criley, a supply station for the Santa Fe railroad, was established here in 1872. Also in this park is a historic band shell and an old stone stile used back in the day to help women mount their horses.

Post Office: 213 3rd. The red-brick building on the corner was a bank and now serves as the post office. Go in and buy some stamps to help keep this little PO in business. While you're there take a look at the narrow doors. Maybe you'll know their purpose! Monday-Friday 8 a.m.-12 p.m.; Saturday 8:15-9:15 a.m.

School Memorial:

Porter and School. A classic old bell that once stood on top of the 1917 Garfield School has been preserved as a memorial. The school's history is engraved in a black granite stone beneath the bell. The red-brick auditorium added in 1936 and built by

the WPA stands to the east of the memorial.

Fort Larned Military Road

Marker: From 3rd, 1½ miles southwest on U.S. 56. Near the treeline in the parking area, a marker and a sign indicate that at this point the Fort Larned Military Road intersected with the Santa Fe Trail. The military road linked the fort with the "wet" route of the Santa Fe Trail allowing soldiers to access the trail and protect travelers. This junction of the road and the trail is at the Coon Creek Crossing (NRHP), and wagon ruts are still visible on the north bank of the creek.

LARNED

Population 4,046

Fort Larned National Historic Site (8 Wonders of Kansas History):

1767 K-156. From Broadway, 6½ miles west on K-156. From 1859 to 1878 Fort Larned supplied guard detachments to protect mail stages and wagon trains, and the post became known as one of the principal guardians of Santa Fe

Trail commerce. A video and displays in the visitor center introduce you to the fort, and you'll notice that the interpretation of the fort's original buildings and the attention to detail is

E.E. Frizell: In 1902 E.E. Frizell purchased Fort Larned and developed it into a ranch. Although Frizell used the buildings he tried to preserve their historic importance. In 1966 the family transferred ownership of the fort to the National Park Service.

Sibley's Camp: 502 W. 2nd. The 1825 Santa Fe Trail survey team, headed by George Sibley, camped on this site on August 31. An interpretive marker describes the setting in 1825, and a wayside exhibit provides the site history. Sibley, appointed by President John Quincy Adams as one of three commissioners to oversee the Santa Fe Trail survey, referred in his diary to the Cliffs of Soft Rock (sandstone), the remains of which can still be seen at this site.

Little Red House: 2nd and State, across from Sibley's Camp. In 1872 post trader Henry Booth brought this house, one of Fort Larned's structures, to the future town site of Larned. A sign recounts the different functions this building has served over the years.

Henry Booth Boulevard: Main. Henry Booth was a cavalry officer and a state representative from Riley County before coming to Fort Larned to operate the sutler's store. He later helped choose Larned's town site, developed many of its buildings, and was a director of the soldiers' home at Fort Dodge. Booth's importance to the town was acknowledged by his name being added to Main Street.

excellent. The infantry barracks exhibit guns, hats, and uniforms; he bunks are made up with army issue blankets; the 1868 commissary stocks salt pork, barrels of corn meal, and wooden boxes of potatoes; and boots stand beside the bed in the officers' family quarters. After the fort closed it was sold into private hands in 1884 and again in 1902, when it became a horse and cattle ranch. In 1966 it was transferred to the National Park Service and since that time the fort has become one of the best preserved authentic frontier posts in the American West. It hosts annual reenactments for public education and enjoyment. Daily 8:30 a.m.-4:30 p.m. 620.285.6911. nps.gov/fols/index.htm.

Santa Fe Trail Marker and Ruts: From Fort Larned, just west on K-156, 4 miles south on 180, 1 mile west on J, then ½ mile south on 190. A plaque on an old limestone post notes that the Fort Larned Military Road and the Santa Fe Trail crossed this point. Watch your step as you walk to the lookout to see the wagon ruts—the field is home to prairie dogs!

Santa Fe Trail Center: 1349 K-156. From Broadway, 2¼ miles west on K-156. Exhibits interpret the American Indians' and fur traders' use of the trail and how the coming of the railroad altered its history. The 10 buildings of the museum complex include furnished reproduction sod house and dugout homes, a one-room schoolhouse, a Santa Fe railroad depot, and a 1906 church built by its black congregation. A research library and archives are also available (call ahead). Tuesday-Saturday 9 a.m.-5 p.m. Admission charge. 620.285.2054. santafetrailcenter.org.

Zebulon Pike Plaza: From Broadway, ½ mile southwest on Trail (U.S. 56), then just north on Pawnee. The plaza commemorates Captain Pike crossing the Pawnee River near present Larned in October 1806, and recognizes where he and his men camped during his Red River Expedition. Pike's 1806 journals and maps provided information that helped open the trade route that would become the Santa Fe Trail. Numerous markers interpret the many aspects of Pike's presence in this area, as well as that of other American and Spanish explorers and of Santa Fe Trail travelers. larnedks.org/play.

Larned Cemetery: From Broadway, 1¾ miles west on U.S. 156, then ½ mile south on 130. A limestone marker notes that Santa Fe Trail wagon ruts are visible as depressions along the fence in the cemetery's southeast corner. You will also see Civil War graves, veterans memorials, intriguing

SW

headstones, and plaques. "The Last Alarm" is one of the stand-out memorials and is dedicated to Larned's fallen firefighters.

Historic Homes: Fabulous homes await your admiration in Larned including the Babbitt-Doerr House (NRHP), an 1886 Queen Anne house at 423 W. 5th. Additional impressive homes are an 1912 three-story brick Neoclassical (707 State); an 1886 Victorian (323 W. 6th); an 1885 Italianate with a brick tower (1021 Broadway); and a 1909 Craftsman bungalow (527 W. 4th). Pawnee County Historic Homes brochures are available at the chamber office, 502 Broadway.

Lustron Homes: Larned is teeming with these enamel-coated, all-steel prefabricated homes that popped up after WWII in response to the housing shortage. The Ooten House (NRHP) is at 507 W. 15th, and the Patterson House (NRHP) stands at 841 W. 8th. Additional Lustrons are at 1124 Toles, 1421 State, 823 Starks, 721 Martin, 612 Mann, and 505 W. 5th.

Schnack Lowrey Park: W. 1st and Carroll. This nostalgic area, donated by F.D. Lowrey and Peter Schnack, includes a newly renovated duck pond (originally the city swimming pool), a well-tended rose garden, and a modern

swimming pool with a nearby water fountain that displays a gorgeous underwater colored light show at night (May to October). 620.285.8500.

Scraps: 612 Broadway. It's a scrapbook store and coffee shop and much more. Discover gift items, home decor, jewelry, purses, pastries, and lunch options—salad bar, make your own sandwich, daily specials, and make your own baked potato. It's an artistic venue where coffee and creativity come together. Tuesday-Saturday 7 a.m.-5:30 p.m. 620.285.8977. scrapslarned.com.

Dress It Up: 511 Broadway. Opened in 2011 this community-owned shop came about because area women wanted a clothing store and they made it happen. Dress It Up is a wonderful shopping experience, and your support helps it and the community. Monday-Friday 10 a.m.-6 p.m.; Saturday 10 a.m.-3 p.m. 620.285.6886. FB.

B&B Quality Meats: 508 Broadway. B&B processes its own meat (pork, beef, and more), and you'll find a large selection of deli meats and cheeses too. Monday-Friday 9 a.m.-6 p.m. 620.285.8988.

explorer extras...
In Larned

The Stockwell farm is the birthplace of farm credit. A historical marker tells us that 280 acres were collateral for the first Federal Land Bank loan in the nation, made on April 10, 1917, to farmer-stockman A.L. Stockwell. From Broadway, 1¼ miles south on Trail (U.S. 56).

The 1919 blond-brick Pawnee County courthouse at 715 Broadway was built in the Modern Eclecticism style and features an ionic portico.

A playground featuring a Fort Larned theme, historical signs, and a spray feature is found in Doerr-Vernon Park at K-156 and Carroll. On the park's southeast corner, at Fort Larned Ave.and College, the Pawnee County Area All Veterans Memorial features a twisted metal piece from the south tower of the World Trade Center.

The State Theater at 617 Broadway first opened in 1948 and has now been renovated. Its original yellow, red, and white marquee is sure to catch your attention! The theater is owned by the community and operated completely by volunteers. Friday-Sunday 7 p.m. 620.285.3535. FB.

The red-brick Santa Fe railroad depot at 320 N. Broadway was built in 1905 and is now home to the American State Bank.

Central States Scout Museum suffered a devastating fire in 2016 that destroyed part of the extensive collection housed here. However, some of the collection was salvaged, and artifacts that were in storage are on display at its new location, 215 W. 14th. The museum provides a fascinating glimpse into the history and culture of the Boy Scouts of America. Call ahead, 620.804.0509. **ee**

Rush County

Unincorporated

Historic School:

School and Kepner. From Main, 3 blocks east on Kepner. When you see it, you'll understand why this 100-year-old, two-story Collegiate Gothic school still draws attention from passers-by. Many are so spellbound that they pull over or drive back to take photos. Built in 1916, Alexander School has a distinctive Flemish Bond pattern, made with rough-cut native limestone, on the corners of the facade. The limestone is a beautiful contrast and accent to the red brick on the majority of the building. A 1930 gymnasium that stands to the north was built in the same style. The school closed in 1966, and both buildings are now privately owned. Efforts to preserve the school and restore the gym are ongoing. Call ahead, 785.425.7350.

Fort Hays-Fort Dodge Road Crossing:

From Main, 1 block west on Williams, 1½ blocks north on King, then across the bridge on Walnut Creek. Here a limestone post and a plaque indicate the crossing on the Fort Hays-Fort Dodge Road, and 1867-1868 military supply trail between Fort Hays and Fort Dodge. Learn more about it from the historic marker at the Alexander rest stop along K-96.

Rest Stop: From Main, ¼ mile west on K-96. One of the cleanest rest stops in the state is at Alexander. Take a break, stretch your legs, and meander over to the old windmill and water pump and take a closer look at these icons of the prairie. Near the restrooms a historic marker relates the story of the old Fort Hays-Fort Dodge Road (*see* previous entry).

explorer extras...
In Bison

Even the smallest towns have big history. The Bison yesteryears are preserved through historic photos and area artifacts at the combined Bison library and museum, 202 Main. Tuesday 1-6 p.m.; Wednesday 3-8 p.m.; Thursday 9 a.m.-2 p.m. 785.356.4803.

Bison is proud of its name. Notice the bison-shaped street signs, the metal cutout bison welcome sign, and the bison images on the town's trash cans.

WPA projects include the 1936 native limestone former city hall at 214 Main and the 1937 limestone Bison Grade School at Main and Locust.

Two more architectural points of interest are the 1920 brick high school at Main and Locust and the old brick (painted white) city jail in the alley behind the old city hall, 214 Main. As you drive around town, you'll also see the limestone influence in many structures, especially on E. 1st.

If you have questions about the town, inquire at the Bison State Bank, 223 Main. This 1903 red-brick corner bank still has its original teller cage and pressed-tin ceiling. Monday-Friday 8 a.m.-3 p.m. 785.356.2195.

Population 1,289

Barbed Wire Museum:

120 W. 1st. After hosting a swap and sell convention in 1967, LaCrosse became known as the Barbed Wire Capital of Kansas. Barbed wire has quite a history in Kansas and the West, and here you'll see 2,000 different styles of wire, complete with

their specific names, patent numbers, and patent dates. On exhibit also are trade tools including wire splices, stretchers, and post-hole diggers; liniments for barbed-wire lacerations; and a nest that a crow made from barbed wire. May to mid-September, Monday-Saturday 10 a.m.-4:30 p.m. and Sunday 1-4:30 p.m. 785.222.9900. rushcounty.org.

Post Rock Museum
(8 Wonders of Kansas Customs): 202 W. 1st. The museum building was moved stone by stone to this site from Nekoma. Spending time here will help you further appreciate Kansas native limestone, a beautiful natural resource often known as post rock. The museum houses photographs of limestone being quarried and of area buildings constructed of this native material. An exhibit also demonstrates how to extract limestone from the ground using feathers and wedges. An average post rock fence post is nine inches wide on each of its four sides, five to six feet long, and weighs 250 to 450 pounds. For hours, see Barbed Wire Museum. 785.222.2719. rushcounty.org.

Rush County Historical Museum: 202 W. 1st. The 1887 Santa Fe depot from nearby Timken is now home to this museum that preserves

area history. The Pleasant Point one-room schoolhouse, a new addition to the complex, reflects early education in Rush County and displays artifacts from pioneer educator Howard Barnard. For hours, see Barbed Wire Museum. 785.222.2719. rushcounty.org.

Nekoma Bank Museum:
202 W. 1st. This 1916 bank was transported lock, stock, and vault to this site from the unincorporated county town of Nekoma. Artifacts showcase the area's banking story. For hours, see Barbed Wire Museum. 785.222.2719. rushcounty.org.

Rush County Courthouse
(NRHP): 715 Elm. One of the older courthouses in the state, this 1889 Romanesque Revival building is constructed of red brick with limestone trim. Take time to visit the courtroom, still adorned with its original pressed-tin ceiling.

Howard R. Barnard:
Barnard's life work was with rural schools, mainly in Rush County. He was an innovator and introduced his techniques at his experimental school, Entre Nous College (*see* p. 442), which he started near McCracken. He went on to become a much beloved librarian at the LaCrosse High School and later the public library, which was named for

him. See a collection of his artifacts and books at the Barnard Library, 521 Elm. Monday-Friday 1-4:30 p.m.; Saturday 10 a.m.-1 p.m.

PawPaws: 221 S. Main. Burgers and ice cream have kept customers happy and well fed here since the 1950s. The walk-up window is pure retro. April-December, Monday-Saturday 11 a.m.-8 p.m. 785.222.3353. FB.

Tracy's Pub & Grill:
706 Main. Hand-breaded everything is on this menu, including chicken strips, steak fingers, and chicken-fried steak made the Explorer Way. For healthier fare, fill up at the large salad bar. Tracy's is a favorite stop for Sunday morning breakfasts! Tuesday-Friday 11 a.m.-2 p.m. and 4-9 p.m.; Saturday 11 a.m.-9 p.m.; Sunday 6:30 a.m.-1:30 p.m. 785.222.9994. FB.

**explorer extras...
In LaCrosse**

Late-1930s WPA projects include the 1937 Barnard Library at 521 Elm, a school vocational building at 511 Elm, and a variety of structures (shelter house, restrooms, and pump house) in City Park on S. Main. All are constructed of native limestone.

The Boy Scouts placed a replica Statue of Liberty in City Park on S. Main, and it has been a landmark there since 1951. A tasteful display comprises the statue and a veterans memorial, which includes flags representing each Rush County veteran who died in wartime.

The WPA built the stone double-arch bridge (NRHP) that crosses a Sand Creek tributary. This 1942 picturesque bridge can still be appreciated decades after it was built. From U.S. 183, 2 miles west on K-4, then 1½ mile north on 230.

A drive by 505 Washington reveals how native limestone was utilized on this beautiful residence, including its chimney, solid porch columns, railing, and retaining wall around the yard. **ee**

explorer extras...
In Liebenthal

Population 100

Its single spire pierces the sky, and a red roof draws attention to the exquisite limestone St. Joseph Church, dedicated in 1905. The nearby old parochial school and rectory are also built of native limestone. 202 Main.

Pat says his jerky is the best darned beef jerky in the whole world. We believe him, and encourage you to stop at Pat's Beef Jerky in the former Liebenthal State Bank at 401 Main. Try his regular, peppered, or hot hot jerky, then try to decide which one to take home (or buy some of each!). Pat has been at this trade a long, long time and knows how to do jerky right. Monday-Saturday 9 a.m.-5 p.m. 785.222.3341. patsbeefjerky.com.

Sonny's Tavern & Grill: 405 Main. It's a friendly tavern serving 3.2 beer, egg burgers, onion rings, and a good time. Monday-Saturday 10:30 a.m.-10 p.m.; Sunday 1-8 p.m. 785.514.5088. FB. **ee**

MCCRACKEN

Population 180

McCracken Historical Museum: 200 Main. The 1901 stone city building, complete with jail inside, is home to the local museum. An exhibit about the filming of *Paper Moon* in McCracken includes a hand-written thank you from film star Tatum O'Neal. Also featured are a 1906 Kansas railroad map and information about the Fort Hays-Fort Dodge Road and Entre Nous College (*see* later entry). Hours irregular. Call ahead, 785.394.2446.

Sculpture Garden: Next to the Historical Museum. The radiant sunflower sculpture by Pat Istas stands 12 feet tall and "blooms" with 13 flowers and more than 30 leaves. Other

garden sculptures include three milo stalks and a prickly pear. Istas also designed the garden's post rock sign.

Post Office: 307 Main. It's just a little place, but its stamps are as good as anyone's. Buy them here and keep the PO kickin' in McCracken. Monday-Friday 8:30 a.m.-4 p.m.

SW

St. Mary's Church: 310 W. Ash. Completed in 1926, this ornate brick structure with stone arches and trim closed in 1998. It's still standing tall, however, and invites you to drive by and admire it.

Golf Course: Jefferson and Beech. A nine-hole, sand-green course on the east edge of town welcomes you to tee it up. The locals say it's a fun little course and the creek will give you a challenge every time. Greens fee.

Hampton Cemetery: From 6th, 5 miles east on Elm (becomes I), then 1 mile north on 160. The cemetery is dotted with metal crosses marking graves that were located with a divining rod. Many gravestones signify burial places of early pioneers who came to the area in the 1870s.

Fort Hays-Fort Dodge Road Marker: Across from Hampton Cemetery. A limestone marker indicates where the 1867-1868 military supply trail crossed Snake Creek.

Entre Nous College: From Beech, 3¾ miles north on K-4, then 3 miles east on E. Howard Barnard established this innovative experimental school, which operated from 1906 to 1912. Among other advancements, he pioneered a school transportation system, visual education, physical education, and starting a library. An old bell on a limestone base marks the site of this progressive college. Learn more about its short but fascinating life at the Historical Museum, 202 W. 1st, and the Barnard Library, 521 Elm in LaCrosse.

explorer extras... In McCracken

A handsome gray granite marker proudly lists the players of the McCracken Pee Wee and K-18 Baseball teams who won state championships in 1974 and 1977. The monument stands in City Park at 7th and Washington.

The iron cutouts at the town entrance, made by B&B Metal Arts of Hoisington, are a tip of the hat to McCracken's long-time rodeo. **ee**

explorer extras... In Otis

Population 274

You'll find the Peter Brack memorial band shell in City Park at 101 S. Main. A nearby plaque tells more about Brack, who immigrated from Russia to Rush County in 1876 and became a successful area businessman.

Note the decorative terra cotta entrance above the doors at the 1931 Otis-Bison High School, 3rd and Eagle.

Crazy 8 Stop & Repair, 420 N. Main, is good for a candy bar and a cold pop. And if you have a ping in your engine or need a tire fixed, this is the place to go. Monday-Friday 7 a.m.-7 p.m.; Saturday 8 a.m.-2 p.m. 785.387.2255. **ee**

RUSH CENTER

Population 165

Pedestrian Bridge: A vintage wooden bridge spans a low draw on the west side of

Walnut, 1 block south of K-96. The bridge is flanked on both sides by tall historic street lights accenting the slender pathway.

Effies Place: 122 Union. Don't rush by the faded blue metal building until you check if Effies is open for lunch. Effie Crowell turned 93 in 2017, but that hasn't slowed her down much. She's known for her home-style cooking and grilling what some folks say are the best burgers in the world! Whatever you order, order a red beer to go with it. September-April, Monday-Saturday 11 a.m.-2 p.m. 785.372.4233.

TIMKEN

Population 74

WPA School: From K-96, ½ mile north on Main. The mighty Timken Termites went to grade school in this handsome native stone building constructed in 1937 by the WPA. The Termites were wiped out when the mascot became the Bombers. The school closed in the 1980s and the building is now privately owned.

Timken Hill Bar & Grill: K-96 and Main. A full parking lot attests to the continued popularity of this eatery that opened in 1947. That's when Al Holopirek built the red building as a beer joint, and his brother Ernie built the gas and service station next door. Owners have changed over the years, but in 2008 Paul and Linda Hampton and their sons Marty and Zack reopened the bar and grill and it's been hoppin' ever since. Friday nights are burger nights, with bun-busting big burgers and special toppings. On Saturdays the ribeye and the Explorer Way chicken-fried steak with pan gravy pack the house. The food is fantastic and the view is vast at Timken Hill. Friday 5-9 p.m.; Saturday 11 a.m.-2 p.m. and 5-9 p.m. 785.355.2355. FB.

Bohemian National Cemetery:
From Main, 1 mile west on K-96, then 1½ miles south on 310. This well-tended cemetery in a pastoral setting is filled with granite markers, some inset with photos of the deceased. Reflecting the Old World are ornate iron crosses; engraved names such as Kriklan, Pivonka, Matal, and Serpan; and dates and epitaphs written in German and Czechoslovakian.

Scott County

Scott County consistently ranks in the top agriculture-producing counties in the state and in the nation. Agriculture generated $820 million in revenue in 2016. It's big business! The county contains 17 commercial cattle yards that feed in excess of 400,000 head annually. It also comprises six commercial swine operations, one dairy, and cropland that produces grain sorghum, wheat, corn, soybeans, and sunflowers.

AROUND THE COUNTY

Western Vistas Historic Byway:
This 100-mile drive from Lake Scott on U.S. 83 to Oakley and then west to Sharon Springs on U.S. 40 takes you through chalk formations, buttes, and valleys—all buried under the sea 80 million years ago. Buffalo, American Indians, pioneers, early military, Wild West characters, and

paleontologists were deeply connected to this prodigious and legendary land. 785.671.1000. travelks.com/ksbyways.com.

Lake Scott and State Park:
101 W. Scott Lake. From K-96, 9¾ miles north on U.S. 83, then 3 miles west and north on K-95. When in the midst of the High Plains prairie, it's hard to believe you're near a spring-fed lake with deep wooded canyons and craggy Ogallala limestone bluffs. It is an oasis on the prairie. All the usual recreational opportunities, including hiking trails, are available in the park and its rugged 100-acre lake. State park entrance charge. Cabins available, reservations required. Monday-Friday 8 a.m.-12 p.m. and 1-5 p.m. 620.872.2061. ksoutdoors.com.

Battle of Punished Woman's Fork (NRHP):
From K-96, 9¾ miles north on U.S. 83, 1¼ miles west and north on K-95, then ¼ mile west on unnamed gravel road, and follow the signs. In this area Northern Cheyennes clashed with U.S. Army soldiers while attempting to return to their homes in Montana after having been removed to Oklahoma. It was a pivotal event in the larger Northern Cheyenne exodus of 1878-1879. Until recently, access to this area

was restricted, but it is now open to the public. Signage and trails take you to key points of the confrontation and help you understand the events that occurred here. Information and exhibits pertaining to this battle are at the El Quartelejo Museum (see later entry), 902 W. 5th in Scott City. 620.872.5912. tinyurl.com/battlecanyon.

Steele Homestead (NRHP):
520 W. Scott Lake (Lake Scott State Park). Herbert Steele homesteaded here in 1888, and in 1909 he and his wife, Eliza, built their sandstone home just above Ladder Creek. Paths lead you behind the house

SW

to what was once a garden. Graceful old cottonwoods now shade the area. The Steeles wanted their homestead to become a public park and recreation area and sold their 640 acres to the Kansas Forestry, Fish and Game Commission in 1928. To see the inside of the house, inquire at the park office.

Steele Memorial: Across from the Steele homestead. Looking up and across from the Steele house you'll see a monument on top of the ridge. The granite rock with a bronze plaque was placed here in memory of Herbert Steele who homesteaded this area in 1888. The steep path up to the marker offers gorgeous views of the lake and surrounding area.

El Quartelejo Pueblo Indian Ruins (NRHP):

From Lake Scott State Park office (101 W. Scott Lake), 1 mile northwest on Scott Lake. In the late 1600s Taos Indians from the Southwest fled to this area to escape Spanish rule and lived in pueblos here for 20 years. Only lower portions of the stone walls remain, but they show the rooms' interiors.

This northernmost pueblo in the United States had long been buried under drifting soil but was discovered by Herbert Steele in 1898. The ruins were awarded National Historic Landmark Status in 1964. A historical marker provides a detailed story of this unique Kansas site.

Keystone Gallery: From 5th in Scott City, 19 miles north on U.S. 83. (see p. 25).

MODOC

Unincorporated

Scott Cooperative Association: 272 Modoc.

These towns might be small, but their significance to agriculture is great. The elevator and grain bins here can hold 1.6 million bushels of wheat, corn, or milo. You can stop at the co-op office for a pop and a candy bar from the fridge—just leave money in the box on top. If it's harvest time or you see a line of trucks, it's best to come back another time. 620.872.2845.

Modoc Miracles: 2011 S. Beaver. From Modoc, ½ mile west on K-96, then 2 miles south on Beaver. Matt Novak moved back to his hometown of Modoc after earning his horticulture degree, and he set to work

opening a greenhouse business that he named Modoc Miracles. He moved the 130-year-old Modoc train depot to his farm and restored it into a garden center, where he now sells bedding plants from mid-April through mid-June. But he didn't stop there. It took six years, but he restored the 1918 township meeting hall (from Heizer, ½ block north on Modoc) and it is now the community center. Miracles are happening in Modoc. 620.872.2053. FB.

Chicken Coop in a Bank:

Modoc and Heizer. Old buildings are reused for all sorts of things, and the 1917 Modoc Bank is no different. These days deposits come in the way of eggs instead of dollars. Lisa Birney has turned the building into a chicken coop, and added a corral on one side for her horses. It's easy to imagine the horses having a conversation with a friendly teller through the drive-up window!

SCOTT CITY

Population 4,100

El Quartelejo Museum:

902 W. 5th. Cattle and pioneer history, fossils, and American Indian heritage are showcased inside this Southwest style museum. Exhibits feature the archeology of the El Quartelejo pueblo ruins of the late 1600s, the nomadic Indians who camped nearby in the 1500s, and the Battle of Punished Woman's Fork. You'll also learn about Maria DeGeer, who founded the town in 1884 and was the first woman to be admitted to the Kansas Bar Association. Tuesday-Saturday

1-5 p.m. 620.872.5912. elquartelejomuseum.org.

Jerry Thomas Gallery and Collection: 902 W. 5th.

Rich in history are the works of Scott City native and world-renowned artist Jerry Thomas, whose paintings are exhibited in a gallery attached to the El Quartelejo Museum. His painstaking research and attention to detail bring military history, wildlife, and the Old West to life in vivid color and context.

Jerry's personal collection of American Indian, western, and military artifacts, also on display in the gallery, offer a fascinating view into the past and are often depicted in his paintings. Tuesday-Saturday 1-5 p.m. 620.874.0174. jerrythomasart.com.

Scott County Courthouse:

303 Court. Constructed of red brick with limestone trim, this 1924 Modern Eclecticism courthouse occupies a full block square. The courtroom retains its historical integrity with decorative wall panels and pilasters. Monday-Friday 8 a.m.-5 p.m. 620.872.2420.

Downtown: Here are four

reasons, among many, to shop in Scott City. Gifts Etc. (424 S. Main); Bling (409 S. Main); Scott City Antiques (704 W. 5th); and Giftologists (401 S. Main).

Majestic Theatre Restaurant: 420 S. Main.

Fine dining is a majestic experience in this 1922 theatre with a prominent proscenium arch and gold latticework. A prime rib

sandwich, fresh salads with chunky homemade blue cheese dressing, and daily soup and entree specials are a few of the delicious menu choices. No matter what you order, the ambince makes you feel elegant and pampered. Tuesday-Friday 11:30 a.m.-1:30 p.m.; Thursday-Saturday 5:30-8:30 p.m. 620.872.3840. FB.

Tate's: 405 S. Main. Dig in to

fresh, flavorful, and fantastic! Made-from-scratch options include chef's salads with sauteed crab, chicken, and beef kabobs; bison burgers made from Duff Buffalo Ranch bison and served on homemade buns; catfish; and KC strip steaks. Even the grilled cheese sandwich is on homemade bread. If you still have room, the cobbler (homemade of course) is a must! Monday-Saturday 11 a.m.-9 p.m. 620.909.5002. FB.

El Dos de Oros: 1213 S.

Main. Sizzling plates of fajitas; bowls of fresh salsa and chips; mouth-watering beef enchiladas, tacos, and tamales; and the local favorite, the San Juan chicken burrito, are just a few of the dozens of menu choices. Ice cold margaritas in large goblets and other specialty cocktails go perfectly with your meal. Daily 11 a.m.-9 p.m. 620.872.5204.

The Taylor House: 1313 S.

Main. Lynn and Traci Taylor, son Adam, and his wife, Anita, want you to feel like you've stopped by their home for coffee. The Taylor House is a welcoming, warm environment with soft lounge chairs, group gathering spots, and drink options galore. Besides coffee you can enjoy smoothies, chais, and blended drinks. A pastry or the popular homemade breakfast burrito will make you glad you made this house call. Monday-Friday 7 a.m.-1 p.m.; Saturday 8 a.m.-12 p.m. 620.214.1669. FB.

Braun's Butcher Block:

212 N. Main. A cheery, old-fashioned butcher shop is a nice find on Main Street. Friendly and helpful owners Craig and Marcia Braun offer daily lunch specials; deli meats and cheeses; a full line of fresh and frozen beef, pork, and poultry products; and homemade sausage. Pick up local Duff Buffalo Ranch bison here too. Better bring a cooler! Monday-Friday 9 a.m.-1 p.m. and 2-6 p.m.; Saturday 9 a.m.-2 p.m. 620.872.7238. FB.

Duff Buffalo Ranch Tours:

980 W. 100. From K-96, 5 miles south on U.S. 83, then 1 mile west on 100. Bison are the most majestic animals on the Great Plains, and you can arrange a tour on a flatbed trailer into the midst of a herd. It's an experience you won't soon forget. Tours generally mid-May to October. Tour

SW

charge. Reservations required. 620.874.5120. duffmeats.com.

Lodging: The Guest House (620.872.3559); The Vintage Inn (620.872.2164, thevintageinn.net); additional lodging (visitscottcity.com).

explorer extras...
In Scott City

The Charlie Norton bronze sculpture *Cattleman's Harvest* stands in front of the Security State Bank at 506 Main. It portrays a cowboy carrying a calf to safety during a blizzard.

The exquisite entrance to the 1930 Scott City High School, with its terra cotta and colorful relief panels of turquoise, burnt orange, and maize yellow, will catch your attention as you drive down Main. The high school, at 712 Main, also retains the original art deco light fixtures that grace each side of the entrance.

An impressive landscaped plaza honors Scott County veterans and Gold Star Mothers at 415 E. 5th. A touchscreen allows visitors to search names of Scott County veterans.

Kansas Artists AvNell Mayfield and Larry Caldwell were sponsored by the Scott City Arts Council to create an outdoor mural featuring wheat harvest

and the cattle industry with grain elevators on the distant skyline. Volunteers helped paint by using a paint-by-number system. The mural adorns the side of the Harkness Building in the 400 block of W. 5th. ee

SHALLOW WATER

Unincorporated

Adobe School (NRHP):
180 Barclay. Shallow Water School, designed in the Mission and the Spanish Colonial Revival styles, was built with adobe clay blocks covered with stucco on the exterior and plaster on the interior. The construction materials were chosen because of a lack of nearby trees and native stone. Completed in 1942 by the WPA, it is the only known adobe school in the state. The work of many local individuals to construct this school adds up to an impressive community story. The school now serves as a community center.

Seward County

AROUND THE COUNTY

Mighty Samson of the Cimarron:
From Kansas in Liberal, 13 miles east on U.S. 54 between Liberal and Kismet. From 1888 to 1938 the Rock Island railroad had nothing but trouble with the railroad bridge

over the Cimarron River Valley. A hairpin curve and flooding presented endless difficulties, but the crushing blow came in 1938 when the bridge gave way under an engine and 12 railroad cars. To solve the problem once and for all, a concrete and steel bridge 1,269 feet long and 100 feet above the river bed was completed in 1939. Considered an engineering marvel of its day, the bridge was dubbed the Mighty Samson of the Cimarron.

Arkalon Park: 11123 Arkalon Park. From Kansas in Liberal, 10¾ miles east on U.S. 54, then 1¾ miles north and east on Park and Arkalon Park. Drive under the Mighty Samson of the Cimarron and continue on a sandy road past yucca, sand hill plum trees, sage, and shortgrass prairie—all classic High Plains vegetation. Walk the wooded nature trails to feel part of this lovely settings. Camping and RV hookups. April to mid-October. 620.626.0531

LIBERAL

Population 20,956

Tourist Information
Center: 1 Yellow Brick Road. Stop here first to learn about the must-sees and must-dos of Liberal. Monday-Friday 8 a.m.-5 p.m.; Saturday 10 a.m.-4 p.m. 800.542.3725. visitliberal.com.

Mighty Liberal of You:
In the 1880s accessibility to water for travelers was rare. So when S.S. Rogers home-steaded in the area and dug a well, he always let visitors use it. After they had watered

their livestock and restocked their water supply, they asked Rogers how much they owed. When he told them it was free, they responded, "That's mighty liberal of you." The area, a few miles off the Santa Fe Trail, became known as the Liberal Well. Rogers soon added a dry goods store and in 1886 a post office, and the small community became known as Liberal. See a historical marker about Rogers and his liberal well at the west end of North Blue Bonnet Park, 7th and Western.

Coronado Statue: 1 Yellow Brick Road. A bronze statue of Francisco Vázquez de Coronado by sculptor Eldon Tefft stands in front of the visitor information center. The nearby marker recounts Coronado's quest for gold in this area in 1541, and although disappointed in that search, he was impressed with the land itself.

Coronado Museum: 567 E. Cedar. In 1541 Coronado and 36 soldiers came through this area during their search for Quivira, the legendary kingdom of gold. A bit that was used by one of the expedition's horses was found near Liberal and is exhibited at the museum. Housed

in the 1918 Lee Larrabee family home, the museum focuses on the history of Seward County and contains excellent photos of Liberal's early days and a display about area American Indians. Tuesday-Saturday 9 a.m-5 p.m.; Sunday 1-5 p.m. 620.624.7624. dorothyshouse.com.

Dorothy's House, the Land of Oz, and the Yellow Brick Road (8 Wonders of Kansas Customs): 567 E. Cedar. Follow the Yellow Brick Road to Dorothy's House (a replica of the house in the 1939 film *The Wizard of Oz*), and then continue into the Land of Oz. You'll feel like you've stepped into the movie as a Dorothy guide leads you past the Scarecrow in the cornfield, the Munchkins getting ready for the hot-air balloon launch, and much more. The Oz theme is the creation of Linda Windler, who loved the story so much she established this permanent display. Tuesday-Saturday 9 a.m.-5 p.m.; Sunday 1-5 p.m. Admission charge. 620.624.7624. dorothyshouse.com.

International Pancake Day Hall of Fame: 318 N. Lincoln. Every Shrove Tuesday since 1950 the women of Liberal have competed with the women of Olney, England, in a pancake-flipping race. The tradition started in Olney in 1445. Liberal's Hall of Fame features an exhibit about the origins of the England-Kansas competition and generally documents the race over the years. Call ahead, 620.624.6423. pancakeday.net.

Pancake Race Outdoor Mural: 23 W. 4th. Two women running and flipping pancakes is the subject of this Stan Herd mural on the north side of the First National Bank building.

Memorial Library: 519 N. Kansas. A marker on the library grounds notes that this is the official starting point of the International Pancake Day Race. Also on the grounds is a replica Statue of Liberty and a pioneer mother statue. A sculpture of an enormous open book accents the library's front wall.

SW

Mid-America Air Museum: 2000 W. 2nd. One of the premier aviation museums in the nation, Mid-America features detailed exhibits about the 1943-1945 Liberal Army Air Field (a B-24 Liberator training base). You'll see more than 100 aircraft including military planes, helicopters, home-built planes, modern jets, and a starship. Mid-America is the largest air museum in the state! Monday-Friday 8 a.m.-5 p.m.; Saturday 10 a.m.-5 p.m.; Sunday 1-5 p.m. Admission charge. 620.624.5263. FB.

Landmark Center: 303 N. Kansas.
The 1930 Warren Hotel is now the Landmark Center, a beautifully restored office and condominium complex that retains the original building's art deco design and stunning terra cotta detail. Before the hotel was completed, Warren Smither leased it, thus its name. A fountain and a sculpture of Dorothy Gale (of *The Wizard of Oz*) are found on the nicely landscaped southside plaza.

Baker Arts Center:
624 N. Pershing. Inside the 1954 former ranch-style home of Irene Dillon and Francis Baker, the Baker Arts Center has an excellent reputation for its rotating exhibits by local, regional, and national artists. Tuesday-Friday 9 a.m.-5 p.m.; Sunday 1-3 p.m. 620.624.2810. bakerartscenter.org.

Spanish Style Depot (RHKP):
4 Rock Island. After a fire destroyed the original Rock Island depot and the Greer House restaurant, two new red-brick buildings were built in Spanish style in 1911. These structures have now been restored, and one serves as the chamber office. Go inside and look around; you'll find the Mighty Samson of the Cimarron bridge photos most interesting. Monday-Friday 8 a.m.-5 p.m. 620.624.3855. liberalkschamber.com. The second 1911 building houses Ruffino's Italian Restaurant (*see* next entry).

Ruffino's Italian Restaurant: 2 Rock Island.
Housed in the historic Rock Island depot, this restaurant exudes an elegant atmosphere and offers superb cuisine. Eggplant parmigiana, gnocchi tricolore, chicken pomodoro, and pizza provide a little taste of Italy in southwest Kansas. Daily 11 a.m.-9 p.m. 620.626.6300. ruffinosofliberal.com.

Pancake House:
640 E. Pancake (U.S. 54). When you're in Liberal you must eat pancakes! Apple pancakes are the house specialty, but options range from Hawaiian to chocolate chip. Waffles, crepes, and egg dishes also are available. The Kijafa crepes (sour cherries cooked in Kijafa wine) are delicious! Tuesday-Sunday 6 a.m.-1 p.m. 620.624.8585.

Bisteca: 2324 N. Kansas.
Bisteca in many languages translates to steak, and since you're in beef-producing country you're in the right place to order one! The meat is sourced directly from Liberal's National Beef. Tender filet mignons and grilled ribeyes are excellent. Lighter fare includes several salads including the cilantro-lime chicken salad.

Monday-Friday 11 a.m.-10 p.m.; Saturday 4-11 p.m.; Sunday 11 a.m.-3 p.m. 620.624.5255. FB.

Billy's Blue Duck BBQ:
2050 N. Kansas. Billy's is a local favorite with a fun atmosphere and an attached bowling alley and game room. Try any of the barbecue plates or the Big Woody, a deep-fried hot dog wrapped in a flour tortilla and drenched with homemade chili and cheese. Monday-Saturday 11 a.m.-11 p.m.; Sunday 11 a.m.-8 p.m 620.626.4400. billysblueduckbbq.com.

Super Pollo: 150 W. Main.
Don't let the outside fool you. Inside is some of the best Mexican-style smoked chicken you'll find anywhere. Whole-chicken meals, and half- and quarter-sizes are served with beans, rice, pickled onions, and peppers. Thursday-Tuesday 9:30 a.m.-9 p.m. 620.626.4899.

Jac's Kitchen: 1115 N. Kansas.
It's a newcomer but gaining loyal fans fast with its comfort food sandwiches and scrumptious breakfasts. Coffee lovers will appreciate the 50-cents-a-cup price. Monday-Thursday, Sunday 6 a.m.-2 p.m.; Friday-Saturday 6 a.m.-9 p.m. 620.626.5344. jacskitchenliberal.com.

Spencer Browne's Coffee House: 7 Village Plaza.
It might be all the caffeine spiking the air, but whatever the reason Spencer Browne's is a vibrant coffeehouse filled with positive energy. Healthy alternative edibles and dynamite drinks make it a flavorful choice. The namesake, Elmira Spencer Browne, was the county's first superintendent of schools and the great-great-grandmother

of co-owner Carol Francis. Monday-Saturday 7 a.m.-7 p.m. 620.626.5556. FB.

The Hamburger Place:
720 N. Kansas. A food truck? Yes it is, and folks rave about the burgers! Try Maria's special with grilled jalapenos and onions. Daily 11 a.m.-10 p.m. 620.626.5450.

La Pastorcito: Near Pancake and Kansas. The gringos respectfully refer to this food truck as the Mexican Sonic, and they say the tacos are the best ever. Pull into the parking lot and someone will come out and take your order. Daily 11 a.m.-10 p.m.

Mexican and El Salvadoran Restaurants:
El Amigo Chavez (250 W. Pancake); El Mezcal (780 E. Pancake); Santa Rosa Market and Pupuseria (160 W. Pancake).

Lodging: visitliberal.com.

explorer extras...
In Liberal

WPA projects kept 1930s laborers employed at the Seward County Fairgrounds, Western and 8th. By the time the job was finished in 1937, three buildings, a grandstand, and race-track wall were sturdy rock additions that are still used today.

At the entrance to Light Park, 1100 N. Kansas, a plaque notes that the stone pillars were a 1937 National Youth Administration project. Once inside the gates you're only steps away from Adventure Bay, an entertaining water park with a pirate theme. Mid-May through July. Admission charge. 620.626.0187. FB. **ee**

In Liberal Memorial Cemetery, the Fallen Soldier Memorial, with a plaque explaining the symbolism, and an Old Soldiers Monument dedicated in 1916 pay tribute to those who served their country. From Kansas, 1½ miles west on 15th. **ee**

Stanton County

Population 1,462

Stanton County Museum: 104 E. Highland. Inside a handsome sandstone shop built by the WPA in 1935, county exhibits focus on WPA projects, including Manter Dam (*see* later entry). Dust Bowl photographs bring a reality to the 1930s, and additional displays provide a general background of early county life. This well-landscaped complex includes a 1923

Santa Fe depot, a caboose, an 1887 jail, a 1920s home, the 1920s Scott Garage that houses antique vehicles, and a Vosberg tin-clad grain elevator. Monday-Friday 10:30 a.m.-5 p.m.; Sunday 1-4 p.m. 620.492.1526. FB.

Stanton County Courthouse: 201 N. Main. Multicolored brick creates the handsome exterior of this 1926 Modern Eclecticism structure. A monument on the corner of the square features an etched stone image of the 1888 former

Johnson City High School, which is no longer standing. 620.492.2140.

Camp Amache Officers' Barracks: 207 W. Greenwood, 400 block of N. Long, and 200 block of W. Weaver. A piece of WWII history not often remembered are the Japanese American internment camps that sprang up after Pearl Harbor. Fearing that Japanese Americans would side with their homeland, the government built 10 camps across the United States to confine these citizens during the war years. After the camps closed in 1945, many of the buildings were demolished or relocated. Three officers' barracks from the internment facility at Camp Amache near Granada, Colorado, were relocated here for use as apartments. One still functions for that purpose, and the other two are now a church and a fellowship hall.

Lustron Homes: Prefabricated, all-steel homes were popularized after WWII for their affordable efficiency. Two Lustrons can be seen in Johnson City at 303 and 406 N. Long.

Architecture: The Southwest influence is evident in the terra cotta design on the Stanton County Middle School (502 Main), and in the pillars and entry detail of the 1949 Neoclassical Masonic lodge hall (213 S. Main).

SW

County Fare: 105 S. Main. Chicken wraps, Mexican cheeseburger steaks, and grilled chicken Caesar salads are the house specialties. You can count on good fare at fair prices. Monday-Friday 11 a.m.-8 p.m.; Saturday-Sunday 11 a.m.-1:30 p.m. 620.492.1701. FB.

The Old Store: 112 S. Main. The ice cream, old-fashioned sodas, and other yesteryear treats capture a nostalgic flavor at this 1950s Stanley Knight soda fountain with an original 1920 oak back bar. Monday-Friday 2.-5:30 p.m. 620.492.1478. FB.

MANTER

Population 171

WPA Manter Dam: From Main, 6¾ miles west on U.S. 160, 1½ miles north on X, 1 mile west on 17, ¾ mile north on unnamed road, then ¼ mile northeast on a field road. Consider your vehicle as the roads can be pretty rough. At your destination you'll see remnants of stone, concrete, and rebar left from the 1935 Manter Dam construction, but the dam was never completed. A hike takes you through rocky outcroppings overlooking the Buffalo Creek bed, and wandering among wildflowers and looking for fossils makes for a pleasant day. At the same time, this area has an eerie, otherworldly feel to it, almost as if you've gone back to a prehistoric time. An exhibit at the Stanton County Museum tells more about the dam that never was.

Stevens County

HUGOTON

Population 3,979

Stevens County Gas and Historical Museum: 905 S. Adams. This museum was established as a tribute to the Hugoton Gas Field, once the largest in the world. The gas well, drilled in 1945, is still producing, and vintage equipment is displayed at the well site on the museum grounds. Inside the museum, exhibits focus on American Indians, farming, and domestic life. Monday-Friday 1-4 p.m. 620.544.8751.

Stevens County Courthouse: 200 E. 6th. Built in the Modern Movement style, this 1951 two-story courthouse is almost completely without exterior decoration, and its severe vertical and horizontal

lines create an appearance of authority. Inside, the walls and staircases are made from beautiful rose-colored marble. Monday-Friday 9 a.m.-5 p.m. 620.544.2541.

Veterans Memorial: Stevens County veterans who served in times of conflict and in peace are duly honored on this large memorial comprising five polished black panels. The impressive monument stands west of the courthouse.

Hugoton High School: 215 W. 11th. A center tower is the focal point of the blends of Italian Renaissance and Tudor Revival styles evident in the original part of the 1931 high school. The red-tile roof provides a colorful accent to this building, which still functions as the high school.

Jet Drive-In: 401 S. Main. The vintage clock on the roof says it's time to eat! This little spot (totally retro, from the clock and the signs to the building itself) has been in business since 1964. Owned by Lana Slocum since 1978, it is known for big breakfasts, especially the pancakes with a side of bacon. Jet in and enjoy! Tuesday-Friday 6 a.m.-2 p.m. and 5-8 p.m.; Saturday 6 a.m.-2 p.m.; Sunday 6 a.m.-1 p.m. 620.544.8726. FB.

Nieto's Cafe: 110 W. 4th. The green chili enchiladas are especially popular at this long-standing Mexican restaurant. And if you find yourself up the road to the north, you can stop in at a second Nieto's in Satanta. Monday-Saturday 10:30 a.m.-2 p.m. and 4:30-8 p.m. 620.544.4004.

Lodging: Shady Lane Bed and Breakfast (620.544.7747).

explorer extras...
In Moscow

Population 320

Steaks and burgers are the crowd pleasers at Antler's Sports Bar & Grill and have been since 2002. This bar and grill, at 100 Antler on U.S. 56, specializes in prime rib and ribeye but offers a wide selection of steaks. Monday-Saturday 11 a.m.-2 p.m. and 5-10 p.m. 620.598.2078. FB. **ee**

Wichita County

LEOTI

Population 1,503

Museum of the Great Plains:
201 N. 4th. If you're looking for diverse history, look no more! Where else will you find the many fossil discoveries of local paleontologist Marion Bonner, witness an exhibit of more than 20 violins, and "meet up" with notorious bank robbers Jake and Ralph Fleagle? If that's not enough, you'll learn about

the bloody county seat war between Leoti and Coronado, admire the helmet and jersey of native son and Buffalo Bills football legend Steve Tasker, see an extensive military exhibit, and view cowboy artifacts including brands, saddles, and guns. All of this is inside a former municipal auditorium built by the WPA in 1940. Tuesday-Friday 1-5 p.m.; Saturday-Sunday 2-5 p.m. 620.375.2316. FB.

Washington-Ames House (NRHP):
110 N. 3rd. The Wichita County Historical Society took on a large and commendable project restoring the 1892 Victorian home originally owned by prominent Leoti attorney William Washington and his wife, Julia. The house turned out to be a treasure and now exhibits period furnishings and clothing including a large collection of ladies' hats. Call ahead, 620.375.2316.

Wichita County Courthouse: 206 S. 4th. White pillars add stately elegance to this red-brick courthouse built in the Modern Eclecticism style in 1917. A short distance away is the Charlie Norton bronze *Buffalo*

Woman, which portrays an American Indian woman with her papoose. Monday-Friday 9 a.m.-5 p.m. 620.375.2731.

Prairie Flower Quilt Company:
102 S. Indian. It is a haven for quilters throughout the region! In stock are 2,500-plus bolts of fabric, books, patterns, notions, Baby Lock A-Line sewing machines, and machine quilting services. Monday 12-6 p.m.; Tuesday-Friday 10 a.m.-6 p.m.; Saturday 10 a.m.-4 p.m. 620.375.2044. FB.

Double Bar One:
108 N. 5th. This shop, the only full farrier supply store in Kansas, carries horseshoes from pony to draft horse sizes, plus all the tools needed to care for horses' feet. The farrier craft, once but no longer synonymous with blacksmithing, is a centuries-old trade. Stop in and ask questions at this unique Kansas business. Monday-Friday 7:30 a.m.-5:30 p.m.; Saturday 7:30 a.m.-4 p.m. 620.375.4934. doublebarone.com.

Leoti Foods:
123 E. 4th. The third generation of the Gooch family has expanded the business to Leoti (you'll find Gooch's Foods in Tribune). Buying a few supplies at this clean, neat, and well-stocked small-town market supports both it and the community. Monday-Saturday 7 a.m.-8 p.m.; Sunday 8 a.m.-5 p.m. 620.375.4319. FB.

SW

Fortanel Bakery:

219 N. 4th. A double-duty Mexican bakery, it makes traditional panaderia goods such as empanadas and conchas as well as American-style donuts, cakes, cookies, and pastries. You'll also find made-from-scratch pizza and sandwiches on homemade bread. Monday-Friday 8 a.m.-1 p.m. and 4-8 p.m.; Saturday 9 a.m.-6 p.m. 620.214.1868. FB.

Charlie's Mexican Restaurant:

510 E. Broadway. The pork chili and freshly made hot sauce are staples at Charlie's, which has been a popular stop since 1962. The special is a fried flour tortilla with refried beans, pork chili, lettuce, tomato, and cheese. Delicious! Monday-Saturday 5-9 p.m. 620.375.4541. FB.

Dairy King: 412 W Broadway. It's a nostalgic visit to a time when the pace of life was a little slower. So take time to pull off the road for a burger, corn dog, or old-fashioned ice cream treat—sundaes, banana splits, and shakes. A favorite is the Brown Derby, a vanilla ice cream cone dipped in chocolate. Monday-Saturday 11 a.m.-7 p.m. 620.375.2313.

explorer extras... In Leoti

Near 4th and Broadway at the new Downtown Art Park, a large wooden pergola stands over a colorful mural depicting county images. Brenna Downs Castor designed the mural, which was painted by volunteers.

A bright bouquet of sunflowers appears to burst from the former Boy Scout building in City Park. This mural was painted by local artist Gina Mazanec for a city beautification project. From Kansas, 3 blocks south on 1st.

Carnival rides and games for only 25 cents! Area folks operating the Wichita County Amusement Association

Carnival say it's the best deal for the most fun you'll have for four days at the county fair held the last week in July. You can see the rides at 206 S. 4th while they hibernate during their off-months. 620.375.2182. wichitacounty.org. **ee**

MARIENTHAL

Unincorporated

Heartland Mill: 124 N. K-167. Since 1985 owners Mark and Barbara Nightengale have operated their mill to process and manufacture certified organic milled grains, flours, and meal. Their products are used nationwide by top bakers and notable restaurants. You can buy their commodities at the Country Oven Bakery (*see* next entry) or at heartlandmill.com. 620.379.4472.

Blue Bird Inn: 105 N. 3rd. Open the vintage screen door with the Rainbo Bread handle and step into the past. This little 3.2 beer joint, a fixture since 1948, opens at 5 p.m. and closes when the cows come home. Home-style lunch is served on Saturday at noon until the food is gone. 620.379.4604.

Country Oven Bakery:

124 N. K-167. The Nightengale's son Ashlyn, a well-known baker in the area, opened this bakery in 2016, just south of the Heart-

land Mill. He uses his family's quality-milled products in everything he makes. You'll enjoy choosing from a wide selection of fresh-baked goods—breads, rolls, pies, cookies, granola, and cakes, as well as egg noodles, jams, jellies, and much more. Monday-Friday 8:30 a.m.-6 p.m. 620.379.4472. FB.

SELKIRK

Unincorporated

Hand-Dug Well: From K-25, 10 miles west on K-96, 300 feet north on Main, then 550 feet east on unnamed gravel road.

The 1887 Selkirk Well is believed to be the last hand-dug railroad well in existence. A wrought-iron fence surrounds the 102-foot-deep, 24-foot-circumference well, and wire panels cover the opening, but you can still look down and see the bottom. A nearby 1909 Santa Fe depot and caboose lend a bit more history to this site.

Wayside Chapel: From K-25, 10 miles west on K-96, ¾ mile north on Main, then ¾ mile west on P. Deep in a foxhole in Germany during WWII, Willis Reimer promised himself that if he made it back to Kansas alive, he'd build a chapel. This 8x12-foot redwood sanctuary with vaulted ceiling is the result. Always open.

Enjoy your journey.

M

P

S